D0744506

A SHORT HISTORY OF OPERA

A
SHORT HISTORY
OF
OPERA

THIRD EDITION

DONALD JAY GROUT
with Hermine Weigel Williams

COLUMBIA UNIVERSITY PRESS

New York

Columbia University Press
New York   Oxford
Copyright © 1988 Columbia University Press
All rights reserved

Printed in the United States of America

Library of Congress Cataloging-in-Publication Data

Grout, Donald Jay.
A short history of opera.

Bibliography: p.
Includes index.
1. Opera.   I. 3rd edition with Williams, Hermine
Weigel.   II. Title.
ML1700.C83   1987   782.1'09   87-9374
ISBN 0-231-06192-7

Hardback editions of Columbia University Press books are
Smyth-sewn and printed on permanent and durable acid-free paper

Book design by J. S. Roberts

c 10 9 8 7 6 5 4 3

Ad majorem Dei gloriam

CONTENTS

LIST OF
ILLUSTRATIONS

PREFACE TO THE THIRD EDITION

Almost a quarter of a century has passed since the second edition of this book was prepared for publication. During this period, the creation and production of operas has proceeded at a feverish pace. This period has also seen a burgeoning of opera scholarship and a broadening of the perimeters involved in a survey of the genre.

The present volume seeks to take into account these developments. The text has been revised in light of the scholarly research of the past two decades. The chapter on national opera has been expanded into a separate part and includes a section on opera in China. Part 6 has been completely reorganized; operas produced between 1900 and 1950 are discussed in chapter 25 and those produced after 1950, in chapter 26.

To preserve a degree of continuity between the second (English, 1965; Italian, 1985) and third editions, the musical examples of the former have been retained, but several new examples have been added to illustrate twentieth-century operas. Dates of operas refer to first performance unless otherwise specified. A list of modern editions of operas composed before 1800 (included in the second edition) has not been provided in this edition, since that information is readily available from a variety of sources.

The most radical departure from the second (English) edition is in the bibliography. Although the same seven subdivisions are used, the present volume, because of space limitations, confines the bibliographic references to works cited in the notes to the text. Books that cover more than one chronological period are listed either in the general section or in the section where they are first cited in the notes. Books cited for more than one section are cross-referenced for the reader's convenience.

We are indebted to many friends and colleagues for help at various stages in the preparation of this edition. Particular thanks are due to Professor Rey M. Longyear and to our spouses, Margaret and Jay, for their patience and encouragement.

Acknowledgment is made to the following publishers for permission to use copyrighted material for the musical examples added to this edition: B. Schott's Soehne (examples 26.3a, 26.3b); Merion Music, Inc. (example 26.5); Boosey & Hawkes, Inc. (examples 25.5, 25.6, 26.4); European American Music Distributors Corporation (examples 25.9, 25.10, 25.17, 25.18, 26.1).

Donald Jay Grout
Skaneateles, New York
December 1984

Hermine Weigel Williams
Clinton, New York
December 1984

PREFACE TO THE SECOND EDITION

The present edition aims to incorporate the results of recent reseach and to bring the history of opera forward to about 1960. As in the first edition, the main divisions are chronological and based primarily on considerations of musical style. Revisions, more or less extensive, have been made in all chapters; a few judgments have been revised; new illustrations and musical examples have been provided.

The bibliography has been subdivided in accordance with the larger subdivisions of the text. Books that cover more than one chronological period are listed either in the "general" section or under the earliest period with which they deal. Dates of operas refer to first performance unless otherwise specified. Modern editions of operas before 1800 are listed on pages 769 to 786; some of these editions contain, in addition to the music, valuable critical or historical essays.

Grateful acknowledgment is made to the Graduate School of Cornell University and to the American Council of Learned Socieities for grants in aid of research.

I am indebted to many friends and colleagues for help at various stages in the preparation of this edition. Particular thanks are due to Professor Anna Amalie Abert of Kiel for advice, to Mr. Harold Rosenthal of London for illustrations, and to Mr. James Bossert of Ithaca for assistance in reading proof.

Acknowledgment is made to the following publishers for permission to use copyrighted material in the musical examples added for this edition: Boosey & Hawkes, Ltd., London (Exs. 25.7, 25.8, 25.15); J. & W. Chester, Ltd., London (Ex. 24.3); Heugel et Cie, Paris (Ex. 25.12); Möseler Verlag, Wolfenbüttel and Zurich (Exs. 9.2 and 9.4); G. Ricordi & Co., Milan (Exs.

23.2 and 25.13); B. Schott's Soehne, Mainz, and Associated Music Publishers Inc., New York (Ex. 26.1); Universal Editions, A.G., Vienna (Exs. 25.9, 25.10, 25.17, 25.18); Edizioni Suvini Zerboni, Milan (Ex. 26.2).

Donald Jay Grout

Ithaca, New York
September 15, 1963

PREFACE TO THE
FIRST EDITION

Volumes almost beyond counting have been written about opera, but no systematic historical survey since the publication of Hermann Kretzschmar's *Geschichte der Oper* in 1919. This work, though valuable for the early periods of opera history, ends to all intents and purposes with Wagner; moreover, it has never been translated. Most books in English which profess to deal historically with opera are either mere collections of plot synopses strung on a thin thread of continuity, or else obvious bids for popular success without serious pretensions to accuracy or thoroughness. There are a few excellent books which treat of opera in a nonhistorical manner, among which may be especially mentioned Edward J. Dent's *Opera* (New York, Penguin Books, 1940). But the bulk of serious writing about opera at the present time is in the form of specialized studies of limited scope and is read for the most part only by specialists.

Recognizing this fact, it would seem that there might be room for a book which has for its purpose to offer a comprehensive report on the present state of our knowledge about the history of opera. In compressing such a long and diversified history into the compass of a single book it is obvious that many things must be omitted. The reader will not find here, for example, many synopses of opera plots or much gossip about the personal affairs of composers and singers; no attempt has been made to furnish complete statistical information about the output of composers or complete records of performances; biographies have been treated summarily; and digressions on the relation of opera to contemporary production in literature and the other arts, to politics, economics, and the *Zeitgeist* generally have been regretfully held to a minimum. On the other hand, a conscientious effort has been made to present the essential points in the history of opera clearly, fairly, in proper proportion, and with constant reference to the music. Musical examples have been provided, especially for the earlier periods from which scores are not readily available, and some technical analysis of important representative works or passages is included. The bibliographical material has been made full enough, it is hoped, to provide the student with adequate information for beginning research on almost any desired special topic. An elementary acquaintance on the reader's part with the history of music is assumed, though this is perhaps not essential; knowledge of music theory will be found necessary for understanding some of the technical analyses.

Generous help has been given by many friends in the course of preparation of this work. The author wishes especially to express his thanks to the Trustees of the Wesley Weyman Fund, Harvard University, for a grant of one thousand dollars for aid in research. Professor Otto Kinkeldey kindly read the manuscript and made many suggestions which are gratefully acknowledged. Advice on various special topics has been most cheerfully given by Mr. Gilbert Chase, Professor Archibald T. Davison, Mr. Richard S. Hill, Professor Scott Goldthwaite, Dr. Henry L. Clarke, Dr. Walter Rubsamen, Professor Chase Baromeo, and many others. To Mr. Lawrence Apgar, Mr. Leonard Burkat, and their helpers, thanks are due for skilled and devoted labor on bibliographical problems, and to Mr. John Scabia for preparation of the musical examples. Lastly to my wife, who typed most of the manuscript and who has been both a patient sufferer and an encouraging companion throughout the entire labor, a special debt of gratitude must always stand.

Acknowledgment is made to the following publishers for permission to use copyrighted material in the musical examples: Edwin Arnold & Co., London (Ex. 12.2); E. de Boccard, Paris (Ex. 7.10); Choudens, Editeur, Paris (Ex. 18.3); Durand & Cie., Paris (Exs. 12.9, 23.1, 25.1, 25.2); Novello & Co., Ltd., London (Exs. 11.4, 11.5, 11.6, 18.1, 20.3, 20.5); G. Schirmer, Inc., New York (Ex. 20.60); and Joseph Williams, Ltd., London (Exs. 11.1, 11.2, 11.3).

It is perhaps not out of order to warn the reader against the delusion that the history of any kind of music can be learned simply by reading a book. The principal use of any book about music is to serve as an introduction to the music itself, which must always be the central object of study. If beyond this essential point it is possible to suggest some of the implications of the music, some of its relation to the culture of which it is a part and some of its significance for our own time, so much the better. The landscape of history is not alone the solid earth of fact; above must spread the rolling cloudbanks of imagination.

Donald Jay Grout

Skaneateles Lake, New York
September 1, 1947

A SHORT HISTORY OF OPERA

That day the sky was cloudless; the
wind blew softly where we sat. Above
us stretched in its hugeness the vault
and compass of the World; around us
crowded in green newness the myriad
tribes of Spring. Here chimed around
us every music that can soothe the ear;
was spread before us every color that
can delight the eye. Yet we were sad.
For it is so with all men: a little while
(some by the fireside talking of
homely matters with their friends,
others by wild ecstasies of mystic
thought swept far beyond the bound-
aries of carnal life) they may be easy
and forget their doom. But soon their
fancy strays; they grow dull and list-
less, for they are fallen to thinking that
all these things which so mightily
pleased them will in the space of a
nod be old things of yesterday.

WANG XI-CHI (A.D. 353)

INTRODUCTION

The custom of using music in connection with dramatic presentations is universal. It is found throughout the history of all cultures and among primitive and civilized peoples alike. This is perhaps because the desire to add music to drama is really part of the dramatic instinct itself. The motives may be either religious or secular: drama with music may have as its end either edification or entertainment. Of religious dramatic music we know today such forms as the cantata, the oratorio, and the Passion; the two last (aside from their subject matter) differ from opera essentially only in that they include some narrative portions and that they do not require scenery, costumes, or stage action. Even this difference is little more than a historical accident; it arises from the traditional antipathy between church and theater which has existed especially since the period of the Renaissance. The dramatic impulse is retained in these types of sacred music but divested of those external trappings most closely associated with its secular manifestations. The opera itself is, with rare exceptions, a secular form. Its aim is like that of all the secular arts: the enrichment and embellishment of civilized life.

The first work now known as an "opera" was performed in 1598.[1] The word itself, however, was not used in its present sense before 1634. It means literally a "work" (compare "opus") and is a shortened form of the Italian *opera in musica*, that is, a "work of music." Dozens of other designations have been used at different times and places, and new ones are still being invented. The earliest Italian operas were called *favola* ("fable"), *tragedia*

1. This date is often given as 1597, in accordance with the Florentine calendar. For a review of important regional differences in the calendar and in the dating of the New Year, see Donington, *The Rise of Opera*, pp. 307–16.

("tragedy"), or *dramma*, usually with a qualifying word: *favola in musica, favola pastorale, dramma per musica* ("drama by means of music"), or the like. The word "opera" came into general use first in England (from 1656); it was not common in France or Germany until the eighteenth century and is still relatively infrequent in Italy.[2]

It is remarkable not only that both music and the theater had existed for hundreds of years before an opera was written, but also that both music and drama have since flourished during periods and in countries in which opera has shown no comparable vitality. In eighteenth-century Italy, on the other hand, the production of operas far exceeded, in both quantity and quality, that of other musical or dramatic forms. It seems necessary, therefore, to consider what special inherent features of opera may account for such anomalies.

The first is undoubtedly its luxuriousness. Opera is an expensive affair because it is so difficult to stage and perform. It involves the cooperation of a large number of experts, from the librettist and composer through the conductor, the singers, the orchestra, the stage designers, managers, technicians, and so on. All these people must be persuaded or compelled to work together harmoniously, and they must be paid. A large theatre, with all kinds of special equipment, has to be maintained. Since there have seldom been enough persons in any community who are both able and willing to pay the high admission prices necessary to make opera self-supporting, some form of patronage is necessary. The patron may be a wealthy noble maintaining an opera company for the amusement of himself and his friends; or it may be a private association of individuals who attempt with greater or less success to sell opera to the public by exploiting it both as an art work and as a prestige symbol; or again, the state may be the patron, supporting opera by means of subsidies from the public funds. In any case, the result is the same: opera is conditioned poetically, musically, scenically, and to the last detail by the ideals and desires of those upon whom it depends, and this to a degree and in

2. A list of designations used for operas in the seventeenth and eighteenth centuries is given in Haas, "Geschichtliche Opernbezeichnungen." See also Dent, "The Nomenclature of Opera," and "Opera" in *The New Grove Dictionary*. On the use of "opera" and "music drama" to designate types of theatrical entertainment in China, see ch. 24 of the present work.

a manner not true of any other musical form. The opera is the visible and audible projection of the power, wealth, and taste of the society that supports it. For this reason, the study of its history is of value for the light it sheds on the history of culture in general.

Another inherent feature of opera is its artificiality, or stylization. Opera is always laden with certain conventions, which people agree to accept while at the same time acknowledging them to be unnatural or even ridiculous. Take, for example, the practice of singing instead of talking. Nothing could be more "unnatural," yet it is accepted as a matter of course, just as the equally "unnatural" blank verse is accepted as the form of speech in Shakespeare's tragedies. Not only are there such timeless conventions in opera, but every age has a set of them peculiar to itself, which the second or third generation following begins to find old-fashioned and the generation after that finds insupportable. It is not that the music of these operas is inferior; rather, it is bound up with a hundred details which interfere with our understanding of it—operatic conventions which, passing out of knowledge, all too often carry the music with them to oblivion.

All of this points to the necessity for approaching the study of an opera, particularly one of a past period, with especial care. An opera score must be studied with imagination as well as attention. It will not do merely to read the music as if it were a symphony or a series of songs accompanied by an orchestra. One must also imagine the work as it appears in performance, with the stage action, the costumes, and the scenery; and one must be aware of the operatic conventions by which librettist and composer were governed, so as not to judge them according to the conventions of a different period, committing the absurdity, for example, of condemning an opera of Lully or Handel merely because it is not like the operas of Verdi or Wagner.

The luxuriousness and stylization of opera have always provoked reactions. Just as every age has its own kind of opera, so every age has its own humbler counterparts of the form, designed to appeal to persons of less wealth or less cultivation. These stepchildren of opera have been known by many different names: *opera buffa, opéra comique,* ballad opera, "intermezzo," comic opera, vaudeville, operetta, musical comedy, and so on. Whatever the name, all have certain common features: they are less expensive than the opera, their social standing is lower, their tone is more familiar, and many of them caricature or parody the serious opera. They are the poor man's opera, even (as the title of one of the most famous of them has it) *The Beggar's Opera*. So far as artistic merit goes, they may be equal or even superior to the more pretentious form and must certainly be considered along with it in any historical treatment.

An opera, briefly defined, is a *drama in music:* a dramatic action, performed on a stage with scenery by actors in costume, the words conveyed entirely or for the most part by singing, and the whole sustained and amplified by orchestral music. There is an essential difference between a good opera libretto, as the words of the action are called, and the script of a good play. If there were not, conceivably any of Shakespeare's tragedies could be set to music exactly as it stands—a feat which has rarely been attempted. The difference is one of emphasis.

A play centers about characters and a plot; it may contain episodes which could be omitted without damaging its unity or continuity, but if this is the case, it is, strictly speaking, a defect in the structure. An opera libretto, on the other hand, may almost be said to center about the episodes; at least, it admits and even requires many portions which contribute little or nothing to characterization or to development of the action, such as dances, choruses, instrumental or vocal ensembles, and spectacular stage effects. Even the solo songs (arias) are often, from the dramatic point of view, mere lyrical interruptions of the plot; they correspond, in a way, to soliloquies in spoken drama. All these things, which (on a comparable scale at least) would be out of place in a spoken drama, are the very lifeblood of opera. Composers may accept them frankly as episodes or may try to make them contribute in a greater or lesser degree to the depiction of character or the development of the dramatic idea; but they are so much a part of opera that it is difficult to find an example which does not include them to some extent, even among the so-called realistic operas of the late nineteenth and twentieth centuries.

On the other hand, plot and characterization in an opera libretto are likely to be sketched in broad outline rather than in detail. The action is usually simpler than in a play, with fewer events and less complex interconnections among them. Subtle characterization, if it exists at all, is accomplished by means of music rather than dialogue. Most important of all, the entire dramatic tempo is slower, so as to allow time for the necessary episodic scenes and especially for the deployment and development of the musical ideas.

There is another kind of difference between a play and a libretto, one which has to do with the poetic idiom employed, the choice of words and images. It is a commonplace that not all poetry is suitable for music; it would require a composer of genius equal to Shakespeare's to add music to such lines as

> The cloud-capp'd towers, the gorgeous palaces,
> The solemn temples, the great globe itself,
> Yea, all which it inherit, shall dissolve
> And, like this insubstantial pageant faded,
> Leave not a rack behind.

But consider the following:

> When I am laid in earth, [may] my wrongs create
> No trouble in thy breast. Remember me, but ah!
> Forget my fate.

Judged merely as poetry this passage, from Nahum Tate's *Dido and Aeneas*, could hardly merit high praise. Yet it is excellent poetry for music. It suggests in simple terms the image of a woman desolated by an emotion which the words by themselves cannot completely convey, an emotion so overpowering that only with the aid of music can it be given full expression. Moreover, the passage has a maximum of the appropriate dark vowel sounds and liquid consonants, with few sibilants. The important words (laid, earth, wrongs, trouble, remember, fate) are not only well adapted for singing but also are full of emotional suggestion. The very imperfections of the passage considered purely as poetry are its great merit for singing, so strongly do they invite completion by means of music.

Making due allowance for the special requirements of the form, an opera libretto will usually reflect the prevailing ideas of its time with regard to drama. Similarly, opera music will be, in general, very much like other music of the same period. It must be remembered that in an opera, music is only one of several factors. It is necessarily always a kind of program music, in that it must (even if only to a slight degree) adapt itself to the dramatic and scenic requirements instead of developing in accordance with purely musical principles. As a rule, it is somewhat simpler, more popular in style than contemporary larger forms of nondramatic music, more tuneful, more obvious in its rhythms, less contrapuntal in texture—though there are some exceptions to this, notably the music dramas of Wagner. On the other hand, an opera score is apt to be more varied and original in instrumental color, partly because an opera is so long that more variety is needed, and partly in consequence of the composer's constant search after new dramatic effects by means of instrumentation. Thus, trombones had been used in opera two hundred years before they were admitted to symphonic combinations; the devices of string tremolo and pizzicato were first used in dramatic music; Wagner introduced a whole new group of instruments, the so-called Wagner tubas, in his *Ring*.

Neither the poetry nor the music of an opera is to be judged as if it existed by itself. The music is good not if it happens to make a successful concert piece but primarily if it is appropriate and adequate to the particular situation in the opera where it occurs, and if it contributes something which the other elements cannot supply. If it sounds well in concert form, so much the better, but this is not essential. Similarly, the poetry is good not because it reads well by itself but primarily if, while embodying a sound dramatic idea, it furnishes opportunity for effective musical and scenic treatment. Both poetry and music are to be understood only in combination with each other and with the other elements of the work. True, they may be considered separately, but only for purposes of analysis. In actuality they are united as the elements of hydrogen and oxygen are united in water. "It is . . . not simply the combination of elements that gives opera its peculiar fascination; it is the fusion produced by the mutual analogy of words and music—a union further enriched and clarified by the visual action."[3]

3. Cone, "Music: A View from Delft," p. 447. Cf. René Leibowitz: "La musique dramatique ne reproduit nullement l'action pour l'élever . . . sur un plan symbolique, mais le son qui pénètre l'action signifie que celle-ci se trouve absorbée par celui-là." In "Alban

Throughout the history of opera, in all its many varieties, two fundamental types may be distinguished: that in which the music is the main issue, and that in which there is more or less parity between the music and the other factors. The former kind is sometimes called "singer's opera," a term to which some undeserved opprobrium is attached. Examples of this type are the operas of Rossini, Bellini, Verdi, and indeed of most Italian composers; Mozart's *Magic Flute* also is a singer's opera, in which a complicated, inconsistent, and fantastic libretto is redeemed by some of the most beautiful music ever written. On the other hand, such operas as those of Lully, Rameau, and Gluck, not to mention the music dramas of Wagner, depend for their effect on a balance of interest among many different factors of which music is only one, albeit the most important.

Theoretically, it would seem that there should be a third kind of opera, one in which the music is definitely subordinated to the other features. As a matter of fact, the very earliest operas were of this kind, but it was found that their appeal was limited and that it was necessary to admit a fuller participation of music in order to establish the form on a sound basis. Consequently, an opera is not only a drama but also a type of musical composition, and this holds even for those works which include spoken dialogue. The exact point at which such a work ceases to be an opera and becomes a play with musical interludes is sometimes difficult to determine; no rule can be given except to say that if the omission of the music makes it impossible to perform the work at all, or alters its fundamental character, then it must be regarded as an opera.

Throughout its career, opera has been both praised and censured in the strongest terms. It was lauded by its creators as "the delight of princes," "the noblest spectacle ever devised by man."[4] In contrast, Saint-Evremond, a French critic of the late seventeenth century, defined an opera as "a bizarre affair made up of poetry and music, in which the poet and the musician, each equally obstructed by the other, give themselves no end of trouble

Berg et l'essence de l'opéra," *L'Arche* (March 1946), p. 164. On this whole subject, see also the introductory chapter of Kerman, *Opera as Drama*.

4. Marco da Gagliano, preface to *Dafne*, in Solerti, ed., *Le origini del melodramma*, p. 82.

to produce a wretched work."[5] Opera has been criticized on moral as well as on aesthetic grounds; the respectable Mr. Haweis in 1872 regarded it "musically, philosophically, and ethically, as an almost unmixed evil."[6] Despite both enemies and friends, however, it has continued to flourish and indeed shows every sign of vitality at the present time; there is every reason to expect that opera, in one shape or another, will be with us for a long time to come. Like all other forms of art, it contains many things today which cannot be understood without a knowledge of its history. It is hoped that this book will not only serve as an introduction to the opera of the past but may thereby contribute as well to an understanding of the opera of the present.

5. Saint-Evremond, *Œuvres* (1740 ed.), 3:249.

6. Haweis, *Music and Morals*, p. 423.

PART I

*Music and Drama
to the End
of the Sixteenth Century*

CHAPTER ONE

The Lyric Theater
of the Greeks

It is indispensable for a student of the history of opera to know something of the history, literature, and mythology of the ancient world, if only because so many opera subjects have been drawn from these sources. The myth of Orpheus and Eurydice has been used for over thirty operas, the story of Iphigenia (first dramatized by Euripides toward the end of the fifth century B.C.) for at least fifty, and the myth of Hercules for probably twice that number. Over half of the ninety-four operas of J. A. Hasse (1699–1783) are on classical themes. Berlioz's masterpiece, *Les Troyens*, is an outstanding nineteenth-century example. Since then, there have been such works as Richard Strauss' *Elektra* (1909), Fauré's *Pénélope* (1913), Wellesz's *Alkestis* (1924), Milhaud's *Médée* (1939), Malipiero's *Ecuba* (1941), and Orff's *Antigonae* (1948), though on the whole the preference for classical subjects is now much less pronounced than in former times.[1]

Greek drama, however, is of particular interest to us for the reason that it was the model on which the creators of modern opera at the end of the sixteenth century based their own works; it was the supposed music of Greek tragedy which they sought to revive in their "monodic style." Unfortunately, they did not know (nor do we) just how this music sounded. There are a few surviving specimens of Greek dramatic music, including a very short mutilated fragment of unison melody from a chorus of Euripides'

---

1. See Zinar, "The Use of Greek Tragedy."

Orestes (408 B.C.),[2] but these were not known to the early Florentine opera composers.

That music did play an important part in Greek tragedy we may learn from Aristotle's definitions in the *Poetics*, written about a century later than the works of Sophocles and Euripides, which still served as models:

> Tragedy, then, is an imitation of some *action* that is *important*, *entire*, and of a proper *magnitude*—by language, embellished and rendered *pleasurable*, but by different *means* in different parts. . . .
>
> By *pleasurable language*, I mean language that has the embellishments of rhythm, melody, and metre. And I add, by *different means in different parts*, because in some parts metre alone is employed, in others, melody.[3]

The last sentence of this passage would seem to indicate that the tragedies were not sung in their entirety, as has sometimes been stated. It is believed, however, that some kind of musical declamation was employed for at least part of the dialogue, and the fact that the plays were given in large open-air theaters makes this probable on acoustical grounds, if for no other reason. Such declamation may have been a kind of sustained, semimusical speech, perhaps like the *Sprechstimme* of Schoenberg's *Pierrot Lunaire* or Berg's *Wozzeck*, but moving within a more limited range of pitch. It is also probable that regular melodic settings were used in certain places.

Whatever may have been the manner of performing the dialogue, there can be no doubt that the choruses were really sung, not merely musically declaimed. When Greek drama developed out of the earlier ceremonies of Bacchus worship, it took over from them the choral group (dithyrambs) and solemn figured choral dances which have such an important place in the trage-

2. A reproduction of this papyrus fragment (A-Wn G 2315), which dates from about 200 B.C., is in *The New Grove Dictionary*, 6:295. A transcription of the melody is in Sachs, *Die Musik der Antike*, pp. 17–18. See also Mountford, "Greek Music in the Papyri"; Richter, "Das Musikfragment"; Mathiesen, "New Fragments of Ancient Greek Music." A fragment from a late tragedy of Euripides was discovered in 1973 and may constitute the earliest specimen among some forty extant examples of Greek music.

3. Aristotle, *Poetics*, 1449b20.

dies.[4] The role of the chorus in these works is largely that of the "articulate spectator," voicing the audience's response to the events portrayed in the action, remonstrating, warning, or sympathizing with the hero. Formally, the choruses are generally so placed as to divide the action into parts, similar to the division of a modern play into acts or scenes, resulting in an alternation of drama with the comparatively static or reflective choral portions. It is significant that this same formal arrangement is characteristic of opera in the seventeenth and eighteenth centuries, with its clear distinction between the dramatic action (recitative or spoken dialogue) and the lyrical or decorative scenes (arias, choruses, ballets) to which the action gives rise. The typical use of the chorus in Greek drama is best seen in the tragedies of Sophocles (495–406 B.C.) and Euripides (484–407 B.C.), the choruses of the latter's *Iphigenia in Tauris* being particularly beautiful examples. In Aeschylus (525–456 B.C.), the choruses are more numerous and sometimes serve to narrate preceding events *(Agamemnon)* or take a direct part in the action *(Eumenides)*.

All the actors in Greek tragedy were men, and the chorus was no exception. Although in later ages it numbered no more than twelve or fifteen singers, in Periclean times it was undoubtedly larger;[5] the chorus of Furies in Aeschylus' *Eumenides* numbered fifty, and their singing and dancing were said to have had such a terrifying effect that children in the audience were thrown into convulsions from fright. The leader of the chorus *(choregos, choryphaios)* was chosen from among the wealthiest and most prominent citizens of the community. The position was regarded as a distinction, but since the leader had to train and equip the chorus at his own expense he sometimes found himself ruined by the honor, which the satirist listed among the possible calamities of life, like lawsuits and taxes.

The choral songs were unison melodies (like all Greek music), one note to a syllable, with accompaniment of instruments of the kithara or aulos type. The kithara was an instrument like the lyre, the strings being plucked either with the fingers or with

4. See Webster, *The Greek Chorus.*
5. See Hamilton, "The Greek Chorus."

a plectrum. The aulos was a reed-blown instrument, the tone of which probably resembled that of the oboe but with a more piercing character. These instruments may have played short introductions and interludes to the choral songs. The "accompaniments" consisted in either doubling the voices at the unison or embellishing the vocal melody, a practice known as "heterophony." Theorists prescribed certain modes or types of melody as appropriate for certain kinds of scenes, the Dorian being generally favored for majestic verses and the Mixolydian for lamentations in dialogue between the chorus and a soloist. Such dialogues are quite frequent. There are also dialogues between the *choregos* and one of the actors; occasionally (as in the *Alcestis* of Euripides), various members of the chorus have short solo parts. In some cases the choruses have a refrain, a passage recurring several times in "ritornello" fashion (Aeschylus, *Eumenides*).

No composers are mentioned, but poets are sometimes stated to have composed the music for their own plays. This does not mean so much as it would in the present day, for it is probable that the declamatory solo portions of the drama were for the most part improvised, only slight general indications of the rise and fall of the voice being given by the poet; the choruses may possibly have employed certain standard melodies *(nomoi)*, though on occasion new melodies might be composed.

The Greek comedy assigned to music a much less important role than did the tragedy, although Aristophanes (ca. 448–385 B.C.) had choruses of Clouds, Wasps, Birds, and Frogs. In keeping with the general satirical spirit of the comedies, the chorus was dressed in fantastic costumes and indulged in imitation of animal and bird sounds. There was probably very little if any solo singing in the comedies.

By the second century B.C., the chorus had disappeared from Greek drama altogether. As early as the fourth century, Aristotle had spoken of its decline and complained that the poets of that day introduced choral songs which "have no more connection with their subject, than with that of any Tragedy: and hence, they are now become detached pieces, inserted at pleasure."[6] Solo singing remained a feature of the Roman drama, as we learn from a pas-

6. Aristotle, *Poetics*, 1456a25.

sage in Lucian's dialogue "On the Dance," written about 165 A.D., describing an actor in tragedy "bawling out, bending forward and backward, sometimes actually singing his lines, and (what is surely the height of unseemliness) melodising his calamities. . . . To be sure, as long as he is an Andromache or a Hecuba, his singing can be tolerated; but when he enters as Hercules in person and warbles a ditty . . . a man in his right mind may properly term the thing a solecism."[7]

There are still many unanswered questions about the way in which Greek drama was performed, but we may be certain that, although it was not precisely like a modern opera, neither was it entirely in spoken dialogue like a modern play. The function of music was that of an embellishment, though a very important one.[8] It was this conception which Gluck expressed as his theory of the relation of music to drama, namely, that its purpose should be to "animate the figures without altering their contours."

7. *Lucianus*, 5:240.

8. See Aristotle: "Music . . . of all the pleasurable accompaniments and embellishments of tragedy, the most delightful." *Poetics*, 1450b15.

CHAPTER TWO

Medieval Dramatic Music

The history of the theater during the Middle Ages is obscure. Ancient drama seems to have disappeared, although it is possible that traces of Roman comedy may have been retained in the popular farces and other pieces performed by strolling bands of players and (later) by the jongleurs. So far as our actual knowledge goes, however, the significant theater of the Middle Ages is religious.[1] It develops within the liturgy and emerges only partially from the church in the fifteenth century. In the West, two stages of this religious theater are to be distinguished: the liturgical drama (from the eleventh to the thirteenth century and later) and the mysteries (chiefly from the fourteenth to the sixteenth century, with later revivals).[2] We shall give first a brief summary of their course and then a somewhat more detailed description of the features of each.

The origin of the religious theater appears to have been the practice of performing certain portions of the service dramatically—that is, the officiating priests actually representing the characters rather than merely narrating the events. This technique was first applied to the story of the Resurrection, and soon after to that of the Nativity. Around the original kernel there was a steady growth by accretion: in the Resurrection dramas the episode of the two Marys at the tomb of Christ (Matt. 28:1–7) was preceded by the scene of the buying of the ointment and followed

1. Leading works in English on this period include: Chambers, *The Medieval Stage*; Young, *The Drama of the Medieval Church* (on liturgical dramas only); Hardison, *Christian Rite and Christian Drama*; Smoldon, *The Music of the Medieval Church Dramas*; Collins, *The Production of Medieval Church Music-Drama*; idem, *Medieval Church Music-Dramas*. See also Mantzius, *A History of Theatrical Art*, vol. 2.

2. Cf. Stevens, "Medieval Drama" (which includes a notably complete bibliography).

by scenes representing the appearance of the risen Christ to the women and later to the apostles; the story was then extended backward to include the Crucifixion, the trial, and eventually all the events of Passion Week. Similarly, in the Nativity dramas the scene of the shepherds worshiping at the manger was expanded by taking in the Annunciation, the flight into Egypt, the Massacre of the Innocents, and so on. Before this process of accretion was completed, the drama had been removed from its primitive position as part of the church service and reserved as a special feature of feast days, often coming as the climax of a procession and being performed on the church porch or steps—still, however, with priests and clerics as the actors, though the people might take part as a chorus. Next, the vernacular began to replace Latin; stage properties and costumes grew more elaborate; and with the constantly increasing size of the spectacle, the charge of the performances was finally given over to guilds of professional actors, and the arena of the action changed from the church to the market place. This transformation of the liturgical drama from an ecclesiastical to a municipal function was completed by about the middle of the fourteenth century and led into the mysteries, a typical late medieval form of sacred drama. But alongside the latter, the tradition of the older, simpler form survived; its traces are to be found in such works as the "school dramas" (plays on sacred subjects performed in schools and colleges), the oratorio, and certain aspects of opera in the seventeenth century, especially in Rome and northern Germany.

The Liturgical Drama

Like Greek tragedy, the liturgical drama grew out of religious ceremonies.[3] The origin of the principal group of these, the Resurrec-

---

3. It has been suggested that the name "liturgical drama" is not appropriate when applied to plays developed from paraliturgical material and tropes (passages added to the regular liturgy); however, since this term is well established, there seems little point in attempting to replace it by the more accurate designation of "ecclesiastical drama" or "church drama."

tion dramas, is found in the *Quem quaeritis* dialogue, of which
the earliest surviving examples come from the tenth century:

> Interrogatio: Quem quaeritis in sepulchro, o Cristicolae?
> Responsio: Ihesum Nazarenum crucifixum, o celicolae.
> Responsio: Non est hic, surrexit sicut praedixerat; ite,
>   nunciate quia surrexit.[4]

This dialogue seems to have constituted an independent ceremony, for it is not uncommon to find it associated with more than
one liturgical situation within the Easter rites. In one tenth-cen-
tury manuscript, for instance, the *Quem quaeritis* dialogue appears as part of the *Collecta* ceremony; in another, it occurs at
the end of Matins, just before the *Te Deum laudamus*.[5] The *Quem
quaeritis* dialogue was sung, not spoken. In fact, in the earliest
liturgical dramas, everything was sung; the further these plays
grew away from the church, the more speaking and the less music
they included, thus approaching in form the later mysteries.

The music of the liturgical dramas is of two kinds: (1)
Nonmetrical plainsong of a simple though not purely syllabic type.
For texts taken from the liturgy or the tropes, the existing melodies were usually retained, either intact or in a "mosaic" made
by selecting and combining fragments of the traditional chants.
For the added portions, other melodies were selected or composed. (2) Songs of a more or less distinctly metrical character,
either hymn melodies or perhaps tunes of popular origin. These
are less common, but they tend to occur more frequently in the

---

4.

> Question: Whom do you seek in the tomb, O fol-
>   lowers of Christ?
> Response: Jesus of Nazareth who was crucified, O
>   dwellers in heaven.
> Response: He is not here, he has risen as was
>   foretold; go, make known he has risen.

In some manuscripts, *de sepulchro* (from the tomb) is added; see, for example, St. Gall
MS 339.

5. McGee, in "The Liturgical Placements of the *Quem quaeritis* Dialogue," pp. 5–6, defines the *Collecta* ceremony as a service "occurring before important liturgical ceremonies
at a church known as a *Collecta* where congregations and celebrants assembled for a short
collect before processing to the stational church." Cf. Hardison, "Gregorian Easter Vespers and Early Liturgical Drama"; Flanigan, "The Liturgical Context of the *Quem quaeritis* Trope."

later dramas. Their rhythm is not evident from the original notation but is apparent from the metrical form and presence of a
rhyme scheme in the texts. The latter are usually strophic, with
two or fifteen or more stanzas, and may be either in Latin or in
the vernacular. It is possible that some of these songs were sung
by the congregation.

There are songs for both soloists and chorus. In the earlier dramas they may have been accompanied by the organ; occasionally other instruments are mentioned and it is probable that
instruments of many kinds were used much more extensively in
performance than the manuscripts themselves indicate.[6] Most of
the music is written as single-line melody, though there are occasional passages in two or more parts. The term "conductus," which
sometimes occurs, refers not to a musical form but to the procession from one part of the stage to another, marking the division
of the drama into scenes.

Over two hundred liturgical dramas have been preserved, many of them available in modern editions.[7] The subjects
of these cover a wide range: the Resurrection, the Nativity, miracles of saints, the prophets (for example, *Daniel*), a melodrama
with a kidnaping *(Le Fils de Guédron)*, and a comedy *(Le Juif
volé)*. Adolphe Didron has pointed out that the liturgical drama
must have represented for the medieval church a visible embodiment of the sacred stories commemorated in the statues and stained-
glass windows of the cathedrals, as though the figures in these
monuments "descended from their niches and panes . . . to play
their drama in the nave and choir of the vast edifice."[8] There is
about them certainly an air of profound and simple piety, a naïve
blending of sacred and profane without the least sense of incongruity, which is one of the most engaging features of medieval art.

6. See Bowles, "The Role of Musical Instruments."

7. Modern editions of liturgical dramas with music include: Coussemaker, *Drames liturgiques du moyen âge*; G. Vecchi, *Uffici dramatici padovani*; Krieg, *Das lateinische Osterspiel von Tours*; Kühl, "Die Bordesholmer Marienklage"; *Sacre rappresentazioni nel
manoscritto . . . di Orléans*; Smits van Waesberghe, "A Dutch Easter Play"; Greenberg,
ed., *The Play of Daniel*; Smoldon and Greenberg, eds., *The Play of Herod*.

8. Coussemaker, *Drames liturgiques*, p. ix.

The Mysteries

The mysteries (the word is probably derived from the Latin *min-isterium*, "service") flourished during the fifteenth and sixteenth centuries. They differed considerably from the earlier liturgical dramas. Although the church still collaborated and the bishop's permission was necessary for a performance, the sponsor was the community as a whole and the actors were recruited from professional guilds, such as the Confrérie de la Passion in France and the Compagnia del Gonfalone in Italy. National differentiations are evident, and the vernacular is used consistently. The Italian works of this class were known as *rappresentazioni sacre*,[9] and are generally regarded as forerunners of the oratorio, though their influence is apparent in some seventeenth-century Italian operas as well. The subjects of the mysteries are sacred but of even greater scope than those of the liturgical dramas; thus, there was the *Mystery of the Old Testament*, which ran for twenty-five days consecutively,[10] and the *Mystery of the Acts of the Apostles* performed at Bourges in 1536, which lasted forty days. The performance was usually on a large outdoor stage, using the principle of "simultaneous décor," that is, with all the scenes disposed in various places about the stage and each being used as required. Paradise was always placed at a higher level, and it was here that the singers and players were stationed, whence the hauntingly beautiful recurrent phrase in the stage directions, "Adoncques se doit resonner une melodye en Paradis" (Now shall a melody be sounded in Paradise). The middle level was for Earth, and there might be a still lower stage to represent Hell. The walls of Jerusalem, Herod's palace, Noah's Ark, the hill of Golgotha, the Garden of Eden, limbo, purgatory, and scores of other scenes were represented. All the miracles had to be shown visibly: descents and ascents of angels, Lucifer on a fire-breathing dragon, Aaron's rod blossoming, the souls of Herod and Judas carried off by dev-

---

9. For the other Italian names for these pieces, and a general account of them in Italy, see D'Ancona, *Origini del teatro italiano*, 1:370ff.; Becherini, "La musica nell 'Sacre rappresentazioni' Florentine"; and the examples in Bartholomaeis, ed., *Laude drammatiche*; D'Ancona, *Sacre rappresentazioni*; Bonfantini, *Le sacre rappresentazioni italiane*.

10. Modern edition by Rothschild, *Le Mistère du Viel Testament*.

ils, water changed to wine, eclipses, earthquakes, the Deluge, even tortures and beheadings took place on the stage.[11] The juxtaposition of sacred scenes and crude displays no longer gives the impression of naïve piety, as in the liturgical dramas, but rather of almost blasphemous incongruity; the large number of characters and the grotesque, disorderly crowding of episodes make of the mysteries a typically Gothic spectacle, reminiscent of the sprawling confusion of incidents and personages in the medieval epics and romances. There were also comic insertions, improvised antics or farces, often of an indecent nature. Finally, the mysteries went so far as to permit mockery of the church and priests and the introduction of pagan deities on the stage. The awakened conscience of the church, together with the revival of classic ideals of the drama, eventually led to the condemnation of the mysteries on both moral and aesthetic grounds. By the end of the sixteenth century they were virtually extinct, though some remnants of the medieval love of profusion and grotesquerie survived in the operas and ballets of the seventeenth century.

Music in the mysteries was less extensive than in the liturgical dramas. In most cases its function was incidental, and since little of it has come down to us we learn of its existence only by references in the stage directions and from other indirect sources. Hymns and other parts of the liturgy were sung, as in the *Mystery of the Resurrection* (fifteenth century), where at the moment when Christ descends into Hell all the spirits sing "Veni creator spiritus."[12] Most of these selections were probably simple plainsong, but there were occasionally pieces in polyphonic style. In the *Mystery of the Passion* (Angiers, 1486), the voice of God is represented by three singers, soprano, tenor, and bass[13]—this doubtless being intended to symbolize the Trinity. Sometimes the angels in Paradise sing three-part motets, as in the *Mystery of the*

11. Dr. Charles Burney describes a scene of this kind which he witnessed in the performance of a popular mystery play near Florence in 1770 (*The Present State of Music in France and Italy*, entry for Tuesday, September 4).

12. Jubinal, *Mystères inédits du quinzième siècle*, 2:339.

13. "Et est à noter que la loquence de Dieu le père se doit pronuncer entendiblement et bien atraict en trois voix cest assavoir une hault dessus, une hault contre et une basse contre bien accordées et en cest armonie se doit dire toute la clause qui s'ensuit . . ." Quoted in Cohen, *Histoire de la mise en scène*, p. 140, from a 1491 edition of *La Passion de Jean Michel*.

Incarnation (Rouen, 1474). In addition to music of this kind, the mysteries included popular airs, in the singing of which the audience joined. In Germany, where the Nativity plays were especially cultivated, one such song was the well-known "In dulci jubilo."[14]

There was also a considerable amount of instrumental music in the mysteries. Before the performance there would be a procession *(monstre)* through the town, with music by pipe and tabor. Entrances of important personages were announced by a *silete*, similar to the "flourish of trumpets" in Shakespeare. Instrumental music accompanied the procession of the actors to a different scene on the stage. Angels played concerts of harps—or rather pretended to play them while musicians concealed behind the scenes furnished the music. Instruments were also played for dancing: in the *Mystery of the Passion*, Herod's daughter dances a *moresca* to the accompaniment of a tambourine; in Italy we learn of morescas, galliards, pavanes, and many other dances in these spectacles, which frequently concluded with a general dance. For the monstre of the *Mystery of the Acts of the Apostles*, there was an orchestra of flutes, harps, lutes, rebecs, and viols. Trumpets, *bucinae*, bagpipes, cornemuses, drums, and organs are also mentioned; in the *Mystery of the Passion*, the march of Jesus to the temple is accompanied by "a soft thunder of one of the large organ pipes," and in the *Mystery of the Resurrection*, the descent of the Holy Ghost is similarly signalized.[15]

There was at least one mystery in which music, instead of being merely incidental, was used throughout. This was the *Festa d'Elche*, a Spanish mystery performed in the sixteenth century, which had instrumental pieces, unaccompanied plainsong solos, and a number of three- and four-part choruses by the Spanish composers Ribera, Pérez, and Lluis Vich.[16] This instance of continuous music in the mysteries is probably not unique. Some of the Italian rappresentazioni sacre and similar pieces of the fifteenth century seem to have been sung throughout.[17]

---

14. Moser, *Geschichte der deutschen Musik*, 1:320; Hoffman von Fallersleben, *In dulci jubilo.*

15. Cohen, *Histoire de la mise en scène*, pp. 136, 159.

16. Ambros, *Geschichte der Musik*, p. 274; Pedrell, "La Festa d'Elche"; Trend, "The Mystery of Elche."

17. Rolland, *Musiciens d'autrefois*, p. 24; Becherini, "La musica nelle 'Sacre rappresentazioni' Fiorentine."

The medieval liturgical dramas and mysteries, although they did not lead directly into the opera, are more than merely isolated precursors of the form. The Italian rappresentazioni sacre were the models from which the first pastoral dramas with music were derived. We shall have occasion later to see how the traditions and practices of such works manifest themselves in some of the operas of the seventeenth century. But their music was completely unsuited to modern dramatic expression. The immediate predecessors of the opera must be sought in the secular theater of the late Middle Ages and the Renaissance.

Secular Dramatic Music

Aside from the dramas of antiquity, the earliest known secular play which used music extensively is Adam de la Halle's *Le jeu de Robin et de Marion*, performed probably at the court of the king of Naples in 1283 or 1284.[18] Although this work is sometimes called

Example 2.1: *Le jeu de Robin et de Marion*

18. Adam de la Halle, *Œuvres complètes*, edited by Coussemaker (1872). (Other modern editions by Langlois [1896], Cohen [1935], Varty [1960], and Gennrich [1962]. See also Guy, *Essai sur la vie et les oeuvres littéraires du trouvère Adan de la Hale*; Axton, comp., *Medieval French Plays*.

the first *opéra comique*, it actually has no historical connection with the later genre, and indeed differs in no way from other *pastourelles* of its period, except that Adam chose to omit the customary narrative portions and make it simply a little pastoral comedy, in which the spoken dialogue is interspersed with a number of short songs or refrains, dances, and some instrumental music. It is probable that Adam himself wrote neither the words nor the music of the songs, but simply selected them from a current common repertoire.[19] Their charmingly naïve character is illustrated in example 2.1.

Le jeu de Robin et de Marion is an early example of the use of chansons in a dramatic framework. Chansons, for the most part of popular nature and uncertain origin, were frequently inserted in moralities, farces, *sotties*, and like entertainments of the fifteenth and early sixteenth centuries in France.[20]

19. Chailley, "La Nature musicale du *Jeu de Robin et Marion*."

20. Brown, *Music in the French Secular Theater, 1400–1550*; Cohen, ed. *Recueil de farces françaises inédites du XVe siècle*.

CHAPTER THREE

The Immediate Forerunners
of Opera

With the coming of the Renaissance, interest in all forms of secular music increased. Throughout the fifteenth and sixteenth centuries, music was a feature of courtly entertainments, banquets, tourneys, festivals, triumphal entrances, and similar brilliant occasions.[1] This music cannot properly be called "dramatic," since it did not serve to carry on the action of a drama; nevertheless, its connection with the history of opera is important, for these courtly displays of the Renaissance established the practice of bringing together many different artistic resources—singing, playing, dancing, scenery, costumes, stage effects—in a single spectacle calculated to appeal equally to the eye, the ear, and the imagination. Scenes of this kind, nondramatic displays with accompaniment of music, came into opera very early in the seventeenth century and have remained characteristic of opera ever since. In the sixteenth century the most important of the many types of entertainment in which music served were the ballet and the *intermedio*.

The Ballet

The ancestor of the ballet was the masquerade (French *mascarade*, Italian *mascherata*, English masque). Originally a popular

1. See Nolhac and Solerti, *Il viaggio in Italia di Enrico III, re di Francia* [1574], for some notable instances. Comparatively little of this music has been preserved; some examples are published in Ghisi, *Feste musicali della Firenze Medicea*. A comprehensive general treatment of all this pre-operatic music is in Ambros, *Geschichte der Musik*, pp. 161–346.

spectacle associated with carnival time, the Italian *mascherata* had developed into a favorite court amusement, which was imitated by the French and English in the sixteenth century. The French *mascarades* frequently formed part of the ceremonies of welcome to a distinguished personage, as on the occasion of a visit of Charles IX to Bar-le-Duc in 1564, when actors representing the four elements, the four planets, and various allegorical and mythological personages, including the god Jupiter, united in a sumptuous ceremony of homage to the king. *Mascarades* of this sort later became the models for the French opera prologues. By the sixteenth century, as these *mascarades* show, aristocratic poetry had taken over the whole panoply of ancient pagan deities, demigods, nymphs, satyrs, and heroes, together with scores of figures from the pages of medieval epics and romances; all these were freely introduced on the stage, usually more lavishly than logically. In those *mascarades* where the purpose was the entertainment of an entire company rather than the complimenting of an illustrious guest, dancing was the chief attraction, and it was from *mascarades* of this sort that the characteristic French form of the ballet was derived. The English masque, somewhat similar to the *mascarade*, developed later in the sixteenth century, and its heyday was the time of James I and Charles I (1603–1649).

The French word *ballet* comes from the Italian *balletto*, the diminutive of *ballo* (dance). The most famous ballet of the period was *Circe ou le Balet comique de la royne*, which was performed at the Petit-Bourbon palace in Paris, October 15, 1581, on the occasion of the marriage of Mademoiselle de Vaudemont, the queen's sister, to the Duc de Joyeuse. A complete account of this incredibly lavish production (it cost the equivalent of nearly half a million dollars) was published with the score in the following year.[2] The principal author and director, Balthasar de Beaujoyeulx, explains in his introduction that the word "comique" refers to the fact that here for the first time an attempt was made

---

2. Beaujoyeulx et al., *Circe ou le Balet comique de la royne*, Paris, 1582; facsimile editions by MacClintock and McGowan. See also Yates, *The French Academies*, chap. 11; idem, "Poésie et musique pour les magnificences"; Anthony, *French Baroque Music*; McGowan, *L'Art du ballet de cour*; Christout, *Le Ballet de cour de Louis* XIV; Donington, *The Rise of Opera*; Demuth, *French Opera*. (On the importance of the Beaujoyeulx edition for an understanding of the Valois tapestries, see Yates, *The Valois Tapestries*.)

Scene from *Circe ou le Balet comique de la royne* (Paris 1581).

(Niessen, *Das Bühnenbild*)

to unify all the elements of the ballet by means of a coherent plot
(comédie), a simple dramatic framework which gave occasion for
the introduction of many different stage settings and dances. Slight
as it was, this introduction of a dramatic action into the ballet
might have led at once to the creation of French opera if only the
musicians had undertaken to solve the problem of setting dramatic dialogue, thereby making continuous music possible. But
neither their interest nor that of their audiences lay in this direction. The dramatic ballet survived for a few decades in France,
but by 1620 all pretense of a unified plot was abandoned, and the
ballet reverted to a mere diversified spectacle for the amusement
of the court.

The music for *Circe* was by Lambert de Beaulieu and
Jacques Salmon. It consists of six choruses, two dialogues with
choral refrains, two solos, and two sets of instrumental dances.
The choruses are strictly homophonic and rather dull, partly because their musical rhythm is slavishly bound to that of the words,
with long and short notes for the "long" and "short" syllables
according to the principles of *musique measurée à l'antique*. The
bass solos, as was customary in the period, simply follow the bass
of the harmony. Some of the soprano airs are highly ornamented—a style of writing frequently found in solo madrigals and
also used by Monteverdi for one aria in his *Orfeo*. The most in-

Example 3.1: *Circe ou le Balet comique de la royne*

teresting pieces are the dances, with their formal, stately, geo-
metrical rhythms. One of them, "Le Son de la clochette," is still
played today (example 3.1).

Both the ballet and the masque exercised a strong influence on the formation of the respective French and English national operas, as we shall see later.

The Intermedio

In such pieces as the masquerades and ballets, the function of
music was essentially that of adjunct to a visual spectacle. There
is another class of sixteenth-century works in which the role of
music was to offer diversion in connection with a regular spoken
play. As is well known, one of the features of the Renaissance was
the revival of secular drama. The movement began in Italy toward
the end of the fifteenth century with performances of Latin plays,
in the original or in translation, under courtly auspices, at various centers, of which Ferrara, Rome, Florence, Mantua, and
Venice were particularly prominent. Many new plays were written, in Latin or Italian, imitating classical models. Practically all
these plays made use of music to some extent, though often in a
subordinate, decorative fashion.[3] There were occasional solos or
duets, choruses (these especially in tragedies based on Greek originals), madrigals, and instrumental pieces.

The general tendency was to separate the musical numbers from the play itself by placing them in the prologue and at
the ends of the acts, so that each appeared as an *intermedio*, that
is, something "intermediate" in the action of the play. Their subjects were, as a rule, connected in some allegorical way with the
subject of the drama: "that which is enacted by the Gods in the
fable of the Intermedii, is likewise enacted—as it were, under
constraint of a higher power—by the mortals in the comedy."[4]

3. See Rubsamen, *Literary Sources of Secular Music*, chap. 6; Einstein, *The Italian Madrigal*, pp. 161, 234, 250, 283ff., 301, 550, and passim.

4. Il Lasca, forword to the *intermedi Psyche ed Amore*, reprinted in Sonneck, *Miscellaneous Studies*, pp. 269–86, and in *MA* (1911), 3:40–53.

On especially festive occasions, such as princely marriages, the *intermedi* might be very elaborate. Those performed at Florence in 1539 at the marriage of Cosimo I and Eleonora of Toledo, with music by Francesco Corteccia (1502–1571), included three solo songs and four madrigals for four to eight voices with varied instrumental accompaniment.[5] The *intermedi* by Corteccia and Alessandro Striggio for Francesco d'Ambra's *La cofanaria* (Florence, 1565) had solos, madrigals, and other ensemble pieces, with accompaniments by large and varied orchestral groups.[6] Striggio's *intermedi* for *L'amico fido* (Florence, 1569) were presented with a pomp of staging and music that foreshadowed many seventeenth-century operas.[7] Other composers of *intermedi* include Alfonso della Viola (Giraldi's *Orbecche*, Ferrara, 1541, and several others), Antonio dal Cornetto (Giraldi's *Eglè*, Ferrara, 1545), and Claudio Merulo (Dolce's *Marianna*, Venice, 1565, *Troiana*, 1566, and others). Andrea Gabrieli's settings of four of the choruses in an Italian translation of Sophocles' *Oedipus Rex* (Vicenza, 1585) were long famous.[8]

Perhaps the most elaborate *intermedi* of the sixteenth century were those for Girolamo Bargagli's comedy *La pellegrina*, performed at Florence in May 1589 as part of the festivities for the wedding of Grand Duke Ferdinand de' Medici and Christine of Lorraine.[9] The six intermedi were planned by Count Giovanni Bardi; some of the texts were by Ottavio Rinuccini, and the music was by several different composers, including Luca Marenzio, Emilio de' Cavalieri, and Cristofano Malvezzi.[10] Forty-one of the

---

5. See Schering, "Zur Geschichte des begleiteten Sologesangs" and *Aufführungspraxis alter Musik*, p. 67. See also Pirrotta, *Music and Theatre*, pp. 154–69, for musical examples of the *intermedi* by F. Corteccia for Landi's *Il commodo*.

6. Sonneck, *Miscellaneous Studies*, pp. 276–86. Pirrotta, *Music and Theatre*, p. 176, considers the six *intermedi* for *La cofanaria* to represent the first known instance in which a single plot pervades all of them.

7. See description by Balduccini in Ambros, *Geschichte der Musik*, pp. 245–51.

8. See Schrade, *La Représentation d' "Edipo Tiranno" au Teatro Olimpico*.

9. See Solerti, *Musica, ballo e drammatica alla corte Medicea*, pp. 12–22; idem, *Gli albori del melodramma*, 2:15–42; *Atti dell' accademia del R. Istituto musicale di Firenze* (1895), pp. 103ff.; Einstein, *The Italian Madrigal*, p. 730. The two principal source documents differ in some details as to the composers.

10. Unlike most sixteenth-century *intermedi*, the music of these was printed (Venice, 1591). See *Les Fêtes du mariage* for the music that was originally printed by Malvezzi in Venice.

most celebrated musicians of the time took part in the performance. There were five- and six-part madrigals, double and triple
choruses, and a final madrigal calling for seven different vocal
ensembles in a total of thirty parts, each part sung by two voices.
These songs were accompanied by various groups of instruments,
which also played a number of "sinfonie." The orchestra included
organs, lutes, lyres, harps, viols, trombones, cornetts,[11] and other
instruments, used in different combinations for each number.[12]
Three of the six solos are in ordinary madrigal style, with the
lower voices played on instruments. The others exemplify the florid
solo style of the sixteenth century, the voice ornamenting a melodic line which is given simultaneously in unornamented form in
the accompaniment. Example 3.2, for soprano with accompaniment of a *chitarrone* (bass lute), is by Cavalieri.

   With *intermedi* on such a scale as this, we can well imagine that the audience must have had little attention to give to the
play itself, and this was no doubt often the case with such performances in Italy in the sixteenth century. "For the majority of the
audience the dances and pageants formed the chief attraction. It
is therefore no marvel if the drama, considered as a branch of
high poetic art, was suffocated by the growth of its mere accesso-
ries."[13]

Example 3.2: *Intermedio VI*

11. The cornett (Italian *cornetto*, German *Zinke*) is not to be confused with the modern
cornet. See "Cornett," *The New Grove Dictionary*, 4:788.

12. This instrumentation is similar to that found in Monteverdi's *Orfeo*; for a comparison
of the two, see the table in chap. 5. See also Ghisi, "L'orchestra in Monteverdi," and
Beat, "Monteverdi and the Opera Orchestra of His Time."

13. Symonds, *Renaissance in Italy*, 2:143.

(Example 3.2 continued)

It must not be imagined that the coming of opera at once put an end to the *intermedi* and similar spectacles. On the contrary, they remained popular at Italian courts well into the seventeenth century; the opera gradually took over many features of the earlier form and eventually supplanted it. The *intermedio* is important as a forerunner of opera for two reasons: first, because it kept alive in the minds of Italian poets and musicians the idea of close collaboration between drama and music; and second, because in these works, as in the French dramatic ballet, the external form of the future opera is already outlined—a drama with interludes of music and with dancing, splendid scenery, and spectacular stage effects. As soon as the drama itself could be set to music and sung instead of spoken, opera would be achieved.

It is evident that the theater music of the sixteenth century, far from being a mere tentative and imperfect experiment, was a well-developed, essential feature of the entire Renaissance movement. The academies of Italy and France quite naturally interested themselves in music as one aspect of their interest in the revival of ancient art and letters. The texts of the ballets and *intermedi* imply a degree of familiarity with Greek mythology on the part of their audiences which is hardly conceivable at the present day; and mingled with this, as a heritage from the Middle Ages, is a pervasive, subtle use of allegory and personification. Yet these works were not intended only for the erudite. They were a common part of the luxurious, pleasure-loving court life of cultivated persons. Princes and nobles, poets, painters, and musicians, amateur and professional alike, all participated in their composition and performed in them side by side. The music itself, as has been said, was not dramatic; all the action and passion of the drama were in spoken dialogue, leaving for music only the adornment of the spectacular, reflective, or lyrical scenes. But in these, the important musical forms of the sixteenth century found their place: instrumental dances, airs, madrigals, choruses, chansons, canzonets—everything that music had to offer, with one notable exception: the learned contrapuntal art of the Netherlanders. By the last decade of the sixteenth century, Europe was on the verge of opera. It remained only to transform the relation between drama and music from a mere association into an organic union. For this end, two things were necessary: a kind of drama which should be suitable for continuous music, and a kind of music capable of dramatic expression. The former was found in the pastorale, and the latter in the monodic recitative of the Florentine composers Jacopo Peri (1561–1633) and Giulio Caccini (1546–1618).

The Pastorale

Toward the middle of the sixteenth century, the pastorale began to displace all other types of dramatic poetry in Italy.[14] So complete did its dominance become that Angelo Ingegneri, the foremost writer on the theater in the latter part of the century, remarked that "if it were not for the pastorales, it might almost be said that the theater was extinct."[15] A dramatic pastorale is a poem, lyric in substance but dramatic in form, intended for either reading or stage presentation, with shepherds, shepherdesses, and sylvan deities for the chief characters, and with a background of fields, forests, or other idyllic and pleasant scenes of nature. The dramatic action is restricted to mild love adventures and a few incidents arising out of the circumstances of pastoral life, and it usually ends happily. The attraction of the pastorale consisted, therefore, not in the plot but in the scenes and moods, the sensuous charm of the language, and the delicately voluptuous imagery, at which the Italian Renaissance poets excelled. The sources of the pastoral ideal lay partly in literary studies (Theocritus, Vergil), but it was redeemed from affectation by the sincere and profound Italian feeling for the beauties of "nature humanized by industry."

The vision of a Golden Age idealized man's actual enjoyment of the country, and hallowed, as with inexplicable pathos, the details of ordinary rustic life. Weary with courts and worldly pleasures, in

14. Three works dealing with the history of this genre are Guarini, *Compendio della poesia tragicomica;* Crescimbeni, *Commentarii intorno all' "Istoria della Poesia Italiana";* and Greg, *Pastoral Poetry.* See also Harris, *Handel and the Pastoral Tradition.*

15. Ingegneri, *Della poesia rappresentativa,* p. 8.

moments of revolt against the passions and ambitions that wasted their best energies, the poets of that century, who were nearly always also men of state and public office, sighed for the good old times, when honor was an unknown name, and truth was spoken, and love sincere, and steel lay hidden in the earth, and ships sailed not the sea, and old age led the way to death unterrified by coming doom. As time advanced, their ideal took form and substance. There rose into existence, for the rhymesters to wander in, and for the readers of romance to dream about, a region called Arcadia, where all that was imagined of the Golden Age was found in combination with refined society and manners proper to the civil state.[16]

One of the earliest pastoral plays is *La favola d'Orfeo*, by Angelo Poliziano. Based upon Ovid's *Metamorphoses*,[17] this play was performed sometime between 1471 and 1480 at Mantua,[18] with music consisting of at least three solo songs and one chorus, interspersed with the spoken dialogue.[19] It is a relatively short work, consisting of some 400 lines, and adheres closely to its Ovidian model.

The pastoral poem was firmly established by Sannazaro's *Arcadia* (1504), but the real beginning of the pastoral drama is usually dated from the performance of Agostino Beccari's *Il Sacrificio d'Abramo* at Ferrara in 1554. The music of this work, by Alfonso della Viola, has been reprinted.[20] In the third scene of Act III occurs a strophic monologue for bass, with a choral refrain. The solo part is a kind of psalmodic recitative on the bass

16. Symonds, *Renaissance in Italy*, 2:196–97 (paraphrased in part from the closing chorus of Act I of Tasso's *Aminta*, which in turn is paraphrased from Ovid's *Metamorphoses* 1, verses 89–112).

17. Ovid (43 B.C.–17 A.D.), a Roman poet, wrote *Metamorphoses* between 1 and 8 A.D. It is a long poem subdivided into a series of stories suitable for dramatic presentation. The Ovidian story of *Orfeo* forms the basis for many opera librettos, beginning with Rinuccini's *Orfeo* of 1600.

18. Four possible dates for performance—1471, 1472, 1474, and 1480—are mentioned by Pirrotta, *Li due Orfei*, p. 5. Donington, *The Rise of Opera*, p. 32, writes that *Orfeo* was performed "probably in 1478 (rather than in 1472 as previously supposed but certainly no later than 1483)." Sternfeld, "The Birth of Opera," states that Poliziano's *Orfeo* was performed first in 1480, printed in 1494, and reprinted up until 1600.

19. Poliziano, *Le stanze, l'Orfeo e le rime*, pp. 369–507; see also Symonds, *Renaissance in Italy*, 1:409–15, and Henderson, *Some Forerunners of the Italian Opera*, chaps. 4–9.

20. For an edition of all the extant music, see Kaufman, "Music for a Favola Pastorale (1554)." See also Solerti, "Precedenti del melodramma" and *Gli albori del melodramma*, 1:12–13.

Example 3.3: *Il Sacrificio d'Abramo*

ALFONSO DELLA VIOLA

Tu c'haile cor-na ri-guar-dan-iil cie-lo Fis-se ne l'am-pia fronte. e spa-ci-o-sa

Refrain:

O Pan Li - ce - o, O Pan Li - ce - o!

notes of the harmonies, which were undoubtedly filled in (perhaps improvised) by a lute or similar instrument (example 3.3).

The finest examples of the pastorale, and indeed two of the most beautiful poems in all sixteenth-century Italian literature, are Torquato Tasso's *Aminta* (Ferrara, 1573) and Battista Guarini's *Il pastor fido* (written at Ferrara between 1581 and 1590).[21] The pastorales lent themselves naturally to musical treatment not only because of their preponderantly lyric content, their brevity, and their use of choruses, songs, and dances, but also because of the very language, "flowery and sweet . . . so that one may even admit that it has melody in its every part, since there are shown deities, nymphs, and shepherds from that most remote age when music was natural and speech like poetry."[22] In *Aminta*, the words are hovering on the edge of song at every moment; every phrase is filled with that unheard music which Tasso himself called "the sweetness and, so to speak, the soul of poetry."[23] Tasso, like all the Italian artists and poets of his time, was an amateur of music and particularly admired Gesualdo, who made settings of a number of his madrigals. He was a friend of Cavalieri, who composed the incidental music for a performance of

21. See Solerti, *Vita di Torquato Tasso*; Brand, *Torquato Tasso*; Neri, "Gli intermezzi del *Pastor fido*." On the significance of Ferrara and the ducal family of the Este in the history of Italian sixteenth-century music, see Solerti, ed., *Ferrara e la corte Estense*.

22. Doni, "Trattato della musica scenica," chap. 6, quoted in Solerti, ed., *Le origini del melodramma*, p. 203.

23. "La dolcezza, e quasi l'anima della poesia." Tasso, *Dialoghi* 3:111.

Aminta at Florence in 1590.[24] Rinuccini, the librettist of the first operas, was a disciple of Tasso, and his poems *Dafne* and *Euridice*, as well as Striggio's *Orfeo* (set by Monteverdi in 1607) and many of the other early operas, are simply pastorales on the model of Tasso's and Guarini's works.

> Great tragedy and great comedy were denied to the Italians. But they produced a novel species in the pastoral drama, which testified to their artistic originality, and led by natural transitions to the opera. Poetry was on the point of expiring; but music was rising to take her place. And the imaginative medium prepared by the lyrical scenes of the Arcadian play, afforded just that generality and aloofness from actual conditions of life, which were needed by the new art in its first dramatic essays. . . . *Aminta* and *Pastor fido* . . . complete and close the Renaissance, bequeathing in a new species of art its form and pressure to succeeding generations.[25]

The Madrigal Comedy

In studies of sixteenth-century Italian music as a whole, attention is usually concentrated on two fields: the sacred polyphonic music stemming from the Netherlands tradition and brought to its culmination by Palestrina, and the polyphonic madrigal, represented at its height by Marenzio, Gesualdo, and Monteverdi. With the great body of sixteenth-century church music, the history of opera has simply nothing to do. With the madrigal, however, the case is different. The experiments of the latter part of the century include a number of works now known as madrigal comedies, which represent attempts to adapt the madrigal to dramatic requirements.[26] The most famous of these was Orazio Vecchi's *L'Amfi-*

---

24. The music of two other pastorales by this composer—*Il satiro* and *La disperazione di Fileno* (Florence, 1590)—has not been preserved. According to Doni ("Trattato della musica scenica," chap. 9), the pastorales were not in recitative style.

25. Symonds, *Renaissance in Italy*, 2:241, 245.

26. A famous predecessor of these works, Striggio's *Cicalamento delle donne* (1567), is reprinted in Solerti, "Primi saggi del melodramma giocoso."

parnaso, published in 1597.[27] *L'Amfiparnaso* was not staged, but only sung as a madrigal cycle. Vecchi's pupil, Adriano Banchieri, in the preface to his madrigal comedy *La saviezza giovanile* (1598), gives directions which indicate that in this work the singers and players were placed behind the scenes, while the actors on the stage mimed their parts. (It is not clear whether there was also spoken dialogue by the actors.) *L'Amfiparnaso* and similar works show clearly in their plots, character types (Pantalone, Pedrolino, Isabella, and the like), and use of dialect their derivation from the *commedia dell' arte*.[28] In *L'Amfiparnaso* there are eleven dialogues and three monologues, the same kind of musical setting being used for all—namely, five-part (one four-part) madrigal ensembles. In the monologues, all five voices sing; in the dialogues, the differentiation of persons is commonly suggested by contrasting the three highest with the three lowest voices (the *quinto* or middle part being in both groups), though at times all five are used even here. The music of the comic characters is mostly in simple note-against-note style, with a fine sense of the animation of comic dialogue. On the other hand, some of the five-voice pieces are beautiful examples of the serious Italian madrigal style.

The madrigal comedies were an early attempt to combine farce comedy with music, to exploit the lively, popular commedia dell' arte as against the languid, aristocratic pastorales. But they were suites of madrigals, not theater music. So far as their contribution to opera is concerned, their chief usefulness may have been to prove that madrigals alone were not suitable for dramatic purposes. It has even been surmised that Vecchi intended *L'Amfiparnaso* (the title has been freely translated "The Lower Slopes of Parnassus") as a satire on the early attempts at operatic music. In the hands of Banchieri and other later composers, the madrigal comedies soon declined and eventually disappeared.

---

27. For a new edition, with important introductory essays, see Vecchi, *L'Amfiparnaso*, edited by Adkins. See also Dent, "The *Amfiparnaso*"; idem, "Notes on the *Amfiparnaso*'; Hol, "Horatio Vecchi et l'évolution créatrice"; Camillucci, "*L'Amfiparnaso*"; Ronga, "Lettura storica dell' *Amfiparnaso*."

28. Beginning with the early decades of the sixteenth century, the term "commedia dell' arte" refers to plays performed by professional *comici dell' arte*. These plays had *scenari* (plot-outlines), stock characters, and a mode of performance involving masks and improvisation. See Apollonio, *Storia della commedia dell' arte*; Nicoll, *The Development of the Theatre*; Pirrotta, "Commedia dell' arte."

The Florentine "Camerata"
and the Monodic Recitative

There can be no doubt that the first composers of dramatic recitative at Florence toward the end of the sixteenth century believed that they were renewing a musical practice of the ancient
Greeks and that, in so doing, they were accomplishing something
of revolutionary importance. Yet the mere singing of solos to instrumental accompaniment was nothing revolutionary. Even in the
performance of polyphonic madrigals, it was not uncommon for
one part to be sung while the others were played, perhaps by the
singer himself, in a simplified version on a lute. The prevalence
of solo singing in sixteenth-century Italy has the character of a
national reaction against the Netherlands polyphony, which had
been implanted there in the early part of the century. It is a manifestation of certain deep-rooted Italian traits which have remained constant throughout the musical history of that nation: an
aversion to complexity and obscurity, a profound feeling for melody as constituting the essence of music, and (this partly as a
result of the whole mental attitude of the Renaissance) a preference for the individual artist as against the communal group represented by the church choir or the madrigal vocal ensemble.

It is a fact provable by many examples in the history of
music that the establishment of a new practice, particularly if it
be in conflict with an older practice, sooner or later calls forth a
theory by which the new practice is sought to be justified. In the
present case, the development of the theory, as well as its practical applications, was the work of scholars, poets, musicians, and
amateurs in Florence who, from the late 1560s until the early
1600s, organized themselves into groups and academies. One group,
commonly known as the "Florentine Camerata," had as its leading spirit Count Giovanni Bardi di Vernio (1534–1612), a distinguished patron of arts and letters, in whose house the members
met.[29] Among them was Vincenzo Galilei (ca. 1532–1591), father

---

29. Martin, "La 'Camerata' du Comte Bardi"; Pirrotta, "Temperaments and Tendencies
in the Florentine Camerata"; idem, "Tragédie et comédie dans la 'Camerata fiorentina' ";
Palisca, "Girolamo Mei."

of the famous astronomer and himself a singer and a composer of lute music and madrigals.[30] Galilei, having become interested in the study of ancient Greek music, applied for enlightenment on certain questions to a Roman scholar, Girolamo Mei (1519–1594). In a series of letters and conversations between 1572 and 1581, Mei communicated to Galilei his discoveries and conclusions about Greek music and musical theory.[31] Galilei embodied these in a "Dialogue about Ancient and Modern Music," published under his own name at Florence in 1581, a work containing, among other matters, an explicit "declaration of war against counterpoint."[32]

In the writings of Galilei, Caccini, and other members of the Florentine Camerata, the theory of the "new music" was developed.[33] Since the music is to some extent a result of the theory, it will be well to outline the latter before proceeding to a study of the music itself. Like most Renaissance philosophers, the Camerata appealed for authority to the ancient Greeks. But the actual Greek music was unknown to them; Galilei had published three examples in his *Dialogo* but had not been able to transcribe them. Consequently, it was necessary to deduce the character of the music from such writings of the ancients as were available. Long study and discussion of these writings led to the formulation of a basic principle, namely, that the secret of Greek music lay in the perfect union of words and melody, a union to be achieved by making the former dominate and control the latter. "Plato and other philosophers . . . declare that music is none other than words and rhythm, and sound last of all, and not the reverse."[34] From this principle three corollaries followed.

First, *the text must be clearly understood.* Therefore, the performance must be by a solo voice with the simplest possible accompaniment, preferably a lute or similar instrument played by the singer himself. There must be no contrapuntal writing, for

---

30. See Fano, ed., *La camerata fiorentina: Vincenzo Galilei*; Palisca, "Vincenzo Galilei and . . . Monody."

31. The letters are published in Palisca, *Girolamo Mei*.

32. Galilei, *Dialogo*; excerpts in Strunk, ed., *Source Readings*, pp. 302–22.

33. For a list of these writings, see Ambros, *Geschichte der Musik*, p. 292, n. 1. The most important documents are reprinted in Solerti, ed., *Le origini del melodramma*.

34. Caccini, foreword to *Le nuove musiche* (Solerti, ed., *Le origini del melodramma*, p. 56); entire foreword translated in Strunk, ed., *Source Readings*, pp. 377–92.

this distracts the mind and produces confusion, owing to different words being heard at the same time with different rhythms in different parts, leading to distortion of pronunciation (in Caccini's phrase, "laceramento della poesia") and in general appealing not to the intelligence at all but only to the sense of hearing. (This wholesale condemnation of counterpoint was due rather to the exigencies of the theory than to ignorance or lack of appreciation and need not be taken altogether seriously.)

The second corollary was that *the words must be sung with correct and natural declamation*, as they would be spoken, avoiding on the one hand the regular dancelike meters of popular songs such as the villanelle, and on the other the textual repetitions and subservience to contrapuntal necessities found in madrigal and motet writing. Caccini writes:

> The idea came to me to introduce a kind of music whereby people could as it were speak in tones *[in armonia favellare]*, using therein . . . a certain noble negligence of melody *[sprezzatura di canto]*, now and then running over some dissonant tones *[false]*, but holding firmly to the chord in the bass.[35]

Peri is even more explicit:

> I believe that the ancient Greeks and Romans (who, according to the opinion of many, sang their tragedies throughout) used a kind of music more advanced than ordinary speech, but less than the melody of singing, thus taking a middle position between the two.[36]

The third and final corollary had to do with the relation between music and words: *The melody must not depict mere graphic details in the text but must interpret the feeling of the whole passage*, by imitating and intensifying the intonations and accents proper to the voice of a person who is speaking the words under the influence of the emotion which gives rise to them.[37] This

---

35. Caccini, *Le nuove musiche*. Similarly, in the dedicatory letter to his *Euridice*, Caccini writes: "Nella quale maniere di canto, ho io usata una certa sprezzatura, che io ho stimato, che habbia del nobile, parendomi conessi di essermi appressato quel più alla natural favella." The entire letter is translated in Strunk, ed., *Source Readings*, pp. 370–72.

36. Peri, foreword to *Euridice*, printed in Solerti, ed., *Le origini del melodramma*, pp. 45–46, and translated in Strunk, ed., *Source readings*, pp. 373–76.

37. Galilei, *Dialogo*, pp. 88–89; Strunk, ed., *Source Readings*, pp. 315–19.

pronouncement was evidently directed against certain aspects of textual treatment in the sixteenth-century madrigals and motets.

It was in these aesthetic principles and their practical consequences, not in the mere employment of the solo voice, that the revolutionary character of the Florentine reform consisted. They formed the necessary foundation for true dramatic music and thus made possible the creation of opera. Tentative experiments in the new style were made by Galilei as early as 1582, when he composed a setting of Ugolino's monologue from Dante's *Inferno* (canto XXIII, verses 4–75), which he sang to the accompaniment of four viols; neither this music nor his setting of part of the Lamentations of Jeremiah from about the same date has been preserved. It seems that the new ideas must have made their way very slowly at first, for no trace of them is to be found in the music of the famous *intermedi* of 1589.

While Count Bardi was playing host to the Camerata, he himself was being stimulated intellectually at the Accademia degli Alterati, a Florentine literary academy founded in 1569.[38] Documents concerning Bardi's association with the Alterati from as early as 1574 reveal his active participation in their scholarly sessions. Many of the topics discussed were the very ones that concerned other groups in Florence, including the Camerata. Thus, it is apparent that no single group or person can claim credit for formulating the theory or theories of the "new music."

In 1592, when Bardi went to Rome, taking Caccini as his secretary, Jacopo Corsi (1561–1602) emerged as the principal patron of the arts in Florence. His name figures prominently in the early history of opera; he was a composer, harpsichordist, member of the Accademia degli Alterati, and leader of an artistic group which frequented his palace. Members of his group included Tasso, Chiabrera, Monteverdi, Rinuccini, and Peri, some of whom were rivals of those in Bardi's Camerata.

Early in 1598, the first opera, *Dafne*—Rinuccini's libretto set to music by Peri, with some parts by Corsi[39]—was played

---

38. Palisca, "The *Alterati* of Florence," p. 15.

39. Marco da Gagliano, in the preface to his *Dafne* (1608), states that Corsi wrote some of the music. Two excerpts by Corsi are extant. See Porter, "Peri and Corsi's *Dafne*."

before a small audience in Corsi's palace, and it was repeated, with changes and additions, for several years thereafter.[40] In view of the great historical interest of this score, it is singularly unfortunate that none of the music has survived, with the exception of a few short excerpts.

The earliest extant examples of Florentine monody are undoubtedly some of the songs in Caccini's *Le nuove musiche*, which, although not published until 1601, were composed at least ten years previously.[41] The collection consists of "arias" and "madrigals" for solo voice with accompaniment of a lute or other stringed instrument. The music is in the *stile recitativo* ("reciting style"), which, unlike the *stile rappresentativo* ("theater style") of the operas,[42] permits a more symmetrical organization of phrases and a certain amount of textual repetition and vocal embellishment—in other words, a free *arioso* type of melody. The arias, which are strophic in form, have simpler and more regular rhythms than the madrigals.

One other early work must be mentioned before going on to a discussion of the first operas. *La rappresentazione di anima e di corpo* ("The Representation of the Soul and the Body"), by Emilio de' Cavalieri (1550–1601), was performed before the Congregazione dell' Oratorio at Rome in 1600. It was one of the first attempts to apply the principle of monody in a sacred composition.[43] The text, with its moralizing purpose and allegorical figures (Soul, Body, Pleasure, Intellect, and the like), shows its connection with the sacred dramas and morality plays of the sixteenth century.[44] The chorus is used more extensively than in the

40. Performances are known to have occurred in 1598 (1597 by the Florentine calendar), 1599, 1600, and 1604. A libretto (no date or publisher, now in the New York Public Library) may have been printed for the 1598 performance. If so, this would be the earliest known printed libretto. Cf. Sternfeld, "The First Printed Libretto."

41. Caccini, *Le nuove musiche*. See also Mantica, ed., *Prime fioriture*, vol. 2.

42. The distinction between "reciting" and "theater" styles was first made explicit about 1635 by Doni, on his "Trattato della musica scenica," chap. 11. (See his *Lyra Barberina* 2:28–30.)

43. In the preface to the *Rappresentazione*, Cavalieri provides instructions for performing sacred dramatic music and pastorales. Presumably, his comments were meant to apply to his own pastorales, which are no longer extant: *Il satiro* (1595), *La disperatione di Fileno* (1598), and *Il giuoco della cieca* (1599).

44. The text was written by Padre Agostino Manni, a disciple of San Filippo Neri; see Alaleona, "Su Emilio de' Cavalieri."

earliest operas, and several of the solo songs are not in monodic recitative but are distinctly tuneful and popular in character. Dances and instrumental interludes also occur. The prologue is spoken; the alternation of speaking and singing, as in the medieval mysteries, remained during the first half of the seventeenth century a characteristic feature of the sacred dramas which flourished at Rome and Florence.[45]

The "new music" immediately found imitators all over Italy and soon spread to other countries. The older contrapuntal art of the sixteenth century did not, of course, disappear; but the first half of the seventeenth century witnessed a gradual modification of the language of music, owing to the interaction of the monodic idea with the contrapuntal principles and to the efforts of composers to find a means of reconciling the two. For a long time they existed side by side. Christoph Bernhard, in his *Tractatus compositionis* (written about 1648), distinguished between the *stylus gravis* or *antiquus* (marked by slow notes, little use of dissonance, "music mistress of poetry") and *stylus luxurians* or *modernus* (some fast notes, unusual skips, more dissonance, more ornamentation, more tuneful melody); the latter in turn he subdivided into *communis*, in which poetry and music were of equal importance, and *theatralis*, in which poetry was the "absolute mistress" of music.[46] The integration of monody with the traditional practices of music and the earliest adaptation of the resultant new style to opera were achieved during the first half of the seventeenth century.

45. For a theoretical justification of this practice, see Doni, "Trattato della musica scenica," chap. 4–6, and the two "lezioni" following chap. 49 of this same work.

46. Müller-Blattau, ed., *Die Kompositionslehre Heinrich Schützens.*

PART II

The Seventeenth Century

CHAPTER FOUR

The Beginnings

The earliest opera of which the music has survived is *Euridice*. Two complete settings of Rinuccini's poem exist, one by Peri and one by Caccini. Peri's version, with some added numbers by Caccini, was performed on October 6, 1600, at the Pitti Palace in Florence as part of the festivities attending the wedding of Henri IV of France and Marie de' Medici;[1] it was published four months later. Caccini's setting was published at about the same time, but not performed in its entirety until 1602.[2] The poem is a pastorale on the myth of Orpheus and Eurydice—a favorite subject for operas, owing not only to the fact that the mythical hero is himself a singer, but also to the combination of a simple action with a variety of emotional situations (love, death, suspense, rescue from danger) and possibilities for striking scenic effects. In the classic version of the myth, it will be remembered, the condition of the rescue of Eurydice from Hades is that Orpheus shall not look back or speak to his wife until they arrive at the upper world; but in his anxiety he looks back, and Eurydice is returned to death irredeemably. Poets have invented all sorts of expedients to avoid this tragic outcome.[3] Rinuccini's solution is simplicity itself: no condition at all is attached to the rescue, and Eurydice is happily restored to life. The divisions of Rinuccini's poem are as follows:

1. Cf. Palisca, "The First Performance of *Euridice*," and Brown, "How Opera Began." See also Brown's edition (1981) of Peri's *Euridice*.

2. See Solerti, *Musica, ballo e drammatica*; Ehrichs, *Giulio Caccini*; and *Atti dell' accademia del R. Istituto musicale di Firenze*; Strunk, ed., *Source Readings*, pp. 363–76; Hanning, *Of Poetry and Music's Power*.

3. Poliziano's *Orfeo* retains the tragic ending.

Prologue. "Tragedy," in a solo of seven strophes, announces the subject and makes flattering allusions to the noble auditors.

Rejoicings. Shepherds and nymphs celebrate the wedding day of Orpheus and Eurydice. Choruses; entrance of Eurydice; at her invitation, all join in a dance ("Al canto, al ballo"). Entrance of Orpheus (solo, "Antri, ch'a miei lamenti") with his friends Arcetro and Tirsi.

Death of Eurydice. As usual in pastoral poetry, this is not enacted on the stage but narrated by a Messenger (represented in Peri's version of 1600 by a boy soprano).

Lamentations. A long scene, beginning with a solo by Orpheus and climaxing in a choral threnody with a recurring phrase ("Sospirate, aure celeste").

Epiphany. Arcetro as Messenger relates how Orpheus in his grief wished to kill himself; but the goddess Venus came down from heaven to console him and encourage him to demand Eurydice from Pluto in Hades.

Descent into Hell (change of scene). After a brief dialogue between Orpheus and Venus, there follows a solo by Orpheus ("Funeste piagge"). Then, supported by some of the deities of Hades, he argues and pleads with Pluto until the latter yields. The scene closes with a solemn antiphonal chorus of the infernal spirits.

Resurrection (return to the opening scene). A Messenger (Aminta) announces the happy return of Orpheus and Eurydice. Solo by Orpheus ("Gioite al canto mio"); closing choruses and dances.

The two versions of Peri and Caccini are similar. Peri is somewhat more forceful in tragic expression, whereas Caccini is more tuneful, excels in elegiac moods, and gives more occasion for virtuoso singing. Neither score has an overture, and there is almost no independent instrumental music. At the first performance of Peri's work, as we learn from his foreword, there were at least four accompanying instruments, placed behind the scenes: a *gravicembalo* (harpsichord), *chitarrone* (bass lute), *lira grande* (large lyre, a bowed chord-instrument with as many as twenty-four strings), and *liuto grosso* (literally "large lute," that is, probably a theorbo).[4] Doubtless these continuo instruments alternated

---

4. For a contemporary commentary upon the musicians who performed Peri's *Euridice*, see Vincenzo Giustiniani, "Discorsi sopra la musica de' suoi tempi," in Solerti, ed., *Le*

or were used in various combinations, making possible a considerable variety of tonal color. What notes did they play? The score gives only the bass, with a few figures, below the melody of the solo part; the exact realization of the bass is a matter about which editors have differed, and it is essential to keep this in mind when dealing with modern editions of early operas.[5] In the case of Peri and Caccini, the probability is that the harmonies were simple, with few nonharmonic tones or chromatics; certainly the basses do not suggest many contrapuntal possibilities in the texture of the inner parts. The bass has no importance as a line, as may be recognized not only by its stationary, harmonic character but also by the absence of any sustaining bass instrument in the orchestra.

The action in both *Euridice* operas is carried on by solo voices in the new Florentine theater style (stile rappresentativo), consisting of a melodic line not so formal as an aria or even an arioso, yet on the other hand not at all like the recitative of eighteenth- and nineteenth-century Italian opera, which is characterized by many repeated notes and an extremely rapid delivery.[6] The operatic monody of Peri and Caccini is different from all these. Its basis is an absolutely faithful adherence to the natural rhythms, accents, and inflections of the text, following it in these respects even to the extent of placing a full cadence regularly at the end of every verse.[7] Occasionally a solo will be given musical form by using the same bass for two or more strophes, and long scenes are commonly unified by means of choral ritornellos. But the prevailing impression in the solo portions is one of almost rhapsodic freedom, as though the melodic line existed solely to add the ultimate fulfillment of song to a poetic language already itself more than half music. Rarely—too rarely—the song will rise to picturesque and pathetic expression, as at the end of the Messenger's narration of the death of Eurydice in Caccini's setting

origini del melodramma; for an English translation by Carol MacClintock, see *MD* (1961), vol. 15, or *MSD* (1962), vol. 9.

5. On the figuring of the basses and their realization in the early monodists, see Arnold, *The Art of Accompaniment from a Thorough-Bass*, chap. 1, secs. 5–8. See also Wellesz, "Die Aussetzung des Basso Continuo"; Torchi, "L'accompagnamento degli istrumenti nei melodrammi italiani"; Goldschmidt, "Die Instrumentalbegleitung."

6. See Neumann, *Die Aesthetik des Rezitativs.*

7. Cf. Paoli, "*Difesa del primo melodramma*," and Pirrotta, "*Early Opera and Aria.*"

Example 4.1: *Euridice*

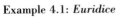

Example 4.2: *Euridice*

(example 4.1) or the heartbroken exclamation of Dafne in Peri's version (example 4.2).

In contrast to the free-rhythmed portions are a few songs in regular meter, either solos or solos alternating with chorus. These songs are in the nature of lyrical interludes in the action; they are placed usually at the ends of scenes, where the effect of dropping into a metrical pattern is similar to the effect produced by a pair of rhymed verses at the end of a scene in Shakespeare, contrasting with the preceding blank verse. One such air is the well-known "Gioite al canto mio" of Peri's setting, sung by Orpheus in the closing scene.

The "chorus"—consisting of probably not more than ten or twelve persons—is on stage during nearly all of the action and plays an important part both dramatically and musically. From time to time it engages in the dialogue, but its principle functions are to lend unity to a scene (as already mentioned) by means of short phrases in refrain and to provide sonorous and animated climaxes, with combined singing and dancing. Such a climax occurs, for example, with the choral ballet "Al canto, al ballo," after the first entrance of Eurydice (example 4.3).

Another notable early opera is the *Dafne* of Marco da Gagliano (1582–1643), founder of the Accademia degli Elevati of Florence in 1607.[8] *Dafne* was first performed at Mantua in 1608, and it was published later that same year. The libretto of this work is adapted from Rinuccini's poem of 1594, which in turn had been taken in part from one of the *intermedi* of 1589. The action is divided into two parts: Apollo slays the Python with his arrows but is himself in turn wounded by the arrows of Love; he vainly pursues the nymph Daphne, who is changed into a laurel tree just as he is about to seize her. The latter episode does not take place on the stage but is narrated by a messenger. The prologue is sung by Ovid, from whose *Metamorphoses* the story is taken. The music is essentially like that of the Florentine monodists, to whose doctrines Gagliano professed adherence, but is more animated in the melodic line and supported by more logical basses and richer harmonies. The free monody occasionally alternates

8. Strainchamps, "New Light on the *Accademia degli Elevati* of Florence." See also Vogel, "Marco da Gagliano."

Example 4.3: *Euridice*

with aria-like sections, and it is possible to see in certain places the outline of the future "recitative and aria" grouping. An "echo song" exemplifies a musical and poetic conceit which long remained popular in opera. Some of the arias have instrumental ritornellos, and there is an instrumental dance (ballo) at the end, as in Peri's *Euridice*. There is no overture, but Gagliano in his

Example 4.4: *Dafne*

preface states that a "sinfonia of the various instruments which accompany the choruses and play the ritornellos" should be played before the prologue—a direction which suggests that similar introductory pieces may have been performed before the earlier operas of Peri and Caccini. The chorus is very prominent in Gagliano's work, sometimes associated with the action and sometimes in purely contemplative passages. Solos, duets, and short instrumental interludes lend variety to the choral numbers. The whole score, in sum, shows abundant musical resources, drawing on the tradition of the old *intermedi* as well as the new monodic recitative. An air with choral refrain is illustrated in example 4.4.

Gagliano also wrote several stage works for Florence, but the only opera among them for which the music survives is *La Flora*, written in collaboration with Peri in 1628. Another Florentine opera, or rather opera-ballet, was *La liberazione di Ruggiero dall' isola d'Alcina*, by Francesca Caccini (1587–ca. 1640), a daughter of Giulio Caccini.[9] *La liberazione*, first performed in 1625, was later performed in Warsaw in 1682, becoming one of the first Italian operas to be staged outside Italy.[10] With these exceptions, the city that saw the birth of opera played little part in its subsequent history until after the middle of the seventeenth century.[11]

The defects of Peri's and Caccini's operas, which came to be recognized as soon as the novelty of the stile rappresentativo had worn off, were the weakness of characterization, the limited range of emotions expressed, the lack of clear, consistent musical organization, and above all the monotony of the solo style. Especially for this last reason, G. B. Doni, the foremost opera theorist of the early seventeenth century, not only advocated the plentiful use of arias and choruses to relieve the "tedium" of the recitative, but as late as 1635 argued that the ideal dramatic work was one in which music alternated with spoken dialogue.[12]

Opera in the beginning was the outgrowth of a limited musical theory applied to an artificial, stylized poetic form. There were no first-rate musicians among the founders but only noble amateurs, poets, and singers, all actuated by an enthusiastic misconception of antiquity. They have often been compared to Columbus, who set out to find the East Indies and accidentally discovered a new continent: so the Florentines, seeking to revive Greek drama, opened the way to modern opera. Like all pioneers, they were soon outdistanced; it was left to others to exploit and develop the new form. The first composer fully to realize its possibilities was Monteverdi.

9. For a modern edition, see Caccini, *La liberazione*, in *Smith College Music Archives* (1945), vol. 7; other Florentine theater music of the early seventeenth century may be found in *Smith College Music Archives* (1957), vol. 13. See also Silbert, "Francesca Caccini."

10. "Caccini, F.," *The New Grove Dictionary* (1980), 3:581.

11. This can be attributed, in part, to a decline in lavish court entertainment following the death of Cosimo II, grand duke of Florence, in 1620/21. For a list of musical spectacles in Florence, see Solerti, *Musica, ballo e drammatica*; and Weaver, *A Chronology of Music in the Florentine Theater*.

12. Doni, "Trattato," chaps. 4–6, in Solerti, ed., *Le origini del melodramma*.

CHAPTER FIVE

Monteverdi's Orfeo

Claudio Monteverdi (1567–1643), the greatest composer of the early seventeenth century, is perhaps better entitled than either Peri or Caccini to be called the founder of opera.[1] At his hands, the new form passed out of the experimental stage, acquiring a wealth of musical resource and a power and depth of expression, that make his music dramas still living works after more than three hundred years. Of his nineteen dramatic or semidramatic compositions, only six, including three operas, have been preserved in their entirety.[2]

Monteverdi's first opera, *Orfeo*, was performed in 1607 at Mantua, where he served the court as "maestro di cappella." The poem, by Alessandro Striggio (ca. 1560-after 1628), is on the same subject as Rinuccini's *Euridice* but considerably expanded and with a different ending.

Prologue. Five strophes, sung by "Music"—a significant contrast to Rinuccini's prologue, sung by "Tragedy."

Rejoicings (Act I and first half of Act II). Broadly arched poetic and musical structures, combining solo arias, recitatives, duets, choruses, and orchestral ritornellos.

Death of Eurydice (this and the next section comprise the second half of Act II). Introductory recitatives, narration by the Messenger (Silvia).

Lamentations. Solo of Orpheus ("Tu se' morta"); orches-

---

1. Fundamental works on Monteverdi as an opera composer are Fabbri, *Monteverdi,* and Abert, *Claudio Monteverdi* (which also includes analyses of many operas by other composers contemporary with Monteverdi). Other important studies are those of Schrade, Redlich, Sartori, Arnold and Fortune, eds., and Covell.

2. References to Monteverdi's works will be to the complete edition (C. E.) by Malipiero: 11, *Orfeo;* 12, *Il ritorno d'Ulisse;* and 13, *L'incoronazione di Poppea.*

tral interlude; finale, duets with choral refrain ("Ahi, caso acer-
bo").

    Epiphany (this and the next section comprise Act III).
"Hope" consoles and encourages Orpheus.

    Descent into Hell. Aria of Orpheus ("Possente spirto");
recitatives, orchestral interludes, closing chorus.

    Resurrection (first half of Act IV). Orpheus and the in-
fernal deities (recitatives).

    Second Death of Eurydice (second half of Act IV). Scena:
recitatives by Orpheus, with short phrases by others; solemn reflective closing chorus.

    Second Lamentation (first part of Act V). Solo scena, Or-
pheus (with an "echo" song).

    Ascent into Heaven (last part of Act V). Apollo takes Or-
pheus with him to dwell forever in heaven. Duet ("Saliam can-
tando"), short closing chorus and ballet (moresca).

    In his original libretto Striggio had followed the ancient
form of the myth, according to which Orpheus met his death by
being torn to pieces by a band of women in a Dionysiac frenzy.
For obviously good dramatic reasons, Monteverdi changed this
ending; he also shortened Striggio's choruses at the close of the
second and fourth acts, and probably made other changes as well.
At any rate, the resulting "favola in musica" is a work of extraordinary and impressive symmetry. All the essential dramatic action
takes place in Acts II–IV; Act I is a prelude, Act V an epilogue.
The musical and dramatic center of the whole is Orpheus' aria
"Possente spirto" in Act III, where he opens his way into the
underworld by the charm of music.

    Equal care for the grand lines of symmetry is evident in
each separate act and subdivision. The first part of Act I, for
example, is shaped as in the chart on the next page.

    The music of *Orfeo* was greeted by contemporaries as a
new example of the Florentine style, and indeed the general plan
of the opera—a pastorale, with monodic declamation—justified
this view. Nevertheless, the differences are fundamental. Monteverdi was a musician of genius, soundly trained in technique, concerned very much with musical and dramatic truth and very little
with antiquarian theories. He combined the madrigal style of the
late sixteenth century with the orchestral and scenic apparatus of

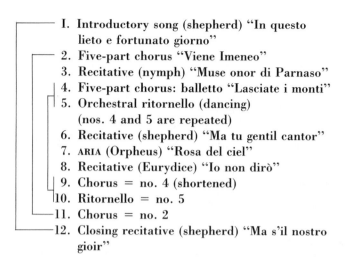

1. Introductory song (shepherd) "In questo lieto e fortunato giorno"
2. Five-part chorus "Viene Imeneo"
3. Recitative (nymph) "Muse onor di Parnaso"
4. Five-part chorus: balletto "Lasciate i monti"
5. Orchestral ritornello (dancing) (nos. 4 and 5 are repeated)
6. Recitative (shepherd) "Ma tu gentil cantor"
7. ARIA (Orpheus) "Rosa del ciel"
8. Recitative (Eurydice) "Io non dirò"
9. Chorus = no. 4 (shortened)
10. Ritornello = no. 5
11. Chorus = no. 2
12. Closing recitative (shepherd) "Ma s'il nostro gioir"

the old *intermedi* and a new conception of the possibilities of monodic singing. *Orfeo* represents the first attempt to apply the full resources of the art of music to drama, unhampered by artificial limitations.

The imposing list of orchestral instruments at the front of the score gives an idea of the extent and importance of the instrumental music of *Orfeo*.[3] The similarity of this orchestra to those of the earlier *intermedi* may be seen by a glance at the table below. The great number and variety of "fundament" (chord-playing) instruments is characteristic of the sixteenth century. Of course, not all the instruments were used at once, and undoubtedly many of the players doubled, so that there were not so many performers as there were different instruments. All the players united for certain numbers (for example, the opening toccata, some of the sinfonias, accompaniments of some of the choruses), but at many places Monteverdi indicated in the score precisely what instruments were to be used, his choice obviously being dictated not only by the desire to secure variety of color but to help characterize the dramatic situation as well. A detailed study of the score in this respect is extremely interesting. For example, in Act III,

3. The exact nature of all these instruments and of the various combinations is not yet definitely established. See Goldschmidt, *Studien*, 1:132–38; Westrup, "Monteverdi and the Orchestra"; Collaer, "L'orchestra di Claudio Monteverdi"; Ghisi, "L'orchestra in Monteverdi"; Beat, "Monteverdi and the Opera Orchestra of His Time."

MONTEVERDI'S ORCHESTRA AND ITS PREDECESSORS

Monteverdi's Orfeo, 1607	Intermedi of 1589	Circe, 1581	Psyche ed Amore, 1565
FUNDAMENT INSTRUMENTS			
2 clavicembalos	1 small cembalo	lutes	4 clavicem-
1 double harp (one	2 harps	lyres	balos
more needed in	6 lutes	harps	4 lutes
performance?)	2 chitarrones	organ with	1 lyre
2 chitarrones	2 guitars	wood pipes	1 bass lyre
(one more called	1 psaltery		1 small rebec
for in score)	1 cither		
2 bass cithers (not	1 mandola		
listed, but called	1 viola bastarda		
for in score)	2 lyres		
3 bass gambas	1 organ with wood		
2 organs with wood	pipes		
(flute) pipes	1 *organo di pivette*		
1 organ with reed	(probably a *re-*		
pipes (*regale*)	*gale*)		
STRINGED INSTRUMENTS			
2 small violins	1 small violin	*violons* (generic	1 soprano
alla francese	(*sopranino di*	name for all	viol
10 viole da braccio	*viola*)	bowed	4 "bowed
(i.e., a string en-	1 *violino*	instruments)	viols"
semble, possibly 4	3 tenor viols		4 bass viols
violins, 4 violas, 2	2 bass viols		1 contrabass
violoncellos)	1 contrabass viol		viol
2 contrabass viols	(and perhaps ad-		
	ditional viols)		
WIND INSTRUMENTS			
4 trombones (one	4 trombones	trombones	4 trombones
more called for in	2 cornetts	cornetts	1 large cor-
score)	1 traverse flute	flutes	nett
2 cornetts	1 (or more) tenor	oboes	2 soft-toned
1 *flautino alla Vige-*	oboes		cornetts
sima seconda	bassoons		2 recorders
(i.e., a high re-			4 traverse
corder; one			flutes
more(?) called for			2 tenor flutes
in score)			1 tenor oboe
1 high trumpet			5 (1) serpents
(*clarino*; possibly			
referring to use of			
high range of or-			
dinary trumpet)			
3 soft trumpets			
(*trombe sordine*)			
PERCUSSION INSTRUMENTS			
None	None	None	2 drums

the voice of Charon, the ferryman of the Styx, is accompanied by the *regale*, or organ with reed pipes; Orpheus' aria "Possente spirto" has with each strophe a different set of instruments; Charon's slumber is depicted by the strings with organ of wood pipes, playing "very softly"; the same organ alone accompanies Orpheus' song as he crosses the Styx; and the final chorus of infernal spirits (two altos, tenor, two basses) is accompanied by a combination of reed and wood organs, five trombones, two bass gambas, and contrabass viol—this in accordance with the traditional usage in the sixteenth-century *intermedi* for such scenes.[4]

The overture to *Orfeo*, called "toccata," is probably a dressed-up version of the customary opening fanfare; it consists of a brilliant flourish on the chord of C major, played three times by the full orchestra. In addition, the score contains ten short instrumental pieces called "ritornello" and five called "sinfonia"; some of these pieces recur one or more times at different places. In early seventeenth-century opera the distinction between "ritornello" and "sinfonia" is not always clear, nor are the designations consistent.[5] In principle a ritornello is, as the name suggests, a recurring interlude in connection with a song. Thus, the prologue to *Orfeo* opens with a ritornello (example 5.1) which is repeated four times in a shortened form after each stanza and once in its original form at the end of the prologue. Morever, Monteverdi brings in the same ritornello at the end of Act II, the turning point of the drama, and again at the end of Act IV, the close of the significant dramatic action—thus making it a kind of leitmotif symbolizing the "power of music," the central idea of the opera as announced in the prologue:

> Io la musica son, ch'ai dolci accenti
> so far tranquillo ogni turbato core.

A sinfonia, on the other hand, is generally a more or less independent instrumental piece used for an introduction or postlude or for depicting events on the stage. The sinfonias in *Orfeo* are serious, solidly chordal pieces, with occasional short points of im-

---

4. See Weaver, "Sixteenth-Century Instrumentation," and Pirrotta, *Music and Theatre*, p. 179.

5. See Abert, *Monteverdi*, pp. 254, 260, 304; Heuss, *Die Instrumental-Stücke des "Orfeo,"* appendix 3; Wellesz, "Cavalli."

Example 5.1: *Orfeo*, Ritornello from prologue

MONTEVERDI

itation, full texture, and much crossing of parts. The ritornellos are more lightly scored, sequential in structure, and more contrapuntal in texture.

The aria "Possente spirto" in Act III is a remarkable example of the florid solo style of the period. It has six strophes, of which all but the fifth are melodic variations over an essentially identical bass. For each of the first four strophes Monteverdi wrote out a different set of vocal embellishments, which he incorporated in the score on an additional staff; these embellishments are doubtless similar to those an accomplished singer of the time would have been expected to add to a plain melodic line. The practice of having solo instruments "concertize"—that is, collaborate and compete—with the voice, as Monteverdi does here, was one destined to become important in later seventeenth- and eighteenth-century opera arias. The employment of such elaborate vocal and

Example 5.2: *Orfeo*, Act II

MONTEVERDI

Vi ri - cor - da o bos-chi om - bro - si Vi ri - cor - da o bos-chi om - bro - si de' miei lungh' as - pri tor - men - ti

instrumental effects at this place is not merely for purposes of display but is calculated to suggest the supreme effort of Orpheus to overcome the powers of Hades by all the strength of his divine art; at the same time, the wild, fantastic figures of the music seem to depict the supernatural character of the scene.

Quite different kinds of songs are found in the first part of Act II. The act begins with a little air by Orpheus in periodic phrasing and three-part form—a miniature *da capo* aria. This whole scene is a lyric interlude, containing no dramatic action; and appropriate to the joyous pastoral atmosphere are the duet of the shepherds ("In questo prato adorno"), with its ritornellos for two high recorders played behind the scenes, and Orpheus' strophic solo "Vi ricorda, o boschi ombrosi," with its effect of alternating 6/8 and 3/4 meters (example 5.2).[6]

Songs of this sort, which show the traits of popular style, establish the background for the abrupt contrast at the entrance of the messenger with the news of Eurydice's death. Nowhere is Monteverdi's superiority over the early Florentine composers more manifest than in the startling change of mood which he achieves at this point and in the dialogue immediately following, with the alternating E-major and G-minor harmonies at Orpheus' exclamations (example 5.3). The harmonic contrast here was undoubtedly underlined by contrast of tone color in the instruments used for the realization of the *basso continuo*.

The ending of the messenger's account (example 5.4) may be compared with the corresponding passage in Caccini's *Euridice*

---

6. This is Jeppesen's "type A" of Laude melodies (*Die Mehrstimmige italienische Laude*, p. xxxi) and is common also in *frottole* (Einstein, *The Italian Madrigal*, p. 80).

Example 5.3: *Orfeo*, Act II

(example 4.1), as showing Monteverdi's grasp of the dramatic possibilities of the monodic style.[7]

    The choruses of *Orfeo* are more numerous and important than those in the early Florentine operas. Some are intended to accompany dancing, such as the chorus "Lasciate i monti" in Act I; others are in madrigal style, such as the ritornello chorus "Ahi, caso acerbo" at the end of the second act. The choruses of spirits at the end of the third and fourth acts exploit the somber color of the lower voices in a thick texture, supported by the trombones.

7. As a warning of the way in which editors can make practically two different pieces out of the same given bass and melody, the reader is invited to compare a facsimile edition of examples 5.3 and 5.4 with the realization made by Leichtentritt (Ambros, *Geschichte der Musik*, 564, 567) and one by Malipiero (C.E. 11:59, 61). An equally instructive comparison may be made between the versions of Orpheus' "Tu se' morta" by Riemann (*Handbuch der Musikgeschichte*, vol. 2, part 2, pp. 200ff.) and Malipiero (C.E. 11:62–64). See also Respighi's edition of Monteverdi's *Orfeo*.

Example 5.4: *Orfeo*, Act II

Perhaps the most remarkable feature of *Orfeo* is Monteverdi's sense of form, of a logically articulated, planned musical structure. This is apparent not only in the use of such devices as strophic songs and instrumental ritornellos and in the broad symmetrical structure of the large units, but even in the monodic portions, such as the entire recitative of the messenger in Act II, from which example 5.4 is quoted. Such places in Peri and Caccini were nearly formless vocal rhapsodies; here, they are organized into musical units in which the freedom of declamation is admirably balanced by the careful plan of the passage as a whole.

Monteverdi's second opera, *Arianna* (Mantua, 1608), was on the same large scale as *Orfeo*, insofar as can be judged from the libretto. The only music that has been preserved is the famous "lament" of the heroine.[8] This song was probably the most cele-

8. Malipiero, C. E. 11:159. See Epstein, "Dichtung und Musik in Monteverdi's *Lamento d'Arianna*"; Tomlinson, "Madrigal, Monody, and Monteverdi's *Via naturale alla immitatione*"; Rosand, "The Descending Tetrachord."

brated monodic composition of the early seventeenth century and was declared by Gagliano to be a living modern example of the power of ancient (that is, Greek) music, since it was said to have moved the audience to tears.[9] Monteverdi later arranged it as a five-part madrigal (1614) and used the music again for a sacred text (1640).

In 1613, Monteverdi received an appointment as choirmaster of St. Mark's at Venice, in which city he remained for the rest of his life. Of his dozen or so operas after *Arianna*, only the last two have been preserved; these will be considered later (chapter 7). One other work, the dramatic cantata *Il combattimento di Tancredi e Clorinda* (performed at Venice in 1624), may be briefly mentioned here because of its significance in the development of a new type of musical expression and because of its use of two new devices of instrumental technique. In the preface to his *Madrigali guerrieri ed amorosi* ("Madrigals of War and Love," the collection in which *Il combattimento* was first published, in 1638), Monteverdi explains that music hitherto has not developed a technique for the expression of anger or excitement and that he has supplied this need by the invention of the *stile concitato* ("agitated style"), based on the meter of the pyrrhic foot (two short syllables).[10] This is a typical Renaissance theory, to justify the use of rapidly reiterated sixteenth notes on one tone. Monteverdi claims credit for the discovery of this device, as well as for the pizzicato, which he likewise uses in this work to depict the clashing of weapons in combat. The orchestra of *Il combattimento* consists of only strings and continuo, an instance of the trend during the early seventeenth century toward reducing the number and variety of instrumental groups and centering interest on the strings.

9. Dramatically interesting laments were written by other composers of this period—for example, Sigismondo d'India (ca. 1582–1629).

10. Kreidler, *Heinrich Schütz und der Stile concitato von Claudio Monteverdi.*

CHAPTER SIX

Other Italian Court Operas
of the Early
Seventeenth Century

Marco da Gagliano called opera "the delight of princes." For the first four decades of its existence, it was exclusively that; indeed, up to the end of the eighteenth century some operas continued to be produced that were primarily for the delectation or glorification of rulers, nobles, or other wealthy patrons and only incidentally if at all for the entertainment of the public. The majority of such operas between 1610 and 1650 appeared at Rome. Most of them, like the earlier operas at Florence and Mantua, were created as special events for festal occasions and hence were mounted with little regard for expense. The scores were usually printed and have come down to us, so that this period of opera is fairly well known to historians.[1] Moreover, the available financial resources permitted elaborate stage effects and a sufficiently large cast to allow for ballets and extensive musical ensembles. These ensembles—called "choruses," though they were in reality madrigal-like pieces for a comparatively small group of singers—are characteristic of the so-called Roman opera of the early seventeenth century.

---

1. See Goldschmidt, *Studien zur Geschichte der italienischen Oper*, vol. 1; Ademollo, *I teatri di Roma*; Pirrotta, "Early Opera and Aria."

The Roman Operas

The monodic style was introduced at Rome in 1600 with Cavalieri's *La rappresentazione di anima e di corpo* and soon found a number of adherents, notably Agostino Agazzari (1578-ca. 1640), Stefano Landi (ca. 1586-ca. 1639), and Domenico Mazzocchi (1592–1665). Agazzari, author of an important treatise on the thoroughbass, served briefly as *maestro di cappella* for the German College of San Apollinare (1602–3) before accepting a similar appointment at the Roman Seminary, a Jesuit institution. For the pre-Lenten entertainment of students enrolled in this seminary, Agazzari composed *Eumelio*, a pastorale performed and printed in Venice in the year 1606.[2]

One student who could have heard the 1606 performance of *Eumelio* was Stefano Landi, for he was enrolled in the Roman Seminary from 1602 to 1607.[3] Landi's appointment as maestro di cappella to the bishop of Padua in 1618 did not deter him from composing operas. His first work in this genre was *La morte d'Orfeo* ("The Death of Orpheus," 1619) which introduces large "scene-complexes," carefully organized with solos and choral ensembles, at the close of each act, the largest one of all coming at the end of Act V.[4] There had been scene-complexes of this sort, of course, in the Florentine *Euridice* operas and in Monteverdi's *Orfeo*, but there they were essentially connected with the drama; in Landi's *La morte d'Orfeo* and the later operas at Rome, on the other hand, the big finales do not as a rule grow organically out of the plot but seem rather like *intermedi*, spectacular visual and vocal displays only loosely related to the action.

The leading patrons of opera at Rome were the powerful family of the Barberini, princes of the church. Their palace had a theater with a capacity of over three thousand;[5] it was opened

---

2. See Johnson, "Agazzari's *Eumelio*"; Donington, *The Rise of Opera*, pp. 128–30.

3. Carfagno, "The Life and Dramatic Music of Stefano Landi."

4. See Grout, "The Chorus in Early Opera."

5. Pope Urban VIII, a member of the Barberini family, commissioned Bernini to design the palace.

Example 6.1: *Sant' Alessio*

(8 more measures)

in 1632 with Stefano Landi's *Sant' Alessio*,[6] one of the most important operas of the Roman school and one of the first operas to be written about the life of a saint.[7] The libretto for this sacred opera was written by Giulio Rospigliosi (1600–1669), friend of the Barberini family, distinguished man of letters, papal secretary, later cardinal, and finally pope under the name of Clement IX (1667–69).[8] It is based on the legend of the fifth-century Saint Alexis, but the persons and scenes, both serious and comic, are obviously drawn from the contemporary life of seventeenth-century Rome.

The opera is divided into a prologue and three acts, with its structural divisions clearly articulated by instrumental and choral numbers. The opera is introduced by a fairly long and well-developed orchestral sinfonia consisting of a solid chordal introduction, evidently in slow tempo (example 6.1),[9] followed by a

6. Rolland, "La Première Représentation du *San Alessio*." See also Pastor, *History of the Popes*, 29:408–544. There is some evidence for a previous performance of *Sant' Alessio* at Rome in 1631. See *The New Grove Dictionary*, 13:622, for an illustration of a 1634 engraving of the stage set for this opera.

7. Sigismondo d'India's opera on the life of saint, *Sant' Eustachio*, was performed in Rome, 1625; the score is no longer extant.

8. See Ademollo, *I teatri di Roma*; Salza, "Drammi inediti di Giulio Rospigliosi"; Pastor, *History of the Popes*, 31: 314–37; Murata, *Operas for the Papal Court, 1631–1668*.

9. Colin Timms, in *The New Grove Dictionary*, 10:425–28, suggests that the sinfonias in this opera are "the first real 'overtures' in the history of opera."

Example 6.2: *Sant' Alessio*

S. Landi

canzona beginning as shown in example 6.2: The canzona continues for sixty measures in contrapuntal style to the end, with the
exception of one more homophonic section consisting of alternating forte and piano phrases and one interlude in the rhythm of a
saraband, in strict note-against-note writing. The piece is then
brought to a close with a stretto-like passage in eighth notes and
a final broad cadence in G major.[10] The formal resemblance of
this canzona overture to the later *sonata da chiesa* is obvious;
and it has further historical importance as being the model for
the type of "French overture" perfected about thirty years later
by Lully. The prelude to the second act of *Sant' Alessio* is likewise
a canzona in three movements but without a slow introduction,
thus giving it a superficial resemblance to the later "Italian overture" pattern (fast-slow-fast).

In the orchestra of *Sant' Alessio*, the old-fashioned viols
are replaced throughout by violins (in three parts) and violon-
cellos. Harps, lutes, and theorbos go for the most part with the
strings, but the harpsichords have a separate staff in many of the
instrumental numbers. It will be noted that the outlines of the
modern orchestra are here distinct; only the number and variety
of "fundament" instruments remind us of the earlier practice,
and these will remain in the orchestra, though in decreasing numbers, until the time of Haydn and Mozart. The wind and percussion instruments will become from now on ever less conspicuous,

10. The overture to Francesca Caccini's *La liberazione di Ruggiero* (1625) begins with a
theme in canzona rhythm but does not have the fugal entrances. An overture similar to
that of *Sant' Alessio* is M. Rossi's "sinfonia" to *Erminia sul Giordano* (1633). See DeLage,
"The Overture in Seventeenth-Century Italian Opera."

Example 6.3: *Sant' Alessio*, Act II, sc. 7

being used in opera only for special effects or in full subordination to the string group.

The vocal writing in *Sant' Alessio* shows signs of moving away from the early Florentine operas. The many repeated notes and frequent cadences in the recitatives (example 6.3) are characteristic features of a later style. There are few distinct solo arias, but many ensemble and choral scenes, among which the finale of the last act is particularly impressive.

The extremely high range of Alessio's part is typical of many roles in early seventeenth-century opera for male sopranos. Such singers, called *castrati*, had first appeared in some of the earliest Florentine operas. Despite efforts to abolish the custom, it became increasingly prevalent, most notably in Italy, during the seventeenth century.[11] Castrati sang not only female roles, espe-

---

11. Maugars, "Response faite à un curieux." See chap. 13 for further discussion.

Example 6.4: Aria from *La catena d'Adone*, Act I, sc. 3

D. Mazzocchi

Ri-da l'au-retta a - man- -te Al bel se - ren del tuo di-vin sem-bian - te, E trà bal- lie trà can - ti Ti si sco - pra gio - con- do No-vo ciel, no-va ter - ra e no- vo mon - do.

(rit.)

(sic)

cially in those cities where there was a papal ban on women appearing on stage, but also male roles in Italian *opera seria*.[12]

Still further departure from the Florentine ideal is evident in Domenico Mazzocchi's *La catena d'Adone* ("The Chain of Adonis"), which was presented at Rome in 1626.[13] The libretto, based on an episode in Marino's epic *Adone*, tells the story of the rescue of Adonis by Venus from the wiles of the enchantress Falsirena. (According to the "allegory" printed at the end of the score, this is supposed to symbolize the rescue of Man by heavenly grace from the bonds of sensuality and error.) The various mythological personages on the stage are no longer the statuesque and serious figures of early Florentine opera but conduct themselves like characters in a bedroom farce; the complicated intrigue is bolstered by all kinds of magic tricks and particularly by the use of disguises—credulity in this respect knowing no bounds in opera from this early day to the present—and by sudden transformations of scene, conjurations, descents of gods, and the familiar pastoral background. The typical later baroque opera plot, with its multitude of characters, fantastic scenes, and incongruous episodes, is already foreshadowed in this work.

Musically, *La catena d'Adone* is important for its many vocal ensembles and also for its embryonic line of demarcation between monodic recitatives and songs of a more definite melodic profile and musical form. The term "aria" appears for the first time in the history of opera in this score, being applied, however, not only to solo songs but also to duets and larger ensembles. Some of the solo "arias" are hardly different from the monodic recitatives; others, however, are organized into clear-cut sections with distinct melodic contours. An aria of Falsirena in the finale of Act I, over a bass in steady movement of quarter notes ("walking bass"), introduces coloratura passages for the expression of joy (example 6.4).

One of the castrato roles in *La catena d'Adone* was sung by Loreto Vittori (ca. 1600–1670), a papal court singer and com-

---

12. Castrato roles continued to be present in operas for almost two hundred years. Late examples include *Idomeneo* (1781) and *La clemenza di Tito* (1791) by Mozart and *Trajano in Dacia* (1807) by Giuseppe Niccolini.

13. This is the one surviving opera by D. Mazzocchi. See Witzenmann, "Domenico Mazzochi."

Example 6.5: *La Galatea*, Act III, sc. 3

(Example 6.5 continued)

poser, who in 1643 also became an ordained priest.[14] Vittori was associated with Cardinal Antonio Barberini, to whom he dedicated the only surviving example of his dramatic work, *La Galatea* (1639). This Italian pastoral opera, one of the last from this period, has both text and music written by Vittori. Musically, *La Galatea* is a superior work, and Romain Rolland calls it "the finest lyric drama of the first half of the seventeenth century."[15] The arias show progress in the direction of formal organization based on a clear system of tonal relationships; the recitatives include occasional expressive dissonances but on the whole tend toward the *secco* style. Some of the finest music of this opera is found in its ensembles (example 6.5).

Conditions at Rome on the whole did not favor the growth of serious opera on secular themes. The influence of the church tended rather to the cultivation of the oratorio or similar quasi-dramatic forms, or at most permitted operas of a pious allegorical or moralizing nature, such as *Sant' Alessio*, already described; *L'innocenza difesa* (1641), by Virgilio Mazzocchi (1597–1646);[16] and *La vita humana* (1656), by Marco Marazzoli (ca. 1602–1662), one of the last operas to be produced at the Barberini theater.[17] Secular productions were represented chiefly by the harmless, diverting genre of the pastorale, of which Vittori's *La Galatea* and Michelangelo Rossi's (1601/2-1656) *Erminia sul Giordano* ("Erminia at the Jordan") are prime examples.

Erminia sul Giordano was performed in Rome at the Palazzo Barberini in 1633. The libertto for this pastoral opera is by Rospigliosi and is based on the sixth and seventh cantos of Tasso's *Gerusalemme liberata*, with episodes from other parts of the poem. Its musical interest is concentrated in the choruses, which include a hunting chorus with echo effects and a chorus of soldiers on a trumpet-like motif to the words "All' armi." *Erminia* consists of an imperfectly connected series of scenes with elaborate stage settings and machines, a feature of the Barberini productions.

14. Vittori sang the castrato roles in many operas, including Luigi Rossi's *Il palazzo incantato*. See Rau, *Loreto Vittori*.

15. R. Rolland, "L'Opéra au XVIIᵉ siècle en Italie," in Lavignac, *Encyclopédie*, 2:711.

16. Virgilio was the brother of Domenico Mazzocchi.

17. Cf. Witzenmann, "Die römische Barockoper *La vita humana*."

The last important Roman composer of serious opera in this period was Luigi Rossi (ca. 1597–1653), a singer who also composed oratorios and over four hundred cantatas and songs. Only two operas by Rossi are known.[18] His first opera, *Il palazzo incantato* ("The Enchanted Palace"),[19] is based on a libretto by Rospigliosi; it was commissioned by Cardinal Antonio Barberini for the 1642 Carnival season at the Barberini theater. The second was *Orfeo*, given in Italian at Paris in 1647. This Paris performance was the consequence of political changes at Rome resulting in the election of Pope Innocent X in 1644, which forced the Barberini family to emigrate. At the invitation of Cardinal Mazarin, many of their musicians, including Rossi, went with the Barberinis to Paris to give the French public a taste of Italian opera.[20] The poem of *Orfeo*, though based faithfully on the ancient myth, introduces many more or less irrelevant episodes, resulting in a hodgepodge of serious and comic scenes intermingled with ballets and spectacular stage effects. The only way a composer can deal with such a libretto is to ignore the drama (or lack of it) and concentrate on the musical opportunities offered by each scene.

The score of *Orfeo* is as variegated as its poem, and it is especially remarkable as being the first opera in which the arias outnumber the recitatives. There are strophic arias over an *ostinato* bass, two-part arias, *buffo* (comic) arias, and da capo arias, as well as many ensembles of different kinds. The music is distinguished by that grace and perfection of style, that refinement of sensuous effect, for which its composer, along with Carissimi and Cesti, was so greatly admired in the seventeenth century. Eurydice's aria "Mio ben" in Act II is an excellent example of a "lament," with long-breathed, mournful coloraturas streaming above a repeated descending bass figure. Another lament, in Act III, is built like the celebrated one from Monteverdi's *Arianna*, in an expressive monodic recitative with a refrain—slightly varied at each recurrence—on the words "Uccidetemi, ò pene" ("Kill me, O sorrows": example 6.6).

18. See Ghislanzoni, *Luigi Rossi*, which contains analyses of these two operas, with many short musical examples.

19. In some sources, this work is entitled *Il palazzo d'Atlante*. See Prunières, "Les Représentations du *Palazzo d'Atlante*."

20. Rolland, *Musiciens d'autrefois*, pp. 55–105; Pastor, *History of the Popes*, 30:48–72.

Example 6.6: *Orfeo*, Act III, sc. 3

(Example 6.6 continued)

With all its beauty of detail, however, Rossi's *Orfeo* as a whole is no more a dramatic entity than Berlioz's *Damnation de Faust*; it is a succession of lyrical and scenic moments in which the beauty of music and décor successfully conceals the absence of any serious dramatic purpose. As such, it illustrates the extent to which opera in the course of forty years had moved away from the early Florentine ideal in the direction of the formal exterior of the later baroque opera.

The First Comic Operas

There were no comic scenes in the earliest operas. Italian popular comedy at this period was represented by the commedia dell' arte, which found its musical counterpart in the madrigal comedies of Vecchi and Banchieri. It is in the Italian pastorales that comic episodes begin to appear. The scenes in Landi's *La morte d'Orfeo*, for example, are of the sort common to other Italian pastorales. *Sant' Alessio*, the first opera to be written about the inner life of a human character, is not without its comic episodes, most notably a duet of ridicule sung by the pages. Here the pages and the nurse represent more realistic comic characters, obviously patterned after the stock characters of the commedia dell' arte.

Diana schernita ("Diana ridiculed," 1629), by Giacinto Cornacchioli (ca. 1598–1673), which parodies contemporary Florentine monody, is considered to be one of the earliest comic operas. But the creation of comic opera, the foundation of the long Italian opera buffa tradition which was to culminate in Mozart and Rossini, was the work of Giulio Rospigliosi. In addition to his opera poems already cited *(Sant' Alessio, Il palazzo incantato, Erminia sul Giordano)*, Rospigliosi wrote several others, including two highly successful comedies; *Il falcone* (better known as *Chi soffre, speri*, "Who Suffers May Hope") and *Dal male il bene* ("Good from Evil"). *Chi soffre, speri*, performed at the Palazzo Barberini in 1639, is a revision of *Il falcone*, which was performed two years earlier at the same theater. It is generally agreed that the second version (the only one of which the music is now known) represents the musical collaboration of Virgilio Mazzocchi and Marco Marazzoli. The extent of that collaboration, however, is open to question, although Marazzoli usually is credited with the composition of *La fiera di Farfa*, the *intermedio* for Act II.[21]

Chi soffre, speri has a romantic plot, with comic scenes featuring character types of the commedia dell' arte and figures from the common walks of Italian life, in the manner established by Michelangelo Buonarroti with his comedies *La Tancia* (1612) and *La Fiera* (1618) and already used by Rospigliosi in his own opera poem *Sant' Alessio*. The dialogue of *Chi soffre, speri* is conveyed in a kind of recitative that differs essentially from the quasi-melodic monody of the Florentines; it is the style which later came to be called *recitativo secco*: a quick-moving, narrow-ranged, sharply accented, irregularly punctuated, semimusical speech, with many repeated notes sustained only by occasional chords—a style for which the Italian language alone is perfectly adapted and which has always been a familiar feature of Italian opera.[22] Although tendencies toward this type of recitative were manifest in earlier Roman works, the necessity of finding a musical setting for realistic comic dialogue led to its fuller development here (example 6.7).

Apart from the recitative and one lively ensemble scene (in an intermezzo depicting the bustle of a fair), the music of *Chi soffre, speri* is surpassed in quality of both libretto and songs by *Dal male il bene*. This comic opera, with music by Antonio Maria Abbatini (?1609–1679) and Marco Marazzoli,[23] was performed in 1653 to mark the return of the Barberini to Rome and the subsequent reopening of the Palazzo Barberini theater. It also marked the celebration of Maffeo Barberini's marriage to Olimpia Giustinani. Rospigliosi, who had served as papal legate in Madrid from 1646 to 1653, showed in the construction of his libretto some influence of the Spanish playwright Pedro Calderón de la Barca

21. See Reiner, "Collaboration in *Chi soffre speri*" and "V. Mazzocchi" in *The New Grove Dictionary*.

22. For a discussion of the terms *secco* and simple recitative, see Bauman, "Benda . . . and Simple Recitative."

23. The exact contribution of each composer is not entirely clear, although Acts I and III are usually attributed to Abbatini and Act II to Marazzoli. Cf. Witzenmann, "Die römische Barockoper," and Holmes, "Comedy–Opera–Comic Opera."

Example 6.7: *Chi soffre, speri*, Act I, sc. 1

(1600–1681), especially the latter's *La dama duende* (1629). *Dal male il bene* is a romantic comedy in which, after complications and misunderstandings, two pairs of lovers are happily united. The servant characters are evidently drawn from life, except for one of them, the comic servant Tabacco, who is obviously taken over from the commedia dell' arte masks. This character type, incidentally, appears again and again in operas of the seventeenth and eighteenth centuries; Leporello in Mozart's *Don Giovanni* is probably the most familiar example. The music of *Dal male il bene* is notable for the skill of the recitatives and for another

Example 6.8: *Dal male il bene*, Act I, sc. 7

A. M. ABBATINI

(Ritornello: strings and continuo)

Aria

In che dà, in che dà il cer-car con tan-to af-fa-no tut-to

l'an-no di sa-per quel ch'al-tri fa? In che dà, in che dà? in che

(7♯6)

dà? Mi par pro - pio fre - ne - si-a lam-bi - car sem pre il cer-

4♯3   4 ♯3   (7) (4♯3)

-vel-lo per in-ten-der quel che si-a hor di que-sto e hor di quel-lo

4♯3

(15 more measures, followed by the Ritornello and a "2a parte" = last 20 measures of part one)

feature which later became characteristic of the opera buffa— namely the solo ensembles, especially the trio at the end of Act I and the sextet which forms the finale of the opera. Tabacco's aria "In che dà?" from Act I shows a well-developed tonal and formal scheme, together with a good sense of comic style (example 6.8).

Another excellent comic opera, with libretto by Andrea Moniglia (1624–1700) and music by Jacopo Melani (1623–1676), is *Il podestà di Colognole* ("The Mayor of Colognole"), performed in 1657 at Florence.[24] This performance in Florence is noteworthy because it makes clear that comic opera productions were no longer exclusively associated with Rome.[25] In fact, almost all of Moniglia's comic librettos were written for a Florentine audience.

Il podestà contains many more arias in proportion to the recitative than did earlier comic works, and it is possible to observe some of the standardized forms into which the aria, in both serious and comic opera, was settling down during the latter half of the seventeenth century. These forms divide themselves, with few exceptions, into three groups:

1. *Strophic songs*, in which the solo part may be either literally repeated for each stanza or more or less varied. The style in many of these is light and simple, frequently showing traces of popular song-types or dance meters. Others are more serious in mood. There is usually an orchestral ritornello or a short section of recitative between the stanzas. (Example: Tancia's "S'io miro il volto," Act I, scene 9.)[26]

2. *Through-composed arias*. These occur in a wide variety of types, both serious and comic, but all have a broader formal pattern and are less regular in melodic and rhythmic structure than the strophic songs. They consist of a number of sections, each ending with a full cadence in the tonic or a related key, and separated by orchestral ritornellos. (Examples: Isabella's "Son le piume acuti strali," Act I, scene 1; Leandro's "Sovra il banco di speranza," Act I, scene 8.[27] The basic form of these arias is two-part, without marked contrast of thematic material. Sometimes, however, the second section may be more contrasting, followed by a

---

24. Also known as *La Tancia, overo il podestà di Colognole.*

25. See Weaver, "Florentine Comic Operas"; Ademollo, *I primi fasti del teatro.*

26. Goldschmidt, *Studien,* 1:357.

27. Ibid., 1:349; 1:355.

repetition of the first, resulting in a three-part form. (Example: Lisa's "Se d'amore un cor legato," Act I, scene 1.)[28]

Arias of this second group represent the main channel of development of operatic style in the later seventeenth century. In the course of time, the formal scheme is expanded, the orchestra enters into the accompaniment proper as well as at the ritornellos, concertizing instruments appear, a fully developed da capo form gradually replaces the simple two-part structure, and eventually a number of stereotypes develop—arias of definite categories, each distinguished by certain stylistic procedures and appearing in the opera in a more or less rigidly fixed order of succession. This final degree of stylization, however, is not achieved until the early part of the eighteenth century.

3. *Arias over an ostinato bass.* Most arias of this group are serious in mood and belong to a recognized type known as the lament. (Example: Isabella's "Lungi la vostra sfera," Act I, scene 20.)[29] They are most often in triple meter, with slow tempo, and the usual bass figure is the passacaglia theme consisting of a diatonic or chromatic stepwise descent of a fourth from the tonic to the dominant, or some variant of this.[30]

By the middle of the seventeenth century, opera had come a long way from its beginnings as a pastoral play with monodic singing based on a supposed imitation of ancient Greek drama. Extensive ensemble numbers, typical of the earliest operas, survived after 1650 only in works destined for special aristocratic or state occasions. More significant historically, therefore, were the steps taken in the early seventeenth century toward establishing the main outlines of the structure of opera as a whole, founded on the separation of recitative from aria and the working out of musical forms for the latter, with distinct tonal relationships. Along with this formal progress went the discovery of new types of expression: the comic opera began its career, with its secco recitative and solo ensemble numbers, while for serious opera the possibility of successful musical treatment of subject matter other than the conventional pastorale was demonstrated by Rospigliosi

28. Ibid., 1:352.

29. Ibid., 1:360.

30. A familiar example of this kind of aria is the lament of Dido, "When I am laid in earth," from Purcell's *Dido and Aeneas*.

and Landi. Finally, the modern orchestra, centering around violin instruments and continuo, was established, and an important type of overture originated. Changes already begun in the first few decades were accelerated as opera moved out of the shelter of aristocratic salons onto the stage of public theaters.

CHAPTER SEVEN

Italian Opera in the
Later Seventeenth Century:
In Italy

Although the beginning of opera is commonly reckoned from the Florentine performances of 1600, it would be almost more appropriate to date it from the opening of the first public opera house in Venice in 1637. Itinerant troupes of singers, rivaling the troupes of the commedia dell' arte and borrowing from them many features of both libretto and music, had begun to circulate in Italy before this date; but the destined center of the new kind of musical drama, based on a combination of broad popular support and prestige appeal to the upper social classes, was Venice.[1] Court operas of the early seventeenth century had always kept a certain reserve, a refinement, almost a preciosity of form and content. After 1640, as opera became increasingly a public spectacle, changes were inevitable. The popularity of the new form of entertainment at Venice was amazing. Between 1637 and the end of the century, more than 350 operas were produced in the new theaters in Venice itself and probably at least as many more by Venetian composers in other cities. No fewer than nine opera houses were opened

1. On Venetian opera, see *Mercure galant* (Paris, 1672–74, 1677–1714); Bonlini, *Le glorie della poesie*; Groppo, *Catalogo di tutti i drammi*; [Salvioli], *I teatri musicali*; Zorzi et al., *I teatri pubblici*; Wiel, *I codici*; Solerti, "I rappresentazioni . . . dal 1571 al 1605" (*intermedi*, pastorales, etc., at the ducal court; no music preserved); Kretzschmar, "Die venetianische Oper"; idem, "Beiträge zur . . . Oper"; Wolff, *Die venezianische Oper*; idem, *Oper: Szene und Darstellung*; Worsthorne, *Venetian Opera*; Prunières, *Cavalli et l'opéra vénitien*; Wellesz, "Cavalli"; Pirrotta, *"Commedia dell' arte* and Opera"; Rommel, *Die Alt-Wiener Volkskomödie*; Rolland, "L'Opéra populaire à Venise"; Westrup, "The Cadence in Baroque Recitative"; Petrobelli, "Francesco Manelli."

in Venice during this period; after 1650, never fewer than four were in operation at once, and for the last two decades of the century this city of 125,000 people supported six opera troupes continuously, the usual seasons filling from twelve to thirty weeks of the year. Citizens were admitted on payment of the equivalent of about fifty cents, and wealthy families rented loges by the season.

The transformation which took place in the character of both libretto and music is attributable in part to these new circumstances; yet signs of the change had already become apparent in Rome, and the whole movement was part and parcel of the changing literary and musical tastes of the time. The genuine Renaissance interest in antiquity being exhausted, only the shell of classical subject matter remained, and even this was frequently abandoned in favor of episodes from medieval romances, especially as embodied in the epics of Ariosto and Tasso. Moreover, the outlines of history or legend were overlaid with so-called *accidenti verissimi*—incidents invented and added by the poets—to the point of being no longer recognizable. Perseus, Hercules, Medea, Alcestis, Scipio, Leonidas, Tancred and Clorinda, Rinaldo and Armida were, in these operas, not so much human (or superhuman) persons as mere personified passions, moving through the drama with the stiff, unreal air of abstract figures (despite the vehemence with which their emotions were expressed), preoccupied with little more than their eternal political or amorous intrigues and caricatured in comic episodes which might take up half the opera. Mistaken identity—a device rendered somewhat less implausible by the presence of castrati in male roles—was a dramatic stock in trade. The Aristotelian unities gave way before a bewildering succession of scenes, sometimes as many as fifteen or twenty in a single act, full of strong feeling and suspense, abounding in sharp contrast and effects of all kinds. Lavish scenic backgrounds added to the spectacle. Pastoral idylls, dreams, oracles, incantations, spectral apparitions, descents of gods, shipwrecks, sieges, and battles filled the stage. In particular, the machines—ingenious mechanical contrivances for the production of sudden miraculous changes and supernatural appearances—attained a degree of development never since surpassed. Heritage of the medieval mysteries, beloved adjunct of the Renaissance *in-*

termedi and the seventeenth-century court spectacles, the machines formed an indispensable part of opera in this period, though
their magnificence declined before the end of the century.[2]

A striking feature of the scores after about 1645 is the
virtual disappearance of the chorus. There are a few choruses in
operas from around this time, and occasional indications that more
were planned but apparently never composed. The mystery of these
missing choruses has not yet been satisfactorily solved, but it is
possible that they were replaced by ballets the music of which was
written by some other composer and consequently not included in
the regular score. At any rate, the absence of a chorus was primarily a matter of aesthetic propriety, for the stately, antique
choral group of the Florentine pastorales had no place in the lusty
melodrama of later seventeenth-century opera. Moreover, the public
cared little for choral singing on the stage, preferring to hear soloists. Giovanni Andrea Angelini-Bontempi (1624–1705), in the
preface to his opera *Il Paride* (Dresden, 1662), stated bluntly that
the chorus belonged in the oratorio,[3] and the managers soon found
that the money it cost to maintain such a large body of singers
could be more advantageously spent for other purposes. Only in
the *festa teatrale* or *festa musicale*, for which extraordinary sums
of money were available, did the chorus remain.[4] Its place was
taken by ensemble solo voices, particularly in the prologues and
epilogues, where divinities and allegorical figures of all kinds came
forward to sing greetings to distinguished spectators or make general moral observations and topical allusions to events of the day.
The decline of the chorus was followed by the rise of a typical
operatic phenomenon, the virtuoso soloist, for whose sake numerous songs having no connection with the drama were interpolated
in the score.

Along with these external changes, the music of Italian
opera in the course of the seventeenth century developed some

2. Sabbattini, *Pratica di fabricar scene*; Haas, *Die Musik des Barocks*; idem, *Aufführungspraxis*, pp. 163ff. See also Burnacini's stage designs in the edition of Cesti's *Il pomo
d'oro* (DTOe III², IV²); *Denkmäler des Theaters*, part 2; Kinsky, *History of Music in
Pictures*; Zucker. *Theaterdekoration des Barock*.

3. Kretzschmar, "Die venetianische Oper," p. 22.

4. Many of these festival operas were written to celebrate a patron's birthday or name
day. See chap. 13.

fundamentally new features of style. The works of the Florentines and early Romans were essentially chamber operas: relatively short, with a limited range of musical effects, sophisticated in feeling and declamation, calculated to appeal to invited guests of aristocratic tastes and education. The later operas, on the other hand, were destined for performance in public theaters before a mixed audience who had paid admission. Box-office appeal was essential. Broad effects by simple means, direct and vivid musical characterization, continual sharp contrasts of mood were required. Tuneful melodies, unmistakable major-minor harmonies, a solid but uncomplicated texture, strong rhythms in easily grasped patterns, above all clear formal structure founded on the sequential repetition of basic motifs—these became the elements of a new operatic style.

Monteverdi

A glance at the scores of the two Venetian operas of Monteverdi which have been preserved, *Il ritorno d'Ulisse in patria* ("The Return of Ulysses to His Country," 1640) and *L'incoronazione di Poppea* ("The Coronation of Poppea," 1642), shows what striking changes had taken place in the generation since his *Orfeo*.[5] The recitative in *Il ritorno d'Ulisse* is no mere rhapsodic declamation of the text, with dramatic high points underlined by startling shifts of harmony; it is constantly organized into patterns, with sequences and canonic imitation between the solo voice and the bass. Sections of free *parlando* on a single note alternate with melodic phrases at the cadences. The recitative frequently gives way to short arias, mostly in triple meter and strophic form. There are several arias on a ground bass. The parts of the gods and goddesses are filled with elaborate coloraturas. Ensembles, particularly duets, are abundant. Conventional word painting is evident—long-held notes over a moving bass for words like "costanza,"

5. See Osthoff, *Das dramatische Spätwerk Claudio Monteverdis*, and idem, "Zur Bologneser Aufführung," for a discussion of the 1640 date for *Il ritorno d' Ulisse*.

melismatic runs on "lieto," long coloratura phrases on "aria," and the like. Serious, comic, and spectacular scenes follow one another closely. Every possible occasion for emotional effect is exploited. From beginning to end, one senses the effort to be immediately understood, along with an almost nervous dread of monotony, of that *tedio del recitativo* which had been so severely criticized in the early Florentine operas. There is little instrumental music: a few sinfonias which recur in the same fashion as the ritornellos in *Orfeo*, and one *sinfonia da guerra* to depict the combat between Ulysses and the suitors at the end of Act II. The high points of the opera are undoubtedly the monologue of Penelope in the first scene of Act I (reminiscent of the famous lament of Arianna) and the opening solo of Ulysses in the seventh scene of this act. At the beginning of Act III, there is a comic lament, a clever parody of this favorite type of scene. Some of the little strophic songs in popular style, such as Minerva's "Cara, cara e lieta" (Act I, scene 8), are very attractive.

On the whole, however, *Il ritorno d'Ulisse* is not to be compared with Monteverdi's next (and last) opera, *L'incoronazione di Poppea*,[6] a masterpiece of the composer's old age paralleled only by the last two operas of Verdi. The libretto of this work, by Francesco Busenello, deals with the love of the Roman emperor Nero for Poppea, the wife of Nero's general Ottone; Nero banishes Ottone and divorces his own wife Ottavia in order to make Poppea his empress. This rather sordid subject is handled by the poet with consistency, good taste, and dramatic insight. Monteverdi altered many details of the libretto in the course of composition, for the sake of more effective musical treatment. The music is not spectacular; there are no display scenes and few ensembles except duets. The composer's greatness lies in his power of interpreting human character and passions—a power which ranks him among the foremost musical dramatists of all times. One example is the dialogue between Nero and Seneca in Act I, scene 9, where the grave admonitions of the philosopher contrast

---

6. See Goldschmidt, *Studien*, vol. 2; Kretzschmar, "Monteverdi's *Incoronazione*"; Covell, "Monteverdi's *L'incoronazione*"; Day, "The Theater of SS. Giovanni . . . *Poppea*"; Rosand, "Seneca and the Interpretation . . . *Poppea*." On the interpretation of the time values in Malipiero's edition of the score, see Redlich, "Notationsprobleme," and Osthoff, *Das dramatische Spätwerk*, pp. 211ff.

Example 7.1: *Poppea*, Act I, sc. 9

with the petulant outbursts of the willful young emperor (example 7.1).

The delineation of comic characters is delightful. The song of the *valletto* or page boy (example 7.2) has a naïveté comparable to Mozart's music for Cherubino. Not less remarkable is the power of pathetic expression, as in the profound grief of Ottavia's lament "Disprezzata regina" (Act II, scene 5), or the noble resignation of Ottone's "E pur io torno" (Act I, scene 1), the characteristic motif of which is deliberately recalled in scene 12 and again in Act II, scene 11. The love passages in *Poppea* can be compared only to Wagner's *Tristan* or Verdi's *Otello*. The frankly sensuous passion of Nero and Poppea is matched by voluptuous, incandescent music, as in the closing duet (da capo form over a passacaglia bass),[7] or in the third and tenth scenes of the

---

7. This duet may have been composed by someone other than Monteverdi; see Chiarelli, "*L'incoronazione di Poppea*."

Example 7.2: *Poppea*, Act II, sc. 5

MONTEVERDI

Se sto te - coil cor mi bat - - - - te, se tu parti io sto me - len - so, al tuo sen di vi - vo lat - te sem-pre aspir - ro e sem - pre pen - so.

first act, which are in a free mixture of recitative and arioso (example 7.3).

No operatic score of the seventeenth century is more
worthy of study and revival than *Poppea*, as recent modern performances have amply shown.[8] In it, Monteverdi applied the full
resources of a mature technique to a dramatically valid subject,
creating in a great variety of musical forms and effects a unified,
moving whole. The perfect balance between drama and music here
achieved was soon to be upset by a trend toward musical elabo-
ration at the expense of dramatic truth and consistency. Yet the

8. These performances, however, call attention to the performance-practice problems inherent in the staging of baroque opera for contemporary audiences. The reader is encouraged to compare the interpretations of *Poppea* by Raymond Leppard and Nikolaus Har-
noncourt, among others, in their respective recordings of the opera. For Monteverdi's own
ideas on performance practice, see Monteverdi, *Letters*.

Example 7.3: *Poppea*, Act I, sc. 10

Monteverdi

influence of the work was far-reaching. Just as *Orfeo* marked the climax of the old-style pastorale, so *Poppea* marked a definitive step (foreshadowed ten years earlier in Landi's *Sant' Alessio*) in the establishment of modern opera, centering about the personalities and emotions of human characters instead of the artificial figures of an ideal world.

Cavalli

The leading figure in the first period of opera at Venice was Monteverdi's pupil Pier Francesco Caletti-Bruni (1602–1676), who (following a common practice of the time) took the name of his patron, Cavalli.[9] About thirty of his operas appeared in the Venetian theaters between 1639 and 1669.[10] Cavalli's fame during his lifetime is attested to by the fact that many of his works were performed also in other cities, including Paris. His best-known opera was *Giasone* (1649), based on the legend of Jason, Medea, and the Golden Fleece.

In the works of Cavalli and later Venetian composers, a standard type of overture developed, consisting of a solemn, pompous, chordal opening movement followed by one or more movements in contrasting tempo, which occasionally introduced themes that would reappear in the prologue or elsewhere in the opera.[11] In addition to the overtures and a few descriptive sinfonias, the orchestra accompanied some of the songs or played short ritornellos between sections of them.

Solo arias were of course a regular feature of opera by this time, and they grew constantly more numerous in proportion to the whole as the century went on. At first, arias were given mainly to secondary personages; they were usually quite short, easily singable, mostly in triple meter with rhythmic patterns characteristic of popular dances or songs. Some were elegiac, minor in tone, with gently curving melodic lines, as in the beautiful "Delizie contente" from the first act of Cavalli's *Giasone*. Others were more lively, sometimes introducing trumpet-like motives for expression of rejoicing (example 7.4). Many arias of these and other types were strophic in form, with orchestral ritornellos. An-

9. On Cavalli, see the literature in n. 1 above, and Goldschmidt, "Cavalli als dramatischer Komponist"; Wiel, "Cavalli"; Hjelmborg, "Aspects of the Aria"; Glover, *Cavalli*.

10. For a list of Cavalli's operas, see appendix 1 of Glover, *Cavalli*. See also Jeffrey, "The Autograph Manuscripts."

11. Cf. Heuss, *Die Instrumental-Stücke . . . die venetianischen Opern-Sinfonien*, pp. 85, 118, 120; Wolff, *Die venezianische Oper*, appendix no. 67; Worsthorne, *Venetian Opera*, pp. 106ff.

Example 7.4: Aria from *Egisto* (1643), Act III, sc. 7

CAVALLI

(*Example 7.4 continued*)

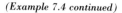

sol di lie-ti. di lie-ti. di lie-ti ar-mo-ni-e rim-bom- ba-te, rim-bom-

- ba-te. rim-bom- ba-te, rim-bom- ba-te, rim-bom - ba - te. ca - no-ri, a me

Li - dio ri - tor-na e la - - scia Clo - ri.

*This broadening at the final cadence — a "built-in" *ritardando* — was a common device in baroque music in triple metre. It was usually notated, as here, by "blackening" the notes affected, resulting in a change from 2 × 3 to 3 × 2 beats (𝄴 ♩♩|♩♩ ♩=𝄴 ♩ ♩ ♩) but without change of duration of the individual notes.

Example 7.5: Aria from *Egisto*, Act II, sc. 6

other favorite form was the lament on a ground bass (example 7.5), in which the contrast of passionate expression with one of the most rigid of musical forms gives rise to a typically baroque species of tension.[12] Toward the end of the century, as arias came to be assigned more and more frequently to principal characters in the drama, the three-part da capo form became more common, and more arias were written in difficult virtuoso style.

Certain traits of style peculiar to Cavalli may be especially mentioned. His comic scenes are marked by robustness, even crudity. Quite unlike the badinage of Monteverdi's page boy and maid-in-waiting is the scene in *Giasone* between Orestes and Demo, who is a stutterer—a typical farce figure, one of many such characters which were always welcomed on the Venetian stage. Cavalli's characteristic way of establishing a mood is to reiterate one striking figure, as in the conjuration scene in *Giasone*, where the

12. The lament became an increasingly prevalent feature of Cavalli's opera; *Statira* (1656), for example, has four laments. Cf. Glover, *Cavalli*, pp. 77, 87–88.

Example 7.6: *Giasone*, Act I, sc. 14

motif ♩ ♩ ♩ | ♩ is repeated twenty-one times with hardly a break, using (except at the cadences) only the chords of E minor and C major (example 7.6). This scene remained famous for a long time; it was parodied at Venice as late as 1677, in Legrenzi's *Totila*.[13]

Despite the presence of well-marked arias and distinct sections of recitative, the formal separation of the styles is by no means complete in the operas of Cavalli. Most of the scenes are a mixture, or rather a free alternation of the two, as in Monteverdi, except that the arias in Cavalli form a somewhat larger proportion of the whole than is the case with the older composer. The method is not fixed; the form arises in each case out of the dramatic requirements. A typical example is the scene from *Ormindo* (1644), which consists of (*a*) a dialogue in recitative, C minor,

13. A parody of the incantation scene from *Giasone* can be found among the ensembles to *Il podestà* by Melani (cited in chap. 6).

eighteen measures; (*b*) an eight-measure solo recitative, ending in G minor; (*c*) a lament on a ground bass, in E-flat major, fifty-six measures; and (*d*) a closing solo recitative in G minor, thirteen measures.[14] The constant use of "scene-complexes" of this sort (that is, scenes made up of different musical elements freely assembled) shows that opera in Cavalli's time had not yet altogether sacrificed dramatic values to the demands of abstract, symmetrical musical form. Cavalli, while not critical of details, showed sound judgment in choosing dramatically effective librettos. He was not an artist of Monteverdi's caliber, but his music has virility and a kind of elemental directness in dramatic expression comparable to Musorgsky—qualities which justify his position in history as the first great popular composer of opera.

Cesti

The most celebrated composer of opera after Cavalli was Pietro Antonio Cesti (1623–1669),[15] whose dozen or so extant operas were written for various Italian and South German cities between 1649 and 1669. They include *Orontea*,[16] *La Dori*,[17] and *Il pomo d'oro* ("The Golden Apple"). Cesti's music is more facile than Cavalli's, less vigorous, more feminine; he excels in the setting of idyllic, tender scenes; his melodies are clearly defined and graceful; his harmony is more conventional than Cavalli's—that is, it sounds less bold and experimental, more like the style of the eighteenth century; and his rhythmic patterns are more regular, sometimes almost stereotyped. In his operas, the already growing fissure between recitative and aria is noticeably widened: the center of mu-

14. Reprinted in Schering, ed., *Geschichte der Musik in Beispielen*, no. 200; see also a similar scene in *HAM*, no. 206.

15. See Coradini, "P. Antonio Cesti"; Wellesz, "Zwei Studien"; Sandberger, "Beziehungen der Königin Christine;" C. Schmidt, "The Operas of Antonio Cesti."

16. *Orontea* (Venice, ca. 1649) was the first opera to be performed at the court of Hanover (1678). For a modern edition of this comic opera, see Holmes, Wellesley Edition, no. 11.

17. *La Dori* was performed first in Innsbruck (1657) and then in Florence (1661).

sical interest moves away from the former, and the chief attention of composer and audience shifts toward the lyrical songs. The latter achieve larger proportions and clearer outlines, blossoming forth in an unprecedented variety of forms and types, offering frequent opportunities for vocal display. Thus the outline of the future "singer's opera" begins to come into focus in the works of Cesti.

This step, involving as it did a complete reorientation of operatic ideals, was of capital importance for the evolution of opera. The doctrines of the Camerata had emphasized poetic values at the expense of music. Monteverdi, by means of organizing the recitative, deepening its content, and introducing arioso or aria forms at critical points in the action, had made the music an equal partner with the text. But by the middle of the century, as composers were becoming more familiar with the new musical idiom, their interest in problems of form began to outweigh their concern for dramatic propriety. It must be said in their defense that the type of libretto which the poets supplied justified this attitude in some measure. As audiences demanded more and more music, they cared less and less about the poetry. The trend was hastened, moreover, by another influence, that of the cantata, a genre in which both Cesti and his teacher, Carissimi, excelled. The cantata, although semidramatic in form and employing recitatives and arias like the opera, was not theater music.[18] Designed for performance before a small audience, the cantata was a vehicle for fine singing rather than for dramatic expression. Its virtues were those appropriate to the chamber: symmetrical forms, correctly balanced phrases, pleasing melodies, unadventurous harmonies; logic, clarity, elegance, and moderation. It was a musical style founded on these ideals, a style for which the widespread popularity of the cantata had already prepared both composers and audiences and which Cesti introduced into the opera.[19] With him may be said to begin the reign of the composer over the dramatist, and of the virtuoso singer over both, which was to characterize Italian opera for the next hundred years.

18. "Eine Cantata siehet aus, wie ein Stück aus einer Opera." [Hunold,] *Die allerneueste Art*, p. 285.

19. Rolland, "L'Opéra au XVIIe siècle en Italie," in Lavignac, *Encyclopédie*, 2:722; Dent, "Italian Chamber Cantatas."

Cesti's *Il pomo d'oro* is one of the most famous examples of a baroque court opera in the grand style.[20] Francesco Sbarra's libretto for this opera was commissioned by Emperor Leopold I of Austria to celebrate his forthcoming marriage to Infanta Margherita of Spain. The wedding was planned for December 1666. Although Cesti began work on the score in the summer of 1666 and presumably completed it by the end of that year, *Il pomo d'oro* was not performed in connection with the wedding festivities.

The first known performance of *Il pomo d'oro* occurred on July 13 and 14, 1668, in honor of Empress Margherita on her birthday. The division of the production into two days was necessitated by the length of the opera.[21] According to contemporary documents, Cesti's opera was presented in a new theater designed specifically for this production, and it was staged with a magnificence appropriate to an imperial court desirous of not being outdone by the royal festivals of Louis XIV at Versailles.[22] The five acts included sixty-six scenes, in the course of which more than twenty different stage sets were required, some of them involving exceedingly elaborate machines.[23] There were several ballets in each act and a grand triple ballet at the end. Ballets, a regular feature of Italian opera, were of course staged with especial magnificence in court spectacles. Often the music for them was written by a different composer.[24]

The story of *Il pomo d'oro* was based on the myth of Paris and the golden apple; in the epilogue *(licenza)*, the god Jupiter presents this prize of beauty to the new empress, as being more worthy of it than the goddesses whose contention for it had

20. A less well-known but equally magnificent festival opera of the same period was Bontempi's *Il Paride*; see Briganti, *Gio. Andrea Angelini-Bontempi*.

21. Although no complete score of this opera is available, it is estimated that the production lasted eight hours. In addition to the extant Prologue and Acts I, II, and IV, an important manuscript collection has come to light that contains some of the musical material from Acts III and V. For a discussion of this manuscript, see C. Schmidt, "Antonio Cesti's *Il pomo d'oro*."

22. See Wellesz, *Essays on Opera*, pp. 54–81; Hadamowsky, *Barocktheater am Wiener Kaiserhof*.

23. For a complete set of these engravings, see DTOe III² and IV².

24. For some of the ballets in the Vienna court operas, see DTOe XXVIII².

brought about the Trojan War. In addition to the chorus there were forty-eight roles, though not necessarily this number of singers, since doubling was customary. All the gods of Olympus, as well as a host of heroes and other legendary personages, were represented in the cast. All the parts were sung by men, with the quaint consequence that some of the male characters in the opera have higher voices than the female ones—a situation not uncommon in Italian seventeenth-century opera even when there were women singers, for the composers favored the woman's alto voice and commonly reserved the soprano roles for castrati. The orchestra consisted of six violins, twelve viols (alto, tenor, and bass), two flutes (for pastoral scenes), trumpets in two parts (used chiefly in sinfonias and choruses), a *gravicembalo* (harpsichord), which was occasionally replaced by a *graviorgano* (a theater organ— that is, probably a *positiv* or one-manual organ with wood pipes), and other continuo instruments (lutes, theorbo). There was also a special group of instruments for infernal scenes, consisting of two cornetts, three trombones, a bassoon, and a *regale*.

The prologue and each act are opened by stately instrumental "sonatas," and there are also many short sinfonias and ritornellos in the course of the opera. Choruses, found chiefly in the prologue, epilogue, and ballet scenes, are of comparatively little musical interest. The recitatives are for the most part mere perfunctory settings of dialogue, with the usual continuo accompaniment; there are, however, a few very beautiful accompanied (continuo and strings) recitatives, notably that of Aurindo in Act I, which show what Cesti could do in the expressive style when he had occasion.[25] The recitatives in *La Dori* are on the whole more flexible and expressive, more closely related to the earlier style of Cavalli, than those of *Il pomo d'oro*.

The favorite ensemble in seventeenth-century Italian opera was the duet. With Monteverdi and (to a lesser degree) Cavalli, the duet, when not merely a recitative dialogue, showed, by its imitative style, the derivation from the older madrigal. In Cesti, the contrapuntal feature is less favored, often being only suggested in the opening phrase and then giving way to melismatic

25. DTOe III², 97, 100ff. Also Lavignac, *Encyclopédie*, 2:729–31.

Example 7.7: *La Dori*, Act I, sc. 9

passages in thirds or sixths. The opening measures of "Se perfido Amore" from *La Dori* (example 7.7) are typical of this graceful, amiable style.

Cesti's arias are not usually of large dimensions, but they show a remarkable variety of types and much care in planning the order in which these occur. There are serene, long-breathed, noble Handelian melodies; playful airs with graceful and piquant rhythms, such as Arsete's "Non scherzi con amore" from *La Dori*, a complete da capo form with the ritornello repeated between the first and second parts and again at the end; martial airs with strong rhythms and much bravura passage work; and buffo arias, lively, moving by wide intervals, exploiting the virtuoso powers and comic possibilities of the bass voice (example 7.8).

The traditional strophic air is also represented in Cesti's operas; the characteristic form of each strophe in these airs is two-part, frequently with the second part repeated (*a–b–b*). Arias on a ground bass are also used, and there is a considerable number of complete da capo arias. Yet the forms are not stereo-

Example 7.8: *Il pomo d'oro*, Act I, sc. 11

Example 7.9: *La Dori*, Act I, sc. 9

typed; subtleties of detail abound. One feature of Cesti's melody, found typically in slow-moving airs of an elegiac character, is the melodic interval of the diminished third at cadences—or, harmonically expressed, the Neapolitan sixth followed by the dominant (example 7.9).[26]

Although Venice by no means had a monopoly of opera in the second half of the seventeenth century, it was preeminent among Italian cities and always had a certain glamour for foreign visitors interested in opera. Some of their observations are worth noting at some length. John Evelyn recorded his experiences at a Venetian theater in 1645:

> This night, having . . . taken our places, we went to the Opera, where comedies and other plays are represented in recitative music, by the most excellent musicians, vocal and instrumental, with variety of scenes painted and contrived with no less art of perspective, and machines for flying in the air, and other wonderful motions; taken together, it is one of the most magnificent and expensive diversions the wit of man can invent. The history was, Hercules in Lydia; the scenes changed thirteen times.[27]

In 1680, the French traveler Limojon de St. Didier reported as follows:

> At Venice they Act in several Opera's at a time: The Theaters are Large and Stately, the Decorations Noble, and the Alterations of them good: But they are very badly Illuminated: The

26. "Les italiens en mettant Bemol au ton favory [i.e., by flatting the supertonic in the melody at a ii–V–VI cadence] évitent la fausse relation [e.g., *d* soprano–*A-flat* bass, which with the flat becomes *d-flat–A-flat*] mais c'est pour exprimer les douleurs ou la faiblesse des moribonds." M.-A. Charpentier, MS treatise on the rules of composition (ca. 1692), quoted in Crussard, "Marc-Antoine Charpentier, théoricien," p. 53.

27. Evelyn, *Diary*, 1:202. The opera referred to was presumably *Ercole in Lidia*, with music by G. Rovetta.

Machines are sometimes passable and as often ridiculous. . . . These Opera's are long, yet they would divert the Four Hours which they last, if they were composed by better Poets, that were a little more conversant with the Rules of the Theater. . . . The Ballets or Dancings between the Acts are generally so pittiful, that they would be much better omitted; for one would imagine these Dancers wore Lead in their Shoes, yet the Assembly bestow their Applauses on them, which is meerly for want of having seen better.

The Charms of their Voices do make amends for all imperfections: These Men without Beards [that is, the castrati] have delicate Voices *(des voix argentines)* besides which they are admirably suitable to the greatness of the Theater. They commonly have the best Women Singers of all *Italy*. . . . Their Airs are languishing and touching; the whole composition is mingl'd with agreeable songs *(chansonettes)* that raise the Attention; the Symphony [orchestra] is mean[,] inspiring rather Melancholy than Gaiety: It is compos'd of Lutes, Theorbos and Harpsichords, yet they keep time to the Voices with the greatest exactness imaginable. . . .

They that compose the Musick of the Opera, endeavor to conclude the Scenes of the Principal Actors with Airs that Charm and Elevate, that so they may acquire the Applause of the Audience, which succeeds so well to their intentions, that one hears nothing but a Thousand *Benissimo's* together; yet nothing is so remarkable as the pleasant Benedictions and the Ridiculous Wishes of the *Gondoliers* in the Pit to the Women-Singers . . . for those impudent Fellows *(canailles)* say whatever they please, as being assured to make the Assembly rather Laugh than Angry.[28]

Ten years later, Maximilien Misson, obviously no enthusiastic devotee, had this to say about the Venetian opera:

The Habits are poor, there are no Dances, and commonly no fine Machines, nor any fine Illuminations; only some Candles here and there, which deserve not to be mentioned . . . they have most excellent Ayres . . . but I cannot forbear telling you, that I find a certain Confusion and Unpleasantness in several Parts of their Singing in those Opera's: They dwell many times longer on one Quavering, than in singing Four whole Lines; and oftentimes they run so fast, that 'tis hard to tell whether they sing or Speak, or whether they do neither of the Two and both together. . . . The

28. [Limojon de St. Didier], *The City and Republick of Venice*, part 3, pp. 61–63.

Symphony is much smaller than at *Paris*; but perhaps, it is never the worse for that. There is also one Thing which charms them, which I believe would not please you; I mean those unhappy Men who basely suffer themselves to be maimed, that they may have the finer Voices. The silly Figure! which, in my Opinion, such a mutilated Fellow makes, who sometimes acts the Bully, and sometimes the Passionate Lover, with his Effeminate Voice, and wither'd Chin[,] is such a thing to be endured? . . . There are at present Seven several Opera's at *Venice*, which Strangers, as we are, are in a manner oblig'd to frequent, knowing not, some times, how to spend an Evening any where else.[29]

Later Italian Composers

The leading composers in this period who worked principally at Venice were Antonio Sartorio (ca. 1620–1681), Giovanni Legrenzi (1626–1690),[30] Pietro Andrea Ziani (ca 1620–1684), Giovanni Domenico Freschi (1640–1690), and Carlo Francesco Pollarolo (1653–1722). Sartorio's chief work was the serious "heroic opera" *Adelaide* (1672). Legrenzi excelled in the genre of the "heroic-comic" opera, which intermingled serious and comic scenes; and he was noted for the unusual care he gave to the orchestra, both in independent instrumental numbers and in accompaniments. His principal operas were *Totila* (1677) and *Il Giustino* (1683). At the hands of these later composers the trend was toward comedy or parody, with lightening of the musical texture, lessening musical importance of the recitative, increasing dominance of the aria, and larger use of the orchestra for accompaniments.

The songs of the earliest operas had been accompanied only by the continuo instruments, improvising in a more or less elaborate texture over a figured bass. Orchestral ritornellos, first used on an extensive scale by Monteverdi in *Orfeo*, were eventually brought into close relation with the vocal part by the simple

29. Misson, *A New Voyage to Italy*, 1:269–70.
30. See Fogaccia, *Giovanni Legrenzi*.

device of using the same thematic material in both.[31] A further
step was taken when the orchestral instruments, instead of being
confined to the pauses between sections or stanzas of the aria,
played with the voice, either as a continuous supporting accompaniment or constantly alternating with the vocal phrases in echoes
or imitations.[32] During the latter part of the seventeenth century
the simple continuo accompaniment of arias declined in favor. In
Cavalli's *Giasone* (1649), only 9 out of 27 arias had been accompanied by the orchestra; in Cesti's *La Dori* (1661), only 5 out of
32; in Stradella's *La forza d'amor paterno* (1678), 35 out of 51;
and in Steffani's *Servio Tullio* (1686), 23 out of 52. The number
varied according to circumstances; the Vienna opera had a large
orchestra, and we consequently find many orchestral accompaniments in the works of Antonio Draghi (see chapter 8). The later
Venetians, especially Pollarolo, introduced the orchestra more
frequently, while Handel in his *Agrippina* (Venice, 1709) has 31
of the 40 arias accompanied by the orchestra, and Scarlatti in
Telemaco (Rome, 1718) dispenses with the continuo-accompanied
arias altogether.[33]

 After 1650, when many other Italian cities opened public
opera theaters,[34] the style developed by Cavalli, Cesti, and their
followers at Venice came to be experienced as a national and even
an international possession. Operas by the Venetian composers
were given performances in other cities—Freschi's, for example,
at Bologna; Cavalli's *Giasone* in at least fourteen other Italian
cities within eighteen years; Cesti's *Argia* (Innsbruck, 1655) at
Rome, Naples, Venice, Milan, Siena, Genoa, Reggio, and Udine.

 When Cesti's *Argia* was performed at Venice in 1670, it
was provided with an unusual prologue. The scene is the interior
of a library; the five characters are seen browsing through the
collection. Each, in turn, selects a volume of music from the shelves

31. As in Landi's *Sant' Alessio* (Goldschmidt, *Studien*, 1:211); Rossi's *Orfeo* (Goldschmidt,
Studien, 1:301); Monteverdi's *Il ritorno* (finale of Act III) and *Poppea* (see Wellesz, "Cavalli," p. 32).

32. An example of continuous supporting accompaniment is found in Oronte's aria "Ren-
ditimi il mio bene," in Act I of Cesti's *La Dori*, in Eitner, ed., *Publikationen*, 12:129ff.

33. Mattheson, in his *Die neueste Untersuchung der Singspiele* (p. 162), written in 1744,
laments the passing of the continuo arias, which he says had long since gone out of fashion.

34. For a list of the local histories dealing with these theaters, see Bustico, *Bibliografia
. . . dei teatri italiani.*

Scene from *Servio Tullio* (Act II, scene 19) by Steffani, performed in Munich, 1686; designed by Domenico Mauro.

and sings an aria from it. Among those arias are two by Draghi, taken from his opera *Il ratto delle Sabine* ("The Rape of the Sabine Women"), which was written presumably for a Venetian production in 1670 but was not staged until 1674 in Vienna.[35]

In addition to the composers already named, there were others in this period who had either limited connection or none at all with Venice. Carlo Pallavicino (1630?–1688) began at Venice, where twenty of his operas were staged, but later he worked principally at Dresden.[36] At the Teatro San Bartolomeo, the first public opera house in Naples, the repertoire included a number of Venetian works along with those written by two Neapolitan composers of importance, Francesco Cirillo (1623–1656) and Francesco Provenzale (1627–1704).[37] Cirillo, whose *Orontea regina d'Egitto* ("Oronte, Queen of Egypt," 1654) and *Il ratto d'Elena* ("The Rape of Helen," 1655) were among the first operas performed at the new theater, was actively involved with Venetian opera as a singer and member of the Febiarmonici and also as a director, arranger, and producer of the Venetian repertoire.[38] In contrast, Provenzale seems to have had little connection with Venice. Only two of his operas are extant, but the music from them shows a fine quality of expressiveness and a subtle use of chromatic harmony comparable to the best Italian style of the period (example 7.10).[39]

Another notable late seventeenth-century composer was Alessandro Stradella (1644–1682), whose roving and adventurous life, spent mainly in Rome and Genoa, has furnished the subject of operas by Flotow (1844) and others. His stage works as well as some two hundred and fifty cantatas show a facility and sensuous grace of melodic invention that justify his position in history as an important predecessor of Scarlatti and the Italian school of the eighteenth century.[40] Stradella's best-known stage works are

35. Glover, *Cavalli*, pp. 114–15.

36. For further discussion of Pallavicino, see chap. 8.

37. Goldschmidt, "Francesco Provenzale."

38. See Stalnaker, "The Beginnings of Opera in Naples"; Bianconi and Walker, "Dalla *Finta pazza* alla *Veremonde*."

39. A facsimile edition of Provenzale's *Il schiavo* is in Brown, ed., *Italian Opera 1640–1770*, vol. 7.

40. See Giazotto, *Vita di Alessandro Stradella*; Hess, *Zur Geschichte des musikalischen Dramas*; and other studies by Allam, Gianturco, Gentili, Richard, Catelani, Roncaglia, Della Corte, and Jander.

Example 7.10: *Il schiavo di sua moglie*, Act I, sc. 8

the comic opera *Il trespolo tutore* (ca. 1677; see example 7.11)[41] and *La forza d'amor paterno* (Genoa, 1678). His connection with Venice, however, is limited to the new prologues and intermezzos which he composed for revivals of Venetian operas staged in other cities. Among these were Cavalli's *Giasone*, Freschi's *Helena*, Melani's *Il Girello*, and Cesti's *La Dori*.[42]

---

41. Gianturco, "A Possible Date for Stradella's *Il trespolo tutore*."

42. Jander, "The Prologues and Intermezzos of Alessandro Stradella."

Example 7.11: *Il trespolo tutore*, Act II, sc. 9

STRADELLA

Che pen - si mio co - re che ru - mi - ni tu, che pen - si mio

be - ne che ru - mi - ni tu? Già per - so èil tuo

be - ne e se - co og - ni spe - me se - co og - ni spe - me d'ha - ver - lo mai

più, già per - so èil tuo be - ne e se - co o - gni spe - me e se - co o - gni

spe - me d'ha - ver - lo mai più. Che pen - si mio co - re che ru - mi - ni

tu, che pen - si mio co - re che ru - mi - ni tu, che ru - mi - ni tu?

CHAPTER EIGHT

Italian Opera in the Later Seventeenth Century: In Germany

The South German courts were not slow to import Italian opera. Performances are recorded in Salzburg as early as 1618; Vienna and Prague soon followed (1626, 1627). Cesti's works were performed at Innsbruck from 1655 to 1665, and there was Italian opera at Regensburg and Munich from 1653.

Vienna

The chief center, as might be expected, was Vienna.[1] Monteverdi, Cavalli, and Cesti were heard there by the middle of the century; subsequent composers included Antonio Bertali (1605–1669), Giovanni Felice Sances (ca. 1600–1679), Pietro Andrea Ziani (ca. 1620–1684), Emperor Leopold I (reigned 1658–1705), and the most prolific of all, Antonio Draghi (1635–1700), who between 1663 and 1699 contributed more than one hundred dramatic pieces of

---

1. See Köchel, *Die kaiserliche Hofmusikkapelle*; Nettl, "Zur Geschichte der kaiserlichen Hofkapelle"; idem, "Exzerpte aus der Raudnitzer Textbüchersammlung"; Weilen, *Zur Wiener Theatergeschichte*; idem, *Geschichte des Wiener Theaterwesens*; Haas, *Die Wiener Oper*; Adler, "Die Kaiser . . . als Tonsetzer"; Wellesz, "Die Opern und Oratorien in Wien"; idem, *Essays on Opera*, nos. 2–5; Bauer, *Opern und Operetten in Wien*; Brockpähler, *Handbuch zur Geschichte der Barockoper*.

Scene from *Il fuoco eterno* (1674) by A. Draghi; designed by Lodovico Burnacini.

(From *Denkmäler des Theaters*, Mappe 7, no. 5)

various kinds to the Viennese repertoire.[2] Draghi, his librettist Nicolo Minato, and the court architect Ludovico Burnacini were the leaders of opera at Vienna during the last three decades of the century.

Draghi was a court composer of skill and facility, if not distinction. The airs of his early works are usually short and in strophic form, typically with the first part returning after a middle section in the dominant (or relative major), either with or without thematic contrast. In his later works this evolved into a full da capo form, with much textual repetition and extremely difficult bravura passages. His recitatives are of the parlando variety, generally barren of musical interest, though occasionally a few measures of arioso are introduced, as in the older Venetian style. His overtures also follow the Venetian model and frequently have dance movements at the end.

Dresden

A style similar to Draghi's is found in the later works of Carlo Pallavicino, director of the first permanent opera theatre at Dresden from 1686.[3] The libretto of his *Gerusalemme liberata* ("Jerusalem Liberated"), composed for Dresden in 1687, combines three episodes from Tasso with a number of newly invented incidents in considerable confusion but with opportunity for several of the favorite spectacular scenes.[4] Comic episodes are less conspicuous than in most contemporary operas, and each of the three acts ends with a ballet. Despite its melodic inventiveness and surety of style, the music gives a total impression of monotony. With the exception of two duets, everything is for solo voice. The sixty-six arias are for the most part very short and preponderantly in

2. Cf. Neuhaus, "Antonio Draghi" (with catalogue of works and many musical examples), and Seifert, *Neues zu Antonio Draghis Weltlichen Werken* (on the authenticity of Draghi's secular works).

3. Although the first opera house in Dresden was opened in 1667, Italian singers were not engaged to sing there on a regular basis until the 1680s.

4. See H. Abert's introduction to the edition of this work in DdT, vol. 50.

Example 8.1: *Gerusalemme liberata*, Act II, sc. 12

da capo form; the orchestral ritornello, played either at the beginning or end, is based on a motif from the aria itself. Certain mannerisms obtrude: phrases are constantly repeated in echo style,[5] whether or not the text justifies such a procedure (example 8.1). The device of sequence is ever present; there are many passages of brilliant coloratura, especially in the larger arias accompanied by the full orchestra. On the other hand, many of the smaller arias are in simple, popular style, including examples of the barcarole and siciliano types. The formal balance is always clear; the middle section of the da capo arias are shorter than the first part and usually offer contrast of key, material, phrase structure, and general design (example 8.2).

There are three accompanied recitatives and two ostinato bass arias. One of the latter (Act I, scene 1), in genuine passacaglia style, is nevertheless in *a–b–a* form, the third and last variation being a literal repetition of the first—a striking instance of the imposition of the da capo idea on the older form.

One feature of the instrumental music in Pallavicino is the frequent repetition of phrases. Sometimes this is merely the echo effect common in the songs, but the repetition may also involve a contrast of instrumentation. The second movement of the overture, for example, consists only of five two-measure phrases, each of which is first played by the continuo instruments alone and then immediately repeated by the full orchestra. Similar places are found in many of the ritornellos: usually (as in the overture) a mere antiphony of short phrases between different instrumental groups, but occasionally a more freely developed concerto-like

5. Cf. Kretzschmar, "Einige Bemerkungen."

Example 8.2: *Gerusalemme liberata*, Act II, sc. 3

PALLAVICINO

* These six measures are repeated.

structure in miniature.[6] Essentially, this procedure amounts to no more than taking over into the instrumental field a practice already established in the orchestrally accompanied arias, with their interplay of solo voice and orchestra. Yet it is worth noting that the appearance of the concerto principle in the instrumental music of opera at this time coincides with the earliest independent compositions for string orchestra in concerto style. The trumpet concerto, a favorite of a slightly earlier period, is represented in the overture to Pallavicino's *Diocletiano* (Venice, 1675) and in a sinfonia from the first act of M. A. Sartorio's *Adelaide* (Venice, 1672).[7]

Munich, Hanover, Düsseldorf

One of the leading Italian composers in Germany was Agostino Steffani (1654–1728), whose eighteen operas were written between 1681 and 1709. Steffani was at Munich from 1667 to 1672 and again from 1674 to 1688, with an occasional sojourn in such cities as Rome and Paris. After this he went to Hanover to serve Duke Ernst August both as a musician and as a diplomat. In this fifteen-year period (1688–1703) he composed eight or nine operas, which were performed in Hanover's newest theater, built in 1688 for the benefit of a resident Italian opera company. During the same period he became increasingly involved with affairs of state, to the extent that his diplomatic missions ultimately brought about a change in the direction of his career. One manifestation of this change was his move to Düsseldorf, where his duties were primarily of a diplomatic and administrative nature. Although his musical activities continued, as evidenced by the production of three operas in this Düsseldorf period, the majority of his compositions, including the excellent chamber duets and the sacred works, were written before 1703. He was the principal intermediary between

6. See also the overture to *L'amazone corsara* (1688) in Heuss, *Die Instrumental-Stücke . . . venetianischen Opern-Sinfonien*, p. 121.

7. Cf. Schering, *Geschichte des Instrumentalkonzerts*, pp. 27ff.

the Italian opera of the late seventeenth century and the German operas of Keiser and Handel so that, even apart from his own achievements as a composer, his historical position is an important one.[8]

The librettos of Steffani's operas differ from Pallavicino's and other contemporary Italian composers' only in their use of subjects from German history and a diminished emphasis on mythological and spectacular elements. The musical form shows the usual regular alternation of recitative and aria, relieved only by an occasional accompanied recitative or duet. But the contrapuntal texture of the music marks a profound break with the prevailing tendencies in Italy, which were toward the homophonic style. Steffani's basses in the continuo arias are independently moving contrapuntal lines. In the orchestrally accompanied arias, the voice is treated as one instrument among several, yet without ever sacrificing its position as "chief among equals" or taking on any nonvocal traits. Concertizing instruments (solo flutes, oboes, violins, bassoon, or trumpet) weave strands of melody about the vocal part, while the full orchestra joins in at the cadences. The characteristic arias are lyrical rather than dramatic, noble and serious in expression—long-breathed, leisurely melodies, effortlessly flowing (example 8.3).

Attention must be called in example 8.3 to the way in which the voice makes a false start, beginning the first phrase of the aria only to abandon it during a short instrumental interlude, after which the phrase is begun again and continued normally. This peculiarity—called by German writers *Devise* and often rendered in English as the "motto beginning"[9]—first came prominently into operatic music with Legrenzi: twenty-six of the arias in his *Eteocle e Polinice* (Venice, 1675) begin in this way. Instances may be found also in Cesti and earlier; it was very commonly used by Pallavicino and P. A. Ziani and by the end of the century had become an almost unconscious mannerism of style, constantly present in the arias of Steffani, Handel, Fux, and other

8. For writings about Steffani, see Untersteiner, De Rensis, Einstein, and Baxter. See also Chrysander, *G. F. Händel*, 1:309–73; Fischer, *Musik in Hannover*; Werner, "Agostino Steffanis Operntheater"; Keppler, "Agostino Steffani's Hannover Operas."

9. See G. F. Schmidt, *Die frühdeutsche Oper*, 2:382–97, for a critical definition, history, and examples of this device.

Example 8.3: *Alcibiade*, Act I, sc. 3

(Example 8.3 continued)

Example 8.4: *Tassilone* (1709), Act III, sc. 6

STEFFANI

(Largo)

Tut-ta tre - mo e per le ve-ne___ Fred-do scor-re un gel mor-

ta - - - - - - - - le.

composers. In many of Scarlatti's arias, the first word or phrase of the text will be repeated but with different music—the first statement being like a mere prelude or announcement, whereas the second is the real beginning of the song.

The fundamental simplicity of Steffani's arias does not exclude melismatic passages, many of which have no particular justification in the text but seem to well forth as the natural completion of the musical idea (example 8.4).

The bravura aria is less characteristic of Steffani, though it was a favorite of Cesti, P. A. Ziani, Sartorio, and other Italian composers. Written for texts of stirring or martial character,[10] these airs abounded in virtuoso passage work; trumpet-like figures in the melody or the addition of a trumpet obbligato rendered the effect even more brilliant (example 8.5).

Steffani's arias are nearly all in da capo form. In keeping with the contrapuntal character of his music, there is an unusually high proportion of arias on a ground bass, which sometimes itself determines the form but more often is simply incorporated in the da capo pattern. In many instances, the ostinato principle is modified, leaving a bass consisting of a steady movement in quarter or eighth notes (walking bass), or of a characteristic rhythmic motif constantly repeated.[11] The accompanied recitatives, with their flexible structure and free mingling of declamatory and arioso phrases, recall the old Monteverdi-Cavalli ideal of purely dramatic song.

Steffani's overtures are obviously modeled on those of Lully, with whose music he had become acquainted on a visit to

10. Cf. Bücken, *Der heroische Stil.*
11. Cf. Riemann, *"Basso ostinato* und *Basso* quasi *ostinato."*

Example 8.5: *Tassilone*, Act IV, sc. 8

STEFFANI

Paris in 1678–79. Steffani is credited with being the first to introduce trio sections in the fast movement of the overture—short interludes for solo instruments, contrasting with the *tutti* in the manner of the *concerto grosso*.

      Steffani stands at one of the culminating points of operatic style at the end of the seventeenth century. He was a spontaneous genius on the order of Mozart or Schubert rather than a dramatist like Cavalli or Handel, and his works represent in perfection the goal of musical opera toward which the whole century had been moving. In his music at last is achieved the reconciliation of the monodic principle with the contrapuntal tradition. Steffani's operas, like the (contemporary) trio sonatas of Corelli, exemplify that balanced classical style of the late baroque which led the way in the next generation to the monumental achievements of Bach and Handel. The aristocratic, dignified, musically serious style of Steffani found successors in the early eighteenth century only in the works of a few exceptional northern composers—for example, Johann Christoph Pez (1664–1716) at Munich and Bonn, and more notably in the works of Keiser and Handel. In Italy it was a stranger; there the demand for simplicity and melody, always immanent in the Italian temperament as well as in the nature of opera itself as a large public spectacle, led ineluctably to the *galanteries* of the eighteenth century.

Echoes of the older style can be heard in the ceremonial operas or *feste teatrali* of Johann Josef Fux (1660–1741), court music director at Vienna from 1713, composer of eighteen operas and much church music, and author of a famous treatise on counterpoint, the *Gradus ad Parnassum*.[12] His *Costanza e fortezza* ("Constancy and Fortitude") was performed at Prague in 1723 to celebrate at the same time the coronation of Emperor Charles VI and the birthday of the empress. Like Fux's other operatic works of the 1720s, *Costanza e fortezza* is filled with elaborate scenic effects, machines, and choruses—all the apparatus, in short, appropriate to festive occasions. The nature of these occasions, as well as Fux's official position, dictated a conservative, somewhat stiff, old-fashioned style in his music; yet he was not without progressive traits. His earlier operas consist almost entirely of solo numbers. Even in the later ceremonial works, the arias and ensembles are in the full da capo form characteristic of the eighteenth century; contrapuntal elements are present but not predominant, and the general baroque severity is lightened by graceful melodies and dancelike rhythms.

12. Köchel, *Johann Josef Fux*; Meer, *Johann Josef Fux als Opernkomponist*.

Proscenio della festa Teatrale intitolata COSTANZA e FORTEZZA rappresentata nel Reale Castello di Praga L'anno MDCCXXIII.

Scene from *Costanza e Fortezza* (Prague, 1723), by J. J. Fux; designed
by Giuseppe Galli Bibiena.

CHAPTER NINE

Early German Opera

The early history of opera in Germany is not one of a comparatively unified development, as in France or England, or even of the evolution of a comparatively consistent musical style, as in Italy. The numerous political subdivisions of Germany in the seventeenth century, the many different cultural traditions, the conflicting elements in both the dramatic and the musical background, and the extremely strong infusion of foreign styles (chiefly Italian, but some French) to different degrees in different parts of the country—all combine to produce a complicated task for the historian.

Abstractly speaking, a purely "German" opera is one written for performance by German artists for German audiences, with an original libretto in the German language and on a German (or, at least, not a typically foreign) subject, composed by a German, and with music in a German (or, at least, not predominantly foreign) style. In actuality, there are few, if any, operas of the early period which correspond to this admittedly narrow definition. What we find are foreign conductors and singers performing before German courts whose tastes are often formed on Italian and French models; librettos in Italian or in German translations or paraphrases of Italian or French texts; Italian composers, or German composers aping the Italian manner; and all possible permutations and combinations of these elements. Add to these conditions the fact that many composers were active in different places; that frequently the same opera poem appeared under different names, and different poems under the same name; that composers habitually used music from their own earlier works or inserted in their scores music from other sources; and finally that the scores themselves, a study of which alone could resolve many of the problems, are in the great majority of cases utterly lost or survive only in fragments—and it will be readily seen that a complete history of German opera in the seventeenth and early eighteenth centuries is, if not quite impossible, at least far beyond the scope of the present work. It has seemed best, therefore, to begin this chapter with a brief survey of the political and social conditions under which German opera was composed and of the dramatic and musical factors which entered into it, to indicate some of the principal developments at important centers, and then to concentrate on the most distinctive of the many local schools, that of Hamburg.[1]

In the seventeenth century, Germany was not a nation but a loose confederation of some 1,700 more or less independent states. Most of these were petty "knights' dominions," but there were also fifty-one free imperial cities (of which the chief were Hamburg, Bremen, Frankfurt am Main, Nuremberg, Augsburg, Ulm, and Strassburg), sixty-three ecclesiastical holdings, and nearly two hundred secular principalities and counties, a few of which were of considerable size and importance. The semblance of unity arising from an ill-defined allegiance to the Holy Roman Empire was disrupted by the Thirty Years War (1618–1648), a calamity which left the country economically prostrated and bereft of almost all pride in its national heritage. Like a body weakened by illness, German culture was invaded by foreign elements. The language became filled with French and Spanish words; French became the common tongue of polite society;[2] the little local courts,

1. The conditions of early German opera are reflected in the fact that the great majority of the studies in this field are in the form of local or regional histories, embodying chronicles and statistics. References to this extensive literature will be found in the three chief general surveys of the period: Kretzschmar, "Das erste Jahrhundert der deutschen Oper," in his *Geschichte der Oper*, pp. 133–57; Moser, *Geschichte der deutschen Musik*, 2: book 2, chap. 3; and Schiedermair, *Die deutsche Oper*, part 1. See also Bolte, *Die Singspiele der englischen Komödianten*; Haas, "Die Oper in Deutschland bis 1750"; Schletterer, *Das deutsche Singspiel*; G. F. Schmidt, "Zur Geschichte, Dramaturgie und Statistik"; Schreiber, *Dichtung und Musik der deutschen Opernarien*; Huber, "Das Textbuch der frühdeutschen Oper"; Brockpähler, *Handbuch zur Geschichte der Barockoper in Deutschland*. A bibliography of regional and local histories of German music will be found in *MGG*, vol. 3, s.v. "Deutschland," cols. 364–90. Biographies of many composers are to be found in Mattheson, *Grundlage einer Ehrenpforte* (1740).

2. A proverb at the Brunswick court in the latter part of the seventeenth century ran: "Wer nicht französisch kann, Der kommt bei Hof nicht an." Hartmann, *Sechs Bücher*, p. 85. See also *Braunschweigischer Magazin* (1903), 9:116–17.

narrow, paternalistic, and extravagant, aspired to imitate the glories of Versailles. Italian opera thus made its appearance as a courtly show, particularly in southern Germany, where we have already seen some of its manifestations at Vienna, Dresden, Munich, Hanover, and Düsseldorf.

The German equivalent of the term "opera" was *Singspiel*, a literal translation of the Italian *dramma per musica*.[3] Ayrer's comedies on popular song-tunes at Nuremberg (from 1598) bear the designation *singets Spil*; the first operas at Hamburg were called *Sing-Spiele*. The term was applied in the seventeenth and early eighteenth centuries both to works sung in their entirety and to those having some spoken dialogue. In the second half of the eighteenth century, its meaning was restricted to works of the latter type. (It may be added that, in the absence of scores, it is not always possible to ascertain in the case of some seventeenth-century German operas whether the recitatives were sung or spoken.) The word "opera" does not often occur in German scores before 1720.[4]

Many courts tried at first to encourage German talent. For example, the "first German opera," *Dafne*, was created and performed in Torgau in 1627 to celebrate the marriage of Princess Luise of Saxony and Landgraf Georg von Hessen-Darmstadt. This work was the old *Dafne* of Rinuccini, translated and adapted by the leading German poet of the time, Martin Opitz, with music by Heinrich Schütz (1585–1672). The score has not survived. In Vienna, the early Italian operas occasionally had German songs inserted. Dresden also staged a few works in German before the establishment of the Italian opera company in the 1680s.[5] One of these, another *Dafne* (1671), with music by Giovanni Bontempi and Marco Peranda (1625–1675), is the earliest German opera for which the full score is extant.[6]

At Brunswick-Wolfenbüttel, the court opera employed

---

3. Cf. [Hunold:] "Eine *Opera* oder ein Sing-Spiel ist gewiss das galanteste Stück der Poesie, so man heut zutage aestimieren pfleget." *Die allerneueste Art* (1707), p. 394.

4. See G. F. Schmidt, *Die frühdeutsche Oper*, 2:45–54.

5. Among them were four other operatic works by Schütz for which only the librettos survive. For a listing of baroque opera in Germany, see Brockpähler, *Handbuch*.

6. Engländer, "Zur Frage der *Dafne*."

native poets, subjects, and composers (Erlebach, Philipp Krieger, Bronner, Kusser, Keiser), but with the opening of a public theater in 1690, the demand for foreign goods became so strong that French and Italian works had to be added to the repertoire. A temporary revival of native opera in the early eighteenth century was led by Georg Caspar Schürmann (ca. 1672–1751), one of the most significant of the German composers, whose dignified, serious musical style has much in common with that of Keiser, Handel, and Bach. Between 1700 and 1730, he composed about forty operas, including *Endimione* (1700), the sacred operas *Salomon* (1701) and *David* (1701), and *Ludwig der Fromme* ("Louis the Pious," 1726), considered to be Schürmann's chief work in this genre.[7] Few of his opera scores have been preserved.

At Leipzig, an opera house was founded by Nikolaus Adam Strungk (1640–1700), opening in 1693 with a performance of his *Alceste*. Here, where operas were played during the Fair season from 1693 to 1720, the texts were mostly translations of Venetian librettos. Poets and composers, players and singers were largely recruited from the students of the school of St. Thomas's church, and so successfully that Kuhnau in 1709 complained that church music suffered from the competition.[8] The general enthusiasm for opera at Leipzig was such that even J. S. Bach did not altogether escape its influence.[9] Another center of German opera was Weissenfels; here the leading composer was Johann Philipp Krieger (1649–1725), whose opera songs were in the tradition of the simple German *lieder*. The subject matter of the Weissenfels operas, however, was not distinctively German; the repertoire shows a strong preponderance of mythological dramas and ballets. A similarly ambiguous picture is presented at many of the lesser courts—German elements struggling against a rising tide of Italian opera, which by the fourth decade of the eighteenth century had won the field everywhere.

7. See G. F. Schmidt, *Die frühdeutsche Oper.*

8. Spitta, *Johann Sebastian Bach,* 2:854.

9. The most obviously dramatic work of Bach is *Phoebus und Pan* (composed for the Leipzig Collegium Musicum in 1731), which one contemporary called a "Gesprächspiel" (Spitta, *Bach,* 2:740). Several of the so-called secular cantatas actually bear the designation "Drama" or "Drama per Musica," and others (e.g., the "Coffee Cantata") are semi-dramatic—not to mention the Passions and oratorios, in which the influence of dramatic forms is clearly evident.

The most likely German forerunner of opera was the school drama, a play in Latin or German, usually of a moral or religious nature, didactic in aim, performed by the students of a school or seminary. Many of these dramas in the sixteenth century included instrumental dances, solo odes, and choral pieces.[10] In the early seventeenth century, the musical portions became more extensive. Although the Thirty Years War put an end to the most flourishing era of the school drama, its influence may be seen in the earliest German opera whose music has been preserved: *Seelewig*, a "spiritual pastorale" by Georg Philipp Harsdörffer, set to music by Sigmund Theophil Staden (1607–1655),[11] and published at Nuremberg in 1644 in a family periodical.[12] As with the first Hamburg opera, nearly thirty-five years later, the subject matter of this singular extant example for Nuremberg is religious. The form is allegorical. "Seelewig" is the soul; the villain of the piece is one Trügewalt, who attempts to ensnare Seelewig with the help of other characters representing Art, the Senses, and so on, while Wisdom and Conscience act as her defenders. The final triumph of virtue is celebrated by an invisible chorus of angels. This highly moral drama is placed in a fashionable pastoral setting: the sylvan scenes are described in poetry filled with moral symbolism, and Seelewig's companions are nymphs and shepherds, while Trügewalt is portrayed as a satyr. Each of the three acts is introduced by a symphony, and there are a few other short instrumental pieces, together with the composer's direction that more may be added if necessary in order to avoid pauses during the changing of the scenery. The second and third acts conclude with a choral movement, a feature characteristic of the German pastorale. The solo songs, which constitute most of the music, have short melodies, and nearly all are in strophic form. Perhaps the best of these songs is Seelewig's outburst of thanksgiving in the closing scene (example 9.1).

10. See Flemming, *Geschichte des Jesuitentheaters*; Liliencron, "Die Chorgesänge des lateinischen-deutschen Schuldramas"; Schünemann, *Geschichte der deutschen Schulmusik*, pp. 67ff., 137; Culley, *Jesuits and Music*.

11. Cf. Keller, "Stadens Oper *Seelewig*"; Harris, *Handel and the Pastoral Tradition*, chap. 3.

12. *Frauenzimmer Gesprächspiele*, 4:31–165, 489–622. Cf. Narciss, *Studien zu den Frauenzimmergesprächspielen*, pp. 93–96; Tittmann, *Kleine Schriften zur deutschen Literatur*; E. Schmitz, "Zur musikgeschichtlichen Bedeutung."

Example 9.1: *Seelewig*, Act III, sc. 6

STADEN

Ach wun-der star - ker Gott der du durch man-

- che Nacht mich gnä-dig - lich ___ ge- führ - et. Es ist kein

Un-ge-lück kein Aug-undHert-zen-blickda ich mich wol re - gi - ret.

(Three more stanzas)

   Seelewig was not the only effort of Harsdörffer along
operatic lines. If in that work he showed himself a follower of the
Italian pastorale, in *Die Tugendsterne* ("The Stars of Virtue") he
sought to turn to moral purposes another favorite genre, the ballet with machines;[13] still another play, *Von der Welt Eitelkeit* ("Of
Worldly Vanity"), consists of four allegorical scenes, each representing a worldly Vanity, with an epilogue sung by Death.[14] No
doubt such works are exceptional, in that they were designed primarily for reading rather than performance; but they show what
kind of stage spectacles presumably interested the citizens of Nuremberg at this period. A later Nuremberg composer, Johann

13. *Frauenzimmer Gesprächspiele*, 5:280–310; see also Haar, "Astral Music in Seventeenth-Century Nuremberg."

14. *Frauenzimmer Gesprächspiele*, 3:170–242. A nearly complete reprint, with the music,
appears in Schmitz, "Zur musikgeschichtlichen Bedeutung," pp. 264–75.

Löhner (1645–1705), is represented for us by some surviving arias but no complete scores.

With the increase of Italian opera everywhere in the south, the native school found a home not in one of the courts but in the free imperial north German city of Hamburg. Here for sixty years (1678–1738) flourished with varying fortunes a public opera house, the first in Europe outside Italy, where German composers were able for a time to combine contributions from Italian and French sources with their own genius to make an original, truly national form.[15]

The earliest Hamburg operas show the influence of the school drama. The initial work performed in the new opera house presented the story of Adam and Eve, under the title *Der erschaffene, gefallene und wieder aufgerichtete Mensch* ("The Creation, Fall, and Redemption of Man," 1678), with music by Schütz's pupil, Johann Theile (1646–1724).[16] Many similar titles appeared in the next few years. Such material was not only traditional but also useful in retaining the good will of the Lutheran church authorities and providing a defense of the opera against frequent attacks on the ground of its worldly and immoral character. Despite sporadic opposition, secular operas soon gained the ascendancy. Composers and poets began to introduce subjects from the Italian and French stages—chiefly translations or adaptations from Venetian librettists (especially Minato), but also occasionally from Corneille (*Andromeda und Perseus,* 1679), from Quinault (*Alceste,* 1680), and from Italian comedies. In addition, a few foreign operas were performed in French (Lully's *Acis et Galatée,* 1689, and Colasse's *Achille et Polyxène,* 1692) or Italian (Cesti's *La schiava fortunata,* 1693,[17] Pallavicino's *Gerusalemme liberata,* 1693, and others). Many of Steffani's works were presented in German translation, and a number of German composers chiefly

15. See Wolff, *Die Barockoper in Hamburg* (the second volume consists entirely of musical examples); Becker, review of Wolff; Marx, "Geschichte der Hamburger Barock Oper"; Zelm, "Die Sänger"; Flemming, ed., *Die Oper,* introduction; Lindner, *Die erste stehende deutsche Oper;* Chrysander, articles on the Hamburg opera (1678–1706) in *AMZ;* Kleefeld, "Das Orchester der Hamburger Oper"; Moller, *Cimbria literata.*

16. Zelle, *Johann Theile und Nikolaus Adam Strungk.*

17. Probably performed in M. A. Ziani's version. Cesti's *La Semirami* (Vienna, 1667) was adapted as *La schiava fortunata* for Modena (1674) and Venice (1674/76), the latter with additional music by Ziani. See "Cesti," *The New Grove Dictionary,* 4:93.

associated with other cities or courts were also represented in the Hamburg repertoire, notably Schürmann, Strungk,[18] and Krieger.

So far as their literary quality is concerned, the Hamburg librettos were on the average neither worse nor better than

Example 9.2: Aria from *Cara Mustapha* (1686)

J. W. FRANCK

18. Berend, *Nicolaus Adam Strungk*.

(Example 9.2 continued)

durch das gar   zu schwe-re zu schwe - re Lei - den,

durch das gar_____   zu schwe-re Lei - den,   *(8 more measures)*

those of contemporary Italian opera, on which they were modeled. (As in Venice, the machines played a conspicuous role.) The
leading poets were Christian Heinrich Postel (1658–1705), Friedrich Christian Bressand (ca. 1670–1699; also active at Brunswick), Lucas von Bostel (1649–1716), and Barthold Feind (1678–
1721), the last of whom took the lead in cultivating caricature and
parody. Chief among those who composed the music for the Hamburg stage were Johann Wolfgang Franck (1644–ca. 1710),[19]
Johann Philipp Förtsch (1652–1732),[20] and Johann Sigismund
Kusser (1660–1727).[21]

19. Zelle, *Johann Wolfgang Franck*; Squire, "J. W. Franck in England"; Sachs, "Die
Ansbacher Hofkapelle"; G. F. Schmidt, "Johann Wolfgang Francks Singspiel *Die drey
Töchter Cecrops*"; Günther Schmidt, *Die Musik am Hofe der Markgrafen von
Brandenburg-Ansbach*; Klages, *Johann Wolfgang Franck*.

20. His opera scores have not been preserved. See Zelle, *Johann Philippe Förtsch*;
Wiedemann, *Leben und Wirken des Johann Philipp Förtsch*.

21. The name is sometimes spelled Cousser or Cusser. See Scholz, *Kusser*; Samuel, "Kusser."

Example 9.3: *Die drey Töchter Cecrops*, Act V, sc. 4

FRANCK

Wenn man sei - nen Zweck er - hält, muss man sich um nich-tes küm-mern, und da-durch sein Glück ver-schlim-mern, das doch, eh' man's meynt, ver-fällt, _____ das doch, eh' man's meynt, ver-fällt.

Franck composed fourteen operas for Hamburg between 1679 and 1686. His music is serious in tone and shows a fine feeling for long-breathed, expressive lines (example 9.2) as well as for melodies in a lighter, more popular vein (example 9.3). He writes arias in a variety of musical forms, including the da capo. He uses a wide range of keys and—exceptional for this time—his scores seem to show evidence of consciously designed tonal architecture. Franck's recitative is more melodic, slower in tempo, and altogether of more musical significance than that of contemporary Italian opera; its style rather resembles the recitative of German seventeenth-century church composers, half declamation and half arioso, measured and dignified in tone, composed with great care for both the rhythm and the expressive content of the text. Altogether, Franck's is a full-textured, stiff-rhythmed baroque music, unmistakably Italian in inspiration but tinged with the serious, heavy formality of Lutheran Germany.

Kusser, on the other hand, had acquired a taste for

Example 9.4: Duet from *Erindo*, Act III

French music from his studies under Lully during a sojourn of eight years at Paris, and so represented a more cosmopolitan style. Kusser's operas were performed at Brunswick and Stuttgart as well as at Hamburg, where he worked from 1694 to 1696. His *Erindo* (1694) is a pastorale on the model of Guarini's *Il Pastor fido*—a choice of libretto attributable perhaps to the composer's French background, since pastorales were uncommon in Italian opera at this period. Kusser's music, as far as can be judged from the extant materials of *Erindo*,[22] is distinguished by attractive *cantabile* melodies, clear formal and tonal schemes, skillful use of concertizing instruments, and numerous little songs in French dance rhythms, such as the passepied (example 9.4), minuet, and gavotte. His importance for the history of German opera is apparently due less to his standing as a composer than to his influence as a conductor and impresario. By making the German public better acquainted with French and Italian music, he was instrumental in preparing the way for the international style of Mattheson, Keiser, and Handel, the leading composers of opera at Hamburg in the early part of the eighteenth century.

22. Notably lacking from the extant items are many of the choral numbers. For a discussion of *Erindo*, see Harris, *Handel and the Pastoral Tradition*, pp. 75–80.

CHAPTER TEN

Lully and the Opera in France

Frrench opera as a continuous institution began only in 1671. This late date is surprising if we reflect that throughout the first part of the seventeenth century (that is, during the reigns of Henri IV and Louis XIII, and the minority of Louis XIV, who assumed power on the death of Mazarin in 1661), close political and cultural relations existed between Italy and the French court. But opera was not congenial to the Gallic spirit, with its rationalistic bias and its quick awareness of absurdities; furthermore, the French for many years held that their language was not suited to recitative, which is the foundation of musical drama. They preferred their drama unadulterated and regarded music in the theater as only an auxiliary to dancing and spectacle. Having their tragedy and their ballet, each the best of its kind in the world, they were of no mind to risk spoiling both by trying to combine them in the form of opera. Yet once launched, the French opera was the only national school in Europe able to maintain itself unbroken through the eighteenth century in the face of Italian competition.[1]

The explanation of this is to be found partly in political circumstances but chiefly in the extraordinary personality of the founder of the French school, Jean-Baptiste Lully (1632–1687).[2]

1. General works on French opera include Blaze, *De l'opéra en France*; Choquet, *Histoire de la musique dramatique en France*; Lajarte, *Bibliothèque musicale du théâtre de l'opéra*; Campardon, *L'Académie royale de musique au XVIIIe siècle*; Borland, "French Opera Before 1750"; Vallas, *Un Siècle de musique et de théâtre à Lyon*; Liuzzi, *I musicisti in Francia*; Anthony, *French Baroque Music*; Isherwood, *Music in the Service of the King*. See also works cited in nn. 2 and 3.

2. See biographies by La Laurencie and Prunières, in which references to sources and other bibliographical material will be found; see also *Lully et l'opéra français*; Rolland,

Italian by birth, Lully came to Paris at the age of fourteen. Having been trained as a ballet dancer and violinist, he rapidly developed into a skillful conductor and composer; a combination of musical talent, ruthlessness, commercial shrewdness, and obsequious manners assured him a brilliant career under the patronage of Louis XIV. In establishing the fundamental pattern of French opera, Lully created a type which incorporated elements from every musical and dramatic form that had already proved itself in France. Those forms were the French classical tragedy as exemplified by the works of Corneille and Racine, the pastorale, the Italian opera, and the French ballet.[3]

Lully's librettist, Philippe Quinault, had begun his career as a playwright.[4] In general form and dramatic framework, his operas are similar to French tragedies of the time. The subject matter, however, is restricted to mythology or legend, including three works *(Roland, Amadis,* and *Armide)* derived from romantic sources. The pastorale genre, which had remained popular in France long after its decline in Italy, and which Lully had used with success in some of his early works, came into his operas especially in the prologues, though in *Isis* and *Roland* there are long pastoral scenes in the body of the opera as well.

Italian opera was known in France from a half-dozen works performed at Paris by visiting troupes between 1645 and 1662, including L. Rossi's *Orfeo* and Cavalli's *Egisto, Serse,* and *Ercole amante* ("Hercules in Love").[5] The last-named work showed evidence of Cavalli's efforts to adapt his music to French taste both in the style of the melodies and recitatives and in the inclusion of many ballet scenes, for which the music was furnished by Lully and other French composers. Italian opera, however, was not a success in France. Undoubtedly audiences were intrigued by the discovery that an entire drama could be set to music, and they enjoyed the ballets; but their real enthusiasm was for the

"Notes sur Lully," in his *Musiciens d'autrefois,* pp. 107–202; Lavignac, *Encyclopédie,* 3:1343–1425; Borrel, *Jean-Baptiste Lully;* Howard, "The Operas of Lully"; Newman, *Jean-Baptiste de Lully and His Tragédies lyriques.*

3. Schletterer, *Vorgeschichte . . . der französischen Oper;* Grout, "Some Forerunners of the Lully Opera"; Anthony, *French Baroque Music.*

4. Gros, *Philippe Quinault.*

5. Prunières, *L'Opéra italien en France.*

stage machines invented by Giacomo Torelli,[6] the like of which had not been seen on such a scale in France since the sixteenth century. The influence of Italian opera was therefore indirect: it stimulated the French to emulate the Italians by trying to create an opera of their own, and it probably led them to favor a large proportion of machine scenes.

The determining factor in the background of French opera, however, was the ballet, which had flourished in France steadily since the famous 1581 production of *Circe ou le Balet comique de la royne*.[7] The accession of the young Louis XIV stimulated a revival of the ballet under Benserade and Lully from 1653 to 1668,[8] as well as a series of "comedy ballets" which Lully wrote in collaboration with Molière, including *Georges Dandin* in 1668, *Monsieur de Pourceaugnac* in 1669, *Les Amants magnifiques* and *Le Bourgeois Gentilhomme* in 1670, and *Psyché* (by Molière, Quinault, and Corneille) in 1671. During these years, Lully perfected all the elements of his mature style; indeed, some of the later ballets and comedy ballets had such elaborate musical and scenic interludes as to be little short of full operas, lacking only a continuous dramatic action developed musically, that is, in recitative.

The official existence of French opera dates from the founding of the Académie Royale de Musique in 1669, under the direction of Pierre Perrin and Robert Cambert (ca. 1628–1677). They staged two operas, or rather pastorales, with music by Cambert, before going bankrupt three years later. Lully, who had hitherto loudly maintained that opera in French was impossible, changed his opinion when his favor with the king enabled him to seize control of the academy and establish a monopoly of operatic performances in France.[9] From 1673 until his death, he produced

6. On Torelli, see Bjurström, *Giacomo Torelli*; Bragaglia, "Celebrazioni Marchigiane"; Torrefranca, "Il *grande stregone* Giacomo Torelli." See also Nicoll, *The Development of the Theatre*, pp. 215–28.

7. Prunières, *Le Ballet de cour*; Ménestrier, *Des Ballets anciens et modernes*. See also references cited in chap. 3, n. 2.

8. Silin, *Benserade and His Ballets de Cour*.

9. See La Laurencie, *Les Créateurs de l'opéra français*; [Truinet and Roquet], *Les Origines de l'opéra français*. The account by Pougin in *Les Vrais Créateurs de l'opéra français* makes Lully seem more of a scoundrel than he really was in this matter, according to Prunières.

an opera nearly every year.[10] These works, all perfectly consistent in form and style, established a type of French national opera destined to endure for a hundred years, essentially unchanged
by Rameau and hardly dethroned even by Gluck.

The nature of opera as conceived by Lully is expressed
in his designation of the form as a *tragédie en musique*—that is,
a tragedy first and foremost, which is then set to music. Interest
in the poem of an opera, and insistence that it be of respectable
dramatic quality, were among the basic differences between the
French and Italian viewpoints in the seventeenth and eighteenth
centuries and indeed (though perhaps to a lesser degree) ever since.
Contemporary French criticism was directed fully as much to
Quinault's texts as to Lully's music. The operas, divided into five
acts, always had a prologue devoted to the glorification of Louis
XIV, with allusions to important recent events of his reign. The
action, unrolling with majestic indifference to realism, presented
a series of personages discoursing lengthily on *l'amour* or *la gloire*
in the intervals of all kinds of improbable adventures. There were
no comic figures, except in *Cadmus* and *Alceste*; everything was
stately, formal, and detached from ordinary life—the kingly opera par excellence, designed not for a general public as in Venice,
not even for an aristocracy as in Rome and Florence, but for a
single individual who was conceived to embody the perfection of
national artistic taste and whose approbation alone was sufficient
to guarantee success: what Louis approved, few dared to con-
demn.

The music was in keeping with this ideal. Its fundamental character may be described by the word "conventional": aspiring not to be new or different but to create the accepted effects
supremely well. There were no startling intervals, chords, or
modulations; everything was kept within moderate bounds, avoiding violence or passion. At its best, therefore, early French opera
was impressive, noble, rich, and dignified; at its worst, barren,
stereotyped, pale, and thin. Considered solely as music, it is likely
to be less appealing to modern ears than contemporary Italian

10. Facsimile editions of seven operas by Lully are included in Brook, ed., *French Opera
in the Seventeenth and Eighteenth Centuries: Ballet de Flore, Le Bourgeois Gentilhomme,
Les Festes de l'Amour et de Bacchus, Atys, Le Triomphe de l'amour, Persée, Armide.*

scores; but considered as opera, and in its proper setting, the French school stands comparison with the Italian very well.

One of Lully's achievements was the creation of musical recitative suited to the French language. His model for the recitative is said to have been the declamation employed in tragedies at the Comédie Française.[11] Almost strictly syllabic, it often falls into a monotony of rhythmic and melodic patterns; yet where the feeling of the text permits, the recitative may display extraordinary variety and naturalness, necessitating for its notation continual changes of time signature. The relatively complex notation of French recitative has sometimes led to an exaggerated view of the contrast between it and the Italian recitative. To a considerable degree, this is a matter of notation rather than of actual sound, although naturally the differences in accent and tempo of the two languages determine the characteristics of the recitative in each case. Modern singers need to be cautioned against taking Lully's recitative too slowly and songfully, forgetting the composer's dictum, "Mon récitatif n'est fait que pour parler."[12]

Occasionally, at points where the emotion expressed by the words is more lofty or concentrated, the recitative gives way to a melodic phrase, which may recur several times in rondo fashion—a procedure analogous to that of Monteverdi or Cavalli, welding recitative and arioso into a unified and expressive whole. A beautiful example of this is the lament in *Persée*, in which the recurring vocal phrase is first announced in the orchestral introduction (example 10.1).

A word is necessary on the interpretation of the time

Example 10.1: *Persée*, Act V, sc. 1

11. Le Cerf de la Viéville, *Comparaison*, 3:188.

12. "My recitative is made only for speaking." Quoted in Le Cerf de la Viéville, *Comparaison*, 3:188.

signatures in Lully. The signs 2 ($=2/2$) and ₵ are two-beat measures, in which theoretically the beat is *half as fast* as in C (a four-beat measure). Thus, where the signatures alternate in the same piece, changing from 2 or ₵ to C, two quarter notes in the latter would have the same value as one half note in the former. The same holds true if the change is from 2 or ₵ to 3 ($=3/4$), or from 3/2 to 3 or C. In other words, the duration of a quarter note is theoretically the same whether the measure is divided into two beats or four, the different signatures being indications of different meters rather than different tempos. Nevertheless, the signatures do serve in some degree as tempo indications, especially in instrumental pieces.[13] In example 10.1, the half notes after 2/2 should not be quite twice as long as the preceding quarters; the change of signature is a way of indicating an *allargando* effect at the cadence rather than an abrupt shift to a slower tempo.

The vocal airs in Lully's operas differ considerably from Italian arias. As a rule, they are not strongly set apart as separate numbers, but are continually interspersed in a scene along with recitatives, duets, choruses, and dances. For the most part these airs are short, narrow in range, and subject to piquant irregularities of phrasing. They do not use coloratura, except for conventional short passages on such picture words as *lancer, briller,* and the like, though the vocal line is ornamented by a multitude of *agréments* (short trills, grace notes, passing tones, and so on). These are seldom indicated in the score, unless by a little *t* or cross above the note affected, which signifies only that some kind of agrément is expected without specifying which one. Their choice and placing were largely a matter of custom and taste, both for singers and for instrumentalists.[14] Thus for the French singer less technical vocal cultivation was required than for the Italian, but a clearer enunciation and a more intelligent grasp of the text.

A favorite type of air in Lully, derived in part from the French popular chanson and in part from instrumental dance music, is illustrated in example 10.2a,b. Part A of this example is from the edition in full score of 1689; part B shows the same air

---

13. See Muffat, *Florileguim*, part 2, introduction.

14. See Aldrich, "The Principal Agréments"; Goldschmidt, *Die Lehre von der vokalen Ornamentik.*

Example 10.2a: *Atys,* Act I

as notated in an edition of 1720. It will be seen that the latter, besides giving fuller directions for realization of the bass and correcting what is probably an error in measure eight, is careful to indicate precisely to which notes the agréments are to be applied. This tune was one of many from Lully's operas that passed into the repertoire of popular chansons and remained familiar to the public for many years (see example 15.3a). Dance rhythms are common in Lully's airs, as is the rondo-like recurrence of the opening phrase in the middle and again at the end of the song.

Example 10.2b: *Atys*, Act I

Lully

Quand le pé - ril est a - gré - a - ble Le moy-

- en de s'en al - lar - mer; Est-ce un grand mal de trop ay -

mer, Ce que l'on trouve ay - ma - ble! Est-ce un grand

mal de trop ay - mer Ce que l'on trouve ai - ma - ble.

A more serious type of air goes back to the French *air de cour*, cultivated in the early and middle seventeenth century by such composers as Antoine Boesset and Michel Lambert.[15] The well-known "Bois épais" from *Amadis* (example 10.3) and the equally famous "Plus j'observe ces lieux" from *Armide*, both occurring in pastoral scenes, show this style at its best.

Lully's operas are filled with long scenes having nothing

15. Gérold, *L'Art du chant en France au XVIIe siècle*.

Example 10.3: *Amadis*, Act II, sc. 4

to do with furthering the action but existing solely to furnish pleasure to eye and ear—pastoral episodes, sacrifices, combats, descents of gods, infernal scenes, funeral and triumphal processions. These pompous displays are the heritage of the seventeenth-
century ballet, and the generic French term *divertissement* well
describes their place in the scheme of the opera. They give occasion for most of the choruses, instrumental numbers, and dances
which are so prominent in Lully. The choruses are generally homophonic and massive, those sung to accompany dancing are characterized by strongly marked rhythms.[16] Scenes with choruses are
particularly numerous in *Bellérophon* (1679), a *tragédie lyrique*.

---

16. Choral parts are frequently subdivided into a *petit choeur* (two sopranos and a
countertenor) and a *grand choeur* (soprano, countertenor, tenor, and bass). See Anthony,
French Baroque Music, pp. 86–88.

Lully's orchestra consists chiefly of the strings (in five parts),[17] which play the ritornellos and overtures, double the chorus parts, and occasionally accompany solos. Flutes or oboes are used especially in pastoral scenes, either in combination with the strings or playing short episodes in trio style with continuo. Bassoons may be added to the ensemble, and the martial scenes employ trumpets and drums. The orchestra of the Paris opera, carefully selected and strictly drilled by Lully himself, achieved a quality of performance that made it celebrated throughout Europe.

Instrumental ritornellos are usually placed at the opening of acts or scenes, and descriptive symphonies (for example, the "Songes agréables" in *Atys*, Act III, scene 4) are common. For the ballets, there are dances and airs. The most frequent dances are the minuet, gavotte, and chaconne; an instrumental "air" in French ballet or opera of this period is a piece played to accompany any dance or other movement on the stage which does not fall into one of the standard dance categories.

The overture, descended from the older canzona, the sonata da chiesa, and the early Venetian overture, and first definitively established by Lully,[18] is a large two-part (not three-part) form. The introductory section, in duple meter, is slow, sonorous, and majestic, marked always by dotted rhythms and usually by suspensions;[19] it cadences on the dominant and is repeated. The second section, the theme of which may be derived from the introduction, is lively and in either triple or duple meter; it begins with imitative entries in the manner of a canzona, but, once the voices have come in, all pretense of systematic imitation is abandoned, though a pseudocontrapuntal texture is maintained throughout, with much sequential treatment (example 10.4). This part, which is also usually repeated, may conclude with a broad allargando somewhat in the style of the opening section, though not necessarily having any thematic resemblance to it. The French

17. There is some debate about whether two or three violas are required for his five-part scoring. For a discussion of the problem, see Riley, *The History of the Viola*, chap. 4.

18. In the ballet *Alcidiane*, 1658. Cf. Prunières, "Notes sur les origines de l'ouverture française."

19. See Neumann, *Essays in Performance Practice*, for a discussion of the dotted note in French baroque music. Essays offering viewpoints that differ from those presented by Neumann are included in his bibliography.

Example 10.4: *Phaëton*, Overture

overture form was one of the most influential musical patterns of
the late baroque period, being taken over into the oratorio and
the instrumental suite. Later opera composers (for example, Handel), borrowing from the suite, often introduced one or more dance
movements at the end of a French overture.

Lully's operas continued to be performed at Paris for many years after his death. *Thésée* and *Amadis* were revived as late as 1779 and 1771 respectively, and nearly all the others lasted until the middle of the eighteenth century. Every successful French opera in this period called forth comic parodies or burlesques at the popular theatres of Paris. *Roland* accumulated ten of these satellites between 1685 and 1755; *Atys*, *Amadis*, and *Armide* each had nine.

The dignified, formal splendor of Lully's works, veritable embodiments of the glory of the age of Louis XIV, offered a model to be imitated at lesser European courts. The serious quality of the librettos, the careful composition of the recitative, the prominence of instrumental music, and the importance of chorus and ballet—all contrasting with the prevailing tendencies in Italy—helped to characterize a distinctive national type of opera which eventually made its influence felt on composers of other countries.

In France itself, Lully established the opera as an institution of the state. This was a source at once of weakness and of strength: of weakness, because it tended to perpetuate forms which, whatever meaning they may have had during the great days of the Sun King, became mere empty show when that triumphal age was past; yet of strength, for without such a foundation French opera might never have survived the series of second-rate composers and the general relaxation of taste which set in toward the end of the century.

One of Lully's first successors was his pupil Pascal Colasse (1649–1709). Colasse's best opera was *Thétis et Pélée* (1689), which remained in the repertoire at Paris until 1754. The *Médée* of Marc-Antoine Charpentier (ca. 1645–1704),[20] produced in 1693, was never revived, though contemporary critics wrote favorably of it.[21] André-Cardinal Destouches (1672–1749) was distinguished for *Issé*, a *pastorale héröique* produced at Fontainebleau in 1697, and for the opera *Omphale* (1700), the last revival of which in 1752 set off a notorious literary quarrel known

20. Crussard, *Un Musicien français oublié*. The exact date of Charpentier's birth is not known; some give it as 1634, in the belief that he was 68 at the time of his death.

21. A facsimile edition of *Médée* is in Brook, ed., *French Opera*. In addition to his works for the Academy, Charpentier also wrote for the *collèges*; his *David and Jonathas*, its subject taken from the Bible, was staged at Louis Le Grand Collège in 1688.

as the *guerre des bouffons.*[22] Another opera composer of this period was Marin Marais (1656–1728); his *Alcyone* (1706) contains
an orchestral representation of a "tempête" (storm), one of the
early examples of this kind of musical realism in opera.[23]

The period between the death of Lully in 1687 and the
first opera of Rameau in 1733 was marked by a gradual change
from the grave pomp and formality of the age of Louis XIV toward
the *galanteries* of the Regency (1713–1723) and the reign of Louis
XV. The dramatic integrity of Lully's and Quinault's tragédie lyrique was undermined by the growing popularity of the pastorale
and by the rise of a new form, the *opéra-ballet.* The latter differed from the traditional *ballet de cour* in that it was purely a
spectators' show, with professional performers, and was set to music
throughout. It contained at least one divertissement, and each act
(entrée) had its own independent action and self-contained little
plot, with all the acts vaguely connected by some central idea.[24]
Thus, the first important opéra-ballet, *L'Europe galante*, by André
Campra (1660–1744),[25] given at Paris in 1697, had each of its
four entrées set in a different country—France, Spain, Italy, and
Turkey. Even so tenuous a bond of unity disappeared from many
later opéra-ballets, in which the poem existed only to provide occasion for dances, airs, choruses, and scenic effects. At the same
time, the tragédie lyrique itself became invaded by irrelevant ballet and display scenes to an extent never imagined by Lully.

Another sign of change in this period was the infiltration
of Italian characteristics—a tendency stoutly opposed by conservative critics, who remained loyal to the pure tradition of French
opera as represented by Lully. The conflict between French and
Italian styles flared up many times in the course of the eighteenth

22. See chap. 15.

23. Barthélemy, "Les Opéras de Marin Marais." Earlier examples of storm music in opera
are found in Locke's *Macbeth* and Colasse's *Thétis et Pélée.*

24. ". . . un spectacle composé d'actes détachés quant à l'action, mais réunis sous une
idée collective, comme les Sens, les Élémens." Marmontel, *Élémens de littérature* (s.v.
"Prologue"), 5:528.

25. Barthélemy, *André Campra.* See also Anthony, "Printed Editions of André Campra's
L'Europe galante." A facsimile edition of the 1724 score of *L'Europe galante* is available
(1967).

century and led to a tremendous amount of polemical writing.[26] The Italian taste was represented by the use of Italian background in scenes of operas and ballets (for example, Campra's *Les Festes vénitiennes*, 1710), by the insertion of whole Italian arias and cantatas or of "ariettes" with French words set to music of Italian style, by occasional use of the da capo form, and particularly by certain harmonic innovations foreign to the idiom of Lully but common in the music of Scarlatti and other Italian composers, such as freer modulations, a more liberal use of appoggiaturas, seventh chords (especially the diminished seventh), chromatic alterations, and more florid or expressive vocal writing.[27]

26. The two chief polemical essays of the early part of the century were Raguenet's *Parallèle des Italiens et des Français* (1702) and Le Cerf de la Viéville's *Comparaison de la musique italienne et de la musique françoise* (1705–6); see translations in Strunk, ed., *Source Readings*, pp. 473–507.

27. Examples in the music of Campra and especially of Destouches. See La Laurencie in Lavignac, *Encyclopédie*, 3:1374, 1382–84.

CHAPTER ELEVEN

English Opera

As in France opera grew out of the ballet, so in England it was rooted in the masque. English opera, like the French, developed late in the seventeenth century into a distinct national type retaining many traces of the parent form.[1] Unlike the French, however, English national opera succumbed to Italian taste soon after 1700. The untimely death of its master, Henry Purcell, is symbolic of its own fate—"a spring never followed by summer."

The English masque was an entertainment something like the French court ballet, allegorical in character, with the main interest in costumes and spectacle, but including spoken dialogue, songs, and instrumental music.[2] The principal author of masques in the early seventeenth-century period was Ben Jonson, and one of his colleagues was Inigo Jones, who designed costumes and scenery. None of the great Elizabethan composers wrote masque music, but the form became a proving ground for experiments in solo singing soon after the beginning of the seventeenth century. This was also the age of the "solo ayre," beginning with the publication of John Dowland's first collection in 1597. Among the earliest composers of masques were Alfonso Ferrabosco (ca. 1575–1628) and Thomas Campion (1567–1620), but the first recitative in England was probably written by Nicolas Lanier (1588–1666)

1. Dent, *Foundations of English Opera*; White, *The Rise of English Opera*; Parry, *The Music of the Seventeenth Century*; Forsyth, *Music and Nationalism*; Nalbach, *The King's Theatre 1704–1867*; Luckett, "Exotick but Rational Entertainments."

2. Reyher, *Les Masques anglais*; Mark, "The Jonsonian Masque"; Noyes, *Ben Jonson on the English Stage*; Cutts, "Le Rôle de la musique dans les masques de Ben Jonson"; Lawrence, "Notes on a Collection of Masque Music"; H. Evans, *English Masques*; W. Evans, *Ben Jonson and Elizabethan Music*; Prendergast, "The Masque of the Seventeenth Century"; Gombosi, "Some Musical Aspects of the English Court Masque"; Finney, "*Comus*, Dramma per musica."

in his music (now lost) for Ben Jonson's *Lovers Made Men* in 1617. This and similar efforts to adapt the new Italian stile recitativo to English words were of no immediate importance for English music, which in the course of the seventeenth century developed its own style in the airs and songs, preferring to leave most of the rest of the masque (that is, those portions which in an Italian opera would have made up the recitative) in spoken dialogue. The songs, being simply inserted pieces and not organically connected with recitative as were the early Italian arias, retained a simple and even popular flavor, which gave a distinctive national stamp to English masque music and, by inheritance, to later English opera.[3]

The masque flourished especially during the reigns of James I (1603–1625) and Charles I (1625–1649). Under the Commonwealth (1649–1660), there were few public masques, though some were still given privately: for example, Shirley's *Cupid and Death* (1643) with music by Matthew Locke (ca. 1630–1677) and Christopher Gibbons (1615–1676). Masques were also performed in schools during this period. The professional theater flourished briefly under the management of William D'Avenant, who in about 1656 presented a five-act work entirely in music, *The Siege of Rhodes*.[4] The music (which has not been preserved) included recitatives and arias; it was written by a number of different composers, among whom were Locke and Henry Lawes (1596–1662). Apparently in order to avoid trouble with the Puritan authorities, the acts were called "entries" and the whole spectacle was known not as an opera (which word, in any case, was still new in England at the time) but as "A Representation by the art of Prospective in Scenes and the Story sung in Recitative Musick." Nevertheless, *The Siege of Rhodes* probably should be regarded as the first English opera. Though successful, it was not followed up, for the Restoration soon brought influences to bear that gave a different direction to English dramatic music.

The Puritans had not sought to suppress secular music,

---

3. The song "Back, shepherd, back" in Henry Lawes' setting of Milton's *Comus* (perf. 1634) is typical of this style.

4. Cf. Zimmerman, *Henry Purcell*, and White, *The History of English Opera*, concerning the premiere. See also Emslie, "Nicholas Lanier's Innovations."

but they did oppose the theater,[5] and this resulted in an attempt to evade their prohibition by disguising a theatrical spectacle as a musical concert. English opera, therefore, as represented by *The Siege of Rhodes*, was born four years before the return of Charles II in 1660. Paradoxically, the result of that event was to put a stop to opera by removing the prohibition against stage plays. English audiences preferred spoken drama, and once this was permitted they no longer had any interest in maintaining a form which to them represented only a makeshift, called forth by special circumstances. Theater music, to be sure, was composed after the Restoration, but not in the form of opera; it was confined for the most part to masques and incidental music for plays, and the style in both these fields was affected by foreign influences.

The tendency of the English to underrate their own music in comparison with that of continental composers has been a bane of their musical history ever since Elizabethan times. That a true English style in dramatic music survived as long as it did— that is, until the end of the seventeenth century—was due partly to the strength of the old tradition, partly to the Commonwealth (which had decidedly not welcomed continental artists), and partly to the genius of a very small number of English composers who were either conservative enough or of sufficiently original genius to resist foreign domination. In the sixteenth and early seventeenth centuries, the predominant foreign influence had been Italian. A number of Italian musicians appeared in the first years of the Restoration: there were Italian operas at the court in 1660; G. B. Draghi arrived in 1667;[6] Nicola Matteis in about 1672 introduced the works of the Italian school of violin composers;[7] a celebrated castrato, Giovanni Francesco Grossi (known as "Siface"), tarried briefly in London in 1687 and probably introduced there some of the music of Scarlatti.[8] But Charles II, who had learned to admire French music at the court of Versailles during his exile, and who soon after his restoration organized a band of

5. Scholes, *The Puritans and Music*, chap. 13 and passim; Bannard, "Music of the Commonwealth."

6. Pepys, *Diary*, February 12, 1667. See West, "Italian Opera in England (1660–1740)."

7. Cf. Evelyn, *Diary*, 2:97.

8. Ibid., 2:268; Dent, *Alessandro Scarlatti*, p. 37.

twenty-four violins (that is, a string orchestra) in emulation of the
vingt-quatre violons of Louis XIV, showed himself disposed to encourage French composers rather than Italian. Thus, in 1666 a
Frenchman, one Louis Grabu (fl. 1665–1694), was appointed Master
of the King's Music, the highest official musical post in England.
Grabu was undoubtedly a better courtier than a composer, if we
may judge by his chief work, a setting of Dryden's *Albion and
Albanius* (1685) in three acts, along the lines of a French opera
prologue. The music, a feeble imitation of Lully, dealt the death
blow to that "monument of stupidity"[9] as far as public success
was concerned. King Charles tried to lure Lully from Paris but
failing in the attempt was obliged to be content with Cambert (see
chapter 10), who found himself out of employment when Lully
took over the Académie de Musique in 1672. Cambert was in London from 1673 until his death in 1677, and two of his operas were
performed there in 1674.[10] In addition to these and other impor-
tations, Charles sent a number of young English musicians, among
them Pelham Humfrey (1647–1674), to acquire a French polish
under Lully at Paris.[11] In spite of foreign influences, however, the
vitality of English music was preserved in the latter part of the
seventeenth century by three composers: Matthew Locke, John
Blow, and Henry Purcell.

Locke, the eldest of the three, had received his training
during the Commonwealth and was at the height of his powers
during the early years of the Restoration. He composed portions
of the music for revivals of Shakespeare's *Macbeth* in 1672 and
The Tempest in 1674.[12] These and similar Shakespearean performances were decked out with machines and added songs, ballets,
and instrumental pieces; the language was altered, the order of
scenes changed, and prologues and even new episodes and characters were added to make an operatic entertainment of a sort
frequently burlesqued in the popular theaters. Nevertheless, this
tradition of plays with music is important, since it was for such

9. Dent, *Foundations of English Opera*, p. 165. (The music is extant.)

10 *Ariane ou le mariage de Bacchus* (probably with revisions by Grabu) and *Pomone.*
See Tessier, "Robert Cambert à Londres"; Flood, "Cambert et Grabu à Londres."

11. Pepys, *Diary*, November 15, 1667.

12. McManaway, "Songs and Masques in *The Tempest*."

productions that Purcell later wrote most of his dramatic compositions. Another work for which Locke furnished some of the music was *Psyche* (1674?), an adaptation by Shadwell of Lully's "tragi-comedy-ballet" of the same name. The music of *Psyche* was published in 1675 under the title "The English Opera." It is of interest as showing the strong French influence in English theater music at this time and for the skillful setting of English recitative; but on the whole, it lacks distinction and is generally regarded as inferior to Locke's earlier dramatic pieces or his instrumental works.

Although he produced only one complete work for the stage, John Blow (1649–1708) is the most important English dramatic composer before Purcell.[13] His *Venus and Adonis* (ca. 1682), although subtitled "a masque," is really a little pastoral opera, with the simplest possible plot and continuous music. The first act, after a long dialogue between Venus and Adonis, ends with a chorus of huntsmen and a dance. The entire second act is an interlude: first a scene in which Cupid instructs all the little Cupids (in the form of a spelling lesson) in the art of causing the wrong people to fall in love with each other; then a half-serious conversation between Venus and Cupid, ending with a dance of Cupid and the three Graces. The farewell of Venus and Adonis, and the latter's death, are set to pathetic strains in the third act; Venus bids Cupid bear Adonis to heaven, and the chorus calls on Echo and the Nymphs to mourn his death.

In its musical style and proportions, *Venus and Adonis* shows the influence of the Italian cantata rather than the opera; certain details, however, suggest that Blow was well acquainted with Cambert's works and with at least the instrumental portions of Lully's. The overture is on the French pattern, though with a rather more contrapuntal style and an individual harmonic idiom. The prologue, like many of Lully's, introduces allegorical figures discoursing on love in general terms, and it ends with an "entry," that is, a ballet. Little coloratura phrases on descriptive words in the recitatives and songs are reminiscent of the French practice, as is also the common device of echoing the final phrase of a chorus or solo. An important part is given to ballets and

13. See Clarke, "Dr. John Blow."

Example 11.1: *Venus and Adonis*, Act II

choruses, and there is a relatively large amount of instrumental music, including particularly a "ground" (that is, a passacaglia) in the finale of Act II and a lovely "saraband" in the same scene, beginning with a descending chromatic bass (example 11.1).[14]

Typically English are the forthright melodies, such as the duet "O let him not from hence remove" in Act I (example 11.2). Above all, Blow's music has a quality of sincerity, direct-

Example 11.2: *Venus and Adonis*, Prologue

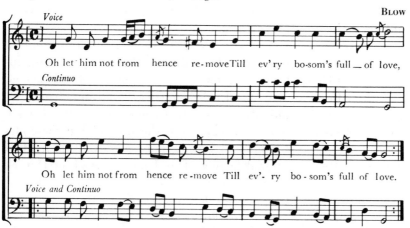

14. For a discussion of the "ground," see Lewis, "Purcell and Blow's *Venus and Adonis*," pp. 266–69.

Example 11.3: *Venus and Adonis*, Act III

ness, and independence, an "air of owing nothing to anyone,"[15] which lifts it out of the realm of mere courtly show and gives to his characters a living human likeness beside which the conventional figures of French opera seem like puppets. The lamenting cry of Venus on hearing of Adonis' death (example 11.3) and the nobly elegiac final chorus exemplify this quality, which has marked so much of English music, whether in the national folk songs, the motets of Thomas Tallis, or the madrigals of John Wilbye, and which at the end of the seventeenth century is incarnated in Blow and his great pupil, Henry Purcell.

The music of Henry Purcell (1659–1695) represents a fusion of different national style qualities.[16] His early training under Captain Henry Cooke, master of the boys of the Royal Chapel, made him familiar with the English musical tradition; from Pelham Humfrey he undoubtedly learned something of the French manner of composition, and from Blow the Italian, but these elements were always dominated by a genius essentially individual and imbued with national feeling. The dramatic work of Purcell

15. H. Watkins Shaw, "Blow," in *Grove's Dictionary* (5th ed.).

16. See Moore, *Henry Purcell and the Restoration Theatre*; Westrup, *Purcell*; Price, *Henry Purcell and the London Stage*; Zimmerman, *Henry Purcell*; Holst, ed., *Henry Purcell*; relevant sections in the histories of Hawkins (4:495–539) and Burney; last three chapters of Dent, *Foundations of English Opera*; White, *The History of English Opera*.

includes only one opera in the strict sense—that is, sung through-out—namely, *Dido and Aeneas*.[17] Composed for performance at a girls' school in 1689, it is on the scale of a chamber opera rather than a full stage work, though exquisite in detail and effective in performance. The rest of Purcell's theater music consists of over-tures, interludes, masques, songs, dances, choruses, and other music for plays;[18] but in some cases the extent and importance of the musical numbers are so great that the works may rightly be considered operas, and indeed were commonly so called in En-gland at the time.[19]

It will readily be seen that such productions are similar to the Renaissance Italian plays with *intermedi* and the French dramatic ballets, though of course their immediate forebears are the masque and the comedy-ballets of Molière and Lully. It is remarkable how long it took before poets and composers worked out fully the implications of the ideal of *dramma per musica*, drama carried on wholly by means of music. To be sure, in Italian opera all the dialogue was sung and, at least with composers like Monte-verdi and Cavalli, often sung in appropriately flexible and ex-pressive recitative. Nevertheless, the Italian tendency, as we have seen, was constantly toward sharpening the contrast in musical style between action dialogue on the one hand and verses express-ing emotion on the other. Even the arias and duets, in regular closed musical forms with periodic melody, were at first treated almost like interpolations and given only to subordinate charac-ters, while larger musical units involving choruses and dances were kept quite distinct from the development of the action itself. By and large, this was the state of affairs in Lully's tragédies lyriques also. But often in early German opera, always in the French comedy-ballet, and in early English opera with only two or three exceptions, the distinction was absolute: spoken dialogue for the action, music only for "set numbers."

When we examine Purcell's music, we are impressed first

17. Cf. White, "New Light on *Dido and Aeneas*," and Harris, *Handel and the Pastoral Tradition*.

18. The principal ones are: *Dioclesian*, 1690; *King Arthur*, 1691; *The Fairy Queen*, 1692; *The Indian Queen*, 1695; *The Tempest*, 1695; *Bonduca*, 1695; and the masque in *Timon of Athens*, 1694.

19. See Locke's preface to *Psyche*, 1675.

of all by the fresh, engaging quality of his melodies, so like in feeling to English folk songs. The air "Pursue thy conquest, love" from Act I of *Dido and Aeneas*, with its horn-call figures and constant lively echoing between melody and bass, suggests the sounds and bustle of the chase. In *King Arthur*, the martial "Come if you dare" shows an English adaptation of the popular trumpet aria of Italian opera, with two of these instruments concertizing in the introduction and interlude, and with the characteristic rhythmic motif ♩ ♩ common in French music and so appropriate to the declamation of English words (example 11.4).

Example 11.4: *King Arthur*, Act I

The duet "Fear no danger" in Act I of *Dido and Aeneas* is similar in rhythm and style to the duets of Lully. No less characteristic, though in a different mood, is an aria such as "Charon the peaceful shade invites" from *Dioclesian*, with the two concertizing flutes, the three- and six-measure phrases, the delicate cross-relations, and the word painting on "hastes" (example 11.5). There are also many fine comic airs and duets, particularly in the lesser theater pieces.[20] Da capo arias are not frequent in Purcell, but he uses most effectively the older form of the passacaglia or ground, the best example of which is Dido's "When I am laid in earth" in the last act of *Dido and Aeneas*, one of the most affecting expressions of tragic grief in all opera. Another air of this kind is the "plaint," "O let me weep," in Act V of *The Fairy Queen*.

Purcell's recitative is found at its best in *Dido and Aeneas*, the only one of his operas that gives opportunity for genuine dramatic dialogue. The treatment, as Dent points out, has nothing in common with the Italian recitativo secco;[21] rather, the style is

20. Examples are "Dear pretty youth" *(The Tempest)*, "Celia has a thousand charms" *(The Rival Sisters)*, "I'l sail upon the dogstar" *(A Fool's Preferment)*, "Celimene, pray tell me" *(Oroonoko)*, and the song of the drunken poet, "Fi-fi-fi-fill up the bowl" *(The Fairy Queen, Act I)*.

21. Dent, *Foundations of English Opera*, pp. 188–92.

Example 11.5: *Dioclesian*, Act II

Example 11.6: *The Indian Queen*, Act III

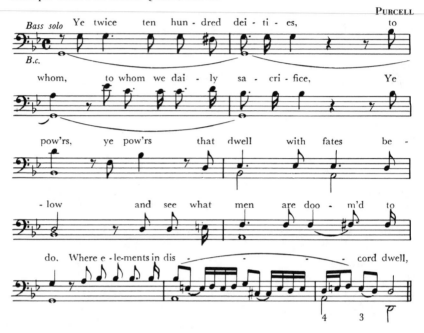

that of free arioso, admitting expressive florid passages, and always maintaining a clear rhythmic, formal, and harmonic organization, yet without sacrificing correctness of declamation or expressive power. The dialogue in the parting scene between Dido and Aeneas (Act III) and the beautiful arioso phrase which introduces Dido's last aria show what can be done by way of dramatic musical setting of the English language, that despised tongue which has been so often condemned as "unsuitable for opera." In Purcell's other works there are isolated examples of recitative phrases, including one from *The Indian Queen* (example 11.6) which Dr. Burney called "the best piece of recitative in our language."[22]

The overtures to Purcell's operas are in the same general form as the French overtures of Lully; one of the finest examples is found in *Dioclesian*. Other instrumental music includes "act tunes" (that is, interludes or introductions), and there are some interesting examples of the canzona and other forms.[23] There

22. Burney, *A General History of Music*, 2:392.

23. *Indian Queen*, Acts II and III; *Fairy Queen*, Act IV; *King Arthur*, Act V.

are dance pieces of all kinds, including the hornpipe, *paspe* (French *passepied*), canaries, and special descriptive dances as in Lully; a favorite type (also common in French opera) is the chaconne or ground, which is often placed for climax toward the end of a scene and in which dancing is combined with solo and choral singing as well as with instrumental accompaniment.[24] Descriptive symphonies occur, such as the introduction to the song "Ye blustering bretheren" in Act V of *King Arthur* or the famous "Cold" symphony and chorus "See, see, we assemble" in Act III—a scene perhaps suggested by the chorus of *trembleurs* in Lully's *Isis*.

The choruses in Purcell's operas contain some of his best music. Such numbers as "Sing Io's" in Act II of *Dioclesian*, with stately vigorous rhythms, brilliant voice groupings, orchestral interludes, and passages of harmony contrasting with contrapuntal sections, foreshadow the broad, sonorous choral movements in Handel's oratorios. Other choruses in Purell are more like those of Lully, in strict chordal style with piquant rhythms;[25] still others show the influences of the English madrigal tradition.[26] Finally, there are the choruses of lamentation, such as "With drooping wings" in *Dido and Aeneas*, which (like many other features of this opera) has a worthy predecessor in the closing number of Blow's *Venus and Adonis*. Except for *Dido and Aeneas*, where the chorus has a part in the action, Purcell's choral numbers usually occur in scenes devoted to spectacle or entertainment, corresponding to the ceremonies, ballets, and the like in French opera. There are scenes of this kind in *Bonduca* (Act III), *King Arthur* (Acts I and III), and *The Indian Queen* (Act V). The masques, of which examples may be found particularly in *Timon of Athens* and *The Fairy Queen*, also contain many choruses and dances; for parallels to these masques, with their fantastic settings and characters, we must look not only in the French opera but also in the contemporary popular plays of the Italian Theater at Paris, which contain many scenes of a similar nature.[27]

On the whole, it is difficult to accept Romain Rolland's

24. Examples in *King Arthur*, Act III; *Dioclesian*, Act III (in canon form).

25. E.g., " 'Tis love that hath warmed us," in *King Arthur*, Act III.

26. "In these delightful pleasant groves," in *The Libertine*.

27. Gherardi, *Le Théâtre italien*.

estimate of Purell's genius as "frail" or "incomplete."[28] The composer of the closing scenes of *Dido and Aeneas* could surely have created a true national opera in England if he had not been frustrated by the lack of an adequate librettist and by his apparently inescapable servitude to an undeveloped public taste.[29] As it was, however, Purcell's death in 1695 put an end to any hope for the development of English musical drama in the foreseeable future. London was even then full of Italian musicians; audiences became fascinated with Italian opera, and English composers did little to counter this trend. Not even George Granville's *The British Enchanters*,[30] which enjoyed a dozen or more performances at the Haymarket Theatre beginning in February 1706, could prevent Italian opera from dominating English opera. The successful production, in English, of *Il trionfo di Camilla, regina de' Volsci* ("The Triumph of Camilla, Queen of the Volsci") by Giovanni Bononcini (1670–1747) at the Drury Lane Theatre in March 1706 marked the capitulation,[31] and the fashion was completely established by the time of Handel's arrival and the performance of his *Rinaldo* in 1711.

There was at least one Englishman who viewed this state of operatic affairs with regret. Joseph Addison in the *Spectator* frequently alluded to the absurdities of Italian opera in England, and in one issue he wrote a long essay in criticism of Italian recitative, with acute observations on the relation of language to national style in music and an exhortation to English composers to emulate Lully by inventing a recitative proper to their own language: "I would allow the *Italian* Opera to lend our *English* Musick as much as may grace and soften it, but never entirely to annihilate and destroy it."[32] That this was a faint hope, Addison had virtually admitted in an earlier letter which so well and so

28. Rolland in Lavignac, *Encyclopédie*, 3:1894.

29. See Purcell's preface to *The Fairy Queen*.

30. Music by John Eccles and William Corbett.

31. This opera, composed for Naples in 1696, received no less than sixty-four performances in London between 1706 and 1709. Recent research credits Giovanni Bononcini rather than his younger brother, Marc Antonio, with the composition of *Camilla*; see Lindgren, "The Three Great Noises."

32. *The Spectator*, no. 29, April 3, 1711.

wittily sums up the situation of opera in England at the beginning of the eighteenth century that it deserves to be quoted at length:

It is my Design in this Paper to deliver down to Posterity a faithful Account of the Italian Opera, and of the gradual Progress which it has made upon the English Stage: For there is no Question but our great Grand-children will be very curious to know the Reason why their Forefathers used to sit together like an Audience of Foreigners in their own Country, and to hear whole Plays acted before them in a Tongue which they did not understand.

Arsinoe[33] was the first Opera that gave us a Taste of Italian Musick. The great Success which this Opera met with, produced some Attempts of forming Pieces upon Italian Plans, that should give a more natural and reasonable Entertainment than what can be met with in the elaborate Trifles of that Nation. This alarm'd the Poetasters and Fiddlers of the Town, who were used to deal in a more ordinary Kind of Ware; and therefore laid down as an established Rule, which is receiv'd as such to this very day, *That nothing is capable of being well set to Musick, that is not Nonsense.*

This Maxim was no sooner receiv'd, but we immediately fell to translating the Italian Operas; and as there was no great Danger of hurting the Sense of those extraordinary Pieces, our Authors would often make Words of their own, that were entirely foreign to the Meaning of the Passages which they pretended to translate. [Here Addison gives some instances of inept translations, and then he continues:] By this Means the soft Notes that were adapted to Pity in the Italian, fell upon the Word Rage in the English; and the angry Sounds that were turn'd to Rage in the Original, were made to express Pity in the Translation. It oftentimes happen'd likewise, that the finest Notes in the Air fell upon the most insignificant Words in the Sentence. I have known the word *And* pursu'd through the whole Gamut, have been entertain'd with many a melodious *The*, and have heard the most beautiful Graces Quavers and Divisions bestow'd upon *Then, For*, and *From*; to the eternal Honour of our English Particles.

The next Step to our Refinement, was the introducing of Italian Actors into our Opera; who sung their Parts in their own

33. *Arsinoe* was performed at Drury Lane in January 1705 and continued to be staged for several years. The text of *Arsinoe* was a translation from the Italian; the music was by Thomas Clayton. See Burney, *History*, 2:655; Fassini, "Gli albori del melodramma italiano a Londra"; Nicoll, "Italian Opera in England."

Language, at the same Time that our Countrymen perform'd theirs in our native Tongue. The King or Hero of the Play generally spoke in Italian, and his Slaves answer'd him in English: The Lover frequently made his Court, and gain'd the Heart of his Princess in a Language which she did not understand. One would have thought it very difficult to have carry'd on Dialogues after this Manner, without an Interpreter between the Persons that convers'd together; but this was the State of the English Stage for about three Years.

At length the Audience grew tir'd of understanding Half the Opera, and therefore to ease themselves intirely of the Fatigue of Thinking, have so order'd it at Present that the whole Opera is perform'd in an unknown Tongue. We no longer understand the Language of our own Stage. . . .

It does not want any great Measure of Sense to see the Ridicule of this monstrous Practice; but what makes it the more astonishing, it is not the Taste of the Rabble, but of Persons of the greatest Politeness, which has establish'd it. . . .

At present, our Notions of Musick are so very uncertain, that we do not know what it is we like, only, in general, we are transported with anything that is not English: so if it be of a foreign Growth, let it be Italian, French, or High-Dutch, it is the same thing. In short, our English Musick is quite rooted out, and nothing yet planted in its stead.[34]

34. *The Spectator*, no. 18, March 21, 1711. See also two essays from *The Spectator* in Strunk, ed., *Source Readings*, pp. 511–17; and the accounts quoted in Lowens, "The *Touch-Stone* (1728): A Neglected View of London Opera." For a study of the influence that Italian opera had upon the productions staged at the Drury Lane and Haymarket theaters from 1704 to 1710, see Price, *Music in the Restoration Theatre*.

PART III

The Eighteenth Century

CHAPTER TWELVE

Masters of the Early Eighteenth Century

During the early part of the eighteenth century, the younger librettists and composers in Italy were gradually evolving a new type of serious opera that was to dominate the scene for over a hundred years. This new Italian opera seria will be the subject of the next chapter. The present one is concerned with certain composers of the first half of the century who in the main kept to types of opera already long established and whose works include some of the best dramatic music of the period. The principal composers of this group are A. Scarlatti in Italy, Keiser in Germany, Handel in England, and Rameau in France.

Scarlatti

Alessandro Scarlatti (1660–1725) once figured in the history of opera as the founder of the so-called Neapolitan school of the eighteenth century. Investigations of the past several decades, however, have shown that his importance in this connection was considerably less than had been supposed and that he is probably better to be understood as one of the last masters of an older tradition than as the initiator of a new movement. Scarlatti was in Naples from 1685 to 1702 and again for shorter periods after 1709; he wrote operas not only for Naples but also for Rome (including some of his most important works), Venice, and Florence. It is not known exactly how many operas he produced; about eighty-five are traceable, of which number less than half are extant, some incompletely.[1]

Scarlatti began work in the style of Legrenzi and Stradella; their influence is apparent in his first operas performed at Rome before 1684. The small forms, the free mixture of recitative and aria passages, and the use of the ground-bass are all characteristic of this period. During his first stay in Naples, Scarlatti began to develop more individual characteristics. Comic roles occur in his librettos with considerable regularity. The comic characters, usually cast as servants and portrayed by a bass and a soprano, form an integral part of the plot. They also have scenes for themselves—comic scenes that are a clear contrast in musical style with the rest of the opera.[2] The number and placement of these scenes within the opera vary. In *La caduta de' decemviri* ("The Fall of Ten Men," 1697), for example, there are two comic scenes in each of the first two acts and one in the third act. In the later operas, it is Scarlatti's custom to end each of the first two acts with a comic duet in lively style, clearly the ancestor of the later opera buffa finale.[3] Even in his comic opera *Il trionfo dell' onore* ("The Triumph of Honor," 1718), Scarlatti retains the servant roles, creating for them farcical situations which contrast with the more subdued comedy of the main plot.[4]

By 1700, Scarlatti had definitely established the new Italian overture, with its quick opening movement, short slow interlude, and closing movement in two-part form with marked dance rhythms. During this period, there is also evident a growing differentiation between Scarlatti's cantata and opera styles. *La Rosaura* (1690) has many details that suggest the cantata. Most of the arias are of small dimensions, and the harmonies are often intricate and subtle. The recitatives, carefully composed, are far from mere stereotypes, and there are many scenes in which recitative, arioso, and aria passages are freely intermingled. The mu-

1. See Dent, *Alessandro Scarlatti*; Lorenz, *Alessandro Scarlattis Jugendoper*; Grout, *Alessandro Scarlatti*; and studies by Borren, Prota-Giurleo, Pagano and Bianchi, Holmes, D'Accone, Bianconi, and Lindgren. See also the introductory material for each volume in Grout, ed., *The Operas of Alessandro Scarlatti*.

2. See Grout, *Alessandro Scarlatti*; Troy, *The Comic Intermezzo*; Hunter, "Comic Scenes."

3. See *Tigrane*, in Grout, ed., *The Operas of Alessandro Scarlatti*, vol. 8.

4. A modern edition by Hermine Williams (St. Louis: MMB Music, 1986) makes available, for the first time, all three acts of this opera.

sic shows to perfection the quality of pleasure in sensuous effect which is such a strong characteristic of the Italian composers. The moods range from tender melancholy to charming playfulness, occasionally touching vehement grief on the one hand or outright broad comedy on the other. The whole is suffused with an aristocratic elegance, avoidance of excess, and perfect understanding of the powers of the solo voice for dramatic expression.

In contrast to *La Rosaura*, *La Statira* (performed at Rome in the same year) is "a very fine example of the grand manner."[5] Some of the arias are on a broad scale, impressive in their rhythms, showy and effective in a masterful way, with copious use of coloratura passages after an opening phrase in long notes with wide melodic intervals. This eminently theatrical style is further exemplified in *Eraclea* (1700), *La principessa fedele* ("The Faithful Princess," Naples, 1710), and *Tigrane* (Naples, 1715). In contrast to this popularizing tendency is *Mitridate Eupatore*, composed for Venice in 1707. This work, with its dignified, deeply expressive music, shows Scarlatti as a worthy representative of the serious Italian opera in late baroque style (example 12.1). The recitative "O Mitridate mio" from Act IV is a remarkable example of passionate declamation, supported by skillful chromatic harmonies with sudden, though always appropriate, modulations (example 12.2). The aria in B minor which follows ("Cara tomba") is marked by many suspensions between the voice and the concertizing solo violin; in its mood of mingled pathos and resignation it is similar to many of the lyrical effusions of Steffani and equally beautiful.[6]

The popular or folk element in Scarlatti is represented by the realistic dialogue and the occasional use of local dialect in the comic scenes of his serious work. In addition, there are many tunes which in their strongly characteristic rhythms and melodic turns are clearly of popular derivation. Perhaps the most common of these are the rather insinuating, languid, minor melodies in 12/8 meter to which the name *siciliano* is generally applied,[7] though it is notable that Scarlatti himself restricts this term to

5. Dent, *Scarlatti*, p. 63. For a study of *La Statira*, see Holmes, "*La Statira*".

6. Both recitative and aria are reprinted (incomplete) in Dent, *Scarlatti*, pp. 109–12.

7. This type of melody is not original with Scarlatti. Early examples occur in Monteverdi's *Orfeo* and in P. A. Ziani's *Galatea* (1660). Their predecessors may be found in the slower barcarole arias in 3/2 meter typical of Steffani and Pallavicino (see DdT, 55:ix).

Example 12.1: *Mitridate Eupatore*, Act II, sc. 1

(Example 12.1 continued)

(Example 12.1 continued)

(Example 12.1 continued)

those airs in which the flatted supertonic is a prominent feature. This note and its harmonization by means of the Neapolitan sixth are not confined to the siciliano-type airs but form a conspicuous mannerism of Scarlatti's style.[8]

    The later operas show an increasing emphasis on vocal ensembles (especially *Griselda*, 1721) and growth in the size and importance of the orchestra.[9] In *Tigrane*, horns are introduced for the first time. The orchestra of *Telemaco* (1718) is large, and in this work there is not a single aria with simple continuo accompaniment. The beginning of the overture to *Griselda* shows evidence not only of a homophonic style in orchestral writing but also of the typical later classical division between strings and winds according to function—the strings having arpeggios and tremolandos while oboes and trumpets reinforce with chords on the strong beats.[10] An even more significant development in the later works is the accompanied recitative, which evinces a growing recognition of the essential feature of this style—namely, antiphonal dialogue

8. Dent, *Scarlatti*, pp. 146–47.

9. This trend had already been established in Scarlatti's serenatas, in which greater emphasis was placed upon vocal ensembles and upon imaginative orchestral scoring for the arias. See Griffin, "The Late Baroque Serenata in Rome and Naples."

10. For a modern edition of *Griselda*, see Grout, ed., *The Operas of Alessandro Scarlatti*, vol. 3.

Example 12.2: *Mitridate Eupatore*, Act IV

A. SCARLATTI

O va - na spe - me! o rot - ta fe - de! o bre - ve.

lu - sin-ghie - ra, fu - nes - ta, em-pïaal-le-grez-za! Da chi più

cer-coai-u - to, o più con - for - to? oin cie - lo o in

ma-reo in ter-ra,o ne-gli ab-bis-si? Ahi! ahi! Mi-tri-da - te è mor-to!

effects between voice and orchestra, in free declamatory rhythms and irregularly recurring motifs. An interesting example of the influence of the accompanied recitative on the aria itself is found in Act II of *Griselda*, where the aria "Figlio! Tiranno," although accompanied throughout in steady rhythm of eighths or six-teenths, is nevertheless so broken and interjectional, with its phrases alternately echoed by the strings or interrupted by rushing scale

Scene from *Teofane* (Dresden 1719) by A. Lotti; designed by Alessandro Mauro.

passages, as to give almost the impression of being a recitative—
an original and highly dramatic treatment. In *Marco Attilio regolo* (1719), toward the end of Act I the arias "Finiscila ragazza"
and "Da fine al disprezzo" are both interrupted by recitatives.[11]
The scene closes with a dialogue-duet for alto and bass, which has
been immediately preceded by a dramatic soliloquy-recitative and
a big aria, "Son qual nave." This entire scene, though not altogether unrelated to the plot of the opera, nevertheless functions
as a kind of comic pendant to the first act.

Fundamentally, Scarlatti in his operas remained a conservative composer, though not altogether unaffected by the currents of the times. Like his contemporaries, he came to use the
full da capo pattern almost exclusively in his arias. Yet there is
much evidence to show that he deplored the extremes toward which
music, especially in Italy, was then tending. That evidence is found
not only in the scores themselves but also in the attitude of Scarlatti's noble patrons (who were constantly urging him to write down
to the level of his audience) and in the significant fact that for the
last four years of his life, during which he resided in Naples, he
wrote no operas, but only cantatas and church music. His fate,
like Bach's, was to be outmoded before his death, "a great man
. . . forgotten by his own generation." His influence upon other
composers may at best have been only partial and indirect. His
own happy combination of strength and sweetness, of passion and
humor, was not to be heard again in music until the time of Mozart.

Three Italian contemporaries of Scarlatti must be briefly
mentioned here. Francesco Gasparini (1661–1727), who possibly
began his studies with Legrenzi, was associated first with Venice,
where he was *maestro di coro* at the Ospedale della Pietà, and
then with Rome, where he settled after 1713. Although his talents
as a teacher and theorist have been duly recognized, his abilities
as an opera composer have until recently been largely over-
looked.[12] A number of his operas—*Statira, Ciro, La principessa
fedele, Tigrane*—are based upon the same librettos set by Scarlatti, a fact that would facilitate a comparison of these two com-

11. See ibid., vol. 2.

12. See Lindgren, "Le opere drammatiche *romane* di Francesco Gasparini (1689–1699)."

posers. Antonio Lotti (1667–1740), a pupil of Legrenzi, produced about twenty operas at Venice and others at Dresden and Vienna.[13] Antonio Vivaldi (1678–1741) was also a composer of operas.[14] Just how prolific and successful he was in this area of composition has been a matter of debate for many years. In a letter written on January 2, 1737, to his patron in Ferrara, Vivaldi claims to have composed ninety-four operas.[15] Evidence to substantiate this claim, however, has not come to light. Researchers have been able to account for only forty-eight of his operas being performed between 1713 and 1739, the majority of these being staged in Venice. Contemporary reports present conflicting views of Vivaldi's success in the theater. On the one hand, his operas and his talents as an impresario were in great demand not only in Venice and other Italian cities but also in Prague. On the other hand, Quantz and Tartini include in their writings derogatory comments about Vivaldi's vocal works, which they deem inferior to his instrumental works. Even Benedetto Marcello's satire *Il teatro alla moda* seems directed, in part, against the Venetian operas of Vivaldi.

Keiser

Reinhard Keiser (1674–1739) was the most talented of the Hamburg group of composers.[16] He is reputed to have written over one hundred operas, of which approximately twenty-five have been preserved. Writing with a sureness of style and a fertility of in-

13. Spitz, *Antonio Lotti*; idem, "Die Opern *Ottone* von G. F. Händel und *Teofane* von A. Lotti."

14. See Pincherle, *Vivaldi*; Rowell, "Four Operas of Antonio Vivaldi"; Kolneder, *Antonio Vivaldi*; Volek and Skalická, "Vivaldis Beziehungen zu den böhmischen Ländern"; Cross, *The Late Operas*; Ryom, "La Situation actuelle." A new critical edition of the works of Vivaldi is being prepared under the guidance of Ricordi of Milan and the Istituto Italiano Antonio Vivaldi, which also publishes the annual *Informazioni e Studi Vivaldiani*.

15. See Kolneder, *Vivaldi*, p. 208; and the facsimile edition of *Griselda* in H. M. Brown, ed., *Italian Opera*, vol. 35.

16. Wolff, *Die Barockoper in Hamburg*; Leichtentritt, *Reinhard Keiser in seinen Opern*; Voigt, "Reinhard Keiser"; Lindner, *Die erste stehende deutsche Oper*; Zelm, *Die Opern Reinhard Keisers*.

vention which remind one of Mozart, Keiser completed the process begun by Franck and Kusser, taking over a full measure of contemporary Italian and French operatic achievements but uniting them in a highly individual way with fundamental German qualities. A worldly, adventurous, impulsive, energetic personality, a musician who commanded the deepest respect of other musicians, Keiser was important historically not only for his own work but also for his direct influence on Handel, whose early Hamburg success stung the older composer at one time to open rivalry.[17] Keiser in the course of his works traversed the road from the heavy-textured music of the late baroque toward the light, thin, and playful *style galant* of the eighteenth century. His career was thus an epitome of an age of transition. It was also, unfortunately, an epitome of the declining fortunes of the Hamburg opera. The librettos of his later works (*Prinz Jodelet* is an example) show an increasing tendency toward the burlesque, the trivial, the vulgar, and the indecent; unskillful poets, pandering to the lowest tastes of an ignorant public, led the way to extinction of German opera, and Keiser lacked either the will or the greatness of soul to fight against the current.

Yet at its best the music of Keiser will stand comparison with that of the greatest of his contemporaries—Purcell, Steffani, Scarlatti, even Handel. The influence of Lully and the French school may be traced in his choruses, ballets, and instrumental pieces. He made no fundamental changes in opera, but his work is remarkable for three features: the flexibility of form in the arias, the skill and elaborateness of the orchestral accompaniments, and the mastery of effect in lyrical and tragic scenes. The da capo does not predominate in Keiser's arias, as it did in those of his Italian contemporaries; when used, it is often modified in subtle ways which suggest the freedom of the earlier Venetian period.[18] In addition, there are many shorter types—arioso melodies and German lieder—occurring at places where the dramatic situation requires something other than the da capo pattern. On the whole,

---

17. Chrysander, *Händel*, 1:129–34. For a list of some of Handel's thematic "borrowings" from Keiser, see the preface to the Händelgesellschaft edition of *Octavia*. See also Roberts, ed., *Handel Sources*, which lists other Handel borrowings from Keiser's *Adonis*, *Janus*, *La Forza della virtu*, *Claudius*, and *Nebucadnezar* and includes facsimiles of the works cited.

18. See, for example, the aria "Hoffe noch" in *Croesus*, Act I, sc. 2.

Keiser's melodic lines, although certainly not unvocal, do not show that instinctive adaptation to the qualities and limitations of the voice which is the gift of nearly all Italian composers: there are more wide intervals, angular phrases, and instrumental idioms. The characteristic mood is more energetic and aggressive than in Steffani. No composer of opera demands a higher degree of virtuosity in bravura-type arias; this is especially true in those arias with Italian texts which are often found in the midst of otherwise German operas—a peculiar practice beginning with *Claudius* in 1703 and increasing in the later works, and for which parallels may be found in both France and England at the same period. There are some arias with simple continuo accompaniment and a very few in which the continuo instruments are omitted from the orchestra. A special effect is created in the arias *all' unisono*, where the violins or violas in unison (sometimes with an oboe added), or all the strings in octaves, concertize with the voice, while the continuo fills in the harmonies. Accompaniments of this sort were fashionable in Italian opera around 1700; examples may be found in the works of Scarlatti and Handel. With Keiser, the vocal line will sometimes be doubled at the unison by a solo instrument or by all the strings. Repeated chords or broken-chord figures are frequent in the orchestral accompaniments. The orchestral parts are particularly noteworthy in the many arias with obligato solo instruments, which appear sometimes in novel combinations (for example, four bassoons or three oboes), producing great richness and variety of texture. Instruments are used effectively for descriptive touches, as in the title character's aria "Wallet nicht zu laut" from *Octavia* (example 12.3) and in some of Nero's arias in the same opera which feature the viola.[19]

Keiser's recitative is somewhat short-breathed, cadencing frequently; it is no mere colorless declamation of text, however, but freely introduces expressive phrases and arioso passages, thus harking back to the older Venetian practice. Such phrases are sometimes used in recurring fashion to give point to the dramatic situation, as for example in *Octavia*, Act I, scene 4

---

19. Use of the viola as a featured instrument is characteristic of operas by Hamburg composers contemporary with Keiser—namely, Graupner, Mattheson, and Handel. See Riley, *The History of the Viola*.

Example 12.3: *Octavia*, Act II, sc. 6

(example 12.4; note the descent from the third at the cadence, which is characteristic). The vitality of Keiser's treatment of the text is well summed up by Mattheson: "I believe assuredly that in the time he flourished there was no composer who . . . had set words to music so richly, naturally, flowingly, attractively, or (above all) so distinctly, understandably, and eloquently."[20]

Keiser's chief opera is *Der hochmütige, gestürtzte und*

---

20. Mattheson, *Ehrenpforte*, p. 129.

Example 12.4: *Octavia*, Act I, sc. 4

wieder erhabene Croesus ("Croesus Haughty, Overthrown, and Again Raised Up"), on one of the most popular librettos of the Venetian poet Minato, translated and arranged by Von Bostel.[21] The plot is an amusing hodgepodge of impossible melodramatic situations, but it has the operatic virtue of providing many opportunities for strong expression of moods *(Affekten)* as well as for pastoral scenes in the second act. There are two versions of this work, one from 1710 and the other a revision by Keiser for a revival in 1730. The two versions show some interesting differences in detail, aside from generally higher quality of music in the latter. For example, the ballets were omitted in 1730. In the original version, the overture was on the French pattern; in 1730, an overture of the Italian type was substituted: a fanfare-like opening movement in simple texture, with musical material and formal treatment like the first movement of an early symphony; a short adagio, consisting of broken-chord figures over a sequential series of seventh chords; and a "third" movement which is nothing but a da capo repetition of the first.

Examples of Keiser's lyrical and tragic power are plentiful in *Croesus:* the spontaneous charm of Elmira's "Sobald dich nur mein Auge sah," with the clever cadence at which Atis (a mute personage in this scene) responds to her question by a gesture on the chord of resolution, is unequaled (example 12.5); the pastoral solo and ensemble "Mein Kätchen ist ein Mädchen" (Act II, scene 3) is in the purest German lied style; Croesus' aria "Götter, übt Barmherzigkeit," over a recurring bass motif, is filled with noble pathos (example 12.6). Altogether, there is ample justification in the music for Mattheson's punning laudatory refer-

21. See Beare, *The German Popular Play "Atis" and the Venetian Opera.*

Example 12.5: *Croesus*, Act I, sc. 6

Example 12.6: *Croesus*, Act III, sc. 12

ence to the composer as "ein Kaiser des Gesangs" ("an emperor of song").[22] Mattheson also praised Keiser for his works embracing the pastorale, citing *Ismene* (ca. 1697) as a fine example of this type of entertainment.[23] Although the score for *Ismene* is not extant, some indication of Keiser's adaptation of the Italian pastorale for the German stage can be learned from his *L'Inganno fedele*. This opera was performed in Hamburg in 1714; its prologue and epilogue express a communal thanksgiving for the end of the plague in that city.

Most of the Hamburg composers contemporary with Keiser need not detain us long. Christopher Graupner (1683–1760) is noted more for his church works and instrumental pieces than for his operas.[24] G. C. Schürmann, Handel, and K. H. Graun all appear in the Hamburg list, but their work chiefly centered else-

22. Mattheson, *Ehrenpforte*, p. 133.

23. Harris, *Handel and the Pastoral Tradition*, p.. 90.

24. See Noack, "Die Opern von Christoph Graupner in Darmstadt."

where. Johann Mattheson (1681–1764), however, was an important figure in the musical life of Hamburg, though his significance as a theorist and historian has overshadowed his other contributions.[25] For some fifteen years he was actively involved with the Hamburg opera as a singer and as a composer. At times both of these roles were simultaneously represented within a single production, as in the case of his third opera, *Cleopatra* (1704), for which he sang the role of Antonius.

The change in musical style announced by Keiser's *Prinz Jodelet* and other later works was completed by Georg Philipp Telemann (1681–1767), whose fabulous productivity included some twenty operas for Hamburg and an even larger number for Leipzig and other cities. Telemann was the most progressive German composer of his day and was far more renowned than Bach.[26] From 1722 until 1738 he served as musical director of the Hamburg Opera. In his works for the Hamburg stage he excelled in the comic style. His full-length comic opera, *Der geduldige Socrates* (1721), and his intermezzo *Pimpinone* (1725)—whose text is a mixture of Italian and German—are models of Italian opera buffa style. *Pimpinone* is strikingly similar in both subject and musical idiom to the more famous *La serva padrona* of Pergolesi, which appeared eight years later.[27]

The closing of the Hamburg opera in 1738 marked the end of German opera for nearly half a century. Although scattered native companies held on for a few years in other cities, the creative impulse that had called them into being was spent. The spirit of common-sense rationalism, the decline of the court-centered life of the wealthy bourgeoisie, and the rise of a com-

25. See his autobiography in Mattheson, *Ehrenpforte*; Cannon, *Mattheson*; Meinardus, "Mattheson und seine Verdienste um die deutsche Tonkunst"; H. Schmidt, *Mattheson*; Haberl, "Mattheson"; Buelow, "An Evaluation of . . . *Cleopatra*."

26. See Mattheson, *Ehrenpforte*; Rolland, "L'Autobiographie d'un illustre oublié"; Ottzenn, *Telemann als Opernkomponist*; Valentin, *Telemann*; Schering, *Musikgeschichte Leipzigs*, 2:437–71; Menke, *Das Vocalwerk Georg Philipp Telemanns*; T. W. Werner, "Zum Neudruck von . . . *Pimpinone*"; Peckham, "The Operas of Georg Philipp Telemann."

27. The German title is *Die ungleiche Heyrath oder Das herrsch-süchtige Camer Mädgen*. This work may not be entirely Telemann's: he may have incorporated or adapted music from a *Pimpinone* (Venice, 1708) by Tomaso Albinoni (1671–1750), only setting the German recitatives and adding a few German arias. Loewenberg, *Annals of Opera*, col. 152.

mercially minded middle class, all contributed to this outcome. As
in England, so in Germany, opera became an exotic; national opera was abandoned in favor of the imported product from Italy.

Handel

There was a time, not many years ago, when the operas of George
Frideric Handel (1685–1759) did not loom large in the estimation
of many of his admirers. Passage of time and changes in operatic
style had thrust them into ill-deserved oblivion. That trend, however, has been reversed; it is not uncommon to find major opera
companies including in their repertoire one or more of Handel's
works.[28] These modern revivals, while revealing a multitude of
beauties, at the same time have raised many questions with regard
to the proper "adjustment" of these works for twentieth-century
audiences.[29] They conform to the conventions of their time, and
the music, much of which was composed under extremely unfavorable conditions, is not always at the highest level of inspiration. Nevertheless, the best of Handel in this field is not only superior to anything his contemporaries were writing but also forms
historically a culminating point which makes the works of Steffani
and Keiser seem almost like preliminary stages. Like Bach at
Leipzig, Handel in London worked in comparative isolation from
the so-called advanced currents of the day—an isolation due not

28. As a recent example, *Rinaldo* was staged at the Metropolitan Opera in New York on
February 11, 1984. On the operas of Handel, see the standard biographies by Mainwaring,
Chrysander, Leichtentritt (with plot synopses of all the operas), Rolland, Dent, Rockstro,
Flower, and Siegmund-Schultze; Burney, *History of Music* (2nd ed.), 2:672–835; Hawkins,
A General History, vol. 5, book 3, chaps. 6–7; Mattheson, *Ehrenpforte*, pp. 93–101;
Deutsch, *Handel: A Documentary Biography*; Dean, *Handel's Dramatic Oratorios and
Masques*; idem, *Handel and the Opera seria*; Poladian, "Handel as an Opera Composer";
Dent, "The Operas," in Abraham, ed., *Handel: A Symposium*; Powers, "*Il Serse trasfor-
mato*"; Lang, *George Frideric Handel*; Harris, *Handel and the Pastoral Tradition*; *Hän-
del-Jahrbuch*, passim.

29. For a discussion of this problem, see Dean, "The Recovery of Handel's Operas," and
idem, *Handel and the Opera seria*, pp. 200–14. See also Wolff, *Die Händel-Oper auf der
modernen Bühne*; Loewenberg, *Annals of Opera*, col. 152; Steglich, articles in *ZfMw* and
Zeitschrift für Musik; idem, "Die neue Händel-Opern-Bewegung"; *Händel-Festspiele*;
Festschrift zur Händel-Ehrung.

to ignorance but to independence; and though his later operas make some concessions to the fashionable modern style, he never capitulated to it entirely and indeed abandoned opera for oratorio when it became evident that his own way of writing could not hold the favor of the London opera-going public against the combined competition of the new ballad operas on the one hand and the modern Italian music of Porpora, Hasse, and Galuppi on the other.

Handel was in Hamburg from 1703 to 1706, during which time his position as violinist and harpsichordist with the opera orchestra brought him into close association with Keiser, director of the opera company, and Mattheson. Handel's first opera, *Almira*, was performed at Hamburg in 1705. The poem, a typical Hamburg libretto with comic scenes and ballets, is a mixture of German and Italian, and the music shows many traces of Keiser's influence, not the least of which is the prominence given the viola in the scoring of several arias.

Equally evident is Mattheson's influence upon Handel. During a visit to Italy from 1707 to 1709, Handel composed a number of stage works, Italian cantatas, and the operas *Rodrigo* (1707) and *Agrippina* (1709).[30] These Italian operas show characteristics of Mattheson's style of writing (especially the tonal unity of the dramatic structure); they also contain material borrowed from Mattheson's own operas.[31]

In 1710, Handel accepted a position as director of music at the court of Hanover. The maturity of style evident in *Agrippina* came to even fuller realization in *Rinaldo* (1711), the work by which he was first introduced to London and one of the most popular of all his operas.[32] The London visit was so successful that Handel obtained permission from his master, the elector of Hanover, to return in 1712; and this time, whether by intention

30. The place and date of the first performance of *Rodrigo* have usually been listed as "Florence, 1707," but this has been questioned by some scholars. Dean, *Handel and the Opera seria*, p. 26, states that "no one knows when, where, or even if *Rodrigo* was performed." See also Strohm, "Händel in Italia."

31. For a discussion of these and other borrowings, see Buelow, "An Evaluation of . . . *Cleopatra*"; Harris, "The Italian in Handel"; Roberts, ed., *Handel Sources*.

32. *Rinaldo* was revised in 1731. On the original London performances see *The Spectator*, no. 5 (March 6, 1711) and no. 14 (March 16, 1711); both essays in Deutsch, *Handel*, pp. 35–37. Cf. Babcock, "Francis Coleman's *Register of Operas*."

or negligence, he overstayed his leave. With the sudden death of Queen Anne in 1714 the elector ascended the English throne as George I, and the famous "reconciliation" between king and composer took place shortly afterwards.[33] Between 1712 and 1741, Handel produced thirty-six operas in London, of which the most notable were *Radamisto* (1720), *Ottone* (1723), *Giulio Cesare* and *Tamerlano* (1724), and *Rodelinde* (1725). The later works (for example, *Orlando*, 1733; *Serse*, 1738, his only comic opera) show a tendency toward a more facile kind of music, influenced to some extent by the newer Italian style, with which Handel had refreshed his acquaintance on a trip to Italy in 1728–29.

During much of the time in London, Handel was not only composer and conductor but manager and impresario as well, with all the troubles incident to such a position. The Royal Academy of Music, which had been opened in 1720, was for a time highly successful but finally had to close its doors in 1728. A new company, founded under Handel's direction the following year, soon fell into difficulties; reorganized in 1733, it was opposed by a rival group (the "Opera of the Nobility"), and both undertakings ended in complete bankruptcy four years later. A breakdown in health forced Handel to retire from active work for some months, and his last operas were produced in London between 1738 and 1741 by the Swiss impresario Heidegger. A blow to the prosperity of Italian opera in London was the fabulous success of *The Beggar's Opera* (1728) and its numerous offspring, with their satirical tendencies, evidencing a reaction in England against the "foreign growth" of which Addison had complained twenty years earlier. Wearied by the material difficulties and discouraged by the waning fortunes of opera, Handel had already begun in the 1730s to turn his attention to oratorio; *Saul* and *Israel in Egypt* were performed by the end of that decade, and in the following years came the other masterpieces by which the composer is best known today.

Handel's operas will not be understood if they are regarded merely as examples of an outworn operatic formula, composed because such was the fashionable thing to do or the best

33. The story (possibly apocryphal) of the reconciliation and the subsequent composition of the "Water Music" is told in Mainwaring, *Memoirs*, pp. 89–92.

way to make money, and unworthy of remembrance except for a few arias to be sung in recital programs. Such views have been advanced by persons who should know better; unqualified acceptance of them can be founded only on ignorance of the nature of this type of opera, on insufficient knowledge of the scores, or on a misunderstanding of Handel's character. These operas, as Leichtentritt has pointed out,[34] are based on the presentation of moods not mixed and modified as in "real" life, but each pure, so that a character at any given moment of expression is for the time being simply the incarnation of a certain state of mind and feeling; thus, the complete picture of the character is to be obtained by the synthesis of all these expressive moments rather than, as in modern drama, by the analysis of a complex of moods expressed in a single aria or scene. For such an aesthetic, the questions of consistency and plausibility in the plot are secondary: it is of little importance what a situation is or how it comes about, provided that it gives occasion for expression of a mood. On the other hand, the music, being free to devote itself to its peculiar function of unmixed emotional expression, expands freely into forms conditioned only by its own nature, unrestricted by requirements of so-called naturalness on the stage. Once this fundamental idea is grasped—and it is difficult only because it happens to be different from modern dramatic principles—then it is easy to perceive that the form of a Handel opera, with its continual succession of recitative and aria, its ubiquitous da capos, and all the other apparently artificial features, is in reality a musical structure of perfect artistic validity, whose restrictions, far from being arbitrary, exist only to assure freedom in essential matters.[35]

Handel was not a revolutionist in opera; he accepted the forms he found but filled them with his own inimitable genius. The subject matter is conventional, drawn from history *(Tolomeo)*, mythology *(Admeto)*, or romantic legend *(Orlando)*. His chief librettists were Nicola Haym *(Radamisto, Giulio Cesare, Ottone, Tamerlano,* and others) and Paolo Rolli *(Floridante, Scipione, Deidamia,* and others); Handel also set three of Metastasio's texts: *Siroe, Poro* (from *Alessandro nell' Indie*), and *Ezio*.

---

34. Leichtentritt, *Händel*, pp. 592ff.; idem, *Music, History, and Ideas*, pp. 150–51.

35. Cf. H. Abert, "Händel," in *Gesammelte Schriften*, pp. 232–63.

The overtures are for the most part of the French type, frequently with added movements after the allegro; one of the best of them is that to *Agrippina*. In *Ottone*, the allegro is followed by a gavotte, and the overture then closes with a fast movement in concerto grosso style with solo passages for two oboes. The sinfonias, marches, and the like, which are used to introduce an act or scene or to accompany some stage business, are neither numerous nor distinctive, and the same may be said of the choruses, as a general rule; dramatic use of the chorus—as in the pastorale *Acis and Galatea* and the operas *Ariodante* and *Alcina*—is exceptional. Ballets are few and of little importance.[36] The favorite ensemble form is the duet, for which Handel learned much from the example of Steffani.

The recitatives are remarkable for the richness and variety of their harmonic patterns, taking full advantage of modulatory possibilities and of the expressive quality of chords such as the Neapolitan sixth and the diminished seventh to underline the dramatic situation. In the comparatively rare accompanied recitatives (see example 12.8) and even occasionally in the recitativo secco, the dramatic element is more prominent.[37] At times, the recitative encloses distinct arioso passages or is combined with an aria in a free manner, which relieves the prevailing regular alternation between the two styles,[38] recalling the scene-complex technique of Cavalli and other seventeenth-century composers.

With few exceptions, Handel's opera arias follow the da capo pattern, but within this framework there is inexhaustible variety.[39] The principle of musical development is the unified working out of one or two basic motives, by voice and instruments jointly, in a continuous flow, within which the various periods are organized by a clear key scheme and a systematic use of sequences. In many of the longer arias, a fairly distinct binary form may be perceived in the principal section. The middle section most often uses the same or similar thematic material, though it is usu-

36. Roth, "Händel's Ballettmusiken."

37. E.g., *Agrippina*, Act II, sc. 4.

38. E.g., in *Poro*, Act I, sc. 9; *Serse*, Act I, sc. 2; and (on a greater scale) *Tamerlano*, Act III, sc. 10.

39. Flögel, "Studien zur Arientechnik in den Opern Händels."

ally shorter than the first section and somewhat contrasting in mood, accompaniment, and tonality. Even where at first glance the middle part of a da capo aria appears to be in complete contrast with the first, often subtle thematic relationships may be discovered. In sum, the whole formal treatment of the aria in Handel may be regarded as a climax of perfection in a style of which Steffani and Keiser were the forerunners. For details, one can only refer the student to the scores themselves, a careful study of which will be found to be both fascinating and rewarding.

The orchestra in Handel's operas is important chiefly (aside from the overtures) for its part in the accompaniment of the solo voice. Here it functions, as in Steffani and Keiser, as an equal partner with the singer. The basic instrumental group is formed by the strings and continuo, to which various instruments are frequently joined for obbligato parts (for example, solo violin, flutes, oboes, bassoons). The principle of opposition between *ripieno* and *concertino* is retained; accompaniments during the singing are entrusted to the smaller group, while the full orchestra joins in at cadences and for the ritornellos. Horns, trumpets, and trombones are used only with the chorus or for special effects. Many of the shorter arias are accompanied only by the continuo and one or two solo instruments, or by continuo and unison violins. A few have accompaniment by continuo alone. In general, the cembalo parts are very sparsely indicated in the originals, since Handel usually played this instrument himself and needed notes only as a reminder. There are even occasionally some blank measures, marked only "cembalo" in the score, at which places we are to understand that the composer improvised.

Handel's use of tonality is a subject which has received considerable attention. Of the importance of the tonal scheme as a formal element within the aria, there can be no doubt. Leichtentritt has also emphasized the composer's tendency to associate certain keys with certain moods, as F major with calm, pastoral, or idyllic sentiments, G major for arias of cheerful character, F-sharp minor for the expression of suffering, and so on.[40] Similar

---

40. Leichentritt, "Handel's Harmonic Art."

concepts were fairly widespread in the eighteenth century.[41] But an interesting question is raised by what often looks like evidence of a tonal plan extending over not merely a single aria or scene but entire acts and even entire operas. The first act of *Amadigi* has a symmetrical tonal structure which it is difficult to believe could be accidental.[42] Many of the operas show a preference for one tonality, which is established in the overture or at the beginning of the first act, returns briefly perhaps somewhere in the second, and is strongly confirmed in the finale.[43] A similar procedure is found in Keiser's *Croesus*, where the overture and first chorus are in D major, and each of the three acts ends in the same key. Purcell's *Dioclesian* seems to be in C major, but his *Dido and Aeneas* is not unified in this way, though there is an evident tonal plan for each act.[44] But these observations, whatever significance they may have, are far from establishing any kind of general rule. Indeed, it hardly seems probable that we should find consistent, conscious tonal architecture throughout many operas of this period, where the choice of key for a given number was so often dictated by external considerations, such as the limitations of wind instruments, the presence of a certain singer, the transference of entire numbers from earlier compositions, or the mood suggested by the text. Nevertheless, the question remains open; a comprehensive study of operas, oratorios, and other large composite works of the late seventeenth and early eighteenth

41. Borrel, "Un Paradoxe musical." Crussard, "Marc-Antoine Charpentier," gives Charpentier's and Rameau's tables of the qualities of the various major and minor keys, with reference to similar tables by Zarlino (1558), Mersenne (1627), Gantez (1643), Parran (1646), De Gouz (1650), Masson (1705), and Saint-Lambert (1707), and to later ones by Grétry, Le Sueur, Lacombe, and J.-J. Rousseau.

42. Leichtentritt, *Händel*, p. 643; idem, *Music, History, and Ideas*, p. 145; Rudolf Steglich, "Händels Opern," in Adler, *Handbuch*, 2:663–67.

43. Examples are *Almira* (B-flat), *Scipione* (G), *Alessandro* (D), *Alcina* (B-flat, with instrumental pieces and chorus in G at the end, corresponding to similar forms in the same key in the second scene of Act I), *Atalanta* (D), *Silla* (G, with closing chorus in D), *Floridante* (A minor and major, closing chorus in D), *Flavio* (B-flat), *Ottone* (B-flat), *Tolomeo* (F), *Ricardo* (D), *Siroe* (F), *Ezio* (F), *Arianna* (D minor and major), and *Ariodante* (G minor and major).

44. Act I: C–F; Act II: D–A; Act III: B-flat–G minor. Cf. Dent, *Foundations of English Opera*, pp. 180–83.

centuries from this point of view might lead to more definite conclusions.[45]

One trait which Handel shares with all composers of his epoch is the frequent use of tone painting and musical symbolism. This ranges all the way from naïve, playful imitation of natural sounds[46] through the brilliant trumpet arias[47] to such awe-inspiring effects as Claudio's "Cade il mondo" ("Let the world fall") in *Agrippina* (Act II, scene 4), with its downward plunge through two octaves to the low bass D (example 12.7). Such devices show

Example 12.7: *Agrippina*, Act II, sc. 4

Ca - de il mon - do,

the play of fancy, now whimsical, now earnest, on the surface of baroque musical forms, but they are no mere externals. All these picturesque or conventional figures are part of the music itself, inseparable from the structure they adorn—so much so that though, as in the London performance of *Rinaldo*, live birds may be released to flutter about the stage while flutes twitter in the orchestra, and the unreflecting person may hear only that the music is imitating the birds, yet the musician feels that this is not so, but rather that it is the birds who are imitating the music. Handel's art, like that of Bach, has the power of glorifying the apparently trivial by showing it to be a manifestation of the eternal; as the rhythm of walking feet becomes in Bach's chorale prelude the rhythm of the soul's march to Heaven, so in Handel the song of the birds is a magic window opening on a glimpse of pastoral Eden.

This universal quality is, of course, most apparent in

45. Cf. G. F. Schmidt, *Die frühdeutsche Oper* 2:315–17. Lorenz, after an exhaustive examination of Scarlatti's operas, could find no evidence of a consistently applied tonal plan, though in certain works (especially among the earlier ones) there are traces of it (*Alessandro Scarlattis Jugendoper*, p. 177 and passim). Gerber, *Der Operntypus Johann Adolf Hasses*, pp. 39–42, finds no evidence whatever in Hasse. The evidence for Rameau has been examined in Ahnell, "The Concept of Tonality," likewise with inconclusive results as far as a definite overall tonal structure is concerned.

46. E.g., *Rinaldo*, Act I, sc. 6, "Augelletti, che cantate."

47. E.g., *Radamisto*, Act I, sc. 3, "Stragi, morti."

those arias that are pure expression of moods, with few or no picturesque external details. The number and variety of these arias is so great, and the power of capturing the most subtle nuances of feeling so astounding, that one is tempted to believe there is no emotion of which humanity is capable that has not found musical expression somewhere in Handel's operas. Referring once more to the only adequate source of information, the scores themselves, let us note a half-dozen examples: (1) the famous "Ombra mai fù" (*Serse*, Act I, scene 1),[48] known universally (in transcriptions, alas) as the "Largo from Xerxes"; (2) the nobly mournful "Lascio ch'io pianga" (*Rinaldo*, Act II, scene 4); (3) the deeply moving "Cara sposa" (*Rinaldo*, Act I, scene 7), "one of the best airs in that style that was ever composed by [Handel] or any other master; and by many degrees the most pathetic song, and with the richest accompaniment, which had been then heard in England";[49] (4) a whole class of arias of the siciliano type, adopted by Handel from the example of Scarlatti and other Italian composers, elegant in contour, elegiac in feeling, moving in languorous 12/8 meter (such as "Con saggio tuo consiglio," *Agrippina*, Act I, scene 1); (5) the idyllic arias, musical pastorales, and landscapes of tranquil charm, filled with sunlight ("Se in un fiorito ameno prato," *Giulio Cesare*, Act II, scene 2); (6) the light, playful "Un cenno leggiadretto" (*Serse*, Act I, scene 15), representative of a less numerous class of arias appropriate to the comic style (in a similar category may be mentioned also the bass songs of Polyphemus in *Acis and Galatea*).

A fine example of the energetic, passionate, displayful aria is Radamisto's "Perfido" (*Radamisto*, revised version, Act I, scene 6), with its recurring rhythmic figure ($\sqcap$) curiously prophetic of the motif of the Scherzo in Beethoven's Ninth Symphony. Coloratura passages such as we find in this aria are frequent in Handel; often they were composed to show off a particular singer, and Handel's mastery of his craft is evident in the virtuosity of this vocal writing. Yet he seldom employed such passages solely for display; they spring naturally from the tension of the

48. The source of the aria is one with the same name by Bononcini; see Powers, "*Il Serse trasformato*," p. 87.

49. Burney, *History of Music*, 2:674.

Example 12.8: *Giulio Cesare*, Act II, sc. 8

(Example 12.8 continued)

(Example 12.8 continued)

music or from some obvious image in the text and are strictly
organized within the musical structure. Occasionally there occurs
a melismatic passage that recalls the softer style of Steffani.[50]

    Surely one of the most beautiful of Handel's arias is
Cleopatra's "Se pietà di me non senti" (*Giulio Cesare*, Act II,

---

50. See the end of example 12.6; also, the beautiful closing cadence of the first part of
"Forte e lieto" (*Tamerlano*, Act I, sc. 1).

scene 8), which is preceded by an accompanied recitative (notable for its wide range of modulations) and introduced by an orchestral ritornello, from which the characteristic "drooping" motif of the obbligato violin is derived (example 12.8).

It must be emphasized that in every case the realization not only of mood but also of personality comes from the music. Caesar in Haym's libretto is a stage hero in the manner of the early eighteenth century; only through Handel's music does his character receive those qualities which make him a truly dramatic figure. Caesar and Cleopatra, Radamisto and Zenobia, Bajazet (in *Tamerlano*), and others of Handel's dramatic creations are universal, ideal types of humanity, moving and thinking on a vast scale, the analogue in opera of the great tragic personages of Corneille. This quality is more than the reflection of a certain musical style or a consummate technique; it is the direct emanation of Handel's own spirit, expressed in music with an immediacy that has no parallel outside Beethoven. It is the incarnation of a great soul. If his characters suffer, the music gives full, eloquent expression to their sorrows—but it never whines; there is not a note in it of self-pity. We are moved by the spectacle of suffering, but our compassion is mingled with admiration at suffering so nobly endured, with pride that we ourselves belong to a species capable of such heroism.

Rameau

Conditions in France were not favorable for serious musical drama in the early eighteenth century. The tendency, as has already been mentioned, was toward the nondramatic entertainment spectacle of the opéra-ballet. A glance at the statistics of new works staged at the Paris Opéra shows this: from 1700 to 1715 there were twenty-seven new tragédies lyriques and ten new ballets; from 1716 to 1740 there were twenty-one new tragédies lyriques and forty-one new ballets of various kinds.[51] The ballet pieces were not only

51. Chouquet, *Histoire de la musique dramatique*, pp. 327–42.

becoming more numerous; they were always more popular as well. Among the hits of the early eighteenth century were *Les Fêtes de Thalie* (1714), an opéra-ballet with music by Jean-Joseph Mouret (1682–1738),[52] which enjoyed revivals until 1764 and was parodied; and a *ballet héroique*,[53] *Les Fêtes grecques et romaines* (1723) by Colin de Blamont (1690–1760), which lasted till 1770. The only opera of this period that approached such popularity was *Jephté* (1732), the biblical subject with music by Michel Pignolet de Montéclair (1667–1737).

Jean-Philippe Rameau (1683–1764) was already known as an organist, theorist, and composer of keyboard music before he presented his tragédie lyrique *Hippolyte et Aricie* in 1733.[54] More than twenty other works for the theatre followed, the most important of which were the operas *Castor et Pollux* (1737), *Dardanus* (1739), and *Zoroastre* (1749) and the opéras-ballets *Les Fêtes d'Hébé* (1739), *Platée* (1745), and *Zaïs* (1748). In general, these works do not depart from the fundamental outlines established by Lully and Quinault: mythological or legendary subject matter, frequent large display scenes with choruses and ballets, and carefully notated recitative intermingled with short airs. Nevertheless, Rameau's operas immediately raised a storm of controversy. He was hailed by progressives as the savior of French opera, and condemned by conservatives as a hopeless pedant, a *distillateur d'accords baroques*, whose capitulation to Italian style was tantamount to musical treason. The reasons for this criticism are not to be sought in the outward aspects of his operas but rather in the music itself, which represents the late baroque style in France as Bach represented it in Germany and Handel in England. Tonalities are absolutely clear, often being emphasized by Rameau's predilection for outlining triads in the melody; large-

52. Viollier, *Jean-Joseph Mouret.*

53. Ballet héroïque, pastorale héroïque, comédie lyrique, comédie ballet, and similar designations were used in France at this time for works partaking of the character of both opera and ballet; to avoid unnecessary complexity, we shall refer to such works under the generic name "opéra-ballet." For the distinctions, see Masson, *L'Opéra de Rameau*, pp. 20ff., and Anthony, "The French Opéra-Ballet."

54. See the biographies by La Laurencie and Girdlestone; La Laurencie, "La Musique française," in Lavignac, *Encyclopédie*, 3:1362–1562; Masson, *L'Opéra de Rameau*; Leclerc, "*Les Indes galantes*"; Anthony, *French Baroque Music*; Cyr, "Rameau's *Les fêtes d'Hébé*" Wolf, "Jean-Philippe Rameau's Comédie Lyrique"; La Gorce, "Twenty Set Models."

scale forms are common, supported by definite modulatory schemes with systematic use of secondary sevenths (a particularly fine example is the great chaconne in the finale of *Castor et Pollux*). The whole style is more contrapuntal than Lully's, though not so much so as that of Bach. Some of Rameau's longer airs are formally set apart from the recitative, and the Italian-inspired ariettes in particular make use of coloratura passages.[55] Other large arias occasionally foreshadow the profound, serious moods of Gluck (example 12.9).

The contrast between Lully and Rameau is particularly evident in the choruses, which are more numerous and varied in the latter and often extremely brilliant, recalling the style of Handel (for example, "Brillant soleil" in *Les Indes galantes*, Act II, scene 5). In his use of the chorus for dramatic purposes (as in the impressive opening of Act I of *Castor et Pollux*), Rameau showed the way for developments which were to culminate in the later operas of Gluck.

Above all, Rameau is distinguished for the instrumental music in his operas. The Paris opera orchestra in 1756 numbered forty-seven players, comprising two flutes, four oboes, five bassoons, one trumpet, and percussion, in addition to the strings and continuo instruments;[56] extra players were hired when needed for musettes, horns, and clarinets (from 1749). The three main types of instrumental pieces in Rameau are the overtures, the descriptive symphonies, and the dances.

The overtures of the earlier operas are in the conventional form, but in certain cases Rameau, unlike Lully, connects the overture with the particular opera for which it is written. Thus, the opening theme of the overture to *Castor et Pollux*, in G minor, reappears in the finale in A major for the scene of the apotheosis of the two heroes. *Zoroastre* has a program overture aiming to summarize the main outlines of the plot of the opera. In his later works, Rameau experimented with different overture forms: that of *Zoroastre* is in three movements (fast–slow–fast), approaching not only in general outline but also in many details— the texture of the music, the nature of the themes, the form of the

55. See examples in the closing scenes of *Hippolyte et Aricie* and *Castor et Pollux*.

56. Masson, *L'Opéra de Rameau*, p. 513.

last two movements, the rhythms, the methods of motivic development, and the use of devices like parallel thirds, unison passages, and echoes—the style of the early classical symphony.

The descriptive symphonies are short instrumental pieces intended to depict in music certain scenes or happenings on the

Example 12.9: *Dardanus*, Act IV, sc. 1

(Example 12.9 continued)

stage. They are typical of an age whose music aesthetic was based
on the ideal of imitation of nature, thus leading to a whole conventional language of musical images for conveying landscapes,
sunrises, babbling brooks, thunderstorms, earthquakes, or other
natural phenomena.[57] Rameau never wrote a piece of music that
was more perfectly expressive of pastoral tranquillity than the
slumber scene in Lully's *Armide*, but he excelled in more violent

---

57. DuBos, *Critical Reflections on Poetry, Painting, and Music*, part 1, sec. 45.

episodes, of which the earthquake in the second entrée of *Les Indes galantes* is a good example. There are in his operas also many short symphonies for filling awkward pauses in the action (such as descents of celestial beings) or suggesting offstage battles.

Most numerous of all are the dances, which comprise all types from the simple minuet to the elaborate chaconne, with an astounding variety, freshness, and fertility of rhythmic invention. These are a noble flowering of the oldest instrumental tradition in France, a line descending from the sixteenth-century ballet through Chambonnières, Lully, Francçois Couperin, and many other distinguished composers. In Rameau perhaps more than in any of his countrymen the music has the strange power of vividly suggesting the movements of the dancers; it is in truth "gesture made audible." The common dance types in duple meter are: gavotte, bourrée, *rigaudon*, tambourin, and contredanse; in triple meter: saraband, chaconne, minuet, and passepied; in compound meter: *loure*, *forlane*, and gigue; others, variable in meter and form: musette, march, entrée, and air (the last usually qualified by a descriptive term, as *air majestueux* or *grave*, *air pour les Fleurs*, *pour les Ombres*, and so on). The principal forms are two-part, rondo, and chaconne. Many of these dances are sung by solo, ensemble, or chorus as well as played by the orchestra. Examples are too numerous and varied to warrant mention of any in particular. Only a study of the scores can give an idea of Rameau's inexhaustible richness in this field.

Rameau is not to be regarded as a mere way station between Lully and Gluck; any conception of him as no more than a composer of graceful dance trifles is completely false. On the contrary, he is one of the very few first-rank composers whose work happens to fall largely in the realm of opera. If he is less consistently a dramatist than Lully, the fault is that of the age in which he worked; as a musician, he is by far Lully's superior. His limited success in France is to be attributed to the poor quality of his librettos (for which his own indifference was partly responsible) and to the fact that in his day the old French opera itself, encumbered by so many conventions of a bygone era, was on its way toward decline. Rameau's music went down to obscurity with it. For a number of years, Rameau's operas were classic examples of great music forgotten. Today that has changed. The operas are

receiving attention from scholars and performers who, on the basis of the requisite knowledge and imagination, not only appreciate their greatness but also breathe new life into scores that once
delighted Paris under the *ancien régime*.

CHAPTER THIRTEEN

The Opera Seria

We have seen how, from its earliest beginnings at Florence and Rome, Italian opera in the course of the seventeenth century passed out of the experimental stage. Radiating from Venice with its public opera houses, it established itself on a firm basis of public interest and support which made it by the end of the century the most widespread and most popular of all musical forms. We have also seen how, in the course of this development, three important national schools of opera rose outside Italy. One of these, the French, maintained its existence and individuality; the English school died with Purcell, while the German gradually lost its identity by absorption into the Italian style. At the beginning of the eighteenth century, therefore, it is possible practically to perceive one single operatic type which dominated all western Europe except France—a type which, despite variations in different countries and composers, showed certain fundamental common features everywhere. From the standpoint of the libretto, we identify this type as the opera of moods or *affects*.[1] Its intention was to present a series of discrete expressive moments, each devoted exclusively to a particular mood; in order to call forth the necessary variety and intensity of moods, situations were contrived with little attention to unity or consistency of plot and with corresponding indifference to realism either in subject matter or in details of dramatic development. The form in which this intention was realized was one which we may call the "aria opera"; musically speaking, that is to say, it consisted of a series of arias separated by passages of recitative. Throughout the latter half of the seventeenth century, the tendency had been more and more to dif-

---

1. Kretzschmar, "Allgemeines und Besonderes zur Affektenlehre."

ferentiate these two styles and, in general, to concentrate the musical interest more and more on the aria. Ensembles, ballets, and instrumental pieces were of only incidental importance.

Within this general type of Italian opera, two distinct directions were perceptible by the end of the seventeenth century. These have been designated by German historians as "aristocratic" and "democratic"; we may also refer to them, in terms corresponding to the usual divisions of music history, as the "late baroque" and the "preclassical" styles of opera. The distinction involves many criteria, applying to both libretto and music.[2] The aim of baroque opera had been to excite admiration and astonishment, to overwhelm, *far stupire:* hence the machines and marvels, the multitude of characters, the sensational disorderly plots, extravagant language, and comic episodes. The newer style came to be refined, polished, regulated; poets envisioned the drama as a school of virtue, teaching devotion to duty and loyalty to the higher impulses of man's nature. They eschewed supernatural interventions and miracles; comic scenes were abolished; the cast was reduced to six stereotyped personages; plots became orderly and formalized, emotions restrained, language conventional and courtly.

Not less sweeping were the differences in the music. In the older style, the harmony was comparatively rich and changeable, the bass lines fairly active, the melody spun out in long phrases of variable length (except in pieces based on dance rhythms), and the forms still somewhat free despite the tendency toward exclusive use of the da capo pattern. In the newer style, harmony was simplified to a few fundamental chords with the bass changing relatively seldom and the whole texture functioning solely as a support for the melody; the latter came to be organized in symmetrical short phrases, though with considerable variety of rhythmic patterns within the phrase. Variety of form gave way to the almost exclusive dominance of the full five-part da capo scheme.[3] The older style admitted the orchestra as a more nearly equal partner with the voice, aiming at a contrapuntal kind of bass and,

2. See Downes, "The Operas of Johann Christian Bach," which contains a thorough survey of Italian opera seria between 1720 and 1780.

3. This scheme will be described later in the chapter.

in the case of composers like Steffani, Keiser, or Handel, sometimes interweaving the vocal line with one or more strands of instrumental melody; the newer style tended to relegate the orchestra to a subordinate position, with a bass whose function was
entirely harmonic, concentrating all musical attention on the singer.
Mattheson remarks on the contrast in this respect between his
own time and the seventeenth century: in the earlier period "hardly
anyone gave a thought to melody, but everything was centered
simply on harmony."[4] Quantz laments that, though most Italian
composers of the day (that is, 1752) are talented, they start writing operas before they have learned the rules of musical composition; that they do not take time to ground themselves properly;
and that they work too fast.[5] To these criticisms, with their implications of frivolousness and lack of counterpoint in Italy, may
be opposed, as representing the Italian viewpoint, Galuppi's classic definition of good music: "Vaghezza, chiarezza, e buona modu-
lazione," which Dr. Burney translates "beauty, clearness, and good
modulation,"[6] though there are really no words in English capable of conveying the exact sense of the original.

The older opera was represented by Legrenzi, Steffani,
Keiser, Handel, and, to a considerable extent, Scarlatti; the newer
tendencies were developed in the works of most Italian composers
after 1700 and became dominant by 1720. One way to illustrate
the distinction is to consider the contrasting types of operatic
overture associated with each of the two schools. The older type
was the French *ouverture*, first outlined by the early Venetians,
given definitive form by Lully, and adopted in its essential features by Steffani, Keiser, and Handel; the newer type was the
Italian *sinfonia*, first established by Scarlatti about 1700,[7] and
gradually ousting the French overture everywhere as the eighteenth century went on. The difference between these two kinds
of overture is usually stated in terms of the order of movements—
the French beginning (and often also ending) in slow tempo, whereas

4. Mattheson, *Ehrenpforte*, p. 93.

5. Quantz, *Versuch*, XVIII. Hauptstück, par. 63.

6. Burney, *The Present State of Music in France and Italy*, p. 177.

7. For modern editions of representative overtures by A. Scarlatti, see Grout, ed., *The Operas of Alessandro Scarlatti*, and Brook, ed., *The Symphony 1720–1840*.

the Italian began fast, had a slow movement in the middle, and ended with an allegro or presto. This distinction, however, is superficial; the essential difference was a matter of musical texture. The French overture was a creation of the late baroque, having a rich texture of sound, some quasi-contrapuntal independence of the inner voices, and a musical momentum bound to the non-periodic progression of the bass and harmonies. The Italian overture was a characteristic preclassical form, light in texture, with busy activity of the upper voices accompanied by simple, standardized harmonic formulas. The French overture looked to the past, the Italian to the future; the latter represented those principles of texture, form, nature of thematic material, and methods of motivic development which were to lead eventually to the style of the classical symphony.[8]

Both the older and the newer type of Italian opera existed in the early part of the eighteenth century, but the former was obviously on the decline as far as popularity was concerned. The general change in the language of music which took place in the middle of the century, and which led through the rococo or gallant style to the later classical idiom, was evident in opera as it was everywhere else. The growing taste for simplicity, ease, lightness of texture, tuneful melody, and facile ornamentation brought to the fore a kind of opera, Italian in origin but international in practice, that has often been called "Neapolitan." This term came into use originally because many of the composers associated with early eighteenth-century opera lived or were trained in Naples. But the implications of "Neapolitan," when used to denote a certain type or style of opera, lead to confusion;[9] so altogether it seems best to abandon the use of the word as a descriptive term, at least until further research shall show whether a strictly Neapolitan kind of opera (as distinct from Venetian or Roman, for example) actually existed in the eighteenth century.

One division within the general field of eighteenth-

8. This trend can be observed in the opera overtures of Francesco Conti, especially those exhibiting the basic elements of sonata forms. See Brook, ed., *The Symphony*, ser. B, vol. 2, for examples of his music. On the early history of the Italian overture, see Heuss, *Die Instrumental-Stücke . . . die venetianischen Opern-Sinfonien*, pp. 88–92.

9. See Downes, "The Neapolitan Tradition in Opera," and Hucke, "Die neapolitanische Tradition in der Oper."

century Italian opera, however, must be kept in mind: namely, that between the serious opera *(opera seria)* and the comic opera *(opera buffa)*. The latter is, at least in the beginning, a quite distinct form and will be treated later. At present we are concerned exclusively with the opera seria, the characteristic type of the age, cultivated in all countries by imported Italians as well as by native composers and singers imitating the Italian style, maintaining itself throughout the eighteenth century and continuing its influence far into the nineteenth. We shall attempt first to give a general idea of this operatic type and to dispose of certain misconceptions regarding it; afterwards, we shall study the music of particular composers. The latter undertaking is still hampered by the paucity of available scores. Almost none of this music was printed; hundreds of manuscripts have been lost, and hundreds of others exist only in rare copies; only an infinitesimal fraction of it is accessible in modern editions.

The Libretto

The foundation of the eighteenth-century opera seria rests upon a literary reform movement which developed at the end of the seventeenth century.[10] The principal target of this reform was the *eroicomico* libretto which had dominated the Venetian stage throughout the second half of the seventeenth century. Led by Gian Vincenzo Gravina (1664–1708) and supported by other members of the Arcadian academy in Rome, this reform movement sought, among other things, to reduce the multiplicity of arias and to eliminate the intermingling of tragic-heroic and comic elements—characteristics of the librettos of Giovanni Cicognini and his contemporaries. First steps toward the reform were taken by Silvio Stampiglia (1664–1725).[11] He tightened the structure of his

10. Giazotto, *Poesia melodrammatica;* idem, "Apostolo Zeno, Pietro Metastasio e la critica del Settecento"; Burt, "Opera in Arcadia"; Vetter, "Deutschland und das Formgefühl Italiens"; Freeman, *Opera Without Drama.*

11. Cf. *Giornale de' letterati d'Italia,* vol. 38, part 2, pp. 117–34, and Giazotto, *Poesia melodrammatica.*

librettos by limiting the number of acts, scenes, and characters, and he heightened the dramatic action through a more creative use of language. Stampiglia was reluctant, however, to eliminate the servants and their integral comic scenes, to discard the happy ending, and to reverse the dominant role of music over poetry. As a result, he succeeded merely in remolding rather than reforming the *eroicomico* libretto, replacing it with his *tragicommedia*. In so doing, he kept alive a type of libretto that was to remain in vogue for several decades in the eighteenth century, most especially in Vienna, where Pietro Pariati (1665–1733) was active as court poet.[12]

The two poets chiefly associated with actually enacting the "reform" as set forth by Gravina were Apostolo Zeno (1688–1750) and Pietro Metastasio (1698–1782).[13] Zeno, under the influence of the French dramatists, favored historical subject matter and sought to purge the opera of erratically motivated plots, supernatural interventions, machines, irrelevant comic episodes, and the bombastic declamation which had reigned in the seventeenth century.[14] this movement was brought to fulfillment by Metastasio, the guiding genius of eighteenth-century Italian opera and a literary figure of such stature that his contemporaries seriously compared him with Homer and Dante. Metastasio became court poet at Vienna in 1730, succeeding Stampiglia and Zeno, who had held that position since 1705 and 1718, respectively. His twenty-seven *drammi per musica* and other theater works were given over a thousand musical settings in the eighteenth century, some of them being composed as many as seventy times. The composers chiefly associated with his works were Leo, Vinci, and Hasse. A modern reader is apt to find Metastasio's plays mannered and artificial, elegant rather than powerful; his characters seem more

12. Cf. Campanini, *Un precursore del Metastasio*, and Williams, "Francesco Bartolomeo Conti: His Life and Operas."

13. On Zeno, see biographies by Negri and Fehr, and Wotquenne, *Alphabetisches Verzeichnis*. On Metastasio, see Brunelli, ed., *Tutte le opere di Pietro Metastasio*. See also Burney, *Memoirs*; Calzabigi, "Dissertazione"; Mattei, *Memorie*; Stendhal, *Vies de Haydn, de Mozart et de Métastase*; Callegari, "Il melodramma e Pietro Metastasio"; Rolland, "Métastase, précurseur de Gluck"; Della Corte, "Appunti sull' estetica musicale di Pietro Metastasio"; Gerber, *Der Operntypus Johann Adolf Hasses*, chap. 1.

14. Metastasio, letter of Fabroni, December 7, 1767; in Burney, *Memoirs* 3:19. See also Wellesz, introduction to Fux's *Costanza e fortezza*, DTOe, 37:xiii.

like eighteenth-century courtiers than the ancient Romans they were supposed to be; "sentimental quandaries" make up most of the situations in these dramas of amorous and political intrigue; there is almost always a *lieto fine,* a happy ending, and the stock figure of the magnanimous tyrant is often in evidence. Yet in spite of all this, if one is willing to allow for the dramatic conventions of the time, some of Metastasio's plays may still be read with pleasure. His achievement consisted in the creation of a consistent dramatic structure conforming to the rationalistic ideals of the period, but incorporating lyrical elements suited for musical setting in such a way as to form an organic whole.

As an example of the Metastasian libretto let us take *Attilio regolo* (1740). Attilio, having been taken captive by the Carthaginians, is offered his freedom if he will use his influence with the Roman Senate to obtain certain advantages for Carthage. Under parole to return if unsuccessful, he is permitted to go to Rome; but once there, he urges the Senate to stand firm, scorning to purchase his own life by betraying the interests of his country. Resisting the entreaties of his friends and family, of the Senate (which is willing to make national sacrifices to save him), and of the entire populace, he voluntarily boards the ship which will take him back to captivity and death. This tragic ending was something of an innovation with Metastasio; it had appeared in only two other works of his, *Didone abbandonata* (1724) and the original version of *Catone in Utica* (1728, revised in 1729), and is exceedingly rare in earlier Italian opera—Busenello's *Didone* of 1641 (music by Cavalli) being one instance.

One may well ask where, in such a drama as this, there is any place for lyricism. The answer is to be found in the peculiar construction of the scenes. In seventeenth-century opera, recitatives, arioso passages, and arias were intermingled according to the composer's fancy or the requirements of the action. There was no standard procedure; very often a scene might end with a recitative. Metastasio standardized the form. In his operas, a typical scene consists of two distinct parts: first, dramatic action in recitative; and second, expression of sentiments by the chief actor in an aria. In the first part of the scene, the actor is a character in the drama, carrying on dialogue with other actors; in the second part, he is a person expressing his emotions or conveying some general sentiments or reflections appropriate to the current situation—not to his fellows on the stage but to the audience. While this goes on, the progress of the drama usually comes to a complete stop. Consequently, the play is made up of regularly alternating periods of movement and repose, the former representing the rights of the drama (recitative) and the latter the rights of the music (aria): the former occupying the larger part of the scene in the libretto, but the latter far exceeding it in the score, by reason of the extended musical structure of the aria, usually built on only two stanzas of four lines each. There results from this scheme an endlessly repeated pattern of tension and release, each recitative building up an emotional situation which finds outlet in the following aria. "The recitative loads the gun, the aria fires it."[15] This is the classical compromise of operatic form, in which drama and music each yield certain rights and thereby find a means of living together compatibly. It permits free development of both elements within conventional limits. So long as these limits were tolerable (as they were to the early and middle eighteenth century), the form was found satisfactory; it lost favor only when other ideals of drama began to prevail. Moreover, the stiffness of the scheme was mitigated in Metastasio's operas by the naturalness of the transition from recitative to aria, by the musical quality of the language in the recitative, and by the variety of verse forms in the aria.

It may be remarked that, whereas with respect to the dramatic action tension is greatest in the recitative and least in the aria, with respect to the music the exact opposite obtains. Musical tension is at a minimum in recitative and becomes strongest in the aria. Thus, the two forces, drama and music, tend to "cancel" one another and the result is a certain neutrality, a remoteness or *generality* of expression in these works, which agrees well with the highly formal pattern of their design.

One paramount fact emerges: the central position of the aria as a musical unit. Musically speaking, that is to say, an opera is a succession of arias; other elements—recitatives, ensembles, instrumental numbers—are nothing but background. From this

---

15. Flemming, ed., *Die Oper*, p. 58. See also the admirably clear exposition of this aesthetic in Grimm, "Poëme lyrique."

fact stem certain consequences: (1) the variety and degree of stylization of aria types, (2) a corresponding looseness of structure in the opera as a whole, and (3) the importance of the singer not only as an interpreter but also as a creative partner of the composer.

Aria Types

Eighteenth-century writers on opera classified arias into certain well-defined types, having distinct characteristics. For example, the Englishman John Brown mentioned five traditional varieties:

> *Aria cantabile*,—by pre-eminence so called, as if it alone were Song: And, indeed, it is the only kind of song which gives the singer an opportunity of displaying at once, and in the highest degree, all his powers. . . . The proper subjects for this Air are sentiments of tenderness.
>
> *Aria di portamento* . . . chiefly composed of long notes, such as the singer can dwell on, and have, thereby, an opportunity of more effectually displaying the beauties, and calling forth the powers of his voice. . . . The subjects proper to this Air are sentiments of dignity.
>
> *Aria di mezzo carattere* . . . a species of Air, which, though expressive neither of the dignity of this last, nor of the pathos of the former, is, however, serious and pleasing.
>
> *Aria parlante*,—speaking Air, is that which . . . admits neither of long notes in the composition, nor of many ornaments in the execution. The rapidity of motion of this Air is proportioned to the violence of the passion which is expressed by it. This species of Air goes sometimes by the name of *aria di nota e parola*, and likewise of *aria agitata*. . . .
>
> *Aria di bravura, aria di agilita*,—is that which is composed *chiefly*, indeed, too often, *merely* to indulge the singer in the display of certain powers in the execution, particularly extraordinary agility or compass of voice.[16]

16. J. Brown, *Letters on the Italian Opera* (2d ed., 1791), pp. 36–39.

A less scientific tabulation is given by the Frenchman Charles de Brosses, writing from Rome about 1740:

> The Italians . . . have airs of great agitation, full of music and harmony, for brilliant voices; others are of a pleasant sound and charming outlines, for delicate and supple voices; still others are passionate, tender, affecting, truly following the natural expression of emotions, strong or full of feeling for stage effect and for bringing out the best points of the actor. The "agitato" airs are those presenting pictures of storms, tempests, torrents, thunderclaps, a lion pursued by hunters, a war-horse hearing the sound of the trumpet, the terror of a silent night, etc.—all images quite appropriate to music, but out of place in tragedy. This kind of air devoted to large effects is almost always accompanied by wind instruments—oboes, trumpets, and horns—which make an excellent effect, especially in airs having to do with storms at sea. . . .
>
> Airs of the second kind are madrigals, pretty little songs with ingenious and delicate ideas or comparisons drawn from pleasant objects, such as zephyrs, birds, murmuring waves, country life, etc. . . .
>
> As to airs of the third kind, which express only feeling, Metastasio takes great care to place them at the most lively and interesting point of his drama, and to connect them closely with the subject. The musician then does not seek for embellishments or passage-work, but tries simply to portray the feeling, whatever it may be, with all his power. . . . I should also place in this class the airs of spectres and visions, to which the music lends a surprising power.[17]

It goes without saying that these and similar classifications cannot always be applied in all their details to the actual music; but their very existence is of interest as showing the high degree of organization—of stylization—which the aria reached in this period. there were other conventions as well, notably the one which decreed that practically every aria must be in the da capo form. Even the order and distribution of the different types were prescribed: every performer was to have at least one aria in each act, but no one might have two arias in succession; no aria could be followed immediately by another of the same type, even though

17. Brosses, *Lettres familières sur l'Italie*, 2:348–51 (translation by Grout).

performed by a different singer; the subordinate singers must have fewer and less important arias than the stars; and so on.[18] At first glance, the whole system seems artificial to the point of absurdity; later in the century, in fact, it was attacked on this very ground. Yet, given the postulates of early eighteenth-century opera aesthetic, it was quite logical, and justification could be found for every rule. (Moreover, the composers did not hesitate to break the rules if it suited their purposes to do so.) It was one of the secrets of Metastasio's success that he could construct a drama which met these rigid requirements without being too obviously constrained by them.

The "Pasticcio"

A second consequence of overconcentration on the aria was a certain looseness of structure in the opera as a whole. With few exceptions, the composer's responsibility for formal unity was limited to each single number. Apart from the libretto, there was nothing to bind these into a larger musical unit except the general requirements as to variety and the custom of placing the two most important arias at the end of each of the first two acts. To use familiar analogies, the arias were not like figures in a painting, each fulfilling a certain role in the composition and each in some measure conditioned by the others; rather, they were like a row of statues in a hall, symmetrically arranged but lacking any closer bond of aesthetic union. The conception corresponded to the baroque ideal of dynamics, where the various degrees of loudness or softness were distinct, without transitions of crescendo or diminuendo; or to forms such as the sonata and concerto, in which each movement was a complete, thematically independent unit. The arias were like Leibniz's monads, each closed off from the others and all held together only by the "preestablished har-

---

18. Hogarth, *Memoirs of the Opera*, vol. 2, chap. 3; Goldoni, *Mémoires*, chap. 28. See also the letter of Giuseppe Riva to Muratori in 1725, on the requirements for a London libretto, quoted in Streatfeild, "Handel, Rolli"; see also Hucke, "Die neapolitanische Tradition," pp. 262ff.

mony" of the libretto. Thus, their order could be changed, new numbers added, or others taken away, without really doing violence to the musical plan of the opera as a whole—though, needless to say, the drama might suffer. Composers therefore freely substituted new arias for old in revivals of their works, or for performances with a different cast. A composer at Rome, for example, who had orders to revise a Venetian opera to suit the taste of the Roman singers and public, would have no compunction about replacing some of the original composer's arias with some of his own, perhaps taken from an earlier work where they had been sung to different words. Indeed, it was exceptional for an opera to be given in exactly the same form in two different cities.

This working of new materials into old garments, if carried far enough, resulted in a kind of opera known as a *pasticcio*—literally, a "pie," but perhaps translatable more expressively for modern readers as "patchwork." There were two distinct kinds of pasticcio. One is illustrated by the opera *Muzio Scevola* (London, 1721), the first act of which was composed by F. Amadei (also known as Mattei), the second by Giovanni Bononcini, and the third by Handel. But the typical pasticcio was the result of a more haphazard process; it was an opera which had migrated from city to city, undergoing patching and alteration at every stage, until it might one day arrive at London (its usual final home) with a libretto in which Metastasio shared honors with "Zeno, Goldoni, Stampiglia, Rossi, and other librettists," while "Gluck, Ciampi, Galuppi, Cocchi, Jommelli, Latilla, Handel and several more might be pasted together" in the same musical score.[19]

The Singers

A third effect—which operated at the same time as a cause—of the importance of the aria was the glorification of the singer. The virtuoso singer was to the eighteenth century what the virtuoso

19. Sonneck, "Ciampi's *Bertoldo*." See also Walker, "*Orazio:* The History of a Pasticcio."

pianist was to the nineteenth, or the virtuoso conductor to the twentieth. The operatic songbirds of that age have been so often and so unsparingly condemned that it seems worthwhile to try to correct this judgment by quoting a passage from Vernon Lee's *Studies of the Eighteenth Century in Italy*, a book naïve in many of its musical opinions and perhaps too uncritical in its enthusiasm for everything Italian but which nevertheless states the case for the singer with sympathy and insight:

> The singer was a much more important personage in the musical system of the eighteenth century than he is now-a-days. He was not merely one of the wheels of the mechanism, he was its main pivot. For in a nation so practically, spontaneously musical as the Italian, the desire to sing preceded the existence of what could be sung: performers were not called into existence because men wished to hear such and such a composition, but the composition was produced because men wished to sing. The singers were therefore not trained with a view to executing any peculiar sort of music, but the music was composed to suit the powers of the singers. Thus, ever since the beginning of the seventeenth century, when music first left the church and the palace for the theatre, composition and vocal performance had developed simultaneously, narrowly linked together; composers always learning first of all to sing, and singers always finishing their studies with that of composition; Scarlatti and Porpora teaching great singers, Stradella and Pistocchi forming great composers; the two branches . . . acting and reacting on each other so as to become perfectly homogeneous and equal. . . .
>
> The singer, therefore, was neither a fiddle for other men to play upon, nor a musical box wound up by mechanism. He was an individual voice, an individual mind, developed to the utmost; a perfectly balanced organization; and to him was confided the work of embodying the composer's ideas, of moulding matter to suit the thought, of adapting the thought to suit the matter, of giving real existence to the form which existed only as an abstraction in the composer's mind. The full responsibility of this work rested on him; the fullest liberty of action was therefore given him to execute it. Music, according to the notions of the eighteenth century, was no more the mere written score than a plan on white paper would have seemed architecture to the Greeks. Music was to be the result of the combination of the abstract written note with the concrete voice, of the ideal thought of the composer with the

individuality of the performer. The composer was to give only the general, the abstract; while all that depended upon individual differences, and material peculiarities, was given up to the singer. The composer gave the unchangeable, the big notes, constituting the essential, immutable form, expressing the stable, unvarying character; the singer added the small notes, which filled up and perfected the part of the form which depended on the physical material, which expressed the minutely subtle, ever-changing mood. In short, while the composer represented the typical, the singer represented the individual.[20]

We read much about abuses on the part of the eighteenth-century opera singers, but we are seldom told why these abuses were tolerated, being tacitly allowed to infer that audiences and composers were either blind to the evil or too supine to resent it. This was not so. The abuses were recognized, but they were endured because they seemed to be inseparable from the system out of which they grew and because, on the whole, people liked the system. The principle of absolute dominance of the aria in the form entailed the absolute dominance of the singer in performance; and in their submission to this principle audiences, composers, and poets alike allowed excesses on the part of the singers which would not have been endured in another age. Only rarely was even an autocrat like Handel (who had the incidental advantage of combining the offices of composer and manager in one person) able to control them, and then only by an extraordinary combination of tact, patience, humor, personal force, and even threats of physical violence. But usually the singers reigned supreme. Metastasio might insist all he pleased that poetry should be the "dictator" in opera, and complain of the mutilation of his dramas by "those ignorant and vain vocal heroes and heroines, who having substituted the imitation of flageolets and nightingales for human affections, render the Italian stage a national disgrace,"[21] but he was powerless to alter a situation which his own works had contributed so much to bring about.

A lively, though unquestionably exaggerated, picture of the singers may be drawn from the critical and satirical writings

---

20. Lee, *Studies*, pp. 117–18.

21. Burney, *Memoirs*, 2:325; 3:43.

of the seventeenth and early eighteenth centuries.[22] The most famous satire was *Il teatro alla moda*, by Benedetto Marcello (1686–1739), himself a composer.[23] Marcello's work is in the form of ironically worded counsels to everyone connected with opera, from the poets and composers down to the stagehands and singing teachers. The composer, he says, "will hurry or slow down the pace of an aria, according to the caprice of the singers, and will conceal the displeasure which their insolence causes him by the reflection that his reputation, his solvency, and all his interest are in their hands."[24] As for the director, he "will see that all the best songs go to the *prima donna*, and if it becomes necessary to shorten the opera he will never allow her arias to be cut, but rather other entire scenes."[25] If a singer

> has a scene with another actor, whom he is supposed to address when singing an air, he will take care to pay no attention to him, but will bow to the spectators in the loges, smile at the orchestra and the other players, in order that the audience may clearly understand that he is the *Signor Alipi Forconi, Musico*, and not the Prince Zoroaster, whom he is representing. . . . All the while the ritornello of his air is being played the singer should walk about the stage, take snuff, complain to his friends that he is in bad voice, that he has a cold, etc., and while singing his aria he shall take care to remember that at the cadence he may pause as long as he pleases, and make runs, decorations, and ornaments according to his fancy; during which time the leader of the orchestra shall leave his place at the harpsichord, take a pinch of snuff, and wait until it shall please the singer to finish. The latter shall take breath several times before finally coming to a close on a trill, which he will be sure to sing as rapidly as possible from the beginning, with-

---

22. Rosa, "La musica"; Adimari, "Satira quarta"; Muratori, *Della perfetta poesia*, 2:30–45 (but see the refutation in Mattheson, *Die neueste Untersuchung*); memoirs of Da Ponte, Goldoni, and others; H. Abert, *Niccolo Jommelli*, p. 426. See also Goldschmidt, "Die Oper und ihre Literatur bis 1752," in his *Die Musikästhetik des 18. Jahrhunderts*, pp. 272–87; Cametti, "Critiche e satire"; Frati, "Satire"; Monnier, *Venise au XVIIIe siècle*, pp. 48ff.

23. Modern editions in Italian (E. Fondi, 1913; A. D'Angeli, 1927), French (E. David, 1890), German (A. Einstein, 1917), and English (R. Pauly, 1948); selections in Strunk, ed., *Source Readings*, pp. 518–31. See also Pauly, "Benedetto Marcello's Satire"; D'Angeli, *Benedetto Marcello*.

24. Marcello, *Il teatro alla moda*, pp. 19–20.

25. Ibid., p. 23.

out preparing it by placing his voice properly, and all the time using the highest notes of which he is capable.[26]

The cadenzas and ornaments to which Marcello here alludes were carefully prepared beforehand:

If [a singer] have a role in a new opera, she will at the first possible moment take all her arias (which in order to save time she has had copied without the bass part) to her Maestro *Crica* so that he may write in the passages, the variations, the beautiful ornaments, etc.—and Maestro Crica, without knowing the first thing about the intentions of the composer either with regard to the tempo of the arias, or the bass, or the instrumentation, will write below them in the empty spaces of the bass staff everything he can think of, and in very great quantity, so that the *Virtuosa* may be able to sing her song in a different way at every performance . . . and if her variations have nothing in common with the bass, with the violins which are to play in unison with her, or with the concertizing instruments, even if they are not in the same key, that will be of no consequence, since it is understood that the modern opera director is both deaf and dumb.[27]

More serious critics also viewed with alarm the overemphasis on vocal virtuosity, as attracting attention at the expense of both drama and music. Thus, Metastasio writes:

The singers of the present times wholly forget, that their business is to imitate the speech of man, with numbers and harmony: on the contrary, they believe themselves more perfect, in proportion as their performance is remote from human nature. . . . When they have played their Symphony with the throat, they believe they have fulfilled all the duties of their art. Hence the audience keep their hearts in the most perfect tranquillity, and expect the performers merely to tickle their ears

—to which Dr. Burney adds, "If forty years ago, Metastasio speaks with so much indignation of the abuse of execution, which has been increasing ever since, what would he say now?[28]

26. Ibid., pp. 26–27. The singer would be able to "complain to his friends" while walking about the stage by virtue of the eighteenth-century custom of seating spectators on the stage.

27. Ibid., pp. 39, 41.

28. Burney, *Memoirs*, 2:135–36.

The technique of singing seems to have reached a level in the eighteenth century that has never since been equaled. In the nature of things, it is difficult to find out much about the details of this art in specific cases, for the singers' greatest displays of skill were improvised, and consequently almost no examples of written-out da capo ornamentation remain in the scores. In general, however, it may be said that there were two related practices, one having to do with ornamentation of the given melodic line (coloratura), and the other with the insertion of improvised passages at the cadences (cadenzas). Both of these practices can be observed in a unique example afforded by an early eighteenth-century manuscript containing the aria "Sciolta dal lido" by Giuseppe Vignati. Notated below the vocal staff is an ornamented version of the soprano part, believed to represent a 1720 performance by Faustina Bordoni.[29]

Ornamentation of the melodic line by solo singers was a custom inherited from the Renaissance and carried on through the whole baroque period.[30] It rose to special prominence in the latter part of the seventeenth century in Italy, as the aria was coming into its commanding position at the expense of the accompaniment. The climax was reached in the eighteenth century, the age of the great Italian singing schools. Particularly in the da capo repetition of the first part of an aria, the singer was expected to show his full powers:

> Among the Things worthy of Consideration, the first to be taken Notice of, is the Manner in which all *Airs* divided into three Parts are to be sung. In the first they require nothing but the simplest Ornaments, of a good Taste and few, that the Composition may remain simple, plain, and pure; in the second they expect, that to this Purity some artful Graces be added, by which the Judicious may hear, that the Ability of the Singer is greater; and, in repeating the *Air*, he that does not vary it for the better, is no great Master.[31]

29. See Buelow, "A Lesson in Operatic Performance Practice," with its illustrative musical examples.

30. For a general survey of this subject, see Haas, *Aufführungspraxis*. See also Aldrich, "The Principal Agréments," which gives full reference to the sources, and Goldschmidt, *Die Lehre von der vokalen Ornamentik*.

31. Tosi, *Observations on the Florid Song*, pp. 93–94.

Example 13.1: *Serse*, Act I, sc. 1

In the rapid bravura arias, opportunity for improvised ornamentation was less than in arias in slower tempo. The well-known "Largo" from Handel's *Serse* would probably have been ornamented by the singer somewhat as shown in example 13.1.[32]

The practice of improvising cadenzas likewise originated in the sixteenth-century solo song and was revived in the eighteenth-century opera. Examples are found in Scarlatti. The natural place for a cadenza was on the $^6_4$ chord of an important cadence, just as we find it commonly in the concertos of the classical period. Inserted in arias, where they served par excellence for the display of the singers' powers, the cadenzas were often extended to ridiculous lengths. Ange Goudar quotes a burlesque petition supposed to have been presented to the management of the Paris Opéra "by the Italian eunuchs" (the castrati) which includes the statement, "A cadenza, to be according to the rules, must last seven minutes and thirty-six seconds, all without drawing breath; for the whole of this must be done in one breath even though the actor should faint on the stage."[33] Tosi criticizes the cadenzas in these words:

> Every *Air* has (at least) three *Cadences*, that are all three final. Generally speaking, the Study of the Singers of the present Times consists in terminating the *Cadence* of the first Part with an overflowing of *Passages* and *Divisions* at Pleasure, and the *Orchestre* waits; in that of the second the Dose is encreased, and the *Orchestre* grows tired; but on the last Cadence, the Throat is set a going, like a Weather-cock in a Whirlwind, and the *Orchestre* yawns.[34]

Examples of cadenzas sung by Farinelli in Giacomelli's *Merope* (Venice, 1734) have been preserved in a manuscript dedicated to Empress Maria Theresa and now in the Vienna library; one of

---

32. For this realization of an ornamented melodic line, I am indebted to Dr. Putman Aldrich. An example of vocal embellishment supplied by Handel can be seen in Dean, "Vocal Embellishment in a Handel Aria." For examples of elaborate bravura arias, see Haböck, *Die Gesangskunst der Kastraten*; Burney, *History of Music*, 2:833–37; *OHM*, 4:221–32.

33. "Une cadenza, pour être dans les regles, doit durer sept minutes & trente-six seconds, le tout sans prendre respiration; car il faut que toute cette tirade soit d'une seule haleine, l'acteur en dût crever sur la scene." Goudar, *Le Brigandage*, p. 127.

34. Tosi, *Observations*, pp. 128–29.

Example 13.2: Cadenza in Giacomelli's *Merope*

them, shown in example 13.2, well illustrates these remarks of Tosi.[35]

35. An autograph manuscript page of Mozart's cadenzas and ornaments to arias from the operas of J. C. Bach (K. 293e), formerly preserved in the Mozarteum at Salzburg, disappeared during the Second World War. Fortunately, however, it had previously been photographed by Edward Downes, who, in "The Operas of Johann Christian Bach," appendix B, reproduces and transcribes Mozart's embellishments for the aria "Cara la dolce fiamma" from Bach's *Adriano in Siria* (London, 1765).

All this outburst of virtuosity was bound up with the peculiar seventeenth- and eighteenth-century Italian institution of the castrato.[36] There are many references to the presence of eunuchs among the singers of Italian and German chapels of the sixteenth century; they are found at Florence in 1534 and in the papal chapel at Rome by 1562. They came into opera during the first decade of the seventeenth century, most notably with Monteverdi's *Orfeo*; by the end of that century they were a usual feature in Italian churches, despite periodic pronouncements by the popes against the custom. Castrato singers flourished especially during the period 1650–1750, both male and female roles in the opera being entrusted to them. Their popularity began to decline in the latter part of the eighteenth century, and the last Italian opera castrato died in 1861.[37] Their extraordinary vogue was due in part to the shortage of women singers after the first few years of the seventeenth century, coupled with the fact that for a long time (especially at Rome), women were forbidden to appear on the public stage;[38] and where women did take part in opera, as at Paris (there were no castrati in the French opera), they were generally regarded as morally outside the pale of respectable society. But the castrati held their ground even in the eighteenth century, a period when there was no dearth of first-rate women singers (such as Faustina Bordoni, wife of the composer Hasse, and Francesca Cuzzoni), by reason of the sheer excellence of their art. Educated as the castrati were from early childhood in the famous conservatories of the Italian cities, their long training gave them a solid grounding in musicianship, in addition to developing a miraculous vocal technique. Their voices (known as *voci bianche*, literally "white voices") were more powerful and flexible, if less sweet and expressive, than those of women,

36. Haböck, *Die Kastraten und ihre Gesangskunst*; Raguenet, *Défense du parallèle des Italiens et des François*; Villeneuve, *Lettre sur le méchanisme de l'opéra italien* (1756); Lalande, *Voyage d'un François en Italie*, vol. 6, chap. 16; Parini, "La evirazione (La musica)" (1769); Foscolo, *Dei sepolcri* (1807), vv. 73–74; Heriot, *The Castrati in Opera*; Petty, *Italian Opera in London 1760–1800*, pp. 80–85.

37. Parolari, "Giambattista Velluti." See also Hogarth, *Memoirs of The Opera*, 2:306–13.

38. See Lalande, *Voyage*, 5:179.

and the quality often remained unimpaired after as many as forty years of singing. So great were the rewards of a successful career that even the slightest sign of a promising voice was often sufficient to induce hopeful parents to offer a boy for emasculation, with the inevitable result that (according to Dr. Burney) in every great town in Italy could be found numbers of these pathetic creatures "without any voice at all, or at least without one sufficient to compensate for such a loss."[39]

Of all the Italian castrati, the most renowned was Carlo Broschi (1705–1782), known as Farinelli, who had a legendary career in Europe. Brilliantly successful as a singer in many countries, the friend of princes and emperors, for twenty-four years the confidant of two successive Spanish kings and virtually prime minister of Spain, the hero of popular tales, and the subject of an opera, he was a figure in the public imagination of the eighteenth century comparable to Liszt or Paganini in the nineteenth.[40]

Composers and Audiences

The number of operas written by eighteenth-century composers testifies to the popularity of this form of entertainment.[41] A tabulation of forty leading composers of the period shows nearly two thousand works, or an average of about fifty operas each. The sum total of the production of all composers would, of course, be much greater. One reason for this was that audiences insisted on new music each season, while they also welcomed the old familiar librettos year after year.[42] Then, too, the writing out of the score

39. Burney, *The Present State of Music in France and Italy*, p. 303. See also Lalande, *Voyage*, vol. 6, chap. 16, and Parini, "La evirazione."

40. For an account of Farinelli, see Burney, *Present State of Music in France and Italy*, pp. 202–17. See also Monaldi, *Cantanti evirati celebri*; Haböck, *Die Gesangskunst der Kastraten*.

41. Cf. Monnier, *Venise au XVIIIe siècle*, chap. 6; Grosley, *New Observations on Italy*; Villeneuve, *Lettre sur le méchanisme*.

42. Lalande, *Voyage*, 6:352.

was not the time-consuming process that it is in modern days, since so much was left to be improvised. The score was really little more than a memorandum of the composer's intentions, to be filled in by the performers. A composer commonly completed a score in a month or six weeks, and received for it a sum amounting to $100 or $150, plus the price of the first copy of the arias—in manuscript usually, though favorite airs of popular operas were often published in London. Once the first copy was sold, the composer's income from his work ended, for there was no copyright protection.

Contemporary audiences, far from regarding the opera as a serious dramatic spectacle, looked upon it merely as an amusement. Brosses reports that the performances in Rome began at eight or nine in the evening and lasted until midnight. Everyone of any consequence had a box, which was a social gathering place for friends. "The pleasure these people take in music and the theatre is more evidenced by their presence than by the attention they bestow on the performance." After the first few times, no one listened at all, except to a few favorite songs. The boxes were comfortably furnished and lighted so that their occupants could indulge in cards and other games. "Chess is marvellously well adapted to filling in the monotony of the recitatives, and the arias are equally good for interrupting a too assiduous concentration on chess.[43] Dr. Burney mentions the faro tables at the Milan opera;[44] at Venice, where the pit was usually filled with gondoliers and workmen, "there is a constant noise of people laughing, drinking, and joking, while sellers of baked goods and fruit cry their wares aloud from box to box";[45] at Florence, it was the custom to serve hot suppers in the boxes during the performance.[46]

This description of the manner in which operas were performed will explain why we of today often fail to see what it was that aroused enthusiasm on the part of the audiences. We must realize that those things which were the very life of the per-

43. Brosses, *Lettres . . . sur l'Italie*, 2:36 and passim. But see also Lalande, *Voyage*, vol. 5, chap. 10.

44. Burney, *Present State of Music in France and Italy*, pp. 81–82.

45. Maier, *Beschreibung von Venedig*, 2:284.

46. Doran, "*Mann*" and Manners at the Court of Florence.

formance were just the things which could never be written in the score—the marvelous, constantly varied embellishments by the singers, the glamour of famous names, the intoxication of the lights and scenery, above all the gay, careless society of the eighteenth century, the game of chess during the recitatives, and the gabble of conversation, hushed only for the favorite aria and the following rapturous applause.

Other Elements of Opera Seria

Although the arias were the chief musical feature, there were a few other elements. The chorus was limited in its function, especially in operas based upon librettos by Zeno and Metastasio.[47] Besides occasional interjections into the dramatic action, most often immediately preceding or following a change of scenery, the chorus was used at the end of an opera to provide a festive conclusion. The only theater works that used choruses at all extensively were of the type known as *feste teatrali*, written for special occasions like the festival operas of an earlier period (see chapter 8). Hardly more important than the chorus was the overture, since the composer knew there would be too much noise in the house for it to be heard. (A notable exception to this situation was the atmosphere in the court theater of Vienna, which differed markedly from the clamor in the public theaters of Venice.) The orchestral accompaniments for the arias, however, were carefully managed so as to support the singer without obscuring the vocal line. The first violins frequently played in unison with the voice—or rather, they played the simple written version of the melody which the singer was ornamenting. Ensembles were few; in the early part of the century, there was usually no more than a perfunctory closing number for all the singers, though later this feature took on more importance, largely under the influence of the comic opera ensembles. Duets were more common, but even here much of the writing was a mere alternation rather than a combination of the two voices;

47. The function of the chorus in these librettos is discussed in Freeman, *Opera Without Drama*, pp. 240–51.

a duet would be placed, like an aria, at the close of a scene, and was usually in da capo form.

Two distinct types of recitative in eighteenth-century opera were inherited from the preceding age. The recitative *semplice* ("simple"), later called *secco* ("dry"), was accompanied only by the continuo instruments. Its function was to carry on the action in dialogue with the slightest possible musical accompaniment.[48] Although audiences as a rule gave it little attention, the secco recitative was not altogether a perfunctory matter. Certain conventions of harmony and certain melodic formulas appear in it regularly, in accordance with the fluctuating emotions of the text; and since the singers allowably took all sorts of rhythmic and melodic liberties with the score in the interest of "natural" expression, it is probable that the secco recitative had in performance considerably more dramatic impact than the bare written notes suggest.

The other kind of recitative was the *recitativo accompagnato* or *stromentato* ("accompanied recitative"), so called because it was accompanied either by the strings or the full orchestra in addition to the continuo. These recitatives were reserved for the two or three most dramatic points in the opera, for monologues expressing strong emotion at the climaxes of the action. The voice, declaiming in flexible, varied, and expressive phrases, alternated with orchestral outbursts of chords, tremolando figures, or rhythmic motifs. Sudden changes of mood, abrupt modulations, were featured. The essential function of the orchestra, indeed, was not so much to accompany the singer as to express, during the pauses in the song, the emotions which words were insufficient to convey—to suggest, in combination with the attitudes and gestures of the actor, those further depths of feeling which only music and movement, transcending the too definite ideas and images of a text, could adequately render.[49] The close union between words and music, together with the natural freedom of form, gave these places great dramatic power, and all contemporaries speak of them with enthusiasm. They were almost the only relief from the monotony of the secco recitative on the one

48. On the performance of such accompaniment in the eighteenth century, see M. Schneider, "Die Begleitung des Secco-Rezitativs um 1750"; Downes "Secco Recitative."

49. Cf. Rousseau, "Récitatif obligé," in his *Dictionnaire de musique*.

hand and the strict formality of the aria on the other, and it is significant that the accompanied recitative was especially cultivated by such later composers as Hasse, Graun, and Terradellas, and above all by Jommelli, Gluck, and Traetta, who were striving to break down the rigidity of the old operatic framework.

The Composers

Naples in the eighteenth century was as preeminent for its music as Venice had been in the seventeenth century.[50] Lalande wrote in 1769:

> Music is the special triumph of the Neapolitans. It seems as if in that country the membranes of the eardrum are more taut, more harmonious, more sonorous than elsewhere in Europe. The whole nation sings; gesture, tone of voice, rhythm of syllables, the very conversation—all breathe music and harmony. Thus Naples is the principal source of Italian music, of great composers and excellent operas; it is there that Corelli, Vinci, Rinaldo [di Capua], Jommelli, Durante (learned in harmony above all the rest), Leo, Pergolesi, Galuppi, Perez, Terradeglias, and so many other famous composers have brought forth their masterpieces.[51]

Among the opera composers active at Naples immediately after the time of Alessandro Scarlatti were Leonardo Vinci (1690–1730) and Leonardo Leo (1694–1744), two of the earliest composers of comic opera in Neapolitan dialect.[52] Vinci is also one of the first in whose music the traits of the new opera seria are

50. Florimo, *La scuola musicale di Napoli* (the basic work, a thoroughgoing study of the Neapolitan conservatories, teachers, composers, and singers up to the middle of the nineteenth century); Croce, *I teatri di Napoli*; Roberti, "La musica in Italia"; Grosley, *New Observations on Italy* (1769); Schletterer, "Die Opernhäuser Neapels"; Robinson, *Naples and Neapolitan Opera*; Hell, *Die Neapolitanische Opernsinfonie*.

51. Lalande, *Voyage*, 6:345. Of the composers named, all but two, Corelli and Durante, were famous chiefly for operas. Francesco Durante (1684–1755), though he wrote no operas himself, was the teacher of many of the most important Italian opera composers of the eighteenth century.

52. On Vinci, see Silva, *Illustri musicisti calabresi*; Dent, "Notes on Leonardo Vinci"; Meikle, "Leonardo Vinci's *Artaserse*." On Leo, see G. Leo, *Leonardo Leo*; idem, *Leonardo Leo . . . e le sue opere musicali*; Pastore, *Leonardo Leo*; Hardie, "Leonardo Leo and His Comic Operas."

fully apparent. His setting of Metastasio's *Didone abbandonata*
led to a brief but fruitful period of collaboration between composer and librettist culminating in their production of *Artaserse*
(1730). Example 13.3 shows the beginning (after an orchestral introduction) of a da capo aria from this opera, typical for its fresh,
clear melody, simple harmonic vocabulary, and thin texture in

Example 13.3: Aria from *Artaserse*, Act III, sc. 1

(Example 13.3 continued)

the string orchestra, colored by a few passages from the horns, doubtless to suggest the rural landscape depicted in the text. One of Leo's most successful serious operas was *Demofoonte* (1738), also based upon a libretto by Metastasio. *Demofoonte* was first staged in the San Bartolomeo theater in January 1735 as a pasticcio with only Act III by Leo. Three years later, Leo set *Demo-*

foonte in its entirety, retaining his original Act III, with the aria "Misero pargoletto," which in later years was acclaimed for its dramatic pathos.

The immensely facile Nicola Porpora (1686–1768), the greatest singing teacher of his time, worked at Naples and Venice, and at various times also in London, Dresden, and Vienna.[53] Dr. Burney remarked about one of his arias that it seemed to have been composed "in a shivering fit,"[54] so full was it of vocal pyrotechnics; but this probably does injustice to Porpora, whose music, if not especially distinguished, is workmanlike and no more extreme in its demands on the singers than that of other composers of the time.

One of the very few Neapolitan opera composers in this period whose name and music are at all well known today is Giovanni Battista Pergolesi (1710–1736).[55] Though remembered now chiefly for his *Stabat Mater* and his comic intermezzos, Pergolesi in his short lifetime also produced one of the finest *opere serie* of the early eighteenth century. This was *L'Olimpiade* (Rome, 1735), one of Metastasio's most popular dramas. An aria from this opera (example 13.4) illustrates the "tenderness of sentiment . . . noble, attractive, enthusiastic feeling, an innocent, touching, childlike quality" that characterizes Pergolesi's music.[56] Note particularly the use of "Lombardic rhythm" in the melody at measure four and elsewhere, and the triplet divisions of the eighth-note beat, both typical of the style of this period. Pergolesi's serious operas, despite their merit, procured him no popular success among his contemporaries.

One of the remarkable phenomena of the eighteenth century was the way Italian opera, both serious and comic, spread to every country of Europe. This movement involved the importation not only of scores and singers but frequently of composers as well. Italian-born or Italian-trained composers would go for a season, or for a few years, to a foreign city or court, where they would conduct their operas and compose new ones tailored to lo-

53. See Villarosa, *Memorie dei compositori*; Di Giacomo, *Il conservatorio dei poveri*; idem, *Il conservatorio di Sant' Onofrio*; Fassini, *Il melodramma italiano a Londra*.

54. Burney, *History of Music*, 2:842.

55. See Radiciotti, *Pergolesi*; Brook and Paymer, "The Pergolesi Hand"; Degrada, "L'opera napoletana"; and Pergolesi, *Complete Works*.

56. Kretzschmar, *Geschichte der Oper*, p. 172.

cal requirements. Thus, Attilio Ariosti (1666–1729?) of Bologna worked at Berlin, Vienna, and London.[57] Giovanni Bononcini of Modena and his brother Marc Antonio Bononcini (1677–1726) also worked in Vienna and London.[58] The former's *Il trionfo di Camilla, regina de' Volsci* (1696) was one of the most popular works of the early eighteenth century; it was heard in Italian cities as late as 1715 and held the stage in London from 1706 to 1728.[59]

As in the seventeenth century so in the eighteenth, the South German courts attracted many of the best Italian opera composers. At Vienna, the principal composers, besides Johann Josef Fux, were Francesco Conti (1682–1732) and Antonio Caldara (1670?–1736). Conti was probably born in Florence and came to Vienna in 1701 to serve the court as a theorbist.[60] Within a few years, he earned for himself the added position of court composer. One of his most successful operas was *Don Chisciotte in Sierra Morena* (1719), a "tragicommedia per musica" on a libretto by Pariati and Zeno after Cervantes.[61] This work, together with his other *tragicommedie*, intermezzos, and comic scenes in his serious operas, exemplifies well the comic style for which Conti was justly lauded by his contemporaries. Caldara, a Venetian by birth and a pupil of Legrenzi, was appointed to the Habsburg court in 1716. There, he set the librettos of Zeno and Metastasio, completing some twenty-five works for the Vienna stage.[62] In the music of Conti and Caldara, the change from baroque to pre-classical traits is manifest. Their operas, however, continued to retain something of the formal style, the magnificence of staging, and the participation of chorus and ballet which have already been noted in the ceremonial operas of Fux.[63]

The most thoroughly representative composer of Italian opera around the middle of the eighteenth century was not an Italian but a German, Johann Adolph Hasse (1699–1783).[64] Hasse

57. Ebert, *Attilio Ariosti in Berlin*; Frati, "Attilio Ottavio Ariosti"; Bose, "Ariosti und Bononcini"; Lindgren, "Ariosti's London Years."

58. Valdrighi, *I Bononcini da Modena*; Ford, "Music and Drama in the Operas of Giovanni Bononcini"; Lindgren, "A Bibliographic Scrutiny."

59. Lindgren, "I trionfi di Camillo." See also chap. 11, n. 31.

60. Williams, "Francesco Bartolomeo Conti: His Life and Operas."

61. For a facsimile edition, see H. M. Brown, ed., *Italian Opera 1640–1770*, vol. 69.

62. See Gmeyner, "Die Opern Antonio Caldaras"; Kirkendale, *Antonio Caldara*.

63. See Lady Montagu's letter of September 14 (O.S.), 1716, in her *Letters*, 1:239.

Example 13.4: *L'Olimpiade*, Act I, sc. 8

PERGOLESI

begin his musical career as a tenor singer at the Hamburg and
Brunswick opera houses. His first opera was produced at the lat-

64. Gerber, *Der Operntypus Johann Adolf Hasses*; Mennicke, *Hasse und die Brüder Graun*;
idem, "Johann Adolph Hasse"; Zeller, *Das recitativo accompagnato in den Opern Johann*

(Example 13.4 continued)

ter city in 1721. He then studied at Naples under Porpora and A. Scarlatti and had several works performed there before moving to Venice in 1727. There he met and married a famous singer,

Adolf Hasses; Burney, *The Present State of Music in Germany*, vol. 1; Millner, *The Operas of Johann Adolf Hasse*; Heartz, "Hasse, Galuppi, and Metastasio."

Faustina Bordoni, and their two careers were joined from then on. In 1731, Hasse was appointed musical director of the Dresden opera, where his wife was the prima donna. He continued to hold his position at Dresden until 1763, while taking frequent travel leaves in order to present his operas elsewhere—at London, Warsaw, Vienna, and various Italian cities. Between 1721 and 1771 Hasse wrote more than fifty operas, the majority of them on librettos of Metastasio, with whom he enjoyed a close friendship. The joint works of these two men exemplify the type of eighteenth-century opera seria that has been described in the first part of this chapter. Hasse had so thoroughly assimilated the Italian spirit that he was known familiarly in Italy as *il caro Sassone*—"the beloved Saxon." His operas were given all over Europe; during his prime he was acclaimed as the greatest living master of vocal music.[65]

Hasse's style is marked by an easy flow of elegant, tasteful, and singable melody. No doubt there is much in his music to justify criticism that he was merely another composer gifted with facility and understanding of the voice but without dramatic insight and uninterested in the instrumental parts of his operas; nevertheless, such criticism must be tempered by an understanding of the operatic ideals of his time and of the peculiar qualities of the Metastasian librettos. These qualities Hasse completely understood, and he wrote music to correspond to them, untroubled by any revolutionary impulses. His arias are models of that musical feeling which transmutes everything into beautiful melody, flowering naturally into long smooth curves of coloratura—superficial perhaps, but with a surface of such perfection that it seems captious to demand more (example 13.5). Yet even within this style, Hasse occasionally displays certain traits which foreshadow a change in operatic ideals. His arias, though usually in the prevailing da capo form, are well constructed, with a feeling for real development rather than mere repetition of the themes. In the later works, even the da capo form itself becomes more plastic. His respect for the integrity of the drama is in contrast to the carelessness of some earlier Italians in this regard; he is no slave to the conventional pattern of regular alternation of arias

65. See Burney, *Present State of Music in Germany*, 1:234.

Example 13.5: *Didone abbandonata*, Act II, sc. 10

and secco recitatives but will on occasion freely intermingle passages in different styles as the situation demands. His handling of the orchestra is above the general level of opera composers of his time.[66] Moreover, and particularly in the accompanied recitatives for which he was so celebrated, he sometimes shows a depth of expression which may be attributable to his Germanic origin (as German historians are fond of pointing out), but which in any case is not a quality for which most Italian composers of the early eighteenth century, except Scarlatti, were distinguished.

66. See diagram of the Dresden Opera orchestra under Hasse in Rousseau, *Dictionnaire de musique*, s.v. "Orchestre."

The typical full or five-part da capo aria as found at its highest point of development in Hasse has the following scheme:

A (first four-line stanza): ritornello I; first section, cadencing on the dominant or relative major; ritornello II; second section, in the nature of a development of the material of the first, with extended coloratura passages, modulating back to the tonic and sometimes with a return of the theme of the first section; cadenza; ritornello III.

B (second four-line stanza): in one section, shorter than A, in a related key, and with material either (1) continuing and developing that of A or (2) contrasting with A; ending with cadenza, then ritornello IV (usually the same as ritornello I).

A da capo (usually without ritornello I), with additional improvised coloraturas and a longer cadenza.

The above scheme is frequently shortened in later composers (for example, Majo) by omitting a portion of part A in the da capo, or by setting both stanzas in a one-movement ABA' form. The da capo aria in one shape or another, however, persists through the whole eighteenth-century opera seria, along with other aria forms.

Another Italianized German, contemporary with Hasse, was Karl Heinrich Graun (1704–1759), the official composer of Frederick the Great of Prussia (1712–1768).[67] This monarch supervised with the closest interest all musical productions at his court and was personally responsible for the creation of the Berlin Opera House, which opened in 1742. Ever since his attendance at the Dresden production (1728) of *Cleofide* by Hasse, Frederick the Great was enamored of Hasse's operas and, as a natural consequence, Graun's music for the Berlin operas tended to imitate the style of his famous compatriot. The libretto of Graun's *Montezuma* (1755), written by King Frederick himself in French prose and translated into Italian verse by the court poet, is remarkable as being one of the comparatively rare modern subjects in eighteenth-century opera—the conquest of Mexico by Cortez.[68] (The

---

67. See Mayer-Reinach, "Carl Heinrich Graun als Opernkomponist"; idem, "Zur Herausgabe des *Montezuma*"; Yorke-Long, *Music at Court*, chap. 4; Strunk, ed., *Source Readings*, pp. 699–710; Helm, *Music at the Court of Frederick the Great*.

68. Most of the librettos set to music by Graun were tragedies, but *Montezuma* was an exception.

ballets even make some attempt at local color, though with rather feeble results.) *Montezuma* is also historically important because in it "cavatinas" replaced the traditional da capo aria.

The word *cavatina*, the diminutive of *cavata*, comes from the Italian *cavare*, "to draw out, to excavate"; hence, one meaning is that of something buried or concealed. Thus, in vocal compositions of the fifteenth and sixteenth centuries there were, for example, *soggetti cavati*—themes (in the tenor) which "concealed" a name, each vowel of which was represented by a note (*a* by fa, *e* by re, *i* by mi, and so on). Walther's *Lexikon* (1732) defines cavata as "a short arioso passage, occurring usually at the end of a recitative, in which the mood or meaning of the recitative is concentrated or drawn forth." Cavatina was used in the eighteenth century as opposed to aria, in the sense of a vocal number which "gathers together" an aria (that is, a da capo aria) in shorter and simpler form, without much text repetition or coloratura. In general, the word defines a type of song rather than any particular formal scheme.[69]

The cavatinas in *Montezuma* are in two-part form without repeats and with the following key scheme: tonic → dominant ‖ dominant → (modulations) → tonic, the ending of the second part repeating that of the first more or less exactly but in the tonic key. Thus, the scheme is that already exemplified in the principal section of many of the large-scale da capo arias in the works of Vinci, Schürmann, and Hasse, corresponding to the typical contemporary instrumental sonata first-movement form. It may be regarded as a truncated da capo aria: an elaborate first section, but without the traditional middle (contrasting) section or the traditional recapitulation of part *A*. The decline of the da capo had already begun in Germany by the 1730s; many of the German scores of that period bear the direction *senza da capo* ("without da capo") at the end of the arias.[70]

It is uncertain whether the large number of cavatinas in *Montezuma* is due to the librettist or the composer. Graun had

69. On the history and significance of the cavatina, see Pirrotta, "Falsirena," and Osthoff, "Mozarts Cavatinen." See also chap. 20.

70. See G. F. Schmidt, *Die frühdeutsche Oper*, 2:397ff.

used the form in earlier works (*Artaserse*, 1743; *Europa galante*, 1748),[71] but Frederick claims most of the credit, as indicated by one of several letters on this subject written to his sister:

> As for the cavatinas, I have seen some by Hasse which are infinitely more beautiful than the arias [that is, da capo arias]. . . . There is no need of repetition, except when the singers know how to make variations [note that "except"!]; but it seems to me, in any case, that it is an abuse to repeat the same thing four times. Your actors . . . were never obliged to do such a stupid thing.[72]

This statement is interesting not only as the comment of an intelligent contemporary on one of the conventions of eighteenth-century opera but also as an anticipation of the theories of Gluck on the same subject.

Graun's music for *Montezuma* is in typical mid-eighteenth-century style. The overture is of the Italian type,[73] in three movements, with homophonic texture, short themes, a simple harmonic vocabulary, many repetitions and sequential patterns, broken-chord figures, and the "Lombardic rhythm" (♫.), a device very common in the music of this period.[74] The arias are well written and show forth the beautiful vocal melodies for which Graun was justly famous. Only occasionally, as in Keiser, are there figures which suggest the instrumental rather than the vocal idiom. The secco recitatives show some harmonic variety and are enlivened by the use of deceptive cadences. (Musical improvement of the secco recitative is a noticeable feature in the work of many composers by the middle of the century.) The accompanied recitatives are excellent examples of this style (example 13.6).

Among the Italianized German composers after Hasse and Graun we may mention Johann Gottlieb Naumann (1741–1801) of Dresden, a celebrity in his time and a typical representative of

71. Helm, *Music at the Court of Frederick the Great*, p. 69.

72. Letter of May 4, 1754, quoted in DdT, 15:ix.

73. This was typical of Graun's overtures after 1745. On the overtures to his other operas, see Mennicke, *Hasse und die Brüder Graun*, chaps. 3 and 4.

74. Quantz, *Versuch*, p. 241, says this rhythm was introduced "about the year 1722." Burney, *History*, 2:847, complains of its abuse in operas sung at London in 1748.

the *Empfindsamkeit* of the late eighteenth century.[75] Curiously
enough, Naumann's best-remembered opera is *Cora och Alonzo*,
composed on a Swedish text in 1779 and performed for the inauguration of a new opera house at Stockholm in 1782. This work
was frequently revived at Stockholm until 1832, and it also appeared on many German stages in translation.

Certain writers in the past have tended to regard everything in eighteenth-century opera before Gluck as being somewhat
in the nature of a necessary but regrettable episode, declining
about the middle of the century to a hopelessly low state of affairs, which Gluck, practically single-handed, redeemed through
his so-called reforms—the very word carrying with it an aura of
moral uplift, implying that something bad was replaced by something better. This point of view, a relic of the evolutionary philosophy of history, has led to the neglect of early and middle
eighteenth-century Italian opera composers, out of a failure to
appreciate their real merits and the qualities of their music in
relation to its period and the circumstances for which it was composed. The situation has been aggravated by the fact that Italian
scholars, who should be most concerned to set this matter in its
true light, have so far not made much of the music of their own
composers available in modern editions. The German musicolo-
gists, understandably enough, have concerned themselves chiefly
with either composers of German birth or composers who were
active in Germany, and even here they have been more attentive
to those aspects of the music which seem to appeal to Germans—
more serious quality of expressiveness, richer texture, greater importance of the orchestra—than to the fundamentally vocal and
melodic traits characteristic of Italy. The result is that the importance of Gluck, great as it unquestionably is, has been exaggerated by inadequate conceptions both of the real nature of the
situation against which he was striving and of the contributions of
other composers who to some extent anticipated his doctrines.[76]
Nor did the reform of opera begin with Gluck. Opera is always

75. Breitholtz, *Studier i operan "Gustaf Wasa"*; Engländer, *Johann Gottlieb Naumann
als Operkomponist.*

76. Goldschmidt, "Die Reform der italienischen Oper."

being reformed; that is to say, it is always changing, and one is presumably entitled to bestow the name of reform on any marked change regarded as being in the "right" direction. A more objective viewpoint is neatly stated by Martin Cooper:

Example 13.6: *Montezuma*, Act III, sc. 1

GRAUN

Opera is constructed of three elements—the musical, the literary, and the spectacular; and at different times each of these three elements has in fact gained an undue supremacy over the other two. For this reason the history of opera is the history of a series of reformations and counter-reformations, no two countries and no

(Example 13.6 continued)

two epochs agreeing on the role that each element should ideally play in the constitution of the whole. Neither evolutionary nor unified, it is the history of perpetually recurring schools of thought, one never victorious over the other, though occasionally gaining the majority of popular opinion.[77]

Granting, then, that in much of the Italian opera of the early eighteenth century the elements of melody and display of singers' virtuosity had usurped too large a place in the scheme, it could be expected that a reaction should take place calculated to restore the balance. Then, too, by the middle of the century there was a general turning away from the frivolities of the age of the Regency, and with this went a desire to make music more serious and expressive. The new Empfindsamkeit, which was at first nothing more than an infusion of a tender and pretty sentimentality into the fabric of rococo music, prepared the way for the classical style of the later eighteenth century. A deepening of the texture, an increased attention to harmonic variety and to the inner voices in the composition, were natural concomitants of this change. French opera, with its informal mingling of recitative and aria and its emphasis on ballet, chorus, and spectacle, began to exert some influence on composers in other countries. Finally, the comic opera, constantly increasing in popularity, acted as a goad through parody and satire and at the same time provided a living example of the effects to be gained through simplicity and variety of style with new types of subject matter, forcing the creators of serious opera to take stock and adapt themselves to a new generation of audiences.

Not all the influences came from the side of music. The rise of sentimental novels such as those of Samuel Richardson, and above all the cult of "naturalness" popularized by Rousseau wrought such changes in literary thought and expression that the opera libretto, and consequently opera music, could not possibly remain aloof. But as these changes are to be more clearly observed in the field of comic opera (through which in large measure their effects were transmitted to the serious opera), we shall defer a more detailed consideration of them until later.

We have already intimated that Gluck was not the only

77. Cooper, *Gluck*, p. 4. Quoted by permission of the publisher.

reformer in the eighteenth century. As a matter of fact, there was hardly a composer of serious opera after 1750 who was not touched by the general movement of reaction against the older type. As in all such changes, there were moderates and radicals. The radical reform movement took place almost wholly outside Italy and, as far as its consequences for Italian opera went, was short-lived; it will be dealt with later. First, we shall consider the moderate or evolutionary changes that came into opera seria everywhere after the middle of the eighteenth century.

These changes affected both the libretto and the music.[78] It was typical of the more moderate composers that they continued to use Metastasio's librettos, although he wrote only four new ones between 1754 and his death in 1782. But in the settings of the later eighteenth century, the earlier Metastasian librettos were altered: many recitatives and arias were deleted, and ensembles and occasionally choruses were added. The whole tendency was to make an opera a less regular but more organic whole, with arias and ensembles more often carrying on the action instead of being merely static moments in its flow. The distinction between recitative and aria was still maintained; but accompanied recitatives became longer and more elaborate, and some scenes were composed in a free alternation of recitative, arioso, aria, and ensemble. The five-part da capo aria virtually disappeared in favor of various more compact versions of the basic da capo scheme; other aria forms were also used, among them a two-movement form, generally in the order slow–fast. Within the general pattern, the music came to be organized in longer and more complex phrases. More attention was given to the orchestra: the texture was enriched, and greater variety of color and more thematic independence were sought. All three movements of the Italian overture became longer and more elaborate; occasionally, overtures might be in one movement, usually a sonata-allegro form. Moreover, in the last part of the century, and especially after Gluck had set the example in his first "reform" works, it became increasingly common to relate the overture to the particular opera it introduced, sometimes only by foreshadowing the general mood,

---

78. For a detailed treatment of this topic, with musical examples, see Downes, "The Operas of Johann Christian Bach," vol. 1.

sometimes by using themes that would later appear in the body of the opera.[79] This was a contrast to the practice of the early eighteenth century, when as a rule the overture was a neutral, independent composition that might have served equally well for almost any opera.

Among the moderate reformers in the eighteenth century we may certainly class Hasse and Graun, the extent of whose innovations has already been noted. A slightly younger and more progressive composer in this group was David Perez (1711–1778), whose scores are remarkable for their wealth of feeling as well as for the skill of their instrumental music.[80] His most important opera was *Solimano*, first performed at Lisbon in 1757. Another Spanish composer active in Italy, Domingo Terradellas (1713–1751), was noted for his depiction of violent emotions and for the daring quality of his modulations.[81] His principal work was a setting of Metastasio's *Artaserse* (Venice, 1744).

Three composers of a later generation may be briefly mentioned. Gian Francesco di Majo (1732–1770) ranks with Perez and Terradellas as one who brought into the regular tradition of Italian opera certain individual qualities, particularly in the expression of sorrowful emotions and in the fineness and elegance of his style, of which the aria "Se mai più saro geloso" from *Alessandro* (Naples, 1767) is an example.[82] Other important operas of Majo are *Cajo Fabricio* (Naples, 1760) and *Ifigenia in Tauride* (1764), which comes close to the advanced reform ideals of Gluck. (It may be noted that this last-named opera was composed not for an Italian audience but for the German court of Mannheim.) Johann Christian Bach (1735–1782), known as the "Milan" or the "London" Bach, was the youngest surviving son of the great Johann Sebastian. Having moved to Milan shortly after his father's death, he turned Catholic and became as completely Italianized

79. See Botstiber, *Geschichte der Ouvertüre*, chaps. 5–7; Mennicke, *Hasse und die Brüder Graun*, chap. 6.

80. Jackson, "The Operas of David Perez."

81. Carreras y Bulbena, *Domenech Terradellas* (contains musical examples); Volkmann, "Domenico Terradellas"; Mitjana y Gordón, "Les Espagnols italianisants," in Lavignac, *Encyclopédie*, 4:2195–2209.

82. Printed in Bücken, *Rokoko und Klassik*, p. 115. See also Di Chiera, "The Life and Operas of Gian Francesco di Majo."

in his music as Graun or Hasse.[83] Bach was one of the most popular of the later composers in the Italian style. Among his operas are *Alessandro nell' Indie* (Naples, 1762), *Lucio Silla* (Mannheim, 1774), *La clemenza di Scipione* ("The Clemency of Sciopone," London, 1778), and one on a revised version of Quinault's *Amadis de Gaule* (Paris, 1779), in which he endeavored to adapt his style to the French requirements. Bach's music, elegant and expressive (if seldom profoundly emotional), clear in form, expert in detail, most characteristic in lyrical moods and cantabile melodies, was much admired by the young Mozart.[84] Dr. Burney states that in his arias "the richness of the accompaniments perhaps deserve [sic] more praise than the originality of the melodies; which, however, are always natural, elegant, and in the best taste of Italy at the time he came over."[85]

One of the last composers of opera seria in the eighteenth-century tradition was Giuseppe Sarti (1729–1802), whose career, like that of many of his contemporaries, took him to foreign courts: Copenhagen for most of the period 1755–1775 and St. Petersburg from 1784 to the end of his life.[86] The most successful of his serious operas was *Giulio Sabino* (Venice, 1781), but he was longer remembered for his works in a lighter vein, particularly for the opera buffa *Fra due litiganti il terzo gode* (Milan, 1782), from which Mozart quoted a phrase in *Don Giovanni*. Sarti's serious operas show, along with many traditional features, some influence of newer ideas, especially in their powerful accompanied recitatives. His graceful melodies and the profusion of his ideas often suggest the style of Mozart.

An Italian contemporary of Mozart was Nicola Antonio Zingarelli (1752–1837), one of the last of the eighteenth-century Neapolitan composers. His principal opera, *Giulietta e Romeo*,

83. Downes, "The Operas of Johann Christian Bach"; Terry, *Johann Christian Bach* (see also review in *ZfMw* [1934], 16:182–88); Schwarz, "Johann Christian Bach"; H. Abert, "Johann Christian Bach's italienische Opern"; Geiringer, *The Bach Family*; Warburton, "A Study of J. C. Bach's Operas."

84. H. Abert, *W. A. Mozart*, 1:58, 242–49; cf. Köchel, *Chronologisch-thematisches Verzeichnis*, no. 293e.

85. Burney, *History of Music*, 2:866.

86. See Scudo, *Le Chevalier Sarti*, and the sequel "Frédérique," *Revue des deux mondes* (1863–64); Rivalta, *Giuseppe Sarti*; Mooser, *Annales*, 2:415–50, 463–79.

with a libretto based on Shakespeare, was performed at Milan in 1796 and continued to be played for more than twenty-five years. Most of Zingarelli's dramatic works were serious, but he also had some success with a comic opera, *Il mercato di Monfregoso* ("The Marketplace of Monfregoso," Milan, 1792).

The radical reform movement in eighteenth-century opera, as already noted, took its course mainly outside Italy. The two Italian composers chiefly associated with this movement were Niccolò Jommelli (1714–1774) and Tommaso Traetta (1727–1779). Jommelli produced a large number of operas, both serious and comic, in Italy beginning in 1737.[87] His earliest works were quite in traditional style, but signs of change and experimentation became evident by 1750. Perhaps unfortunately, in 1749 Jommelli became acquainted with Metastasio at Vienna and remained under his spell ever thereafter, with the result that he was never moved to make a fundamental break with the older type of opera libretto. Two of his most successful works were settings of Metastasian texts: *Demofoonte* (Padua, 1743) and *Didone abbandonata* (Rome, 1747). The climax of Jommelli's life was his period of service (1753–1769) as chapelmaster to the Duke of Württemberg at Stuttgart—a German court, but one in which French taste was an important factor. It was in the works written in Germany that Jommelli's innovations were most marked, and particularly in *Fetonte* (Ludwigsburg, 1768), on a libretto by M. Verazi. His last operas, written after he had returned to Naples in 1769, were received coldly by his countrymen, who found his new style "too German." So strong was the admixture of northern elements in his music that he has been called "the Italian Gluck."

Traetta, by both temperament and circumstances, was led to even greater departure from the accepted Italian models of his time.[88] Like Jommelli, he began with successes in Italian theaters, including two operas on librettos of Metastasio: *Didone abbandonata* (Venice, 1757) and *Olimpiade* (Verona, 1758). An im-

87. H. Abert, *Niccolo Jommelli als Opernkomponist*; idem, "Zur Geschichte der Oper in Württemberg"; Alfieri, *Notizie biografiche*; Yorke-Long, *Music at Court*; McClymonds, *Niccolo Jommelli: The Last Years 1769–1774*.

88. On Traetta, see studies by Nuovo, Damerini, Raeli, Casavola, and Schlitzer, ed.; also Yorke-Long, *Music at Court*; Mooser, *Annales*, 2:87–132.

portant influence in Traetta's career was his term of service from 1758 to 1765 at the court of Parma, which was dominated by French ideas of opera. Some of his most important later works were written for the German stage: *Armida* (1761) and *Ifigenia in Tauride* (1763) for Vienna, *Sofonisba* (1762) for Mannheim. From 1768 to 1775, Traetta was at the court of St. Petersburg.

What are the qualities in the operas of Jommelli and Traetta—qualities most strongly evident in their works for non-Italian theaters—that have caused their composers to be numbered among the reformers in the eighteenth century?

The first is their international character. Earlier Italian composers, though they traveled a great deal, always took with them the Italian tradition and preserved it untouched by foreign musical influences, even of those countries in which they worked. At this time, there was only one school of opera in Europe outside Italy, that of France, which had been preserved by virtue of almost complete isolation from Italian music in the first half of the century. By 1750, the French opera had begun, though slightly, to make itself felt by composers in those courts and cities which in other respects also were touched by French culture—meaning, in effect, the German courts and a few in northern Italy. French influence was still strong on German life throughout the eighteenth century up to the time of Lessing, Herder, and Goethe, as witness in literature the doctrines of Gottsched (1700–1766) and in manners those of Frederick the Great, the great friend of Voltaire, who habitually spoke and wrote French and despised German as "the language of boors." It happened that both Jommelli and Traetta came into this French orbit, the former at Stuttgart and the latter at Parma. The very subjects of some of Traetta's operas are significant—for example, *I tintaridi* (1760), a translation of Rameau's *Castor et Pollux*; *Le Feste d'Imeneo* (1760), a festa teatrale or opéra-ballet similar to Rameau's *Fêtes d'Hébé*; and *Ippolito ed Arice* (1759), the same subject as Rameau's *Hippolyte et Aricie*. Traetta's principal librettists, Marco Coltellini (ca. 1740–1775) and Carlo Frugoni (1692–1768), were well acquainted with Rameau's works. Coltellini was a pupil of Calzabigi;[89] in 1765

---

89. The eighteenth-century spelling of his name was Calsabigi. For more on this important poet, see chap. 14.

he was engaged to prepare the libretto of *Telemaco* for Gluck, and in 1772 Calzabigi designated him as his successor at the Vienna court. The importance of the ballets in both Jommelli's and Traetta's operas is another sign of French influence. At Stuttgart, the ballet master was Jean-Georges Noverre (1720–1810), author of a celebrated treatise on the dance and ballet master at the Paris Opéra, who advocated a return to Greek ideals of the dance, with naturalness of movements, simplicity of costume, and emphasis on the dramatic content of the ballet rather than on abstract figures or the virtuosity of the dancers.[90] Another evidence of French taste in Traetta and Jommelli is the greater prominence of the spectacular element in their operas, as in Traetta's *Sofonisba*, with temple scenes, battle scenes, the undersea palace of Thetis, the transformations of Proteus—all reminiscent of Lully and Rameau. Equally French are the pictorial details in the music, touches of that imitation of nature so dear to eighteenth-century aestheticians: storms, battles, pastoral idyls, even the rhythm of a horse's gallop imitated in the second violins throughout an aria,[91] or the realistic direction *urlo francese* ("French howl"), a cry rather than a musical note, literally imitating the sound of the voice under stress of emotion.[92]

The German influence on Jommelli and Traetta is seen in their treatment of the orchestra, showing a greater complexity of texture and increased attention to idiomatic use of the instruments. The orchestra was the medium through which German music in the eighteenth century began its conquering career in Europe: the Mannheim orchestra was famous by 1745, while those of Dresden under Hasse and Stuttgart under Jommelli (there were forty-seven players for his *Fetonte* in 1768) were hardly less celebrated. Likewise owing to German influence is the greater richness and variety of the harmonies in both Jommelli and Traetta, as compared with their Italian contemporaries.

Another aspect of their operas is the way in which Jommelli and Traetta consistently aim at a closer coordination of mu-

90. Noverre. *Lettres sur la danse. et sur les ballets*. See also H. Abert. "J. G. Noverre." in his *Gesammelte Schriften*. pp. 264–86.

91. "Quel destriere" in Jommelli's *L'Olimpiade*.

92. Traetta's *Sofonisba*.

sic and drama. One sign of this is the decreased proportion of secco recitative, a style which by its very nature excludes any thorough participation of music in the action. To a greater extent than ever before, secco recitatives are replaced by the accompanied variety. In the second act of Jommelli's *Demofoonte*, only two of the eleven scenes are secco, all the rest being accompanied by full orchestra; this is an extreme instance, but it illustrates the whole tendency of the century which culminated in the later works of Gluck, where the secco recitative is eliminated altogether. Among the accompanied recitatives in these operas are some splendid examples of dramatic power, such as the tenth scene of Act III of Traetta's *Sofonisba*. The treatment of the aria also undergoes a change: many are so contrived as to further the action rather than interrupt it as in the older Italian opera; the melodic style is more expressive and covers a wider range of emotions. A distinctly Mozartean quality is apparent in some of the cantabile arias, such as "Non piangete" from Traetta's *Antigona* (1772) (example 13.7). A sense of climax and proportion, a sure grasp of

Example 13.7: *Antigona*, Act III, sc. 2

the principles of musical form and their adaptation to the dramatic situation, are everywhere evident.[93] The tendency is constantly toward greater fluidity, toward breaking down the old hard-and-fast boundaries between recitative and aria. We often find long scene-complexes in which accompanied recitative, arioso, aria,

93. See, for example, Jommelli's *Fetonte*, Act II, scs. 8–9.

ensemble, and chorus all participate freely. Even the conventional da capo pattern of the arias is artfully concealed: more prominence is given to the middle (contrasting) section, especially in Traetta; on repetition, the principal section is shortened or otherwise altered; changes of mood, of meter, and of tempo are incorporated; declamatory (recitative) sections occur in the midst of an aria; or an accompanied recitative and the following aria will use the same thematic material—all changes from the old order, even though some of them had been anticipated by earlier composers.

The changing conception of the overture is another eighteenth-century tendency which finds reflection in the works of Jommelli and Traetta. One of the points of Gluck's reform manifesto of 1769 is a statement of the new ideal of an overture which should be specifically connected with the drama following; though neither Jommelli nor Traetta consistently aimed at this ideal, their operas do show certain marks of it. Thus, in Traetta's *Sofonisba* the theme of the slow movement of the overture recurs in a quintet in the last scene of the opera—a device similar to that employed by Rameau in *Castor et Pollux* twenty-five years earlier— and the finale leads without pause directly into the first scene of Act I. Both here and in Jommelli's *Fetonte* the overture evidently suggests the general course of the drama—as in Rameau's *Zoroastre* of 1749. In *Fetonte*, the very short first movement of the overture leads at once into the first scene of the opera (an andante solo with chorus), which replaces the usual second movement; then follows the "third" movement, a musical depiction of an earthquake (as in many French operas), after which, with the second scene of Act I, the opera proper begins. The overture to Majo's *Ifigenia in Tauride* is a similar compromise between the old Italian concert overture and the later nineteenth-century program type, which was first exemplified in Gluck's *Iphigénie en Aulide* (1772).

The French example, and the departure from the Italian norm, are most clearly evidenced in Jommelli and Traetta by the return of the chorus to an important place in their operas not written for Italian performance. Choruses are numerous and often of large dimensions; they do not merely appear in the spectacle scenes but also form part of the action. Perhaps the most notable instance is the fourth scene of Act II of Traetta's *Ifigenie in Tauride*, in which the pleadings of Orestes are interrupted by outbursts of the Chorus of Furies. Although the librettos are not the same, an interesting comparison may be made between this and the parallel scene in Gluck's *Iphigénie en Tauride* (Act II), written twenty years later. In spite of their impressive scale and appearance, the choruses in Traetta never attain the real solemnity and impact of the great choral scenes of Rameau and Gluck, or of Mozart's *Idomeneo*. The eighteenth-century Italians apparently lacked feeling for the full dramatic possibilities of the chorus.

In sum, while the operas of Jommelli and Traetta show many important differences from what may be called the orthodox Italian opera seria of the eighteenth century, they still do not make a complete break with it. In Jommelli particularly, and in Traetta to a lesser degree, the old type of libretto still prevails. The duality of poem and music is weakened but not overcome. In spite of all changes in detail, the works remain singers' operas, with the old virtuoso display, improvised embellishments, and cadenzas.[94]

94. Several operas by composers mentioned in this section are discussed and analyzed in part 2 of Heinse's novel, *Hildegard von Hohenthal*. See Lauppert, *Die Musikästhetik Wilhelm Heinses*.

CHAPTER FOURTEEN

The Operas of Gluck

Christoph Willibald Gluck was born in 1714, the son of a Bohemian forester. After acquiring some knowledge of music in the elementary schools he went to Prague, where he remained from 1732 to 1736. After a short spell at Vienna as a chamber musician in the employ of Prince Ferdinand Philip Lobkowitz, he was sent by another noble patron to study with Sammartini at Milan. No details of his early musical education are known for certain; he must have become acquainted in Prague with the current Italian opera as represented by Hasse, while at Vienna he would have heard the older style of Caldara. At Vienna likewise he met Metastasio, whose poetry appealed to him as to every other opera composer; seventeen of Gluck's operas were on Metastasian librettos. His studies with Sammartini opened to him the new world of modern symphonic music. His first ten operas were successfully performed at Milan and other Italian cities between 1741 and 1745. They are distinguished from those of contemporary Italian composers by a certain melodic freedom and individual energy of expression, but they show no traces of the revolutionary principles for which he later became famous.[1] In the season of 1745–46, Gluck visited London, where he presented two operas with no

1. Of Gluck's approximately one hundred dramatic works, about half have been preserved either wholly or in part. For editions, see Hopkinson, *A Bibliography*, and Gluck, *Sämtliche Werke*, ed. by Gerber. See also Wotquenne, *Catalogue thématique*; *Gluck-Gesellschaft* (4 vols., 1913–18); Wortsmann, *Die deutsche Gluckliteratur*; Croll, "*Gluck-forschung und Gluck-Gesamtausgabe*"; the special issue of *Chigiana* (1975) devoted to Gluck; and "Gluck," in *The New Grove Dictionary*, for an extensive bibliography. Biographies include those by A. Abert, A. Schmid, Marx, Newman, Cooper, Einstein, Gerber, and Felix. For a technical study of all the operas before *Orfeo*, with musical examples, see Kurth, "Die Jugendopern Glucks"; also H. Abert, "Glucks italienische Opern," *Gluck-Jahrbuch* (1915), 2:1-25, and the same author's introduction to *Le nozze d'Ercole e d'Ebe* in DTB, vol. 26.

particular success and drew upon himself the oft-quoted remark of Handel to the effect that "he [Gluck] knows no more of counterpoint than Waltz, my cook." Nevertheless, Gluck made friends with the older composer and was undoubtedly impressed by his music,[2] though the influence exerted itself only considerably later and then indirectly, in the form of an ideal of grandeur which Gluck embodied in his own particular way in the reform operas. The two years following the visit to London were spent in touring Germany as conductor with a traveling opera company. *Le nozze d'Ercole e d'Ebe* ("The Marriage of Hercules and Hebe"), a *serenata* performed at a wedding in Pillnitz (near Dresden) in 1747, shows Gluck as an accomplished composer in a rather pretty, trifling Italian style.[3] In this work, as indeed in all his operas, Gluck followed the eighteenth-century custom of borrowing numbers from his own previous works or even from those of other composers; several arias are from earlier Gluck operas, and the first movement of the overture is taken from a symphony of Sammartini, with only slight alterations. The aria "Così come si accese," from the epilogue, is typical of the graceful, tuneful, Pergolesi-like melodies in which this work abounds (example 14.1).

In 1750 Gluck was married in Vienna. The substantial dowry his wife brought him undoubtedly encouraged a certain

Example 14.1: *Le nozze d'Ercole e d'Ebe*

2. Kelly. *Reminiscences of the King's Theatre*, 1:255.

3. "Serenata" is the eighteenth-century name for a small opera or dramatic cantata, often of a pastoral nature and employing few characters, composed for a special occasion (such as a birthday or wedding) in a patron's household.

independence which Gluck began to manifest about this time. Concrete evidence of the new attitude is found in the scores of *Ezio* (Prague, 1750) and *La clemenza di Tito* ("The Mercy of Titus," Naples, 1752), both on librettos of Metastasio. In carefulness of orchestral writing, nobility of melody, and seriousness of expression, these works surpass not only the earlier operas but also most of the Italian ones of the next ten years. The characteristic vigor which had always been remarked in Gluck's music, and the growing individuality of his methods, may have been what caused Metastasio about this time to describe him as a composer of "surprising fire, but . . . mad."[4] It was the cry of the conservative, instinctively recognizing the presence of a force inimical to the settled state of affairs. Yet it was to be ten years before Gluck composed *Orfeo*; and during that time he still produced some works in the old manner, as well as a sparkling one-act comic piece, *Le cinesi* ("The Chinese Ladies"), on a libretto of Metastasio, for the entertainment of the imperial court in 1754. The success of this work was instrumental in securing for him the position of official court composer of theater and chamber music under the superintendency of Count Durazzo, whose influence and encouragement played a large part in determining the new artistic ideals which were then developing in Gluck's mind. Their first collaborative work, the one-act *Innocenza giustificata* ("Innocence Vindicated," 1755), although apparently conforming to the Metastasian type of libretto, is in actuality a forerunner of the monumental simplicity of *Orfeo*, with the musical resources (including a chorus) largely subordinated to the dramatic aims. This work was revised by Gluck in 1768 under the title *La vestale*; it is the same subject as that of Spontini's opera of 1807.

Another important influence on Gluck in the years immediately preceding the composition of *Orfeo* was his contact with the *opéra comique*, which made its appearance in Vienna as early as 1752.[5] This distinctive national form of comic opera had grown up at Paris, at first using only popular melodies to which poets fitted their words but coming toward the middle of the century to make use of more and more original music and at the same time

---

4. Letter to Farinelli, Nov. 16, 1751, in Burney, *Memoirs*, 1:402.

5. Haas, *Gluck and Durazzo*; Holzer, "Die komische Opern Glucks."

improving in poetic quality and musical interest. The Viennese court being curious to hear these pieces, Durazzo arranged for some to be sent from Paris. Gluck was charged with the duty of conducting the performances, which entailed arranging the music and composing new numbers where it was thought the original melodies might not be suited to the Viennese taste. As the number of performances of opéras comiques in Vienna steadily increased, so too did the proportion of new music, until in *La Rencontre imprévue* ("The Unexpected Meeting," 1764) not one of the original French airs was retained, the entire text having been newly composed by Gluck.[6] Thus, as it were by accident, the composer in his forties went to school to the French opéra comique, learning a syllabic style of text setting, a melodic restraint, a freedom of phrase structure, and a close adaptation of music to poetry which contrasted with the typical Italian arias in an extreme degree. How thoroughly he assimilated the French musical idiom may be gathered not only from the scores but also from the testimony of the French poet and manager Favart, who speaks with highest praise of Gluck's settings of his librettos: "They leave nothing to be desired in the expression, the taste, the harmony, even in the French prosody."[7]

A final stage of preparation for *Orfeo* was the composition of music for Angiolini's ballet *Don Juan* in 1761,[8] a work which seems as though designed to illustrate the new principles outlined by Noverre in his book on the dance that had been published only a year previously. As in the opéras comiques Gluck had learned to subordinate music to text, so here he adapted his art to the service of pantomime. There is in this music something of Rameau's wonderful power of depicting gesture in sound; and, as in the older opera, the score is divided into many short numbers, each complete in itself. But the music is more than mere accompaniment to patterns of motion; it enters into the action and becomes a partner of the drama figured forth by the dancers.

6. Gluck's involvement with the Viennese opéra comique extends from *La fausse esclave* ("The False Slave," 1758) to *La Rencontre imprévue*. See B. A. Brown, "Gluck's *Rencontre Imprévue*."

7. Letter to Durazzo, Nov. 19, 1763; in Favart, *Memoires*, 2:169.

8. Cf. Haas, "Die Wiener Ballet-Pantomime im 18. Jahrhundert"; Testa, "Il binomio Gluck-Angiolini."

Example 14.2: *Don Juan*, No. 30

Part of the closing scene between Don Juan and the Statue will serve to show this quality and also to suggest how Mozart must have remembered, perhaps unconsciously, the music of Gluck when composing his own *Don Giovanni* (example 14.2). Indeed, comparison between the two works is almost inevitable, though it is not in superficial thematic resemblances but rather in the whole spirit of the music that Mozart's indebtedness to the older composer is evident.

With the composition of *Don Juan*, Gluck stood at the parting of the ways. Having begun with the conventional Italian operatic formulas and having reached the point of instilling into this framework a new breath of dramatic life, he might have continued along the lines of Jommelli and Traetta, toward the type of opera which Mozart eventually brought to unsurpassable heights. That Gluck's genius now took a different turn was not owing to any inner compulsion of Gluck the musician but rather to a quite unexpected development of Gluck the dramatist—a development for which at this moment external forces were largely responsible. These forces were immanent in the whole intellectual and artistic atmosphere of the later eighteenth century.[9] Fundamental was the profound yearning for free, simple, unaffected expression of human feelings. The baroque had been an age of order, authority, and formality, to which the early eighteenth century had reacted with the critical and skeptical philosophy of rationalism, summed up in the works of Voltaire. Into the vacuum created by this essentially negative criticism, there rushed the earlier manifestations of mannered sentimentality and capricious, superficial ornamentation, extending through all the details of life and mirrored in music of the gallant style. But mere caprice was not enough. To the gallant ideal succeeded that of naturalness, whose great prophet was Jean Jacques Rousseau with his *Nouvelle Héloïse* (1760) and *Emile* (1762), the fountains of the romantic movement in literature.

Yet naturalness, however valid as an ideal, was too vague to furnish by itself a sure foundation for art; not only an ideal but a form as well was needed, and the form, the regulating, ordering principle without which great artistic creation is impossible, was sought now, as it had been at the time of the Renaissance, in the models of the classical age of ancient Greece. In 1764, a German archaeologist, Johann Joachim Winckelmann, published his *Geschichte der Kunst des Alterthums* ("History of

9. Cf. H. Abert, "Gluck, Mozart und der Rationalismus," in his *Gesammelte Schriften*, pp. 311–45.

Ancient Art"), embodying the fruits of nearly twenty years of study and meditation; from this publication may be said to date the epoch of European art known as the "neoclassical" period. Winckelmann's work was not only a history but also a philosophy of art, which served in some degree to counteract the dangers of unrestrained individualism implicit in the doctrines of Rousseau. Beauty, according to this philosophy, can be attained only when individual characteristic details are subordinated to the general plan of the whole, thus creating an ideal, suprapersonal work marked by harmonious proportions and a certain repose in the total effect—in Winckelmann's phrase, "noble simplicity and calm greatness."[10]

It may be doubted whether Gluck ever read either Rousseau's or Winckelmann's books, though he probably had met Winckelmann at Rome in 1756. In any case, the question is not important, for the ideas which both men expressed were so much in the air at this time that no thinking person could possibly have escaped them. With regard to the classic models, of course, the same difficulty was present as in the Renaissance, namely, the lack of actual specimens of ancient music. But theorists in the eighteenth century did not trouble to speculate, as the Florentine Camerata had done, on the nature of Greek music; rather, they attacked the problem of opera at its root, advocating fundamental changes in the libretto and in the relations among composer, poet, and performing artists. The most influential writer in this field was the Italian Francesco Algarotti, a highly esteemed philosopher, a friend of Voltaire and Frederick the Great, and artistic adviser to the court of Parma, where Traetta was working. His *Saggio sopra l'opera in musica* ("Treatise on the Opera"), first issued in 1755, became the manifesto of operatic reform, influencing even in details both the practice and the theory of Gluck.[11] The resemblance between Algarotti's book and Gluck's preface to *Alceste* (1769) leaves no room for doubt on this point.

10. Winckelmann, *Sämtliche Werke*, 1:1–58. He may have obtained the phrase from Gottsched: "Man sollte in der Opernmusik mehr auf eine edle Einfalt sehen, als auf die unförmlichen Ausschweifungen der Italiener" (*Versuch einer kritischen Dichtkunst*, 3:1734, quoted in Reichel, "Gottsched und Johann Adolf Scheibe," p. 665).

11. See Strunk, ed., *Source Readings*, pp. 657–72. A summary of Algarotti's teachings, with copious quotations, will be found in Newman, *Gluck and the Opera*, part 2, chap. 2.

The fundamental impulse, the suggestion of a model, and the aesthetic theory were thus present, and at this moment appeared the poet Ranieri de Calzabigi (1714–1795), from whose collaboration with Gluck *Orfeo* and *Alceste* resulted.[12] Calzabigi was the real standard-bearer of the revolt against Metastasio,[13] in spite of the fact that he had earlier brought out at Paris an edition of the latter's works which in the preface he characterized as "perfect tragedies." He had led an adventurous life in Italy, Paris, and elsewhere; he was known as a literary amateur and aesthetician and was an admirer of Shakespeare. Gluck handsomely acknowledged his indebtedness to Calzabigi:

> If my music has had some success, I think it my duty to recognize that I am beholden for it to him. . . . However much talent a composer may have, he will never produce any but mediocre music, if the poet does not awaken in him that enthusiasm without which the productions of all the arts are but feeble and drooping.[14]

Calzabigi himself went so far as to claim, without contradiction from Gluck, that it was he who had taught the composer exactly how to write his recitatives and had persuaded him to banish both coloratura passages and the secco accompaniment of recitative from his operas.[15]

Orfeo ed Euridice, the first joint work of Calzabigi and Gluck, was performed at Vienna on October 5, 1762, to celebrate the emperor's nameday.[16] Thus, the new reform began with the same subject as that of the first Florentine operas of 1600. Aside from two incongruous features—the irrelevant overture and the artificial happy ending (both due to the festive occasion for which the opera was written, where too much tragedy would have been out of place)—the work is a profound contrast to the contemporary Italian operas. On the title page of the libretto for the first

12. Cf. Michel, "Ranieri Calzabigi," *Gluck-Jahrbuch* (1918), 4:99-171; Hammelmann and Rose, "New Light on Calzabigi and Gluck."

13. Cf. Einstein, "Calzabigi's 'Erwiderung' von 1790," *Gluck-Jahrbuch* (1915), 2:56-102; (1917), 3:25-50.

14. Letter in the *Mercure de France*, 1781, quoted in Einstein, *Gluck* (1936 ed.), pp. 67–68.

15. Letter in the *Mercure de France*, August 1784, p. 135.

16. See Tiersot, "Etude sur *Orphée*"; Heartz, "*Orfeo ed Euridice*."

production, as well as in the first engraved edition of the score, it is called an *azione teatrale*—a designation commonly used with eighteenth-century Italian works which, unlike the regular dramma per musica, made considerable use of the chorus. The plot is simplified to the verge of austerity, and it is presented in a series of tableaux rather than as a connected story. Eurydice has died before the action begins, and the curtain rises to show Orpheus and the chorus lamenting over her bier; this was a favorite type of scene in French opera, the *tombeau*, a fine example of which may be found at the opening of Act I of Rameau's *Castor et Pollux*. The choral lament is intensified by Orpheus' moving cries of "Euridice!" There follows a short recitative and a ballo, that is, a solemn dance, after which the lament is resumed. At its conclusion, Orpheus sings his aria "Chiamo il mio ben così," in F major, three strophes separated by short recitatives, a simple expression of grief made more poignant through echo repetitions of the closing phrases by a second orchestra behind the scenes. A final outburst of sorrow is interrupted by the appearance of the God of Love, who in pity directs Orpheus to seek his departed wife in the realms of the dead.

The opening of Act II shows the Furies guarding the gates of the underworld; their fierce denials Orpheus overcomes by the magic power of his singing. A gradual lessening of tension leads naturally into the next scene of the Elysian Fields, where a mood of bright, serene happiness is sustained throughout with remarkable consistency. This scene is introduced by the famous "Ballet of the Happy Spirits" and the lovely aria "Che puro ciel," with its delicately pictorial accompaniment. Eurydice appears, conducted by a train of Blessed Spirits. Everything moves with a still, unearthly, dreamlike motion. With the third act, the mood is abruptly broken; we suddenly find ourselves watching a human-interest drama. The first part of this act is less interesting musically, though it brings the catastrophe of the action. Orpheus, no longer able to withstand the pleadings of Eurydice, looks back; and her death is followed by that ideal, classic outpouring of grief "Che faro senza Euridice?" which in its profoundly simple feeling is matched in opera only by the closing solo of Purcell's *Dido and Aeneas*. Here the action properly concludes; but since the occasion required a happy ending, the God of Love once more appears and restores Eurydice to life. General rejoicings, with ballets and chorus, furnish the closing scene, which thus, with the overture, frames this antique myth for presentation to a European court of the eighteenth century.

In no other work did Gluck realize so consciously and so fully the effect of classic, statuesque repose as in *Orfeo*. The music, like the libretto, is denuded of all unnecessary ornament; nothing in it calls attention to itself. The forms are clearly perceived but freely intermingled and always appropriate to the moods and situations; the extremes of secco recitative on the one hand and of coloratura aria on the other are abolished; always the simplest means are used, and yet these produce an effect apparently out of all proportion to their simplicity. It can hardly be said that the music is in any degree suppressed in favor of poetry, even in the recitatives, which are certainly more musical and expressive than those of Lully or Rameau.[17] Rather, the music is purified; it is as though Gluck, by voluntarily abandoning the outward charms of Italian operatic melody, stimulated the sources of inward beauty.

The full score was printed at Paris in 1764—one of the very few Italian operas to be published since 1639. Its popularity may be inferred both from this fact and from the number of parodies which appeared in the latter half of the eighteenth century.[18] A decade later, in 1774, *Orfeo* was performed at Paris with a French libretto, some added ballets, and a change of the role of Orpheus from contralto to tenor, which also involved some changes in the key scheme.

The five years after *Orfeo* were occupied with the composition of two other Italian operas, *Il trionfo di Clelia* and *Alceste*, and a number of lesser works.[19] *Alceste*, the second opera on which Gluck and Calzabigi collaborated, was first performed in Vienna on December 26, 1767. It is based upon a Greek subject first dramatized by Euripides. Like *Orfeo*, the opera exists in both the original form and a revision made for Paris (in 1776). The differences between the two versions are more extensive than in

---

17. See Meyer, *Die Behandlung des Rezitatives in Glucks italienischen Reformopern.*

18. Cucuel, "Les Opéras de Gluck dans les parodies."

19. *Il trionfo di Clelia* was commissioned for the opening in 1763 of the Teatro Comunale in Bologna. See Unger, "Zur Entstehungsgeschichte des *Trionfo di Clelia.*"

Orfeo, but, as in the earlier work, it is hardly possible to decide which is superior. Both have certain faults of dramatic construction, chiefly the artificial ending. King Admetus lies at the point of death; an oracle decrees his life may be spared if another will die in his stead. His wife, Alcestis, offers herself as the victim but is rescued and restored to Admetus—in Calzabigi's poem by Apollo, and in the Paris version by Hercules. The latter accords with the Greek original, but in both librettos the interference has the character of a mere arbitrary act of magnanimity on the part of a conventional eighteenth-century *deus ex machina* instead of being motivated, as in Euripides, by a feeling of gratitude for hospitality. Still, as Einstein points out, the strength of this motive, however it may have been appreciated by the Athenians, could not have been made clear to a modern audience, for whom the spectacle of Alcestis' sacrificial devotion was bound to overshadow all other interests. Thus, the opera centers around the heroine, in comparison with whom the other figures count for little.

Gluck had called *Orfeo* an "azione teatrale"; *Alceste* he designated a *tragedia per musica*. The entire action is on a grander scale than in *Orfeo*. It is organized, in a manner similar to Traetta, into monumental scene-complexes with large choruses, which are the most prominent features of the score. The first act is the most unified and satisfactory, from the truly tragic overture which leads directly into the opening outburst of the chorus, the announcement by the herald of Admetus' impending death, and the choruses of mourning, proceeding in an unbroken crescendo of interest through the pronouncement of the oracle, and climaxing with Alcestis' heroic resolve and her famous aria "Divinités du Styx." The second act (in the Paris version) opens with the needed contrast, the dances and choruses of rejoicing over Admetus' recovery. The dramatic entrance of Alcestis, and the revelation to the king of the identity of his rescuer, lead to some remarkable recitative dialogue, ending with Alcestis' cavatina "Ah! malgré moi," the agitated second part of which is broken by a short choral interlude. The third act is dramatically an anticlimax, the action remaining for a long while just where it was at the end of Act II; but the music is notable for the choruses, the strangely calm and yet moving aria of Alcestis, "Ah, divinités implacables," and a fine passionate aria of Admetus, "Alceste, au nom des Dieux."[20] After a banal final chorus, the opera closes with the customary suite of ballets.

When the score of *Alceste* was published at Vienna in 1769, it contained a dedicatory preface which is the clearest and fullest statement of Gluck's and Calzabigi's new ideals for opera. This preface has been reproduced so many times, and is so easily accessible in translation, that it does not seem necessary to quote it in full here.[21] Like many history-making documents, it embodied no ideas that had not been stated before; it was a defense of a *fait accompli* rather than a program for the future. It voiced the usual arguments against the caprice and vanity of singers and against the domination of musical stereotypes over the requirements of the text, and it set forth the purpose of the overture in much the same way that Algarotti had done. Most significantly, it enunciated Gluck's musical aesthetic in a famous simile:

> I have striven to restrict music to its true office of serving poetry by means of expression and by following the situations of the story, without interrupting the action or stifling it with a useless superfluity of ornaments; and I believed that it should do this in the same way as telling colors affect a correct and well-ordered drawing; by a well-assorted contrast of light and shade, which serves to animate the figures without altering their contours.[22]

Such self-abasement would have been inconceivable to an Italian composer of the old school, for whom the story existed only as a pretext for the music. In the preface to *Paride et Elena* (1770), Gluck (or Calzabigi) was even more explicit: "He who is concerned with truthfulness must model himself to his subject, and the noblest beauties of harmony and melody become serious faults if they are misplaced."[23] Such a theory strongly suggests the later doctrines of Wagner, and it has sometimes been cited as evidence of the latter's ignorance of operatic history, or of his egoistic jealousy, that he failed to recognize the fundamental kinship of Gluck's ideas with his own when he proclaimed that "the famous revolu-

20. The aria of Hercules, "C'est en vain que l'enfer," was probably arranged (by Gossec) from an aria in Gluck's *Ezio*.

21. See, for example, Strunk, ed., *Source Readings*, pp. 673–75.

22. As translated in Einstein, *Gluck* (1936 ed.), pp. 98–99.

23. Quoted in Cooper, *Gluck*, p. 143.

tion of Gluck . . . really consisted only in the revolt of the composer against the arbitrariness of the singer."[24] But Wagner was
right inasmuch as he was judging by results, not by professed
intentions, for Gluck did not fully carry out the implications of
his own theories. How far the comparative simplicity of his music
was the result of his aesthetic beliefs, and how far the beliefs were
ex post facto attempts to justify his practice, is not easy to say.
He was not a great technician; and though he probably did know
more about counterpoint than Handel's cook, he certainly was
not a match for either Hasse or Jommelli in facility of invention
or power of sustained thematic development in long arias. Moreover, the art of singing was already on the decline; there were no
more artists of the caliber of Farinelli, even if Gluck could or
would have written for them. By way of compensation, orchestral
technique was steadily improving. One cannot therefore totally
exclude the possibility that Gluck's ideas of the subordination of
music, of formal freedom, plainness of diction, and importance of
orchestration were, if not actually inspired, at least supported by
very practical considerations. At any rate, they had a certain
measure of success. When Dr. Burney visited Vienna in 1772, he
reported the operatic situation in these words:

> Party runs as high among poets, musicians, and their adherents,
> at Vienna as elsewhere. Metastasio, and Hasse, may be said, to be
> at the head of one of the principal sects; and Calzabigi and Gluck
> of another. The first, regarding all innovations as quackery, ad-
> here to the ancient form of the musical drama, in which the poet
> and musician claim equal attention from an audience; the bard in
> the recitatives and narrative parts; and the composer in the airs,
> duos, and choruses. The second party depend more on theatrical
> effects, propriety of character, simplicity of diction, and of musical
> execution, than on, what *they* style, flowery descriptions, superflu-
> ous similes, sententious and cold morality, on one side, with tire-
> some symphonies, and long divisions, on the other.[25]

The chevalier Gluck is simplifying music . . . he tries all he can
to keep his music chaste and sober, his three operas of *Orfeo*,

24. Wagner, *Gesammelte Schriften*, 3:237.

25. Paraphrased from the preface to *Alceste*.

Alceste, and *Paride* are proof of this, as they contain few difficulties of execution, though many of expression.[26]

I cannot quit Hasse and Gluck, without saying that it is very necessary to use discrimination in comparing them together. Hasse may be regarded as the Raphael, and . . . Gluck the Michael Angelo of living composers. If the affected French expression of *le grand simple* can ever mean anything, it must be when applied to the productions of such a composer as Hasse, who succeeds better perhaps in expressing, with clearness and propriety, whatever is graceful, elegant, and tender, than what is boisterous and violent; whereas Gluck's genius seems more calculated for exciting terror in painting difficult situations, occasioned by complicated misery, and the tempestuous fury of unbridled passions.[27]

Reading between the lines, it is easy to see that Dr. Burney's sympathies are temperamentally with Hasse rather than with Gluck, and this lends added weight to his testimony as to the enthusiasm with which both *Orfeo* and *Alceste* were received at Vienna. By comparison, *Paride ed Elena*, the next production of Gluck and Calzabigi, was a failure, and whether for this reason or another, they collaborated no more.

Gluck remained dissatisfied. His new style met with no understanding and but little attention outside the Vienna circle. Durazzo, meanwhile, had gone as ambassador to Venice in 1764; Calzabigi left Vienna sometime in 1772 to take up residence in Italy.[28] Gluck's native tenacity rebelled at the prospect of only an incomplete triumph. Moreover, he had suffered financial reverses and doubtless felt the need to recoup his fortunes. Paris was the only city in Europe that offered the possibilities he sought, and his inclination to try his luck there was strengthened by the fact that the new dauphine of France, Marie Antoinette, who had formerly been his singing pupil at the imperial court, was still interested in his career. Fortunately also, the situation in Paris was favorable for him. The old French opera, incurably conservative, had declined steadily in prestige since the middle of the century

26. Burney, *The Present State of Music in Germany*, 2:232-33, 237.

27. *Ibid.*, 2:349-50.

28. *The New Grove Dictionary*, 3:635.

and was under constant critical attack from the partisans of Italian music, led by Rousseau. Although Gluck himself was probably not well known in Paris, the works of the German symphonists had been favorably received there for many years. In 1772, Gluck began the composition of *Iphigénie en Aulide*, a "tragédie opéra" on a libretto adapted from Racine's tragedy by Du Roullet, a member of the French embassy staff at Vienna. By a combination of skillful diplomacy and the powerful intercession of Marie Antoinette, the score was accepted; Gluck directed the carefully rehearsed first performance at Paris on April 19, 1774, and the work had an immediate success.

What chiefly distinguishes *Iphigénie en Aulide* from *Orfeo* and *Alceste* is the greater rapidity and decisiveness of the action; it is a drama of events rather than a series of comparatively static pictures. As a consequence, the rhythm is more animated, the declamation more pointed, and the musical units shorter, more continuous, more completely intermingled, less self-sufficient than in the earlier works. When Dr. Burney visited Gluck at Vienna, the composer sang for him almost the whole of *Iphigénie en Aulide*, which he had (according to his custom) already composed in his mind though not yet set down on paper; and it was doubtless this work which led Burney to remark that "it seldom happens that a single air of his operas can be taken out of its niche, and sung singly, with much effect; the whole is a chain, of which a detached single link is but of small importance."[29] Gluck himself expressed the same idea: lamenting the insufficiency of melody and even of harmony for the expression of certain emotions, and speaking particularly of Achilles' air "Calchas, d'un trait mortel percé" in *Iphigénie en Aulide*, he said, "My magic consists only in the nature of the song that precedes this and the choice of instruments that accompany it."[30] Burney's observation is especially applicable to the great scene at the end of Act II, where Agamemnon, wavering between his supposed duty to his country and his love for his daughter, in a magnificent monologue finally resolves to save Iphigenia's life. Gluck's power as a dramatist in

29. Burney, *The Present State of Music in Germany*, 2:262.

30. Reported in *Le Journal de Paris*, August 21, 1788, p. 1010, and quoted in Downes, "The Operas of Johann Christian Bach," 1:202.

this scene is surpassed only by some of the pages of his own later *Iphigénie en Tauride*. Another beautiful place is the farewell of Iphigenia in the third act ("Adieu! conservez dans votre âme"), surely, as Newman says, "one of the most perfect emotional utterances of the eighteenth century."[31] The overture to *Iphigénie en Aulide*, Gluck's finest instrumental composition, still holds a place on symphonic programs.

The triumph of *Iphigénie en Aulide* was followed by Paris performances of the revised versions of *Orfeo* (1774) and *Alceste* (1776), as well as by unsuccessful revivals of two of Gluck's French opéras comiques. Meanwhile, the inevitable happened. A group of literati, headed by Jean François Marmontel, determined to furnish Paris the spectacle of a musical combat between the new lion and a representative of the Italian school. Their chosen champion was Niccolò Piccinni (1728–1800), a prolific composer of Italian operas,[32] trained at Naples, and famous throughout Europe for his comic opera *La buona figliuola* (see chapter 15). Piccinni lent himself in all innocence to the proposed competition and came out of the affair a distressed and chastened man.[33] The excitement in Paris over the "Quarrel of the Gluckists and Piccinnists," as over that of the Bouffonists twenty-five years earlier (also dealt with in chapter 15), manifested a side of the Gallic temperament that usually leaves the Anglo-Saxon cold. Benjamin Franklin, then commissioner of the United States of America in Paris, was moved in 1778 to pen a satire in the manner of Swift:

We had been shown numberless skeletons of a kind of little fly, called an ephemera, whose successive generations, we were told, were bred and expired within the day. I happened to see a living company of them on a leaf, who appeared to be engaged in conversation. You know I understand all the inferior animal tongues. . . . I listened through curiosity to the discourse of these little creatures; but as they, in their national vivacity, spoke three or four together, I could make but little of their conversation. I found,

31. Newman, *Gluck and the Opera*, p. 128.

32. Cametti, "Saggio cronologico"; H. Abert, "Piccinni als Buffokomponist," in his *Gesammelte Schriften*, pp. 346–64; biographies and studies by Pascazio, Guingené, Della Corte, and La Rotella.

33. For details, see Desnoiresterres, *Gluck et Piccinni*; Strunk, ed., *Source Readings*, pp. 676–83.

however, by some broken expressions that I heard now and then, they were disputing warmly on the merit of two foreign musicians, one a *cousin*, the other a *moscheto*; in which dispute they spent their time, seemingly as regardless of the shortness of life as if they had been sure of living a month. Happy people! thought I, you live certainly under a wise, just, and mild government, since you have no public grievances to complain of, nor any subject of contention but the perfections and imperfections of foreign music.[34]

Franklin's badinage is less withering than the straight-faced observation of Symonds: "At times when politics have been dull, theology dormant, and science undemonstrative, even music has been found sufficient to excite a nation."[35]

The pleasant idea was conceived of having both Gluck and Piccinni compose music for the same libretto, Quinault's *Roland*. When Gluck found that Piccinni was already working on such a project, he refused and produced instead a setting of Quinault's *Armide*, which was performed in September 1777, four months before Piccinni was ready with his *Roland*. The latter had a better reception than its composer had hoped for, though his reputation in French opera was not made secure until later. Meanwhile, Gluck's *Armide* was received with enthusiasm by his friends and disparagement by his enemies. The score is indeed uneven, partly because of the old-fashioned five-act libretto, which included many scenes not capable of stimulating the composer to his best efforts. Comparisons with Lully were to be expected, and verdicts were freely rendered in favor of one or the other according to the prepossessions of the critic. The most remarkable feature of the music is its idyllic, sensuous charm, giving a foretaste of the romantic style. This may be heard particularly in the air "Plus j'observe ces lieux" (Act II, scene 3) and in the scene of parting between Armide and Renaud (Act V, scene 1), a surprisingly passionate love duet for the eighteenth century. The chaconne in the following scene is one of Gluck's noblest instrumental creations, a worthy companion to the chaconne in Rameau's *Castor et Pollux*.

The last important work of Gluck, and his masterpiece,

34. Franklin, "The Ephemera," p. 207. Quoted by permission of the publisher.

35. Symonds, *Renaissance in Italy*, p. 244.

was *Iphigénie en Tauride*, first performed at Paris on May 18, 1779. The libretto, written by Nicolas-François Guillard on the model of Euripides, is the best poem Gluck ever set, and the entire work, a real drama in music, probably comes as close as possible to the ideal of a modern revival of the spirit of Greek tragedy.[36] It is an extraordinary and happy mixture of ancient and modern motifs. The sense of an inexorable Fate which drives human beings on to catastrophe is combined with vivid, contrasting characterization and masterly depiction of emotion: the noble pathos of Iphigenia, the sullen, superstitious cruelty of Thoas, the fearful remorse of Orestes, the friendship between him and Pylades, and the mysterious brother-sister love between Orestes and Iphigenia. All these were things calculated to call forth Gluck's highest powers. These are displayed in the accompanied recitative near the beginning of the first act, "Cette nuit j'ai rêvu le palais de mon père," where Iphigenia relates her dream which obscurely prefigures the course of the entire tragedy and serves in a manner as a substitute for the prologue of Euripides. It is not difficult to see in the music of these pages the source and model for nineteenth-century composers of similar scenes—Cherubini, Weber, Berlioz, even Wagner and Richard Strauss. Equally powerful is the gloomy air of Thoas, "De noirs pressentiments," with its heavy dotted rhythm and rising arpeggio figures in the bass reaching up "like tentacles of the underworld."[37] The choruses intensify by contrast the outlines of these individual characters. Unlike *Alceste* and the earlier *Iphigénie*, the chorus here takes no direct part in the action, except for a moment at the climax of the last act; the priestesses of Diana (sopranos and altos) furnish an immobile, neutral-colored background for Iphigenia; the chorus of Scythians (tenors and basses) is little else than spectacle, closely connected with a series of ballets whose descent from the exotic scenes of the traditional French ballet is obvious despite the conventional "Turkish" instruments of the late eighteenth century; the chorus of the Eumenides in Act II is the personification of Orestes' conscience, haunting him in a symbolic and terrible dream.

36. See Rushton, "Iphigénie en Tauride: The Operas of Gluck and Piccinni."

37. Marx, *Gluck and die Oper*, 2:273. This rising broken-chord figure in the bass is a characteristic device of Gluck's to suggest the supernatural.

Iphigénie en Tauride has no formal overture but rather an introduction depicting first "the calm," then a "storm"—no mere tour de force of nature painting (as often in earlier French opera) but a prelude leading naturally into the first scene, which opens with the cry of Iphigenia and the chorus, "Grands dieux! soyez-nous secourables!" Of the many fine details of the orchestral accompaniment in the course of the opera, one in particular may be mentioned: Orestes, left alone after Pylades has been arrested by the temple guards, falls into a half stupor; in pitiable self-delusion he tries to encourage the feeling of peace which descends upon him momentarily, singing "Le calme rentre dans mon cœur." But the accompaniment, with a subdued, agitated sixteenth-note reiteration of one tone, and with a sforzando accent at the first beat of every measure, betrays the troubled state of his mind, from which he cannot banish the pangs of remorse for his past crime. It is perhaps the first occurrence in opera of this device of using the orchestra to reveal the inward truth of a situation, in distinction from, even in contradiction to, the words of the text—a practice which Wagner was later to incorporate in a complete system.

One feature of this opera is the way in which Gluck returns to long-breathed, purely musical, even lyrical forms in the arias. It is as though the extreme of revolt against the dominance of music over poetry had passed, and the two were coming together again on equal terms. It is an example of the final stage of artistic revolutions, which usually end by taking over much of that which at first they had rejected. We are accustomed to regard Monteverdi, Gluck, and Wagner as three revolutionary figures in the history of opera; but we tend too much to emphasize what each rejected of the past and to lose sight of the fact that the end result in every case was an enrichment of the musical substance of opera by the incorporation of many earlier musical achievements, though in a new guise or with new significance. Gluck, as has already been mentioned, often used numbers from his earlier operas when composing a new score; borrowings of this sort are especially frequent in his reform operas, and we are thus confronted with the realization that the works in which he is supposed to have renounced the ways of Italian opera are, to a considerable degree, made up of music from his own Italian operas

Interior view of the Drottningholm Court Theater (Sweden). This eighteenth-century theater, still in use today, houses more than 30 original eighteenth-century stage sets, including some for the productions of operas by Handel and Gluck. Photo shows a 1774 stage set designed by Carlo Galli Bibiena.

(Drottningholms Theatermuseum, Sweden)

of an earlier date.[38] The opening of the overture and the aria "Diane impitoyable" in *Iphigénie en Aulide* borrows material from *Le Fête d'Apollo* and *Telemaco*. The last-named work likewise supplied the overture to *Armide*. In *Iphigénie en Tauride*, the chorus of the Eumenides is taken from *Semiramide*, Iphigenia's aria "O malheureuse Iphigénie" from *La clemenza di Tito*, and other portions from *Telemaco*. The reversion to musical opera, however, is more than a matter of a few borrowed numbers. The whole score of *Iphigénie en Tauride*, particularly the arias, shows a tendency toward gathering the music into longer, more continuous, and more highly developed units. Even the old da capo appears in Orestes' "Dieux qui me poursuivez," a fine instance of the dramatically appropriate use of this form; and two of the other arias have the same pattern. Altogether, we may see in this work a reconciliation of the two elements, words and music, the conflict of which had so much occupied the thoughts of Gluck and his contemporaries.

Gluck's last opera, *Echo et Narcisse* (1779), was not a success at Paris, in spite of some beautiful individual numbers, and he took the disappointment badly. He returned at once to Vienna, where he died in 1787.

It is difficult to define Gluck's true significance for the history of opera. His essential achievement was the restoration of a more even balance between music and poetry, between what we may call the audible surface of opera and its dramatic content. His goal was to elevate the drama to a more important place and to reduce the musical excrescences of the preceding period. Paradoxically, he accomplished this by simplifying the libretto and enriching the music, by replacing the intricacies of Metastasian intrigue with the elemental actions of Greek drama, the roulades and ornaments of Hasse with his own harmonically conceived, orchestrally supported, oratorically molded melody, for which he obtained many suggestions from French opera. Gluck had a genius for achieving effects of sublimity by apparently simple means. At the same time, he enriched opera by bringing into it elements from both the ballet and the oratorio and by utilizing all re-

---

38. For a tabulation of these borrowings, see Hortschansky, *Parodie und Entlehnung im Schaffen . . . Glucks*, appendix 4.

sources of the operatic style in long complex scenes held together by broad principles of musical form.[39] His reform works combined the simplicity of the opéra comique, the grandeur of the tragédie lyrique, the vocal charm of Italian opera seria, and the symphonic achievements of the Italian and German schools in an international, or rather supranational, opera, which corresponded at once to the demand of his contemporaries for naturalness, their interest in classical forms, and their passion for art with the moral aim of offering great models of heroism for contemplation. His success was due not only to his fiery temperament and his powers as a musician but also to his intellectual grasp of the moving ideas of his age, his gift for taking practical advantage of the means at hand, his willingness to compromise when necessary, and a certain peasantlike obstinacy in the pursuit of his fundamental aims.

Nothing could be more misleading on the subject of Gluck than his own oft-quoted statement to the effect that when composing an opera he endeavored above all things to forget that he was a musician. Such a remark has all the characteristics of an épigram for the benefit of the French literary critics whom it was his interest to conciliate. Even if he himself by any chance believed there was an atom of meaning in it, there is no reason for us to take it seriously. On the contrary, he never forgot he was a musician; but he also never forgot that it was a drama he was composing, and, so far as the later works are concerned, he composed it so carefully, his settings were so uniquely right, that he marks the beginning of the end of that era that regarded any libretto as any composer's property and saw nothing extraordinary in seventy different settings of the same poem, all, if not perhaps equally good, at least equally suitable to the words. Gluck's operas survive not because of their poems or because of anyone's theories, but because of Gluck's music; and his music survives while that of many cleverer composers is forgotten because it is in itself the drama, not a mere fashionable dress to cover a text.

The influence of Gluck on later composers was largely indirect. Something of his spirit may be sensed in Mozart's *Ido-*

---

39. Similar constructions are found in operas and oratorios earlier in the eighteenth century: see for example Handel's *Semele* (1744), Act I, scenes 1–4.

meneo of 1780 and Haydn's *Armida* of 1784, but only at Paris did his operas become part of the regular repertoire. Here too were presented some works by other composers in a style clearly derived from Gluck. Such were Piccinni's *Didon;* two operas, *Les Danaïdes* and *Tarare,* by Antonio Salieri (1750–1825), an Italian composer chiefly resident at Vienna;[40] and *Oedipe à Colone,* by another Italian, Antonio Sacchini (1730–1786), who worked at Paris after 1781.[41] We may trace the influence of Gluck in the French operas of Méhul, Cherubini, and Spontini, continuing on to the greatest of his nineteenth-century spiritual descendants, Berlioz. But the line, particularly as regards Berlioz, is through similarity of dramatic aims and ideals rather than in actual musical idiom. Outside France, Gluck made little permanent impression. Italy practically ignored him; there were a few performances of his later works in Germany in the eighteenth century,[42] but on the whole that country remained under the Italian spell until a national opera began to develop with the approach of romanticism. Gluck was, like Handel, the end of an epoch rather than the beginning. He sums up the classical age of serious opera as Handel does that of the late baroque. The qualities of sincerity, uprightness, and honest dealing with the art of music are common to both men.

40. See Jullien, *La Cour et l'opéra sous Louis XVI;* biographies by Mosel and Magnani; Angermüller, *Antonio Salieri.*

41. Jullien, *La Cour et l'opéra sous Louis XVI;* Thierstein, "Five French Operas of Sacchini." *Oedipe à Colone* was first performed at Paris in 1787, the year following Sacchini's death.

42. For example, *Iphigénie en Tauride* was performed at the Weimar court theater in 1796 under the direction of Friedrich Schiller; see Longyear, "Schiller and Opera."

CHAPTER FIFTEEN

The Comic Opera

In seventeenth-century opera, comic episodes of all kinds were regularly mingled with serious scenes. The comic scenes, dramatically related to the operas with which they were performed, could also be excerpted and performed as if they were independent intermezzi.[1] The practice of commingling comic and serious scenes continued into the eighteenth century, especially in Naples and Vienna. At the same time, comic and serious operas were emerging as separate types. The separation of styles was brought about, in part, by Zeno and Metastasio, whose reform of the opera libretto in the early eighteenth century called for the abolition of the comic as being irrelevant to the plot and incongruous with the tragic style.

Comic opera grew up independently in each country, creating a number of quite diverse national forms, such as the Italian opera buffa, the French opéra comique, the English ballad opera, and, after the middle of the century, the German singspiel and the Spanish *tonadilla*.[2] Certain features were common to all these works in the early stages of their history: all showed signs of their humble origin in the choice of light or farcical subjects and the preference for scenes, personages, and dialogue taken from familiar popular comedies or from the everyday life of the common people (if fantasy was present, it was treated comically); all were performed by comparatively unskilled singers, often by in-

1. A representative collection of *scene buffe*, excerpted from eighteen different operas, originally performed in Naples from 1697 to 1702, is contained in two manuscript volumes at the Sächsische Landesbibliothek in Dresden. The contents of these volumes are cited in Troy, *The Comic Intermezzo*, pp. 23–24.

2. See chap. 9 for the use of the term singspiel in the seventeenth and early eighteenth centuries.

ferior actors for whom music was, to say the least, only an avocation;[3] all except the Italian opera buffa used spoken dialogue; all occasionally parodied the serious opera; and all cultivated a simple, easily grasped musical style in which national popular idioms played a prominent part. Finally, in the course of the eighteenth century, all underwent a radical change in character, from low-class farce to middle-class comedy of various sorts, acquiring in the process so many new features, both in the libretto and in the music, that by the end of the century the original distinction between serious and comic operas no longer had much meaning. Comic opera in its beginning was a "low-brow" entertainment, regarded by operagoers as something about on the level of a circus midway show; within a little over fifty years it became of equal respectability and importance with serious opera; and in less than fifty years more, it dominated the stage, having supplanted or absorbed the old opera seria almost completely.

Opera Buffa

The term "opera buffa" is used somewhat loosely as a general designation for Italian operas of the early and middle eighteenth century that cannot be classified as opera seria.[4] Two distinct kinds of comic opera existed in Italy at the beginning of the century. First, there were full-length operas based on nonserious librettos, works similar to Rospigliosi's *Dal male il bene* and other comic and pastoral pieces which had been produced, though not in large numbers, all through the seventeenth century. Most composers of Italian opera seria also produced works in the comic genre. Alessandro Scarlatti exemplifies this well with his *Il trionfo dell' onore,*

---

3. The castrato, that symbol of opera seria, appeared only rarely in comic opera, but male roles were sometimes sung by women.

4. Other terms used for the genre include *commedia per musica* and *dramma giocoso*. Carlo Goldoni used *dramma giocoso* to indicate an opera buffa which combined *parti serie* with *parti buffe*; Heartz, "Goldoni, Don Giovanni, and *Dramma Giocoso*." General works on the opera buffa are D'Arienzo, "Le origini dell' opera comica"; Della Corte, *L'opera comica*; Scherillo, *L'opera buffa napoletana*; H. Abert, *W. A. Mozart*, 1:400-458; Roncaglia, *Il melodioso settecento italiano*; Robinson, *Naples and Neapolitan Opera*.

a "commedia" in which the roles range from serious to farcical. This comic opera was composed for the Teatro dei Fiorentini, a small theater in Naples known for its productions of a special type of "comedy in music," one using Neapolitan dialect and drawing some of its character types from the commedia dell' arte.[5] Vinci and Leo each produced a half-dozen or more pieces of this sort in the 1720s.[6] *Li Zite 'n galera* (1722), with music in a simple style, is the only one of Vinci's works in this genre known to survive.

The second kind of Italian comic opera at the beginning of the eighteenth century was in the form of intermezzi, that is, short pieces in one act, intended to be performed between the acts of a serious opera. These intermezzi were, in a way, the descendants of the comic scenes that had been scattered through the plots of seventeenth-century operas. Although the reforms of Zeno and Metastasio banished comic episodes from the opera seria libretto, the comic element continued to find refuge in the intermezzi and in various other dramatic forms.

Between 1700 and 1730, a sizable repertoire of intermezzi dramatically independent of the opera serie with which they were performed developed first in Venice and then in Naples and Vienna.[7] It was the custom for the intermezzi required for an opera seria to form a continuous plot, so that performances in effect consisted of two operas, one serious and one comic, in alternation. Understandably, foreigners sometimes complained of the resultant confusion.[8] Subdivision of the intermezzi into two, three, or four parts was often determined more by local preference than by the number of acts in the attendant opera seria. In Naples, for example, preference for the two-part intermezzo was well established by 1730. Sometimes the intermezzi were performed at the

5. The earliest known comic opera in Neapolitan dialect is *La Cilla* (1706), with libretto by F. A. Tullio and music (lost) by M. Fazzioli (1666–1733). Seven arias from A. Orefice's *Le finte zingare* (1717) are among the earliest extant examples of music from a comic opera in Neapolitan dialect. *Patrò Calienno della costa*, staged at the Teatro dei Fiorentini in 1709, was one of the earliest three-act operas of this kind; the music, by Orefice and other composers, is lost, but for a discussion of the libretto, see Scherillo, *L'opera buffa napoletano*.

6. Hardie, "Leonardo Leo (1694–1744) and His Comic Operas."

7. Lazarevich, "The Role of the Neapolitan Intermezzo"; Troy, *The Comic Intermezzo*.

8. Cf. Wright, *Some Observations Made in Travelling*, p. 85.

end of the opera as an afterpiece, thus becoming to all intents and purposes independent works. Among the hundreds of intermezzi produced by famous as well as obscure composers in the first half of the eighteenth century, Pergolesi's *La serva padrona* ("The Maid Mistress," 1733) has deservedly maintained its popularity down to our own time. It is characteristic of such works in its economy of musical resources: only two singers (soprano and bass) and a third mute character, with an orchestra of strings and continuo. The musical style is likewise typical: predominantly major, rapid in movement, with much repetition of short motifs, a disjunct melodic line, comic effects produced by sudden offbeat accents, wide skips, and an infectious gaiety and vigor of utterance, offering much to the tone and gesture of the actor (example 15.1).

Example 15.1: *La serva padrona*, Act I

Beside the more common allegro arias, there is found in the intermezzi a slower, cantabile style, sometimes in minor, which often features chromatic melodies and harmonies for mock-pathetic effects. Folk-songish canzonettas and bass-buffo patter songs frequently appear; duets conclude the structural divisions within the intermezzi. Throughout the scores, one is impressed by the absolute fidelity of music to text; the singing seems to be simply a highly flexible, sensitive, melodic declamation of the words, preserving and heightening every detail that might contribute to the comic effect. At the same time, there is never a suggestion that the words impede the spontaneous flow of the music; textual repetition is a constant feature but somehow never gives the impression of artificiality. One consequence of this perfect union of text and music is the extraordinary variety of forms in the arias of the intermezzi, in marked contrast to the stock da capo pattern of the opera seria of the time. This variety is well represented in Johann Adolf Hasse's eight intermezzi, composed between 1726 and 1730.[9]

Around 1740, the two previously distinct kinds of Italian comic opera began to lose their peculiar characteristics and merge into a common type. This process was facilitated as the intermezzi became detached from their original connection with serious operas and came to be regarded as a separate and independent form. One traditional characteristic of the comic scenes and intermezzi had been the use of the bass voice, which practically never appeared in opera seria. The presence of basses along with the higher voices made possible one of the most distinctive features of Italian comic opera—the ensembles, particularly those at the end of each act.[10] Opera seria, with its emphasis on solo singing, had not developed the ensemble forms, with the exception of the duet. A composer who is reputed to have made important contributions to the ensemble finale is Nicola Logroscino (1698-ca. 1765); he produced a considerable number of comic operas at Naples in the 1740s and 1750s, but so little of his music has been preserved that it is difficult to know how far his reputation as the founder of the *buffo finale* is deserved.[11] The ideal aim in these comic operas was an ensemble finale which would not be a mere closing set-piece but rather would carry on the action of the drama while at the same time evolving a satisfactory musical form. Although this aim was not to be fully achieved before Mozart, some progress was made toward it after the middle of the century. One of the most prolific composers of the day was Baldassare Galuppi (1706–1785), called "Il Buranello" from the name of his birthplace, an island near Venice. Galuppi's operas, nearly a hundred in number, both serious and comic, were presented for the most part at Venice, but he was famous all over Europe and worked at the court of

9. Some of Hasse's intermezzi have been edited by Lazarevich. See Recent Researches in the Music of the Classical Era (1979) and Concentus Musicus (1985). See also Lazarevich, "J. A. Hasse as a Comic Dramatist"; idem, "Pasticcio Revisited."

10. M. Fuchs, "Die Entwicklung des Finales"; Dent, "Ensembles and Finales"; Heartz, "The Creation of the *buffo* Finale."

11. See Kretzschmar, "Zwei Opern"; Prota-Giurleo, *Nicola Logroscino*.

St. Petersburg from 1765 to 1768.[12] Galuppi frequently composed the finales of his comic operas in the form of a chain of short sections, by means of which he was able to relate the music closely to the ongoing action.

About the middle of the century, Galuppi began an association with the dramatist Carlo Goldoni (1707–1793) at Venice;[13] one of the most successful of their joint productions was *Il filosofo di campagna* ("The Peasant Philosopher," 1754). Goldoni was the leading figure in the reform of Italian drama in the eighteenth century. His comedies, rejecting the stock character types and plots as well as the improvised dialogue of the old commedia dell' arte, are models of natural characterization and spontaneous action. His influence on the libretto marked a turning point in the history of the opera buffa, which from this time on became more dignified, more orderly in structure, and more refined in action and language. New kinds of comic opera librettos began to appear—works which must be called dramas rather than farces and were often sentimental or even pathetic in character. These newer tendencies did not replace the old comic elements altogether but rather existed side by side or intermingled with them, so that the comic opera libretto in the second half of the eighteenth century was distinctly varied and, on the whole, much more interesting than that of the opera seria.

One of the best and most popular comic operas of this period was *La buona figliuola* ("The Good Girl"), composed by Niccolò Piccinni for Rome in 1760. It enjoyed a two-year run there and soon became known all over Europe. The opera is based upon a libretto which Goldoni wrote in 1756, soon after his arrival in Parma.[14] The story for this *melodramma giocoso* was taken from Richardson's *Pamela; or, Virtue Rewarded*, which had become a favorite novel of readers in every country since its publi-

12. Wotquenne, "Baldassare Galuppi"; Piovano, "Baldassare Galuppi"; Bollert, *Die Buffoopern Baldassare Galuppis*; Della Corte, *Baldassare Galuppi*. Mooser, *Annales*, 2:69-86.

13. See Goldoni, *Mémoires*, and biographies and studies by Chatfield-Taylor, Torre, Spinelli, Rabany.

14. Another opera based upon Goldoni's *La Cecchina, ossia La buona figliuola* had been composed by Egidio Duni for the Parma stage in 1756. This production concluded the Italian phase of Dunni's operatic works. See K. M. Smith, "The Life and Music of Egidio R. Duni."

cation in 1740.[15] Piccinni's score is remarkable for the long, complex, and carefully planned finales of each act. Piccinni was probably the first composer to try to unify these sections by means of a recurring musical theme *(rondo finale)*, thus taking a step toward the highly organized symphonic finale which was to be perfected by Mozart. In other ways also—for example, in the assigning of independent motifs to the orchestra and in the relatively greater continuity and self-sufficiency of the instrumental parts—Piccinni advanced the style of opera buffa.

As the century went on, the music of comic opera grew more ambitious, broadening its range of expression in accordance with the broadening subject matter of the librettos. One notable work of the 1770s was *L'incognita perseguitata* ("The Persecuted Incognita," Rome, 1773) by Piccinni's pupil Pasquale Anfossi (1727–1797). A more important composer of the late eighteenth century was Giovanni Paisiello (1740–1816), who worked principally at Naples except for a period at St. Petersburg from 1776 to 1784.[16] His *Il rè Teodoro in Venezia* ("King Theodore in Venice"), first given at Vienna in 1784, had many performances over the next thirty years and was revived at New York in 1961; the most remarkable features of this opera are the lively ensemble finales. Paisiello's *Il barbiere di Siviglia* ("The Barber of Seville," 1782), composed for St. Petersburg, remained such a favorite in Italy that even in 1816 Rossini had to overcome popular prejudice against the presumption of any other composer attempting to set the same libretto. *Socrate immaginario* ("The Man Who Thought He Was Socrates," Naples, 1775) is an example of parody, a frequent resource of comic opera librettists. The objects in this case are the classicist movement in general and Gluck's *Orfeo* in particular—the scene between Orpheus and the Furies being burlesqued in broad, though clever, fashion. In *La molinara* ("The Maid of the Mill," Naples, 1788), Paisiello displays many of those expressive qualities and turns of phrase which we are accustomed to associate with Mozart, and his *Nina* (Naples, 1789) is one of the best examples of sentimental comedy in this whole period (ex-

15. See Holmes, "Pamela Transformed."

16. See Hunt, *Giovanni Paisiello*; H. Abert, *Gesammelte Schriften*, pp. 365–96; biographies and studies by Della Corte, Pupino-Carbonelli, Speziale, Faustini-Fasini, and Cortese; Mooser, *Annales*, 2:191-244, 355-62.

Example 15.2: *Nina*

ample 15.2). Paisiello was a master of musical characterization, perhaps the most important figure in eighteenth-century opera buffa next to Mozart himself and one who exercised a strong influence on the musical style of the latter. Paisiello's gifts are apparent in his orchestral writing, which is more varied and more important dramatically than in any earlier buffo composer. In his finales, Paisiello rivaled Piccinni both in scope and in the skill with which musical forms were adapted to the action of the text. He also was one of the first composers to introduce into serious opera ensemble finales which advanced the action of the drama.

An immediate forerunner of Mozart at Vienna was Florian Leopold Gassmann (1729–1774), whose two most celebrated comic operas were *L'amore artigiano* ("Love Among the Laborers," 1767) and *La contessina* ("The Countess," 1770), both on librettos by Goldoni. Gassmann's ensemble finales are remarkable

for the way in which the orchestra carries on the music in continuous fashion, giving unity and direction to the entire scene.
The orchestral part is important also in the arias, sometimes even
having greater melodic interest than the voice.[17]

Also active as a composer of Italian operas was Franz
Joseph Haydn (1732–1809), though his works for the theater are
little known today in comparison with his symphonies, quartets,
and oratorios.[18] Yet one of Haydn's prime concerns during his
long years of service under Prince Esterházy was the preparation
and conducting of operas, the composition of new arias to be inserted in others composers operas performed at Eszterháza, and
the composition of new operas of his own.[19] Nor did he lack success: more performances of Haydn's operas took place during his
lifetime than of Mozart's during *his* lifetime.

The music of Haydn's six singspiels and of two of his
four pieces for marionettes is no longer extant. The rest of his
operatic output, all on Italian librettos, consists of eight comic
operas; four others of serious or semiserious character, the most
successful of which was *Armida*, staged for the Esterházy family
in 1784; and one dramma per musica, *Orfeo ed Euridice* (also
known as *L'anima del filosofo*), composed for London in 1791 but
not performed.[20] *Orfeo* contains some beautiful music, but the
libretto (by C. F. Badini) is certainly one of the worst specimens
of its kind in the whole history of opera—no mean distinction.
More satisfactory as far as balance of interest between text and
music goes are Haydn's operatic works of the 1760s and 1770s,
from *Lo speziale* ("The Druggist," 1768), a chamber opera with

---

17. Donath, "Florian Gassmann als Opernkomponist."

18. Larsen, *Die Haydn-Ueberlieferungen*; Geiringer, *Joseph Haydn*; Wirth, *Joseph Haydn als Dramatiker*; idem, "The Operas of Joseph Haydn before *Orfeo*"; Lawner, "Form and Drama in the Operas of Joseph Haydn"; Bartha and Somfai, *Haydn als Opernkapell-meister*, Harich, "Das Repertoire des Opernkapellmeisters J. Haydn in Eszterháza"; Landon, "Haydn's Marionette Operas." See also Feder, "A Special Feature of Neapolitan Opera Tradition in Haydn's Vocal Works," and Lazarevich, "Haydn and the Italian Comic Intermezzo Tradition."

19. Prince Esterházy's theater was far more important than has been generally acknowledged. See Landon, "Out of Haydn"; Bartha, "Haydn's Opera Repertory."

20. The score was reconstructed and the opera recorded by the Haydn Society in 1950. Other Haydn operas have been revived since that date.

text by Goldoni, to *L'infedeltà delusa* ("Infidelity Deluded," 1773), *L'incontro improvviso* ("The Unexpected Meeting," 1775), and *Il mondo della luna* ("The World of the Moon," 1777). *La vera costanza* ("True Constancy"), a *dramma giocoso* performed in 1779, is a particularly good example of the way in which Haydn could combine comic and serious elements in the new kind of mixed musical drama that was gradually replacing both the strictly comic opera buffa and the old-fashioned opera seria everywhere in the last three decades of the eighteenth century.

The comic opera in Italy at the end of the eighteenth century is best represented by Domenico Cimarosa (1749–1801), a prolific composer with some eighty operas to his credit.[21] Like many of his compatriots, Cimarosa was called for a time to St. Petersburg (1787–1791). On his return, he stopped over at Vienna and there produced his masterpiece, *Il matrimonio segreto* ("The Secret Marriage"), in 1792. The success of this work was immediate and has continued to the present day. Cimarosa's music fairly rivals Mozart's in tunefulness and spontaneity, though lacking Mozart's profundity and musical constructive power. But profundity was far from being an Italian ideal in this field; the qualities of wit, liveliness, melodic flow, and a never-ending vein of loquacity and good humor constituted the charm of Cimarosa as of his Italian confreres. He continued the tradition of Paisiello and the other eighteenth-century buffo composers in that inimitable musical style which led in the nineteenth century to Rossini, Donizetti, and ultimately Verdi's *Falstaff*.

Opéra Comique

The founders of the French comic opera were Molière and Lully, whose comedy ballets, pieces in which spoken dialogue alternated

---

21. Biographies by Vitale and Tibaldi Chiesa; see also essays in *Per il bicentenario della nascita di Domenico Cimarosa*, especially Schlitzer, "Annali delle opere"; Chailly, *Il matrimonio segreto*; Mooser, *Annales*, 2:451-55.

with songs and dances, were presented before Louis XIV during the 1660s.[22] When Lully assumed control of the Academy of Music in 1672, his monopoly cut off all but the barest musical resources from other Paris theaters, and the death of Molière in the following year put an end to the first stage of the comedy ballet.[23] At this juncture, the Italian Theater, which had been established on a permanent basis at Paris in 1661, began to intermingle French scenes, including music, with its improvised Italian comedies. In the course of the next two decades, the French language gradually replaced Italian; eventually, the "Italian" troupe gave nothing but comedies and farces (of a rather low sort) in French, which still retained many traces of their commedia dell' arte predecessors and which were embellished by fanciful displays with ballets and songs.[24] After the Italians were expelled from Paris in 1697, their repertoire was taken over, in a still cruder form, by various small popular theaters, which played a few weeks in each year at the two large fairs of Paris. Practical exigencies forced these groups to simplify their music to an extreme degree. They used for the most part little popular tunes ("vaudevilles"—see example 15.3) to which the authors adapted new words—a process known technically as "parody." Little by little, the fortunes of the "fair theaters" improved, until in 1715 they were brought under one management and formally established as the Théâtre de l'Opéra-comique. For a long time, they continued presenting popular comedies in which the vaudevilles were the principal source of music and burlesque of the serious opera a frequent device.[25] They had a competitor in the so-called New Italian Theater, which had been

22. Cucuel, *Les Créateurs de l'opéra-comique*; idem, "Sources et documents"; Genest, *L'Opéra-comique*; Campardon, *Les Comédiens*; idem, *Les Spectacles des foires*; La Laurencie, "L'Opéra-comique," in Lavignac, *Encyclopédie*, 3:1457ff.; Grout, "Origins of the Opéra-comique"; Cooper, *Opéra comique*.

23. Tiersot, *La Musique dans la comédie de Molière*; Bötther, *Die "Comédie-Ballet" von Molière-Lully*.

24. Parfaict, *Histoire de l'ancien théâtre italien*; Du Gérard, *Tables*; Gherardi, *Théâtre italien*; Grout, "The Music of the Italian Theatre at Paris, 1682–1697"; idem, "Seventeenth Century Parodies of French Opera."

25. Carmody, *Le Repertoire de l'opéra-comique en vaudevilles*; Parfaict, *Mémoires*; Le Sage, *Le Théâtre de la foire*; Barberet, *Lesage et la théâtre de la foire*; Calmus, *Zwei Opernburlesken*; Cucuel, "La Critique musicale"; Grannis, *Dramatic Parody*.

Example 15.3: Vaudeville Airs from *Théâtre de la Foire*, Vol. I

*This first part of the example is taken from Lully's *Atys*. (f. example 10.2a.)

reestablished in Paris after the death of Louis XIV in 1715.[26] Among the literary talents attracted to the latter theater was Charles-Simon Favart, who during the 1740s raised the vaudeville comedy to its highest level and at the same time encouraged the introduction of new music—airs parodied from operas and even some originally composed songs—in place of the old-fashioned vaude-

26. *Le Nouveau Théâtre italien*; *Les Parodies du nouveau théâtre italien* (with supplement); Geulette, *Notes et souvenirs*; Desboulmiers, *Histoire anecdotique*; Origny, *Annales du théâtre-italien*; Cucuel, "Notes sur la comédie italienne de 1717 à 1789."

villes.[27] From 1752 to 1754, the performance at Paris of a dozen Italian buffo operas, including Pergolesi's *La serva padrona*, by a visiting troupe gave rise to a famous quarrel, the "War of the Bouffons," in the course of which the relative merits of French and Italian music were argued ad nauseam.[28] One of the peculiar features of this quarrel was that no one seemed to realize that all the comparisons were being made between French *serious* opera and Italian *comic* opera, and therefore the real point at issue was missed. However, the results of the Italians' visit were important, for they led a new generation of French composers to create a national comic opera with original music, in which the native popular idiom of the vaudeville was overlaid and enriched by a more refined, varied, and expressive style.

A forerunner of the new opéra comique was *Le Devin du village* ("The Village Soothsayer"), which was performed at the Academy of Music in 1752 and remained in the repertoire for sixty years.[29] This charming little work by Jean Jacques Rousseau (1712–1778) is Italian in form—that is, it has continuous music, with recitatives—but French in style and feeling. The melodies show kinship with both the vaudeville and the popular romances of the day, while the harmonizations are amusingly naïve. Rousseau's attempt to found a French comic opera had no immediate results; he himself, with typical inconsistency, declared in the following year that "the French have no music and never can have any—or if they ever do, so much the worse for them."[30] Yet after a few years of experimentation, the new French comic opera came to full growth in the works of three composers: Egidio Romualdo

27. Favart, *Théâtre*; idem, *Mémoires*; Monnet, *Mémoires*; Font, *Favart*; Iacuzzi, *The European Vogue of Favart*.

28. Richebourg, *Contribution à l'histoire de la "Querelle des Bouffons,"* contains a bibliography of the principal documents in this affair. See Grimm, "Lettre sur Omphale"; idem, *Le Petit Prophète de Boemischbroda*; idem, *Correspondance littéraire*; Kretzschmar, "Die *Correspondance littéraire*"; Rousseau, *Lettre sur la musique française*; Diderot, *Le Neveu de Rameau*; La Laurencie, "La Grande Saison italienne de 1752"; Hirschberg, *Die Enzyklopädisten*; Boyer, *La Guerre des bouffons*; Oliver, *The Encyclopedists as Critics*; Strunk, ed., *Source Readings*, pp. 619–55.

29. Tiersot, *Jean-Jacques Rousseau*; Masson, "Les Idées de Rousseau"; Pougin, *Jean-Jacques Rousseau, musicien*; Arnheim, "*Le Devin du village*"; Strauss, "Jean Jacques Rousseau"; Lowinsky, "Taste, Style, and Ideology."

30. The ending of his *Lettre sur la musique française*.

Duni (1708–1775), an Italian who came to Paris in 1757 after having tried his hand at French comic operas at the court of Parma;[31] François-André Danican Philidor (1726–1795), the last of a distinguished family of musicians and equally renowned as a chess master;[32] and Pierre-Alexandre Monsigny (1729–1817), who, though not a trained musician, succeeded on the strength of his natural melodic gift, which lay in the direction of tender and sentimental expression.[33] While these three composers were writing opéras comiques at Paris, Gluck was producing a series of similar pieces at Vienna.

The new opéra comique differed in many ways from both the earlier vaudeville comedies and the Italian opera buffa. The form was known as a *comédie mêlée d'ariettes*, a "comedy [in spoken dialogue] mingled with songs." The term "ariette" was used as the diminutive of the Italian "aria" to distinguish a newly composed song from the traditional vaudeville melodies. The subject matter was varied: Gluck's *La Rencontre imprévue*, given at Vienna in 1764, was a romantic comedy in an oriental setting; Duni's *Isle des foux* ("The Island of Madmen," 1760) and *La Fée Urgèle* (1765) were respectively farce and fairy tale; Philidor's *Tom Jones* (1765) was based on Fielding's picaresque novel; Monsigny in *On ne s'avise jamais de tout* ("You Never Know All," 1761) produced an intrigue comedy of the Italian sort and in *Le Déserteur* (1769), his best work, a sentimental drama. An important class of opéras comiques were those with scenes and characters representing an idealized peasantry, with a naïve heroine (a character type inherited from Favart) and a manly young hero who, oppressed by a wicked noble, are finally saved either by virtue of their own innocence and honesty or by the intervention of a more powerful noble or the king himself. Monsigny's *Le Roy et le fermier* ("The King and the Farmer," 1762) was of this type, and the same motif entered into many other opéras comiques. The "advanced" ideas of the day, the currently fashionable criticism

---

31. K. M. Smith, "The Life and Music of . . . Duni," and Rushton, "Music and Drama at the Académie Royale."

32. Bonnet, *Philidor*; Carroll, "François-André Danican Philidor."

33. Pougin, *Monsigny et son temps*. See also Arnoldson, *Sedaine et les musiciens de son temps*; Druilhe, *Monsigny*.

Example 15.4: *Le Déserteur*, Act, sc. 1

MONSIGNY

Peut - on af - fli - ger ce qu'on ai - me? Pour - quoi cher -
cher _____ à le fâ - cher? _____ Peut -
on af - fli - ger ce qu'on ai - me? C'est bien en vou -
- loir à soi mê - me, c'est bien en vou -
- loir à soi mê - - me.

of the social order, and the doctrines of Rousseau and the other
encyclopedists were reflected, though in a harmless enough fashion, in these works.

The music of the opéra comique was seldom profound
but often tuneful and charming (see example 15.4). Ensembles,
especially duets, were common, though the French never developed the dramatic ensemble finale to the extent the Italians did.
Short descriptive orchestral background pieces were frequent—a
heritage from Lully and Rameau. Most opéras comiques ended
with a "vaudeville final," a strophic song with refrain, the tune
either a popular vaudeville or in imitation of that style. The form
of the vaudeville final established itself not only in the later French
opéra comique but in other countries as well; the finales of Gluck's
Orfeo, Mozart's *Die Entführung aus dem Serail*, and Rossini's *Il
barbiere di Siviglia* are of this type.

The leading composer of opéras comiques in the latter
part of the eighteenth century was André Ernest Modeste Grétry
(1741–1813).[34] Grétry was a Belgian who, after studying at Rome,

34. On Grétry, see his *Mémoires* and *Œuvres complètes*; Strunk, ed., *Source Readings*,
pp. 711–27; biographies by Bobillier, Curzon, and Clercx. See also Jobe, "The Operas of
Grétry"; Pendle, "The Opéras Comiques of Grétry and Marmontel."

Example 15.5: *Richard Coeur-de-Lion*, Act I, sc. 2

GRÉTRY

came to Paris in 1767 and there produced over forty opéras comiques, of which the chief are *Le Tableau parlant* ("The Talking
Picture," 1769), *Zémire et Azor* (1771), and especially *Richard
Coeur-de-Lion* ("Richard the Lion-Hearted," 1784). Grétry's music happily combines the melodic grace of Italy with the delicate
imagination, simplicity, lyricism, and rhythmic finesse of the
French. *Richard Coeur-de-Lion* is a landmark of early romantic
opera, based on the legend of the rescue of King Richard from
prison by his faithful minstrel Blondel. The rescue plot was a
favorite in operas of the late eighteenth and early nineteenth centuries, blending the emotions of suspense, personal loyalty, and
triumph of virtue over evil in an effective dramatic pattern, familiar to us still through Beethoven's *Fidelio*. By way of added
romantic color, Grétry introduced in *Richard* an imitation of a
simple troubadour song, which pervades the work almost like a
leitmotif. The ballad "Que le sultan Saladin" in Act I, introduced
simply as a song external to the action, is the type of many such
interpolations in later opera. Blondel's air "O Richard, O mon
roi" (Act I), by its elevated, earnest, and ardent expression, lifts
this opéra comique into the realm of serious romantic drama, setting an ideal to which many later composers paid homage (example 15.5).

The opéra comique continued to flourish during the revolution and the early years of the nineteenth century,[35] though it
had no composers comparable to Grétry either in ability or popularity until François Adrien Boieldieu (1775–1834), whose greatest success was his *Jean de Paris* (1812). Like the Italian opera
buffa, the French opéra comique in the course of the eighteenth
century had undergone a transformation from low popular comedy to varied, semiserious human drama, from the music of popular song to the effort of able composers. It was destined for greater
triumphs in the nineteenth century and for such further changes
of style and subject matter as to leave the designation "comique"
merely a memento of its origin and a conventional indication of
one vestige of its early days, the use of spoken dialogue.

---

35. Pougin, *L'Opéra-comique pendant la révolution.*

Ballad Opera

When Addison complained in 1711 that "our English Musick is quite rooted out," he uttered no more than the melancholy truth, so far as the theater was concerned. Yet the enthusiasm for Italian opera which prevailed during the first quarter of the eighteenth century eventually provoked a reaction. The English, unable to compete with foreign opera seria on its own ground, took revenge by creating the ballad opera, which ridiculed Italian music and at the same time originated a national comic type as distinctive and popular for the British as opera buffa was for the Italians or opéra comique for the French.[36] The best-known of these works, and one which has survived to our own time, was *The Beggar's Opera*, written by John Gay with music arranged by John Christopher Pepusch (1667–1752) and first performed at London in 1728.[37] The characters are pickpockets, bawds, convicts, and similar gentry (in keeping with Swift's suggested title, "The Newgate Pastoral"), the language is low and racy, and the

Example 15.6: *The Beggar's Opera*, Air XVI,
Over the Hills and Far Away

36. Squire, "An Index of Tunes in the Ballad Operas"; Tufts, "Ballad Operas"; Gagey, *Ballad Opera*; Fiske, *English Theatre Music*; Rubsamen, ed., *The Ballad Opera*.

37. Burney, *History of Music*, 2:985–90; C. Hughes, "John Christopher Pepusch"; Calmus, *Zwei Opernburlesken*; Kephart, "An Unnoticed Forerunner"; and studies of Gay and *The Beggar's Opera* by Benjamin, Kidson, Schultz, and Berger.

play is full of satirical thrusts both at the absurdities of Italian opera and at the reigning Whig politicians of the day. The songs, which alternate with spoken dialogue, are for the most part familiar ballad tunes (example 15.6), though there are some borrowings from other sources (for example, Purcell, Bononcini, and Handel, including his march from *Rinaldo*). The motifs of political and musical satire are particularly congenial to the English in comic opera, as witness Gilbert and Sullivan; neither in the eighteenth nor the nineteenth century were the Londoners inclined to take opera seria with complete seriousness.

The success of *The Beggar's Opera* struck a blow at the fortunes of Handel and marked the beginning of the decline of Italian opera in England. A spate of ballad operas followed during the next ten years, and they continued to be produced throughout the century. The form underwent an evolution similar to that of the vaudeville comedy in France: people tiring of the same old tunes, composers turned to other sources or began to introduce their own songs into the scores, though keeping in general to the ballad style. Indeed, the typical English comic opera of the later eighteenth century is such a hodgepodge of popular tunes, songs from favorite operas, and original music that the elements are hard to disentangle, though the genuine folk ballads of the early days gradually disappeared. The influence of the opera buffa and opéra comique is increasingly apparent after the middle of the century, not only in the outright appropriation of both librettos and music but also in the whole trend from broad comedy and burlesque toward a semiserious, sentimental type of plot with simple half-Italian, half-English music—a singularly innocent, naïve kind of entertainment which was tremendously popular in its day and is still not without a certain appeal.[38]

One of the composers of comic opera was Dr. Thomas Augustine Arne (1710–1778), the most eminent English composer of his generation. Arne's *Thomas and Sally* (1760), on a libretto by Isaac Bickerstaffe, was one of his most successful comic operas and has had frequent revivals up to our own time. *Love in a*

38. Studies of English opera in the second half of the eighteenth century include Winesanker, "The Record of English Musical Drama, 1750–1800"; Kelly, *Reminiscences*, 2:36, 66; Graves, "English Comic Opera"; Petty, *Italian Opera in London 1760–1800*; *The London Stage 1660–1800: A Calendar of Plays*; White, *The History of English Opera*.

Scene from the comic opera *Love in a Village* (London 1762), by T. A. Arne.

(Courtesy of Harold Rosenthal)

Riot protesting against increased prices for Arne's opera *Artaxerxes*,
London, 1763.

(Courtesy of Harold Rosenthal, from his *Two Centuries of Opera at Covent Garden*, p. 15)

Village (1761), also with words by Bickerstaffe, was a typical pasticcio of the period, drawing on music by sixteen different composers; Arne, besides arranging the work, contributed more than a dozen new airs of his own.[39] Arne, incidentally, was the composer of the only successful English serious opera of the eighteenth century: *Artaxerxes* (1762), on a libretto translated and adapted by the composer from Metastasio. The music of *Artaxerxes* is quite a fair specimen of the current Italian style; the opera continued to be performed in England through the early years of the nineteenth century and was revived in London in 1962.

One of the most popular pasticcio operas of the eighteenth century was *The Duenna; or, The Double Elopement* (1775). Based upon Richard Sheridan's comedy, with music selected, arranged, and in part composed by Thomas Linley the Elder (1733–1795) and Thomas Linley the Younger (1751–1778), *The Duenna* was successfully staged in London, Dublin, and the American colonies for more than a quarter of a century, with several hundred performances to its credit.[40] Equally popular was *Midas*, an English *burletta* in which Kara O'Hara's rhymed verses were set to music with recitatives, arias, and ensembles, the whole constituting a comic satire of classical mythology and a burlesque of opera seria. It was produced in both a three-act and a two-act "afterpiece" version.[41]

The principal later composers of English comic opera were Charles Dibdin (1745–1814), William Shield (1748–1829), and Stephen Storace (1763–1796).[42] The most successful of Dibdin's operas were *Lionel and Clarissa* (1768), *The Padlock* (1768), *The Waterman* (1774), *The Quaker* (1775), and *The Seraglio* (1776). Shield was the most gifted, though not the most popular,

39. Parkinson, *An Index to the Vocal Works.*

40. See Fiske, "A Score for *The Duenna*"; Walsh, *Opera in Dublin*; Virga, *The American Opera to 1790*; Beechey, "Thomas Linley, Junior 1756–1778."

41. Performances of the three-act version occurred in Belfast (1760), Dublin (1762), and London (1764); the two-act version was first staged in London (1766). See Rubsamen, ed., *The Ballad Opera*, vol. 23.

42. Sear, "Charles Dibdin"; Hauger, "William Shield"; Fiske, "The Operas of Stephen Storace." See also Kelly, *Reminiscences*, which gives many interesting details on the state of the English stage at the end of the eighteenth century. Dibdin published a five-volume *History of the Stage* (1795), as well as memoirs and several novels.

of these three composers. His *Rosina* (1782) is an excellent example of the English comic opera of this period. Shield's librettos, like those of Storace (*The Haunted Tower*, 1789; *The Pirates*, 1792; *The Cherokee*, 1794), show an expansion of subject matter to include popular supernatural and adventurous tales in the early romantic taste. Storace's music betrays to some extent the influence of Mozart, especially in the use of the concerted finale (as in Act I of *The Pirates*). The comic opera was continued in the early nineteenth century by Sir Henry Rowley Bishop (1786–1855), of whose 120 dramatic compositions or arrangements nothing is known to present-day audiences but a setting of Shakespeare's "Lo, here the gentle lark" and the melody of "Home, sweet home," from the comic opera *Clari, the Maid of Milan* (1823).

English opera, unlike that of either Italy or France, remained a local development, with little influence on the course of serious opera anywhere. Although it flourished for a time in Ireland, most notably from 1770 to 1777, it was of greatest historical consequence for opera in the American colonies. Beginning in the 1730s, the majority of operas staged in America were either from England or written by Americans in the style of English opera. In a century which, to speak mildly, was not the Golden Age of British music, the ballad opera appeared as a vigorous but solitary gesture of revolt against foreign musical domination; but it lacked a principle of growth within itself, nor did external conditions favor the rise of an independent serious national opera on the basis of the popular comic-opera style.

The Singspiel

The collapse of German opera in the first half of the eighteenth century discouraged any systematic attempt at native musical drama for many years. Even the regular theater, though spurred on by the reforms of Gottsched, did not succeed in shaking off its baroque crudities and its later subservience to French tragedy until after the middle of the century. As for opera, with a few insignificant exceptions, nothing corresponding to the Italian opera seria or the French tragédie lyrique appeared. Yet the seeds of a new growth were present, and the soil in which they were to flourish was the same that had nurtured comic opera in Italy, France, and England—namely, the theater of the common people. Bands of strolling players discovered that they could attract larger audiences by mingling music with their plays, and so the new German singspiel arose, somewhat like the French opéra comique, as a spoken comedy with interspersed lyrical songs.[43] The latter, since they were to be performed by actors not skilled in music, had to be of the simplest possible kind. A model was at hand in the German "lied," which, from the publication of Sperontes' collection *Die Singende Muse an der Pleisse* (1736–1745), entered upon a revival destined to continue uninterruptedly through the century and eventually lead up to the works of Schubert.[44]

Although there were earlier instances of popular comic music in cantatas, school dramas, and intermezzi,[45] the first definite impulse to the new singspiel came from England. In 1743, Charles Coffey's ballad opera, *The Devil To Pay; or, The Wives Metamorphos'd*, was performed at Berlin, in German translation ("Der Teufel ist los; oder, Die verwandelten Weiber") but with the original English music as arranged by Seedo (ca. 1700-ca. 1754).[46] In a new arrangement by Christian Felix Weisse, and with new music by J. C. Standfuss,[47] it was given again at Leipzig in 1752 with great success. Another singspiel by Weisse and Standfuss, likewise based on a ballad opera, *The Merry Cobbler (Der lustige Schuster)*, was presented at Lübeck in 1759. The music of Standfuss is fresh and jolly, with the true breath of German folk song. His successor, and the most important early composer

43. Schletterer, *Das deutsche Singspiel*; Eitner, "Die deutsche komische Oper"; Lüthge, *Die deutsche Spieloper*.

44. Friedländer, *Das deutsche Lied im 18. Jahrhundert*; Kretzschmar, *Geschichte des neuen deutschen Liedes*.

45. Cf. Moser, *Geschichte der deutschen Musik*, 2:371; Schering, "Zwei Singspiele des Sperontes."

46. *The Devil To Pay*, in its shortened "afterpiece" version, enjoyed almost as much success as *The Beggar's Opera*. Its American premiere occurred in 1736 in Charleston, South Carolina, along with John Hipplesley's *Flora*, another highly successful ballad opera. For facsimile editions, see Rubsamen, ed., *The Ballad Opera*. See also Virga, *The American Opera to 1790*.

47. Calmus, *Die ersten deutschen Singspiele*; Minor, *Christian Felix Weisse*; Rubsamen, "Mr. Seedo, Ballad Opera, and the Singspiel."

of the singspiel, was Johann Adam Hiller (1728–1804), who was the first conductor of the famous Gewandhaus concerts at Leipzig and editor of an important musical periodical, the *Wöchentliche Nachrichten*.[48] Hiller's singspiels were produced in collaboration with Weisse at Leipzig, beginning with a new version of *Der Teufel ist los* in 1766 and climaxing with *Die Jagd* ("The Hunt") in 1770, the most popular German opera before Weber's *Der Freischütz*. Although Hiller's early works show some Italian influence, the music of *Die Jagd* is characteristically German; the score is filled with melodies of the purest folk-song type, contrasting (as in all his singspiels) with the intentionally more elaborate and Italianate arias which Hiller considered appropriate for kings and other highly placed characters.[49] Some of the songs, without departing from the prevailing simple style, have a sweep of line which almost reminds one of Beethoven (example 15.7). There are nine

Example 15.7: *Die Jagd*, Act II

ensembles, including three with chorus, and an orchestral "storm," in addition to the usual three-movement overture.

The success of Hiller's singspiels was not due to the music alone. Weisse's librettos, nearly every one adapted from contemporary French opéras comiques,[50] reflected the same preoc-

---

48. On Hiller, see his autobiography and the biography by Peiser; Calmus, *Die ersten deutschen Singspiele*.

49. The complete score and libretto for *Die Jagd* are included in Bauman, ed., *German Opera 1770–1800*. For a comprehensive study of North German opera composers, see Bauman, *North German Opera*.

50. The derivation of the principal librettos is as follows: *Lisuart und Dariolette* (1766) from Favart's *Fée Urgèle, ou Ce qui plait aux dames*, music by Duni, 1765; *Lottchen am Hofe* (1767) from Favart's *Ninette à la cour*, pasticcio, 1755; *Die Liebe auf dem Lande* (1768) from Mme Favart's *Annette et Lubin*, music mostly from vaudevilles, 1762, and Anseaume's *Clochette*, music by Duni, 1766; *Die Jagd* (1770) from Sedaine's *Le Roi et le fermier*, music by Monsigny, 1762; *Der Dorfbarbier* (1771) from Sedaine's *Blaise le savetier*, music by Philidor, 1759.

cupation with scenes and characters from common life, the same touches of romantic fancy, the same exaltation of sentiment and glorification of the peasantry, the same inevitable triumph of simple virtue over the wickedness of the nobles, and the same motif of devotion to the king as protector and father of the innocent— in short, all those ideas which made such a deep appeal to the feelings of the people in this prerevolutionary period and which made the comic opera of both nations a genuine popular manifestation. The folk basis is even more pronounced in Germany than in France; many of Hiller's melodies became national folk songs.[51] French opéras comiques, or translations and imitations, with the original music or in new settings by German composers, appeared in Germany with considerable frequency after 1770.[52] The growth of the singspiel went hand in hand with the ever-increasing popularity of the lied; authors and composers, professional and amateur alike, all over the country, joined in a universal outpouring of song; for sheer quantity, it was one of the most productive periods in the history of German music.

Two distinct branches of the singspiel developed. In the north, where the influence of Weisse and Hiller predominated, the literary framework remained that of the idyllic, sentimental, lyrical comedy on the model of the French opéra comique, with music of a simple melodic type closely allied to folk song. The adherence to a national musical language and the increase of romantic elements in the libretto led naturally in the nineteenth century to the romantic German opera of Weber.[53]

Of the many North German composers after Hiller, we may mention particularly Georg Benda (1722–1795), who was noted not only for his singspiels but also for his "melodramas."[54] A melodrama is a stage piece without singing, but with action and speaking by one or two performers accompanied by or alternating

51. Burney, *The Present State of Music in Germany*, 1:84; Hoffmann von Fallersleben, *Unsere volkstümlichen Lieder*, nos. 48, 265, 304, 947.

52. *Theater-Kalendar*, passim.

53. One example of this development is Kunzen's *Holger Danske* (Copenhagen, 1789), from Wieland's *Oberon*. See L. Schmidt, *Zur Geschichte der Märchenoper*.

54. See the studies by Hodermann and Brückner, and also Istel, *Die Entstehung des deutschen Melodrams*; musical examples in Martens, *Das Melodram*; Garrett, "Georg Benda."

with the orchestra (there may also be choral interludes). Rousseau had written a melodrama, *Pygmalion* (performed 1770, with music by Coignet),[55] but Benda's *Ariadne auf Naxos* (1775) was the first important German work in this form and had many successors.[56] The chief historical importance of the melodrama lay in the effective use made of the style by later composers for special scenes in opera: the grave-digging scene in *Fidelio* and the Wolf's Glen scene in *Der Freischütz* are familiar examples. Beethoven also has a melodrama in his music to *King Stephen*, and Schubert makes good use of the technique in his operas *Die Zauberharfe* and *Fierrabras*.

Other notable North German singspiels include *Die Dorfgala* ("The Village Festival," 1772) by Anton Schweitzer (1735–1787);[57] *Das tartarische Gesetz* ("The Law of the Tartars," 1789) by Johann André (1741–1799); and *Die Apotheke* ("The Apothecary," 1771) by Christian Gottlob Neefe (1748–1798), pupil of Hiller and teacher of Beethoven.[58] Johann Friedrich Reichardt (1752–1814), Goethe's favorite composer and an important figure in the history of German song, invented a new form which he called the *Liederspiel*, a comedy with familiar popular songs, similar to the early French vaudeville comedy or English ballad opera. Reichardt was also of some importance for the development of opera at Berlin; his *Claudine von Villa Bella* (Goethe's text) and his Italian opera *Brenno* were presented there in 1789. A revival of the latter in 1798, in translation and in concert form, was the first occasion on which opera was sung at Berlin with German words.

A Danish branch of the singspiel had as its leading composers Johann Abraham Peter Schulz (1747–1800) and Friedrich Ludwig Aemilius Kunzen (1761–1817). Two other composers prepared the way for Danish national opera in the nineteenth cen-

---

55. On the debated question of Rousseau's own music for his Pygmalion, see Istel, *Studien zur Geschichte des Melodrams*; Hirschberg, *Die Enzyklopädisten*, pp. 88–90; Mason, "The Melodrama in France."

56. A reproduction of the eighteenth-century publication of this one-act melodrama is in Bauman, ed., *German Opera 1770–1800*. See also Schletterer, *Das deutsche Singspiel*, p. 225; Subirá, *El compositor Iriarte*.

57. Maurer, *Anton Schweitzer als dramatischer Komponist*.

58. Leux, *Christian Gottlob Neefe*.

tury: Christoph Ernst Friedrich Weyse (1774–1842) and Friedrich Kuhlau (1786–1832).[59]

In South Germany, the singspiel took on a different character, owing in part to the strong influence of Italian opera buffa. The Viennese found the quiet, lyrical melodies of the north "too Lutheran" and demanded more liveliness and display. Hence, the librettos at Vienna tended to be gay and farcical, with not a hint of social significance; the supernatural, which in the north was an accepted means of romantic expression, here became usually an object of spectacle or of ridicule. A national opera theater, founded at Vienna by Emperor Josef II, was opened in 1778 with a performance of *Die Bergknappen* ("The Miners") by Ignaz Umlauf (1746–1796). A repertoire for this new theatre was quickly developed and included Umlauf's *Die schöne Schusterin* ("The Beautiful Shoemaker," 1779), Salieri's *Der Rauchfangkehrer* ("The Chimney Sweep," 1781), and, most importantly, Mozart's *Die Entführung aus dem Serail* (1782).[60]

The leading Viennese singspiel composer, however, was Karl Ditters von Dittersdorf (1739–1799), composer of fifteen Italian and twenty-nine German comic operas as well as a huge amount of symphonic and other instrumental music.[61] Dittersdorf's singspiels show traces of the Italian comic style in their vivacious rhythms, bravura passages, chromatic touches, short-phrased interjectional melodic lines, long ensembles which continue the action, and lively comic details of all sorts. Yet Dittersdorf is no mere imitator of the Italians; many of his melodies, as in his *Das rote Käppchen* ("The Little Red Cap," 1788), are unmistakably Viennese (example 15.8). His facility, energy, and humor, together with his melodic gift, his imaginative use of the orchestra, and his grasp of formal structure, make it easy to understand the

59. Krogh, *Zur Geschichte des dänischen Singspiels*; Behrend, "Weyse und Kuhlau"; Thrane, *Danske Komponister*.

60. On the history of the singspiel at Vienna, see R. Haas, introduction to Umlauf's *Bergknappen* in DTOe, vol. 18, Part 1; idem, "Die Musik in der Wiener deutscher Stegreifkomödie"; idem, "Wiener deutsche Parodieopern um 1730"; Helfert, "Zur Geschichte des Wiener Singspiels." For examples of the music, see (in addition to works of separate composers) *Deutsche Komödienarien 1754–1758* (DTOe, vol. 33) and Glossy and Haas, eds., *Wiener Komödienlieder*.

61. See Ditters von Dittersdorf's autobiography; also studies by Krebs, Holl, and Riedinger.

Example 15.8: *Das rote Käppchen*, Act II, finale

DITTERSDORF

1. Herr Schultz auf ein Wort warum bleibt er zu
2. Ich dan - ke fürs Es - sen, ich dan - ke fürs

Haus, und will nicht er - schei - nen beim heu - ti - gen Schmaus? Da
Trin-ken, wenn Män - ner be - trunk-en vom Stuhl her- ab sinken.

Orch.

mögt' es wohl ü - bel den Wei - bern er - geh'n,

mögt' es ü - bel den Wei - bern schon geh'n, doch

bleibt man zu Hau - se, da kann nichts ge - scheh'n

success of his works at Vienna and show him as a composer of comic opera not unworthy to be named along with Mozart.

Another composer associated with Vienna was Peter Winter (1754–1825),[62] whose Mozartean singspiel *Das unterbrochene Opferfest* ("The Interrupted Sacrificial Feast," 1796) was one of the most successful German operas to be staged in that city around the turn of the century. Other works in this genre include his *Der Bettelstudent oder Das Donnerwetter* ("The Beggar Student, or The Thunderstorm," 1785), fashioned from the writings of Cervantes, and *Der Sänger und der Schneider* ("The Singer and the Tailor," 1820), both of which were staged in Munich, where Winter was court conductor and Kapellmeister. Other Viennese singspiel composers were Johann Schenk (1753–1836),[63] whose *Dorfbarbier* ("The Village Barber," 1796) looks forward to the comic style of Lortzing; and Wenzel Müller (1767–1835),[64] in whose works there is apparent an increasing popularization of both libretto and musical idiom, in a manner destined to lead to the nineteenth-century Viennese operetta. The operetta is, indeed, the natural successor of the lighthearted melodious singspiel of the eighteenth century.

Early Spanish Opera

From its beginnings in the fifteenth century, the Spanish secular theater, like the Italian, called on music to adorn and supplement the spoken dialogue of its dramas.[65] Most of the plays of Juan del Encina (1469?-ca. 1529) end with a *villancico*, a little song for four voices (somewhat similar to the Italian *frottola*) which was both sung and danced.[66] The plays of Gil Vicente (d. 1557) and

62. For bibliographic references, see chap. 21.

63. Autobiography in *SzMw* (1924), 11:75-85.

64. See studies by Krone and Raab.

65. Shergold, *A History of the Spanish Stage.*

66. Examples of the music may be found in Asenjo y Barbieri, *Cancionero musical.* Cf. Subirá, *La participación musical*; Livermore, "The Spanish Dramatists"; Beau, "Die Musik im Werk des Gil Vicente."

Diego Sanchez de Badajoz (1479-ca. 1550) commonly used music, not only at the beginning and end but sometimes also intermingled with the action. In the sixteenth century also flourished the *ensalada* (literally "salad," that is, "hodgepodge"), a humorous type of piece reflecting popular scenes and character types and having many features in common with the Italian madrigal comedy.[67] Among the Spanish dramas of the next century, a few were sung throughout. The earliest was Lope de Vega's *La selva sin amor* ("The Forest Without Love," 1629), the music of which is not known.

During the Golden Age of Spanish drama, the seventeenth century, there arose the characteristic national *zarzuela*.[68] The name comes from the Palacio de la Zarzuela, a hunting lodge near Madrid which was refurbished by Philip IV in 1634. It housed a new theater, where pieces called *fiestas de la Zarzuela* were first performed. The zarzuela of this period, of which Pedro Calderón's *El golfo de las Sirenas* (1657) is a typical example, was in two acts,[69] usually on pastoral or mythological subjects and with emphasis on very elaborate scenic effects; it used spoken dialogue but also included much music, in the form of solos, dialogues, dances, and choruses. In general plan, it corresponded most closely to the contemporary comedy ballet of Molière and Lully, but its vitality and significance were greater. All the major Spanish playwrights of the seventeenth century interested themselves in the zarzuela and similar forms, such as the *comedia harmónica* (comedy with music), the *egloga* (pastorale), and the *auto sacramentale* (a religious play). Most of the musical scores of these plays seem to have been lost, and if we may judge from the published examples of those that survive, it is a loss greatly to be regretted.

An important zarzuela composer serving the court at Madrid during the seventeenth century was Juan Hidalgo (ca. 1612–1685). He is remembered especially for his collaborations with Calderón, but surviving examples of his music, beginning with *Triunfos de amor y fortuna* ("The Triumphs of Love and For-

---

67. See Mateo Flecha, *Las Ensaladas* (1581).

68. Cotarelo y Mori, *Historia de la zarzuela*; Sage, "Nouvelles lumières sur la genèse de l'opéra."

69. One-act zarzuelas appeared with some frequency after 1850.

tune," 1658), show that he also was associated with a number of other dramatists. Of particular interest is Hidalgo's music for Juan Vélez de Guevara's *Los celos hacen estrellas* (1672), one of the earliest zarzuelas for which most of the original music is extant.[70] Equally important is Hidalgo's setting of Calderón's *Celos aun del aire matan* ("Jealousy, Even of the Air, Kills," 1660), which is considered by many to be the earliest score available of a Spanish opera.[71] The music for this work in three acts consists chiefly of solo songs in through-composed or strophic forms *(coplas)* and simple songs in dancelike triple meter *(seguidillas)*, with frequently recurring themes connected by secco recitatives; there are also brief homophonic choruses.

Although Italian opera was known to Hidalgo, its influence upon his music was modest in comparison with that exercised by the zarzuelas of Sebastián Durón (1650–1720), who was appointed to the court as Hidalgo's successor in 1691. Durón's late-baroque style of writing contains a mixture of Spanish and Italian elements. Typically Spanish is his use of women instead of castrati to sing the male roles in the soprano range, his inclusion of guitars, castanets, and the *vihuela de arco* in the instrumental scoring, his continuation of the strophic forms for the solo songs, and his conspicuous flavoring of the musical fabric with syncopation (in a unique form of notation)[72] rhythmically suggestive of various Spanish dances. Balancing these indigenous traits are elements drawn from Italian opera which focused upon closer text-music relationships. They include instrumentally accompanied recitatives, bolder harmonic progressions in the basso continuo, melismatic rather than syllabic vocal lines, and the gradual introduction of da capo arias and concerted ensembles.

The historical career of the zarzuela is strikingly parallel to that of the national English and German operas of the same

70. Vélez de Guevara, *Los celos hacen estrellas.*

71. See the edition by Subirá. See also Ursprung, *"Celos"*; Pitts, "Don Juan Hidalgo." Some categorize this work as a zarzuela, and indeed a clear differentiation between the terms "opera" and "zarzuela" was not observed during this period. Calderón's *La púrpura de la rosa* (1660) was initially called an opera but later, when printed, was designated a "fiesta de la Zarzuela." For a discussion of the terminology, see Bussey, *French and Italian Influence on the Zarzuela,* chap. 1.

72. Bussey, *French and Italian Influence,* chap. 2.

period. In the course of the eighteenth century, after attaining the height of its first phase of development around 1700, the zarzuela was temporarily abandoned, owing to the popularity of Italian opera and drama in Madrid. Beginning in 1703 with the arrival of an Italian company of actors and continuing throughout the reign of Philip V (1700–1746), interest and support for Italian theatrical entertainment increased at the court while that for the *zarzuela heróica* declined.[73] By the 1760s, a reaction to foreign influence gave rise to a new spirit of nationalism which found expression in the *zarzuela burlesca* and the tonadilla.

The musical numbers in the zarzuelas and plays of the seventeenth and early eighteenth centuries appeared in various forms, some of which developed considerable importance of their own. Among these was the *entremés* (intermezzo), which was usually performed as an interlude between the acts of a play.[74] Frequently the entremés ended with a song called a tonadilla (diminutive of *tonada*, a word applied in the seventeenth century to a solo song with accompaniment). About the middle of the eighteenth century, this finale of the entremés, this tonadilla, began to be expanded to include two or more separate numbers, and even a little dramatic framework. Eventually the tonadilla, thus expanded, was detached from the entremés and launched on a career of its own; it flourished especially at Madrid throughout the second half of the eighteenth century as the national Spanish form, corresponding to the English ballad opera or the French opéra comique.[75] One of the earliest composers, though not the originator, of the tonadilla was Luis Misón (d. 1766), who established the independence of the form and the use of the orchestra for accompaniment. The chief later composers were Pablo Esteve y Grimau (d. 1794) and Blas de Laserna (1751–1816).[76]

The tonadilla was usually performed between the first

---

73. Cotarelo y Mori, *Orígenes*; Carmena y Millán, *Crónica de la ópera italiana*; Virella Cassañes, *La ópera en Barcelona*.

74. Cotarelo y Mori, ed., *Colección de entremeses*. The form was also known as a *sainete*.

75. The chief study of the tonadilla is Subirá, *La tonadilla escénica*, which contains many musical examples. Further examples may be found in the same author's *Tonadillas teatrales inéditas* and *Los maestros de la tonadilla escénica*. See also Nin, *Sept Chants lyriques* and *Sept Chansons*, and Pedrell, *Cancionero musical*, vol. 4, for modern editions.

76. See the biographical study of Blas de Laserna by Gómez.

and second acts of a comedy; it was seldom more than twenty minutes long and consisted almost entirely of solo songs or dialogues, sometimes with dancing, and with occasional short spoken phrases. The later tonadillas became longer and had a larger proportion of spoken parts, though they still kept to the basic plan

Example 15.9: Una mesoñera y un arriero, *(Tonadilla a duo)*

of a series of songs in contrasting tempos, with occasional duets or ensembles. There were no independent instrumental pieces, though a full orchestra was nearly always used for accompaniment. The cast of singers might comprise one to six persons, or even more in the *tonadilla generale*. The solo tonadillas were mostly on satirical or narrative texts; the others usually consisted of a short comic episode, with scenes and character types from familiar daily life, ending (especially in the later period) with a general moral reflection. In form, the tonadilla was divided into three parts, the *introducción, coplas,* and *final,* the last usually consisting of seguidillas of various types, which might be both sung and danced; seguidillas were also sometimes inserted in the coplas, the body of the tonadilla, by way of interludes.

The music of the early tonadillas was simple, tuneful, and with marked dancelike rhythms, closely derived from folk song, as can be seen in example 15.9, from Misón's *Una mesonera y un arriero* ("A Lady Innkeeper and a Muledriver," ca. 1757). Later it became slightly more sophisticated, often giving evidence of the popularity of Italian opera at Madrid by the inclusion of recitatives and arias in Italian style and even with Italian texts. By the nineteenth century, the national Spanish element had practically disappeared, being replaced by an imitation of Italian opera buffa music. Tonadillas were still produced during the first half of the nineteenth century, but the form finally gave way to a new type of zarzuela in about 1850 (see chapter 24).[77]

77. For studies of early Spanish opera, see Soriano Fuertes, *Historia de la música española;* Chavarri, *Historia de la música;* Mitjana y Gordón, "La Musique en Espagne" (with many musical examples), in Lavignac, *Encyclopédie,* 4:2003-2257; idem, *Histoire du développement du théâtre;* Pedrell, *Teatro lírico español* (many musical examples); Reiff, "Die Anfänge der Oper in Spanien"; Subirá, *La música en la casa de Alba;* idem, "Le Style dans la musique théâtrale espagnole"; idem, *Historia de la música teatral en España;* Chase, *The Music of Spain.*

CHAPTER SIXTEEN

The Operas of Mozart

Most opera composers have been specialists; Wolfgang Amadeus Mozart (1756–1791) was one of the few whose greatness was manifested equally in opera and in other branches of composition. His genius and training led him to conceive of opera as essentially a musical affair, like a symphony, rather than as a drama in which music was merely one means of dramatic expression. In this conception he was at one with the Italian composers of the day, and his work may be regarded in a sense as the ideal toward which the whole eighteenth-century Italian opera had been striving. He overtopped his predecessors not by a changed approach to opera but by the superior beauty, originality, and significance of his musical ideas, by his greater mastery of counterpoint, by his higher constructive powers, and by his ability to write music which not only perfectly portrayed a dramatic situation but at the same time could develop freely in a musical sense, without appearing to be in the least hampered by the presence of a text. The variety of musical forms in Mozart's operas, which can best be appreciated by an analysis of the scores, is paralleled by the skill with which these forms are adapted to the dramatic aims. In this rare combination of dramatic truth and musical beauty, there can be no doubt that the music is the important thing. Without it, none of the operas, except possibly *Figaro*, would be intelligible; with it, even *The Magic Flute* makes sense. So completely does the music absorb the drama, and so perfect is the music itself, that Mozart today not only holds the stage but offers the phenomenon of one composer whose operas are universally enjoyed by operagoers and music lovers alike.[1]

It is no disparagement of Mozart to remark that, like

1. For a comprehensive bibliography on Mozart, see Sadie, *The New Grove Mozart*. Some of the more important works for a study of Mozart's operas are: Köchel, *Chronologisch-*

many another great man, he was born at the right time. Everywhere there were producers ready to stage new operas and audiences ready to listen to them; the classical orchestra and orchestral style were well beyond the experimental stage; the art of singing, though beginning to decline, was still at a high level of virtuosity; the opera itself had the advantage of an established form within which recent developments—the innovations of Gluck, the vitality of opera buffa, and the growing interest in the German singspiel—offered stimulating possibilities to a composer. Mozart's operas were, on the whole, successful; if they did not obtain for him all the reward or recognition which their merits deserved, and for which he hoped, the fault lay not in the conditions of the time so much as in the fact that Mozart personally was always unfortunate in his adjustments to the patronage system and that the Viennese public, which might have sustained him, was not yet capable of appreciating those qualities which set him above Dittersdorf and other popular singspiel composers. In other words, Mozart was slightly in advance of his time, but he was no more a conscious revolutionist in opera than was Handel. His twenty-two dramatic works (twelve of them written before the age of twenty-five) include school dramas, serenatas, and Italian serious operas, but the greater part of his output is in the two fields most cultivated in the later eighteenth century, the Italian opera buffa and the German singspiel.

The Italian Operas

The predominance of an Italian background in Mozart's music is natural, since Italian music was the international standard of his time. The strong early influence of J. C. Bach (London,

thematisches Verzeichnis; H. Abert, *W. A. Mozart;* Einstein, *Mozart; Mozart: Die Dokumente seines Lebens; Mozart und seine Welt in zeitgenössischen Bildern;* Wyzewa and Saint-Foix, *W.-A. Mozart;* Anderson, ed., *The Letters of Mozart; Mozart: Briefe und Aufzeichnungen;* Lert, *Mozart auf dem Theater;* Conrad, *Mozarts Dramaturgie der Oper;* Dent, *Mozart's Operas* (both editions); Abraham, "The Operas"; Deutsch, *Mozart: A Documentary Biography;* Mann, *The Operas of Mozart;* Gianturco, *Mozart's Early Operas;* Lippmann, ed., *Colloquium;* Szabolcsi, "Mozart et la comédie populaire." See also the *Mozart-Jahrbuch* and *Neues Mozart-Jahrbuch.*

1764–65), the three Italian journeys of his boyhood, and a course of contrapuntal studies with Padre Martini in 1770 all strengthened this tendency. Among Mozart's childhood works was an Italian opera buffa, *La finta semplice* ("The Pretended Simpleton"), composed for Vienna in 1768 but not performed until the following year at Salzburg. At the age of fourteen, he composed his first opera seria, *Mitridate, rè di Ponto* ("Mithridates, King of Pontus"), which was performed at Milan in December 1770. Two years later, another work of the same type, *Lucio Silla*, was also produced at Milan. Both are on librettos of the conventional type established by Metastasio and are more remarkable as examples of Mozart's extraordinary precocity than for anything else. His aim—and the aim of his father, who still closely supervised his compositions—was to produce successful operas according to the current Italian standard. We marvel at the degree to which Mozart had assimilated the operatic manner of his time, but the whole effect is similar to that produced by any performance of a child prodigy: brilliant but inappropriate coloratura passages abound in these early scores, and there is little individuality of melody and nothing of the later variety of forms or, except in a few places, true characterization of the text. One aria in *Mitridate*, Aspasia's "Nel sen mi palpitar" (no. 4), foreshadows the Mozartean pathetic style; in *Lucio Silla*, the *ombra* scene with chorus (Act I, scenes 7–8) is an imaginative and even powerful treatment of the situation, while Cecilio's aria "Quest' improvviso tremito" (no. 9), with the preceding accompanied recitative, is an unusually dramatic solo in the grand style. The success of these early works was not great, and, though his interest in the form continued, it was nearly ten years before Mozart had the opportunity to compose another opera seria.

La finta giardiniera ("The Pretended Gardener"), produced at Munich in 1775, was an Italian opera buffa with a libretto that unhappily combined the new sentimental style of Goldoni's *La buona figliuola* with a complicated and cumbersome array of secondary characters, disguises, mistaken identities, and farcical episodes inherited from the older Italian comedy.[2] The music

2. The librettist has not been identified; attributions of authorship include Calzabigi, Coltellini, and Petrosellini. Cf. Angermüller, "Wer war der Librettist von *La finta giardiniera?*," and Gianturco, *Mozart's Early Operas*, chap. 10.

is only too faithful to the text, with the consequence that it not merely lacks dramatic continuity but presents the same characters at different moments in contradictory aspects. Tragedy and comedy rub shoulders, but there is no sign of the synthesis of the two which is so characteristic of Mozart's later dramatic works. Thus, the heroine Sandrina is presented in Act I (no. 4) as a superficial young girl of the usual comic-opera type but in Act II (nos. 21, 22) as a tragic figure appropriate to opera seria. Aside from such inconsistencies, which were so common in this period, the score of *La finta giardiniera* is extraordinarily attractive. The musical material is individual and is treated with imagination and humor. The serious portions mark an important advance in Mozart's handling of this type of expression, however out of place they are dramatically. Another notable feature is the finale of Act I, where the development of the action is combined with character differentiation and musical continuity, giving a foretaste of the finales of *Figaro* and *Don Giovanni*.[3]

The remaining early Italian works may be briefly noted here. *Ascanio in Alba* (Milan, 1771), a serenata in two parts, is notable for its choruses, dances, and accompanied recitatives.[4] The serenata *Il sogno di Scipione* ("The Dream of Scipio," Salzburg, 1772) and the festival opera *Il rè pastore* ("The Shepherd King," Salzburg, 1775) offer nothing of particular interest or significance in Mozart's development. They were occasional pieces composed as part of his duties in the service of the archiepiscopal court and (like many of their kind) were adequate but uninspired—with the exception of one aria with a solo violin obbli-

---

3. *La finta giardiniera* was translated into German and presented as a singspiel by traveling troupes, beginning around 1780. Spoken dialogue was substituted for the secco recitatives; the instrumentally accompanied recitatives were revised by Mozart to accommodate the German text. An eighteenth-century copy of this opera with Italian and German texts for all three acts has recently been discovered. See Gianturco, *Mozart's Early Operas*, and the introduction to *W. A. Mozart: Neue Ausgabe sämtlicher Werke*, ser. 2, vol. 5.

4. The terms "serenata," "cantata," "festa teatrale," and "azione teatrale" were used interchangeably in eighteenth-century writings. For example, *Ascanio in Alba* is subtitled "festa teatrale" by the librettist, Giuseppe Parini. Leopold Mozart, in a letter of July 19, 1771 (*Mozart: Briefe*, 1:424), referred to *Ascanio* as both a serenata and a theatrical cantata, and in a letter of August 31, 1771 (ibid., 1:436), he referred to it as both a serenata and an azione teatrale. Cf. Hortschansky, "Mozarts *Ascanio in Alba*," and Gianturco, *Mozart's Early Operas*, pp. 100–108.

gato, "L'amerò, sarò costante," in Act II of *Il rè pastore*, which is a lovely example of Mozart's lyrical powers.

The influence of Italian opera in Mozart's dramatic career was balanced and modified by his interest in symphonic music. Stemming from Italy and originally based to a large extent on the musical idiom and forms of Italian operas, the preclassical German symphony was at a flourishing stage when Mozart visited one of its chief centers, Mannheim, in 1777–78. Before this date he had already composed many symphonies, two of which especially (K. 183 and 201) showed a sure grasp of the form, but the works of Johann Stamitz and the Mannheim school were among the models which most influenced him in his mature years. His close association with Christian Cannabich (1731–1798), who had succeeded Stamitz as conductor of the famous Mannheim orchestra at the time of Mozart's visit, led to a deeper appreciation of the symphonic style and of the possibilities of orchestral manipulation in general. This is not the place to speak of Mozart as a symphonist, except to point out that his lifelong interest in and mastery of the larger instrumental forms are reflected on every page of his operas—in the way in which voices and instruments are adjusted to one another, in the texture and treatment of the orchestral parts (particularly the independence of the woodwinds), in the broadly symphonic overtures, and in the unerring sense of musical continuity extending over long and complex sections of the score.

At Mannheim Mozart also came into contact with German opera—not the singspiel but the new German opera, raising its head again after a forty-year sleep. In 1773, Wieland's *Alceste*, with music by Anton Schweitzer, was performed at Mannheim with such success that in January 1777 a second German opera, this time on a subject from German history, was presented: *Günther von Schwarzburg*, composed by Ignaz Holzbauer (1711–1783). Mozart wrote enthusiastically of Holzbauer's music, which is indeed fiery and spirited, though both it and the libretto show all too plainly the outlines of Italian opera seria. Neither Schweitzer nor Holzbauer was able to bring about a permanent awakening in Germany; the time was not ripe, and their works, although performed at Mannheim and in several other cities, remained only an episode in the history of national opera.[5] Yet the ideal persisted; Mozart's *Magic Flute*, which has strains reminiscent of *Günther*, was to be the first effective step toward its realization.

From Mannheim, Mozart journeyed to Paris, arriving in March 1778, in the midst of the Gluck-Piccinni controversy. An unknown young foreign musician, he attracted little attention—a disappointing contrast to his reception fifteen years before as a child prodigy. His temperament, converging with the anxious advice of his father, kept him aloof from the current quarrel. Moreover, the whole tone of musical life and society in Paris was discouraging to him, with its endless theorizing and debating about matters which he himself either understood quite simply as a musician or else felt to be of no importance. He had no sympathy for French opera and could not abide French singing; the opéra comique apparently did not interest him, and he does not seem to have made the acquaintance of Grétry. Plans for a French opera came to nothing, and the only theater music of this period was part of a ballet, *Les Petits Riens* (K. Suppl. 10), arranged by Noverre and performed in connection with one of Piccinni's operas. Mozart's joy over the success of his "Paris" Symphony (K. 297) was turned to sadness by the death of his mother; he left Paris in September and returned to Salzburg no richer in either money or prospects than when he had left. Yet the Paris visit was not without importance, for it helped to make Mozart for the first time more fully conscious of his own artistic aims and of his position as a composer in relation to the ideals of Gluck and the French school.

In 1780 came a welcome commission to provide an opera seria for Munich. The result was *Idomeneo, rè di Creta* ("Idomeneus, King of Crete," 1781), the first opera which shows Mozart in the fullness of his powers.[6] The libretto, on a subject first used by the French composer Campra in 1712, was written by the Abbé G. B. Varesco of Salzburg; it is of the old-fashioned Meta-

---

5. Their influence can be felt in Winter's *Das unterbrochene Opferfest* (1796), one of "the most successful German operas between *Zauberflöte* (1791) and *Freischütz* (1821)." See D. G. Henderson, "The *Magic Flute* of Peter Winter."

6. See Heartz, "The Genesis of Mozart's *Idomeneo*."

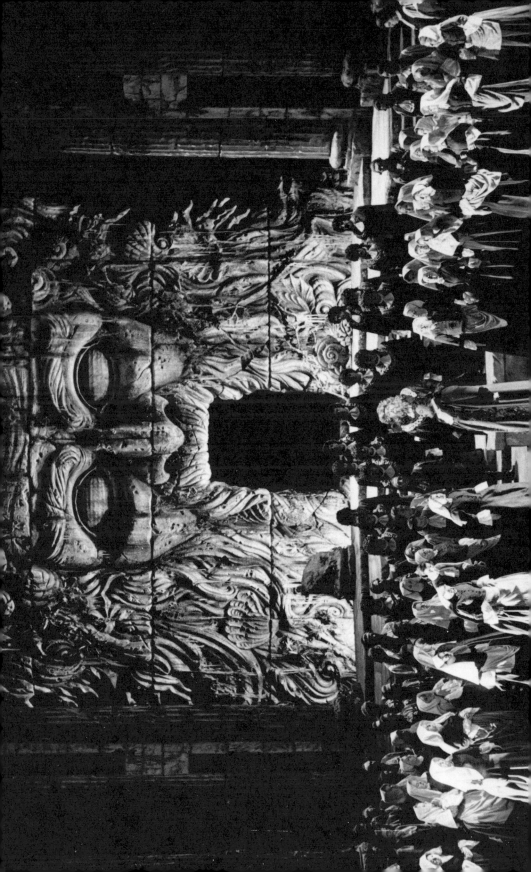

Scene from *Idomeneo* by W. A. Mozart; designed by Jean-Pierre Pon-
nelle for production at the Metropolitan Opera (New York 1982).

stasian type, on a classical subject with amorous intrigues, but including some large choral scenes in the newer style of Coltellini and Frugoni. The music also is old-fashioned in some external details; there is the conventional framework of recitatives alternating with arias, one of the principals is a male soprano, and there are many brilliant coloratura songs with improvised cadenzas, such as Idomeneo's comparison aria "Fuor del mar" in Act II and Electra's "Tutte nel cor vi sento" in Act I, which is especially notable for the striking effect made by the return of the first theme in C minor after the original statement in D minor.[7] Ensembles are few: two duets, one trio, and one quartet, this last considered by Mozart to be one of the finest numbers in the whole opera. In accordance with late eighteenth-century practice, there is relatively little secco recitative but a large number of accompanied recitatives; one of the best of these is the highly dramatic recognition scene between Idomeneo and his son Idamante in Act I ("Spietatissimi Dei"), a masterpiece of psychological perception and effective harmonic treatment.[8] Like the operas of Jommelli, Traetta, and Gluck, *Idomeneo* is filled with large scene-complexes built around recitative, with free musical and dramatic handling, often combined with spectacular effects—for example, the oracle scene in Act III. Many of these scenes introduce ballets, marches, and choruses.[9] The extent and importance of the choral portions are reminiscent of Rameau and Gluck: the last scene of Act I has a march and chorus (*ciacona*) which is similar to the choral scenes of older French operas, as is also the well-known chorus, "Placido è il mar, andiamo," in Act II. More like ancient Greek usage is the scene in Act III between Idomeneo and the chorus, in which the latter comments, warns, and expostulates. The most dramatic choral scene is that at the end of the second act, where the repeated cries of the chorus, "Il reo qual è?" ("Who is the guilty one?"), with the feeling of terror enforced by the strange, swiftly changing tonalities of the music, the tumult of the storm in the

7. The role of Idomeneo was sung by the tenor, Anton Raaff (1714–1797), whose advanced age caused problems for Mozart's setting of his aria texts. See Mann, *The Operas of Mozart*, chap. 13, and Heartz, "Raaff's Last Aria."

8. Here and throughout the opera, Mozart employs the tritone and diminished seventh chords to symbolize evil. See Heartz, "The Great Quartet in Mozart's *Idomeneo*."

9. Contrary to the usual practice of the period, Mozart himself composed the ballet music for *Idomeneo*, as he had done for *Ascanio in Alba*.

orchestra, Idomeneo's anguished confession, and the final disper-
sal and flight of the people all form a great and powerful finale
equal in force to anything of Gluck's and surpassing Gluck in
fertility of musical invention.

Mozart's understanding of the style of opera seria is seen
here in his treatment of the most traditional of operatic forms,
the aria, of which we may single out two examples for special
mention. Ilia's "Se il padre perdei" in Act II is a splendid example of Mozart's sensitiveness to details of the text, of his ability to
unite many different aspects of feeling in one basic mood, and of
his imaginative use of orchestral accompaniment for subtle psychological touches; and Ilia's third aria, "Zeffiretti lusinghieri,"
in Act III, brings a commonplace conceit of eighteenth-century
opera into a setting which simply transfigures the faded sentiments of the poem by the freshness of the music.

Nowhere in his operas did Mozart lavish more care on
the orchestral writing than in *Idomeneo*. This is seen especially in
the independence of the woodwinds and their frequent employment for the most subtle touches of color and expression.[10] The
overture at once sets the tone of lofty seriousness which prevails
throughout the opera. At the end, the music dies away with a
tonic pedal point, over which we hear in the woodwinds a series
of repetitions of a characteristic descending phrase which recurs
several times during the opera, alternating with rising scale-
passages; the final chord of D major, owing to the plagal harmonies, has the effect of a dominant in G, thus leading into the G
minor accompanied recitative with which the first act opens.

It is perfectly clear that in writing *Idomeneo* Mozart had
before his mind not only the most recent developments in the Italian opera seria but likewise the French operas of Gluck, with
which he was well acquainted. In many respects, *Idomeneo* is the
finest opera seria of the late eighteenth century; it shows that Mo-

---

10. Examples are the recurrent descending fifth in the oboes and bassoons in Ilia's aria
"Padre germani" (no. 1); the arpeggio figure for the flute in Electra's "Tutte nel cor vi
sento" (no. 4); the many expressive interludes for woodwinds in Ilia's "Se il padre perdei"
(no. 11), which seem to envelop the solo as if with phrases of consolation; the spirited
interplay of the voice with flutes and oboes in the coloratura passages of Idomeneo's "Fuor
del mar" (no. 12); the repetition of the climactic phrases of the chorus "Qual nuovo ter-
rore" (no. 17) by the brasses and woodwinds; the solemn chorus of trombones and horns
accompanying the voice of the Oracle (no. 28); and the effective contrast of the dominant
seventh chord for flutes, oboes, and bassoons which introduces the recitative immediately
following.

zart had fully appreciated the advances made by Jommelli, Traetta, and Sarti and thus marks an important stage in his own development over his youthful dismissal of Jommelli's *Armide* as "too serious and old-fashioned for the theater."[11] Mozart surpassed Jommelli not only in spontaneity, variety, and richness of invention but even more in his grasp of the emotional content of the text and in his incomparable power of musically characterizing both persons and situations. To the mastery of traditional outward forms he added the quality of psychological insight and a genius for expressing this insight in musical terms. Observing his treatment of the opera seria, we are made aware that a miracle is taking place: the two-dimensional figures of the old dramma per musica suddenly take on a new dimension, and we see them in depth and perspective. Yet all this did not amount to a fundamental reform. *Idomeneo* was not the starting point of a new evolution in opera seria but rather one of the last great examples of a form which was already on the decline.

The presence of choral scenes in *Idomeneo* does not indicate acceptance of Gluck's reform theories. Mozart simply adapted for his own purposes certain practices by which the leading Italian composers of the time were seeking to rejuvenate the opera seria. To regard him as in any sense a disciple of Gluck is to misunderstand both men. As a matter of fact, the contrast between two contemporary opera composers could hardly be greater. Gluck, at least as far as *Orfeo* and later works are concerned, was an artist to whom the conscious perception of aims and rational choice of means were necessary preliminaries to musical creation; every detail of his scores was the result of a previously thought-out plan, and he was always ready to justify his procedures by reference to his intentions. Mozart, on the other hand, was no philosopher; thought and realization were to him indivisible parts of the same creative process; his music was no less logical than Gluck's, but it was the logic of music, not something capable of being detached and discussed in relation to extra-musical conceptions. For him, "in an opera poetry must be altogether the obedient daughter of the music."[12] With Gluck the idea of the drama as a whole came first, and the music was written as

---

11. Anderson, ed., *Letters of Mozart*, 1:211; but cf. ibid., 1:208.
12. Ibid., 3:1150.

part of the means through which the idea was realized; with Mozart the idea took shape immediately and completely as music, the mental steps involved in the process being so smooth and so nearly instantaneous that he has often been called an "instinctive" composer, though that is incorrect—unless we choose to denote by the word "instinct" that sureness, clarity, and speed of reasoning which is characteristic of genius.

In addition to this difference of temperament, there was a fundamental difference between Gluck's and Mozart's conceptions of drama. Gluck's characters are generalized and typical rather than individual; they have a certain classic, superhuman stature; and as they are at the beginning of an opera, so they remain to the end. But Mozart's characters are human persons, each uniquely complex and depicted variously in changing moods rather than statically as a fixed bearer of certain qualities. It is for this reason that Mozart's operas seem to us modern while Gluck's seem old-fashioned; Gluck's dramatic psychology is that of the eighteenth century, while Mozart's is that of our own time. The symbols of the contrast are the Gluck chorus, in which the individual is submerged in the typical, and the Mozart ensemble, in which the individual is all the more sharply defined by means of interaction with other individuals.

Finally, Gluck's music, quite apart from any technical inferiority to Mozart's, is intentionally austere. Its appeal is not to the senses and emotions primarily, but to the entire "rational" man as the eighteenth century conceived him. Much of it therefore (though we must make important exceptions to this statement, especially in *Orfeo*) lacks those qualities of ease and spontaneity which are never absent from Mozart even in his least inspired moments. To appreciate Gluck, one needs to know something about the eighteenth century, but no comparable background is required in the case of Mozart.

With the exception of two unfinished pieces of 1783, Mozart's next Italian opera was *Le nozze di Figaro* ("The Marriage of Figaro"), first performed at Vienna on May 1, 1786. During the five years between *Idomeneo* and *Figaro*, Mozart had become acquainted with the music of Bach and Handel, and he had written *Die Entführung aus dem Serail* ("The Abduction from the Seraglio," 1782), the "Haffner" Symphony, the six "Haydn" quartets, and many of the great piano concertos. He was now a mature artist, at the height of his powers. Moreover, he had a libretto which combined comedy with excellent possibilities for character delineation. Beaumarchais's play *Le Mariage de Figaro* had been written in 1778 but owing to difficulties with the censorship at Paris was not performed until 1784. It was an immediate success, in part because the author had seasoned his comedy with the fashionable revolutionary doctrines of the time. The adaptation for Mozart's libretto was made by Lorenzo da Ponte (1749–1838), then imperial court poet at Vienna and a past master of the craft of writing for the theater.[13] The story is a sequel to Beaumarchais's *Le Barbier de Seville*, which had been so popular in Paisiello's setting four years previously. Needless to say, the subversive aspects of the plot were not unduly emphasized by Da Ponte or Mozart in an opera intended for Vienna, where Beaumarchais's play was still forbidden. The first performance was a great success,[14] and it was therefore all the more disappointing to Mozart that *Figaro* was soon displaced in the affections of the public by newer works—Dittersdorf's *Doktor und Apotheker* and *Una cosa rara* by the popular Spanish-Italian composer Vicente Martín y Soler (1754–1806),[15] which also had a libretto by Da Ponte.

No characters in any opera give more strongly the impression of being real persons than do Figaro and Susanna, the Count and Countess, Cherubino, and even the lesser figures of this score. It is therefore important to point out that this vividness of characterization is due not to Da Ponte or Beaumarchais but to Mozart, whose imagination conceived his characters not as stock figures in opera buffa going through a set of conventional antics travestied from the superficial aspects of current daily life, nor yet as social types in an eighteenth-century political pamphlet, but as human beings, each feeling, speaking, and behaving under certain vital circumstances very much as any other human being of like disposition would under similar conditions, whether

13. On the checkered career of Da Ponte, including the last thirty-three years of his life in the United States, see his *Memorie* (not always reliable) and Fitzlyon, *The Libertine Librettist*.

14. See Kelly, *Reminiscences*, 1:258ff.

15. Mooser, "Un Musicien espagnol en Russie"; idem, *Annales*, 2:455–61.

in the eighteenth century or the twentieth. Just how music succeeds in making us aware of this timeless quality is not easy to
describe, but no one who has read the libretto and then heard
the opera will deny that it does so. It is not merely that the words
are sung, or that through his control of tempo, pitch, and accent
the composer can suggest the inflections of speech necessary to a
given character at a given moment. The secret is rather in the
nature of music itself, in the form created by the extension of a
melodic line in time, and in the simultaneous harmonic combinations, rhythms, and colors of the supporting instruments—all of
which somehow, given a composer like Mozart, convey to us just
those things, inexpressible in words yet infinitely important, which
make the difference between a lifeless figure and a living being.
Consider, for example, the Countess's "Porgi amor" or Cherubino's "Non so più" or "Voi che sapete": note how little the words
alone tell us about the person, and how much the music.[16] Indeed,
it seems that with Cherubino (significant name!) Mozart has
achieved in music what Guillaume de Lorris is said to have achieved
in poetry, "that boy-like blending . . . of innocence and sen-
suousness which could make us believe for a moment that paradise had never been lost."[17]

One of the most remarkable things about the character
delineation in *Figaro* is that more of it is done in ensembles than
in solo arias. Nearly half the numbers in the score are ensembles,
a higher proportion than in the usual Italian opera buffa. The
technique of differentiating the persons is extremely subtle, de-
pending on details of rhythm, harmony, accompaniment, and the
register or even the tone of the voice, rather than on obviously
contrasting melodic lines. Moreover, it all takes place without
causing the slightest impediment to the music, which continues to
develop in its natural way all the time while carrying on the drama.

The highest examples of Mozart's skill are to be found
in the ensemble finales, in which no other composer before or
since has equaled him. This characteristic feature of the opera
buffa had attained by Mozart's time such a high degree of development that Da Ponte could describe it quite correctly as "a sort

16. Levarie, *Mozart's "Le Nozze di Figaro"*; Allanbrook, *Rhythmic Gesture in Mozart*;
Levallois and Souriau, "Caractérologie musicale."

17. Lewis, *The Allegory of Love*, p. 135.

of little comedy in itself,"[18] a section in which all the lines of the action were brought together and driven more and more swiftly to a climax or to the final solution of the plot, involving the appearance on the stage of all the characters, singly and in various combinations, but in increasing numbers and excitement as the end of the act approached. Mozart's music appropriately follows the general pattern indicated, but it differs from that of the typical Italian opera buffa in two important particulars. Whereas the Italian composers as a rule were concerned only with suggesting bustle and activity and exploiting in every way the often crude farcical elements of the finale, Mozart never loses sight of the individuality of his persons; humor is there in abundance, but it is a finer, more penetrating humor than that of the Italians, a humor of character more than of situations, with that intermingling of seriousness which is the mark of all great comedy. Then too, Mozart's music in these finales is not merely a succession of pieces in appropriate tempi but is truly symphonic—that is, a Mozart finale is a composition for voices and orchestra in several movements, with variety of texture within each movement, with the musical material developed by essentially the same technique as in a symphony, with a definite relation between principal and subordinate elements, and with continuity and unity arising from an overall plan of tempo successions and key relationships.

The total plan of the finale as a whole in Mozart is an interesting study. In the first finale of *Figaro*, the principal keys are:

E-flat   B-flat   G C F   B-flat   E-flat

In the last finale, the scheme is:

D G   E-flat   B-flat   G D

The last finale of *Così fan tutte* is more complicated both dramatically and tonally; it begins and ends in C, with the tonality strongly enforced by the dominant-tonic relation of the last two movements, but dwells on the minor mediant (E-flat) and related keys, with an excursion to E, A, and D in the middle. The first finale

18. Da Ponte, *Memoirs* (trans. by Abbott), p. 133. Cf. the tonadilla, which was "a little comedy in itself," growing out of a finale.

of *Don Giovanni* is tonally in rondo form, thus: tonic (C)—subdominant—tonic—dominant—tonic. The second finale is similar: tonic (D)—minor mediants—tonic (minor → major)—subdominant—tonic. The first finale of *The Magic Flute* has the key successions C, G, C, F, C, but with many connecting recitative passages and passing modulations; the second finale (E-flat) is remarkable for having no movement in the dominant, the emphasis instead being on the mediant keys of C and G. It may be noted incidentally that in every opera of Mozart from *Mitridate* on (with the exception of *Il rè pastore* and *Die Entführung*), the last finale is in the same key as the overture.

The unity within each single movement of a finale comes from its key scheme and from the use of a few simple rhythmic motifs throughout, generally in the orchestra. Forms within these movements are infinitely varied, but each is usually a complete unit; only exceptionally (for example, in the first finale of *Figaro*) is a particular theme or motif carried over from one movement to another. Each finale is a unique form, resulting from the translation of a dramatic action into symphonically conceived music by a master of that style. The finales are, consequently, invaluable sources for study of the principles—as distinct from the patterns—of symphonic form in the classical period.[19]

Although *Figaro* did not have a long run in Vienna, it met with an enthusiastic reception at Prague the following winter, and this resulted in a commission to Mozart for a new opera for that city. Da Ponte furnished the libretto for this new opera, *Il dissoluto punito, ossia: Il Don Giovanni* ("The Libertine Punished, or: Don Juan"), a dramma giocoso in two acts, first performed at Prague on October 29, 1787.[20] The ancient Don Juan legends have been used by playwrights and poets since the early seventeenth century—by Tirso de Molina, Molière, Shadwell, Goldoni, Byron, Lenau (whose poem furnished inspiration to R. Strauss), and Shaw, among others. Da Ponte took his version largely from a one-act comic opera, *Il convitato di pietra* ("The

19. This applies only to the Italian operas. The ensembles in *The Magic Flute* are, musically speaking, more in the nature of medleys than symphonic compositions. Cf. Lorenz, "Das Finale in Mozarts Meisteropern"; Engel, "Die Finali der Mozartschen Opern"; Rossell, "The Formal Construction of Mozart's Operatic Ensembles and Finales"; Heartz, "The Creation of the *buffo* Finale."

20. For a discussion of this term, cf. Noske, "*Don Giovanni:* An Interpretation," and Heartz, "Goldoni, Don Giovanni, and *Dramma Giocoso*."

Stone Guest"), by Giovanni Bertati with music by Giuseppe Gazzaniga (1743–1818), which had been first performed at Venice early in 1787.[21] This was the most recent of some half-dozen musical settings of the story in the eighteenth century before Mozart's.

It may seem strange that an action whose catastrophe shows divine vengeance overtaking a libertine and blasphemer should have been treated as a comedy; the reason lies not only in the obvious comic possibilities of the great lover's adventures but fully as much in the grotesque and fanciful aspects of the statue scenes and the final spectacular punishment of the hero. The legend has a dramatic weakness similar to that of Orpheus in that it is impossible to find a satisfactory ending: moral considerations require that the Don be punished, but unfortunately the spectators either feel so sternly about the matter that the customary lighthearted merrymaking of a closing buffo scene would be improper or else sympathize too strongly with the hero to rejoice at his fate. Da Ponte and Mozart compromised by using a device common in the opéra comique: a "closing moral," sung by the entire surviving cast, to the effect that the death which overtakes the wicked is a fit end to their misdeeds.[22] Another weakness of the Don Juan subject matter is that the only really necessary scenes are those in which the hero and the Commander are brought together—the duel, the cemetery scene, and the banquet. To fill out the opera, the librettist has to bring in a great deal of nonessential material. Mozart, however, turned this material to advantage by setting it to some of his most effective music, such as Leporello's "Catalogue" aria, Don Giovanni's "Champagne" aria and serenade ("Deh vieni alla finestra"), Ottavio's "Dalla sua pace" (a later addition to the score, which is unfortunately sometimes omitted in performance), Donna Anna's brilliant "Or sai chi l'onore," and Zerlina's "Batti, batti"—to mention only a few of the outstanding arias in a score particularly rich in unforgettable melodies.

The ensembles in *Don Giovanni* are less important than in *Figaro*. It is significant that not only the duet "Là ci darem la mano," the serenade trio "Ah taci, ingiusto core," and most of

21. See Chrysander, "Die Oper *Don Giovanni*," and cf. Heuss, "Mozart's *Idomeneo*"; Jouve, *Le Don Juan de Mozart*; H. Abert, *Mozart's "Don Giovanni"*; Rushton, *W. A. Mozart's "Don Giovanni"*.

22. On the romantic interpretations of *Don Giovanni* and various "improvements" on the closing scene, see Dent, *Mozart's Operas*, pp. 265ff. (1st ed.), pp. 177ff. (2nd ed.); E. T. A. Hoffmann, *"Don Giovanni"*; Kirkegaard, "The Immediate Stages of the Erotic."

the great sextet in Act II (which Dent conjectures may have been originally intended for one of the finales in a three-act version), but even considerable portions of both finales belong to the class of static ensembles; they are like the quintet in the third act of Wagner's *Die Meistersinger* or the canon in Beethoven's *Fidelio*, where the singing, instead of carrying on the action, is devoted to comment on or contemplation of the dramatic situation, developing its significance by means of music in a manner not possible in ordinary drama but eminently suitable to opera. One amusing touch in the last finale, comparable to the practice of representing actual persons among the figures of an imagined group in a painting, is the brief quotation of three melodies from popular operas of the day—Sarti's *Fra due litiganti il terzo gode*, Martin's *Cosa rara*, and Mozart's own *Figaro*. These inserts, for wind instruments, make a formal counterpart to the little dances in the first finale, which are played by strings.

Although it is misleading to regard *Don Giovanni* as a romantic opera in the nineteenth-century sense, nevertheless we cannot ignore one quality in the music which reveals Mozart in a different light from the all too common misconception of him as a merely elegant and graceful artificer in tones. The very opening measures of the overture—that "sound of dreadful joy to all musicians"—suggest at once the idea of the inexorable, superhuman power which opposes itself to the violent human passion of the hero. The overture does not outline the course of the action, nor does it aim to depict the details of Don Giovanni's character; it simply presents in monumental contrast the two opposing principles whose conflict is the essence of the drama. The demonic element of Mozart's genius is even more strongly evident in the cemetery scene and in the terrifying apparition of the Commander's statue in the last finale.[23] At these places Mozart follows a long tradition of opera by introducing the trombones. The irruption of this peculiar demonic quality in many of Mozart's late works—it is heard in some scenes of *The Magic Flute* and is even more striking in the *Requiem*—suggests interesting speculations as to the possible course of his artistic development had he lived long enough to be fully exposed to the forces which brought about the romantic movement in music in the early nineteenth century.

23. Cf. Heuss, "Das dämonische Element"; Clive, "The Demonic in Mozart."

Mozart's last comic opera was *Così fan tutte ossia La scuola degli amanti* ("Thus Do They All; or, The School for Lovers"), on an original libretto by Da Ponte, first performed at Vienna on January 26, 1790. It is an opera buffa in the Italian manner, with two pairs of lovers, a plot centering about mistaken identities, and a general air of lighthearted confusion and much ado about nothing, with a satisfactorily happy ending. The music is appropriately melodious and cheerful, rather in the vein of Cimarosa, with a large proportion of ensemble numbers. Nowhere does the music suggest that Mozart felt constrained by the somewhat commonplace, old-fashioned libretto; rather, it is as though he were playing with the traditional types and combinations of the opera buffa, making out of them a masterpiece of musical humor lightly touched with irony, avoiding vapid superficiality but never introducing a tone of inappropriate seriousness. The last finale is an especially fine example of his art, an apotheosis of the whole spirit of eighteenth-century comic opera.

If *Così fan tutte* was the very incarnation of opera buffa, *La clemenza di Tito* was only a shadow of the old opera seria, a form and style which Mozart had already long outgrown when he was commissioned to compose Metastasio's libretto (with substantial revision by C. Mazzolà) for the coronation of Leopold II at Prague on September 6, 1791.[24] Although the first performance engendered some criticism (especially from the empress), the opera later attained a considerable degree of popularity.[25] The whole score had been put together at a time when Mozart was preoccupied with work on *The Magic Flute* and the *Requiem*, suffering under financial distress, worried about the health of his wife, and already ill himself.[26] The wonder is that in such circumstances he could summon enough of his old powers of adaptability to produce music such as these arias and duets—music which has a certain stiff, old-fashioned nobility, appropriate to the formality of

24. The revisions involved a consolidation of three acts into two, the elimination of a number of arias, and a reworking of material to increase the number of ensembles (duets, trios, and finales).

25. Interest in this opera waned after 1830, and only recently has it once again found favor with scholars and producers alike; its first performance at the Metropolitan Opera was staged in 1984. See King, *Mozart in Retrospect*; Mann, *The Operas of Mozart*; Moberly, "The Influence of French Classical Drama."

26. The sequence in which Mozart, with the help of Süssmayr, composed the music of *La clemenza di Tito* is discussed in Tyson, "*La clemenza di Tito* and Its Chronology."

the occasion and of the libretto.[27] Of the ensembles, the finale of Act I (which begins "allegro" and ends "andante") is the most dramatic and is incidentally interesting on account of the use of the chorus as background for the soloists—a device which Mozart had not hitherto employed. No less interesting is the festive one-movement overture (composed by Mozart in Prague after he had completed the rest of the score), for here the essence of the opera—dramatic and musical—is captured within an instrumental form.[28]

The German Operas

Mozart's first singspiel was *Bastien und Bastienne*, composed at the age of twelve on a German translation of Favart's vaudeville comedy of 1753 (which in turn had been parodied from Rousseau's *Le devin du village*) and first performed at Vienna in the garden of Dr. Anton Mesmer, the famous hypnotist. The charming songlike melodies and the simplicity of the style, in which some influence of the French opéra comique composers is discernible, have kept this little work alive, and it is still occasionally heard. Mozart had no further occasion to compose theater music to German words until 1779, from which year we have the unfinished singspiel *Zaïde*, evidently intended for performance at Salzburg, and three choruses and five entr'actes for Gebler's play *Thamos, König in Aegypten* ("Thamos, King of Egypt"). Both these works are notable for employing the device of melodrama, which Benda had recently introduced in Germany. *Zaïde*, in both subject matter and musical style, is like a preliminary study for *Die Entführung aus dem Serail*. Mozart himself was particularly fond of the *Thamos* choruses, which have a dignity comparable to what is heard in Gluck and Rameau. (The same religious and mystical mood is heard again in the second act of *The Magic Flute*, which

27. See, for example, Sesto's aria "Deh, per questo istante solo" in Act II.

28. Cf. Floros, "Das 'Programm' in Mozarts Meisterouvertüren," and Heartz, "Mozart's Overture to *Titus*."

deals with similar subject matter.) *Der Schauspieldirektor* ("The Impresario," Vienna, 1786) was a little one-act comedy with music on the model of some of the early French opéras comiques, in which a rehearsal scene serves as a pretext to show off the talents of two rival women singers, who then fall to quarreling while a tenor tries to make peace. The closing number is a vaudeville finale (strophic solos with refrain), like the finale of *Die Entführung*. This piece also is occasionally revived.

What Mozart had done for the opera seria in *Idomeneo* and for the opera buffa in *Così fan tutti* he did for the German singspiel in *Die Entführung aus dem Serail*, which was performed at Vienna on July 16, 1782, with immediate success. The libretto, arranged by Gottlieb Stephanie (the Younger) from a play by Christoph Bretzner, makes use of the Turkish background which was so popular in eighteenth-century opera, both serious and comic.[29] It is not remarkable for originality but offers sufficient possibilities for effective musical setting, especially in the character of Osmin, to whom Mozart required Stephanie to give a much more conspicuous role than he had in the original play, and for whom he wrote two of the best comic bass arias in the whole realm of opera.[30] The music is somewhat inconsistent in style; the hero and heroine sing big arias of the Italian sort, while their two servants have simpler liedlike melodies—a division of labor quite in accordance with the theories of J. A. Hiller. Pedrillo's "romanza" (no. 18), a strophic ballad inserted in the action like "Que le sultan Saladin" in Grétry's *Richard*, has curious modulations by which Mozart perhaps intended to suggest oriental atmosphere. Other concessions to local color are found in the theme of the first chorus and in the addition of "Turkish" instruments (that is, piccolo, triangle, cymbals, and bass drum) to the orchestra for the overture, one duet, and two choruses of Janizaries. The ensembles are not to be compared in either dramatic or musical importance with those of the later Italian comic operas, since the action of *Die Entführung* takes place almost entirely in spoken dialogue. On

29. Cf. Gluck's *Rencontre imprévue*, the plot of which is almost identical with that of *Die Entführung*. See also Engländer, "Glucks *Cinesi*"; Preibisch, "Quellenstudien zu Mozarts *Entführung*"; Szabolsci, "Exoticisms in Mozart."

30. See Mozart's remarks about these arias and other numbers in *Die Entführung* in a letter to his father dated September 26, 1781 (Anderson, ed., *Letters*, no. 426).

the whole, the melodic line is less ornate than in the Italian operas, and the phrases are noticeably shorter and more regular, in conformity with the less flexible construction of the German poetry.

What Mozart accomplished in *Die Entführung* was to raise the Viennese singspiel at one stroke from a comparatively amateur level to a complex work of dramatic art, taking in (though, to be sure, not always fully assimilating) elements of Italian serious and comic opera and of French opéra comique, as well as the warmth and earnestness of German song. Moreover, he created a work which, whatever its stylistic inconsistencies, is fresh and youthful in inspiration, filled with vitality and beauty which have not faded to this day.

We come now to Mozart's last dramatic composition, that sphinx among operas, *Die Zauberflöte* ("The Magic Flute"), first performed on September 30, 1791. It was an immediate and lasting success in Vienna, thus realizing one of Mozart's deepest desires; unfortunately, he did not live to enjoy the triumph for long. The libretto at first sight presents an extraordinary jumble of persons and incidents. The explanation of this state of affairs is somewhat complicated and has been further complicated by various widespread but apocryphal stories about the circumstances under which the work was written.

The author (though even this point has been disputed) was Emanuel Schikaneder (1751–1812), an actor and manager whom Mozart had met at Salzburg in 1780.[31] Schikaneder was in charge of a theater (the Theater auf der Wieden) just outside the city walls of Vienna, where he offered to the public a mixed fare of singspiels and plays. Included in these were plots of fairy tales and magic adventure in exotic settings, featuring spectacular tableaux and scene-transformations and often spiced with allusions to current events and personalities in Viennese life. When Schikaneder proposed the subject of *The Magic Flute*, Mozart accepted it as an opportunity to create a real German opera; in the manuscript, it is called not a singspiel (despite its spoken dialogue) but a *"grosse Oper,"* something that might be translated as "grand opera" if that particular term had not been preempted by historians for a different use (see chapter 18).

31. See biography by Komorzyński (1951).

Schikaneder, a kind of literary magpie, filched characters, scenes, incidents, and situations from others' plays and with Mozart's assistance crammed them into a libretto that ranges all the way from buffoonery to high solemnity, from childish faërie to sublime human aspiration—from the circus to the temple, in short, but never neglecting an opportunity for effective theater along the way. One of the more puzzling features of this work is the way in which the "good" characters apparently change into "bad" ones, and vice versa, beginning with the closing scene of Act I. The explanation usually assumed is that Schikaneder and Mozart at this point suddenly decided, for no evident good reason, to reverse the plot and transform the entire character of the opera. But there is good weight of authority now to discredit this explanation or at least to restrict its scope.[32] In the first place, the inconsistencies between the earlier and later parts of the libretto are not so great as they appear at first sight, not greater than might be expected in a plot that moves altogether in an atmosphere of magic and the marvelous. In the second place, there is no evidence in Mozart's music that he felt a complete reversal of moral values was occurring at the end of Act I. It is rather as though the first part of the opera takes place in a neutral, one might say a premoral, realm; the appearance of Sarastro and the priests signifies the coming of higher, specifically human obligations, the transition from childhood to adulthood. Whether this new element came in as the result of a deliberate change of plan or had been tacitly foreseen from the beginning is a question that probably never will be finally answered.

One thing, however, is certain. Mozart and Schikaneder resolved to depict the realm of moral duties and virtues by means of Masonic symbols. Masonry was a force of great influence and considerable political importance in eighteenth-century Europe, counting among its members such distinguished men as Frederick the Great, Voltaire, Goethe, and Haydn. Both Mozart and Schikaneder were members of the Masonic order, and there is evidence in Mozart's correspondence and his music of the deep

---

32. The arguments on this point and other matters concerning the tangled history of *The Magic Flute* may be read in Dent, *Mozart's Opera "The Magic Flute"*; idem, *Mozart's Operas* (2nd ed.), pp. 209ff.; idem, "Emanuel Schikaneder"; Komorzyński, *Mozart*; idem, *Emmanuel Schikaneder* and *Emmanuel Schikaneder: Ein Beitrag*; idem, articles in *Neues Mozart-Jahrbuch* (1941) and *Mozart-Jahrbuch* (1952, 1953, and 1955).

impression its teachings had made upon him.[33] So the second act of *The Magic Flute* carries its hero Tamino and heroine Pamina through various solemn ordeals, undoubtedly veiled representations of the degrees of Masonic initiation, which they undergo successfully with the help of the priests and are then united.

One cannot hope to understand the libretto of *The Magic Flute* without a willingness to accept its externals as in some sense symbolical of profounder meanings. That such meanings exist is suggested by the respect this opera has always claimed from poets and philosophers as well as musicians. Goethe, for example, not only praised its theatrical effectiveness but also compared it with the second part of his *Faust* as a work "whose higher meaning will not escape the initiated."[34] Was this a reference simply to its Masonic features? Attempts have been made to interpret the opera in detail as representing not merely Masonic doctrines but actual persons and events associated with the lodges of Vienna in Mozart's time.[35] But such an interpretation, even if true, would not by itself account for the peculiar quality of the music. Equally inadmissible is the assumption that Mozart simply poured forth great music in serene disregard of the inconsistencies or frivolous details of the libretto. Such a view can only ignore his whole career as an opera composer, for he was never uncritical of his texts and was always making changes suggested by his own dramatic instinct or experience of the theater.[36] It is more reasonable to conclude that he saw in *The Magic Flute* an expression, partly in the guise of a fairy story and partly by means of Masonic or pseudo-Masonic symbols, of the same great ethical ideal of human ennoblement through enlightened striving in brotherhood which exer-

33. E.g., K. 468, 471, 477, 483, 484, 619, and 623; Anderson, ed., *Letters*, 3:1351. See also H. Abert, *W. A. Mozart*, 2:56–64; Deutsch, *Mozart und die Wiener Logen*; Nettl, *Mozart and Masonry*; Chailley, "*The Magic Flute*".

34. Eckermann, *Gespräche mit Goethe*, 1:175; see also ibid., 2:18. Goethe's second part of *The Magic Flute* was left unfinished for lack of a suitable composer; many of the ideas it contains reappear in the second part of *Faust*, which, itself strongly influenced by the form and style of opera, may be regarded historically as the link between *The Magic Flute* and Wagner's music dramas. See chap. 21 for comments on Winter's sequel to *The Magic Flute*.

35. Zille, "*Die Zauberflöte*."

36. See, for example, the letters exchanged between Mozart and his father during the composition and rehearsals of *Idomeneo* (Anderson, ed., *Letters*, 2:978–1051). See also Moberly, "Mozart and His Librettists."

cised such power over men's minds at the time of the French Revolution and which later inspired Beethoven's Ninth Symphony and the second part of Goethe's *Faust*. The exact interpretation of the significance of each person and event of the opera in this general plan must be largely a subjective matter. What concerns us here is that the idea itself operated so powerfully on Mozart that it not only enabled him to fuse all sorts of contradictory elements into unity—a trait which had always been fundamental to his genius—but furthermore compelled him to seek a new musical language for the stage. With the creation of that language, modern German opera was born. The way lay open to *Fidelio, Der Freischütz*, and the *Ring*.

When we look over the score of *The Magic Flute*, we are struck by the variety of musical types: simple, folklike, strophic songs, elaborate coloratura arias, ensembles, choruses, a chorale, and long accompanied recitatives—a diversity corresponding to the diversity of characters and scenes in the story. Yet in hearing the opera, we are conscious that it is a unit. This homogeneity results not only from the fundamental dramatic idea but also from musical factors. If one excepts the two arias for the Queen of the Night, in which the style of opera seria is adopted for dramatic reasons, the music is essentially German rather than Italian. Little attention is paid to merely picturesque details of the text, and sensuous appeal is treated not as an end in itself but as a means of expression. German folk-song quality is most apparent in the solos of Papageno (nos. 2, 20), in his duet with Pamina (no. 7), in the dance of the slaves (finale I), and in the duet ("Wir wandelten durch Feuergluten") sung by Pamina and Tamino in the last finale. Less naïve in language, more varied in form, richer in harmony, and filled with that combination of German fervor and Italian melodic charm which we recognize as peculiarly Mozartean are airs like Tamino's "Dies' Bildnis ist bezaubernd schön" (no. 3),[37] Sarastro's "In diesen heil'gen Hallen" (no. 15), and Pamina's "Ach, ich fühl's" (no. 17). The Dignified, earnest mood is especially felt in the march at the opening of Act II, the imme-

---

37. An instructive comparison may be made between this aria and one in the same key on a similar text in *La finta giardiniera*, "Welch ein Reiz in diesem Bilde" (Act I, no. 6). The resemblance of melodic outline in the themes makes the contrast in treatment all the more striking—Italian-style coloratura as against simple German melody.

diately following aria "O Isis und Osiris" with its choral refrain, and above all the choruses of the priests, to which the trombones lend a somber color. Elsewhere, too, the dark tone-color of the trombones, and of the bassett horns (tenor clarinets), is a striking feature of this score.[38] A contrasting, though equally original, color effect is heard in the trios for boys' voices at the beginning of each finale and in no. 16. In the duet of the armed men in the second finale, we have the chorale "Ach Gott vom Himmel sich' darein," sung in octaves and in a strict contrapuntal setting—a style novel in opera and producing here a climax of solemnity.

In the recitatives, Mozart solved a problem which the singspiel had hitherto avoided—namely, that of finding an appropriate musical declamation for German dialogue. In the long scene between Tamino and the High Priest in the first finale, we hear how the melodic line—now declamatory, now breaking forth in arioso phrases—is fitted to the accents and rhythm of the language and at the same time suggests most vividly the contrasted feelings of the two interlocutors. Not a note is wasted; there are no meaningless formulae; every phrase plays its part in the dramatic structure of the dialogue, to which the harmonic progressions also contribute a significant share.[39] Such recitative had not been heard in Germany since the time of Bach.

The unity arising from the pervasive national quality of the music is reinforced by various technical means, chief among which is the key scheme. The tonality of the opera as a whole is E-flat, and the principal related keys are the dominant, its dominant, and the two mediants. The first act begins and ends in C, with the middle section (nos. 3–7) in E-flat. The second act is divided, tonally, into three parts: nos. 9–13, C and its dominants; nos. 14–18, distant keys; nos. 19–21, returning to E-flat. The second finale is almost an epitome of the whole tonal plan: E-flat–Cm–F–C–G–C–G–Cm–E-flat.[40]

Particular dramatic significance, as Abert points out,[41]

---

38. Cf. Mozart's use of the basset horn in *La clemenza di Tito*.

39. This recitative may be compared with that preceding the Queen of the Night's first aria (no. 4), which is in the conventional Italian style.

40. Cf. the tonal plan of *La clemenza di Tito*, as discussed by Heartz in "Mozart's Overture to *Titus* as Dramatic Argument."

41. H. Abert, *W. A. Mozart*, 2:687, n. 4; see also Schmitz, "Formgesetze in Mozart's *Zauberflöte*."

attaches to certain keys: E-flat is consistently the tonality of the
basic dramatic idea of the opera, G major that of the comic persons, and G minor that of the expression of pain. F major is the
tonality of the "world of the priests," though also of Papageno's
merry song "Ein Mädchen oder Weibchen"; C minor is the key
of the "inimical dark powers" and also of the chorale.

Several motifs recur at different places in the opera and
thus contribute to the effect of unity. Most conspicuous is the
symbolic "threefold chord" of the overture, which we hear again
at particularly solemn moments in connection with Sarastro and
the ceremonies of initiation. The dotted rhythm of these chords
in some form or other is always associated with the priests, though
dotted rhythms are also employed in situations of danger for the
expression of fear or excitement. Phrases from Sarastro's "O Isis
und Osiris" appear in the quintet no. 5 (at "O Prinz, nimm dies'
Geschenk" and "Zauberflöten sind zu eurem Schutz vonnöthen")
and in the duet no. 7 (at "Wir leben durch die Lieb' allein"). The
opening phrase of "Dies' Bildnis ist bezaubernd schön" turns up
at a half-dozen unexpected places in the second finale. These and
similar melodic reminiscences are not to be regarded as leitmotifs
in the Wagnerian sense but as partly unconscious echoes of musical ideas which were in Mozart's mind throughout the composition of the opera. Such reminiscences, not only within a single
opera but also from one opera to another, are not infrequent in
Mozart; they seem to be motivated by corresponding resemblances of dramatic ideas or situations. Certain stylistic details in
The Magic Flute—the large proportion of themes built on notes
of the triad, the frequent use of first inversions, deceptive cadences, and the melodic interval of the seventh—may be further
mentioned as characteristic.[42]

In the operas of Mozart, the eighteenth and nineteenth
centuries meet. He brought into the inherited traditions, forms,
and musical language a new conception, that of the individual as
a proper subject for operatic treatment. His characters are viewed
from the point which most strongly emphasizes their individuality—namely, their love relationships. No composer has ever sung
of human love in such manifold aspects or with such psychological

---

42. See Chantavoine, *Mozart dans Mozart*; King, *Mozart in Retrospect*, chap. 9; E. Werner, "Leading or Symbolic Formulas in *The Magic Flute*"; Schmitz, "Formgesetze in Mozarts *Zauberflöte*"; Godwin, "Layers of Meaning in *The Magic Flute*."

penetration; and in every instance it is the person, not the abstract emotion, that is central. The change from the expression of an affect to the portrayal of a person is symbolized in the disappearance of the castrato, in the replacement of this impersonal instrument by the natural human voice. It is this shift of emphasis from the typical to the individual that most clearly separates Mozart from earlier opera composers of the eighteenth century and establishes his kinship with the romantics. When finally, as in *The Magic Flute*, sexual love is subordinated to a mystic ideal and the individual begins to be a symbol as well as a person, we may well feel that a path has been opened which will lead ultimately to the music drama of Wagner.

PART IV

The Nineteenth Century

CHAPTER SEVENTEEN

The Turn of the Century

French Operas

During the first half of the nineteenth century, Paris was virtually the European capital of opera. Not only did many composers of eminence live there, but even those residing elsewhere did not feel they had arrived until they had had a Paris success. The origin of this dominance goes back to the time of Gluck. Although Gluck's later operas had a delayed success in Germany and none at all in Italy, their style was so congenial to the French that it attracted disciples, through whom this style of opera maintained itself through the revolutionary period and blossomed anew in the days of the First Empire.

French fondness for public spectacles was gratified during the Revolution by the inauguration of magnificent national festivals, for which music was provided by composers such as Gossec, Méhul, Catel, Le Sueur, and Cherubini, largely in the form of huge choral numbers and "hymns" to be sung by the entire populace.[1] These festivals kept alive the demand for operas with similar large musical numbers and in this way formed a historical link between old French opera and the grand opera of the nineteenth century.[2]

---

1. Pierre, *Les Hymnes et chansons de la révolution*.

2. For a general survey of this period, see NOHM (1982), vol. 7. Facsimiles of opera scores by Cherubini, Auber, Méhul, Le Sueur, Halévy, and Spontini are in Gossett and Rosen, eds., *Early Romantic Opera*. See also Lang, "The Literary Aspects"; Garlington, "The Concept of the Marvelous"; Mongrédien, *Contribution à l'étude d'un demi-siècle de musique française*; Longyear, *Nineteenth-Century Romanticism in Music*; Plantinga, *Romantic Music*.

Maria Luigi Cherubini (1760–1842), a Florentine who had studied under Sarti, proved to be a master of counterpoint, an excellent church musician, and a gifted composer for the theater.[3] He had successfully produced a number of serious and comic operas in Italy and London before taking up residence in Paris, where, in 1788, he staged *Démophoön*, his first opera on a French libretto.[4] Although this work was a failure, due primarily to the ineptness of his setting of the French language, it nevertheless revealed an important aspect of his writing: the dramatic use of the orchestra. In the overture, the incidental music, and the accompaniment of the voices, the orchestra clarifies, intensifies, and even interrupts the dramatic action. Nowhere is this more poignantly felt than in Cherubini's *Médée* (1797). Based upon a classical subject (which shows that interest in this material did not necessarily wane during the Revolution), *Médée* is strongly reminiscent of Gluck in general plan and treatment, though in a musical idiom which is on the dividing line between classicism and romanticism, often suggesting the early style of Beethoven. This opera did not fare particularly well at Paris, but it was given frequently in Germany during the nineteenth century. It was heard in Italy for the first time only in 1909; in an Italian version, with recitatives added in place of the original spoken dialogue, *Médée* has since been revived with considerable success.

The dramatic intensity of Hoffman's libretto for *Medée* focuses unrelentingly upon Medea and demands a similar intensity in the musical setting. Cherubini responds with a score that conveys the unexpected. One of the criticisms voiced about this opera, and to a lesser extent about his other operas as well, was that the music was "overdeveloped," too heavy in texture—"too much accompaniment," Napoleon is said to have complained— and too slow in dramatic pace to be fully effective in the theater. Still, Cherubini was one of the most influential composers of the early nineteenth century; a conservative by nature, an admirer of

3. Biographies of Cherubini include those by Bellasis, Hohenemser, Schemann, Confalonieri, and Deane. See also Damerini, ed., *Luigi Cherubini*; Stomne, "The French Operas of Luigi Cherubini"; Selden, "Cherubini and England"; Kretzschmar, "Über die Bedeutung von Cherubinis Ouvertüren"; Willis, *Luigi Cherubini*.

4. For a facsimile edition of the printed score, see Gossett and Rosen, eds., *Early Romantic Opera*, vol. 32.

Mozart, distrusting Weber, and having apparently no under-standing whatever of the later Beethoven, he was nevertheless al-most universally admired by his professional contemporaries.

Cherubini's importance for the history of opera rests not only on *Médée* but also on four other works: *Lodoïska* (1791), *Eliza ou le Voyage aux glaciers du Mont S. Bernard* ("Eliza, or The Voyage to the Glaciers of Mt. St. Bernard," 1794), *Les Deux Journées* ("The Two Days," 1800), and *Faniska*, presented at Vi-enna in 1806, three months after the first performance of Bee-thoven's *Fidelio*. All four, like *Médée*, have spoken dialogue, and are of the type known as "rescue" operas, an earlier example of which we have already met in Grétry's *Richard*. The natural popular taste for this kind of plot was strengthened in the dis-turbed times of the Revolution, when hairbreadth escapes through the loyalty of friends or servants were of frequent actual occur-rence. The violent events and feelings of this period naturally stimulated the demand for plays and operas exploiting danger, suspense, and the thrilling last-minute rescue; and the emotion accumulated by all these events was discharged in impassioned appeals for the rights of man against tyranny and oppression. Thus, *Les Deux Journées*, for example, is filled with outbursts of the most exemplary sentiments of loyalty, kindness, and general devotion to the ideals of "humanity," with which the "good" characters of the libretto are fully identified.

This infusion into the librettos of a new spirit of ur-gency, of direct concern with the sentiments and the fate of recog-nizably "real" people, making the plot not a remote play of fancy to be enjoyed with detachment but something to grip a contem-porary auditor's feelings by making him think "this might hap-pen, even to me," and by voicing emotions that appealed to masses of people caught up in the excitement of revolutionary times—this kind of plot called for a new kind of musical expression. French critics tend to see in *Lodoïska* a landmark of early romantic style in opera, a work that "opened the way to Méhul, Le Sueur, and Spontini."[5] (See example 17.1)

Les Deux Journées had a successful run in Paris, and it was received even more warmly in Germany, where for many years

5. Clément, *Dictionnaire lyrique*, s.v. "Lodoïska."

Example 17.1: *Lodoïska*, Act II, sc. 1

CHERUBINI

(Example 17.1 continued)

(Example 17.1 continued)

it was performed, in translation, under the title of *Der Wasser-träger* ("The Water-Carrier"). Weber wrote enthusiastically about this opera and Beethoven was much impressed when he heard it at Vienna in 1803. The music consists mostly of ensemble numbers, which are developed usually at some length and with more regard for musical than dramatic considerations. The chorus of soldiers at the beginning of Act II was one of the most popular numbers of the opera, and the bridal chorus in Act III has a folklike quality similar to the bridal chorus in Weber's *Frei-schütz*. The score has two solo numbers, both positioned near the beginning of the opera. One of these is the romance of Anton ("Un Pauvre Petit Savoyard"), the refrain of which (example 17.2)

Example 17.2: *Les Deux Journées*, Act I

recurs several times in the course of the opera, like Blondel's song in *Richard Cœur-de-Lion*. Anton's song is a forerunner of numberless romances and ballads in nineteenth-century opera, including Senta's ballad in *The Flying Dutchman*, which has the same two-part structure and is even in the same key (G minor–G major). In addition to spoken dialogue and recitative, the device of melodrama is used very effectively and constitutes one of the more important features of this score.

One of the most typical rescue operas was *La Caverne*,

by Jean-François Le Sueur (1760–1837),[6] performed at Paris in 1793, the most terrible year of the Revolution. The eminently romantic nature of the plot—it includes a band of picaresque brigands and their mysterious and magnanimous chief—was to find an echo in many operas of the nineteenth century. Le Sueur's predilection for romantic subjects and for the supernatural is evident in some of his other operas, notably *Ossian, ou Les Bardes* (1804), a work highly praised by Napoleon but not overly successful with the critics and public of Paris. Characteristic of Le Sueur's operas are the recurring motifs, often associated with specific characters, as in *La mort d'Adam* ("The Death of Adam," 1809); the enormous performing forces, both vocal and instrumental; the elaborate stage machinery; and the unusual orchestral requirements. His other principal operas are *Télémaque* and *Paul et Virginie* (both 1794). But Le Sueur is remembered chiefly as the teacher of Berlioz, whose *Les Troyens* bears a marked resemblance to *Ossian*.

Another composer of the Revolutionary period was Etienne-Nicolas Méhul (1763–1817), who first turned to dramatic composition on the advice of Gluck.[7] During the two decades from 1790 to 1810, he produced about twenty-five opéras comiques, which show a wide variety of styles and many interesting experiments in orchestration.[8] His *Euphrosine, ou Le Tyran corrigé* ("Euphrosine; or, The Tyrant Rebuked," 1790), with its touch of comedy, was highly praised by Grétry. This work, in its revised form,[9] and *Stratonice* (1792) were important in establishing a type of opéra comique on serious subjects, approaching the musical style of ordinary opera in all respects save for the use of spoken dialogue. The chief works of the following years were *Ariodant* (1799), especially notable for its chromatic harmonies and for its

6. See biographies by Buschkötter and Lamy. See also Fouque, "Le Sueur comme prédécesseur de Berlioz"; Coults, "Jean-François Le Sueur"; Saloman, "Aspects of 'Gluckian' Operatic Thought"; Charlton, *"Ossian"*; Mongrédien, *Catalogue thématique*.

7. See biographies by Pougin and Brancour, and see also Strobel, "Die Opern von E. N. Méhul"; Dean, "Opera Under the French Revolution."

8. The overtures exemplify these experiments in scoring *(Ariodant* and Uthal) and characterization (*Le jeune sage et le vieux fou*, 1793).

9. The revision was in two stages: the original five acts were reduced to three sometime before 1793, and a completely new third act (in which the comedy was eliminated) was supplied by 1795. See NOHM, 7:47, n. 1.

systematic use of a musical leitmotif associated with the central idea of the opera and recurring throughout the work in different scenes;[10] *Une Folie* (1802), Méhul's most popular work in purely comic vein; and *Uthal* (1806), a one-act opera on a subject from Ossian, in which the orchestration is designed to evoke a dark, primeval world.

Méhul's most celebrated opera was *Joseph* (1807), one of the rare examples in the history of opera of a biblical subject treated with good taste and at the same time with real dramatic force.[11] It has no feminine characters, though the part of Benjamin is sung by a soprano and women's voices are heard in many of the choruses. The most noticeable characteristic of the music is the happy combination of classical severity, as in the overture and the chorus "Dieu d'Israël" (on a plainsong motif), with a simple and touching melodic expressiveness in the solos, especially in the two romances of Joseph and Benjamin. Many of the harmonic and rhythmic patterns recall the style of Gluck, but there is throughout a certain personal, direct quality, a rather naïve appeal to the tender emotions, which makes this score another interesting example of the transitional period between classicism and romanticism in music.

Opera in the grand manner attained a climax in the First Empire with the works of Napoleon's favorite composer, Gasparo Spontini (1774–1851), whose masterpiece, *La Vestale* ("The Vestal Virgin,"), triumphed at Paris in 1807 and remained in the repertoire of opera companies almost to the present day.[12] The success of *La Vestale* was due in part to a brilliant libretto by Etienne Jouy, which combined the old rescue motif and a passionate love story with the solemnity of the tragédie lyrique on a huge scale, adding a strong touch of the melodramatic. The many spectacular crowd scenes are climaxed in the third act, where a bolt of lightning rekindles the fire on the altar of Vesta to establish the innocence of Julia, the heroine, and lead to the happy ending.

10. See Bücken, *Der heroische Stil in der Oper*, pp. 81–83.

11. Another is Rossini's *Moïse en Egypte* (Paris version of 1827).

12. See biographies by Ghislanzoni and Fragapane, and see also Belardinelli, ed., *Documenti Spontiniani inedite*; Wagner, "Erinnerungen an Spontini," in his *Gesammelte Schriften*, 5:86–104.

The music, which Spontini revised many times during the rehearsals, was at first condemned by the Opéra jury as "bizarre, defective, and noisy," and the personal intervention of Empress Josephine was required to bring about the performance. It is one of the most effective operas ever written from the theatrical point of view, every opportunity offered by the libretto being exploited to the utmost. The score abounds in beautiful solos and ensembles, the choral numbers are built on a massive scale, and the orchestration is full of fine details. That the music now seems somewhat old-fashioned may be explained in part by the rather stodgy harmonic structure, ponderously swinging between tonic and dominant, while the melodic line flows above in regular, often singsong rhythms, dividing by triplets or dotted figures, with a strong beat invariably at the beginning of each measure. "Expressive" appoggiaturas, often on chromatic tones, are a constant feature. Even where the harmonic rhythm is quickened, as in passages of excitement, the rising sequential phrases and the usual diminished seventh chord at the climax are devices which have lost much of their effect for modern ears.

The second act of *La Vestale* contains the most celebrated numbers of the opera, among which may be mentioned especially Julia's aria "Impitoyables Dieux" (no. 9), Licinius' "Les Dieux prendront pitié" (no. 10), and Julia's solo at the beginning of the finale, "O des infortunés." The finale itself attains a thrilling climax by sheer weight of numbers of volume of sound, intensified at the close by a stretto, that is, an acceleration of the tempo—an effect then relatively new, though later overworked in the operas of Meyerbeer.

The success of *La Vestale* was not equaled two years later by *Fernand Cortez*, which Spontini revived with important changes in 1817. The libretto is not as good as that of *La Vestale*, and the musical style is less even; there are some passages of real distinction (example 17.3) but also many trivial tunes where the poverty of melodic and harmonic invention suggests nineteenth-century Italian opera at its worst. A third work, *Olympie* (1819), long in composition and subjected to many revisions, was slow in making its way at Paris, though it found some favor at Berlin, where Spontini was conductor of the opera and a consequential figure in German musical life from 1819 to 1841. During this time, his only

Example 17.3: *Fernand Cortez*, Act III

important dramatic composition was *Agnes von Hohenstaufen* (1827, revised 1837), his last completed opera.

Spontini was the last of the great opera composers in whose music the dramatic methods of Gluck were still of living force.[13] Although his Parisian masterworks may be regarded as the starting point of the Meyerbeer type of grand opera, Spontini has by comparison a certain restraint, an artistic integrity which keeps sensational elements within bounds and never allows the dramatic purpose to be overwhelmed by irrelevant theatrical or musical effects. His style, despite its pompous rhetoric, has a unity, a massiveness, and a fundamental simplicity which are closer to the classic than to the romantic spirit.

In what sense can the French operas of the period 1790–1815 be called "romantic"?[14] In considering this question, it is important to remember three related social factors: first, the breakdown or at least the radical transformation of many old traditions under the impact of revolutionary ideas; second, the rapid increase of middle-class audiences for opera; and third, the gen-

13. Wagner, *Gesammelte Schriften*, vol. 5, praises Spontini for achieving what Gluck had only dreamed of: a seamless operatic design.

14. See Dent, *The Rise of the Romantic Opera*, chaps. 1–7, 12.

eral intensification of emotion in a long-continued atmosphere of national excitement. To these may be added, under the Empire, the position of Napoleon as patron, toward whom Spontini had much the same sort of relation that Lully had had toward Louis XIV. The grandiose sentiments and the colossal style in French opera of this whole period were largely motivated by the desire to glorify the Revolution, the nation, or the Empire, using for this purpose the traditional form of opera with huge spectacular and choral scenes, a form already long established in France by Lully, Rameau, and Gluck.

But the grandiose, whether in sentiment or in outward form, was not the only characteristic of French opera around the turn of the century. More specifically romantic was the intermixture, in both libretto and music, of elements formerly thought to be incongruous. We have already seen how everywhere in the latter part of the eighteenth century the comic and the serious opera tended to approach one another in style and eventually to merge, as in Mozart's "dramma giocoso" *Don Giovanni* or in *The Magic Flute*, which is a synthesis of many apparently discordant elements. So likewise in French opera of the 1790s we find similar incongruities: the form of the opéra comique (that is, spoken dialogue instead of recitative) used for deadly serious plots—which, however, admit occasional comic scenes and characters; musical numbers in the grand style of the tragédie lyrique side by side with the simple popular song types of the *romance* and *couplets*;[15] magic happenings involving ordinary people and being mixed up with everyday occurrences instead of being relegated to a realm of pure make-believe, as in the eighteenth century; and Christian religious ceremonies and prayers brought onto the stage as a means of theatrical effect. (The prayer in Act III of Méhul's *Mélidor et Phrosine* [1794] is one of the first of a long line of *prière* scenes stretching through the opera of the nineteenth century.) Some elements in the librettos of late eighteenth-century French opera that we may be inclined to think of as particularly romantic—forests, caverns, wild landscapes, storms—are in fact equally common in

---

15. The *romance* is a brief song or instrumental piece having a naïve and graceful character. The *couplets* were originally verses (spoken or sung) inserted in spoken prose dialogue; and thence, a song in popular style, more sophisticated than a *romance*, usually strophic and with a refrain, inserted as a separate number in an opera.

operas of the seventeenth and early eighteenth centuries; the difference is that in the earlier period they were mere decorative background, whereas later they became an essential ingredient in the setting of the plot. The same applies to exoticisms and "local color." An example of the latter was the Swiss mountain setting of Cherubini's *Eliza* (1794); Grétry had used the same background in his *Guillaume Tell* of 1791, and Rossini was to make the most of it in his own opera of the same title in 1829.

It is evident from the foregoing that one cannot easily isolate any single element of the libretto in French opera at the turn of the century and simply say of it, *"This* is romantic." It is in the peculiar combination of the elements and the peculiar function of each in the whole pattern that the romantic quality consists. Much the same may be said of the music. The mixture of musical styles has already been mentioned; popular idioms had long been familiar in comic opera of the eighteenth century, and the only difference now was that these idioms were incorporated into serious opera and in consequence came to be regarded as serious music. Their presence may also be explained in part by reference to the new middle-class audience for opera. This factor, however, is more important in explaining one feature of the music, especially of Cherubini's music, that has become a common subject of present-day criticism, which alleges that the musical ideas are spread too thin, that too much time is taken up with reiterating the obvious and repeating musical clichés. Such criticism is natural to us because we have long since become accustomed to the more concentrated musical style of Mozart and Beethoven, beside whom Cherubini seems unbearably diffuse. But to audiences of the 1790s, for many of whom listening to music of any complexity at all must have been an unfamiliar experience, the thinner, spread-out style of Cherubini and his operatic contemporaries was well adapted; indeed, the very concentration of Mozart's and Beethoven's language was probably one of the factors that operated against an immediate popular success for *Don Giovanni* and *Fidelio.*

Other features in the French opera of this period may be pointed out as being romantic at least in the sense that they were imitated by later nineteenth-century composers. One of these is the large proportion of ensembles and choruses. The former, of

course, came from the Italian opera buffa and the latter from the
French serious opera of Rameau and Gluck. It is significant that
the ensembles and choruses in these French operas at the turn of
the century were often admired far more than the solo numbers.
The solos are, in fact, usually conventional, often declamatory in
style, lacking both the melodic suavity and the coloratura embellishments of Italian arias, but intended to be sung with intense
feeling, a manner of delivery suggested by the occasional directions *"très-concentré"* or *"voix concentrée"* in the score of Le
Sueur's *Télémaque*. Another romantic trait in these operas is the
presence of long descriptive instrumental "symphonies" for scenes
of battles, storms, conflagrations, and the like; these descriptive
symphonies are a heritage from earlier French opera, but they
become much more extensive and important toward the end of
the century. More particularly romantic in the scores of Cherubini and Méhul are occasional touches of special orchestral color—
long solo phrases for flute or horn, cantabile melodies for the
clarinet, the ensemble of harps in Le Sueur's *Ossian*, or the string
section without violins of Méhul's *Uthal*. Finally may be mentioned anticipations of romantic harmony, in the shape of chro-
maticisms or unexpected modulations (although some of Le Sueur's
strange harmonies are probably due to his thinking that he was
writing in the Greek modes).

It must be recalled that the French operas we have been
considering were not confined to France; they occasionally reached
Italy but most of them were much more widely known and more
often performed in German cities than in Paris. The influence of
Cherubini, Méhul, and Spontini on the development of German
romantic opera was considerable; in particular, the rescue opera
of the French revolutionary period was the model for one of the
most important operas of the early nineteenth century, which has
remained in the performing repertoire to the present day.

Beethoven's Fidelio

When Cherubini's operas came to Vienna, Ludwig van Beethoven
(1770--1827) was in search of a libretto for himself. There was,

in fact, hardly a year between 1800 and 1815 that he did not dally with some operatic proposal. In 1803, he had begun work on a libretto by Schikaneder, *Vestas Feuer* ("The Vestal Fire"), some of the music of which he later incorporated in *Fidelio*. His continuing interest in the theater is evidenced not only by this and other abortive projects but also by such works as the ballet *Prometheus* (1801) and the incidental music to plays *(König Stephan, Egmont, Coriolanus)*. His aptitude for dramatic writing was proved in the oratorio *Christus am Ölberg* (1803). But Beethoven was a difficult man to please. He could not bring himself to compose music to the usual buffo libretto and constantly refused any drama which did not conform to his own high standards of the proper subject matter for serious works. He rejected in principle all "magic" subjects and condemned on moral grounds the texts of *Don Giovanni* and *Figaro*. In his opinion, the two best opera librettos were *La Vestale* and *Les Deux Journées*.

This preference brings into relief one characteristic of Beethoven's which is important for the understanding of *Fidelio*. We have already observed that among the effects of the French Revolution on opera were the popularization of the grand style and the demand for dramatic tension, suspense, and strong feeling which brought the typical rescue plot into such favor. But another, even more far-reaching effect came from the tremendous liberation of humanitarian idealism all over Europe at this period. The theories of the eighteenth-century Enlightenment suddenly ceased to be playthings of philosophers, orators, and dramatists and became explosive realities of life, ideas to which powerful emotions were attached, capable of inspiring enthusiasm. Their effect on the music of the early nineteenth century in general and that of Beethoven in particular cannot be ignored.

Fidelio, with its themes of unselfish love, loyalty, courage, sacrifice, and heroic endurance, appealed so strongly to the idealism of Beethoven that he was perhaps blind to the technical faults of the drama. The original French libretto, by Jean Nicolas Bouilly (author of *Les Deux Journées*), under the title *Léonore, ou l'Amour conjugal* ("Leonora, or Married Love"), had been set to music by Pierre Gaveaux in 1798; the German version of Beethoven was prepared by Joseph Ferdinand Sonnleithner. The opera was first performed on November 20, 1805, at Vienna. It was a comparative failure, partly owing to disturbed political conditions and partly because it was too long and not well arranged. Beethoven was persuaded to make some cuts and changes, and the opera was produced again the following spring, but the composer withdrew it after only two performances. In 1814, the libretto was completely revised by G. F. Treitschke, and in this final setting began its successful career.

The outline of the plot, said to be based on an actual event of the French Revolution, is as follows: Florestan has been unjustly imprisoned. His wife, Leonora, disguised as a man under the name of Fidelio, obtains the post of assistant to Rocco, the jailer. There are two subsidiary characters: the jailer's daughter, Marzelline, and her suitor, the porter Jaquino. Pizarro, governor of the prison, has been warned that Don Fernando, the minister of state, is coming to investigate the cases of the prisoners. Pizarro thereupon determines to murder Florestan, but Leonora prevents him. At that moment, Don Fernando arrives, sets Florestan free, and punishes Pizarro.

Fidelio is thus a rescue opera, and the customary touch of horror is introduced by means of an episode in which Rocco and Fidelio are depicted digging a grave for the doomed prisoner (Beethoven opens this scene very effectively with a melodrama). The whole of the dungeon scene, in which Leonora saves Florestan's life, with the superbly theatrical detail of the trumpet call announcing the arrival of Fernando, realizes to the full the suspense and excitement which all opera composers of the time sought. Even the spoken dialogue, so often a stumbling block, is turned to good account. The entrance of Jaquino, the porter, at the climax of this scene, with his excited words, provides an element of almost comic relief after the unbearable tension of the preceding action—one of Beethoven's Shakespearean effects, comparable to the introduction of the Turkish music in the finale of the Ninth Symphony. The characters of Marzelline and Jaquino are descendants of the servant lover pair of eighteenth-century comic operas, and in Fernando we have an echo of the magnanimous king in Metastasio's operas. The significant characters are three: Pizarro, the thoroughly wicked man; Florestan, the just man suffering undeserved cruelty; and above all Leonora, the devoted and courageous wife, one of the truly great heroines of opera. It is obvious from the music that it was these three persons, and the situations arising from their interrelations, that chiefly fired Beethoven's imagination.

The music of *Fidelio* is unique in opera. Every measure bears the stamp of Beethoven's high purpose and painstaking care in composition. The score was a labor of love, but a labor nonetheless, as the endless revisions testify; the introduction to Florestan's aria at the beginning of Act II, for example, was changed at least eighteen times before reaching its final form. All this is a striking contrast to the facility of a composer like Mozart, not to mention the Italian opera composers of both the eighteenth and nineteenth centuries. To be sure, Beethoven was notorious for revising and working over his material, and the composition of any important work was a struggle with him; but *Fidelio* gave him even more trouble than usual. Part of the difficulty was no doubt due to Beethoven's lack of experience with opera; still more may be attributed to the fact that he was not a natural opera composer. It was only by an effort that his mind could concern itself with details of action or characterization that did not form part of the larger ethical and musical plan of the work. Take, for example, Rocco's aria in Act I, "Hat man auch nicht Geld beineben," the burden of which is that money is more necessary than love for a happy marriage. To this banal proposition, Beethoven did his best to write a comic bass aria in the general style of the Viennese singspiel. It cannot be denied that he succeeded, but the effect on the listener is, in a peculiar way, painful, like the spectacle of a profound thinker with no gift of small talk trying to enter cheerfully into a conversation on trivial topics. To save himself from boredom, and because he cannot help it, he pursues and develops ideas in a manner so superior to that of the company in which he finds himself that he remains, despite the most conscientious effort, an outsider. Thus, the music of Rocco's aria, with its fine rhythmic details, its individual harmonic scheme, its welding of three short movements into the strophe, and the little canon between voice and violins in the coda, is perfectly good Beethoven, much too good for the commonplace text, which could have been better suited by someone like Dittersdorf.

The whole approach changes, however, when the drama really gets under way. In the arias of Pizarro, Florestan, and Leonora, the ensembles of Act II, and both finales, Beethoven wrestles with the text, using it as a springborad for the loftiest flights of imagination, setting to music not so much the actual words as their implications, the abstract ideas of wickedness, devotion, endurance, courage, and the final triumph of right. It is in these numbers that we are aware of Beethoven the poet, the idealist, the musician for whom opera is only a vehicle for the expression of his own towering conceptions, in comparison with which the outward dramatic form is of only secondary importance. This is exemplified well in the famous quartet "Mir ist so wunderbar," a four-part canon in G major which is so beautiful that the words are quite superfluous. In all this music, Beethoven, as usual when his "raptus" was upon him, is merciless in his demands on the singers. The thought simply transcends complete expression, and the glory of the music lies not so much in what it says as in its suggestion of things too great for utterance. In *Fidelio*, as in the *Missa Solemnis* and the Ninth Symphony, there are passages which cannot be adequately sung by human beings, though they are nonetheless worthy to be sung by the angles. *Fidelio* is not merely an opera—and this "not merely" is the source of its defects—but, in the last analysis, a hymn to the heroism of Leonora.[16]

16. See Thayer, *Life of Ludwig van Beethoven;* Braunstein, *Beethovens Leonore-Ouvertüren;* Kufferath, *"Fidelio";* Hess, *Beethovens Oper "Fidelio";* Kastner, *Bibliotheca Beethoveniana;* mongraphs in *Neues Beethoven Jahrbuch;* Dean, "Beethoven and Opera"; Lang, *The Experience of Opera,* chap. 4; Ruhnke, "Die Librettisten des *Fidelio*"; *Opera News* (January 7, 1984), 48:12–21.

CHAPTER EIGHTEEN

Grand Opera

For eight years after Spontini's *Olympie* (1819), no significant new works were produced at the Paris Opéra.[1] In 1828 occurred the first performance of Auber's serious opera *La Muette de Portici* ("The Dumb Girl of Portici," known also as *Masaniello*, after the name of its hero). This was followed less than a year later by Rossini's French opera, *Guillaume Tell*. In 1831 appeared Meyerbeer's *Robert le Diable* ("Robert the Devil"), in 1835 Halévy's *La Juive* ("The Jewess"), and the following year Meyerbeer's *Les Huguenots*. These works established a type of musical drama which has come to be generally known under the name of "grand opera." Before considering specific examples, let us attempt to define the essential features of this style.

The term "grand opera" was originally used in contrast to opéra comique, and involved the technical distinction already mentioned: in the former the musical numbers were connected by recitatives and in the latter by spoken dialogue. But the adjective "grand" also implied a serious subject of heroic nature, treated in grandiose proportions and employing the utmost resources of singing, orchestral music, and staging. Grand opera was in the line of descent from Lully, Rameau, Gluck, and Spontini, but in its most flourishing period—the 1830s and 1840s—the traditional features were infused with romantic conceptions in such a way as to give it a special character. Subjects were chosen no longer from classical antiquity but from medieval or modern history, with strong emphasis on local color and often with pointed application to con-

1. The Opéra was known in this period as the Académie Royale de Musique, a company housed at the Salle Le Peletier from 1821 to 1875. The theater had a seating capacity of approximately 1,800 people. See *The New Grove Dictionary*, 14:210, figure 18; Pendle, *Eugène Scribe*, p. 27.

temporary issues *(Guillaume Tell)*; religious motifs were introduced *(Les Huguenots)*, and actions of violence and passion were favored *(La Juive)*.[2] Some parallels in the field of literature may be briefly indicated: the romantic treatment of religious themes by Chateaubriand; the historical novels of Scott and Dumas père; and the romantic dramas of both Dumas *(Henri III et son cour,* 1829) and Victor Hugo *(Hernani,* 1830; *Le Roi s'amuse,* 1832; *Ruy Blas,* 1838; *Les Burgraves,* 1843).

French grand opera was the creation of three men: the director and entrepreneur Louis Véron (1798–1867), who reigned over the Paris Opéra from 1831 to 1835; the librettist Eugène Scribe (1791–1861), author of *La Muette de Portici, La Juive, Robert le Diable,* and *Les Huguenots;* and the composer Giacomo Meyerbeer (1791–1864), in whose works all the best and worst features of grand opera were exemplified. The elements were already present, having been developed in French opera of the late eighteenth and early nineteenth centuries; they were combined under the stimulus of a commercial undertaking that had to pay its own way—and did so, with a little help from the government—by appealing to the *haute bourgeoisie* of Paris in the early days of Louis Philippe. Sheer spectacle, on a scale surpassing anything before attempted, was a basic ingredient in that appeal; but this was amply supported by the nature of the drama and music that went with it. Plots aiming to stimulate excitement through sudden, often grotesque, contrasts and shocks were well adapted for music and indeed required it for their full realization. Scores became longer and more complex than ever before in the history of opera. All kinds of novel orchestral effects were exploited. Ballets became larger and more elaborate. Choruses and crowd scenes abounded. The Mozartean ensemble, with its careful preservation of the individuality of each character, was transformed into a brilliant chorus for solo voices. Solo parts expanded in range, tone color, and expression; coloratura arias, impassioned dramatic outbursts, appeared side by side with simple ballads and

2. Crosten, *French Grand Opera;* Lang, "Grand Opera," in his *Music in Western Civilization,* pp. 825–34; Abry, *Histoire illustrée de la littérature française,* chaps. 51–58; Smith, *The Tenth Muse,* chap. 14; Pendle, *Eugène Scribe* (containing an extensive bibliography); Lang, *The Experience of Opera,* chap. 11; Perris, "French Music in the Time of Louis-Philippe."

romances. Musical forms and idioms were mingled in a luxuriant eclecticism, the object being to dazzle popular audiences who demanded thrills and for whom the aristocratic restraints of the eighteenth century had no meaning. The inevitable consequence was an inflated style of "effects without causes,"[3] of striking and brilliant musical numbers inadequately motivated by the dramatic situation. In short, composers and librettists acted on three principles that are still quite familiar: (1) give the public what it wants; (2) if a little is good, more is better; and (3) the whole (that is, the complete opera) is equal to the sum of its parts (that is, the several musical styles of which the opera is composed). The result, if one can judge from the fame and fortune of Scribe and his collaborators, was undeniably successful at the time and of considerable influence on the future course of opera.

For several decades, the librettist Eugène Scribe dominated the theatrical scene in Paris with works that embraced a variety of genres from comedy to tragedy, from vaudeville to grand opera.[4] Scribe's first work for the Paris Opéra was *La Muette de Portici* (1828), a five-act libretto for which the music was composed by Daniel-François-Esprit Auber (1782–1871), in the style of grand opera.[5] The plot is based on a historical event, the revolution at Naples in 1647, which was led by Masaniello, a fisherman; for good measure, another event—the eruption of Mt. Vesuvius in 1631—is brought in at the climax of the opera. This historical framework, however, belies the immediacy of the political and social events portrayed on the stage. With no intention of Scribe's part, *La Muette* nevertheless has the distinction of having triggered a revolution. A performance of the opera at Brussels on August 25, 1830, touched off the popular uprising which resulted the next year in the establishment of Belgium as an independent state. The Brussels audience undoubtedly was moved by the tragic finale of Act V, in which "good" does not triumph over "evil." Masaniello and his sister, Fenella, the mute girl of the title, are caught between the extremes of the ruling faction and the revo-

3. Wagner's phrase; see his *Opera and Drama*, part 1, chap. 6.

4. See Pendle, *Eugène Scribe*; Longyear, "Political and Social Criticism in French Opera, 1827–1920"; W. Weber, *Music and the Middle Class.*

5. See biographies of Auber by Kohut and Malherbe; Longyear, "D. F. E. Auber."

lutionary mob and become sacrificial victims. Masaniello, the hero, dies at the hands of the people he tried to free from political oppression. His death, in turn, causes Fenella to take her own life. In this unusual score, the heroine is a mute personage, who expresses herself only in pantomime to orchestral accompaniment—an interesting use of dance and the melodrama technique.[6]

Auber's music is on a typical grand-opera scale, filled with choruses, crowd scenes, processions, ballets, and huge finales. There are a few lighter numbers for contrast, such as the barcarole in the finale of Act II and the vivacious marketplace chorus in Act III, but the mood is for the most part serious, pervaded with romantic enthusiasm, rising to patriotic fervor in the celebrated duet of Act II, "Mieux vaut mourir" (example 18.1)— incidentally a good specimen of the "military band" rhythm of the accompaniment that was a common feature in many nineteenth-century operas, a steady four staccato chords per measure in march time, with a whang on the second beat at the cadences.

In spite of its grandiose qualities, the music of *La Muette* seems appropriate to and justified by the libretto; Auber does not fall into the error of striving after effects merely for their own sake. The same observation holds for the next grand opera to be presented at the Opéra, *Guillaume Tell* (1829), by Gioacchino Rossini (1792–1868), which exploits a similar patriotic-revolutionary theme in a spectacular, though dramatically weak, arrangement of Schiller's drama by Etienne Jouy and Hippolyte Bis (with revisions by the composer).[7] *Guillaume Tell* was Rossini's last opera.[8] Its success was not great at first, but the work remained in the repertoire almost to the present day, and the score, the masterpiece of one of the most original geniuses of nineteenth-century opera, has always held the respect of musicians. Undoubtedly it

---

6. The mute as a central character is not, however, unique to *La Muette*; earlier works by Pixérécourt and Weber have similar roles. Stefano Pavesi's *Fenella* (1831) is also based on the story of *La Muette* with the mute as the central character (see chap. 20.). Scribe, in his position as scenarist for the ballet at the Opéra, was well versed in the use of mimed action. See Pendle, *Eugène Scribe*, and Guest, *The Romantic Ballet in Paris*.

7. See Moutoz, *Rossini et son "Guillaume Tell"*; Pendle, *Eugène Scribe*; Gossett, "Gioacchino Rossini."

8. For a discussion of his other operas, see chap. 20.

Example 18.1: *La Muette de Portici*, Act II, no. 8

AUBER

is uneven in quality and, by modern standards, too long. On the
other hand, the overture has a vitality which years of playing by
military bands has failed to quench. The first act is well planned
to furnish contrast between the pastoral music at the beginning,
in which Rossini employed many authentic alpine horn motifs
(Ranze des vaches), and the magnificent finale, ending with an
exciting *veloce* movement in 3/4 rhythm. Act II is the most nearly
perfect both in general arrangement and in the details: Mathilde's
recitative and aria "Sombres forêts," the following duet, and above
all the trio for men's voices "Ces jours, qu'ils ont osé proscrire."
The third act contains long ballets and the too-often-parodied scene
of the apple, as well as many dramatically effective choruses. There
are long arid stretches in both the fourth and fifth acts, but they
are relieved by occasional numbers of great beauty, such as the

introduction to Act IV, Arnold's aria "Asile héréditaire," the canonic trio for women's voices "Je rends a votre amour" (very much like the canon in *Fidelio*), and the final hymn to freedom.

One French grand opera that still holds the stage is *La Juive* (1835) by Jacques-François Fromental Elie Halévy (1799–1862), distinguished composer of some thirty-seven operas, of which the most successful, along with *La Juive*, were *L'Eclair* (1835) and *La Reine de Chypre* (1841).[9] The longevity of *La Juive* is probably due to the fact that by making copious cuts it is possible to eliminate not only much of the repetition which was such a feature of grand opera but also many of the more commonplace melodies, thereby uncovering a score which, in originality of musical ideas, consistency of style, orchestral coloring, and harmonic interest, is distinctly superior to any of its contemporaries, except possibly *Tell*. *La Juive* has all the characteristic devices of grand opera—big ensembles, processions and crowd scenes, ballets (which were staged at the first performances with unusual magnificence), and emotional tension. Among the many effects may be mentioned the use of church style in the Te Deum of Act I (with organ accompaniment) and in the striking choral prayer of the last finale—examples of the common practice in romantic opera of employing religious ceremony for sentimental or theatrical purposes. All the solo roles are expertly written to display the best qualities of the singers. The chief fault of this opera is its monotony of mood, owing to the succession of melodramatic situations almost unrelieved by lighter touches; the choruses and ballets, which offer variety in this respect, are musically among the weakest numbers of the score. Halévy's style in this and other operas was often criticized as too heavy and learned for the theatre, but it has been admired and studied by musicians.

Meyerbeer is the composer who more than any other fixed the distinguishing traits of grand opera.[10] German by birth, he

9. See Halévy, *Souvenirs et portraits* and *Derniers Souvenirs et portraits*; biography by Pougin; Curtiss, "Fromental Halévy."

10. See biography by Kapp; also Meyerbeer, *Briefwechsel und Tagebücher*; H. Abert, *Gesammelte Schriften*, pp. 397–420; Heine, *Sämtliche Werke*, 8:99–116; Becker, *Der Fall Heine-Meyerbeer*; Frese, *Dramaturgie*; *Opera News* (January 1977), 16:10–43; Becker, *Giacomo Meyerbeer*; Cooper, *Ideas and Music*; Gibson, "The Ensemble Technique"; Fulcher, "Meyerbeer and the Music of Society."

was a fellow pupil with C. M. von Weber of the famous organist and teacher Georg Joseph ("Abbé" or "Abt") Vogler (1749–1814). Meyerbeer had written two German operas before going, at Salieri's suggestion, to Venice for further study in 1815. There he soon mastered the Italian style of composition, at the time chiefly represented by Rossini, and had considerable success with a number of Italian operas, especially *Il crociato in Egitto* ("The Crusade in Egypt") at Venice in 1824.[11] But Paris was the goal of his ambition, a goal Rossini helped him achieve in 1826 when he produced *Il crociato in Egitto* at the Théâtre Italien. When in Paris to supervise the preparation of *Il crociato* for performance, Meyerbeer undertook a systematic study of French opera scores. Assimilating this style also, he achieved his own mature idiom in which German harmony, Italian melody, and French declamation were all represented. Meyerbeer's first French opera, *Robert le Diable*, was originally planned as an opéra comique in fulfillment of a commission from Pixérécourt, director of the Opéra-Comique. In the course of its creation, however, Meyerbeer transformed his conception of the Scribe libretto into a grand opera, and it was in this form that *Robert le Diable* was presented at the Paris Opéra in 1831. It was a sensational triumph and an immediate international success. There followed, five years later, *Les Huguenots*, which is generally regarded as his masterpiece.[12] His other two grand operas were *Le Prophète* (first performed at Paris, after many revisions, in 1849) and *L'Africaine* (Paris, 1865). Other notable works of Meyerbeer include two opéras comiques, *L'Etoile du nord* ("The North Star," 1854) and *Le Pardon de Ploermel* ("The Pardon of Ploermel," also known as "Dinorah," 1859). The librettos of all except the last-named work were by Scribe.

Few composers in history have been subject to such diverse and strongly held judgments as Meyerbeer.[13] The extraordinary fascination he exercised over several generations of opera audiences has led with the passage of time to a reaction, so that

11. This was one of the last major operas to require a castrato.

12. For a discussion of Act II, see Grout, *A History of Western Music*, 3rd. ed., p. 612.

13. See the examples in the introduction by Becker to Meyerbeer, *Briefwechsel*, pp. 23–24.

the very qualities that led to his success are those for which he is now most strongly condemned. Whatever opinion one may hold of Meyerbeer's music, there can be no doubt that the operas that he and Scribe wrote corresponded to the taste of the time and consequently are, at the very least, important documents for a phase of European culture of the nineteenth century. *Robert le Diable*, for example, that jumble of medieval legends, romantic passions, grotesque superstitions, and fantastic confrontations, could hardly have been endured save by a generation nourished on the gothic novels of Mrs. Radcliffe and the tales of E. T. A. Hoffmann. Historical subject matter in opera has always been transmuted to suit contemporary ideas; the perversions of history in *Les Huguenots* and *Le Prophète*—based respectively on the St. Bartholomew's Day massacre of 1572 and the career of the Anabaptist fanatic John of Leyden (d. 1536)—are no worse than similar distortions in librettos of the seventeenth and eighteenth centuries, and no less characteristic of their own period.

Meyerbeer's music likewise must be judged in its historical context. He was an exceptionally gifted and versatile composer, one who as a dramatic craftsman has had few equals in the history of opera. A master of effect, he labored conscientiously to realize to the uttermost all the scenic and emotional possibilities of his librettos. Nowhere is this more vividly demonstrated than in the church-related scenes (often staged simultaneously with secular scenes of a political or amorous nature).[14] Magnificent scenery detailing a sixteenth-century cloister or the Münster cathedral becomes realistically enlivened with liturgically appropriate materials: a chorale or choral prière, an instrument (organ or harp) suggestive of sacred and celestial realms. He met dramatic needs with scenic spectacles, musical needs with tableaux.

Meyerbeer's music is tuneful and highly competent technically, his rhythms vigorous, his harmony often original, his orchestration unusual, his choral writing massive but humanized, and his treatment of the solo voices uniformly brilliant. Moreover, his operas are not lacking in numbers that are beautiful, moving, and worthy of all respect: for example, in *Robert le Diable*, the aria "Robert, toi que j'aime"; in *Les Huguenots*, the

---

14. He also used simultaneous staging of indoor and outdoor scenes.

Stage mechanism used to simulate the motion of a ship, for a production at the Bowery Theater (New York ca. 1874) of *L'Africaine* by G. Meyerbeer.

(From Olive Logan, "The Secret Regions of the Stage," in *Harper's New Monthly Magazine* [April 1874], p. 635)

duet in Act IV (particularly the portion from the words "Tu m'aimes?" to the final stretto) and the *scena* and trio in Act V; in *Le Prophète,* the famous aria "Ah! mon fils"; and in *L'Africaine,* the entire finale of Act II.

Nevertheless, Meyerbeer's work is uneven. Numbers like those just mentioned will be found side by side with tunes that can only be described as trivial, no matter how well covered by orchestral color and stage action. Moreover, change in fashion, that nemesis of all opera, has been particularly hard on Meyerbeer. The very length of the scores, the irrelevant ballets and spectacular scenes, the repetitions, the monotony of phrase structure, the overworked device of the sequence, unmotivated coloratura passages, languishing cadenzes—in short, all those features which were practically obligatory in an opera of this period risked becoming outmoded gestures, stale through familiarity.

Meyerbeer's last work, *L'Africaine,* evidences a more sober and more consistent musical style, even though its composition extended over a period of twenty years [15]—a style purged of many of the earlier excesses, rich in melodic beauties, and containing some interesting harmonic refinements (example 18.2); its

Example 18.2: *L'Africaine,* Act II, finale

---

15. The opera was begun in 1837 but not produced until after the composer's death. Revisions of the score were made by Fétis, at which time almost two dozen pieces by Meyerbeer were eliminated.

musical exoticism was not without influence on Verdi when he undertook the composition of *Aida* five years later.

Meyerbeer was primarily a composer for the theater, interested equally in music, scenery, stage management, and choreography; his aim was to present theatrically effective scenes and he never proposed—as Wagner later did—to undertake a fundamental reformation of opera.[16] The high reputation which he enjoyed, and his long-continued influence on the opera everywhere, were not due merely to two or three ephemeral successes in the 1830s.[17] It has been well said that "Meyerbeer's faults remained in his own works; his virtues were transmitted to his successors."[18] His harmony and especially his treatment of the orchestra influenced many later composers.[19] The ideal of grand opera, which he did more than anyone else to embody in concrete form, is evident in Verdi's *Vêpres siciliennes*, *Don Carlos*, and *Aida*, as well as in numberless other operas of the nineteenth and even the twentieth century. One of Meyerbeer's most notable, if ungrateful, disciples was Wagner, whose *Rienzi* (Dresden, 1842), originally designed for Paris audiences, frankly aimed to surpass Meyerbeer and Scribe on their own ground. All the familiar dramatic and scenic apparatus of grand opera was employed in Wagner's libretto, and the music, with its tunes so often repeated, its monotony of phraseology, its massive choruses and ensembles, and its generally huge proportions, is startlingly like Meyerbeer's.[20] Thus Wagner, like Gluck, began his career by demonstrating his mastery of a style of which he later became the most vociferous opponent.

Although he cannot be regarded as in any sense a follower of Meyerbeer, the contributions of Hector Berlioz (1803–1869) to opera may be considered here, since his chief work, *Les Troyens* ("The Trojans," composed 1856–58), is in form a grand

---

16. See the introduction by Becker to Meyerbeer, *Briefwechsel*, p. 25.

17. Throughout the nineteenth century and into the present era, Meyerbeer's operas have been performed in many different countries with repeated success. One of the more recent productions was that of *Le Prophète* at the Metropolitan Opera in 1977.

18. Dauriac, *Meyerbeer*, p. 182.

19. Lavoix, *Histoire de l'instrumentation*, pp. 384–416, especially pp. 402ff.

20. Wagner brought his score of *Rienzi* to Meyerbeer for criticism.

opera and in content and spirit a worthy successor to the musical dramas of Gluck and the romantic operas of Le Sueur.[21] Berlioz wrote only a few other operatic works. His first was *Benvenuto Cellini* (1838), based upon a libretto by Leon de Wailly and Auguste Barbier. Its general plan is a chain of broadly conceived episodes rather than a plot developed in full detail. In form, therefore, it is somewhat like Musorgsky's *Boris Godunov*, and the treatment of the crowd scenes foreshadows both that work and Wagner's *Meistersinger*. Initial productions of *Benvenuto Cellini* did not succeed (in part because the score requires resources that were not readily available in the conventional theaters), but the opera continues to be known through performances of the overture, one of Berlioz's best short instrumental pieces, and the "Roman Carnival" extracted from the finale of Act II.

Béatrice et Bénédict (1862), a two-act opéra comique, was Berlioz's last opera. Based upon Shakespeare's *Much Ado About Nothing*, the opera is in many places lyrical, almost melancholy in mood; it is full of the most exquisite detail, though perhaps too fine in its workmanship for the demands of the theater.[22] *La Damnation de Faust* (1846), based on Goethe's drama, is sometimes given as an opera, though it is perhaps better classified as a symphonic drama. As in *Cellini*, here also Berlioz sets to music only those scenes that he regards as most suitable for musical treatment, omitting unessential connecting episodes. In this music, Berlioz's fantastic imagination and orchestral virtuosity are at their height, and it is these things rather than any specifically operatic qualities that have made *Faust* one of his best-known works.

The libretto of *Les Troyens*, after the second and fourth books of Vergil's *Aeneid*, is by Berlioz himself and represents some of the best French operatic verse of the nineteenth century.[23] Part 1, comprising the first two acts, is entitled *La Prise de Troie* ("The Capture of Troy") and part 2, comprising the last three acts, *Les*

---

21. The tempestuous life and opinions of Berlioz can best be followed in his own *Mémoires*, supplemented by his letters and other writings. See also works by Boschot, Barzun, Crabbe, Primmer, Holoman, and Hopkinson, among others.

22. See especially the duet "Vois soupirez, Madame" (Act I) and Beatrice's recitative and aria "Dieu! Que viens-je d'entendre?" (Act II).

23. Smith, *The Tenth Muse*, p. 307.

Troyens à Carthage ("The Trojans at Carthage"). The second part was performed twenty-one times at Paris in 1863; the first part did not see the stage until 1890, at Karlsruhe. A number of revivals, some complete but more in partial or shortened versions, have occurred since 1920 but only recently has this masterpiece been accorded the performance honors it deserves; it opened the gala centennial season (1983) of the Metropolitan Opera. *Les Troyens* is quite possibly the most important French opera of the nineteenth century, the Latin counterpart of Wagner's Teutonic *Ring*; its strange fate is paralleled by nothing in the history of music unless it be the century-long neglect of Bach's *Passion According to St. Matthew*. One can account for this in the case of Berlioz's work: it is long, it is extremely expensive to stage, and its musical idiom is so original, so different from the conventional operatic style, that managers (no doubt with reason) have been unwilling to take the redoubtable financial risks involved in mounting it. There is no overwhelming public in any country for Berlioz as there is for Wagner, Verdi, and Puccini; and not even all connoisseurs are agreed about *Les Troyens*.[24] But, public or no public, the work ought to be produced regularly until conductors, singers, and audiences are brought to realize its greatness.

The full score of *Les Troyens* was not even published in authentic form until 1969[25]—a serious matter in the case of a composer like Berlioz, whose music is conceived in terms of specific instruments and of whom it may be said, as of Delacroix, that "the color creates the design." A piano-vocal reduction made by Berlioz himself is full of most pathetic suggestions as to how scenes might be cut and the cost of staging and the performance time reduced. How deeply the failure of the work affected him may be seen from those words in his foreword: "O ma noble Cassandre, mon heroïque vierge, il faut donc me résigner, je ne t'entendrai jamais!" ("O my noble Cassandra [the heroine of part 1], my heroic virgin, I must then be resigned, I shall never hear thee!")

24. See, for example, Lang *(Music in Western Civilization*, pp. 850–51. (I [Grout] shall never forget my astonishment at hearing Vaughan Williams describe *Les Troyens* as "the second most boring opera in the world." Of course, I immediately asked him which was the first.)

25. It is vol. 2 in the *New Berlioz Edition* (Kassel, 1967–), ed. by H. J. MacDonald et al. See also L. Goldberg, "A Hundred Years of Berlioz's *Les Troyens*"; Cohen, "Berlioz and the Opera."

In form, *Les Troyens* is a "number" opera, with many large choral and ballet scenes. With these features its resemblance to the typical grand opera ends. Its plot revolves not about individuals' fates but about great historic-legendary motifs: the fall of Troy, the flight of Aeneas, the sojourn at Carthage, the departure of the Trojans for Italy, and the death of Dido. The individuals appear as agents in a cosmic drama, not as persons concerned only with dramatizing their own woes and posturing before a picturesque historical background. Since the average operagoer is not accustomed to associate dramatic emotion with impersonal issues, he is prone to regard a work like *Les Troyens* as an epic (that is, a long and boring narrative relieved by occasional spectacular interludes), especially since he has never been given the opportunity of realizing that here is the one opera of the nineteenth century in which the epic has been successfully dramatized.[26] So strong is this suprapersonal, antique character that the appearances of the god Mercury at the end of Act IV and of the specters of Priam, Hector, and other Trojan warriors in Act V actually seem natural and convincing.

Berlioz's melodic line is in the best French tradition of utter fidelity to the text. It contains not a trace of Italian operatic opulence; nothing is brought out merely to gratify the singer or tickle the ear of the listener. The rhythmic patterns are novel, subtle, and extraordinarily varied. Most notable in *Les Troyens* is the quality of classic restraint, that purification and concentration of style characteristic of the maturity of genius (example 18.3). The harmony occasionally drops into the commonplace (there is unquestionably too much reliance on the chord of the diminished seventh, for example); one remarkable feature is the almost total absence of suspensions and appoggiaturas, making an extreme contrast with the characteristic later Wagnerian style. The chromaticism is much more restrained than in Berlioz's earlier works. There are occasional dull passages, though certainly no more in proportion to the whole than in Wagner. Yet these are surely redeemed by such places as the lament of Cassandra (Act I), the March of the Trojans (Act III, and recurring at various times),

---

26. Wagner's music dramas are not epics, but myths. The only comparable works are from the twentieth century. See, for example, Milhaud's *Christophe Colomb*.

the choruses "Dieux de la ville éternelle" (Act I) and "Gloire, gloire à Didon" (Act III), the song of the sailor (Act V, scene 1), and the magnificent final scene of Dido's immolation—all music that can hardly be excelled in beauty by any score of the nineteenth century.

Example 18.3: *Les Troyens*, Act V

(*Example 18.3 continued*)

Ma ten - dre sœur qui me sui - vis ma ten- dre

sœur, qui me sui - vis er - ran - te; A

poco riten.   *a tempo*

dieu mon peuple A - dieu A - dieu

The principal interlude is the scene of the hunt (Act IV), a complete symphonic poem in Berlioz's most brilliant orchestral style, accompanied by a fantastic pantomime on the stage with wordless vocalizing calls and distant cries of "Italie!"—the recurring motif of the drama, the command of the gods to Aeneas to lead his Trojan warriors to Italy and there found the empire destined to rule the world.

Comparison of Berlioz and Wagner is inevitable and leaps to the mind again and again when studying the score of *Les Troyens*. It is well to remember that *Tristan* had not yet been heard when Berlioz wrote the marvelously delicate and sensuous love music at the end of Act IV: the septet and chorus "Tout n'est que paix et charme" and the duet "Nuit d'ivresse et d'extase infinie!," the dialogue form of which is imitated from Act V, scene I, of *The Merchant of Venice*. The change from G-flat to D at the entrance of Mercury, who strikes Aeneas' shield and utters the solemn warning word "Italie!," and the final dark, unexpected cadence in the remote key of E minor make an effect absolutely unparalleled in tragic power.

In view of the current conception of Berlioz (based on his earlier works and autobiographical writings) as an irrational extremist, a composer who "believed in neither God nor Bach,"[27] it should be pointed out that he never ceased to emphasize the independence of music from literary associations and expressed the hope that his *Symphonie fantastique* would "on its own merits and irrespective of any dramatic aim, offer interest in the musical sense alone." He was no Wagnerian. He cared for none of Wagner's music later than *Lohengrin*, found the *Tristan* prelude incomprehensible, and had only the vaguest notion of Wagner's musico-dramatic theories. He wrote, after outlining what he thought were the doctrines of the "music of the future": "If such is this new religion, I am far from being a devotee; I have never been, I am not, I never shall be. I raise my hand, and I swear: 'non credo.' "[28]

Berlioz, however, did seem to be a devotee of the communal utopia advocated by Saint-Simon and his followers, a form of socialism that affirmed the value of the arts in creating an ideal society. A prominent member of the Saint-Simonism movement who composed music for the communal rites was Félicien David (1810–1876), one of the earliest orientalists in French nineteenth-century music.[29] David's missionary activities led him to Eastern

27. F. Hiller, cited in Berlioz, *Memoirs*, p. 103.

28. Berlioz, *A Travers Chants* (1872), p. 315.

29. See the biography by Brancour, and see also Combarieu, *Histoire de la musique*, vol. 3; Achter, "Félicien David"; Gradenwitz, "Félicien David"; Locke, "Notice biographique sur Félicien David."

countries, where he came into contact with the indigenous music of the regions visited. Works written after his return to Paris show this Eastern influence, beginning with the symphonic ode *Le Désert*, which caused a sensation at its premiere in 1844. His opera *La Perle du Brésil* ("The Pearl of Brazil," 1851) has many points of resemblance to Meyerbeer's *L'Africaine*; another opera, *Herculanum* (1859), won a state prize in 1867. But David's most successful stage work was his two-act opéra comique *Lalla-Roukh* (1862), which held the stage in Paris until the end of the century and even received some performances outside France. David's orientalism was an early example of those exotic tendencies in French romanticism which were to become more prominent in opera of the seventies and eighties.

CHAPTER NINETEEN

Opéra Comique, Operetta, and Lyric Opera

The Evolution of Opéra Comique

Even before the French Revolution, several distinct tendencies had become apparent in the opéra comique.[1] There were those works, such as Monsigny's *Déserteur*, Philidor's *Tom Jones*, and Grétry's *Richard*, in which the comic features were secondary to sentimental or romantic elements. Other early composers who contributed pieces of this type were Nicolas Dezède (ca. 1740–1792),[2] who produced about fifteen opéras comiques at Paris, including *Les Trois Fermiers* ("The Three Farmers," 1777), and Nicolas Dalayrac (1753–1809),[3] an unusually prolific and popular composer whose *Nina* (1786) furnished the libretto for Paisiello's work of the same title and whose *Les Deux Petits Savoyards* ("The Two Little Savoyards," 1789) made its way all over Europe and lasted well into the nineteenth century. During the Revolution and afterwards, this vein of romantic comedy was still cultivated, but it had a strong rival in the many horror and rescue pieces of the same period, to which allusion has already been made. There were

1. Chouquet, *Histoire de la musique dramatique*, chaps. 8–9; Pougin, "La Première Salle Favart"; Soubies, *Histoire de l'opéra-comique*; idem, *Histoire du théâtre-lyrique*; idem, *Le Théâtre-italien de 1801 à 1913*; "L'Opéra-comique au XIXe siécle," special issue of *RM* (1933). See also "Opera: France," in *The New Grove Dictionary*, and Pendle, *Eugène Scribe*, for excellent bibliographies; Bartlet, "Archival Sources for the Opéra-Comique"; Longyear, " 'Le Livret bien fait'."

2. Biography by Pougin, in his *Musiciens francais du XVIIIe siècle*.

3. Biography by Pougin; see also Cucuel, *Les Créateurs de l'opéra-comique*, chap. 8, and Lavignac, *Encyclopédie*, 3:1600–1604.

also, of course, many operas and opéras comiques on patriotic subjects which were of only ephemeral interest. To the composers of opéra comique who have already been mentioned we need add only the names of Daniel Steibelt (1765–1823), with *Roméo et Juliette* (1793), and Henri-Montan Berton (1767–1844), a pupil of Salieri, the most successful of whose forty-seven operas were *Montano et Stéphanie*, *Le Délire* (both 1799), and *Aline, reine de Golconde* (1803). All these works, while never losing the popular touch or pretending to be as grand and formal as the regular opera, assumed a more or less serious attitude toward the subject matter, which in turn was reflected in the style of the music. Cherubini's *Médée* and Méhul's *Joseph* are other examples of this combination of serious themes with the old opéra comique practice of alternating singing with spoken dialogue, a combination found likewise in Germany with Mozart's *Magic Flute* and Beethoven's *Fidelio*. Thus, the opéra comique approached more closely the style of the regular opera, the distinction between the two in many cases resting almost entirely on the technical point of spoken dialogue in the one as against continuous music (with recitatives) in the other.

The rapprochement between the opera and the opéra comique is further illustrated by the fact that practically all the composers of opera at this time were at least equally active in the field of opéra comique. The old Academy of Music, founded under Lully and made illustrious in the eighteenth century by the productions of Rameau and Gluck, was maintained as a national institution by the revolutionary governments and strongly supported by Napoleon. Its leading composers during this period were Cherubini, Le Sueur, Méhul, and Spontini. Lesser figures included François-Joseph Gossec (1734–1829), Belgian by birth and better known as a composer of symphonies and quartets;[4] Jean-Baptiste Lemoyne (1751–1796), a disciple of Piccinni and Sacchini; Rodolphe Kreutzer (1766–1831), the violinist to whom Beethoven dedicated his *Kreutzer* Sonata, who composed a *Lodoïska* opera in competition with Cherubini's in 1791 but whose *Aristippe* (1808) and *Abel* (1810) were more successful;[5] Charles-Simon

4. Biographies by Hédouin, Hellouin, Dufrane, and Prod'homme.
5. Biography by Hardy.

Catel (1773–1830), author of a textbook on harmony;[6] and Louis Luc Loiseau de Persuis (1769–1819), whose most important opera was *Jérusalem delivrée* (1812).

Along with the opera and the serious opéra comique there continued a lighter type of comic opera, with librettos based on amusing intrigues or developments of improbable farcical situations, coupled with music of extreme simplicity and popular appeal, largely in the style of the vaudevilles and romances. Among the specialists in this field may be mentioned François Devienne (1759–1803); Jean-Pierre Solié (1755–1812); Pierre-Antoine-Dominique Della Maria (1769–1800), a pupil of Paisiello and a composer of extraordinary facility, who wrote his chief work, *Le Prisonnier* (1798), in eight days; and especially Nicolo Isouard (1775–1818), a prolific composer who was also endowed with a remarkable flair for effective theater music and ensemble writing.[7] The most successful of his earlier works was *Les Rendez-vous bourgeois* (1807); his style gradually developed along more serious lines, and his best works (*Cendrillon*, 1810; *Joconde*, 1814; *Jeannot et Colin*, 1814) were composed under the stimulus of rivalry with Boieldieu, of whom he was the principal forerunner.

A new phase of the French opéra comique began in the 1820s: a "classical" phase, which on the one hand led to the *opéra lyrique* of the later nineteenth century and on the other, to the operetta. The composer and concert pianist François-Adrien Boieldieu (1775–1834) represented the beginning of this classical phase.[8] His early works in this genre, written for theaters in Rouen (his native city) and Paris, attracted favorable attention and won for him several important appointments. After a sojourn in St. Petersburg (1803–1811), where he served the Russian imperial court and directed the French opera, he returned to Paris, establishing his fame with *Jean de Paris* (1812). Later works included *Le Petit Chaperon rouge* ("Little Red Riding Hood," 1818) and his masterpiece, *La Dame blanche* ("The White Lady," 1825), which had a thousand performances within forty years. To Boiel-

6. Biographies by Carlez and Hellouin. See also Suskin, "The Music of Charles-Simon Catel."

7. Biography of Isouard by Wahl.

8. Excellent biography and study of Boieldieu's works by Favre.

dieu is due the merit of having upheld the national French comic opera almost single-handed for a long time against the blandishments of the Italian opera of Rossini. His music is neither learned nor brilliant; it may easily be criticized for its monotony of phraseology and excessive textual repetition. Nevertheless, it has to a superlative degree the characteristic French traits of clarity, restraint, and simplicity, "de la grâce, de l'esprit, des motifs charmants, une harmonie élégante" (see example 19.1).[9] In *La Dame blanche* these qualities are applied to a libretto by Scribe derived from Sir Walter Scott's *The Lady of the Lake, The Monastery, Guy Mannering,* and *The Abbot,* combining a long-lost hero, a haunted castle, buried treasure, and similar appurtenances in the best tradition.[10] In honor of the Scottish background of the story, the composer included two Scottish tunes: a drinking song in Act I and "Robin Adair" in the famous recognition scene of Act III, wherein the song is introduced by the chorus and completed by the hero, George.

The opéras comiques of Daniel-François-Esprit Auber continued the "classical" phase; they are marked by a sophistication in the librettos and by an increased presence of Italian musical characteristics. Both Auber and his usual librettist, Scribe, were thorough Parisians, and their work has a certain smartness, an air of the boulevards, an alert, nervous, often lightly mocking quality which is one of its principal charms. Their first pronounced success was *Le Maçon* ("The Mason," 1825), and this was followed by a long series of works of which *Fra Diavolo* (1830) and *Le Domino noir)* ("The Black Domino," 1837) were especially popular.[11] Auber's musical style is well suited to comic opera, being for the most part light-textured, tuneful, piquant, and unpretentious. The most characteristic melodies are built on one salient motif in dotted or 6/8 rhythm, which is repeated over and over without undergoing anything like a musical development (Example 19.2). Less common are lyrical melodies of elegant contour, lightly seasoned with chromatics (example 19.3). The favorite solo

9. The tribute was paid by Clément, *Dictionnaire*, p. 375.

10. See Pendle, *Eugène Scribe*, pp. 274–311, for an analysis of Scribe's use of the Scott sources, which were available in French translations after 1816.

11. On *Fra Diavolo*, see Pendle, *Eugène Scribe*, pp. 139–72.

Example 19.1 *Jean de Paris*, Act I (no. 5) Duo

BOIELDIEU

(Example 19.1 continued)

Example 19.2: *Les Diamants de la couronne* (1841)

Example 19.3: *La Part du Diable*, Act III (1843)

AUBER

Re - viens, ma no - ble pro - tec - tri - ce ai -
Bass: A   E

der ton pau - vre ser - vi - teur: du   sort dont je crains le ca -
F♯   B   E   B   E   A

- pri - ce pour moi dé - tour - ne la ri -
F♯   B   E   A

gueur,   pour moi dé - tour - ne le ri - gueur!
                                        E   A

forms are strophic, as in the frequent couplets, romances, and
the like. There are many duets and trios, though the larger ensembles (for example, the finales) are not so extensively developed
either musically or dramatically as in Boieldieu. The chorus is
used freely, most often in combination with soloists. Instrumental
numbers are relatively unimportant, consisting only the overtures
(generally a mere medley of tunes from the opera), entr'actes, and
occasional dances or marches.

With Louis-Joseph-Ferdinand Hérold (1791–1833), the
Italian traits evident in Auber's music become more conspicuous.
Herold was a brilliant young composer who won the Prix de Rome
in 1812 and produced an opera buffa, *La gioventù di Enrico Quinto*
("The Youth of Henry V"), at Naples in 1815.[12] Though endowed
with a real gift for theatrical style, he nevertheless had few triumphs
in French opera within the span of his brief life: *Marie* (1826),
Zampa (1831), and *Le Pré aux clercs* ("The Field of Honor,"
1832). *Zampa*, on a melodramatic and confused libretto, but with
a wide variety of musical expression, was long a favorite in Germany. *Le Pré aux clercs*, more consistent and unified in both text

12. Biographies by Jouvin and Pougin.

Example 19.4: *Le Pré aux clercs*, Act I

HÉROLD

and music, equaled the popularity of Boieldieu's *La Dame blanche*, with a thousand performances at Paris in the first forty years of its existence. Hérold's style is a good illustration of his own axiom: "Remember that *rhythm* does everything." [13] His music is more virile than that of Auber; the melodies, most of which begin on the first beat of the measure, are strongly accented and abound in syncopations, chromatic appoggiaturas, and sudden shifts to the minor submediant or even remoter keys (example 19.4). Every effect is repeated many times, as if to make sure that the listener shall not possibly miss it. There is some coloratura writing. A common device—found also in Rossini,[14] as well as in the early works of Auber—is for the voice to declaim rapid syllables on a single tone while the melody is heard in the orchestra. Lyrical melodies are exceptional in Hérold, though a beautiful example is found in the duet in Act III of *Zampa*, in the form of a barcarole, a type of song almost as popular in early nineteenth-century opera as the siciliano had been a century previous.

The revitalization of French opéra comique was sparked by a reaction to Rossini's domination of the Paris scene; at the same time Rossini himself contributed to this rejuvenation. His *Le Comte Ory* ("Count Ory"), on a libretto by Scribe, was composed for the Opéra in 1828. Although the characters are not representative of the middle or lower classes and the dialogue is orchestrally accompanied rather than spoken, *Le Comte Ory* belongs to the realm of opéra comique. The medieval story centers upon the notorious escapades of Count Ory; its hilarious incongruous situations (the Count disguised as the mother superior of a religious order; the "nuns" showing the effects of drinking too much wine) are balanced by those of a more reflective dramatic nature (unaccompanied female chorus of Act II; the storm scene)— the whole supported by Rossini's remarkable score.

13. Pougin, *Hérold*, p. 32.

14. See, for example, the aria with chorus "Dans ce lieu solitaire" in Act II of *Le Comte Ory*.

The Operetta

Boieldieu's pupil Adolphe-Charles Adam (1803–56),[15] in his *Postillon de Longjumeau* (1836) and some fifty other works for the theater, continued the trend toward a more frivolous type of opéra comique which, growing in popularity during the next two decades, prepared the way for the flourishing of the operetta in the favorable atmosphere of the Second Empire (1852–1870). It is hard to draw a definite dividing line between the lighter opéra comique and the operetta: both have spoken dialogue, both deal with pleasant subjects and have comic elements, both cultivate a comparatively restricted and simple musical style, and both aim at charm, lightness, and esprit.[16] If there is any principle of difference, it is that in the opéra comique the audience is expected to lend a certain amount of credence and sympathy to the story; some appeal is made to the feelings of the spectators, some trace of sentiment exists. In the operetta and similar genres, on the other hand, the aim is simply to amuse, and the means are wit, parody, and satire. Opéra comique, as we have already seen, is a broad term, admitting at one extreme frivolous, operetta-like pieces, but at the other extreme admitting sentimental and serious works which in some cases cannot be called "comic" at all. The mid-nineteenth-century version of this serious opéra comique in France is exemplified by such composers as Thomas and Gounod, who will be dealt with later. Meanwhile, the composers of lighter types, in France and elsewhere, claim our attention.

Among the many French composers of popular stage works in the 1850s were Albert Grisar (1808–1869), with *Bonsoir, M. Pantalon* (1851), and Antoine-Louis Clapisson (1808–1866), with *La Fanchonette* (1856). A longer day of fame was allotted to Victor Massé (1822–1884) for his sentimental *Galatée* (1852) and *Les Noces de Jeannette* ("Jeannette's Wedding," 1853); the latter had received a thousand performances by 1895 and is still given

15. Adam, *Souvenirs d'un musicien* and *Derniers souvenirs d'un musicien*; biography by Pougin.

16. See Bruyas, *Histoire de l'opérette en France*; Harding, *Folies de Paris*.

occasionally. A more serious work of his, *Paul et Virginie*, was produced in 1876 with some success. *Les Dragons de Villars* by Louis Maillart (1817–1871) and *Maître Pathelin* by François Bazin (1816–1878), both produced in 1856, were popular for some years, though Bazin's greatest success came with *Le Voyage en Chine* ("The Voyage to China'") in 1865. The works of Florimond Ronger, called Hervé (1825–1892), represent the French operetta of the 1860s in characteristic fashion (*L'Oeil crevé*, 1867; *Chilpéric*, 1868; *Le Petit Faust*, 1869, a parody of Gounod's opera). But one name overtops all others in this field: Jacques Offenbach (1819–1880), whose witty, melodious, and cleverly orchestrated operettas had a tremendous vogue in the Paris of the Second Empire and have in large part maintained their popularity to this day.[17]

Offenbach arrived in Paris from Cologne in 1833 and soon established his credentials as a cellist and conductor. It took another twenty years, however, for him to find acceptance as a composer, his works having been repeatedly rejected for performance at the Opéra-Comique. With the opening of his own Théâtre des Bouffes-Parisiens in 1855, he was able to stage his *opéras bouffes*, a unique kind of operetta that blends the gay spirit of the eighteenth-century vaudeville comedies and Italian buffa operas with biting satire and brilliant parody. Offenbach's most prominent librettists were Louis Meilhac and Ludovic Halévy; their texts are based on well-known myths, updated to reflect contemporary situations. They thus could parody the tragédie lyrique of a bygone era while simultaneously satirizing political issues and universal conventions of society. Nowhere is this better exemplified than in *Orphée aux enfers* ("Orpheus in the Underworld," 1858, revised 1874), a parody of Gluck's famous opera on the same myth and a satire on the Second Empire. Offenbach's other principal opéras bouffes include *La Belle Hélène* ("The Beautiful Helen," 1864), *La Vie parisienne* ("Parisian Life," 1866), *Barbe-Bleue* ("Bluebeard," 1866), and *La Périchole* (1868). The scores show Offenbach's artistry in the projection of humor (most espe-

---

17. See the composer's own *Offenbach en Amérique*; also Kracauer, *Orpheus in Paris*; Decaux, *Offenbach, roi du second empire*; Folstein, "A Bibliography on Jacques Offenbach."

Scene from *Die Bergknappen* (Burgtheater, Vienna 1778) by I. Umlauf.
(Bildarchivs der Oesterreich Nationalbibliothek)

cially in the quotation of familiar themes from other composers' operas in particularly incongrous incidents). *Les Contes d'Hoffmann* ("The Tales of Hoffman"), a more serious work and his only opera to be sung throughout, was posthumously produced at the Opéra-Comique in 1881, the score having been completed by Ernest Guiraud.

A distinct branch of the operetta stemmed from Offenbach and flourished at Vienna from about 1870.[18] The leading composers of this school were Franz von Suppé (1819–1895), whose overtures, in arrangement, have been the delight of amateur orchestras and village bands;[19] Johann Strauss the Younger, "The Waltz King" (1825–1899),[20] of whose numerous operettas *Die Fledermaus* ("The Bat," 1874) and *Der Zigeunerbaron* ("The Gypsy Baron," 1885) are still heard with pleasure;[21] Karl Millöcker (1842–1899), with *Der Bettelstudent* ("The Beggar Student," 1882); Richard Genée (1823–1895), with *Der Seekadett* ("The Naval Cadet," 1876); Karl Zeller (1842–1898), with *Der Vogelhändler* ("The Bird Dealer," 1891); and Richard Heuberger (1850–1914), conductor and critic as well as composer of *Der Opernball* ("The Opera Ball," 1898) and other operettas.[22]

The influence of French opéra comique was felt in other countries, setting the tone for light opera everywhere for a long period. It was reflected in Germany in the works of Kreutzer, Lortzing, and Flotow, and in Great Britain in the two most popular romantic operas to English texts of the nineteenth century, both the work of Irish composers: *The Bohemian Girl* (1843), by Michael William Balfe (1808–1870),[23] and *Maritana* (1845), by William Vincent Wallace (1812–1865).[24] The apparently immortal operettas of W. S. Gilbert and Arthur Sullivan (1842–1900) were

18. Keller, *Die Operette*; Hadamowsky, *Die Wiener Operette*; Holzer, *Die Wiener Vorstadtbühnen*; Grün, *Kulturgeschichte der Operette*.

19. Keller, *Franz von Suppé*.

20. See studies by Decsey, Jaspert, H. Jacob, and Schenk.

21. The repertoire of Viennese operettas continues to be produced in traditional style by the Volksoper of Vienna.

22. Heuberger, *Im Foyer*, is a collection of his critical essays.

23. Biography by Barrett; Kenney, *A Memoir*.

24. See Flood, *William Vincent Wallace: A Memoir*.

to London of the eighties what Offenbach's works had been to Paris twenty years earlier (*H.M.S. Pinafore*, 1878; *The Pirates of Penzance*, 1880; *The Mikado*, 1885).[25]

Other composers of English opera in the middle nineteenth century were John Barnett (1802–1890), whose *Mountain Sylph* (1834) was sung throughout, thereby earning the distinction of being the first English opera since Arne's *Artaxerxes*; Edward James Loder (1813–1865), whose *Night Dancers* (1846) was highly praised by Hogarth;[26] Sir George Alexander MacFarren (1813–1887), with twelve operas, of which the most successful was *Robin Hood* (1860); and Sir Julius Benedict (1804–1885), whose *Lily of Killarney* (1862) is still remembered.

Lyric Opera

If the opéra comique turned on the one hand in the direction of the operetta, composers were still not lacking who, in the middle decades of the nineteenth century, preferred to cultivate the more serious and lyrical aspects of this characteristic French form of dramatic music and thereby continue the tradition of Cherubini and Boieldieu. Between the pompous grand opera and the merry operetta there was room for a type of piece less heavy and pretentious than the former yet more serious than the latter—a kind of opera that should give scope to the French national genius for measured and refined lyrical expression of serious (or, at all events, not exclusively comic) subject matter, combined with a certain amount of ballet and similar stage entertainment. Such works, although they grew up within the fold of the opéra comique with spoken dialogue, are nevertheless better described by the term "lyric opera." Of course, in one sense all opera is lyric, since by definition it is sung poetry. But the word "lyric" is especially ap-

---

25. The literature on Gilbert and Sullivan is extensive, but see especially Williamson, *Gilbert & Sullivan Opera*, and Jacobs, *Arthur Sullivan*. For other works, see Dunhill, I. Goldberg, Pearson, Hughes, Sullivan and Flower, and Baily.

26. Hogarth, *Memoirs of the Opera*, 2:375–76.

plicable to the kind of opera we are now considering, which is, by comparison with grand opera, more inward in the emotions expressed,[27] smaller in dimensions, and more unified in mood. The leading composers of this kind of opera in France before 1870 were Ambroise Thomas (1811–1896) and Charles Gounod (1818–1893).

Thomas was a pupil of Le Sueur and a teacher of Massenet, thus linking the late eighteenth and late nineteenth centuries in French music.[28] He began his career as an opera composer auspiciously with the opéra comique *La Double Echelle* ("The Double Ladder") in 1837, but his subsequent works obtained no favor until *Le Caïd* (1849), followed in the next year by *Le Songe d'une nuit d'été*, the libretto of which has hardly anything to do with *A Midsummer Night's Dream*, though Shakespeare himself appears in it as one of the principal characters. Thomas's most famous works are opéra comique *Mignon* (1866), derived from Goethe's *Wilhelm Meister*, and the operas *Hamlet* (1868) and *Françoise de Rimini* (1882), with librettos for all three provided by the duo-combination of Jules Barbier and Michel Carré. *Mignon* had attained its 1,600th performance at the Opéra-Comique by 1927.[29] Its music—clear, correct, melodious, and elegantly expressive—is a splendid example of these eminently French qualities as descended from the eighteenth century through the line of Monsigny, Grétry, and Boieldieu. Thomas's talents were hardly equal to the exigencies of tragic drama, and although *Hamlet* has remained in the repertoire, it is rather for the sake of its lyrical virtues than for its adequacy to the Shakespearean subject.

Gounod, the most thoroughly representative French composer of the mid-nineteenth century,[30] was an eclectic yet individual musician, an ingratiating melodist, capable of a certain profundity, endowed with a fine ear for the effects of harmony and color in music, and exceptionally sensitive to the qualities of

---

27. Cf. Hegel's distinction between lyric and epic poetry, in his *Aesthetik*, pp. 419ff.

28. See Achter, "Félicien David."

29. Loewenberg, *Annals of Opera*.

30. See Gounod, *Mémoires*, and the standard biography by Prod'homme. On *Faust* in particular, see Chorley, *Thirty Years' Musical Recollections*, pp. 302ff.; Soubies and De Curzon, *Documents inédits*; Landormy, *Faust*.

a text. Familiarity has tended to breed contempt for Gounod's music, which is sometimes unfairly compared with that of later nineteenth-century composers; it is amusing to note that, after the production of *Faust*, Gounod was accused of Wagnerism and of obscurity, traceable to his fondness for the later Beethoven quartets, "that muddy spring whence have issued all the bad musicians of modern Germany."[31] Such criticisms can be understood only when we remember the opera music which Parisians were accustomed to hearing in 1860. Gounod's style is in fact admirably logical and well proportioned, truly French though tinged to some degree by Italianate feeling, and with occasional touches of solemnity, which remind us that he was a composer for the church as well as the theater. His dramatic masterpiece, *Faust*, was staged as an opéra comique in 1859. The following year, recitatives were substituted for spoken dialogue, and in the new form *Faust* became the most popular French opera ever written, attaining its 2,000th Paris performance in 1934 and having been given besides in at least forty-five different countries and twenty-four different languages.[32]

The legend of Faust received numerous musical treatments in the nineteenth century, including Spohr's opera (1816), Berlioz's *Damnation de Faust*, Schumann's *Szenen aus Goethes Faust*, Liszt's "Faust" Symphony, and Boito's opera *Mefistofele* (1864).[33] The libretto prepared for Gounod by Jules Barbier and Michel Carré is based only on part 1 of Goethe's drama—damnation being a more fascinating subject in the theater than salvation—and consequently the Germans rightly insist on calling this opera *Margarete*, after the name of its heroine. It is well that the subject was limited in this way, for it is hardly conceivable that Gounod could have risen to an appropriate treatment of the second part. Berlioz, unusually for him, highly praised Gounod's music, singling out especially Faust's aria "Salut, demeure chaste et pure" and the closing portion of the love duet (Act III); yet nearly every number of the score is famous.

Of Gounod's other operas, the most popular were *Mir-*

31. See quotations in Combarieu, *Histoire*, 3:371.

32. Loewenberg, *Annals of Opera*.

33. Hoechst, *Faust in Music*; Butler, *The Fortunes of Faust*.

eille (1864) and *Roméo et Juliette* (1867), though the latter called down renewed criticisms of lack of tunefulness (!) and undue subjection to the influence of Meyerbeer and Wagner. A word should be added about the lighter comic operas of Gounod, especially *Philémon et Baucis*, 1860; these are filled with charming melodies which it would be a pleasure to hear more often on concert programs.

Whatever the present verdict on the music of Gounod, it must be remembered that in the decade before the Franco-Prussian War it was he who, almost alone, maintained characteristic French qualities in serious dramatic music. Maurice Ravel has thus estimated his importance for the later French school: "The musical renewal which took place with us towards 1880, has no more weighty precursor than Gounod."[34]

34. Quoted in Hill, *Modern French Music*, p. 45.

CHAPTER TWENTY

Italian Opera:
Verdi and His Contemporaries

In the early part of the eighteenth century, Italian opera had been predominant in every country of Europe except France; by the end of the century, it was one among several national schools. Composers of Italian birth who worked mainly outside their own country—men like Sacchini, Salieri, Cherubini, and Spontini—tended to merge their national characteristics in an international style of which the most conspicuous examples were the works of Gluck's followers in France and, in a later line of development, the French grand opera. Alongside this cosmopolitan opera were the various national types, especially the French opéra comique and the German singspiel, all taking on renewed life from about 1815 and destined for honorable growth during the remainder of the nineteenth century.

The two decades from 1790 to 1810, which saw the production of Mozart's *The Magic Flute* and Beethoven's *Fidelio* at Vienna and of Cherubini's *Les Deux Journées*, Spontini's *La Vestale*, and Méhul's *Joseph* at Paris, were in Italy a time of relative stagnation—not in point of quantity, to be sure, but insofar as progress through acceptance of new ideas was concerned. Cimarosa had to all intents and purposes ended his career with *Il matrimonio segreto* in 1792; Zingarelli never produced anything better than his *Giulietta e Romeo* of 1796. Ferdinando Paer (1771–1839), one of the most talented Italians of this period, spent most of his productive life in Germany and France.[1] His *Camilla, ossia*

---

1. Della Corte, *L'opera comica italiana*, 2:199ff; Engländer, "Paërs *Leonora* and Beethovens *Fidelio*."

Il sotterano ("Camilla; or, The Tunnel"), based on one of the "horror" operas of the French Revolution, was presented at Vienna in 1799, his *Leonora* (the same subject as Beethoven's *Fidelio*) at Dresden in 1804, and an opéra comique, *Le Maître de chapelle* ("The Chapelmaster"), at Paris in 1821. Stefano Pavesi (1779-1850), who in the latter part of his career succeeded Antonio Salieri as music director of the court opera in Vienna, produced some very successful operas in Italy. They included *Ser Marcantonio* (1810) at Milan and *Fenella ovvero La muta di Portici* (1831) at Venice.[2] Various minor masters in Italy supplied the demand for light entertainment with their comic operas, especially a characteristic one-act type, the *farsa in un atto*, an example of which is *Adelina* (Venice, 1810), by Pietro Generali (1773–1832). But the opera seria in Italy held conservatively to the old traditions until signs of change began to appear after 1800 with the works of Giovanni Simone Mayr (1763–1845).[3]

Mayr was a Bavarian who came to Italy at an early age and, after studies at Venice, where his first opera *(Saffo)* was given in 1794, settled at Bergamo. There he directed music in the church of Santa Maria Maggiore and founded, in 1805, a music school, where Donizetti was to receive his training. The most important of his seventy operas were *Lodoïska* (1800), *Ginevra di Scozia* ("Ginevra of Scotland," 1801), *Adelasia ed Aleramo* (1807), *La rosa bianca e la rosa rossa* ("The White Rose and the Red Rose," 1813), and *Medea in Corinto* (1813). Mayr was a thoroughly Italianized German, like Hasse and J. C. Bach, but he was able to accomplish something that Jommelli had vainly attempted fifty years earlier: namely, to induce the Italian public to accept some changes in the forms and style of serious opera music. Like Traetta, Mayr drew often on French sources for his librettos. A case in point is his *Il sacrifizio d'Ifigenia* (1811; revised as *Ifigenia in Aulide*, 1820), in which the libretto follows closely that used for Gluck's *Iphigénie en Aulide*, an opera that did not find acceptance in Italian theaters until the San Carlo performance of 1812. Use of French sources necessarily led him to include a consider-

2. Excerpts from Pavesi's operas are in Gossett, ed., *Italian Opera 1810–1840*, vol. 37.

3. Kretzschmar, "Die musikgeschichtliche Bedeutung Simon Mayrs"; Schiedermair, *Beiträge zur Geschichte der Oper*; Freeman, "Johann Simon Mayr and His *Ifigenia in Aulide*."

able number of ensembles and choruses, a practice to which Mayr introduced one of his later librettists, Felice Romani, who carried it on in the librettos he afterwards wrote for Mercadante, Bellini, and Donizetti. The use of the chorus—sometimes as a set piece, sometimes as part of the dramatic action, sometimes as background to a solo—was only one aspect of the generally greater flexibility of form which began to characterize Italian opera in the early nineteenth century. The old Metastasian opera seria had in principle permitted only three types of solo song—recitativo secco, recitativo accompagnato, and aria—and the three were kept separate. A soloist was seldom interrupted in the course of an aria, and when he had finished he made his exit, thereby bringing that scene to an end. Metastasio's formal pattern, from which eighteenth-century composers of opera seria departed only exceptionally, gradually in nineteenth-century Italian opera came to be modified at will by a more or less thorough intermingling, in the same scene, of several soloists and different types of solo song (such as the cavatina-cabaletta for an entrance aria),[4] perhaps also with ensembles, choruses, and orchestral passages, the whole being organized on a broad musico-dramatic plan. Something of this kind, of course, had already taken place in the opera buffa ensemble finales in the eighteenth century, as well as in the operas of Gluck and his followers in France and Germany; but the idea penetrated only slowly to the more conservative opera seria in Italy. Another eventual new form in nineteenth-century Italian opera was the so-called *scena ed aria* for a single soloist, which consisted usually of a recitativo accompagnato followed by an aria, the whole in contrasting tempi and of a dramatic rather than lyrical or reflective character.

These formal developments were certainly foreshadowed in the works of Mayr, but their full realization was reserved for his successors. A more immediately important innovation of his was to make the orchestra richer in sonority and texture, and to use the woodwinds and brasses, not only in the overtures and set pieces but also in accompaniments, to an extent hitherto unheard of in Italian opera. The variety of instrumental color and the sometimes sheerly overpowering sound of the Italian opera or-

4. These terms are discussed later in this chapter.

chestra of the nineteenth century—as in Verdi's *Aida*, for example—go back ultimately to the example of Mayr.

Rossini

Italian composers of the early *ottocento* was soon to come under the domination of a young genius, Gioacchino Rossini,[5] who began his meteoric career in 1810 with *La cambiale di matrimonio* ("The Marriage Contract"), a one-act farsa staged at the Teatro San Moisè, Venice. There followed in rapid succession a variety of stage works, of which *L'inganno felice* ("The Happy Deception," 1812), another farsa, and *La pietra del paragone* ("The Touchstone," 1812), a melodramma giocoso, were particularly outstanding. European fame began in 1813 with *Tancredi*, an opera seria,[6] and *L'italiana in Algeri* ("The Italian Girl in Algiers"), an opera buffa, and was confirmed for all time by the worldwide success of *Almaviva ossia L'inutile precauzione* ("Almaviva; or, The Useless Precaution")—better known by its later title, *Il barbiere di Siviglia ("The Barber of Seville")*—in spite of the spectacular failure of its first performance at Rome in 1816. *Otello*, produced at Naples in the same year, was given frequently until it fell into oblivion after Verdi's *Otello* came out in 1887. Although the libretto is an incredibly silly caracature of Shakespeare, Rossini's opera contains—especially in the third act—some of the most beautiful music he ever wrote.

Very few composers have equaled Rossini in rhythmic

5. See biographies by Radiciotti, Toye, and Weinstock; see also Stendhal, *Vie de Rossini* (untrustworthy for facts but lively reading); Strunk, ed., *Source Readings*, pp. 808-26; and Gossett, "Gioacchino Rossini," which contains a very complete bibliography.

6. *Tancredi* is based on a play by Voltaire, but Rossi's libretto for the first performance in Venice omitted the final death scene. Instead of having Tancredi die in combat, Rossi permits Tancredi's life to be spared so that he can learn of Amenaide's innocence. When *Tancredi* was staged in Ferrara one month later (March, 1813), it was given a tragic ending together with a new musical setting by Rossini. In all subsequent performances during the nineteenth century, Rossini reinstated the Venetian finale, apparently guided by audience preference for the *lieto fine*. Both versions of *Tancredi* have been published in the new edition of Rossini's operas, the Ferrara version having come to light as recently as 1974. Cf. Gossett, "Happy Ending for a Tragic Finale."

élan and sheer tunefulness. It is difficult to analyze the patent charm of these apparently effortless, seemingly artless Rossinian melodies that well forth in a ceaseless stream from his operas. Held within the frame of a persistent rhythmic motif (typically with dotted notes or in 6/8 meter), cast in short regular phrases of narrow range which are often immediately repeated, crystal clear in their harmonic implications, punctuated by occasional emphasized chromatic notes, and sometimes modulating in their second period to the rather remote mediant key instead of the familiar dominant, they seem to gather up in themselves the whole national genius for pure vocal melody as the elemental mode of musical expression. (See example 20.1, the celebrated cabaletta

Example 20.1: Aria "Di tanti palpiti," *Tancredi,* Act I

from *Tancredi,* which is said to have been adopted as a favorite melody by the gondoliers of Venice.) Such tunes require the lightest possible texture in the accompaniment, and they will not enter into contrapuntal combinations; in places where Rossini gives a melody to the orchestra, the voice is kept in the musical background, having perhaps detached interjections or a patter of words in monotone.

There is some coloratura ornamentation of the melodic line in Rossini, but it is not excessive for the period. In all his operas after 1815, Rossini sought to curb the abuse of ornamentation by writing out the ornaments and cadenzas instead of leaving them to be improvised by the singers, as had been the former practice; and it is one of the minor ironies of musical history that he has sometimes been accused of introducing excessive coloratura into opera, simply because his scores are *in appearance* more florid than those of his predecessors. Moreover, it must be remembered that in Italian serious operas of the nineteenth century, coloratura passages were not intended to be taken at high speed by a light voice but were to be sung rather slowly and expressively by a dramatic coloratura—a type of singer with which the present generation is not familiar. Rossini was one of the last important composers to write castrato roles,[7] and he was also one of the first to appreciate the value of contralto or mezzo-soprano voices in leading parts, as in *L'italiana*, *Il barbiere*, and *Semiramide*.

Already in *Tancredi* Rossini had introduced an unusual number of large ensembles; in *Elisabetta, regina d'Inghilterra* ("Elizabeth, Queen of England," 1815) and *Otello*, he took the further step of having all the recitatives accompanied by the orchestra. His technique of ensemble writing is best exemplified, of course, in the comic operas, above all in *Il barbiere*. His ensembles are always lively, realistic, and full of contrasts; musically, they are kaleidoscopic rather than symphonic as in Mozart. Their principle of unity is mainly that of steadily mounting excitement, sometimes assisted by the famous Rossinian crescendo. This is a deceptively simple device (and one easily abused), consisting in many repetitions of a passage, each time at a higher pitch and with fuller orchestration; the classic example is the "Calunnia" aria in *Il barbiere*.

Rossini's treatment of the orchestra, though criticized by some of his contemporaries as noisy and obtrusive, seems to us now a model of clarity, economy of means, and deft choice of instrumental color. Always kept tactfully subordinate when accompanying solos, it comes into its own in the ensembles and especially in the overtures, many of which are still played today, detached from the operas for which they were originally written.

Rossini's first opera of importance after *Otello* was *La Cenerentola* (1817), a semicomic treatment of the tale of Cinderella, abounding in melodies from the inexhaustible Rossinian

---

7. The castrato role in his *Aureliano in Palmire* (1813) was sung by Giambattista Velluti, one of the last great castrati, who also appeared in Meyerbeer's *Il crociato in Egitto* (1824).

treasure-house, an excellent specimen of that hedonistic manner described by Stendhal as "seldom sublime, but never tiresome." An equally attractive work is *La gazza ladra* ("The Thieving Magpie," 1817), now remembered chiefly for its overture. *Mosè in Egitto* (1818), a "sacred story of tragic impact," is especially notable for the stirring *preghiera con coro* near the end of Act III; this opera, in the extensively revised version given at Paris in 1827, with its generally elevated style and many choral scenes, clearly foreshadows the more famous *Guillaume Tell* of 1829. *La donna del lago* ("The Lady of the Lake," 1819) has a romantic libretto adapted from Scott's poem, but the few romantic touches in the music itself are evidently only skindeep. The last opera for Italy was *Semiramide* (1823), a "tragic melodrama" with a huge score, including one of Rossini's finest overtures (built for the most part on themes from the opera itself), many ensembles and large choruses, and arias in a great variety of forms with much coloratura—all in all, a good illustration of the progress of Italian opera since the beginning of the century. *Semiramide* also has a military band on stage, a novel feature that was frequently imitated by later composers.[8]

After one short season in London, Rossini in 1824 moved to Paris, where he remained for most of the rest of his life. Here he presented, among other operas of his own, *Moïse en Egypte*, the French version of the above-mentioned *Mosè in Egitto;*[9] *Le Siège de Corinthe* ("The Siege of Corinth," 1826), an extensively revised form of another of his Italian operas, *Maometto II* (1820); *Il viaggio à Reims* ("The Journey to Reims," 1825), performed to celebrate the coronation of Charles X; and *Le Comte Ory* (1828), in which music from *Il viaggio à Reims* reappears. As *Moïse* and *Le Siège de Corinthe* were important steps toward the formation of French grand opera, so *Le Comte Ory*, an original and sparkling opéra comique, demonstrated Rossini's mastery of the French comic style and in turn exercised a strong influence on the later course of French opéra comique and operetta (see chapter 20). With *Guillaume Tell*, Rossini reached the climax of both his art

---

8. Cf. Longyear, "The *Banda sul Palco*: Stage Bands in 19th-Century Opera."

9. The French version of *Mosè in Egitto* was also presented in an Italian version and entitled *Mosè e Faraone*. Cf. Conati, "Between Past and Future."

and his fame. He was then thirty-seven. Whether from distrust of his own powers, disgust at the new direction of public taste as evinced by the rage for Meyerbeer, or a combination of these and other motives, he wrote no more operas—though the *Stabat Mater* of 1842 showed that he had not forgotten how to be dramatic in music. But he had carried Italian opera, as Beethoven had carried the symphony, through the transition from the eighteenth to the nineteenth century; and he had furnished in *Il barbiere* an immortal masterpiece of opera buffa and in *Guillaume Tell* one of the finest examples of grand opera of the early nineteenth century.[10]

Donizetti, Bellini, and Mercadante

The course of Italian opera from Rossini to Verdi is summed up in the work of Gaetano Donizetti (1797–1848), Vincenzo Bellini (1801–1835), and Saverio Mercadante (1795–1870). Donizetti, a pupil of Simon Mayr, was a composer of almost incredible fecundity, whose seventy-three operas make up only a fraction of his total musical output.[11] His first important opera was the two-act romantic tragedy *Anna Bolena* (1830), followed two years later by the romantic comedy *L'elisir d'amore* ("The Elixir of Love"). The idyllic, sentimental charm of the familiar aria "Una furtiva lagrima" in the latter of these is all the more effective by contrast with the prevailing lighthearted character of the rest of the music.

    Lucrezia Borgia (1833) and *Lucia di Lammermoor* (1835) may be taken as typical of the more violent sort of romantic Italian operas of this period. *Lucrezia* was adapted from Hugo's drama, *Lucia* from Scott's novel. Both are full of melodramatic situations well adapted to Donizetti's style, and it is undeniable that his mu-

---

10. In 1980, the city of Pesaro (Rossini's birthplace) inaugurated the Rossini Opera Festival, which, in conjunction with Fondazione Rossini, is committed to the presentation of all of Rossini's operas.

11. Biographies by Donati-Petteni, Zavadini, Weinstock, and Ashbrook; see also Ashbrook and Budden, "Gaetano Donizetti," and Ashbrook, *Donizetti and His Operas*, which has an excellent bibliography.

sic at its best has a primitive dramatic power even when its substance is only rudimentary, as in the closing scene of *Lucrezia*. The score of *Lucia* is worked out with more critical care and its effects are less often marred by trivial melodic episodes; the famous sextet in Act II and the "Mad Scene" in Act III are excellent examples of Donizetti's art. He had a Midas gift of turning everything into the kind of melody which people could remember and sing, or at least recognize when they heard it sung next day in the streets. His tunes have a robust swing, with catchy rhythms reinforced by frequent sforzandos on the offbeats.

A common musical form for arias (and sometimes duets) in Donizetti, as in all Italian opera of his time and later in the nineteenth century, is the *cavatina* or *cantabile*, an expressive, melodious slow movement, followed usually by a *cabaletta*, a fiery allegro with virtuoso vocal effects and a climactic close; recitative dialogue and even phrases for the chorus might intervene between the two parts of such an aria, bringing it into connection with the ongoing dramatic action.[12] Frequent ensembles and choruses were the rule in opera by Donizetti's time; he keeps the chorus onstage a great deal of the time, not always for dramatic reasons but sometimes simply to add volume and color to the musical background. Another common device, heard sometimes in Spontini and increasingly often in Rossini, Donizetti, and later composers, is the declaiming of a salient melodic phrase in unison or octaves by both singers of a duet or by a whole ensemble or chorus—an electrifying effect at high moments in a scene.

Like Rossini and Bellini before him, Donizetti was invited to compose for the Paris theaters. Of his five operas originally written to French texts, the most important were the opéra comique *La Fille du régiment* ("The Daughter of the Regiment," 1840) and the four-act grand opera *La Favorite* (1840). The former, still very popular, shows traces of both Rossini and Boieldieu in some of its melodies and rhythms. *La Favorite* is uneven, though the third act is very fine both musically and dramatically,

---

12. *Cavatina* does not define a particular kind of solo song. Its connotations are as varied as the scores in which the term appears, from the cavatina in Graun's *Montezuma* to that in Weber's *Der Freischütz*, from the slow-fast cavatina-cabaletta type in Mayr's operas to the multipurpose application of the term in the works of Donizetti. *Cantabile-mezzo-cabaletta* designates the three-part form with an intervening section.

Example 20.2: *Linda di Chamounix*, Act II

the whole representing a composite of borrowed and newly composed music.[13] Donizetti's last two serious operas were both written for Vienna: *Linda di Chamounix* (1842) and *Maria di Rohan*
(1843). *Linda*, the better of the two, is an "opera semiseria" with
mingled comic, romantic, and pathetic scenes, matched with un-
affectedly expressive music (example 20.2).

Donizetti's opera buffa *Don Pasquale* (Paris, 1843) is
worthy to be named with Rossini's *Il barbiere di Siviglia* and Verdi's *Falstaff* among the masterpieces of nineteenth-century comic
opera. The comedy of *Don Pasquale* is delightful in itself, but it
is also touched with deeper feeling and thus lifted above the level
of mere amusement; this is particularly evident in the duet of
Norina and Don Pasquale in Act III, a poignant juxtaposition of
buffoonery and pathos.

While the music of Donizetti's serious operas represents
the more hearty, extrovert qualities of romanticism, that of Bellini's is marked by the more inward, and lyrical qualities. Bellini's principal early operas were *Il pirata* ("The Pirate," 1827)
and *La straniera* ("The Stranger," 1829). His European fame began with *La sonnambula* ("The Sleepwalker") and the masterwork *Norma*, both of them produced at Milan in 1831. Bellini's
last opera, *I Puritani di Scozia*, ("The Puritans of Scotland") was
written for Paris and performed there in 1835.[14]

When Bellini died at the age of thirty-four, he had written nine operas. At the same age, Rossini had written thirty-four
operas and Donizetti, thirty-five. One reason for this difference
in the rate of production is evident from a glance at the autograph
score of *Norma*, which is full of cancellations and emendations.
Bellini worked more slowly because he was more particular about
his librettos and more fully dedicated to an ideal union of words
and music. He had a loyal collaborator in Felice Romani, who
furnished the librettos for all his important operas except *I Puritani*. One consequence of Bellini's sensitiveness to the text is that

13. Self-borrowings are characteristic of all Donizetti's operas, often involving highly improbable reuse of materials.

14. Recent studies of Bellini's life and works include those by Orrey, Weinstock, Adamo
and Lippmann, and Brunel. See also Bellini, *Epistolario*; Pizzetti, *La musica italiana dell'*
Ottocento; Pastura, *Bellini secondo la storia*; Pannain, *Ottocento musicale italiano*;
Lippmann, "Vincenzo Bellini."

his recitative not only is more correct, musical, and flexible than that of his contemporaries, but also at the right dramatic moments rises to extraordinary intensity of expression, as in the marvelous scene that opens the second act of *Norma*.

Bellini's melodies are of incomparable elegance, evolving in long lines usually without much obvious repetition of motifs but sometimes with subtle irregularities in the length of the phrases. The elegiac, melancholy character of some of Bellini's music (example 20.3)[15] has often been compared to Chopin's, and indeed

Example 20.3: *La sonnambula*, Act II, finale

the two composers are similar not only in this respect but also in that both require a sympathetic interpreter to do them justice. It must never be forgotten, in dealing with Italian opera of this period, that everything depends on the singers. Composers most often wrote their parts with certain singers in mind,[16] and many a melody which looks banal enough on the page becomes luminous with meaning when sung by one who understands the Italian *bel canto* and the traditions of this type of opera. This is especially true of

15. Cf. Dahlhaus, *Die Musik des 19. Jahrhunderts*, pp. 96-98.

16. In Bellini's case, Giovanni Battista Rubini and Guiditta Pasta were the two singers for whom he wrote some of his most famous music.

Bellini, in whose works the whole drama is concentrated in melody to a degree surpassing even Rossini, Donizetti, and Verdi. Yet Bellini's harmony, while never calling attention to itself, is considerably more varied and interesting than that of Donizetti, and his treatment of the orchestra, particularly in the later works, is by no means negligible. The principal place of instrumental music (aside from the overture) in the operas of these two composers is in the introduction to a scena; comparison of any such orchestral passages in Donizetti with the introduction to the first act of Bellini's *Norma* will strikingly demonstrate the latter's superiority. In the accompaniments, Bellini's orchestra is, of course, completely subordinated to the singer. Like all his contemporaries, he frequently gives the melody to both voice and instruments, ornamented for one and plain for the other; or he may realize the melody in unbroken continuity in the orchestra while the voice joins in with fragmentary phrases—but it is always one and the same melody. Another device, found equally in Rossini, Donizetti, and Verdi, is the announcement of an aria by playing the first phrase or two in the orchestra before the singer begins. This has a superficial resemblance to the "false start" of seventeenth- and eighteenth-century opera arias, where the voice sings an opening phrase and then breaks off to begin again, but the difference between the two procedures is significant: in Scarlatti or Handel, the beginning is like a sonorously proclaimed title; in Donizetti or Bellini, it is a seductive appeal for the audience's attention. It has also the practical purpose of giving the singer time to disengage himself from the business of the preceding recitative and come downstage into position for his aria.

With Bellini, as with Donizetti, the chorus is an important factor. It is most conspicuous in *I Puritani,* where Bellini was adapting himself to grand opera on the scale required at Paris, but is is also used effectively in *Norma,* as in the opening scene— a chorus was practically obligatory in the first scene of an opera at this time—and in the cavatina "Casta diva," where the chorus forms part of the quiet musical background for Norma's solo. A few choral scenes in Bellini's earlier operas, notably those in the second act of *La sonnambula,* suggest in some inexplicable way the feeling of Greek drama or the early Florentine *favola in musica.*

One of the most popular composers in Italy in the 1820s and 1830s was Saverio Mercadante (1795–1870), a Neapolitan and pupil of Zingarelli.[17] Mercadante can perhaps be characterized as a Janus-faced composer; his works written before 1837, including the successful *"opera semiseria" Elsia e Claudio* (Milan, 1821) and *I Normanni a Parigi* ("The Normans in Paris," Turin, 1832), are stylistically related to the Italian operas of his contemporaries, whereas those written after 1837, the so-called "reform" operas, point toward the mature style of Verdi. The pivotal work is *Il giuramento* ("The Oath," 1837), composed under the influence of Mercadante's contact with French grand opera during a sojourn in Paris. It initiates some of the "reforms" which Mercadante described in his oft-quoted letter addressed to Florimo, librarian at the Naples Conservatory, where Mercadante served as director from 1840 until his death. Further manifestation of these reforms can be found in what many consider Mercadante's best operas, *Il bravo* ("The Brave Man," Milan, 1839) and *La Vestale* (Naples, 1840). Example 20.4, from the latter work, illustrates the full-bodied, rich texture and lusty melodic sweep of his style, as well as another new trait in nineteenth-century Italian opera—the frequent use of the more remote flat keys.

None of the changes in Italian opera from 1800 to 1840 had overturned the foundations already established. Starting from the axiom that music should prevail over drama, the Italians had always held to two principles of opera: the solo voice, and therefore *melody*, as the essential vehicle of musical expression; and division into distinct numbers, mainly recitatives and arias, as the governing rule of the musical structure. Beginning with Mayr and Rossini, composers in the nineteenth century made the orchestra more colorful and gave it more to do, but they never questioned the supremacy of melody in the total musical scheme; rather, they tried to make the melody more expressive and thus to bring it, with the aid of harmony, rhythm, and instrumental color, into closer relation with the drama. Similarly, while loosening the formal structure of opera by giving prominence to ensembles and

17. Florimo, *La scuola musicale di Napoli*; Notarnicola, *Saverio Mercadante* and *Saverio Mercadante nella gloria*; Ballola, "Mercadante e *Il bravo*"; and (by way of antidote) Walker, "Mercadante and Verdi." Facsimiles of the operas cited are in Gossett, ed., *Italian Opera 1810-1840*, vols. 14–22.

Example 20.4: *La Vestale*, Act II, finale

(Example 20.4 continued)

(Example 20.4 continued)

choruses, they never renounced the general principle of separate numbers; rather, they made the numbers longer and more diversified within themselves, combining soloists and chorus, and replacing the three-part da capo aria with the *cantabile-mezzo-cabaletta*, or the old recitative-aria combination with the more ample and varied *scena ed aria*. The first impulse toward the expansion of the orchestra came from Germany through Simon Mayr; the model for the greater flexibility of form was French opera, but French opera as developed mainly by foreigners resident at Paris—Gluck, Cherubini, Spontini, Paer, Rossini, Meyerbeer—who had brought into French opera certain traits from their own countries. Thus, opera in Italy, which at the turn of the century had been a rather local affair, gradually began to assume a more cosmopolitan character, though without sacrifice of its individuality. This process of adjustment, already well advanced in Donizetti and Bellini, was to be carried to its final stage by Verdi.

Verdi

Don Pasquale, Donizetti's last important work, was produced in 1843. For the next fifty years, the history of Italian opera is dominated by a single figure, that of Giuseppe Verdi (1813–1901). Verdi began where his countrymen left off,[18] brought the older Italian opera to its greatest height, and finally in his own person embodied the change from that style to the more subtle and sophisticated manner of the later nineteenth century. An Italian of the Italians, faithful to their instincts, a clear-sighted and indomitable artist, he maintained almost single-handed the cause of Italian opera against the tide of enthusiasm for Wagner and in the

---

18. Lists of Italian opera composers of the early and middle nineteenth centuries may be found in Adler, *Handbuch der Musikgeschichte*, 2:908, 912–14. The most important of them are P.A. Coppola (1793–1877), composer of *La pazza per amore* (1835); G. Pacini (1796–1867), *Saffo* (1840); the brothers Luigi (1805–1859) and Federico (1809–1877) Ricci, whose best work was the jointly composed *Crispino e la comare* (1850); A. Cagnoni (1828–1896), *Don Bucefalo* (1847); E. Petrella (1813–1877), *Marco Visconti* (1854) and *Jone* (1858); and F. Marchetti (1831–1902), *Ruy Blas* (1869).

end vindicated the tradition of Scarlatti and Rossini alongside that of Keiser and Weber.[19] The old struggle between Latin and German, southern and northern music in opera—the singer against the orchestra, melody against polyphony, simplicity against complexity—was incarnate in the nineteenth century in the works of Verdi and Wagner, who represented the two ideals in all their irreconcilable perfection.

With the exception of *Falstaff* (1893) and one early unsuccessful work, all Verdi's operas are serious. His first triumph was achieved at Milan in 1842 with the biblical opera *Nabucodonosor* (generally known as *Nabucco*), followed a year later by *I Lombardi alla prima crociata* ("The Lombards at the First Crusade")—both works which in their large choruses and melodramatic situations recall Meyerbeer's *Robert le Diable*. International fame began with *Ernani* (1844), on a libretto arranged by Francesco Piave from Victor Hugo's drama. The music of these early operas showed Verdi as a composer with a sure feeling for the theater and a melodic gift in which the facility of Donizetti was combined with greater breadth of phrase and ferocious energy of expression (example 20.5).

Verdi was immensely popular in Italy because he brought to the accepted forms and idiom of opera just that touch of dynamic individuality which was needed; but there was a further reason only indirectly connected with the music itself. Italy during the *Risorgimento* (ca. 1815–1870) was seething with revolution, and Verdi's operas came to play an important part in the patriotic movements of the 1840s and 1850s. Though their scenes and characters ostensibly had no connection with contemporary events, the librettos were filled with conspiracies, political assassinations, appeals to liberty, and exhortations against tyranny, all of which were readily understood in the intended sense by sympathetic audiences. *Nabucco, I Lombardi, Ernani, I due Foscari* ("The Two Foscari," 1844), *Giovanna d'Arco* (1845), and especially *Atilla* (1846) and the "occasional" opera *La battaglia di Legnano* ("The Battle of Legnano," Rome, 1849) all gave rise to

19. See Toye, *Verdi*; Hussey, *Verdi*; Walker, *The Man Verdi*; Budden, *The Operas of Verdi*; Weaver, ed., *Verdi*; Conati, *Encounters with Verdi*; Kimbell, *Verdi in the Age of Italian Romanticism*. See also the bibliography in Porter, "Guiseppe Verdi."

Example 20.5: *Ernani*, Act III

fervent demonstrations and made Verdi's name a rallying-cry for Italian patriots. Even *Rigoletto* (1851), based on a very good adaptation by Piave of Victor Hugo's *Le Roi s'amuse*, was attacked by the censorship,[20] and the names of historical characters (especially King Francis I of France) as well as several other details

20. Censorship was a severe problem for Italian composers, especially those working in Rome, Palermo, and Naples during the *primo ottocento*.

had to be changed before production was permitted. A similar situation arose with regard to *Un ballo in maschera* ("A Masked Ball") at Naples in 1859, where the authorities insisted on the transformation of the original Gustavus III of Sweden into an imaginary Earl of Warwick and the locale of this fantastic and bloody melodrama to the Puritan city of Boston in New England! It was during the popular demonstrations attending the preparation of this opera that crowds in front of his hotel shouted "Viva Verdi"—a cry of double meaning, for the letters of the composer's name formed the initials of "Vittorio Emanuele Re D'Italia," and thus he came to be identified with the cause of Italian national unity as a symbol.

With the production of *Il trovatore* ("The Troubadour") and *La traviata* ("The Erring Woman") in 1853, a climax of Verdi's work in the purely Italian opera was reached. We may therefore pause here to indicate some of the essential characteristics of the style by which Verdi was known and loved in his own land at this time.

Verdi's principal librettists were Temistocle Solera *(Oberto Nabucco, I Lombardi, Giovanna d'Arco, Attila)*, Francesco Piave *(Ernani, I due Foscari, Macbeth, Il corsaro, Stiffelio, Rigoletto, La traviata, Aroldo, Simon Buccanegra, La forza del destino)*, and Salvatore Cammarano *(Luisa Miller, Il trovatore)*. The literary sources of the librettos were various: from Schiller came *Giovanna d'Arco, Luisa Miller (Kabale und Liebe), I masnadieri (Die Räuber),* and *Don Carlos;* from Victor Hugo, *Ernani* and *Rigoletto,;* from Dumas the Younger, *La traviata (La Dame aux camélias);* from Scribe, *Les Vêpres siciliennes* and *Un ballo in maschera;* from Byron, *I due Foscari* and *Il corsaro;* from the Spanish dramatist Gutierrez came *Il trovatore* and *Simon Boccanegra,* and from another Spaniard, the Duke of Rivas, *La forza del destino;* from Shakespeare, Verdi drew *Macbeth, Otello,* and *Falstaff* (the last two arranged by Arrigo Boito), as well as the projected, but never completed, *King Lear* and *Hamlet.*

The plots (except for *Falstaff)* are all serious, gloomy, and violent; the earlier works especially are typical examples of the blood-and-thunder romantic melodrama, marked by situations of strong passion in rapid succession, giving vivid contrasts and a theatrically effective sweep to the action, however questionable the details may be from a dramatist's viewpoint. Influences upon this type of plot may be traced through Meyerbeer in France and through Mayr, Mercadante, and Donizetti in Italy; but whereas in the French operas horror and violence serve to reinforce the humanitarian message, now they are being used for their own sake. The obscurity of many of Verdi's plots is due largely to the extreme condensation upon which the composer insisted, and often a careful reading of the libretto is necessary in order to understand the action. Whatever may be thought of the subject matter, it cannot be denied that it always offered the kind of opportunity which Verdi needed to exercise his special gifts.

The essence of his early style is a certain primitive directness, an uninhibited vigor and naturalness of utterance. This results often in melodies of apparent triviality, which are nevertheless patently sincere and almost invariably appropriate to the dramatic situation. His effects are always obtained by means of voices. His orchestration grew constantly more expert and original from the earliest to the latest operas,[21] but the orchestra never has the symphonic significance or the polyphonic texture of Wagner's. The overtures (especially those for *Luisa Miller, Nabucco, Les Vêpres siciliennes*) are important, but many of his operas begin with only a short orchestral prelude. The ballet music is seldom distinguished, and most of the instrumental music for ball scenes, marches, and the like (often performed by a military band on the stage) is trite. Nature painting and the depiction of the fantastic, so important in contemporary German romantic opera, find little place in Verdi.[22] His interest is in the expression of human passions in song, to which all else is subordinated; and through that medium he creates a musical structure of sensuous beauty and emotional power, basically simple and uncomplicated by philosophical theories, with an appeal so profound, so elemental, that it can hardly be conveyed or even intelligibly discussed in any other language than that of music itself.

The heart of the melodramatic, romantic Verdi is to be found in three works: *Ernani, Rigoletto,* and *Il trovatore.* The

21. See the "Introduzione" to Act I of *Rigoletto,* with its three orchestras, playing together. Cf. Chusid, "Notes on the Performance of *Rigoletto.*"

22. There are, of course, exceptions. See, for example, *Attila.*

last is particularly rich in traits that mark the composer's works in this period: the roaring unison of the "Anvil Chorus"; the unbelievable contrast of moods in the "miserere" scene; the nostalgic sentiment of Azucena's "Ai nostri monti"; Manrico's lusty bravura aria "Di quella pira"—these and other melodies from this opera are so well known that citation or comment is superfluous. *Rigoletto*, almost equally agonizing in its plot and situations, is a more unified whole and superior in character delineation, besides containing the famous quartet, one of the finest serious dramatic ensembles in all opera.

Beside the naked brutality of *Rigoletto, Il trovatore,* and some of the other early works, *La traviata* is a refined drawing-room tragedy; its more restrained, almost intimate musical style had already been foreshadowed in *Luisa Miller* (1849). Several details in *La traviata* are significant in the light of Verdi's future development. The orchestra is of relatively greater dramatic importance: in the ballroom scene of Act I, it furnishes a continuous background of dance music against which a conversation is carried on;[23] the opening strain of the prelude, with its pathetic minor harmonies in the divided violins, recurs most effectively at the beginning of Act III to set the mood for the closing scenes of the opera. Then, too, there is an occasional vocal phrase which demonstrates a greater freedom in the melodic line, a beginning of emancipation from the usually all-too-regular patterns of the early Verdi (example 20.6);[24] the entire scene which culminates in this beautiful passage is a fine example of moving dramatic declamation.

Several of Verdi's operas make systematic use of recurring themes. Mere repetition of previously heard themes was not at all uncommon in operas of the first half of the nineteenth century, and instances may also be found in Mozart, Grétry, and Monteverdi. Verdi's procedure should not be confused either with the simple earlier practice or with Wagner's system of leitmotifs (to be discussed in chapter 22); it consists rather in introducing a

23. Cf. also the last scene of *Un ballo in maschera*, and the waltzes in Strauss's *Rosenkavalier*.

24. The model for the melody in example 20.6 can be found in "O Pia mendace" from *Pia de' Tolomei* (1837) by Donizetti. See Budden, *The Operas of Verdi*, 2:36.

Example 20.6: *La traviata*, Act II

VERDI

A - ma - mi,Al - fre - do, a - ma - mi

quan - t'io t'a - mo, a -

ma - mi,Al - fre - do, quan - t'io t'a - mo,

dim.

quan - t'io t'a - mo Ad - di - o!

musical phrase already associated with a certain dramatic situation into a later situation with the purpose of underlining the similarity—and also perhaps, by implication, the contrast—between the two.[25] Thus, in *Ernani* the motif of the pledge, and in *Rigoletto* that of Monterone's curse, recur at appropriate moments in the opera; *I due Foscari* offers further examples, as do also *Il trovatore* and especially *La traviata*. The use of recurring themes in *Aida* and *Otello* is thus only a continuation and refinement of Verdi's earlier practice and of course has nothing to do with any alleged Wagnerian influence.

With regard to the ensembles in Verdi, one can do little but refer the reader to the scores. Telling declamation, perfect dramatic timing, and an infallible sense of climax mark them all; perhaps the most remarkable feature is the composer's endless inventiveness in sound combinations, his reveling in sweet and powerful sonorities. The *sotto voce* ensembles, such as those in the Paris version of *Macbeth*, have an indescribably mysterious, suggestive quality.

Verdi was not a composer who studied the scores of his rivals with a view to excelling them on their own ground; secure in his own musical and dramatic instincts, he pointedly avoided

25. Cf. Roncaglia, "Il 'tema-cardine' nell' opera di Giuseppe Verdi"; Kerman, *Opera as Drama*, pp. 155ff.

too close acquaintance with other composers' music. Almost the only specific non-Italian influence which can be traced in his works is that of Meyerbeer, for whom he had considerable admiration. *Il trovatore*, in its bewildering array of incidents and musical effects, is very reminiscent of Meyerbeer, and the character of Azucena, the gypsy mother, has often been compared to that of Fidès, the mother of John of Leyden in Meyerbeer's *Prophète*. The magic attraction of Paris for Italian composers was still strong, and it is not surprising that Verdi should have aspired, like Cherubini, Spontini, Rossini, Bellini, and Donizetti before him, to the satisfaction of a Paris success. He made some essays in the grand-opera style in his early career, especially in *Giovanna d'Arco. I Lombardi* had been adapted and successfully performed at Paris in 1847, under the title *Jérusalem*. An even more thorough adoption of grand-opera style occurred in 1855, when Verdi composed *Les Vêpres siciliennes*, using Scribe's five-act libretto based upon the historical subject of the massacre of the French by the Sicilians in 1282. The story reads almost like a travesty of all the devices for which Verdi's operas were famous; the music, with the exception of the overture, is in general inferior to Verdi's usual style. A greater success was obtained with *Don Carlos* (Paris, 1867), another work along grand-opera lines, excessively long in the original version but containing many fine individual numbers.

Other operas of the period between *La traviata* and *Aida* include *Simon Boccanegra*, which failed at its first appearance (1857) but was successful in a thoroughly revised version in 1881.[26] *Un ballo in maschera* is remarkable both for certain experimental details in the instrumental writing (for example, the canonic treatment of one of the themes in the prelude) and for the beginning of Verdi's later buffo style in the music given to Oscar, the page— a new idiom which is carried through the role of Fran Melitone in *La forza del destino* and reaches fruition in the pages of *Falstaff*. *La forza del destino* ("The Power of Destiny," St. Petersburg, 1862) is a somber melodrama distinguished by a score in which we can trace still further the progress of Verdi toward that long-

---

26. Verdi, with the help of Boito, revised *Simon Boccanegra*, eliminating those elements which were not part of his "Italian" vocabulary. A similar revision of *Don Carlos* was made in 1884.

breathed, broadly rhythmed, infinitely expressive melody which we associate with the composer's later style.

Early in 1870, Verdi accepted a commission to write a work for a new opera house at Cairo, to be produced as a festival performance in connection with the opening of the Suez Canal, and this resulted in *Aida*. The plot, based on a story by the French Egyptologist François Mariette, was sketched by Verdi and his friend Camille du Locle and put into poetic shape by Antonio Ghislanzoni. Ghislanzoni's share really amounted to little more than turning Verdi's ideas into verse, for the composer himself dictated the layout of scenes and even details of the dialogue, on the basis of his long experience with the theater.[27] The libretto is even more effective theatrically than the librettos of Verdi's earlier operas, since the details of the plot are clearer, the psychology of the characters more lifelike, and the action simpler and more straightforward. The first performance at Cairo in December 1871 was followed two months later by an equally successful one at La Scala in Milan.

Aida was in every respect the culmination of Verdi's art up to that time, uniting the melodic exuberance, the warmth and color of the Italians with the pageants, ballets, and choruses of grand opera. *Aida* is Italian opera made heroic, grand opera imbued with true human passion, a fusion of two great nineteenth-century styles. Verdi here surpassed himself in his own domain: he had never written better solo arias than Radames' "Celeste Aida" or Aida's soliloquy "Ritorna vincitor"; the finale of Act II exceeds in splendor anything from the earlier operas; and the closing scene is a climax in the expression of that mood of tragic poignancy of which Verdi had always been a master. But beyond such matters as these are still more significant advances. Music and drama are more tightly interwoven, and this in turn affects the form as a whole; for while *Aida* is still a number opera, the score possesses more continuity than any of Verdi's previous works. This is due in part, but not entirely, to two devices: (1) the use of recurring themes, more extensively and systematically than in any of the other operas; and (2) a pervasive, subtle exoticism. The

27. For details, see Verdi, *I copialettere*, pp. 631–75; Werfel and Stefan, eds., *Verdi: The Man in His Letters*, pp. 278–87.

latter is not the product of borrowed Egyptian native tunes but of Verdi's own sensitiveness to color, expressed not only in melodies of modal turn, with chromatic intervals, but also in original harmonies and many details of instrumentation (see, for example, the introduction to Act III). Even the ballet music, usually rather perfunctory with Verdi, here has a richness of harmony and scoring, a freshness of melodic and rhythmic invention, which make it of equal interest with the rest of the opera.

In a word, the production of *Aida* saw Verdi, then aged fifty-eight, at the summit of his career, wealthy, successful, the acknowledged master of Italian opera, the idol of his countrymen, a world-famous figure. Had he never written another note, his high position in the history of opera would have been secure. After the triumphal reception of the *Requiem* (1874), he himself felt that his active days as a composer were over. A mood of depression gripped him in the years around 1880, due to both political and musical conditions in Italy at the time. Wagnerian music and Wagnerian philosophy were threatening the very foundations of Italian art, and while Verdi was far from feeling envy toward Wagner, he was alarmed at what he felt was a false course on the part of many of his countrymen. In 1889, he wrote:

> Our young Italians are not patriots. If the Germans, basing themselves on Bach, have culminated in Wagner they act like good Germans, and it is well. But we, the descendants of Palestrina, commit a musical crime in imitating Wagner, and what we are doing is useless, not to say harmful.[28]

Although Verdi sensed the "irrepressible conflict" between German and Italian opera, he hesitated long before committing himself to battle. He was weary, haunted by distrust of his own powers, and apprehensive of public failure. For sixteen years after *Aida*, no new opera came from his pen. It was not until 1887, when the composer was over seventy years old, that *Otello* appeared, the greatest Italian tragic opera of the nineteenth century and the triumphant answer of Italian art to the threat of German domination.

---

28. Letter to Franco Faccio, 1889, quoted in Toye, *Verdi*, pp. 196ff. The sentiments here expressed dated from many years previous. See also Franz Werfel's novel, *Verdi*, for an imaginative treatment of this phase of the composer's life.

Verdi chose to counter the Nordic myth as operatic subject matter with a return to purely human drama, and he chose
the subjects of *Otello* and *Falstaff* from his favorite dramatist,
Shakespeare. The arrangement of the librettos was the work of
Boito, to whose skill and devotion much of the credit for both
works must be given. Boito's adaptations of Shakespeare are excellent. In *Otello*, especially, the delicate problem of shortening
the poetry so as to leave scope for the development of the music
is handled with skill, and the action of the original is followed
closely. Boito altered only a few details and added only the verses
of Iago's "Credo" in Act II.[29]

As to the music of *Otello*, we must beware of regarding
it as a complete break with Verdi's earlier style. It is rather the
culminating point of an evolution. Not all the older practices are
abandoned: there are precedents for the storm at the opening of
Act I (compare *Rigoletto*); the drinking song and chorus in the
same act; the serenade in the garden scene of Act II, with its
accompaniment of bagpipes, mandolins, and guitars; the duets,
conventional enough in their placing at the end of Acts I and II;
the ensembles, especially the magnificent one at the end of Act
III; and the superb theatrical close of this act, with Iago's melodramatic "Ecco il Leone!," which is in the best tradition of Italian opera. There are recitatives and arias—for example, Iago's
"Credo," Otello's "Ora e per sempre addio!," Desdemona's "Salce"
and "Ave Maria." But all these forms and styles in *Otello* have a
finish and perfection, a close connection with the drama, surpassing anything previous. Moreover, certain procedures are definitely new with this work. Perhaps the most obvious of these is
the continuity of the music throughout each act—that is, the absence of separate numbers, as in the earlier operas. But closer
attention shows that this does not involve a radical change in
structure; the divisions are still there, only their boundaries are
a little less distinct; instead of a double bar, there is an interlock-
ing or a transition. The sense of unity is also strengthened by the
magnificent use Verdi makes of the recurring motive of "the kiss,"
first heard in the orchestra near the end of the love duet in Act I

---

29. See Kerman, "Verdi's *Otello*, or Shakespeare Explained"; Roncaglia, *L'Otello di Giuseppe Verdi.*

and returning twice with indescribably poignant effect in the closing scene of the opera.

Much of the continuity of style in *Otello* must also be
attributed to the libretto, which offers few opportunities for numbers of the traditional sort, but rather being made up for the most
part of scenes of continuing action which are most appropriately
set to a different kind of music—a flexible, dramatically powerful,
sensitive, and infinitely varied melody, supported by the orchestra with characteristic rhythmic motifs for each scene and organized in long periods by means of the harmonic structure: "dramatic declamation in strict time substituted for classical recitative
on the one hand and Wagnerian polyphony on the other."[30] This
declamation does include both strict recitative (used especially effectively for the dialogue between Otello and Emilia at the end of
the scene of Desdemona's murder in Act IV) but also melodic
phrases of the most pronounced arioso character, with extreme
compression of emotion. No such free, passionate, long-spun melodic line had been heard in Italian opera since Monteverdi's *Poppea*. It is clearly enough the model for Puccini and other later
Italian composers, who constantly aimed at, but seldom attained,
the pathos of Verdi in this style (example 20.7).

Even within the more or less formal arias, the melody is
a long way removed from the singsong, regularly patterned tunes
of some of the early operas. It is no less expressive than these, no
less vocal, but nobler, more plastic, more richly interwoven with
the orchestra, more intimately wedded to the harmony. In the
harmonic idiom itself, Verdi never went to Wagnerian lengths of
chromaticism, though no composer was more alive to the effectiveness of a few judicious chromatic alterations. He was also aware
of the broadening conceptions of tonality which prevailed at this
time, as witness the freedom of his harmonic vocabulary and the
range of his modulations.[31]

Inasmuch as it has been claimed that Verdi in his later
operas was imitating the Wagnerian music drama, it may be well
not only to emphasize again the continuity of the musical style of

---

30. From a review of the first performance in *Secolo*, quoted in Toye, *Verdi*, p. 191.

31. See for example the tonal scheme of the duet at the end of Act I: G-flat–F–C–E–
D-flat.

Example 20.7: *Otello*, Act IV

Otello with that of Verdi's preceding works but also to point out certain fundamental differences which remain between the two composers. In the first place, *Otello* and *Falstaff* are both singer's operas; in spite of the greater independence of the orchestra, it is never made the center of the picture, and the instrumental music does not have either the self-sufficiency or the symphonic range of development that it has in Wagner. Second, Verdi never adopted a system of leading motifs; the formal unity of his operas is like that of the classical symphony rather than the romantic tone poem; that is, a union of relatively independent individual numbers with themes recurring only in a few exceptional cases. Third, Verdi's operas are human dramas, not myths. Their librettos have no hidden world, no symbolism, no set of meanings below the surface. They are free of any trace of the *Gesamtkunstwerk* or other theories. And finally, there is about Verdi's music a simplicity, a certain Latin quality of serenity, which the complex German soul of Wagner could never encompass. It is a classic, Mediterranean art, self-enclosed within limits which by their very existence make possible its perfection.

As *Otello* was the climax of tragic opera, so *Falstaff* (1893) represented the transfiguration of opera buffa. Written on a libretto arranged by Boito from Shakespeare's *Merry Wives of Windsor*, it is not only a remarkable achievement for an octogenarian but a magnificent final crescendo of a great career. Excelling all earlier works in brilliancy of orchestration, wealth of spontaneous melody, and absolute oneness of text and music, it is a technical tour de force, abounding in the most subtle beauties, which often pass so quickly that only a close acquaintance with the score enables the listener to perceive them all. Because of this very fineness of workmanship and perhaps also because of the profound sophistication of the ideas underlying the music,[32] *Falstaff* has never become so popular with the public as any of the other three comic operas with which alone it can be compared— Mozart's *Figaro*, Rossini's *Barbiere*, and Wagner's *Meistersinger*. *Falstaff* is the kind of comedy that can be imagined only by an artist who is mature enough to know human life and still be able to laugh. Verdi parodied himself in the conspiracy scene at the end of the first part of Act III and took his leave of opera with a jest at the whole world, including the art of music: *Falstaff* ends with a fugue, that most learned of all forms of composition, to the words "Tutto nel mondo è burla"—"All the world's a joke."

Arrigo Boito (1842–1918) was more than a librettist; he was also a novelist, composer, and critic.[33] In his writings, he was extremely outspoken about the degree of conformity within the Italian operatic tradition; at the same time, he expressed interest in a type of opera that would permit a union of the arts. Boito admired Wagner and had been one of his ardent Italian disciples but in later years was converted to Verdi by the music of *Aida* and the *Requiem*. The precepts of operatic composition advocated by Boito in prose did not find manifestation in his own opera *Mefistofele* (1868, revised 1875), of which he wrote both libretto

32. Cf. Noske, "Ritual Scenes in Verdi's Operas."

33. See biographical studies by Ballo, Nardi, and Mariani; Boito, *Tutti gli scritti*; Borriello, *Mito, poesia e musica nel "Mefistofele"*; Walker, *The Man Verdi*, chap. 9; Scarsi, *Rapporto poesia-musica*. An important collection of letters is contained in Medici and Conati, eds., *Carteggio Verdi-Boito*, See also Smith, *The Tenth Muse*.

and music. *Mefistofele* holds much closer to the model of Goethe's *Faust* than either Berlioz's or Gounod's settings. The score includes many marginal Wagner-like disquisitions on the characters and events of the drama. Boito's music is interesting and original in many respects but, although *Mefistofele* is still fairly often performed, it has never become as great a popular success as Gounod's more conventional work. *Nerone,* Boito's last opera, was left unfinished at his death but was given in 1924 in a version arranged by Arturo Toscanini and Vicenzo Tommasini.[34]

Whereas Boito was a leader among the "advanced" Italian composers of the 1860s, the chief figure among the "conservative" group, which found its ideal in the operas of Verdi's middle period, was Amilcare Ponchielli (1834-1886).[35] His most famous opera, *La Gioconda* (1876), with libretto by Boito, is an old-fashioned melodramatic work which still holds the stage in Italy and elsewhere.

34. In both *Mefistofele* and *Nerone,* there exists a struggle for supremacy between opposites (the dualism of good and evil, God and the Devil) that defies resolution.

35. Biography by De Napoli.

CHAPTER TWENTY-ONE

The Romantic Opera
in Germany

The rise of nationalism in music, one of the outstanding features of the nineteenth century, is nowhere more striking than in the rapid growth of the romantic opera in Germany.[1] Before 1820, German opera was known outside its own country through a very limited number of singspiels, of which Mozart's *The Magic Flute* was the principle example. With the performances of Weber's operas, especially *Der Freischütz* at Berlin in 1821, German romantic opera became fully established and its ensuing developments culminated in the worldwide triumph of Wagner's music dramas fifty years later. Since Germany displays more clearly and completely than any other country the effects of the romantic doctrines on opera, it will be convenient to summarize here those features of romanticism which came to light particularly in German opera between 1800 and 1870.

If we were to search for the most general principle of difference between the opera of the eighteenth and that of the nineteenth century, we should probably find it in the contrast between the idea of distinctness on the one hand and that of coalescence on the other. The contrast begins with the relation of the composer to his music. The eighteenth-century composer was

---

1. General works are *NOHM*, vol. 8 (1982); Dent, *The Rise of the Romantic Opera*; *19th Century Music* (a journal, initiated in 1977, with excellent articles and reviews); Smith, *The Tenth Muse*; Goslich, *Die deutsche romantische Oper*. See also Chantavoine and Gaudefroy-Demombynes, *Le Romantisme dans la musique européenne*; Istel, *Die Blütezeit der musikalischen Romantik*, chap. 5; Kraus, "Das deutsche Liederspiel"; Goslich, *Beiträge zur Geschichte der deutschen romantischen Oper*; *Almanach der deutschen Musikbücherei*; Schmitz, "Zur Geschichte des Leitmotivs"; Daninger, *Sage und Märchen im Musikdrama*; Ehrenhaus, *Die Operndichtung der deutschen Romantik*; Strunk, ed., *Source Readings*, pp. 782–97.

a craftsman who stood outside the art works which he created; the nineteenth-century composer thought of music rather as a means of self-expression,a projection of his own feelings and ideas. His music has consequently a certain subjective quality which demands that the hearer shall place himself in sympathy with the composer, failing which he may not understand the music. Moreover, the music itself is directed more to the listener's emotions and less to his intellect than in the eighteenth century. The horror and rescue operas, the works of Weber, Meyerbeer, Donizetti, Verdi, and Wagner, all make a direct assault on the nerves and feelings of the audience in a manner which to Hasse, Gluck, or Mozart would have been inconceivable. In pursuit of this aim, and emancipated by the authority of individual freedom from the old restrictions, the nineteenth century proceeded to create a new aesthetic and a new set of musical procedures for opera, all of which, as said before, were dominated by the idea of coalescence as against the eighteenth-century idea of distinctness.

Another example of the difference lies in the relation between libretto and music in the two periods. We have already seen how in the eighteenth-century opera seria these two elements were harnessed together in a kind of marriage of convenience which, provided certain conventions were observed, left each to a great extent free and unimpeded; the same libretto might receive many different musical settings, and the same music might be used for different words. This conception was no longer prevalent in the nineteenth century, even in Italy. Everywhere, and to an increasing degree, the ideal, express or implicit, came to be a complete union of words and music in one perfect whole. But in Germany, this ideal was carried in theory even further to advocate generally the amalgamation of music, poetry, and all the other arts in one supreme art which should be greater than the sum of its individual constituents. The ideal took various and sometimes fantastic forms; thus, August von Schlegel wrote: "The arts should be brought together again, and bridges sought from one to another. Perhaps columns shall come to life as paintings, paintings become poems, poems become music."[2] Poets and painters saw in music

---

2. Quoted in Adler, *Handbuch der Musikgeschichte*, 2:865. Cf. Schelling's well-known definition of architecture as "frozen music" (*Philosophie der Kunst*, pp. 576, 593), and Goethe's similar statement (Eckermann, *Gespräche mit Goethe*, 1:261, March 23, 1829). Such conceptions were not peculiar to the nineteenth century. Compare, for example,

the ideal toward which the other arts were striving—immediate in its expression of feeling, limited in its power to depict the world of objects, but by this very indefiniteness supporting all the more strongly that flight from the outer to the inner world, toward those "somber longings, depressions and joyous elation without any recognizable cause" which are typical of certain romantic temperaments.[3] The arts were united not only in ideal but also in practice: poets and painters composed music, and musicians wrote essays, novels, and poetry. The ultimate stage as far as opera was concerned came with Wagner's theory and realization of the *Gesamtkunstwerk*, the total, all-inclusive work of art.

In the librettos of many German romantic operas we find also that the eighteenth-century distinction between man and nature, and between nature and the supernatural, is broken down. In the eighteenth century, nature appears in opera only as scenery in the background, and the music that depicts nature is of an imitative or descriptive sort, such as bird-song arias, comparison arias, orchestral storms, and the like. The supernatural in eighteenth-century opera is either a dramatic convention (as in Rameau and Gluck) or else a source of farce (Dittersdorf) or pageantry *(The Magic Flute)*. But in much German opera of the nineteenth century, both nature and the supernatural are closely identified with the moods of man, nature becoming as it were a vast sounding board for the murmurs of the unconscious soul, and the "invisible world of spirits" constantly impinging for good or evil on the affairs of everyday life. The storms in Mozart's *Idomeneo* are only incidental; the storm in Wagner's *Fliegende Holländer* is the whole mood of the drama. In Weber's *Freischütz*, both the natural background and the supernatural happenings must be taken seriously or the plot is meaningless; yet here we have scarcely emerged from the fairy-tale stage. In Wagner's *Tannhäuser* and *Lohengrin*, the supernatural begins to have symbolic importance. Finally, in the *Ring*, both nature and humanity become absorbed into a supernatural and superhuman

---

Harsdörffer, *Frauenzimmer Gesprechspiele*, 3:242, and Mattheson, *Die neueste Untersuchung*, pp. 86–87, although the latter clearly asserts not the identity of the arts but only their cooperation.

3. The quotation is from Berlioz's program for the *Symphonie fantastique*.

realm ruled by transcendent moral forces, so that the whole action takes place on a symbolic, mythical plane.

All this fairy tale, legend, and myth in German romantic opera is national in character, as opposed to the earlier use of Greek mythology, medieval epic, or Roman history. The emphasis on national subject matter in opera followed the movement in literature which had begun in England with the publication of Macpherson's "edition" of Ossian and Percy's *Reliques of Ancient English Poetry* in the 1760s. In Germany, Herder's cosmopolitan *Stimmen der Völker in Liedern* (1778–79) was followed in the years 1805–8 by an exclusively German collection, Arnim and Brentano's *Des Knaben Wunderhorn*. Interest in German legends and medieval literature was revived by the brothers Grimm (*Kinder- und Hausmärchen*, 1812–15; *Deutsche Mythologie*, 1835). Folk tales, fairy tales, patriotic odes, and historical novels and dramas were produced by many authors. Much of this literature was not only national but also popular, that is, "of the folk." Glorification of "the folk," of humble scenes and pleasures and the instincts of simple people, is common in the early romantic period; and the imprint of these features remained on German opera even after 1830, when new influences were at work in literature.[4]

Turning now to the music of romantic opera, we find likewise a coalescing of formerly distinct factors. In the eighteenth century, the functions of voice and orchestra were clearly defined. The orchestra accompanied the singers; it was heard by itself only on specified occasions, as in the overture, the ritornellos, and the ballets, marches, or descriptive pieces. In the nineteenth century, the orchestra not only creates moods and provides exotic suggestion but also enters intimately into the pattern of the drama itself. Eventually it becomes a continuous web of instrumental sound, thereby freeing the voice for more realistic, varied, and pointed declamation of the text. The overture achieves a close connection, both thematic and structural, with the opera itself. Improvement of the brass and woodwind instruments, and the introduction of new instruments, make possible an enor-

4. One interesting manifestation of this emphasis on national subject matter appears in *Hans Sachs im vorgerückten Alter* (Dresden, 1834), a successful singspiel on the life of the sixteenth-century poet, Hans Sachs, by Adalbert Gyrowetz (1763–1850), Czech composer and conductor at the Vienna Court Theater.

mously enlarged and variegated color scheme in operatic music. With increasing emphasis on the inner voices and increasing chromaticism in the harmony, the orchestra becomes more and more dominant in the musical texture. Curt Sachs has pointed out how this growth in importance of the orchestra in opera coincides with the rise of non-Italian schools—"the eternal antithesis between the playing North and the singing South."[5] The climax comes with Wagner's music dramas, in which the orchestra develops the entire action in a polyphonic tissue of sound.

Still another contrast between eighteenth- and nineteenth-century opera is seen with respect to musical forms. The older opera consisted of a series of distinct numbers, without thematic interconnection. The tendency throughout the romantic period, as already observed, is for the separate numbers to coalesce into larger units, and this process is finally carried to a point where the music flows uninterruptedly from the beginning of an act to the end. This continuity may be simply a matter of concealing the joints, or it may be the kind of organic unity in Wagner's music dramas, with a number of musical motifs used continually and systematically throughout a whole act, or a whole opera, or even several different operas. What is true of the form as a whole is true also of the details: distinction between aria and recitative becomes less marked; recitatives, arias, ensembles, and choruses combine freely in large form-complexes. In harmony, the boundaries of tonality become less definite, while modulations become more frequent and are made to more distant keys; chromatic alterations, progressions motivated by chromatically moving inner voices, become characteristic. In the later works of Wagner, even distinct cadences are avoided, so that the music seems never to come to a full stop but to move on in an endless melody. Finally, dissonance, especially in the form of suspension or appoggiatura, takes on new and special importance as a leading means of expression, and the indefinite postponement of its final resolution becomes a symbol of the eternal romantic longing after the unattainable.

The actual historical course of opera in early-nineteenth-century Germany was affected by a number of factors which tended

5. Sachs, "The Road to Major," p. 403.

to interfere with the steady development of a truly national type. The original inspiration of German romantic opera, both for the poetry and for the music, came from France—in part directly from late eighteenth- and early nineteenth-century opéra comique and in part indirectly through the singspiel, which, as we have seen, was largely dependent in the beginning on French models. There being no national center of opera in Germany, the singspiel developed in relatively isolated localities, preserving everywhere, however, two traditional characteristics of the form: the choice, indifferently, of either serious or comic subject matter (or of a mixture of the two) and the use of spoken dialogue. One factor that constantly hampered the growth of a national opera was the rooted public favor for foreign works, or works of essentially foreign cast, so that composers who might otherwise have devoted their full energies to the building of German opera often felt induced to write in imitation of French or Italian models. Beethoven's *Fidelio*, for example, was a French revolutionary rescue opera; later, it was the French grand opera or the Italian opera of Rossini, Bellini, and Donizetti that offered the fatal attraction to German composers. Nevertheless, the native singspiel continued to flourish in a modest way and to make progress during the first two decades of the nineteenth century.

Two general types of libretto are discernible in the singspiel at the beginning of the century. One type, specializing in familiar, homely scenes and characters idyllically or sentimentally treated, is illustrated by *Die Schweitzerfamilie* ("The Swiss Family"), first given at Vienna in 1809. The music, by Joseph Weigl (1766–1846),[6] has some romantic orchestral coloring and makes use of Swiss themes and of reminiscence motifs. *Die Schweitzerfamilie* was one of the most popular singspiels ever staged in Germany or abroad. The other type of singspiel libretto in the early nineteenth century emphasized legendary or magic elements, strange happenings to men and women living in a "real" world but ever subject to the mysterious intervention of unseen spiritual powers. It was this eminently romantic kind of subject matter that was to furnish the material of German romantic opera.

6. See De Eisner-Eisenhof, "Giuseppe Weigl"; Bollert, "Joseph Weigl und das deutsche Singspiele"; Angermüller, "Zwei Selbstbiographien."

Important examples representing both types appeared in the period bounded by *Die Zauberflöte* and *Der Freischütz.* Their titles leave no doubt that romantic motifs had become increasingly prevalent in the librettos: *Die Geisterinsel* ("The Isle of Spirits," based on Shakespeare's *The Tempest*), *Der Unsichtbare* ("The Invisible"), *Der Kobold* ("The Goblin"). Two works inspired by *Die Zauberflöte* were given at Vienna in 1797 and 1798 respectively: *Babylons Piramiden* ("The Pyramids of Babylon") and *Das Labyrinth, oder der Kampf mit den Elementen: Zweiter Teil der "Zauberflöte"* ("The Labyrinth, or The Battle with the Elements: Second part of *The Magic Flute*"). Both were on librettos of Schikaneder, with most of the music by Peter Winter, Munich's most celebrated composer at the turn of the century.[7] Winter received Schikaneder's commission to write the music for the sequel to *Die Zauberflöte* presumably because he had become very popular and successful in Vienna, having secured an international reputation with the highly acclaimed productions of *Das unterbrochene Opferfest*, a singspiel with many exotic and magical features. *Das Labyrinth*, based upon a fairy tale of the same title from an anthology by Wieland, involves all the main characters of *Die Zauberflöte* plus a few new ones. Winter's setting, an extravaganza with magnificent choral numbers, shows allegiance to both Mozartean and Gluckian ideals, but it is the influence of French grand opera that dominates. From *Helena und Paris* (1782) to *Colmal* (1809), a through-composed German "reform" opera, Winter's musical style derived from an assimilation of French, German, and Italian influences and contributed to the initial phase of German romantic opera.

Other composers who shared in the formative stages of German romantic opera include Paul Wranitzky (1756–1808), Vienna court conductor whose *Oberon* (1789) for a time rivaled Mozart's singspiels in popularity; George Christoph Grosheim (1764–1841),[8] with *Titania* (1792); Ferdinand Kauer (1751–1831), with *Das Donauweibchen* (1798), which inspired many imitations; Jo-

---

7. Frensdorf, *Peter Winter als Opernkomponist;* Kuckuk, "Peter Winter als deutscher Opernkomponist"; Moser, *Geschichte der deutschen Musik*, vol. 2; Henderson, "The *Magic Flute* of Peter Winter." For more on Winter, see chap. 15. The overture and Act I of *Babylons Piramiden* were composed by Johann Mederitsch.

8. Grosheim, *Selbstbiographie.*

hann Rodulf Zumsteeg (1760–1802), with *Die Geisterinsel;* Friedrich Heinrich Himmel (1765–1814),[9] with *Fanchon das Leiermädchen* (1804), *Die Sylphen* (1806), and *Der Kobold* (1813); and Carl David Eule (1776–1827), with *Der Unsichtbare* (1809).

A decisive stage in the creation of German romantic opera came with two works first performed in 1816: *Undine* by E. T. A. Hoffmann, at Berlin, and *Faust* by Ludwig Spohr, at Prague. Hoffmann (1776–1822), the famous romantic author, is important in the history of German opera for both his writings and his music.[10] The writings contain persuasive arguments for the creation of a German romantic opera, Hoffmann's interest in the subject no doubt having been sparked by his awareness of Carl Theodor's campaign to establish a national opera, by his association with Friedrich Rochlitz (editor from 1798 to 1818 of *Allgemeine musikalische Zeitung*), and by his studious reading of August von Schlegel's *Lectures on Dramatic Art and Literature* (1808–1809).[11] They also reveal Hoffman's concern for the literary quality of texts used for stage works, something generally lacking in the German librettos of the period. And indeed, the libretto for Hoffmann's masterpiece, *Undine*,[12] is an exception, for it is of real literary merit. Adapted by Friedrich Henrich Karl de La Motte-Fouqué from an earlier, merely fanciful play, a fairy tale about a water spirit, the libretto conveys a feeling of human significance, thus achieving some dramatic force in spite of a complex and fantastic plot. The music suffers from some technical faults and the more ambitious arias are the less successful ones, but the romantic mood of Weber's *Der Freischütz* is distinctly foreshadowed. This is especially true in the scenes depicting supernatural beings, in the many folklike melodies and choruses, and in the thematic reminiscences (anticipating the leitmotif principle)—the same features Weber found impressive. He mentions

---

9. Odendahl, *Friedrich Heinrich Himmel;* see also Garlington, "German Romantic Opera."

10. Hoffmann's literary works are published in an edition by Griesebach; his writings on music separately *(Musikalische Novellen und Aufsätze).* See biography by Kroll; Greeff, *E. T. A. Hoffmann als Musiker;* Garlington, "E. T. A. Hoffmann's *Der Dichter und der Komponist*"; Schafer, *E. T. A. Hoffmann and Music.*

11. See Garlington, "August von Schlegel and the German Romantic Opera."

12. Schläder, "*Undine* von E. T. A. Hoffmann"; Hsu, "Weber on Opera."

them in a review of *Undine* along with his definition of "the opera which the German desires—an art work complete in itself, in which the partial contributions of the related and collaborating arts blend together, disappear, and, in disappearing, somehow form a new world."[13]

Spohr (1784–1859) is now remembered chiefly for his oratorios and violin music,[14] but his *Faust* and *Jessonda* are important landmarks in the development of a German romantic musical style. Weber conducted the first performance of *Faust* (1816) and immediately proclaimed its merits, for at long last he had found an opera with the degree of dramatic and musical unity he considered essential for this art form. That this unity was not accidental is made clear in Spohr's preface to the score, where he indicates how the thematic motifs are meant to represent various facets of Faust's personality. These motifs, stated first in the overture, are used as reminiscence motifs throughout the opera. Like *Undine*, the opera has many features that point toward *Der Freischütz*.[15] Though the music is less masculine and forceful than Weber's, it is nonetheless interesting for its freedom of key relationships and chromatic progressions;[16] its expressive suspensions and upward-resolving appogiaturas often suggest the style of Wagner, although the romanticism of Spohr is mostly a matter of such details as these rather than a fundamentally new approach.

Jessonda (1823) is a fully sung opera.[17] Spoken dialogue has been eliminated and in its place Spohr has reinstated the recitative, but in a style that more nearly resembles the arioso. A special affinity with French rescue operas is felt not only in the exotic story of a Portuguese adventurer in India rescuing a widow from suicidal death on a funeral pyre but also in the musical conception of the important arias and grand finales. Given the ro-

---

13. See Strunk, ed., *Source Readings*, pp. 801–7, for a translation of the review, which appeared in the *Allgemeine musikalische Zeitung*.

14. Spohr, *Lebenserinnerungen*; Wassermann, *Ludwig Spohr als Opernkomponist*; Salburg, *Ludwig Spohr*.

15. In his 1852 revision of *Faust*, Spohr provided recitatives for the spoken dialogue.

16. See also the passage from the first finale of *Jessonda*, quoted in Bücken, *Die Musik des 19. Jahrhunderts*, p. 88.

17. Spitta, "Jessonda"; C. Brown, "Spohr's *Jessonda*"; A. Abert, "Webers *Euryanthe* und Spohrs *Jessonda* als grosse Opern."

mantic spirit of Spohr's operas, it is surprising that he was unsympathetic to the music of Weber and the late Beethoven, but he was one of the earliest champions of Wagner in Germany, and in his own *Kreuzfahrer* ("The Crusaders," 1845) he attempted to write a national romantic opera after the model of *Der fliegende Holländer* and *Tannhäuser* (these operas having premiered in Dresden in 1843 and 1845, respectively).

The operatic production of Franz Schubert (1797–1828) extends from 1814 to 1823 and includes sixteen works (counting those that have been preserved incomplete), only three of which ever reached performance during the composer's lifetime.[18] These were the one-act singspiel *Die Zwillingsbrüder* ("The Twin Brothers," 1819); the melodrama *Die Zauberharfe* ("The Magic Harp," 1820), Schubert's first big work for the stage, consisting of choruses and some particularly beautiful orchestral numbers in a fantastic play by G. E. von Hoffmann; and the well-known incidental music for Helmine von Chézy's drama *Rosamunde von Cypern* (1823). But Schubert's principal dramatic works were the two large operas *Alfonso und Estrella* (composed 1822, first performed 1854) and *Fierrabras* (composed 1823, first performed 1897). *Fierrabras* has some spoken dialogue, but *Alfonso und Estrella*—exceptionally for German opera in this period—is sung throughout. Schubert had hoped to see this opera staged at Berlin, but it was rejected because of the alleged difficulty of the music and because the libretto was found "unsuitable." The score contains a wealth of arias in great variety, a generous number of choruses, and a tremendously big finale—altogether a work in the grand romantic style, with characteristic Schubertian harmony and orchestral colors. *Fierrabras* is equally rich in large scene-complexes with intermingled arias, dramatic accompanied recitatives, and choruses, and in addition contains many instances of recurring themes in the orchestra, a device used here with consummate skill and effect. Outstanding numbers in this score are the lovely duet for two sopranos "Weit über Glanz und Erdenschimmer" and the four-part unaccompanied men's chorus "O theures Vaterland" in Act

18. Krott, "Die Singspiele Schuberts"; King, "Music for the Stage"; Deutsch, *Schubert: Thematic Catalogue* and other books on Schubert; M. J. Brown, *Schubert: A Critical Biography.*

II; the melodrama scene near the end of this act; and the finale-complex at the end of Act I. It is indeed tragic that Schubert never had the opportunity to hear these two operas in the theater, for he might then have gone on, with that experience as a guide and with the help of better librettos, to adapt his great lyric genius more fully to the practical requirements of the stage and attain in this field the success that always just eluded him.[19]

Two other romantic composers also attempted opera without much success. Mendelssohn's *Hochzeit des Camacho* ("Camacho's Wedding") was withdrawn after a few performances at Berlin in 1827; he composed a half-dozen smaller stage pieces (of which only the one-act singspiel *Son and Stranger* was published) and left unfinished a large opera, *Loreley*.[20] Schumann's *Genoveva* was performed at Leipzig in 1850 under the composer's direction, but neither then nor since has it obtained enduring public favor.[21] Its libretto is poorly constructed and the music lacks genuine dramatic directness and characterizing power, though there are many beautiful passages (for example, near the beginning of Act IV, Genoveva's recitative and aria from the words "Die letzte Hoffnung schwindet"). Schumann's *Szenen aus Goethes Faust*, for chorus, soloists, and orchestra, is intended for concert performance; it is perhaps, of all *Faust* music, the most appropriate to Goethe's drama and ranks equal with the composer's better-known cantata *Paradise and the Peri*.

Hoffmann and Spohr had prepared the way, but the real founder and hero of German romantic opera was Carl Maria von Weber (1786–1826).[22] Weber's father was a theater director, and the boy was reared in an atmosphere of the stage. His experience as impresario and conductor at Breslau (1804–6) and Prague (1813–17) gave him a firm knowledge of the essentials of dramatic

19. See Liszt's essay on *Alfonso und Estrella*, in his *Dramaturgische Blätter*, 3:68–78.

20. Schünemann, "Mendelssohns Jugendopern."

21. H. Abert, "Robert Schumann's *Genoveva*"; Abraham, "The Dramatic Music," in Abraham, ed., *Schumann: A Symposium*, chap. 7.

22. On Weber, see his diary, letters, and other writings; biographies by his son M. M. von Weber, Kroll, Schnoor, Laux, Saunders, Stebbins and Stebbins, and Warrack. See further Dünnebeil, *C. M. von Weber, ein Brevier* and *Schrifttum über . . . Weber*; thematic catalogue by Jähns; Warrack, ed., *Carl Maria von Weber: Critical Writings on Music*. Moser's edition of Weber's works, begun in 1926, has only three volumes: *Das Waldmädchen, Peter Schmoll* (vol. 1), *Rübezahl, Silvana* (vol. 2), *Preciosa* (vol. 3).

style. At Prague, he staged works by Spontini, Méhul, and Cherubini, Grétry's *Richard*, Mozart's *Figaro, Don Giovanni*, and *Titus*, Beethoven's *Fidelio*, and other leading operas of the current repertoire. Vogler's influence, as well as the whole intellectual milieu of Weber's life, inclined him strongly toward romanticism, and in 1814 his settings of ten songs from Körner's *Leyer und Schwert* ("Lyre and Sword") made him the idol of the patriotic youth of Germany. Weber's first extant dramatic work, of which only fragments remain, was a singspiel, *Das stumme Waldmädchen* ("The Dumb Girl of the Forest," 1800); it was not successful, but parts of the music were incorporated into a later work, *Silvana* (1810).[23] Two comic singspiels, *Peter Schmoll und seine Nachbarn* ("Peter Schmoll and His Neighbors," 1803) and the highly successful *Abu Hassan* (1811), and an unfinished romantic work, *Rübezahl* (ca. 1805),[24] complete the list of Weber's earlier dramatic compositions. Though he showed in these works an original talent for instrumentation, a gift for comic writing and characterization, and a feeling for the quality of German folk melody, there is little in the music to suggest the romantic power later to be unloosed in *Der Freischütz*. *Abu Hassan* may be regarded as a forerunner of *Oberon*, and the medieval-romantic *Silvana* anticipates some features of *Euryanthe*.

Early in the year 1817, Weber, who had just been appointed director of the German opera at Dresden, persuaded his friend Friedrich Kind to write for him a libretto based on the tale, "Der Freischütz," which had appeared in the *Gespensterbuch* ("Book of Ghosts," 1810), by J. A. Apel and Friedrich Laun.[25] The legend itself was at least a hundred years older, and some of its principal themes belong to still more ancient folklore.[26] The

23. Act II of the 1810 production of *Silvana* is missing and thus the only available score is based upon later versions prepared for Berlin and Dresden.

24. "Rübezahl" is the name of a mountain spirit of the Riesengebirge, a prominent figure in the folklore of Silesia and the subject of many folk tales, plays, and operas. Weber's overture is still occasionally played, in a revised form, under the title "The Ruler of the Spirits."

25. So scarce were good German librettos that Weber sometimes had to resort to more than "persuasion." See, for example, his advertisement in the Prague *Allgemeine Musik-Zeitung*, in which he invited German poets to send their manuscripts to him (quoted in Smith, *The Tenth Muse*, p. 251).

26. For a thorough discussion of the sources of the libretto, see Warrack, *Carl Maria von Weber*, chap. 11.

title is difficult to translate: it means literally "The Free Marks-man," but the usual English title "The Charmed Bullet" is suffi-ciently descriptive and certainly more graceful. Interest in the *Gespensterbuch* tale prompted immediate dramatizations. Franz Xavier von Caspar's *Der Freyschütz*, a "romantic tragedy in four acts" with music by Carl Neuner, was one of the earliest, a first version for Munich (1812) followed by a second, five-act version (with a tragic ending) in 1813. The similarities between Caspar's play and Kind's subsequent libretto suggest a strong dependence of the latter upon the former.[27] Weber's music was not completed until 1820, and still another year elapsed before the first perfor-mance, at Berlin, on June 18, 1821. The work was fabulously successful from the start and spread like wildfire all over Ger-many and abroad, being performed in German and in many other translations. After its reception in Vienna, Weber wrote in his diary, "Greater enthusiasm there cannot be, and I tremble to think of the future, for it is scarcely possible to rise higher than this."[28] His words were prophetic, as the fate of *Euryanthe* was to prove; but with *Der Freischütz*, he had set German romantic opera on its road and dealt a blow to the century-long Italian reign in the German theaters.

The popularity of *Der Freischütz* was due not only to the music but also to the libretto, which, for Germany in the early romantic period, literally had everything.[29] Most of its elements were inherited from the late eighteenth-century singspiel: a back-ground of nature and a foreground of humble and happy village life; a pure heroine and a well-intentioned but credulous hero; a villain caught in his own trap; the supernatural in many pictur-esque and shuddery forms; and finally, the time-tested figure of the magnanimous prince as righteous judge and father of his peo-ple. But though the ingredients were old, the mixture was new.

27. Mayerhofer, *Abermals vom Freischützen.*

28. Quoted by Philipp Spitta in his article on Weber in *Grove's Dictionary of Music*, 4th ed., 5:652.

29. For a synopsis, the reader is referred to Warrack, *Carl Maria von Weber* (pp. 216–29), or to any other opera handbook; many editions of the music do not give the spoken dialogue, which is essential to the understanding of the plot. It was, perhaps, the large amount of spoken dialogue that prompted numerous translations of the text within a short time after the initial performance; the opera was staged in English, for example, in London and New York as early as 1824 and 1825 respectively.

For the first time in opera, all these details were convincingly presented as aspects of something important; the trial of marksmanship took on the character of Armageddon, the ultimate battle of good against evil, one sustained by the power of the church and the other aided by the maleficent spirits of ancient heathendom, and the triumph of good was felt as the triumph of the German soul. Thus, the national appeal of *Der Freischütz* was not limited to the romantic period but has remained equally strong to this day. "There never was an opera, and there is no likelihood that there ever will be one, so intimately bound up with the loves, feelings, sentiments, emotions, superstitions, social customs, and racial characteristics of a people." [30]

The overture is a model of its kind. Although made up entirely, except for the opening horn theme, of melodies from the opera, it is not a mere medley but a finished composition in symphonic first-movement form. The mysterious last twelve measures of the introduction (diminished sevenths with low clarinets, strings tremolo, pizzicato basses and kettledrums on the afterbeats) are the quintessence of romanticism in music, and so, in a different way, is the clarinet melody in E-flat of the vivace movement. The return of the closing triumph theme in C major, heralded by a recurrence of the last part of the introduction and three impressive "general pauses," is electrifying. In the larger arias, the music of *Der Freischütz* approaches grand opera, and it is natural to find in Caspar's "Der Hölle Netz" (end of Act I) a resemblance to Italian style, or in the opening section of Max's "Durch die Wälder" a mild echo of Méhul. Both the latter aria and Agathe's "Leise, leise" are complex musical structures, splendidly dramatic and of Beethovenian amplitude. Aennchen's "Kommt ein schlanker Bursch gegangen," with its polacca rhythm, is in keeping with the singspiel tradition of differentiating the social standing of the characters by means of different musical styles and forms. The contrast between Agathe and Aennchen, mistress and maid, so neatly established in their duet at the beginning of Act II, is confirmed and emphasized in their two following arias.

Parts of the score which did much to endear it to the public were those which glorified the songs and dances of the peo-

---

30. Krehbiel, *A Book of Operas*, p. 207.

ple: the hunters' and bridesmaids' choruses, the march and waltzes in Act I, and the shorter pieces (lied, romance, cavatina) in popular form. In *Der Freischütz*, Weber succeeded as no other composer had done in raising the music of the folk to the dignity of serious opera and combining it skillfully with more pretentious elements. The most celebrated part of the opera has always been the finale of the second act, the "Wolf's Glen" scene, one of the most effective evocations of supernatural thrills ever created for the stage. Among the devices Weber uses may be pointed out the mysterious harmonies (tremolo strings) at the beginning, the monotone choruses of the spirits (note the unison of tenors, altos, and sopranos on a'), the dialogue between the singing Caspar and the speaking Samiel, and the melodrama for the casting of the magic bullets, a Walpurgisnacht of legendary phantoms of the dark forest. The C minor themes of the overture, associated throughout the opera with the demonic powers, are much in evidence. The systematic recurrence of these motifs and others, especially the triumph motif (overture, in E-flat and C major; Agathe's aria, E major; last finale again in C major), contributes much to the feeling of unity which is one of the outstanding qualities of the work. The overture gives the musical plan of the whole as it were in embryo, and the structure thus sketched is fully expanded in the course of the three acts.

Weber's incidental music to P. A. Wolff's play *Preciosa* (adapted from a novel by Cervantes) was composed immediately after *Der Freischütz* and came sooner to performance (Berlin, March 14, 1821). At about the same time, he started, but did not finish, a comic opera on another Spanish subject, *Die drei Pintos* ("The Three Pintos").[31]

Weber's *Euryanthe* was first performed at Vienna on October 24, 1823. The source of the plot was a thirteenth-century fabliau which had been employed by Boccaccio in the *Decameron* (day 2, story 9) and by Shakespeare in *Cymbeline*; Schlegel had published a version in 1804 under the title "Die Geschichte der tugendsamen Euryanthe von Savoyen" ("The History of the Virtuous Euryanthe of Savoy"). Helmine von Chézy, after many re-

---

31. It was completed by Gustave Mahler, partly from Weber's sketches and partly from other works of the composer, and performed at Leipzig in 1888. For an excellent discussion of the Mahler reconstruction, see Warrack, *Weber*, chap. 13.

visions and with considerable help from Weber, produced a libretto. In planning the work, Weber, in accordance with his lifelong habit, deliberately tried to correct the faults that critics had found in *Der Freischütz*. The criticisms had been mainly to the effect that the work was deficient in large, highly developed musical forms; that is, that it was too much of a singspiel and not enough of an opera. *Euryanthe*, therefore, Weber set to music throughout (it is the only opera of his that does not have spoken dialogue) and on a greater scale than any of his other works. However, he did not wish to make the music dominant as in Italian opera, but conceived rather a kind of Gesamtkunstwerk, "a purely dramatic attempt, aiming to create its effect by means of the combined effects of all the sister arts."[32] Unfortunately, the results did not correspond to this ideal, nor did the success of the opera come up to Weber's hopes and expectations. It has never become a public favorite, but its interest for musicians is shown by numerous attempts to promote it in revised forms. There can be no doubt that it includes some of Weber's greatest music (for example, the overture); the arias are broad and powerful,[33] and the way the chorus is used in the drama reminds one of Gluck. Weber's usual skillful handling of the orchestra is evident, as well as the same tasteful use of folklike motifs as in *Der Freischütz*. Contrast of key is used as an aid to characterization, and there is a significant employment of reminiscence motifs. All in all, *Euryanthe* is a grand opera both in form and in loftiness of conception, a landmark in the history of German opera between *Fidelio* and *Lohengrin*, and a work that deserves to be performed more frequently.

Weber's last opera, *Oberon*, was composed to an English libretto by J. F. Planché and first performed under the composer's direction at London, April 12, 1826. The fatigue of the journey and the labor of the production hastened Weber's death, which occurred at London on June 4. In some ways, *Oberon* was a backward step: the story, a rambling oriental fantasy with numberless scene changes, gave only limited occasion for development of character or genuine human emotion; there were many nonsinging

---

32. Quoted in Moser, *Geschichte der deutschen Musik*, 3:73, n. 1.

33. See especially Lysiart's aria at the beginning of Act II and Euryanthe's aria with chorus "Zu ihm, und weilet nicht" in Act III.

actors, and so much of the action took place in spoken dialogue
that the music was reduced almost to an incidental position.
Weber intended to rearrange the work for German theaters, and
though he did not live long enough to do so, many more or less
thoroughgoing revisions and additions have been made (some in
accordance with Weber's plan) by later musicians. *Oberon* is historically important chiefly because of its fairy music, such as the
opening chorus of Act I, the finales of the second and third acts,
and above all the beginning of the overture, with its magic horn
call, muted strings, and swift figure in the woodwinds. Such music
was in the air: Mendelssohn's octet with its scherzo had appeared
the year before, and his *Midsummer Night's Dream* overture was
composed in the summer of 1826. Vigorous, ardent, stormy romanticism as in Rezia's aria "Ocean, thou mighty monster" (the
closing theme of which had appeared in the overture), is also well
represented in *Oberon*.

Weber died in midcareer. Had he lived to complete his
work, the history of German opera for the next twenty years might
have been one of steady development. As it was, although *Der
Freischütz* continued its triumphal course, no German work was
produced for nearly a generation that could match it either in
popularity or in musical worth. The early romantics had created
a world of opera in which the lives of simple human beings were
felt to be so intertwined with the processes of nature, and both
man and nature so informed and governed by all-encompassing
spiritual powers, that the three realms seemed as one. This original unity was lost after *Der Freischütz*, with unfortunate results
for both libretto and music. Poets and composers began to exploit
the supernatural for mere sensation and the human for sentiment
or comedy; and periodically they would be distracted by the al-
lurements of grand opera.

If Weber can be said to have had a successor, it was
Heinrich Marschner (1795–1861),[34] who first became widely known
in 1828 for *Der Vampyr*, an opera now remembered mainly because it was one of Wagner's models for *Der fliegende Holländer*
(see especially the ballade in Act III). Marschner's *Templer und*

---

34. Münzer, *Heinrich Marschner*; Fischer, *Musik in Hannover* (2nd ed.) and *Marschner-
Erinnerungen*; Gaartz, *Die Opern Heinrich Marschners*; Gnirs, *Hans Heiling*; Köhler,
"Rezitativ, Szene und Melodram in Heinrich Marchners Opern"; Palmer, *Heinrich August
Marschner*.

Jüdin ("The Templar and the Jewess," 1829) was adapted from Scott's *Ivanhoe*. His masterpiece, *Hans Heiling* (1833), was on a libretto by Eduard Devrient from a story by Körner, originally intended for Mendelssohn. As the central situation of *Templer und Jüdin* is similar to that of *Lohengrin*, so the figure of Hans Heiling, half man and half earth spirit, in love with a mortal woman, has many points of resemblance to Wagner's Dutchman. Yet in the working out of the story as well as in the music, much of the trivial is mingled with the serious. The style for the most part is that of the popular singspiel, with simple tunes in symmetrical patterns, interspersed with spoken dialogue. Echoes of Weber, Italian opera, and Meyerbeer's *Robert le Diable* are heard. In some respects, the music looks ahead to Wagner: the frequent chromatic passing tones in the melody, especially at cadences; the use of modulating sequences; and occasionally a passage of grimly powerful declamation. Many of the choruses are interesting, and the finales of the first and third acts are well constructed. The opening scene, in the Kingdom of Earthly Spirits, is unusual in that the overture follows rather than precedes the choral prologue, a dramatic touch that had its imitators later in the century. The most original number, and one which shows Marschner's gifts to good advantage, is the melodrama and lied at the beginning of the second scene of Act II.[35] Yet, on the whole, his talent was of second rank, the Biedermeier spirit in music. His later works, in which there are many traces of the fashionable Italian and French opera of the time, contributed nothing to his fame.

Along with the romantic traits of Marschner, there survived in German opera a current of sentimental or comic drama, descended from the eighteenth-century singspiel. A very popular opera of this kind was *Nachtlager in Granada* ("The Night-Camp in Granada," Vienna, 1834), by Konradin Kreutzer (1780–1849).[36] The libretto, based on Friedrich Kind's play of the same title, uses the old reliable motif of the good prince in disguise conferring rewards on humble virtue and innocent young love and offers occasion for romances, hunting choruses, a conspirators' chorus, a prayer, airs and ensembles, all somewhat in the manner of Au-

---

35. The melody at the words "Sonst bist du verfallen" is the original for Wagner's death-announcement theme in *Die Walküre*.

36. Riehl, essay in *Musikalische Charakterköpfe*, vol. 1.

ber and Donizetti—light, sometimes trifling, but on the whole pretty and pleasing music in a harmless way. A more spirited comic vein was worked by Gustav Albert Lortzing (1801–1851) in his most successful work, *Zar und Zimmermann* ("Czar and Carpenter," Leipzig, 1837), and especially in *Der Waffenschmied* ("The Armorer," Vienna, 1846).[37] The latter abounds in humorous situations like those of the older Viennese singspiel, with a fresh, pleasant, often witty melodic style and some ensembles that recall the spirit of Mozart. Most characteristic, however, are the simple songs in folk idiom, reminiscent of the tunes of J. A. Hiller. With another three-act comedy, *Der Wildschütz* ("The Poacher," 1842), and even more pronouncedly with his four-act magic opera, *Undine* (1845), Lortzing—who in all these works was his own librettist—ventured on the ground of romantic opera with its supernatural beings and theme of redemption through love. Lortzing was hardly capable of composing music equal to the emotions and characters of this libretto, but his systematic use of recurring motifs and his powers of musical description (especially the watersprites' music, first heard in Act II, scene 5) are interesting both in themselves and as predecessors of the music of Wagner's *Ring*. Another of Lortzing's comic operas, *Hans Sachs* (1840), is one of the numerous sources of *Die Meistersinger*.

Other German operas produced around the middle of the nineteenth century can be mentioned only briefly. *Die lustigen Weiber von Windsor* ("The Merry Wives of Windsor," Berlin, 1849), by Otto Nicolai (1810–1849), is a fine comic work, in which Italian and German characteristics are happily blended.[38] Its sparkling, cosmopolitan style contrasts with the simple "homemade" quality of another popular contemporary work, *Martha* (1847), by Friedrich von Flotow (1812–1883), a sentimental old-fashioned piece which has inexplicably survived while many better operas have been forgotten.[39] An important younger figure of

37. Biographies by Kruse and Killer; Lortzing, *Gesammelte Briefe*; Laue, *Die Operndichtung Lortzings*; Burgmüller, *Die Musen darben*; M. Hoffmann, *Gustav Albert Lortzing, der Meister der Deutschen Volksoper*; Subotnik, "Popularity and Art in Lortzing's Operas" and "Lortzing and the German Romantics."

38. Nicolai, *Tagebücher*; Kruse, *Otto Nicolai* and "Otto Nicolai's italienische Opern."

39. Its style derives from both the singspiel and the opéra comique, but it does not use spoken dialogue. See Flotow, *Friedrich von Flotow's Leben*; Dent, "A Best-Seller in Opera."

this period was Peter Cornelius (1824–1874), disciple of Liszt and champion of Wagner, a poet and composer who wrote his own librettos.[40] His *Barbier von Bagdad* ("The Barber of Bagdad," Weimar, 1858) is a wholly delightful oriental comedy in a sophisticated musical idiom. The rhythms, deriving in part from oriental verse forms, are particularly varied and interesting—for example, the aria "O holdes Bild" (Act II, scene 2) is in alternate 4/4 and 3/4 measures; five-measure phrases are also common throughout the score. Each of the two acts runs continuously, without marked division into numbers. The orchestra has an important role not only in the formal scheme but also in the provision of many humorous details in the accompaniments. A half-dozen recurring motifs are used systematically. *Der Barbier* is not high comedy like *Die Meistersinger* but a farce, cleverly using every resource of music for farcical purposes (see, for example, the canonic duet "Wenn zum Gebet" in Act I). The freedom of rhythm, the declamatory melodies, the frequent wide intervals and chromatic harmonies often foreshadow the style of Strauss's *Rosenkavalier*. There is also some parody of Italian opera, especially in the sentimental unison love duet "So mag kein anders Wort erklingen" in the second scene of Act II. (This scene is also an unintentional parody of the love duet in the second act of *Tristan*, with the Barber filling the role of Brangäne.)

During the 1830s and 1840s, it seemed almost as if the Italians had been driven from German opera houses only to be replaced by the French.[41] The works of Hérold and Adam were particularly popular, while the equally gifted native composers Marschner and Lortzing were neglected. The situation was saved by Wagner, who, after early experiments in the Italian style and that of French grand opera, went on to create a new epoch of national German romantic opera in *Der fliegende Holländer*, *Tannhäuser*, and *Lohengrin*.

40. P. Cornelius, *Literarische Werke*, and musical works in 5 vols. (Breitkopf & Hartel, 1905–6); biographies by Hasse and C. Cornelius. See also Hasse, *Peter Cornelius und sein "Barbier von Bagdad"*; W. Jacob, *Der beschwerliche Weg des Peter Cornelius zu Liszt und Wagner*.

41. For a contemporary account of this period, see Chorley, *Modern German Music*.

CHAPTER
TWENTY·TWO

The Operas of Wagner

From time to time in the history of music, there have been composers whose works summed up the achievement of a whole epoch, making the final synthesis of a style: Palestrina and Bach are the outstanding examples. There have been other composers whose work incorporated not only the end of one style but the beginning of another as well: to this group belong Beethoven and Wagner. The early operas of Richard Wagner (1813–1883) were the consummation of German romantic opera of the nineteenth century; the later music dramas were in a style which, although retaining many features of what had gone before, nevertheless introduced innovations in both theory and practice.[1] These innovations were

1. A tabular list of Wagner's operas and music dramas is given below. Dates of composition include scoring but not preliminary sketches.

Title	Dates	First Performance
Die Feen	1833–34	Munich, 1888
Das Liebesverbot	1835	Magdeburg, 1836
Rienzi	1838–40	Dresden, 1842
Der fliegende Holländer	1841	Dresden, 1843
Tannhäuser	1843–45	Dresden, 1845
Lohengrin	1846–48	Weimar, 1850
Der Ring des Nibelungen	Poem begun 1848, completed 1852	First complete performance, Bayreuth, 1876
I. Das Rheingold	1853–54	Munich, 1869
II. Die Walküre	1854–56	Munich, 1870
III. Siegfried	1856–57, 1864–65, 1869–71	Bayreuth, 1876
IV. Götterdämmerung	1869–74	Bayreuth, 1876
Tristan und Isolde	1857–59	Munich, 1865
Die Meistersinger von Nürnberg	1862–67	Munich, 1868
Parsifal	1877–82	Bayreuth, 1882

not confined to the music but embraced the whole drama, and in working them out Wagner, who perceived all the implications of his ideas and developed them with typical German thoroughness, touched on many issues that were fundamentally involved with nineteenth-century thought. He is the only eminent composer whose writings have been considered important outside the conventional limits of the field of music. For him, indeed, these conventional limits hardly existed; consequently, in order to understand his music, it is necessary to take into account his views on other subjects, including his philosophy of art in general and of the drama in particular. Whether one agrees or disagrees with these views is a question of the same order as whether one likes or dislikes the music; in either case, it is desirable to comprehend as well as judge.

The Early Operas

In music, Wagner was for the most part self-taught.[2] During his days at Leipzig, where his formal musical training was under the guidance of the cantor of St. Thomas's church, he became acquainted with the works of Beethoven and Mozart and heard at the theater the plays of Schiller and Shakespeare as well as the operas of Weber and Marschner.[3] He wrote dramas and some

An incomplete edition of Wagner's *Musikalische Werke* was published in Leipzig (1912–1922) and reprinted in New York (1969). A new and complete edition, *Richard Wagner: Sämtliche Werke*, is in progress (Mainz, 1970–), ed. by C. Dahlhaus, E. Voss, and others. Wagner's prose works were published in German in 1871–1883 and translated into English in 1892–99. A comprehensive bibliography of the Wagner literature can be found in *The New Grove Dictionary* article on Wagner and in Deathridge and Dahlhaus, *The New Grove Wagner*; an annotated bibliography of selected works available before 1965 in Grout, *A Short History of Opera*, 2nd ed., pp. 392–93. The standard biography has been Newman, *The Life of Richard Wagner*; see also biographies by Westernhagen and Gregor-Dellin. See also studies by Bailey, H. Bauer, O. Bauer, Dahlhaus, Deathridge, Donington, Glass, Voss, and Westernhagen; articles in periodicals devoted to Wagner research and in *19th Century Music*.

2. He did study harmony and counterpoint for several years, but he seldom mentioned that aspect of his education.

3. Weber's *Euryanthe* and Marschner's *Der Vampyr* influenced the composition of *Die Feen*, for which Wagner wrote both music and libretto. In his essays, Wagner acknowl-

instrumental music, including a symphony in C major which was performed in 1833. During two seasons as chorus trainer at Würzburg (1833–34), he became familiar with many more works of the current opera repertoire and he composed *Die Feen* ("The Fairies"), his first completed opera. This is a long work, with the usual subdivision into recitatives, arias, ensembles, and the like. A few traits of the music suggest his later works *(Tannhäuser* and *Lohengrin)*, but the style on the whole is modeled after Beethoven and Weber. The romantic idiom of the period is handled with great energy, aiming at big theatrical effects by conventional means. There is no technical reason why this opera could not have been performed; it is by no means an inexpert work, only it lacks individuality.[4] Wagner's libretto, based on a fairy tale by Carlo Gozzi, introduces all the fantastic and decorative apparatus of romantic opera in profusion, but without the unifying power of a really significant dramatic idea.

If *Die Feen* may be regarded as an essay in German romantic opera, *Das Liebesverbot* ("The Ban on Love") showed Wagner eagerly assimilating the Italian style. Bellini's *Montecchi e Capuletti* had aroused much enthusiasm at Leipzig in 1834, and Wagner was temporarily in reaction against the alleged heaviness, lack of dramatic life, and unvocal quality of the typical German operas. His libretto for *Das Liebesverbot* was based on Shakespeare's *Measure for Measure;* it is full of comic scenes and has some spoken dialogue. The music is a blend of Auber, Rossini, and Donizetti, with distinct traces of Meyerbeer in the finales, which often seem to strain terribly for effect. The melodies are florid, often with typically Italian cadenzas, and everything is repeated at great length. The best quality of the score is its liveliness and enthusiasm, though even this becomes wearisome after a time. There is not one really distinguished theme in the whole work; the duet in the first scene of Act II may be taken as typical of the style (example 22.1). Some of the crowd scenes faintly foreshadow the ending of Act II of *Die Meistersinger;* the duet of Isabella and Marianna and the latter's aria in the last act have a

edged that his career and works had been influenced by others; see, for example, his essay "Music of the Future."

4. Although excerpts from *Die Feen* were given in concert performances, the complete opera was not produced during Wagner's lifetime.

Example 22.1: *Das Liebesverbot*, Act II, no. 7

WAGNER

Ha, welch' ein Tod   für Lieb'   und Eh - re,   ihm

(8a sempre -

weih'   ich   mei - ne   Ju - gend-kraft.für die er-hab(ne)

sultry erotic quality which looks forward to Richard Strauss. *Das Liebersverbot* was performed only once, and then very badly, at Magdeburg in 1836, with the composer conducting.

From 1837 to 1839, Wagner was music director of the theater at Riga. There he began the composition of *Rienzi*, based on Bulwer-Lytton's novel and inspired by a performance of Spontini's *Fernand Cortez* which Wagner had witnessed at Berlin in 1836. In the summer of 1839, he went to Paris; the first stage of the trip was the memorable stormy sea voyage to London, the impressions of which later influenced him in the composition of *Der fliegende Holländer* ("The Flying Dutchman"). The two-and-a-half years in Paris were a nightmare of failure, disappointment, and poverty. Even the efforts of Meyerbeer on his behalf did not avail to obtain him a hearing. Yet during this time Wagner completed *Rienzi* and wrote *Der fliegende Holländer*, finishing the latter at the suburb of Meudon in August 1841. *Rienzi* was finally accepted by the Dresden Opera, where the first performance took place on October 20, 1842. Wagner went to Dresden in the summer to supervise the rehearsals. The success of the work was immediate and overwhelming and led to a demand for *Der fliegende*

Holländer, which was produced in January 1843. A month later, Wagner was appointed as a conductor for the Dresden Opera.

Rienzi, as already noted (chap. 18), was a grand opera in the fashion of the time, with just enough novelty to make it extremely popular.[5] The reception of *Der fliegende Holländer* was less flattering: in externals, this work was less brilliant than *Rienzi*, and its inner dramatic significance went for the most part unperceived. This was not altogether the fault of the audiences, for Wagner himself had not yet perfected his technique. *Der fliegende Holländer* is essentially a German romantic opera in the tradition of *Der Vampyr* or *Hans Heiling* (though without spoken dialogue), and is divided into the customary numbers. Some of these are quite successful, while others seem mechanical and forced, monotonous in rhythm, and without marked originality of melody or harmony. Wagner took his version of the medieval legend of the Flying Dutchman from a tale by Heinrich Heine, adding features suggested by Marschner's *Vampyr*. As in *Der Freischütz*, nature, animated by supernatural forces, is all-pervasive. This time it is not the forest but the sea: in the storm music, the steersman's song in Act I, and the sailors' choruses in Act III, Wagner set forth with all his power the impressions gathered in the voyage from Riga to London. These portions are not mere musical descriptions of the sea but are filled with symbolic meaning for the human drama. In the story of the redemption of the Dutchman from the curse of immortality by Senta's love, Wagner for the first time clearly worked out the idea of salvation through love which became fundamental in his later dramas. It is stated in Senta's Ballad (Act II), the central number of the opera and the one first composed. The ballad, a type of song which in earlier nineteenth-century opera had been as a rule only a set piece, here becomes the pivot of the whole dramatic and musical development, and its traditional two-part form is used to contrast the ideas of curse and salvation. The themes chosen are good examples of Wagner's characteristic procedure of representing basic dramatic ideas by specific musical formulae: the opening motif

---

5. It is a heroic-tragic opera in five acts, requiring six hours to perform. In addition to productions in opera houses, both large and small, *Rienzi* has also been accorded lavish open-air performances, which accentuate the crowd spectacle and accommodate the cavalcades of horses called for by the libretto.

forming an empty fifth, the stormy chromatics, and the diminished sevenths are set against the calm diatonic major melody of the second section.[6] The ultimate salvation—already prophesied at the end of the overture—is symbolized in the finale of the opera by using the latter theme for an extended plagal cadence in D major. These two themes (or rather theme groups) and their derivatives are used systematically in many other parts of the opera; Wagner had already adopted the device of the reminiscence motif, but had not yet extended it to every portion of the work. The historical interest of *Der fliegende Holländer* lies not so much in this device—which, as we have seen, was not new with Wagner— as in the quality of the themes themselves, in the individuality of their harmonies, and in the way they seem to embody the essential dramatic idea, completing its expression and giving it depth and emotional power.

Another important number in *Der fliegende Holländer* is the C-minor recitative and aria of the Dutchman in Act I ("Die Frist ist um"), ending with his pathetic appeal for death ("Ew'ge Vernichtung, nimm mich auf!"), which is echoed mysteriously in E major by the voices of the unseen crew—a momentary shift of tonality made more striking by the immediate, implacable return to C minor in the orchestral coda. The long duet of Senta and the Dutchman in the finale of Act II is the climax of the drama, but its operatic style is an unfortunate lapse into an earlier and less individual musical idiom. Of the remaining numbers, it is necessary to mention only the familiar "Spinning Song," which opens the second act, with the women's voices in A major offering a pleasant contrast to the dark colors of Act I and making an ideal prelude to Senta's Ballad.[7]

In *Tannhäuser* (1845), Wagner sought to unite the two elements which he had developed separately in *Der fliegende Holländer* and *Rienzi*, to clothe the dramatic idea of redemption in

6. The first motif has an obvious resemblance to the beginning of Beethoven's Ninth Symphony, which Wagner had heard for the first time adequately played by the Paris Conservatoire orchestra under Habeneck. For the orchestration here, as elsewhere in this opera and also in *Tannhäuser*, Wagner had learned much from Berlioz.

7. Wagner reworked *Der fliegende Holländer* in 1846 and 1860; among other things, he diminished the role of the brass instruments and revised the ending of the overture. For an informative discussion (with illustrations) of the adaptability of this opera to varying interpretations of scene design, see O. Bauer, *Richard Wagner: The Stage Designs.*

the garments of grand opera. His poem combined materials from a number of different sources, treating of the medieval legend of the knight Tannhäuser, who sojourned with Venus in her magic mountain and later went on a pilgrimage to Rome to obtain absolution, which was refused him: "Sooner will this dry staff blossom than your sins be forgiven," he was told by the pope. But the staff miraculously blossomed, a sign of God's mercy. To this story Wagner added the episode of the song contest and the figure of Elizabeth, through whose pure love and intercession the miracle of salvation was effected. All this is cast in the traditional outlines of an opera with the customary theatrical devices. The division into numbers is still clear, though with more sweep and less rigidity than in the earlier works. There are solos (for example, Tannhäuser's song in praise of Venus, Elizabeth's "Dich, teure Halle," her prayer, Wolfram's song to the evening star), ensembles (especially the end of Act II), choruses (for example, the Pilgrims' choruses for men's voices,[8] a favorite medium in nineteenth-century opera), the Venusberg ballet, and the brilliant crowd scene of the entrance of the Knights and the song contest in Act II. Numbers such as these, treated with Wagner's mastery of stage effect and in a style that audiences could easily understand, assured the success of *Tannhäuser*, though the new work did not arouse enthusiasm equal to that which had greeted *Rienzi*. Yet even where *Tannhäuser* is most operatic, it does not sacrifice the drama to outward show. The spectacular scenes are connected with the action and have a serious dramatic purpose; indeed, there are few operas in which form and content are so well balanced.

The portions of *Tannhäuser* that listeners failed to comprehend were just those which were most important in Wagner's estimation, and most significant in view of his later development: namely, the recitatives, of which Tannhäuser's narrative of his pilgrimage to Rome (Act III) is the principal example. Here is a long solo containing some of the central incidents of the drama; it is certainly not an aria with regular melody and balanced phrases, but neither is it recitative of the neutral, declamatory type found in earlier operas (and elsewhere in Wagner also). It is a melody strictly molded to the text, a semirealistic declamation of the words combined with expression of their content by means of a flexible

8. Sopranos and altos are added for climactic effect at the end of Act III.

Example 22.2: *Tannhäuser*, Act III

line supported by an equally important harmonic structure. In addition to providing the harmony, the orchestra has certain musical motifs which, by reason of their character and their association with the text, are heard as a commentary on the words, or as a further and purely musical expression of their meaning (example 22.2). This is the style which came to prevail almost exclusively in Wagner's later works; it was not entirely new with Wagner—Weber had done something similar in *Euryanthe*—but he used it so extensively, wielded it so effectively, and built it so firmly into his whole theory of the music drama that he perhaps rightly ranks as its discoverer. To the original singers of *Tannhäuser*, as well as to the audience, it was a mystery. Even the famous soprano Wilhelmine Schröder-Devrient, Wagner's staunch friend from the beginning and one from whom he received much inspiration, confessed that she could not make head or tail of her role of Venus; and the tenor Tichatschek, though equally devoted to the composer, had not the slightest perception of his new dramatic aims. Little by little, however, a small section of the Dresden public began to sympathize; this group—which, significantly, included few professional musicians—was the nucleus of the future Wagner cult.

The essential dramatic idea in *Tannhäuser* is the opposition of the world of sensual ecstasy and the world of ascetic renunciation, the former represented by Venus and her court, the latter by Elizabeth and the Pilgrims. Both Wagner's expansion of the Venusberg ballet for the disastrous Paris performances of 1861 and his revision of the last finale to include the actual appearance of Venus served to accentuate the contrast between the two basic ideas of the opera.[9] Wagner's music embodies the character of each of these worlds with an imaginative grasp and intensity of utterance which are more remarkable than anything else in the whole score. His greatness as a composer lies just in this power of evoking in the listener's mind such conceptions, in all their emotional depth and complexity, by means of music in which every detail is consciously or unconsciously directed toward the expressive purpose. In pursuit of his aims, Wagner found it necessary to rely more and more on the resources of harmony and instrumental color; as the aria diminished in importance, the orchestra rose correspondingly. This is evident in *Tannhäuser* both in the thematic importance of the accompaniments and in the separate orchestral pieces. The introduction to the third act, depicting Tannhäuser's pilgrimage, is one of those short symphonic poems

9. On the Paris production, see Abbate, "The Parisian 'Vénus' and the 'Paris' *Tannhäuser*."

of which there were to be more in the later works—Siegfried's Rhine Journey in *Götterdämmerung*, for example, or the Good Friday music in *Parsifal*. The overture to *Tannhäuser* is a complete composition in itself and, like those of *Der fliegende Holländer* and *Die Meistersinger*, a synopsis of the larger dramatic and musical form to follow.

It has been noted that the first six completed operas of Wagner are grouped in pairs, and that within each pair, each member is in many ways complementary to the other.[10] This is especially noticeable with *Tannhäuser* and *Lohengrin*. The latter was composed in the years from 1846 to 1848, though not performed until 1850 at Weimar, under Liszt's direction. Its sources, like those of *Tannhäuser*, are found in folklore and Germanic legend, but the treatment is considerably different. In *Lohengrin*, Wagner is less concerned with the tale itself or the historical setting and more with the timeless significance of the events portrayed. The characters, though adequately depicted as human, are at the same time agents or personifications of forces the conflict of which makes the drama. Thus, Lohengrin may be said to represent divine love and its longing for reciprocal love and faith from mankind, while Elsa represents human nature incapable of the necessary unquestioning trust. Whatever meaning one may see in the story, the necessity of some interpretation in the sense suggested is unavoidable. In keeping with this view of the drama, the musical setting of *Lohengrin* is altogether less spectacular than that of *Tannhäuser*; there are no sensational contrasts, and an extraordinary unit of mood prevails throughout. The system of reminiscence motifs is still further developed, not only in extent but also in the changed function of the motifs themselves: they are no longer used simply to recall earlier scenes and actions but to symbolize situations or abstract ideas. For example, the motif which some analysts label "the forbidden question," first sung by Lohengrin as he lays the command on Elsa never to ask for his name or country, is a complete, periodic, eight-measure theme (example 22.3). It recurs, in whole or in part, throughout the opera wherever the situation touches pointedly on this prohibition: in the introduction to Act II, during the dialogue between

10. See Chamberlain, *Das Drama Richard Wagners.*

Example 22.3: *Lohengrin*, Act I

WAGNER

Nie sollst du mich be - fra-gen, noch Wi - ssens Sor - ge tra-gen, wo -
- her ich kam der Fahrt, noch wie mein Nam' und Art!

Ortrud and Friedrich in the first scene, in the second scene at Ortrud's hypocritical warning to Elsa against the "unknown" knight, at Elsa's sign of doubt in the last scene of the act, and in the closing orchestral cadence; it comes into the duet of Act III, rises to full force as Elsa asks the fatal question, echoes again at the end of this scene, and is heard once more at Elsa's entrance in the last finale. Other characteristic motifs are used in a similar way. The principle is not yet that of the *Ring*, where the motifs are shorter, essentially harmonic and rhythmic rather than melodic, and employed continuously in a symphonic web; nevertheless, *Lohengrin* carries the practice further than any preceding opera and clearly points the way to Wagner's later style.

From the formal point of view, *Lohengrin* has shed many traces of the traditional division into numbers, as well as much of the distinction between aria and recitative. The new free declamation is the normal style in this work, except in a few places like Elsa's "Einsam in trüben Tagen"—and even here the three strophes of the solo are separated by choruses and recitatives—and Lohengrin's narrative in Act III, the Bridal Chorus, and the duet following this. The colorful orchestral prelude to Act III is often played as a separate concert number. The prelude to the opera, unlike the overture to *Tannhäuser*, is in one mood and movement, representing (according to Wagner's statement) the descent and return of the Holy Grail, the type of Lohengrin's own mission, as we hear when the same themes and harmonies accompany his narrative in Act III. The A-major tonality of the prelude is associated with Lohengrin throughout the opera, just as the key of F-sharp minor is assigned to Ortrud and, as a rule, the flat keys to Elsa. The harmony of *Lohengrin* is remarkably diatonic;

there is very little chromaticism of the sort found in the middle section of the Pilgrims' Chorus or the Evening Star aria in *Tannhäuser*. The orchestration likewise contrasts with that of *Tannhäuser*: instead of treating the instruments as a homogeneous group, Wagner divides them into antiphonal choirs, often with the violins subdivided and the woodwind section expanded so as to make possible a whole chord of three or four tones in a single color. The effect, while less brilliant than in *Tannhäuser*, is at the same time richer and more subtle. Even in the last scene of Act II, showing the dawn of day heralded by trumpet fanfares, and the procession to the minster, the sonority is restrained in comparison with the usual grand-opera treatment of such episodes.

The skillfully written choruses in *Lohengrin* are an important musical and dramatic factor. For the most part, the chorus is treated either as realistically entering into the action or else as an "articulate spectator" in the manner of Greek tragedy (especially in the second scene of Act I and the finale of Act III). The prominence of the chorus may have been suggested to Wagner by his study of Gluck's *Iphigénie en Aulide*, which he revised for performances at Dresden in 1847.

Lohengrin is generally regarded as the last of the important German romantic operas. It has many resemblances to Weber's *Euryanthe:* in the continuity of the music, the style of declamation, and the use of recurring motifs, as well as in the plot and characters.[11] At the same time, *Lohengrin* functions as a pivotal work, for on the one hand it represents the culmination of a half century of operatic achievements, while on the other it foreshadows the style of Wagner's later music dramas.[12] The juncture between these two phases of Wagner's development is marked by a pause in musical creativity; five years separate *Lohengrin* from *Das Rheingold*, begun in 1853.

11. The basic plot—the test of a wife's love—is common to the two works. The character of Elsa corresponds to Euryanthe, Telramund and Ortrud to Lysiart and Eglantine; the figure of the good king is also in both. Act I of *Lohengrin*, as Bekker points out (*Wagner*, chap. 6), was doubtless also influenced by Marschner's *Templer und Jüdin*.

12. The short musical sketches made in 1850 for *Siegfrieds Tod* are similar in style to the *Lohengrin* music. See Newman, *The Life of Richard Wagner*, 2:159–61.

The Ring *Cycle*

In 1849, as a result of quarrels with his superiors and a multitude of other difficulties climaxing in his active participation in the revolutionary uprising in May of that year, Wagner was obliged to flee from Dresden. He sought refuge at Weimar with Liszt, who helped him escape to Switzerland. Settled at Zurich, Wagner found leisure to clarify in his own mind the new ideas on music and the theater which had already been occupying him at Dresden and of which some intimations may be found in his earlier operas, *Lohengrin* especially. The result of these cogitations was a series of essays, including the important *Oper und Drama* ("Opera and Drama," published in 1851), a systematic account of the philosophy and technical methods by which all his subsequent works were to be governed.[13] A knowledge of *Oper und Drama* is indispensable for anyone who seriously desires to understand these works—the *Ring*, *Tristan*, *Die Meistersinger*, and *Parsifal*—even though Wagner's practice is not always consistent with his theories.[14]

The doctrines of *Oper und Drama* are best exemplified in *Der Ring des Nibelungen* ("The Ring of the Nibelung"), which consists of four consecutive dramas: *Das Rheingold* ("The Rhine Gold"), shorter than the others (it consists of but a single act) and a prelude to them; *Die Walküre* ("The Valkyrie"); *Siegfried*; and *Götterdämmerung* ("Twilight of the Gods"). Altogether, the composition of the *Ring* occupied twenty years of Wagner's life. Its subject combines two distinct Germanic myth cycles, the story of Siegfried and that of the downfall of the gods. Wagner in 1848 wrote a drama, *Siegfrieds Tod* ("Siegfried's Death"), which he expected to set to music at once; but as the subject grew in his mind, he felt the need for another drama to precede this, and accordingly he wrote *Der junge Siegfried* ("Young Siegfried") in 1851.[15] The work expanded still further: *Die Walküre* was required to lead up to *Der junge Siegfried*, and *Das Rheingold* as

13. For English translations, see Wagner, *Prose Works* and *Opera and Drama*. There is a good summary in Abraham, *A Hundred Years of Music*.

14. Various opinions have been expressed about this "consistency." Cf. Stein, *Richard Wagner and the Synthesis of the Arts*, and Glass, *The Fertilizing Seed*.

15. See McCreless, *Wagner's "Siegfried."*

Setting for Act III, scene 1 of the original production of R. Wagner's *Die Walküre* (Bayreuth 1876); designed by Joseph Hoffmann.

(Courtesy Archiv des Hauses Wahnfried, Bayreuth)

Setting for the same scene, (Bayreuth 1960); designed by Wolfgang Wagner.

a general prelude to the whole. These two poems, in this order, were written in 1852, after which *Der junge Siegfried* and *Siegfrieds Tod* were revised into the present *Siegfried* and *Götterdämmerung*, respectively, the whole text being completed by the end of 1852.[16] Meanwhile, some sketches for the music had been made, composition was begun in 1853, and by 1857 the setting was completed through the second act of *Siegfried*. After an interim during which he composed *Tristan* and *Die Meistersinger*, Wagner resumed work on the *Ring* in 1865, though *Götterdämmerung* was not finished until nine years later. The first performances of the whole tetralogy took place at Bayreuth in 1876.

The story of the *Ring* is so familiar—or, at any rate, is so easily accessible in popular books of all sorts, not to mention the scores themselves—that there is no need to recapitulate it here. The material is taken not from folklore (as in *Die Feen*), or history (as in *Rienzi*), or even legend (as in *Der fliegende Holländer* and *Tannhäuser*), but from mythology. The reason is not primarily that the myth is entertaining, but that it is meaningful. According to Wagner, the myth presents, in the simplest, most inclusive, and most concentrated form imaginable, the interplay of eternal forces affecting the relation of human beings to God, to nature, and to each other in society—in other words, living, eternal issues of religious, social, and economic importance, with which it is the duty of art consciously to deal. These issues are set before us in the myth, and consequently in the *Ring*, by means of symbols, either objects (the Gold, Valhalla, the Sword) or persons (Wotan, Siegfried, Brünnhilde). It is the nature of a symbol to be capable of various interpretations; and although Wagner labored hard, both in the poem itself and in other writings, to make clear his own interpretation of the *Ring*, he did not fully succeed—partly because of some inconsistencies in his thinking and the obscurity of his literary style, but more because the symbols were so ambiguous that it was impossible to make a single definitive explanation of them. Many writers have tried to do so, and have argued vehemently, each according to his own convictions, for or against the doctrines conceived to be embodied in the *Ring*. Still

16. On the changes made in the earlier poems, and some resulting inconsistencies in the present text, see Newman, *The Life of Richard Wagner*, vol. 2, chap. 17; on the symbolism, Overhoff, *Richard Wagners germanisch-christlicher Mythos*.

others regard any intentional preaching in art as either of no importance or else downright vicious and inartistic. There is no need at this day to add anything more to the enormous mass of controversial literature about Wagner. It is not within the scope of a book like this to investigate the alleged effects of his teaching, in the *Ring* or elsewhere, on European politics.[17] That he did intend to teach—that his views of art and the theater impelled him in his operas to assume the role of prophet as well as musician—is a fact, whether one approves it or not; but all that concerns us here is the consequences of that fact in his art work itself.

It is not easy to dramatize abstractions. In the *Ring*, Wagner felt obliged to introduce some explanatory passages which slow down or interrupt the action of the play—for example, the long dialogue between Wotan and Brünnhilde in the second scene of Act II of *Die Walküre*. For the benefit of opera audiences, who are not particularly interested in metaphysics, these passages are often cut or shortened in performance. The same is true of the many repetitions of the story which occur from time to time, and other apparent digressions. All these matters have their justification, however, in Wagner's theories; moreover, the leisurely pace of the action suggests the tempo of the long medieval epic poems from which the incidents were taken. Another interesting reminiscence of these poetic models is Wagner's employment of *Stabreim*, or alliteration, instead of the more modern device of end rhymes:

> Gab sein Gold mir Macht ohne Mass,
> nun zeug' sein Zauber Tod dem der ihn trägt!

> (As its gold gave me might without measure,
> Now may its magic deal death to him who wears it!)
> *Das Rheingold*, scene 4.[18]

The relation of music to drama is one of the subjects on which Wagner discourses in much detail in his writings. The first proposition of *Oper und Drama* is: "The error in opera hitherto

---

17. Cf. Donington, *Wagner's "Ring" and Its Symbols.*

18. Wagner's concept of *Stabreim* is expressed in *Oper und Drama*, part 2, chap. 6. *Stabreim* is verse with free rhythms and alliterative rhymes. It pairs words of similar meaning, similar initial consonants, similar final consonants, or even similar initial vowel sounds: a form of poetic writing intended, by its short lines and repeated sounds, to conjure up a feeling of an ancient language.

consisted in this, that a means of expression (the music) has been made an end, while the end itself (the drama) has been made the means."[19] It does not follow, however, that now poetry is to be made primary and music secondary, but rather that both are to grow organically out of the necessities of dramatic expression, not being brought together, but existing as two aspects of one and the same thing. Other arts as well (the dance, architecture, painting) are to be included in this union, making the music drama a composite or total art work. This is not, in Wagner's view, a limitation of any of the arts; on the contrary, only in such a union can the full possibilities of each be realized. The "music of the future," then, will exist not in isolation as heretofore, but as one aspect of the Gesamtkunstwerk, in which situation it will develop new technical and expressive resources and will progress beyond the point at which it has now arrived, a point beyond which it cannot substantially progress in any other way.

This view was the consequence of a typical nineteenth-century philosophy. Wagner regarded the history of music as a process of evolution which must inevitably continue in a certain direction. The theory that the line of progress involved the end of music as a separate art and its absorption into a community of the arts is not without analogy to the communistic and socialistic doctrines of the period, with their emphasis on the absorption of the interests of the individual into those of the community as a whole.[20] It is not surprising that some such view of the future of music should have arisen in the second half of the nineteenth century. It is plain enough to us now that the resources of music— that is, of the kind of music which had been growing up since Beethoven—were approaching their utmost limits at this time, and that these limits were in fact reached in the works of Wagner, Brahms, R. Strauss, and Mahler. It has been the mission of twentieth-century composers to recognize this situation and to create new musical styles, much as the composers of the seventeenth century had to do after the culmination of sixteenth-century polyphony in the works of Palestrina, Byrd, and Lassus. In discerning

19. Wagner, *Gesammelte Schriften*, 3:231; cf. Stein, *Richard Wagner and the Synthesis of the Arts*.

20. Cf. Barzun, *Darwin, Marx, Wagner*.

the approaching end of a musical style, therefore, Wagner was right. His error was in postulating the Gesamtkunstwerk as the only possible road for the future.

Wagner held that music in itself was the immediate expression of feeling, but that it could not designate the particular object toward which feeling was directed. Hence, for him the inner action of the drama existed in the music, while the function of word and gesture was to make definite the outer action.[21] This aesthetic is the theoretical basis of many features of the *Ring* and later works. For example, since the inner action is regarded as being always on a plane of feeling where music is appropriate and necessary, there is no spoken dialogue or simple recitative. Moreover, the inner action (unlike the outer) is continuous; hence the music is continuous. (In this theory, intermissions between the acts, and the performance of the *Ring* on four separate evenings instead of all at once, can be regarded only as one of Wagner's reluctant concessions to human frailty.) Transitions from one scene to the next are made by means of orchestral interludes when necessary, and within each scene the music has a continuity of which the most obvious technical sign is the avoidance of perfect cadences. Continuity in music, however, is more than avoidance of perfect cadences. It is a result of the musical form as a whole, and since form in Wagner (as in any composer) is partly a function of harmonic procedure, this is an appropriate place to consider these two subjects together.

The statements most frequently made about Wagner's harmony are (1) that it is "full of chromatics" and (2) that the music "continually modulates." Both statements are true but superficial. Much of the chromaticism in the earlier works (for example, in the original version of *T'annhüser*) is merely an embellishment of the melodic line or occurs incidentally in the course of modulating sequences. Many of the chromatic passages in the *Ring*, such as the magic sleep motif, are found in the midst of long diatonic sections. The impression that Wagner continually modulates is due in part to a short-breathed method of analysis

21. Cf. Schopenhauer, *Die Welt als Wille und Vorstellung*, vol. 1, book 3, sec. 52; and vol. 2 ("Erganzungen"), chap. 39. See also Reeser, "Audible Staging."

based on a narrow conception of tonality, which tends to see a modulation at every dominant-tonic progression and, preoccupied with such details, overlooks the broader harmonic scheme. A more comprehensive and illuminating view is set forth by Alfred Lorenz in his four studies entitled *Das Geheimnis der Form bei Richard Wagner* ("The Secret of Form in Richard Wagner"). Lorenz, in the enthusiasm of discovery, occasionally strains the facts to make them fit his theory; nevertheless, he does succeed in showing that Wagner's music dramas are cast in definite musical forms, and that the formal clarity is evident not only in each work as a whole but also in the constituent sections, down to the smallest.[22] The structure of the music is inseparable from that of the drama, and one of its fundamental elements is the key scheme. *Das Rheingold*, for example, is regarded as a large *a–b–a* form in D-flat, with an introduction in E-flat (the dominant of the dominant); D-flat, with an introduction in E-flat (the dominant of the dominant); D-flat is also the tonality of the *Ring* as a whole. *Tristan* is likewise in three-part form, Acts I and III corresponding and Act II being the B section—though here the correspondence is one of themes and dramatic action, not of tonality. The three acts of *Die Meistersinger* make a huge *a–a–b* form, the first two being equal in length and the third as long as the first two together. These two forms, the *Bogen* (*a–b–a*, literally "bow") and the *Bar* (*a–a–b*),[23] are frequently exemplified also in the structure of scenes and smaller subdivisions; thus, the fifteenth "period" of Act II of *Siegfried* (three measures before "Noch einmal, liebes Vöglein" to the change of signature to four sharps at "nun sing") is an *a–b–a* or Bogen in E minor (18 + 30 + 21 measures), and the introduction to Act II of *Die Walküre* is a Bar in A minor (introduction, 14 measures; two *Stollen*, 20 + 19 measures; *Abgesang*, 20 measures). Other form types (strophic, rondo) also appear, and many units are composed of two or more of the basic types in various

22. In more recent times, Lorenz's system has been challenged, especially by Carl Dahlhaus. For an overview of current scholarship concerning Wagner's form, see Newcomb, "The Birth of Music."

23. The Bar, consisting of two *Stollen* (*a,a*) and an *Abgesang* (*b*), was the favorite from of the German minnesinger. It is explained by Hans Sachs in *Die Meistersinger*, Act III, sc. 2, and is well illustrated in both versions of Walther's "Prize Song" in the same opera.

modifications and combinations.[24] One may not choose to follow Lorenz in every detail, and it would certainly be in order to question some of his interpretations of the basic formal schemes; but taken as a whole, it is impossible in the face of his demonstration not to be convinced of the essential orderliness, at once minute and all-embracing, of the musical cosmos of the *Ring*, as well as of *Tristan, Die Meistersinger*, and *Parsifal*. It is an orderliness not derived at second hand from the text but inhering in the musical structure itself. Was Wagner fully aware of it? One is tempted to think not, since he says almost nothing about it in his writings. Yet, whether conscious or unconscious, the sheer grasp and creation of such huge and complex organisms is a matter for wonder. It may be unnecessary to remark that the fact (if it is a fact) that Wagner's creative processes were largely instinctive or unconscious does not of itself invalidate any analysis of his music. It is no essential part of a composer's business to be aware, in an analytical sense, of everything he is doing.

Within the larger frameworks of order, and subsidiary to them, take place the various harmonic procedures which have given rise to Wagner's reputation: modulations induced by enharmonic changes in chromatically altered chords and forwarded by modulating sequences; the interchangeable use of major and minor modes and the frequency of the mediants and the flat supertonic as goals of modulation; the determination of chord sequences by chromatic progression of individual voices; the presence of "harmonic parentheses" within a section, related to the tonality of the whole as auxiliary notes or appoggiaturas are related to the fundamental harmony of the chord with which they occur; the systematic treatment of sevenths and even ninths as consonant chords; the resolution of dominants to chords other than the tonic; the combination of melodies in a contrapuntal tissue; and finally, the frequent suspensions and appoggiaturas in the various melodic lines, which contribute as much as any single factor to the peculiar romantic, Wagnerian, "longing" quality of the harmony—a quality heard in perfection in the prelude to *Tristan und Isolde*.

24. Lorenz's system of analysis cannot be adequately illustrated without going into greater detail than is possible here. See his outline of Act I of *Die Walküre* in Abraham, *A Hundred Years of Music*, pp. 122–29, and cf. Dickinson, "The Structural Methods of *The Ring*."

While the musical forms of Wagner's dramas are determined in part by the harmonic structure, a more obvious role is played by the continuous recurrence and variation of a limited number of distinct musical units generally known as "leitmotifs" or leading motifs. The term "leitmotif" is not Wagner's, though he did use the apparently synonymous word *Hauptmotiv* (principal motif). However, it seems likely that Wagner suggested the word, as well as the system of analyzing his music dramas in terms of motifs, to Heinrich Porges, whose book on *Tristan und Isolde*, written in 1866–1877 (though not published before 1902), uses this method. The analysis of Wagner's music in terms of leitmotifs was popularized by Hans von Wolzogen, first editor of the *Bayreuther Blätter* and author of many "guides" to the music dramas.[25]

Different analysts distinguish, and variously name, 70 to 200 leitmotifs in the *Ring*. Each is regarded as the focal point of expression of a certain dramatic idea, with which it remains associated throughout the tetralogy. The clue to the association of motif and idea is to be found at the first appearance of the former;[26] for example, the Valhalla motif is first heard at the opening of the second scene of *Das Rheingold*, as the curtain rises to reveal the castle of Valhalla. Here, as usual at the first statement of a motif, Wagner repeats and spins out the phrase so as to impress it on the memory; moreover, there is an anticipation of the Valhalla motif at the end of the preceding scene, where its derivation from the Ring motif is obvious. The motifs are short and of pronounced individual character; they are often suggested by a pictorial image (as the fire motifs), or by association (as the trumpet figure for the sword motif), but each aims to convey not merely a picture but also the essence of the idea for which the visible symbol stands. In this capacity, the motifs may recur not simply as musical labels but whenever the idea recurs or is suggested in the course of the drama, forming a symphonic web which

25. See, for example, his *Thematischer Leitfaden durch die Musik zu Richard Wagners Festspiel "Der Ring des Nibelungen"* and later similar works; further in Newman, *The Life of Richard Wagner*, 3:382–83. On the early history of recurring themes in opera, see Schmidt, *Die frühdeutsche Oper*, 2:255–80; Bücken, *Der heroische Stil in der Oper*, passim.

26. Exceptions to this occur; see, for example, motifs stated in the preludes to *Tristan* and *Parsifal*, which acquire specific meaning only later in the opera.

Example 22.4: Motifs from the *Ring*

corresponds in theory, and generally also in fact, to the dramatic web of the action. The connection between the musical forms so evolved and the dramatic forms is thus complete. The motifs may be contrapuntally combined, or varied, developed, and transformed in accordance with the changing fortunes of the idea they represent. Relationship of ideas may be shown by thematic relationships among the motifs (example 22.4), though probably some of the resemblances are not intentional. Altogether, the statement, recurrence, variation, development, and transformation of the motifs is analogous to the working out of musical material in a symphony.

Since the inner meaning of the drama is found in the music, it follows in Wagner's theory that the orchestra is the basic medium, rather than the voices. In his phrase, the words "float like a ship on the sea of orchestral harmony." Only rarely are the leitmotifs sung. As a rule, the voice will make a free counterpoint to the instrumental melody. The voice part, however, is always itself melodic, never merely declamatory as in secco recitative; its line is so arranged as not only to give the correct declamation but also to reproduce the accent, tempo, and inflections appropriate to each character. Textual repetition is avoided. In theory there are to be no ensembles, especially in the old-fashioned sense where some voices are used only to supply a harmonic background; but this rule Wagner relaxed on occasion, as in the finale of Act II of *Götterdämmerung* or the quintet in *Die Meistersinger*. Of Wagner's genius as an orchestrator there is no need to speak here.[27] His music is the realization of the full, rich, romantic sound ideal of the nineteenth century. Its peculiar texture is determined in large part by the nature of the melodic lines: long phrased, avoiding periodic cadential points (this in contrast to *Lohengrin* and earlier works), so designed that every note tends to move on without ever quite coming to rest.[28] The full resources of symphonic style—counterpoint, orchestral color, and formal structure—are invoked. This in itself was not new in the history of opera, for many earlier composers (for example, Monteverdi in *Orfeo*) had done the same. But Wagner, besides having the immensely developed instrumental resources of the nineteenth century at his disposal, was conscious as no earlier composer had been of the drama and its "poetic intent" as the generating forces in the whole plan; and he was original in placing the orchestra at the center, with the essential drama going on in the music, while words and gesture furnished only the outer happenings. From this point of view, his music dramas may be regarded as symphonic poems the program of which, instead of being printed and read, is explained and acted out by persons on the stage.

Wagner's music dramas have been as popular as any operas. The source of their appeal is primarily, of course, the music itself. Yet there are certain other factors which have at different

---

27. His changing conception of orchestration, among other things, is revealed in his revisions of *Die fliegende Holländer* and *Tannhäuser*. Cf. Abraham, "Wagner's Second Thoughts," and Abbate, "The Parisian 'Vénus'."

28. This is one meaning of Wagner's term "unending melody"; it has other meanings as well. See Lorenz, *Geheimnis der Form*, 1:61–70; Kurth, *Romantische Harmonik*, part 7.

times made for popular success in opera. One of these factors in the nineteenth century was the appeal to national pride, as in some of Weber's and Verdi's works. Such an appeal is indirectly present in most of Wagner's operas insofar as they are founded on Germanic myths or legends; but this kind of nationalism is of little importance, since Wagner thought of his dramas as universal, dealing with what he called the "purely human," not limited to Germans in the sense in which *Der Freischütz* was. Even *Die Meistersinger*, for all its reference to "holy German art," is not narrowly patriotic or jingoistic in spirit. In his essay "Music of the Future," Wagner makes clear his ideal that art forms should be unencumbered by barriers of nationality: "If differences of language prevent literature from attaining universality, music— that great language all men understand—should have the power, by dissolving verbal concept into feeling, to communicate the innermost secrets of the artist's vision—especially when it is raised through the medium of a dramatic performance to that clarity of expression hitherto reserved to painting alone."[29]

Another and more general basis of popular appeal in opera is stage spectacle. Wagner availed himself of this resource unstintingly, though always maintaining that every one of his effects grew of necessity out of the drama itself. It would be difficult to think of any beguiling, eye-catching, fanciful, sensational device in the whole history of opera from Monteverdi to Meyerbeer which Wagner did not appropriate and use with expert showmanship somewhere in his works.[30] One has only to look at the poem of the *Ring* to see how prominent is this element; it has a large place also in *Parsifal*. In *Tristan* and *Die Meistersinger*, it is less in evidence, for these are dramas of human character and as such appeal directly to fundamental human emotions, with less need of spectacular stage effects. This quality of direct, human appeal is heard at only a few places in the *Ring*, as in the love scenes of Siegmund and Sieglinde (*Die Walküre*, Act I) and of Siegfried and Brünnhilde (*Siegfried*, Act III), or in the scene of Wotan's fare-

29. Wagner, *Three Wagner Essays*, pp. 17–18.

30. In O. Bauer, *Richard Wagner: The Stage Designs*, there are excellent illustrations of the scenery not only for premiere productions but also for subsequent international productions. See also Petzet and Petzet, *Die Richard Wagner-Bühne*, which is beautifully illustrated. For Josef Svoboda's contemporary scenography for Wagner's operas (with analysis of specific problems), see Burian, *Svoboda: Wagner*.

well to Brünnhilde (*Die Walküre*, Act III); and when Wagner, like Wotan in this scene, put aside his concern with godhood to create the truly memorable characters of Walther, Eva, Hans Sachs, Isolde, and Tristan, he created two works that are likely to out-live all the pageantry and symbolism of the *Ring*.

Tristan und Isolde

The poem of *Tristan und Isolde* was begun at Zurich in 1857, and the score was finished in 1859. It is often regarded as a monument to Wagner's love for Mathilde Wesendonck, the wife of one of his most devoted friends during his years of exile. Newman sensibly points out, however, that this view probably confuses cause and effect, that Wagner did not compose *Tristan* because he was in love with Mathilde, but rather that he was in love because he was composing *Tristan*. Either way, the matter is not important. In 1857–58, Wagner composed five songs to poems by Mathilde; two of these ("Träume" and "Im Treibhaus") are made up of the-matic material used in *Tristan*, and Wagner later described them as "studies" for the opera. *Tristan* was undertaken at a time when there appeared no prospect of ever bringing the *Ring* to perfor-mance, and it was Wagner's hope that a less exacting music drama might have better prospects of success. But by now his ideas of what constituted a practicable work had so far outgrown the ac-tual practice of the theater's that *Tristan* for some years could not be produced, either. After more than seventy rehearsals at Vienna in 1862–63, it was abandoned as impossible. Finally, in 1864, the young king Ludwig of Bavaria summoned Wagner to Munich and placed almost unlimited resources at his disposal. After careful preparation, the first performance took place at Munich on June 10, 1865, under the direction of Hans von Bülow.

The legend of Tristan and Isolde is probably of Celtic origin. In the early thirteenth century, it was embodied by Gott-fried of Strassburg in a long epic poem, which was Wagner's prin-cipal source for his drama. Wagner's changes consisted in com-pressing the action, eliminating nonessential personages (for example, the original second Isolde, "of the white hands"), and simplifying the motives. Some details were doubtless borrowed from other sources: the extinction of the torch in Act II from the story of Hero and Leander, the dawning of day at the end of the love scene from Shakespeare's *Romeo and Juliet*, and Tristan's delirium in Act III from Matthew Arnold's poem; the love duet in the second act has some points reminiscent of a dialogue between Faust and Helena in the second part of Goethe's drama, and the figure of Brangäne as watcher was perhaps suggested by Goethe's Lynceus.[31] The prominence of the motif of death, the yearning for fulfillment of love in release and annihilation which broods over the whole drama, were at least partly due to Wagner's absorption in the philosophy of Schopenhauer, with whose works he had first become acquainted in the 1850s.[32] But whatever the contributions of others, *Tristan und Isolde* is Wagner's own. It is owing to him, and to him alone, that this is now one of the great love stories, living in the imagination of millions along with the tales of Romeo and Juliet, Paolo and Francesca, Launcelot and Guinevere.

The peculiar strength of the drama arises from the fact that external events are simplified to the utmost, so that the action is almost all inner and consequently is expressed almost wholly in music. The words themselves often melt into music, losing their very character as intelligible language, nearly superfluous in many places where the plane of expression is purely that of the emotions—as, for example, in Isolde's solo at the end of Act III. "Every theory was quite forgotten," wrote Wagner; "during the working out I myself became aware how far I had outsoared my system."[33]

The three leading ideas of the drama—love, night, and death—are inseparable, but each one in turn is especially emphasized in each of the three acts. The magic potion of Act I is, in Wagner's version, purely a symbol, figuring forth the moment of realization of a love already existing but unacknowledged. Isolde's extinction of the torch is the symbol of Act II; the ecstatic greeting

---

31. *Faust*, part 2, lines 9372–9418, 11288–11337. These literary derivations are suggested with some diffidence. The torch episode is found in Méhul's *Mélidor et Phrosine*; the watcher is a common figure in German medieval love poems. Cf. the introduction to Loomis, ed., *The Romance of Tristram and Ysolt.*

32. There are echoes here also of Novalis and F. von Schlegel. Cf. Mann, *Leiden und Grösse der Meister*, pp. 130–32.

33. Wagner, *Gesammelte Schriften*, 7:119.

of the lovers leads into the duet "Descend upon us, night of love," followed by the love-death music with the words "O could we but die thus together, endless, never to awaken!" The climax of the whole scene is in the song of Brangäne, off stage: "Lonely I watch in the night; you that are lost in the dream of love, heed the lonely one's call: sorrow comes with awakening. Beware! O beware! For the night soon passes." Few artists have so poignantly expressed what many human beings have experienced, the unutterably sorrowful realization in the midst of happiness that this moment cannot last. There is a comparable passage in the *Arabian Nights:*

Presently one of them arose and set meat before me and I ate and they ate with me; whilst others warmed water and washed my hands and feet and changed my clothes, and others made ready sherbets and gave us to drink; and all gathered round me being full of joy and gladness at my coming. Then they sat down and conversed with me till night-fall, when five of them arose and laid the trays and spread them with flowers and fragrant herbs and fruits, fresh and dried, and confections in profusion. At last they brought out a fine wine-service with rich old wine; and we sat down to drink and some sang songs and others played the lute and psaltery and recorders and other instruments, and the bowl went merrily round. Hereupon such gladness possessed me that I forgot the sorrows of the world one and all and said, "This is indeed life; O sad that 'tis fleeting."[34]

The doom fated from the beginning is fulfilled. Tristan, reproached by King Mark, mortally wounded by Melot, is carried home to his castle of Kareol and dies as Isolde comes to him bringing Mark's forgiveness. The love-death of Isolde herself, the celebrated *Liebestod*, brings the tragedy to an end.

Volumes could be, and have been, written about the music of *Tristan und Isolde*. The extreme simplification and condensation of the action, the reduction of the essential characters to only two, and the treatment of these two as bearers of a single all-dominating mood conduce to unity of musical effect and at the same time permit the greatest possible freedom for development of all the musical elements, unchecked by elaborate parapherna-

34. "Tale of the Third Kalendar" (Burton's translation).

lia or the presence of antimusical factors in the libretto. There are comparatively few leitmotifs, and many of the principal ones are so much alike that it is hard to distinguish and label them clearly. The dominant mood is conveyed in a chromatic style of writing which is no longer either a mere decorative adjunct to, or a deliberate contrast with, a fundamentally diatonic idiom, but which is actually the norm, so much so that the few diatonic motifs are felt as deliberate departures, "specters of day" intruding into the all-prevailing night of the love drama. It is impossible here to enter into a comprehensive examination of the technical aspects of this chromaticism;[35] we can only note that history has shown the *"Tristan style"* to be the classical example of the use of a consistent chromatic technique within the limits of the tonal system of the eighteenth and nineteenth centuries. It was not only the climax of all romantic striving in this direction but also the point of departure for Wagner's own later experiments in *Parsifal*, for the more sophisticated, external, ironic chromaticism of Richard Strauss, and for the twelve-tone system of Arnold Schoenberg, the conclusion of the whole style. The power of the *Tristan* chromaticism comes from its being founded in tonality. A feature of it is the ambiguity of the chords, the constant, immanent, felt possibility that almost any chord may resolve in almost any one of a dozen different directions. Yet this very ambiguity could not exist except for underlying tonal relations, the general tendencies of certain chord progressions within the tonal system. The continuous conflict between what *might be*, harmonically, and what actually *is*, makes the music apt at suggesting the inner state of mingled insecurity and passionate longing that pervades the drama. This emotional suggestiveness is accompanied throughout by a luxuriance of purely sensuous effect, a reveling in tone qualities and tone combinations as if for their own sake, evident in both the subdued richness of the orchestration and the whole harmonic fabric.

Such matters as these are felt by even the casual listener to *Tristan und Isolde*. What is less obvious, though it may be dimly sensed, is the complete formal perfection of the work. Here again the reader must be referred for details to the epoch-making

---

35. This task has been performed, with great thoroughness and insight, in Kurth, *Romantische Harmonik und ihre Krise in Wagners "Tristan"*.

Example 22.5: Motif from *Tristan und Isolde*

(a) Prelude.   (b) End of Act III   WAGNER

study of Lorenz.[36] The close correspondence of Acts I and III, with the resulting Bogen form of the opera as a whole, has already been mentioned. As to the tonality, Lorenz holds it to be E major—beginning in the subdominant (A minor) and ending in the dominant (B major). The tonic itself, in this view, is almost never sounded, this being at the same time an instance of the persistent avoidance of resolution in the harmony and a symbol of the nature of the love of Tristan and Isolde, which attains its satisfaction only in the ideal, not the actual world. The only extended E major portion of the opera is the scene of Tristan's vision of Isolde in Act III. The complete first theme as announced in the prelude (measures 1–17) recurs only three times in the course of the opera, once at the climax of each act: at the drinking of the potion in Act I, after Mark's question near the end of Act II, and at Tristan's death in Act III; its function is thus that of a refrain for the whole work. The continuity and formal symmetry, demonstrable in full only by a detailed analysis, are neatly epitomized by the fact that the opening chromatic motif of the prelude receives its final resolution in the closing measures of the last act (example 22.5).

Wagner's Last Works

After completing the score of *Tristan* and spending an unhappy season in Paris, marked by the scandalous rejection of the revised

36. Lorenz, *Das Geheimnis der Form*, vol. 2.

Tannhäuser at the Opéra (March 1861), Wagner lived for a year and a half in Vienna. With the failure of prospects for performing *Tristan* there, his fortunes reached their lowest ebb. His dramatic rescue by King Ludwig of Bavaria brought happier times, but six months after the successful first performance of *Tristan*, Wagner was compelled to leave Munich, owing largely to political jealousies on the part of the king's ministers. He found a home at Hof Triebschen, near Lucerne, where he remained from 1866 to 1872. His first wife having died in 1866, he married in 1870 Cosima von Bülow, daughter of Liszt and former wife of Hans von Bülow, the pianist and conductor. Wagner's chief activity in the early years at Triebschen was the composition of *Die Meistersinger*.

Die Meistersinger von Nürnberg ("The Mastersingers of Nuremberg") had been sketched in 1845, as a kind of comic pendant to *Tannhäuser*, but toward the end of 1861, Wagner planned the work anew, writing some parts of the music before the words.[37] The score was completed in 1867, and the opera was first performed at Munich in the following year. The story has as its historical background the mastersinger guilds of sixteenth-century Nuremberg and their song contests, bound about with traditional rules and customs. Wagner not only incorporated many of these points but also borrowed several names and characters of real mastersingers, notably Hans Sachs, the cobbler-poet-composer who lived from 1494 to 1576.[38] Likewise of historical interest are Wagner's use of an actual mastersinger melody (the march theme beginning at measure forty-one of the overture), the parody of the mastersingers' device of *Blumen* (literally, "flowers") or melodic ornaments in Beckmesser's songs, and the paraphrase of a poem by the real Hans Sachs (the chorale "Wach' auf!" in Act III). Yet *Die Meistersinger* is not a museum of antiquities but a living, sympathetic re-creation in nineteenth-century terms of an epoch of German musical history, with the literal details of the past illu-

---

37. On the differences between the two versions, and some minor inconsistencies in the final draft, see Newman, *The Life of Richard Wagner*, 3:156–64. The various sources of the play are studied in Roethe, "Zum dramatischen Aufbau der Wagnerschen *Meistersinger*." Cf. also Rayner, *Wagner and "Die Meistersinger"*; Thompson, *Wagner and Wagenseil*.

38. Many of Sachs's melodies may be found in Münzer, ed., *Das Singebuch des Adam Puschmann*.

minated by reference to an ever-timely issue, the conflict between tradition and the creative spirit in art. Tradition is represented by the mastersingers' guild; the deadly effect of blind adherence to rules is satirized in the comic figure of Beckmesser, a transparent disguise for the Viennese critic Eduard Hanslick, whose views and influence had made him one of the most persistent and conspicuous of Wagner's opponents. The impetuous, innovating drive of the young artist, impatient of all restraints, is incarnated in the person of Walther von Stolzing, whose conflict with the mastersingers is finally resolved by the wisdom of Hans Sachs, the artist grown wise through experience. Sachs shows that neither tradition nor novelty can suffice by itself; they are reconcilable by one who understands the living spirit behind all rules of art and hence realizes that the new must constantly learn from the old, the old constantly absorb the new.

It is probably not fanciful to suggest that in Walther and Hans Sachs Wagner has drawn idealized portraits of two aspects of himself, and that the views of Sachs represent his own mature philosophy of art, set forth with deep insight and poetic beauty. One feature of this philosophy is the professed reliance on the judgment of "the people" as final arbiter in artistic matters. *Das Volk* was one of Wagner's most beloved abstractions, one which he always carefully distinguished from *das Publikum*. One is sometimes tempted to believe that the distinction in his mind was simply between those who liked Wagner's music dramas and those who preferred Rossini or Meyerbeer: the former comprising all the unspoiled virtues and sound instincts of the race, while the latter were unhealthy, misled, or corrupt. Yet there is fundamental truth in the doctrine of the sovereignty of the people in art which *Die Meistersinger* proclaims, so long as one understands "the people" in the democratic sense of the word—not as a mob but as bearers of a profound, partly unconscious instinct which, in the long run, is apt to perceive and judge rightly.

In the last analysis, however, *Die Meistersinger* is not to be regarded as a treatise on the philosophy of art; its teachings are of little importance in comparison to the drama and the music. It is by far the most human, the most easily accessible, of all Wagner's works. It has every requirement of good comedy: the simple love story of Walther and Eva, the charming scenes of

David and the apprentices, the broadly comic strokes of Beck-messer's serenade and his ridiculous attempt to steal Walther's song for the contest. Above all is to be noted the character of Hans Sachs, Wagner's greatest dramatic figure, who surveys the whole drama from the standpoint of one who through suffering has attained resignation, having learned to find joy in the happiness of others and the triumph of principles.

It is interesting to note that, with such a play as this, Wagner was led to compose a score that more nearly approaches the traditional outlines of opera than had any of his works since *Tannhäuser*. To be sure, the principle of symphonic development of a set of leitmotifs is maintained, and there is no return to the old-fashioned recitative; but withal there is an amount of formalization of which the listener is, perhaps, hardly aware, since it fits so naturally with the dramatic requirements. Like the Orpheus legend, the *Meistersinger* story is essentially musical in conception. Within its framework fall the four "arias" of Walther, the serenade of Beckmesser, Pogner's "Address," David's song in Act III, and Sachs' two monologues, as well as the formal overture and the chorale at the beginning of Act I. Even more operatic, though no less appropriate, are the apprentices' choruses and the huge final ensemble in Act I, the uproariously comic crowd scene at the end of Act II, and the glorified mass finale with ballet and choruses in Act III. Then, too, there is the quintet in the third act, which is as much pure opera as anything in Donizetti or Verdi: an interpolated number in closed form *(a–b–a)* and a remote key (G-flat), which does not directly further the action but does have thematic connection with the rest of the work—a number which, in a word, would be out of place in the strict theoretical form of the music drama, but is justifiable here on the same grounds that justify the canonic quartet in *Fidelio* or some of the ensembles of *Don Giovanni*.[39]

It is a sign of Wagner's versatility that, at the same period of his life, he could compose two works which differ so much not only in dramatic plan but also in musical style as do *Die Meistersinger* and *Tristan*. Both the historical background and the nature of the subject matter of *Die Meistersinger* are reflected

39. See above, chap. 16.

in the diatonic quality of most of the music, in a certain square-
ness of rhythmic structure and simplicity of idiom. The chorales,
the many melodies of folklike cast, the fugal section and the contrapuntal combination of three principal themes in the overture,
as well as the contrapuntal style of the finale and of many other
passages—all seem to contain or suggest the very traits and forms
that have always been most typical of German music. By contrast,
the freer, more chromatic individual Wagnerian touch is heard in
the love scenes and in the monologues of Hans Sachs. The beautiful orchestral prelude to the third act is not only the quintessence of the musical style but also the high point of the drama,
the complete, living description of the noble character of Sachs;
there is no better example of music as the heart of dramatic life,
the true carrier of the inner action of the play.

The essentially musical character of the drama in both
Tristan and *Die Meistersinger* is shown significantly by the fact
that in both these works the musical forms are more clear and
comprehensive than anywhere else in Wagner. This is, of course,
only another way of saying that these two works come as close as
possible to the ideally perfect union of music and drama within
the Wagnerian system. The form type most prevalent in *Die
Meistersinger* is, as we have already mentioned, the Bar, of which
five examples should be especially noted: (1) Beckmesser's serenade in Act II is a pedantically correct example of two identical
Stollen and an Abgesang, the whole being twice repeated to make
a song of three strophes. (2) Walther's first song before the
mastersingers, "Am stillen Herd," is a Bar in which the two Stollen are almost, but not quite, identical. (3) Walther's trial song,
"So rief der Lenz," is a more extended Bar with two distinct themes
in each Stollen, carried on grimly to the end in spite of the uproar
of opposition from his audience. (4) In Walther's dream song, the
first version of the Prize Song, the two Stollen are not identical,
the second being altered so as to cadence in the dominant. (5) In
the final version of the Prize Song, the melody is further extended
and the differences between the two Stollen are likewise greater,
though still without loss of the essential felt likeness.

In addition to many other instances of Bar form, some
shorter and some longer than the above, the opera as a whole
exemplifies the same structure: anyone who will take the trouble

to compare Acts I and II, either with or without the help of Lorenz's outline,[40] will discover that there is a detailed parallelism of the action, and that furthermore in most cases each scene in the second act is a parody of the corresponding scene in Act I—a relationship already foreshadowed by the overture, in which the themes of the middle section parody those of the first. Acts I and II thus form two Stollen, of which Act III is the Abgesang. The whole opera is rounded off by the thematic and tonal correspondence of the beginning and the ending; Lorenz notes that the entire finale, from the entrance of the mastersingers on, is an expanded and varied reprise of the overture.[41]

After *Die Meistersinger*, Wagner turned his attention to completing the *Ring* and building a *Festspielhaus*. Plans for this new kind of theater, dedicated solely to the presentation of his music dramas, had been described by Wagner in letters and essays as early as the 1850s. Those plans materialized in 1872 with the laying of the foundation stone on land donated by the town of Bayreuth. In the same year, Wagner moved his family to Bayreuth and completed the score for the *Ring*, whose first full performance was given in 1876 to inaugurate the festival theater.[42] The premiere was quite successful (even though some of the mechanical items did not operate as well as expected), but the deficit incurred in this undertaking was considerable, causing the second Bayreuth production of the *Ring* to be delayed by twenty years. In the meantime, there occurred many and varied international productions of the *Ring*, some with the original stage sets and costumes on loan from Bayreuth.

Parsifal, Wagner's last music drama, was composed between 1877 and 1882, and first performed at Bayreuth on January 13, 1882, exactly one year and one month before Wagner's death. The sources of the *Parsifal* drama are even more varied than those of the earlier works. The convergence of many lines of philosophic thought and the complex and often obscure symbolism of the persons and events make this the most difficult of all Wagner's music dramas to comprehend, even though the outer action is comparatively simple. The legend of the Holy Grail (al-

40. Lorenz, *Das Geheimnis der Form*, 3:11–13.

41. Ibid., p. 171.

42. See Hartford, *Bayreuth: The Early Years*.

ready touched upon in *Lohengrin* and some other uncomposed dramatic sketches) is combined with speculations on the role of suffering in human life, and the central idea is again that of redemption—this time not through love, but by the savior Parsifal, the Pure Fool, the one "made wise through pity."[43]

No doubt the complexity of the poem is responsible for the music of *Parsifal* being less clear in formal outlines than that of either *Tristan* or *Die Meistersinger*. There is sufficient resemblance between the first and third acts to delineate a general a–b–a structure, but neither the key scheme nor other details of the various scenes are as amenable to analysis as in the case of the other two works. The music, like that of *Tannhäuser*, depicts different worlds of thought and feeling in the sharpest possible contrast; but whereas in *Tannhäuser* there were two such worlds, in *Parsifal* there are three. One of these is the realm of sensual pleasure, exemplified in the second act: the magic garden and the Flower Maidens of Klingsor's castle, with Kundry as seductress under the power of evil magic. The confrontation between Kundry and Parsifal builds to the climactic scene of the "kiss," the dramatic focus of the entire opera. If the music for these scenes is compared with the ebullient eroticism of the Venusberg music in *Tannhäuser* or the glowing ardors of the *Siegfried* finale, there may seem to be a slight falling off in Wagner's earlier elemental power. Nevertheless, the musical setting provides the degree of contrast needed with the first and third acts, in which are opposed and intermingled the worlds of Amfortas and of the Grail, the agonizing penitent and the mystical heavenly kingdom of pity and peace. The Amfortas music is of the utmost intensity of feeling, expressed in richness of orchestral color, plangency of dissonance, complexity and subtlety of harmonic relationships, and a degree of chromaticism which carries it more than once to the verge of atonality. The Grail music, on the other hand, is diatonic and almost churchlike in style. The very opening theme of the prelude (the Last Supper motif), a single-line melody in free rhythm, is reminiscent of Gregorian chant; the Grail motif is an old "Amen" formula in use at the Royal Chapel in Dresden.

One feature of the Grail scenes in *Parsifal* deserves spe-

---

43. See H. Bauer, *Wagners "Parsifal"*; Chailley, *"Parsifal" de Richard Wagner*; Beckett, *Richard Wagner: Parsifal*.

cial emphasis: namely, the expertness of the choral writing. One does not ordinarily look to opera composers for excellence in a field of composition which has always been chiefly associated with the church, and the peculiar technique of which has not always been grasped by even some of the greatest composers. Wagner's distinguished choral writing in *Lohengrin*, *Die Meistersinger*, and above all in *Parsifal* is therefore of interest. In particular, the closing scenes of Acts I and III of *Parsifal*, with their fine choral effects and the device of separated choirs, with the high and low voices giving an impression in music of actual space and depth, recall the Venetian composers of the later sixteenth century.[44]

In 1880, Wagner sent a letter to Ludwig II in Munich, in which he declared that performances of *Parsifal*, his *Bühnen-weihfestspiel*, would be restricted to the Bayreuth theater. He justified his actions by referring to the solemnity of the theme and the use of Christian religious symbols, elements that should not be brought forth on the unhallowed stages of the entertainment world. In his last important essay, "Religion und Kunst" (1880), Wagner further amplified his thoughts on religion and art as the two basic needs of mankind; he also reaffirmed the role of music in communicating feelings and emotions. The "religious" character of the *Parsifal* performances, so much a part of the Bayreuth festivals, has also been carefully maintained in other opera houses, even though the statute of performance limitation expired in 1914.

In attempting to estimate the significance of Wagner in the history of opera, one must first of all acknowledge the man's unswerving idealism and artistic integrity. However open to criticism some aspects of his personal conduct may have been, as an artist he stood uncompromisingly for what he believed to be right. He fought his long battle with such tenacity that his final success left no alternative for future composers but to acknowledge the power of the Wagnerian ideas and methods, whether by imitation, adaptation, or conscious rebellion. His form of the music drama did not, as he had expected, supersede earlier operatic ideals, but certain features of it were of permanent influence. Chief among these was the principle that lay at the basis of the Gesamtkunst-

---

44. It is not always remembered that Wagner greatly admired the music of Palestrina and had made an arrangement of his *Stabat Mater* for a concert in 1848.

werk idea—namely, that every detail of a work must be connected with the dramatic purpose and serve to further that purpose. Wagner is to be numbered among those opera composers who have seriously maintained the dignity of drama in their works. In addition, many of his procedures left their mark on the next generation or two of composers: for example, the parallel position of voice and orchestra, the orchestral continuity, and the symphonic treatment of leitmotifs. Other matters, however, were less capable of being imitated. Wagner's use of Nordic mythology as subject matter, and his symbolism, were so individual that most attempts to copy them resulted only in unintended parody.

It would not have been his wish to be remembered primarily as a musician, but the world has so chosen, and the world in this case has probably understood the genius better than he understood himself. The quality of Wagner's music that has been the cause of its great popularity has been equally the cause of the severest attacks upon it by musicians: that it is not pure, absolute, spontaneous music, created for music's sake and existing in a realm governed only by the laws of sound, rhythm, and musical form. Wagner is not, like Bach or Mozart, a musician's musician. For him no art was self-sustaining. Music, like poetry and gesture, was but one means to a comprehensive end which can perhaps best be defined as "great theater." Granted this end (which may or may not be conceived as a limitation), it is hardly possible to deny the adequacy of Wagner's music in relation to it. Not only does the music possess sensuous beauty. It can suggest, depict, characterize a universe of the most diverse objects and ideas. Above all is its power—by whatever aesthetic theory one seeks to explain it—of embodying or evoking feeling, with a purity, fullness, and intensity surely not surpassed in the music of any other composer. Such emotion is justified by the grandiose intellectual conceptions with which it is connected and by the monumental proportions of the musical forms in which it is expressed. In this monumental quality, as well as in the characteristic moods, aspirations, and technical methods of his music, Wagner is fully representative of the time in which he lived.

CHAPTER
TWENTY-THREE

The Later Nineteenth Century

France

The rise of a new school and a new spirit in French music began in 1871, when the Société Nationale de Musique was founded, with the device *Ars gallica*. Undiscriminating acceptance of incongruous musical styles on the one hand and a frivolous addiction to the trivialities of operetta on the other were succeeded by a strenuous effort to return to the indigenous music of the land— the folksong—and to restore in modern terms the great musical individuality which had belonged to France in the sixteenth, seventeenth, and eighteenth centuries.[1] The range of activity was widened. Whereas before 1870 composers had centered nearly all their efforts on opera, now choral, symphonic, and chamber music began to be undertaken;[2] higher standards of musical education were introduced, and a more cultivated and exacting public gradually came into being. This renewal of national musical life made the opera more vital, original, and adventurous. And although the highest rewards of popular success still went to those composers who were able and willing to bend their talents to the public fancy, nevertheless the best work found hearing and appreciation; there were no scandals like those of the Second Em-

1. The Schola Cantorum, founded in 1894 by Charles Bordes, Alexandre Guilmant, and Vincent d'Indy, augmented this effort. The school, located in Paris, was dedicated to the restoration of church music through performance, study, and training.

2. The Franco-Prussian War had begun in 1870, bringing to a halt the extravagance of the Second Empire and thus contributing to a reduction in the dominance of opera over other forms of musical entertainment.

pire, when *Tannhäuser* was hissed off the stage and *Les Troyens* closed after only twenty-one performances.[3]

It is worth remarking that almost every important new operatic work in Paris after 1870 was produced not at the Opéra but at the more enterprising and progressive Opéra-comique. The old distinction between the forms of opera and opéra comique had practically disappeared by the end of the nineteenth century, for the latter had by then largely abandoned the traditional spoken dialogue; so the repertoire of the two theaters contrasted simply as large-scale, established, conventional works in the one, and new, often experimental works in the other—alternating with the light, operetta-like pieces which continued to flourish. Composers of serious operas that should have been produced at the Paris Opéra frequently had recourse also to the Théâtre de la Monnaie at Brussels for the first performance; and Monte Carlo was the scene of some notable premières as well. How little the term "opéra comique" in this period had to do with "comic" opera will be realized by recalling that Bizet's *Carmen*, Delibes' *Lakmé*, Lalo's *Roi d'Ys*, Massenet's *Manon*, Bruneau's *Attacque du moulin*, D'Indy's *Fervaal*, Charpentier's *Louise*, and Debussy's *Pelléas et Mélisande* were all staged at the Théâtre de l'Opéra-comique in Paris.

One of the first new operas of distinction to be produced in Paris after 1870 was *Carmen*, the last opera of Georges Bizet (1838–1875).[4] *Carmen* was not altogether a failure at first, as is widely believed, but its full success in France did not begin until some eight years after the composer's death. It stands today as the most popular and vital French opera of the later nineteenth century. Its Spanish subject was a reflection of the exotic trend in French music which had begun a generation earlier with Félicien David; but more important than this feature was the realism

3. General works on French music during this period are *Almanach des spectacles; Cinquante Ans de musique française;* Bruneau, *La Musique française;* Rolland, *Musiciens d'aujourd'hui;* Seré, *Musiciens français d'aujourd'hui* (contains excellent bibliographical lists); Hill, *Modern French Music;* Coeuroy, *La Musique française moderne;* Jullien, *Musiciens d'aujourd'hui;* Tiersot, *Un Demi-siècle de musique française* [1870–1917]; Aubry, *La Musique française d'aujourd'hui;* Cooper, *French Music: From the Death of Berlioz to the Death of Fauré.*

4. Biographies by Curtiss and Dean; *RdM* (November 1938), special issue on Bizet; Istel, *Bizet und "Carmen."*

with which scenes and characters were depicted, a psychological realism which the librettists, Henri Meilhac and Ludovic Halévy, had somewhat toned down from Prosper Mérimée's original story (especially with respect to Carmen herself), but which still was strong enough to scandalize Paris in the seventies; never before had an audience at the Theatre de l'Opéra-comique been offered murder and immorality as ingredients for musical entertainment. The tragic ending was also a target of criticism.

Bizet formed his musical style from a variety of sources. He borrowed and adapted a number of melodies from folk songs, from other composers (the habañera tune in Act I from a Spanish-American composer, Sebastian Yradier), and from his own works (the entr'acte music preceding Acts II and III from *L'Arlésienne*). He used Spanish dance rhythms to add local color to his original tunes, of which the Toreador Song (Act II) and the seguidilla "Près des remparts de Seville" (Act I) are well-known examples. Many of the choruses and ensembles are in characteristic operetta style. The occasional repetition of motives associated with characters and situations, such as the two forms of the "fate" motive, is of no more significance in *Carmen* than it was in Verdi's *Rigoletto* a quarter of a century earlier. What is fundamental, however, is the firm, concise, and exact musical expression of every situation in terms which only a French composer would be capable of producing: the typical Gallic union of economy of material, perfect grasp of means, vivid orchestral color, and an electric vitality and rhythmic verve, together with an objective, cool, yet passionate sensualism.

Carmen is divided into conventional arias, ensembles, and other numbers. In its original form, it also had spoken dialogue, like other works of the opéra-comique genre. When it was presented in Vienna seven months after the Paris premiere (and four months after Bizet's death), it was transformed into a "grand opera" by a friend of Bizet's, Ernest Guiraud (1837–1892), who replaced the spoken dialogue with his own newly composed recitatives. This "recitative" version gained wide acceptance outside France and became part of the standard opera repertoire. The changes did not diminish the dramatic power of the original version, which has continued to be performed, with even increasing frequency, to the present day.

The whole structure and aesthetic of *Carmen* was such that Nietzsche, after he had turned against Wagner, could point to it as the ideal opera according to the principles of a properly "Mediterraneanized" European art:

> Yesterday I heard—would you believe it?—Bizet's masterpiece, for the twentieth time. . . . This music seems perfect to me. . . . It is rich. It is precise. It builds, organizes, finishes. . . . With this work one takes leave of the damp north . . . In every respect the climate is changed.[5]

It is hard to imagine what was in the minds of those contemporary critics who found the music untuneful, lacking in definite outlines, and overpowered by a too-rich orchestration—charges, in a word, of Wagnerianism, such as had been leveled earlier at Gounod. So far as Bizet was concerned, Wagner's music dramas and theories might never have existed, but "Wagnerian" was a convenient word in France at this time for damning anything a critic disliked or could not understand. The styles of Gounod and Bizet do, indeed, have much in common, though the affinity is more apparent in Bizet's earlier operas *Les Pêcheurs de perles* ("The Pearl Fishers," 1863) and *Djamileh* (1872). But these works have less musical individuality and interest than *Carmen*; in fact, the only other compositions of Bizet that compare with this opera are his incidental music to Daudet's play *L'Arlésienne* (1872) and his early *Symphony in C* (1855).

The exotic flavor of *Carmen* and *Les Pêcheurs de perles* is found again in *Lakmé* (1883), the best opera of Léo Delibes (1836–91),[6] which takes place in India and has a tragic plot faintly reminiscent of Meyerbeer's *Africaine* and more than faintly foreshadowing Puccini's *Butterfly*. Delibes' music is elegant, graceful, and well orchestrated but lacks the intense quality of Bizet's. In *Lakmé*, the oriental perfume is blended with an otherwise conventional idiom. Delibes' amusing and tuneful opéra comique *Le Roi l'a dit* ("The King Said So," 1873) is still remembered; a more serious work, *Jean de Nivelle* (1880), was almost equally successful at first but has not remained in the repertoire. On the whole,

5. Kaufmann, *Basic Writings of Nietzsche*, pp. 613–14. See also Nietzsche, "Der Fall Wagner," sec. 3, and "Jenseits von Gut und Böse," part 8.

6. See studies by De Curzon and Coquis.

Delibes excelled as a composer of ballets, his best works in this form being *La Source* (1866), *Coppélia* (1870), and *Sylvia* (1876).

A more substantial figure than Delibes in French nineteenth-century opera was Ernest Reyer (1823–1909).[7] Reyer belongs with those composers whose music often compels more respect for its intentions than admiration for its actual sound. He had "genius without talent"[8]—that is, lofty and ideal conceptions without the technique for realizing them fully in an attractive musical form. This incapacity may have been due in part to his defective early training, but it was also a matter of temperament; as a critic, he was a despiser of mere prettiness, a rebel against the superficial judgments of the Paris public,[9] and an early defender of Berlioz and Wagner. Reyer was influenced by the fashionable orientalism in his choice of subjects, as seen in his symphonic ode *Sélam* (1850) and the ballet-pantomime *Sacountala* (1858). His first important operatic work, *La Statue* (1861), is also an oriental story. A similar background is found in his last opera, *Salammbô* (1890), taken with few alterations from Flaubert's novel and treated in an austere oratorio-like style, yet with a grandeur of line recalling the spirit of Berlioz's *Troyens*; the plot in general and the closing scene in particular are reminiscent of Verdi's *Aida*. The most successful of Reyer's operas was *Sigurd* (composed in the 1870s, first performed in 1884); the subject is almost identical with that of Wagner's *Siegfried* (Act III) and *Götterdämmerung*, with a touch of *Tannhäuser* in the shape of a seductive ballet, with a wordless chorus of elves, in Act II. But the resemblance to Wagner is only skin-deep, even in the libretto: Sigurd talks in the accents of Quinault's Renaud rather than in those of the great blond lad of the *Ring*; and the rest of the personages likewise somehow seem more Gallic than Teutonic. In the music there is even less evidence of Wagnerian influence; on the contrary, we find the old separate numbers of grand opera, a distinctly periodic melody, and very little chromaticism. There is some recurrence of motifs, but this is not a distinctly Wagnerian trait. The

7. See Reyer, *Notes de musique* and *Quarante Ans de musique*; also De Curzon, *Ernest Reyer* and *La Légende de Sigurd*.

8. Alfred Bruneau, quoted in Combarieu, *Histoire de la musique*, 3:389.

9. In this, Reyer shared the attitude of César Franck. See Lavignac, *Encyclopédie*, 3:1727–28, and Cooper, *French Music*.

musical style is serious and even has a certain nobility; its model, clearly enough, is *Les Troyens*.

Parisian journalists had been crying wolf for years before any serious reflection of Wagner's ideas or musical style became apparent in French music. The bitterness of the Franco-Prussian War, aggravated by Wagner's silly gibes in his playlet *Eine Kapitulation*, delayed his acceptance still longer. Yet by the early eighties, all was apparently forgiven, and Wagner became the rage in Paris for some ten or twelve years.

> From 1885 Wagner's work acted directly or indirectly on the whole of artistic thought, even on religious and intellectual thought of the most distinguished people of Paris. . . . Writers not only discussed musical subjects, but judged painting, literature, and philosophy, from a Wagnerian point of view. . . . The whole universe was seen and judged by the thought of Bayreuth.[10]

A remarkable evidence of this enthusiasm was the flourishing periodical *La Revue Wagnerienne* (1885–87), contributors to which included Verlaine, Mallarmé, Huysmans, and practically every other important writer in Paris (Baudelaire had been converted already in 1861). This journal (and its successor, *La Revue Indépendante*) was designed primarily to inform the public about the nonmusical aspects of Wagner's compositions, philosophy, and aesthetics. One effect of all this was to introduce the subject of music to many people who would not otherwise have taken an interest in it; another was to stimulate symphonic composition. In opera, the risks involved in the magic garden of Wagnerism were so patent that the composers for the most part withstood temptation, though not always without effort. It is sometimes difficult to decide what is to be called imitation of Wagner and what was simply acceptance of new ideas, such as the abolition of formal separate arias and recitatives. Taken altogether, however, the direct influence of Wagner on French opera, in both literary and musical treatment, is seen most strongly in works by three composers: Chabrier, Chausson, and D'Indy.[11]

Emmanuel Chabrier (1841–1894) was one of the foremost composers of the new movement in France, as well as a

10. Rolland, *Musicians of Today*, p. 253.
11. Cf. D'Indy, *Richard Wagner*.

pianist of exceptional ability.[12] He may seem an unlikely person to be an apostle of Wagner, for the pieces by which he is best known, the orchestral rhapsody *España* and the *Bourrée fantasque*, show him as a composer of typical Gallic vivacity, wit, and rhythmic exuberance. And indeed these qualities are predominant in his first important comic opera, *L'Étoile* ("The Star," 1877),[13] and in his best-known stage work, *Le Roi malgré lui* ("The King in Spite of Himself," 1887), harmonically one of the most original opéras comiques of this period. But in 1879, Chabrier heard a performance of *Tristan und Isolde* at Munich which made a strong impression on him, reinforced by his experience shortly afterwards in directing rehearsals of *Lohengrin* and *Tristan* for performances at Paris. His opera *Gwendoline* (Brussels, 1886) is obviously influenced by Wagnerian elements: the libretto brings echoes of *Der fliegende Holländer*, of the Valhalla mythology, and above all of *Tristan*, even to a love duet in the second act and a love-death at the end of the third. The form is a compromise between continuous drama and the older number opera. The music shows more than a trace of Wagner in its systematic use of leitmotifs, chromatics, chords of the seventh and ninth, and the characteristic appoggiaturas and suspensions. However, this must not be taken to mean that it is a mere copy of Wagner's idiom. Chabrier had an individual harmonic style, one quite advanced for his time, as well as a genuine and sometimes profound gift of serious expressiveness. The most interesting portions of *Gwendoline* are the "Spinning Song" in Act I, which incorporates an air from Moore's *Irish Melodies*; the love duet (strongly reminiscent of *Tristan*); and the orchestral prelude to Act II, the style of which has been well described as one of the links between Wagner and Debussy.[14] The skillful voice writing and the highly poetic orchestration of this opera should also be noted. But the uneven quality of the music as a whole, together with a rather dull and awkwardly proportioned libretto, have worked against its success. In his unfin-

---

12. See Hill, *Modern French Music*, chap. 4; studies by Martineau, Servières, Myers, and Robert.

13. This work has been produced in the United States as *The Merry Monarch* and elsewhere under various titles. See Loewenberg, *Annals*.

14. Abraham, *A Hundred Years of Music*, p. 201.

ished opera *Briseïs* (Act I performed, 1899) Chabrier demonstrated even more daring harmonies than in *Gwendoline*. Somewhat
similar in subject matter to *Gwendoline*, and likewise tinctured
with Wagnerian conceptions, is the only important opera composed by César Franck (1822–1890), *Hulda*, written between 1882
and 1885.[15] This opera and his incomplete *Ghisèle* were performed posthumously in 1894 and 1896, respectively.

A more thorough and at the same time a most personal
adaptation of Wagner's methods to French opera was brought about
by Franck's pupil Vincent d'Indy (1851–1931) in his *Fervaal* (1897)
and *L'Étranger* ("The Stranger," 1903).[16] Like Wagner, D'Indy
wrote his own librettos. The background of *Fervaal* is vaguely
mythological, and the action in both operas is treated as symbolic
of broad moral issues—the conflict between pagan religion and
sacrificial love in *Fervaal* and the expiation of unlawful love through
death in *L'Étranger*. But whereas Wagner's symbolism is nearly
always in practice wielded for theatrical effect, D'Indy's evident
purpose is to make art a vehicle for essentially religious teachings
and to use every possible artistic means toward that end. The
almost medieval combination of this austere ideal with a catholic
breadth of resource, welded into unity by superb technical skill,
is the clue to D'Indy's style.[17] It explains how he was able to take
over many features of Wagner's music dramas without sacrificing
his own individuality: pseudomythology, symbolism, continuity of
the music, harmonic sophistication, symphonic orchestral texture
with cyclical recurrence of motifs, free arioso treatment of the
voice line, Wagnerian instrumental sonorities, even (in the love
music of the first and third acts of *Fervaal*) actual reminiscences
of *Tristan*. The strange suggestiveness of the musical landscape in
the introduction to Act II of *Fervaal* and the sober, mysterious
poetry of the scene that follows are especially noteworthy. So too
is the introduction of choral treatments of Gregorian melodies,

---

15. See the biographies of Franck by D'Indy and Vallas; also Van den Borren, *L'Oeuvre dramatique de César Franck*; Davies, *César Franck and His Circle*.

16. See Vallas, *Vincent d'Indy*; Paul, "Rameau, D'Indy, and French Nationalism"; D'Indy, *Richard Wagner*. See also the following special studies: Bréville and Gauthier-Villars, *"Fervaal"*; Calvocoressi, *"L'Etranger"*; Destranges, *"Le Chant de la cloche"*; idem, *"Fervaal"*; idem, *"L'Etranger."*

17. See Rolland, *Musiciens d'aujourd'hui*, chapter on D'Indy.

Example 23.1: *L'Étranger*, Act II, sc. 3

notably the "Pange lingua" in the transcendently beautiful closing scene of this opera.[18]

D'Indy's indebtedness to Wagner is even more apparent in *L'Étranger* than in the earlier opera. Although the music is

18. See also the quotation of the intonation of the Credo in Act II, sc. 1, of the same opera; and cf. in the finale of Bruneau's *Messidor* (also 1897), the plainsong passage from the Litany.

(Example 23.1 continued)

less Wagnerian, with its conciseness of orchestral scoring and its inclusion of folksong themes, the dramatic intention weighs heavily on the side of Wagner's philosophical ideas, especially those expressed in *Der fliegende Holländer*. In *L'Étranger*, the musical portrayal of the sea—from the prelude to the tragic ending—is remarkable for its imaginative and pictorial power, as shown by the third scene of Act II (example 23.1). That neither this opera nor *Fervaal* has become popular may be due in part to the unusual character of the librettos but more to the music, which lacks the simple, salient, easily perceived qualities necessary for success on the stage. One cannot help feeling that, for the theater, the music has many of the defects of Wagner without the latter's compelling emotional power. Yet *Fervaal* in particular deserves respect as one of the outstanding French operas of the later nineteenth century, in the noble tradition of Berlioz's *Troyens*. D'Indy's *Le Chant de la Cloche* ("The Song of the Bell"), a 1912 stage version of an earlier choral work, and *La Légende de St. Christophe* (composed between 1908 and 1915, performed in 1920), an allegorical opera of sacred history with narrator and a cappella choir, reflect his association with the Schola Cantorum.

The influence of Wagner continues to be noticeable in *Le Roi Arthus* ("King Arthur"), by Ernest Chausson (1855–1899),[19] first performed in 1903. It is a not very successful mixture of old grand-opera formal elements with the new Wagnerian idiom, including the inevitable Tristanesque love duet in Act I. Neither libretto nor music offers any passages of real distinction; indeed, the composer himself regarded *Le Roi Arthus* as only an experiment. This is perhaps the final word for all the attempts by French composers to assimilate Wagner's methods in the nineteenth century, since no consistent or historically important school grew out of them. Along with these experiments, the natural line of French lyric opera in descent from Gounod continued to flourish, and it is the composers of this distinctively national group who next claim our attention.

The first is Camille Saint-Saëns (1835–1921),[20] whose *Princesse jaune* ("The Yellow Princess," 1872) set the fashion for Japanese subjects in comic opera. Saint-Saëns' most famous dramatic work is the biblical *Samson et Dalila* (1877), half opera and half oratorio, like Liszt's *Legende von der heiligen Elisabeth* or D'Indy's *St. Christophe*. Saint-Saëns was not by nature a dramatic composer, but his technical facility and knowledge of many different musical styles enabled him to construct smooth and com-

19. See Gallois, *Ernest Chausson: l'homme et l'oeuvre*.

20. Biographies by Langlois and Chantavoine; see also the composer's own writings, especially *Portraits et souvenirs*; Du Tillet, "A propos du drame lyrique."

petent, if not exciting, works in dramatic form. Of his sixteen stage works, the most successful, next to *Samson et Dalila*, were *Henri VIII* (1883), with orchestration that is suggestive of Debussy and Ravel, *Ascanio* (1890); and the opéra comique *Phryné* (1893).

Another composer of conservative national tendency, who forms a link between Saint-Saëns and Massenet, was Edouard Lalo (1823–1892).[21] He wrote only one opera, *Le Roi d'Ys* (1888); it is based on a Breton legend. The music of this opera is original in style, of remarkable rhythmic vitality, varied in color, and admirably adapted to the stage—qualities that have assured its survival to the present day. Three other French composers of the late nineteenth century should be mentioned in passing, though their work is less important than that of Saint-Saëns or Lalo: Emile Paladilhe (1844–1926; *Patriel*, 1886); Benjamin Godard (1849–1895), a composer of facile and pleasing melodies whose *Jocelyn* (1888) was long remembered because of one number, the "Berceuse"; and Isidore De Lara (1858–1935), English by birth and residence but most of whose operas, including the successful *Messaline* (1899), were written to French texts and produced in France.

The outstanding French opera composer of this era was Jules Massenet (1842–1912),[22] an exceptionally productive worker whose music is marked by characteristic French traits that we have already noticed in earlier composers such as Monsigny, Auber, Thomas (Massenet's teacher), and Gounod. First among these is the quality of the melody. Massenet's melody is of a highly personal sort: lyrical, tender, penetrating, sweetly sensuous, rounded in contours, exact but never violent in interpreting the text, sentimental, often melancholy, sometimes a little vulgar, and always charming. This melody determines the whole texture. The harmonic background is sketched with delicacy and a fine sense of instrumental color, and every detail of the score shows smooth craftsmanship. With no commitment to particular theories of opera, Wagnerian or otherwise, Massenet within the limits of his own style never hesitated to make use of any new device that had proved effective or popular, so that his works are not free of eclecticism and mirror in their own way most of the successive

---

21. Biography by Servières.

22. Biographies by Schneider, Bruneau, and Harding. See also Massenet, *Mes Souvenirs*.

operatic tendencies of his lifetime. The subjects and their treatment also show the composer's sensitiveness to popular taste. Thus *Le Roi de Lahore* (1877) is an oriental story, *Le Cid* (1885) is in the manner of grand opera, *Esclarmonde* (1889) is Wagnerian, *La Navarraise* ("The Girl from Navarre", 1894) shows the influence of Italian verismo, and *Cendrillon* (1899) recalls Humperdinck's *Hänsel und Gretel*.

With *Le Jongleur de Notre Dame* (1902) and its all-male cast, Massenet explored a different kind of opera. It is a miracle play, based upon a medieval legend, for which there could have been no public demand, but which the composer treated with special affection and thereby created one of his best operas. This opera, in particular, should lay to rest the suspicion that Massenet's choice of subjects, as well as his use of certain fashionable musical devices, was motivated by a desire to give his audiences what he knew they wanted rather than by any inner impulsion. But there is no sacrifice of musical individuality in all this; and in the case of a composer whose instincts were so completely of the theater, who always succeeded in achieving so neatly and spontaneously just the effect he intended, it seems a little ungracious to insist too strongly on an issue of artistic sincerity. Massenet excelled in the musical depiction of passionate love, and most of his best works are notable for their heroines—unforgettable ladies all, of doubtful virtue perhaps, but indubitably alive and vivid. To this gallery belong Salomé in *Hérodiade* (1881), the heroines of *Manon* (1884), *Thaïs* (1894), *Sapho* (1897), and Charlotte in *Werther* (1892). With these works should also be mentioned *Thérèse* (1907), one of the last operas of Massenet to obtain general success.

Massenet traveled the main highway of French tradition in opera, and his natural gifts so corresponded to the tastes of his day that success seemed to come almost without effort. Nor was his style without influence, direct or indirect, on later French composers. But he was the last to produce operas so easily. Changing musical idioms and new literary movements had their effect on the next generation, giving its work a less assured, more experimental character. One of these literary movements was that known as "naturalism."

The word "naturalism" and the related word "realism,"

however useful they may be in the study of literature or the graphic arts, are exceedingly vague when applied to music. Unless they refer to the unimportant practice of imitating everyday sounds by voices or instruments in a musical composition (as, for example, the bleating of sheep in Strauss's *Don Quixote*), it is difficult to see what meaning they can have that is related directly to music itself. What some writers call "realistic" or "naturalistic" music is simply, in effect, a certain kind of program music; the realism is deduced not from the music but from an extramusical fact (such as a title) about the composition in question. When we speak of realistic or naturalistic opera, therefore, we have reference primarily to the libretto; we mean that the opera presents persons, scenes, events, and conversations that are recognizably similar to the common daily experience of its audience, and that these things are treated seriously, as becomes matters of real moment, not with persiflage or fantasy as in an operetta.

It goes without saying that such tendencies in late nineteenth-century opera grew out of earlier tendencies in literature. Thus, Bizet's *Carmen*, the first important realistic opera in France and one of the principal sources of the Italian verismo, was based on Mérimée's story. The chief disciples of realism in later nineteenth-century French literature were Guy de Maupassant (1850–1893) and Emile Zola (1840–1902). The latter found a musical interpreter in Alfred Bruneau (1857–1934),[23] Massenet's pupil and rival, the librettos of whose principal operas were either adapted from Zola's books or written especially for the composer by Zola himself. To the former group belong *Le Rêve* ("The Dream," 1891) and *L'Attacque du moulin* ("The Attack on the Mill," 1893); to the latter, *Messidor* (1897), *L'Ouragan* ("The Hurricane," 1901), and *L'Enfant roi* ("The Child King," 1905). These works were concerned with current social and economic problems, presented in compact, tense situations with symbolical overtones, and in prose instead of the customary verse. Unfortunately, the rhythm of Zola's prose did not always inspire Bruneau to achieve correspondingly flexible rhythms in the music; the melodic line is declamatory rather than lyrical, but the regular pattern of accentuation indicated by the bar lines becomes monotonous. The music is aus-

23. Biography by Boschot, and see also Bruneau's own writings.

tere; it is especially apt in the creation of moods through reiterated motifs, but with all its evident sincerity and undoubted dramatic power, the important quality of sensuous charm is often lacking. Nevertheless, Bruneau is significant as a forerunner of some later experiments in harmony and as an independent, healthy force in the growth of modern French opera, counterbalancing to some extent the Wagnerian tendencies of D'Indy and the hedonism of Massenet.

A fuller measure of success in the field of operatic naturalism was granted to another pupil of Massenet, Gustave Charpentier (1860–1956).[24] The "musical novel" *Louise* (1900) is his only important opera, a strange but successful combination of several distinct elements. In scene, characters, and plot, *Louise* is realistic; Charpentier, writing his own libretto, has almost gone out of his way to introduce such homely details as a bourgeois family supper, the reading of a newspaper, and a scene in a dressmaking shop; many of the minor personages are obviously taken "from life," and sing in a marked Parisian dialect. The melodramatic closing scene recalls the mood of the Italian verismo composers. Charpentier, like Bruneau, touches occasionally on social questions: the issue of free love, the obligations of children to their parents, the miseries of poverty. But along with realism there is symbolism, especially in the weird figure of the Noctambulist, personification of "the pleasure of Paris." Paris itself is, as Bruneau remarked,[25] the real hero of this opera. Behind the action is the presence of the great city, seductive, mysterious, and fatal, enveloping persons and events in an atmosphere of poetry like that of the forest in Weber's *Freischütz*. Its hymn is the ensemble of street cries, running like a refrain through the first scene of Act II and echoing elsewhere throughout the opera. To realism and symbolism is added yet a third factor: sentiment. The dialogue between Louise and her father in Act I is of a convincing tenderness, while the love music of Act III, with the often-heard "Depuis le jour," is not only a fine scene of passion but also one of the few of its kind in late nineteenth-century French opera that never reminds us of *Tristan und Isolde*—or hardly ever. It was

24. Delmas, *Gustave Charpentier*; Himonet, *"Louise."*
25. Bruneau, *La Musique française*, p. 154.

the achievement of Charpentier to take all this realism, symbolism, and sentiment, holding together only with difficulty in the libretto itself, and mold them into one powerful whole by means of music.

The score reminds one in many ways of Massenet: there is the same spontaneity and abundance of ideas, the same simple and economical texture, obtaining the maximum effect with the smallest apparent effort. The harmonic idiom is more advanced than Massenet's but less daring than Bruneau's. The orchestral music is continuous, serving as background for spoken as well as sung passages, and is organized by recurring motifs. A number of standard operatic devices are cleverly adapted to the libretto: Julien's serenade with accompaniment of a guitar, the ensemble of working girls in Act II (where the tattoo of the sewing machine replaces the whirr of the old romantic spinning wheel), and the balletlike scene where Louise is crowned as the Muse of Montmartre in Act III. On the whole, it will be seen that when this opera is cited as an example of naturalism, the word needs to be taken with some qualifications. In any case, it is not the naturalism that has caused it to survive, for this was but a passing fashion. *Louise* remains in the repertoire for the same reason that other successful operas do: because it has melodious and moving music wedded to a libretto that permits the music to operate as an effective partner in the projection of the drama.

Fashions in opera might come and go, but the operetta and kindred forms went their way unperturbed. The line of French light opera, established in the nineteenth century by Auber, Adam, and Offenbach, was continued after 1870 by Charles Lecocq (1832–1918),[26] whose best work was *La Fille de Madame Angot* (1872); Jean-Robert Planquette (1848–1903), whose sentimental and still popular *Les Cloches de Corneville* ("The Bells of Corneville") came out in 1877; Edmond Audran (1840–1901), with *La Mascotte* (1880); and Louis Varney (1844–1908), with *Les Mousquetaires au couvent* ("The Musketeers in the Convent," 1880). Somewhat later began the long series of popular operas and operettas by André Messager (1853–1929),[27] distinguished conductor and facile

---

26. Schneider, *Charles Lecocq.*

27. Biographies by Augé-Laribé and Février.

composer in a straightforward, attractively melodious vein (*La Basoche*, 1890; *Les P'tites Michu*, 1897; *Monsieur Beaucaire*, 1919). At the beginning of the twentieth century appeared the operettas of Claude Terrasse (1867–1923), including *Le Sire de Vargy* (1903) and *Monsieur de la Palisse* (1904).

Italy

As Italians in the eighteenth century would have nothing to do with Gluck, so in the nineteenth they cared little for Wagner. It was not until the eighties that even *Lohengrin* began to be accepted. With the exception of Boito, no important out-and-out Wagner disciples appeared in Italy. There was considerable talk about Wagner and considerable skepticism as to the future of Italian opera, but the only result of any consequence was to call forth a vigorous national reaction, of which the greatest monument is Verdi's *Otello*. Italian opera was too secure in its traditions and methods, too deeply rooted in the national life, to be susceptible to radical experiments, especially experiments resulting from aesthetic theories of a sort in which Italians were temperamentally uninterested. A mild influence of German romanticism, but hardly more, may be found in a few Italian opera composers of the late nineteenth century. Alfredo Catalani (1854–1893) is the most distinguished of this group; his principal operas were *Loreley* (1890— a revision of his *Elda*, which had appeared in 1880), *Dejanice* (1883), and *La Wally* (1892),[28] Catalani has a refined melodic style, nearly always free of exaggerated pathos, with interesting harmonies and a good balance of interest between voice and orchestra. Along with traces of Tristanesque chromaticism are experiments in harmony and texture that anticipate some of the favorite devices of Puccini. The robust rhythms are notable, especially in the choruses and dances of *La Wally*. Unfortunately, Catalani appeared at a time when the Italian public was being seduced by

---

28. See Nicolaisen, *Italian Opera in Transition 1871–1893*; biography by Gatti; articles by Klein.

Mascagni and Leoncavallo, so that his reserved and aristocratic music was drowned by the bellow of verismo.

Some influence of Wagner seems to be present in the harmonies and the important position of the orchestra in the operas of Antonio Smareglia (1854–1929), whose chief work, *Nozze istriane* ("Istrian Wedding"), was performed in 1895; but Smareglia lacked the convincing popular touch in his melodies and his operas were not greatly successful.[29] Alberto Franchetti (1860–1942) has been called "the Meyerbeer of Italy" because of his fondness for massive scenic effects, but his music, on the whole, is undistinguished; his principal operas were *Cristoforo Colombo* (1892) and *Germania* (1902). None of these composers was attracted by the verismo movement of the 1890s, which was the popular trend in Italy at that time.

The most explosive reaction against Wagner was launched with the performance of *Cavalleria rusticana* ("Rustic Chivalry") by Pietro Mascagni (1863–1945) in 1890 and *I pagliacci* ("The Clowns") by Ruggiero Leoncavallo (1858–1919) two years later. Neither composer was ever able to duplicate the fantastic success these two works achieved, though Mascagni approached it with *L'amico Fritz* (1891) and *Iris* (1898),[30] while Leoncavallo's *Zaza* (1900) became fairly widely known.[31] But *Cavalleria* and *Pagliacci*, now usually given on the same evening as a double bill, are the classics of *verismo*, or "realism."[32] This typically Italian movement resembles French naturalism in the use of scenes and characters from common life; but the French naturalists used these materials as a means for the development of more general ideas and feelings, idealizing both scene and music, whereas the goal of the Italian realists was simply to present a vivid, melodramatic plot, to arouse sensation by violent contrasts, to paint a cross

---

29. See biographical studies by Nacamuli, A. Smareglia, and M. Smareglia.

30. See studies by De Donno; biography by Jeri; Mascagni, *Mascagni parla.*

31. Leoncavallo wrote his own librettos and shared in the writing of *Manon Lescaut* for Puccini.

32. *Verismo* ("truth") is a term applied to a phase of naturalism in literature and music, emerging in the late nineteenth and early twentieth centuries and characterized by the projection on stage of fierce passions, violence, and death. The relatively few operas which fall into the verismo category tend to be in one act so that a singleness of mood and situation can be presented without interruption. See Lang, *The Experience of Opera*, chap. 9, and Rinaldi, *Musica e verismo.*

section of life without concerning themselves with any general significance the action might have. Verismo is to naturalism what the "shocker" is to the realistic novel, and the music corresponds to this conception. It aims simply and directly at the expression of intense passion thorough melodic or declamatory phrases of the solo voices, to which the orchestra contributes sensational harmonies. Choral or instrumental interludes serve only to establish a mood which is to be rent asunder in the next scene. Everything is so arranged that the moments of excitement follow one another in swift climactic succession. It cannot be denied that there was plenty of precedent in Donizetti and the earlier works of Verdi for melodramatic situations in opera; but by comparison the action of the veristic operas takes place as in an atmosphere from which the nitrogen has been withdrawn, so that everything burns with a fierce, unnatural flame, and moreover quickly burns out. The brevity of these works is due not so much to concentration as to rapid exhaustion of the material. Much the same is true of the verismo movement as a whole, historically considered. It flared like a meteor across the operatic sky of the 1890s, but by the end of the century it was practically dead, though its influence can occasionally be detected in some later operas.

The leading figure in Italian opera of the late nineteenth and the early twentieth century was Giacomo Puccini (1858–1924), who resembles Massenet in his position of mediator between two eras, as well as in many features of his musical style.[33] Puccini's rise to fame began with his third opera, *Manon Lescaut* (1893), which is less effective dramatically than Massenet's opera on the same subject (1884) but rather superior in musical interest—this despite occasional reminiscences of *Tristan*, which few composers in the nineties seemed able to escape. Puccini's world-wide reputation rests chiefly on his next three works: *La Bohême* (1896), *Tosca* (1900), and *Madama Butterfly* (1904). *La Bohême* is a sentimental opera with dramatic touches of realism, on a libretto adapted from Henri Murger's *Scènes de la vie de Bohême*, which had been dramatized in 1849 under the title *La Vie de Bohême*. *Tosca*, taken from Victorien Sardou's drama of the same name (1887), is "a prolonged orgy of lust and crime" made endurable

---

33. Biographies in Marino, Hopkinson, and Carner's "Giacomo Puccini." See also studies by Carner, Sartori, Ashbrook, and Osborne (the last with a synopsis of each opera).

by the beauty of the music, and *Madama Butterfly* is a tale of love and heartbreak in an exotic Japanese setting. The outstanding musical characteristic of Puccini in all these operas is the "sensuous warmth and melting radiance of the vocal line."[34] It is like Massenet without Massenet's urbanity: naked emotion crying out, and persuading the listener's feeling by its very urgency. For illustrations the reader need only recall the aria "Che gelida manina" and the ensuing duet in the first scene of *La Bohême*, the closing scene of the same work, or the familiar arias "Vissi d'arte" in *Tosca* and "Un bel dì" in *Butterfly*.

The history of this type of melody is instructive. It will be remembered that in Verdi we encountered from time to time a melodic phrase of peculiar poignancy which seemed to gather up the whole feeling of a scene in a pure and concentrated moment of expression, such as the "Amami, Alfredo" in *La traviata* (example 20.6), the recitative "E tu, come sei pallida" of *Otello* (example 20.7), or the Kiss motive from the same work. Later composers, perceiving that the high points of effectiveness in Verdi were marked by phrases of this sort, became ambitious to write operas which should consist entirely (or as nearly so as possible) of such melodic high points, just as the verismo composers had tried to write operas consisting entirely of melodramatic shocks. Both tendencies lead to satiety of sensation. These melodic phrases in Verdi are of the sort sometimes described as "pregnant"; their effect depends on the prevalence of a less heated manner of expression elsewhere in the opera, so that they stand out by contrast. But in Puccini we have, as an apparent ideal if not always an actuality, what may be called a kind of perpetual pregnancy in the melody, whether this is sung or entrusted to the orchestra as a background for vocal recitative. The musical utterance is kept at high tension, almost without repose, as though it were to be feared that if the audiences were not continually excited they would go to sleep. This tendency toward compression of language, this nervous stretto of musical style, is characteristic of the *fin de siècle* period.[35]

34. Carner, *Puccini*, p. 273; the entire section is an excellent analysis of the composer's melodic and general musical style.

35. The compression is also characteristic of Puccini's librettos, which often eliminate subplots entirely and usually observe the classical unities of time, place and action.

The sort of melody we have been describing runs through all of Puccini's works. In his earliest and latest operas it tends to be organized in balanced phrases, but in those of the middle period it becomes a freer line, often embodying a set of recurring motifs. These motifs of Puccini, admirably dramatic in conception, are used either simply for recalling earlier moments in the opera or, by reiteration, for establishing a mood, but they do not serve as generating themes for musical development.

Puccini's music was enriched by the composer's constant interest in the new harmonic developments of his time; he was always eager to put current discoveries to use in opera. One example of striking harmonic treatment is the series of three major triads (B-flat, A-flat, E-natural) which opens *Tosca* and is associated throughout the opera with the villainous Scarpia (example 23.2). The harmonic tension of the augmented fourth outlined by

Example 23.2: *Tosca*, The "Scarpia" chords

the first and third chords of this progression is by itself sufficient for Puccini's purpose; he has created his atmosphere with three strokes, and the chord series has no further use but to be repeated intact whenever the dramatic situation requires it. One common trait of Puccini's, found in all his operas from the early *Edgar* (1889) down to his last works, is the "side-slipping" of chords (example 23.3); doubtless this device was learned from Verdi (compare the passage "Oh! come è dolce" in the duet at the end of Act I of *Otello*) or Catalani, but it is based on a practice common in much non-European music and one going back in Western musical history to medieval organum and *faux-bourdon*. Its usual

Example 23.3: *Madama Butterfly*, Act II

PUCCINI

purpose in Puccini is to break a melodic line into a number of parallel strands, like breaking up a beam of light by a prism into parallel bands of color. In a sense it is an effect complementary to that of intensifying a melody by duplication at the unison and octaves—an effect dear to all Italian composers of the nineteenth century and one to which Puccini also frequently resorted. Parallel duplication of the melodic line at the fifth is used to good purpose in the introduction to the third act of *La Bohême* to suggest the bleakness of a cold winter dawn; parallel triads are employed in the introduction to the second act of the same opera, for depicting the lively, crowded street scene (a passage which might have been in the back of Stravinsky's mind when he wrote the music for the first scene of *Petrouchka*); and parallelism of the same sort, extended sometimes to chords of the seventh and ninth (as with Debussy), is found at many places in the later operas.

The most original places in Puccini, however, are not dependent on any single device. Consider, for example, the opening scene of Act III of *Tosca*, with its broad unison melody in the horns, the delicate descending parallel triads over a double pedal in the bass, the Lydian melody of the shepherd boy, and the faint background of bells, with the veiled, intruding threat of the three Scarpia chords from time to time—and inimitably beautiful and suggestive passage, technically perhaps owing something to both Verdi and Debussy, but nevertheless thoroughly individual. Another device used most effectively is silence, the dramatic pause that heightens tension without words or music, as in the silence that follows Scarpia's murder in *Tosca*.

An important source of color effects in Puccini's music

is the use of exotic materials. Exoticism in Puccini was more than a mere borrowing of certain details but rather extended into the very fabric of his melody, harmony, rhythm, and instrumentation.[36] It is naturally most in evidence in the works on oriental subjects, *Madama Butterfly* and *Turandot* (1926). *Turandot*, based on a tragicommedia of the eighteenth century by Carlo Gozzi and completed after Puccini's death by Franco Alfano (1876–1954), shows, side by side, harmonic experimentation (for example, the bitonality at the opening of Acts I and II), the utmost development of Puccinian lyric melody, and the most brilliant orchestration of any of his operas.

Puccini did not escape the influence of verismo, but the realism of his operas is always tempered by, or blended with, romantic and exotic elements. In *La Bohème*, common scenes and characters are invested with a romantic halo; the repulsive melodrama of *Tosca* is glorified by the music; and the few realistic details in *Madama Butterfly* are unimportant. A less convincing attempt to blend realism and romance is found in *La fanciulla del West* ("The Girl of the Golden West"), taken from a play by David Belasco and first performed at the Metropolitan Opera House in 1910. Though enthusiastically received by the first American audiences, *La fanciulla* did not attain as wide or enduring a popularity as the preceding works. The next opera, *La rondine* ("The Swallow," 1917), was even less successful. A return was made, however, with the *trittico*, or triptych, of one-act operas first performed at the Metropolitan in December 1918: *Il tabarro* ("The Cloak"), a veristic melodrama; *Suor Angelica* ("Sister Angelica"), a miracle play; and *Gianni Schicchi*, the most popular of the three, a delightful comedy in the spirit of eighteenth-century opera buffa. Puccini's comic skill, evidenced also in some parts of *La Bohème* and *Turandot*, is here seen at its most spontaneous, incorporating smoothly all the characteristic harmonic devices of his later period. Only the occasional intrusion of sentimental melodies in the old vein breaks the unity of effect.

Puccini was not one of the great composers, but within his own limits—of which he was perfectly aware—he worked honorably and with mastery of his technique. Bill Nye remarked of

36. See Carner, "The Exotic Element in Puccini," with musical examples.

Wagner's music that it "is better than it sounds"; Puccini's music, on the contrary, often sounds better than it is, owing to the perfect adjustment of means to ends. He had the prime requisite for an opera composer, an instinct for the theater; to that he added the Italian gift of knowing how to write effectively for singers, an unusually keen ear for new harmonic and instrumental colors, a mind receptive to musical progress, and a poetic imagination excelling in the evocation of dreamlike, fantastic moods. Even *Turandot*, for all its venturesome harmonies, is a romantic work, an escape into the exotic in both the dramatic and the musical sense.

        A younger contemporary of Puccini was Umberto Giordano (1867–1948),[37] whose *Andrea Chénier* (1896) is like a rescue opera of the French Revolution period without the rescue; both plot and music show the influence of verismo in the exaggerated emphasis on effect at all costs (example 23.4). Apart from its undoubted dramatic qualities, the score offers little of interest; the harmonies are heavy and old-fashioned and there are few notable lyric passages in the voice parts, though some local color is provided by the use of revolutionary songs ("Ça ira," "La Carmagnole," "La Marseillaise"). *Fedora* (1898) and *Siberia* (1903) are in the same style, with Russian instead of French background. In *Madame Sans-Gêne* (New York, 1915), the composer's theatrical talents are applied to a vivacious and tuneful comedy drama. Of Giordano's later operas, *La cena delle beffe* ("The Feast of Jests," 1924), a lurid four-act melodrama, has been the most successful. None of these are of great significance musically; they are the work of a gifted but not profound composer operating within the traditional Italian framework and skillfully adapting it to the current practice of orchestral continuity. A similar but less conspicuous position must be assigned to Francesco Cilèa (1866–1950), who was, incidentally, one of the first Italian composers of this period to have occupied himself much with music in other forms than opera.[38] His *Adriana Lecouvreur* (1902), based on a libretto by Scribe, is an involved drama of the age of Louis XV with expertly contrived music of a lyrical-tragic sort obviously influenced

37. Biography by Cellamare.
38. Biography by T. d'Amico; see also Pilati, "Francesco Cilèa."

Example 23.4: *Andrea Chénier*, sc. 2

by Puccini, unadventurous harmonically or rhythmically but good theater and effective for the singers.

Germany

Wagner affected the course of lyric drama like a new planet hurled into a solar system. The center of the operatic universe shifted; all the old balances were disturbed; regroupings took place, accompanied by erratic movements. These consequences were least marked in Italy, more so in France, and most of all, naturally, in Germany. Yet even there they did not appear quickly; established traditions—romantic opera in the manner of Marschner and grand opera on the model of Meyerbeer—were still strong.[39] *Loreley* (1863), by Max Bruch (1838–1920),[40] composed to a libretto originally written for Mendelssohn, was a romantic opera, conventional in form though with some progressive traits in the musical style. *Die Königin von Saba* ("The Queen of Sheba," 1875), by Karl Goldmark (1830–1915),[41] one of the favorite German works of the later nineteenth century (it was performed at the Metropolitan fifteen times in 1885), is grand opera—agreeable but old-fashioned, complete with set numbers, ballets, pageantry, and some conventional strokes of oriental color. Goldmark had accepted Wagner as a far as *Tannhäuser*, but was evidently not acquainted with, or at any rate not at all influenced by, the later style of *Tristan* and the *Ring*.

Some typically Wagnerian subject matter had come into German opera independently of Wagner. Karl Mangold (1813–1889) had produced a *Tannhäuser* in 1846 and Heinrich Dorn (1804–1892) a *Nibelungen* in 1854, both composed without knowledge of Wagner's corresponding works; Dorn's opera, indeed, was seriously regarded for a time as rivaling Wagner's *Ring*.[42] One of the first composers in whom the direct influence of Wagner can be seen was Franz von Holstein (1826–1878), poet and composer, whose "grand opera" *Der Haideschacht* (1868) was based on Hoffmann's tale *Die Bergwerke zu Falun* ("The Mines at Falun"); but Holstein resented being known as a mere epigone of Wagner and in fact demonstrated considerable independence in his *Hochländer* ("The Highlanders," 1876), a historical grand opera in the tradition of Meyerbeer, which incidentally uses some Scottish melodies.[43] Wagnerian ideas in subject matter and treatment, use of leitmotifs, importance of the orchestra, and attempted musical continuity—all modified, however, by some compromises with older

39. General works on the period are Schiedermair, *Die deutsche Oper*; Louis, *Die deutsche Musik der Gegenwart*; Istel, "German Opera Since Richard Wagner"; idem, *Die moderne Oper*; *Monographien moderner Musiker*; Moser, *Geschichte der deutschen Musik*, 3:351–451; Kroyer, "Die circumpolare Oper"; Dahlhaus, *Between Romanticism and Modernism*.

40. Biography by Gysi.

41. Goldmark was born in Hungary but resided in Austria most of his life. See Goldmark, *Erinnerungen*; biography by Koch.

42. Dorn, *Aus meinem Leben*; Rauh, *Heinrich Dorn als Opernkomponist*.

43. Biography by Glaser.

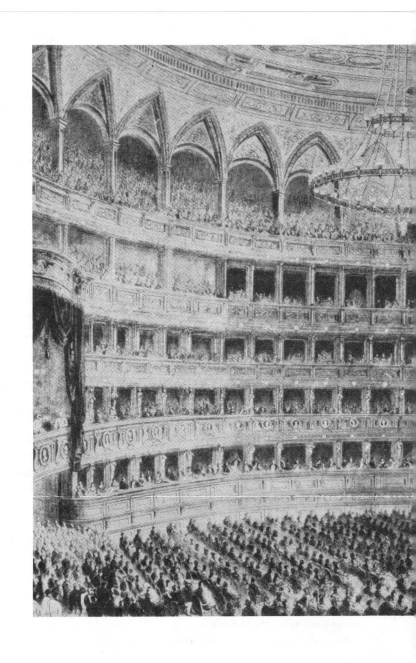

Interior of Vienna Opera House at the inaugural production, May 25, 1869: Mozart's *Don Giovanni*. From an original engraving by L. E. Petrovits.

(Bildarchivs der Oesterreichischen Nationalbibibiliothek)

operatic forms—are evident in *Iwein* (1879) and *Gudrun* (1882), by August Klughardt (1847–1902),[44] and in *Gudrun* (1884) by Felix Draeseke (1835–1913),[45] *Kunihild* (also 1884) by Cyrill Kistler (1848–1907), *Wieland der Schmied* (1880, revised 1894), by Max Zenger (1837–1911); and *Kudrun* (1896), by the Swiss Hans Huber (1852–1921).[46] But some of these composers later managed to shake off the Wagnerian influence and develop along lines more congenial to their own temperaments—Kistler, for example, toward operas of a simple popular style, Zenger (especially in his last opera, *Eros und Psyche*, 1901) toward the classical ideal of Gluck, and Huber, with moderate success, toward romantic opera (*Die schöne Bellinda*, 1916).

The Wagnerian school toward the end of the century is represented by Felix von Weingartner (1863–1942), with *Sakuntala* (1884), *Genesius* (1892), and the trilogy *Orestes* (1902), as well as many later dramatic works in various styles;[47] Heinrich Zöllner (1854–1941), with *Faust* (1887); and especially August Bungert (1845–1915), whose *Homerische Welt* ("The Homeric World"), consisting of two cycles of six operas in all, was the most ambitious musico-dramatic undertaking since the *Ring* but nevertheless failed to make its way with the public, because of appallingly uninteresting music.[48] These composers for the most part followed Wagner in writing their own librettos. Among other Wagnerian works of this period may be mentioned some early operas by other composers who subsequently developed a more personal style: Wilhelm Kienzl's *Urvasi* (1886), Max von Schillings' *Ingwelde* (1894), Richard Strauss's *Guntram* (1894), Hans Pfitzner's *Arme Heinrich* (1896), and Eugen d'Albert's *Kain* (1900).

The inevitable consequence of all this imitation of Wagner was a reaction. Both public and composers, growing tired of repetitions of a style in which Wagner had already said the final word, were ready for something new, and ways out were sought

---

44. Biography by Gerlach.

45. Biography by Röder.

46. Biography by Refardt.

47. See Weingartner's own writings, especially *Lebenserinnerungen* and *Die Lehre von der Wiedergeburt*.

48. Biography by Chop.

in three directions: comic opera, popular opera *(Volksoper)*, and fairy-tale opera *(Märchenoper)*. An outstanding work in the comic genre was *Der Widerspenstigen Zähmung* ("The Taming of the Shrew," 1874), by Hermann Goetz (1840–76),[49] an opera which, like Cornelius's *Barbier von Bagdad*, has never had the wide success it merits by the cleverness of its libretto and the Mozartean humor of its music. A later, more sophisticated school of comic opera, going back for musical inspiration to *Der Barbier* or Wagner's *Meistersinger*, is represented by the celebrated but seldom performed *Corregidor* (1896) of Hugo Wolf (1860–1903).[50] Based on a story by P. A. de Alarcón, *Der Corregidor* is in many respects an inspired attempt to create a gay, original German comic opera "without the gloomy, world-redeeming ghost of a Schopenhauerian philosopher in the background."[51] This laudable intention was frustrated by Wolf's long-standing admiration for Wagner's music: the orchestra of *Der Corregidor* is as heavily polyphonic as that of *Die Meistersinger*, and the music is full of leitmotifs—a style completely unsuited to Wolf's libretto. Moreover, Wolf, like Schubert and Schumann, was not at home in the theater: his invention seems to have been paralyzed by the requirements of the stage; the music goes from one song to the next like a Liederspiel; neither persons nor situations are adequately characterized. This composer, "who could be so dramatic in the lied, here in the drama remained above all a lyricist."[52] *Der Corregidor*, though not lacking in finely wrought details,[53] was a failure as an opera.

Another Spanish subject, from Lope de Vega, was treated by Anton Urspruch (1850–1907) in his comic opera *Das Unmöglichste von allem* ("The Most Impossible of All," 1897), with light

49. Biographies by Kreuzhage and Kruse.

50. Biographies by Decsey, Walker, and Von Graedener-Hattingberg. See also Hellmer, ed., *"Der Corregidor"*.

51. Letter of Wolf to Grohe, 1890. See Istel, "German Opera Since Richard Wagner," pp. 278–79.

52. Moser, *Geschichte der deutschen Musik*, 3:397.

53. Examples are the duet "In solchen Abendfeierstunden," Act II; Frasquita's "In dem Schatten meiner Locken" (Act I), a charming song taken from Wolf's earlier *Spanisches Liederbuch*; Luka's monologue (Act III, sc. 3), the most nearly dramatic music in the opera.

parlando dialogue and intricate contrapuntal ensembles derived from the style of Mozart. A more spirited and dramatic composer in this field was the Austrian Emil Nikolaus von Rezniček (1860–1945),[54] whose *Donna Diana* (1894), again on a Spanish subject, gave promise of a future that was not realized in his next few operas; but with *Ritter Blaubart* ("Knight Bluebeard," 1920), "an eclectic score embodying elements of Italian cantilena style and the technique of French impressionism,"[55] he renewed his reputation.

One of the best German comic operas of the late nineteenth century was D'Albert's *Abreise* ("The Departure," 1898), a fine example of swift-moving dialogue with a tuneful, spontaneous, and deftly orchestrated score, somewhat reminiscent of Cornelius. More in the *Meistersinger* idiom were the comic operas *Das war ich* ("That Was I," 1902) and the more ambitious *Versiegelt* ("Sealed," 1908), by Leo Blech (1871–1958);[56] but these, like Wolf's *Corregidor*, suffered from the music being, as a rule, too heavy and polyphonic for the simple librettos. Two other similar comic operas of this period were Schillings' *Pfeifertag* ("The Parliament of Pipers," 1899) and R. Strauss's *Feuersnot* ("The Fire Famine," 1901), the latter an extraordinary combination of humor, eroticism, and autobiography, with music which shows the composer in transition from his early Wagnerian style to that of *Salome* and *Elektra*. On the whole, however, German comic opera of this type in the late nineteenth and the early twentieth centuries is disappointing. No unified or generally accepted tradition was evolved, and individual works of talent remained isolated experiments which their composers seemed unable to repeat.

It was otherwise with the Volksoper. Two works of this class in the late nineteenth century were *Das goldene Kreuz* ("The Golden Cross," 1875), a pleasant comedy by Ignaz Brüll (1846–1907), with music slightly reminiscent of Auber; and the popular *Trompeter von Säckingen* (1884), by the Alsatian Viktor Nessler (1841–1890), with men's choruses, airs, and dances, all in a simple, tuneful style. Even more successful was *Der Evangelimann*

54. Studies by Chop and Specht.

55. Slonimsky, *Music Since 1900*.

56. W. Jacob, ed., *Leo Blech*.

(1895) by the Austrian Wilhelm Kienzl (1857–1941).[57] The personage of the "Evangelimann" has no English equivalent; he is a wandering mendicant who receives alms in return for reading and telling stories from the Scriptures. Kienzl's appeal is founded on the application of Wagnerian techniques to nonheroic subjects, but much of his musical material has a distinctly folklike flavor (example 23.5). *Der Evangelimann* is, in fact, a kind of anthology

Example 23.5: *Der Evangelimann*, Act I

KIENZL

O Zit-ter-bart, o Zit-ter-bart, o Franz Xa-ve-rius Zit-ter-bart! Du

triffst ja nicht den La-den mehr; die Ku-gel ist für dich zu schwer.

of popular dance and song types, together with sentimental melodies in the vein of Nessler and amusing reminiscences of *Lohengrin, Tristan, Die Meistersinger*, and *Hänsel und Gretel*—all attached to a libretto of the most flagrantly melodramatic-romantic sort. Its popularity in Germany and Austria may be judged by the fact that *Der Evangelimann* had over 5,300 performances in the first forty years of its existence.

Closely related to Kienzl's work is that of another Austrian, Julius Bittner (1874–1939),[58] whose operas (to his own texts) are based on a folklike type of melody, alternating closed numbers with declamatory passages and combining sentiment with hu-

57. Two *Festschriften* (1917, 1937) have been dedicated to Kienzl; see also his autobiography, *Meine Lebenswanderung*; essay by Morold in *Monographien moderner Musiker*, vol. 3. Selections from the autobiography and letters are in *Kienzl-Rosegger*.

58. Biography by Specht.

mor. *Die rote Gred* ("Red-headed Gred," 1907) and *Der Musik-ant* ("The Musician," 1910) show his characteristic style in purest form; *Der Bergsee* ("The Mountain Lake," 1911) has curious post-Wagnerian reminiscences. *Das höllisch Gold* ("The Infernal Gold," 1916), a humorous miracle play, was his most varied and most popular work. Likewise in the field of people's opera must be noted the Viennese Richard Heuberger (1850–1914), with *Barfüssele* (1905), and the Czech Karel Weis (1862–1944), with *Der polnische Jude* (1901), both works popular in their day. Finally may be mentioned the Viennese operetta, which flourished in the early twentieth century with new hits by Franz Lehár (1870–1948),[59] particularly *Die lustige Witwe* ("The Merry Widow," 1905); Oscar Straus (1870–1954),[60] *Ein Walzertraum* ("A Waltz Dream," 1907) and *Der tapfere Soldat* ("The Chocolate Soldier," 1908); and Leo Fall (1873–1925), *Die Dollarprinzessin* ("The Dollar Princess," 1907).

The way of recourse to the Märchenoper as a means of escape from wholesale imitation of Wagner—in effect, a return to one kind of subject matter that had been current in the early romantic era—was discovered almost inadvertently. Alexander Ritter (1833–96),[61] a disciple of Liszt and composer of a number of historically important symphonic poems, had produced at Munich in 1885 a fairy-tale opera, *Der faule Hans* ("Lazy Hans"), which, although it had only a moderate success, is of interest as being a forerunner of a most important fairy-tale opera which came out in 1893: *Hänsel und Gretel*, by Engelbert Humperdinck (1854–1921).[62] Humperdinck first wrote this music for a play for his sister's children to perform at home; made into a full opera, it caught the public fancy to such a degree as to start a whole new school in Germany. People turned with relief from the misty depths of mythology to the homely, familiar, enchanted world of the fairy tale, to subjects like those which their grandparents had enjoyed in the days of Marschner and Lortzing. The transition was made

59. Biographies by Czech and Peteani.

60. Grün, *Prince of Vienna*.

61. Biography by Von Hausegger.

62. Biography by Besch; Kuhlman, *Stil und Form in der Musik von Humperdincks Oper "Hansel und Gretel"*.

easier because Humperdinck kept up an appearance of loyalty to Wagner: the music of *Hänsel und Gretel* is, in fact, a peculiar mixture of German folk melody and Wagnerian polyphony. Perhaps the texture is too complicated for the subject matter, but if this be a fault, it is one easy to forgive in view of the many musical beauties and the heartfelt, simple emotion of the work. The music brings together many qualities rooted in the affections of Germans over generations: the songs and dances of the children, the idyllic forest scenes, just enough of the supernatural (but with a comic touch), and the choral-like feeling of the "evening blessing" melody, which recurs in the finale to the words

> When past bearing is our grief,
> God himself will send relief.

Among the many fairy-tale operas in neo-Wagnerian style that followed *Hänsel und Gretel* were Humperdinck's *Königskinder* ("The Royal Children"), first composed in 1898 as incidental music to a play and made into an opera ten years later; Carl Friedrich Zöllner's best opera, *Die versunkene Glocke* ("The Sunken Bell", 1899); *Lobetanz* (1898), by Ludwig Thuill (1861–1907);[63] *Illsebill* (1903), by Friedrich Klose (1862–1942);[64] *Rübezahl* (1904), by Hans Sommer (1837–1922);[65] and two works by Leo Blech, who had been a pupil of Humperdinck: *Alpenkönig und Menschenfeind* ("Alpine King and Man's Enemy," 1903; revised in 1917 under the title of *Rappelkopf*) and *Aschenbrödel* ("Cinderella," 1905). Here in varying degrees the post-Wagnerian musical idiom was adapted to popular subjects. To this group of composers belongs also Richard Wagner's son Siegfried Wagner (1869–1930), another pupil of Humperdinck, whose *Bärenhäuter* (1899) was the first and best of a long series of fairy-tale operas to his own texts which attempt to combine legend, symbolism, and humor in a popular style.[66] None of the later works, however,

63. Biography by Munter.

64. Biography by Knappe.

65. Biography by Valentin.

66. See S. Wagner, *Erinnerungen*; Glasenapp, *Siegfried Wagner und seine Kunst*; Du Moulin-Eckart, *Wahnfried*; other studies by Rebois, Pretzsch, and Daube. *Der Bärenhäuter* is untranslatable. The story on which it is based will be found under the title "Des Teufels russiger Bruder" in Jacob Grimm and Wilhelm Grimm, *Kinder- und Haus-Märchen* [Berlin, 1815], 2:100–105.

attained the lasting success of *Hänsel und Gretel,* which remains the classic example of late nineteenth-century German Märchen-oper as well as a perennial source of pleasure for children of all ages.

PART V

Nationalism and Opera

C H A P T E R
T W E N T Y - F O U R

National Opera

The eighteenth and nineteenth centuries saw the rise of independent schools of composition in many countries that had previously been tributary to the chief musical nations of Europe or that, like Spain and England, had been for a long time only on the periphery of the main developments. Opera played a leading part in the growth of musical nationalism, as the use of characteristic national subjects, often from patriotic motives, stimulated composers to seek an equally characteristic national expression in their music. National operas, as a rule, were not intended to be exportable, and indeed relatively few of these works have made their way into foreign countries. Nevertheless, the national schools are important in the history of nineteenth- and twentieth-century opera, and the present chapter presents a survey of their development.

Russia and Neighboring Lands

RUSSIA. Native opera began to appear in Russia before the end of the eighteenth century.[1] It had been preceded, as in the coun-

1. General histories of Russian music are Asaf'ev, *Russkaia muzyka ot nachala XIX stoletiia*; Akademiia nauk SSSR, *Istoriia russkoi i sovetskoi muzyki*; Keldysh, *Istoriia russkoi muzyki*; Livanova, *Ocherki i materialy po istorii russkoi muzykal'noi kul'tury*; Calvocoressi and Abraham, *Masters of Russian Music*; Abraham, *Studies in Russian Music*; idem, *On Russian Music*; M. Brown, ed., *Russian and Soviet Music*. See also other titles in the Russian Music Studies series (Ann Arbor, Mich.; UMI Research, 1981–   ).

tries of western Europe, by various types of drama that used music in incidental fashion; religious mystery plays, going back to the sixteenth century or earlier, and school dramas and court pageants in the seventeenth and eighteenth centuries. When the first public theater was opened at St. Petersburg in 1703, its offerings consisted for the most part of foreign plays, which occasionally used incidental music.

The record of Italian opera at the Russian court begins in 1731 with *Calandro* (1726), a commedia per musica by Giovanni Alberto Ristori (1692–1753). Under Catherine the Great (reigned 1762–1796), St. Petersburg became as much of a cosmopolitan center for opera as London, with Galuppi, Paisiello, Cimarosa, Salieri, and others in residence for varying lengths of time, while many other Italians, as well as the leading composers of the French opéra comique and German singspiel, were represented in the repertoires. During the last quarter of the century, nearly 350 operas had their premieres in Russia, over thirty new ones coming out in the year 1778 alone. Most of the operas by foreign composers that were performed in Russia were sung in the original languages, and even some by Russian composers had foreign-language librettos: for example, Dmitry Bortnyansky (1751–1825), who during his years of study in Italy had produced Italian operas, after his return to St. Petersburg in 1779 wrote comic operas to French texts.

By the 1770s, however, operas with original Russian texts began to appear; musical scores of about thirty such works before 1800 have been preserved, and librettos of forty more.[2] Most of them are comic and some are satirical, while sentimental or fairy-tale elements begin to appear toward the end of the century; the usual form is spoken dialogue alternating with solo airs and en-

---

2. General works on Russian opera are Bernandt, *Slovar' oper*; Cheshikhin, *Istoriia russkoi opery*; Druskin, *Voprosy muzykal'noi dramaturgii opery*; Iarustovskii, *Dramaturgiia russkoi opernoi klassiki*; Asaf'ev, *Izbrannye trudy*; Newmarch, *The Russian Opera*. See also articles in *Sovetskaia muzyka*. On the period before Glinka, see Findeisen, *Ocherki po istorii muzyki v Rossii*; idem, "The Earliest Russian Operas"; Ginzburg, *Russkii muzykal'nyi teatr 1700–1835*; Rabinovich, *Russkaia opera do Glinki*; Livanova, *Russkaia muzykal'naia kul'tura XVIII veka*; Gozenpud, *Muzykal'nyi teatr v Rossii*; Lehmann, *Russlands Oper und Singspiel*; Seaman, *History of Russian Music*, vol. 1; idem, "The National Element in Early Russian Opera"; Selden, "Early Roots of Russian Opera"; Mooser, *Opéras, intermezzos, ballets*; Karlinsky, "Russian Comic Opera"; Berkov, *Russkaia komediia*; Druskin, *Ocherki po istorii russkoi muzyki, 1790–1825*.

sembles. The plots typically introduce characteristic Russian scenes and persons and the music may draw on popular folk melodies. In one early comic opera entitled *Melnik-koldun, obmanshchik i svat* ("The Miller-Magician, Deceiver, and Matchmaker," Moscow, 1779), by Mikhail Sokolovsky (flourished ca. 1750–1780), all the songs were set to popular tunes, in the manner of the earliest French opéras comiques. More often, however, the composers incorporated folk song into their own more sophisticated style, which they had learned from Western examples or training. The leading composer of Russian opera before 1800 was the Italian-trained Evstigney Ipatovich Fomin (1761–1800),[3] whose finest work was a melodrama, *Orfey i Evridika* (1792). Between 1786 and 1800, Fomin produced a half-dozen comic operas at St. Petersburg; his *Yamshchiki na podstave* ("The Coachmen," 1787) had a score based entirely on folk material and including choruses in which the composer attempted to transcribe the authentic polyphony of Russian folk song.[4]

Russian opera was thus well under way by the end of the eighteenth century. Under Alexander I (reigned 1801–1825), a great upsurge of national sentiment, imbued in Russia as elsewhere with the spirit of Byronesque romanticism, wonderfully encouraged the production of national opera. Curiously, one of the principal composers of Russian opera in the early nineteenth century was a versatile Venetian, Catterino Cavos (1776–1840), who came to St. Petersburg in 1798 and remained there for the rest of his life. He composed, to Russian, French, or Italian texts, over forty operas. Among those on Russian themes and in the Russian language were *Ilya Bogatyr* (1807), *Ivan Susanin* (1815), and *Zharptitsa* ("The Firebird," 1822). *Ivan Susanin* is Cavos' best work and one that remained a model of musical nationalism in Russia until Glinka's opera on the same subject replaced it twenty years later.[5] Among the native-born composers of the early and middle nineteenth century was Alexey Nikolaevich Verstovsky (1799–

3. See Dobrokhotov, *E. I. Fomin*.

4. The Russian title may also be translated as "The Postdrivers." This opera was revived at Moscow in 1977.

5. An important difference between these two works is Glinka's departure from the lieto fine tradition of early nineteenth-century Russian opera. Cavos spares the life of the heroine; Glinka allows the tragic denouement in Act IV to proceed to its logical conclusion.

1862),[6] whose chief opera, *Askoldova mogila* ("Askold's Grave," Moscow, 1835), held the stage in Russia into the twentieth century.[7]

An important milestone in the history of Russian opera was the performance in 1836 at St. Petersburg of *Zhizn za tsarya* ("A Life for the Tsar"),[8] by Mikhail Ivanovich Glinka (1804–1857).[9] Although it has sometimes been regarded as the very foundation and source of Russian national opera, *A Life for the Tsar* owes its reputation in this respect more to its plot and its immense and long-continued popularity in Russia than to any consistent, strongly pronounced national qualities in the music, which indeed sounds for the most part as much French or Italian as Russian. Quotations from folk song occur in the opening of Susanin's aria no. 3 and in the accompaniments to Susanin's last two solo passages at the end of Act IV, and the choral theme of the epilogue so took hold on popular fancy as to become almost a second national anthem; but, with few exceptions, melodies such as that of the Bridal Chorus in Act III (example 24.1) represent Glinka's nearest approach in this score to a genuinely national idiom. Compensation may be found for the undistinguished quality of much of the mu-

Example 24.1: *A Life for the Tsar*, Act III

GLINKA

---

6. Dobrokhotov, *A. N. Verstovskii*; Abraham, "The Operas of Alexei Verstovsky."

7. It was given at New York in 1869, the first Russian opera to be performed in America.

8. The original title of this opera was *Ivan Susanin*.

9. General works on nineteenth-century Russian opera are Gozenpud, *Russkii opernyi teatr*; Taruskin, *Opera and Drama in Russia*; Ridenour, *Nationalism, Modernism, and Personal Rivalry in Nineteenth-Century Russian Music*; Olkhovsky, *Vladimir Stasov and Russian National Culture*; Stasov, *Selected Essays*. See also studies on Glinka, which include Akademiia nauk SSSR, *Pamiati Glinki*; Glinka, *Literaturnoe nasledie*; idem, *Zapiski*; Livanova, ed., *M. I. Glinka*; Stasov, *Izbrannye stat'i*; idem, *Mikhail Ivanovich Glinka*; Dmitriev, *Muzykal'naia dramaturgiia*; Protopopov, "*Ivan Susanin*" *Glinki*; and biographies in English by Calvocoressi, Montagu-Nathan, and D. Brown.

sic in the clear and varied orchestration, which was a model for all the later Russian nationalists, including Rimsky-Korsakov.

In his extensive use of recurring motives, Glinka was far in advance of any opera composer before Wagner. The quasi-folk-song theme of the opening chorus of *A Life for the Tsar* is used as a leitmotif of Russian heroism, sung by the hero Susanin in Act III as he defies the Polish conspirators. The Polish soldiers are characterized by themes in the national dance rhythms of the polonaise and the mazurka; first heard in the ball scene of Act II, they recur in Act III at the entrance of the Poles, and the mazurka rhythm is heard again at their appearance in Act IV. The opposing national motifs are contrasted in the orchestral introduction to the epilogue. Susanin's last aria (Act IV) is to a large extent made up of previously heard themes, the recurrences here producing a purposeful dramatic effect. The theme of the final chorus, repeated again and again with cumulative power, has been subtly prepared by two or three statements earlier in the opera. This brilliant epilogue is not only a climax of patriotic emotion but also a fine example of the highly colored mass effects of sound and spectacle much beloved in Russian opera.

Although *A Life for the Tsar* was more popular, the significant musical foundations for the future were laid in Glinka's second and last opera, *Ruslan i Lyudmila* (1842). The libretto is a fantastic and incoherent fairy tale adapted from a poem by Pushkin; the music, in spite of some traces of Weber, is more original than that of Glinka's earlier opera, and the musical characterizations are more definite. The system of recurring motives here is almost nonexistent; the one important trace of it is the recurrent descending whole-tone scale associated with the wicked magician Chernomor (example 24.2)—said to be the earliest use of the whole-tone scale in European music. But at least five distinct styles or procedures characteristic of later Russian music appear in *Ruslan and Ludmila*: (1) the heroic, broad, solemn, declamatory style, with modal suggestions and archaic effect (introduction and song of the Bard in Act I); (2) the Russian lyrical style, with expressive melodic lines of a folkish cast, delicately colored harmony featuring the lowered sixth or raised fifth, and chromatically moving inner voices (Finn's ballad and Ruslan's first aria in Act II); (3) depiction of fantastic occurrences by means of

Example 24.2: *Ruslan and Ludmila*, Act IV

GLINKA

unusual harmonies, such as whole-tone passages or chord progressions pivoting about one note (scene of Ludmila's abduction, toward the end of Act I); (4) oriental atmosphere, sometimes using genuine oriental themes (Persian chorus at opening of Act III), sometimes original melodies (Ratmir's romance in Act V), but always characterized by fanciful arabesque figures in the accompaniment and a languorous harmony and orchestration; and (5) the vividly colored choruses and dances, with glittering instrumentation and often daring harmonies (chorus in honor of Lel in the finale of Act I; Chernomor's march and following dances, especially the *lezginka*, in the finale of Act IV)—models for similar scenes in Borodin's *Prince Igor*, Rimsky-Korsakov's *Sadko*, and even Stravinsky's *Le Sacre du Printemps*.

The first important Russian opera after *Ruslan and Ludmila* was by Alexander Sergeevich Dargomyzhsky (1813–

1869): [10] *Rusalka* (1856), likewise on a text from Pushkin and somewhat similar in subject to Glinka's work. Musically, however, it spoke a language intentionally different from *Ruslan*, for Dargomyzhsky sought to develop the dramatic rather than the lyric aspects of a national Russian style. *Rusalka* achieved an important first step in that direction with its realistic declamation of the recitative, a style of declamation Dargomyzhsky proceeded to develop to the highest degree in his last opera, *Kamenny gost* ("The Stone Guest"). This work was completed after Dargomyzhsky's death by César Cui, orchestrated by Rimsky-Korsakov, and first performed in 1872. The libretto for *The Stone Guest* is nothing less than the actual spoken drama by Pushkin, a setting of the Don Juan story. Although this opera is no masterpiece and never had a popular success, it influenced later Russian opera because of the composer's attempt to write the entire work (except for some songs near the beginning of Act II) in a melodic recitative, a vocal line which would be in every detail the equivalent of the words. The result, though accurate in declamation and dramatic on occasion, lacks sharp characterization or melodic interest, and there is no compensation for the melodic poverty in the orchestral part, which is conceived as accompaniment rather than as continuous symphonic tissue. In his repudiation of set musical forms and his high respect for the words, Dargomyzhsky had arrived in his own way at certain features of the Wagnerian music drama, though there is no trace of Wagner in the musical substance. Harmonically, some interest attaches to Dargomyzhsky's use of whole-tone scale fragments as motifs for the Statue and in some passages constructed entirely on this scale.

One of the more explicit and self-conscious disciples of Wagner in Russia was the critic and composer Alexander Nikolaevich Serov (1820–1871),[11] whose works add significantly to an understanding of that enigmatic period separating the 1830s and 1870s. *Yudif* ("Judith," 1863), *Rogneda* (1865), and *Vrazhya sila* ("The Power of Evil," completed by his widow and Nikolay So-

10. See Pekelis, *A. S. Dargomyzhskii i ego okruzhenie*; idem, *Dargomyzhskii i narodnaia pesnia*; Serov, "*Rusalka*"; Baker, "Dargomizhsky, Realism, and *The Stone Guest*."

11. Abraham, "The Operas of Serov"; Gozenpud, *Russkii opernyi teatr*; Taruskin, *Opera and Drama in Russia*. See also biographies by Baskin, Findeisen, and Khubov.

lovyov, and first performed in 1871) are three quite different expressions of Serov's operatic style. *Judith*, based on a story from the Apocrypha, was Serov's first successful opera. The musical material, fashioned to complement scenarios rather than specific words, achieves a continuous flow of emotions through a flexibility of forms and tonal centers. In short, the opera shows the composer's admiration for all the methods of grand opera of the Meyerbeer and early Wagner type. *Rogneda* was even more popular than *Judith*. It concerns the historical Vladimir the Great and his jealous wife, Rogneda, who is sentenced to death for attempted murder but, through the intervention of a chorus of Christian pilgrims, has her life spared. This is grand opera with a new and different degree of operatic realism, one which brought historical realism into the social realm of the theater. In Serov's final work for the stage, there emerges yet another manifestation of realism—the incorporation of folk music as the vehicle of the musical drama. *The Power of Evil* is derived from *Don't Live as You'd Like To, But Live as God Commands*, one of a group of plays from the 1850s by Alexander Nikolaevich Ostrovsky. In this play, Ostrovsky used folk songs to clothe the dramatic events with an aura of national identity. Serov's opera carries forth this nationalistic realism, combining authentic folk songs (mainly those found in Ostrovsky's play) with adaptations of folk songs fashioned to meet the artistic needs of the score.[12] Although Serov's operas won little regard from musicians and critics during his lifetime,[13] they were nevertheless popular enough with the public to remain in the repertoire of Russian opera companies until the First World War.

From about the middle of the nineteenth century, Russian musicians were divided into two groups. In one were the professional, foreign-trained, and officially supported composers who were not primarily interested in musical nationalism but wished to see Russian musical life develop along the same lines as in Western Europe, particularly Germany. The head of this school

12. For a table listing these folk-song sources, see Taruskin, *Opera and Drama in Russia*, p. 171.

13. One of his critics was Vladimir Vasil'evich Stasov (1824–1906); see n. 24 below.

was Anton Rubinstein (1829–1894),[14] the famous pianist and the founder and first director of the Imperial Conservatory at St. Petersburg. Of Rubinstein's nineteen operas (eight on Russian and eleven on German texts), *Demon* ("The Demon," 1875) had a considerable success both in Russia and abroad. Its libretto strongly recalls Wagner's *Fliegende Holländer*, but the forms are conventional and the musical style is that of pre-Wagnerian romanticism mingled with some oriental elements. Musically more interesting, though less popular, was *Kupets Kalashnikov* ("The Merchant Kalashnikov," 1880). Rubinstein's biblical operas, or rather stage oratorios (for example, *Die Makkabäer*, "The Maccabees," 1875), are remembered now only for a few separate numbers.

The leading composer of the non-nationalist school was Pyotr Ilyich Tchaikovsky (1840–1893), in whom Slavic temperament and German training were leavened by lyrical genius and a lively appreciation of Italian opera and French ballet.[15] Reckoned by bulk, if not also by musical excellence, Tchaikovsky's achievement is as important in the field of opera as in that of the symphony. After three early works in which he experimented with the then-fashionable nationalism—*Voevoda* (1869),[16] *Oprichnik* (1874), and *Kuznets Vakula* ("Vakula the Smith," 1876),[17]—Tchaikovsky produced his masterpiece, *Eugene Onegin*, at Moscow in 1879. In both the libretto (after Pushkin) and the musical style, this is an old-fashioned romantic opera, but the music is in Tchaikovsky's happiest vein, with graceful melodies, expressive harmonies, transparent and imaginative orchestration—true and living in expression without the hysterical emotionalism of some of the later symphonic works. The character of the heroine, Tatyana, is delineated with especial sympathy, and that of Onegin himself is scarcely less vivid. The ballet music (particularly the waltz in Act

14. Biographies by Alexeyev and Barenboim.

15. Iarustovskii, *Opernaia dramaturgiia Chaikovskogo; Myzykal'noe nasledie Chaikovskogo;* biographies in English by Evans, Hanson and Hanson, Warrach, and D. Brown. See also P. Tchaikovsky, *Diaries;* Abraham, ed., *Tchaikovsky: A Symposium;* Bowen and Von Meck, *"Beloved Friend"*; Zagiba, *Tschaikovskij;* Al'shvang, *P. I. Chaikovskii;* Berliand-Chernaia, *Puskin i Chaikovskii;* Iakovlev, *Pushkin i muzyka.*

16. Abraham, "Tchaikovsky's First Opera."

17. *Vakula the Smith* was revised in 1885 as *Cherevichki* ("The Slippers").

II) is tuneful and charming, as are also the choruses in Act I.
Tchaikovsky's next three operas were in a more heavily dramatic
style. *Orleanskaya deva* ("The Maid of Orleans," 1881), with a
libretto after Schiller, was less successful than *Mazepa* (1884),
from a poem by Pushkin. The latter contains two of the composer's finest dramatic moments: the monologue of Kochubey and the
extremely pathetic final scene. *Charodeyka* ("The Enchantress,"
1887) had such a disappointing reception that Tchaikovsky returned to his more characteristic lyrical style for his last two operatic works: *Pikovaya dama* ("The Queen of Spades," 1890), his
most popular opera next to *Eugene Onegin*, and *Iolanta* (1892).
In *The Queen of Spades*, based on a melodramatic tale by Pushkin, Tchaikovsky attained a more nearly perfect balance than in
any of his other operas among dramatic declamation, lyrical expressiveness, and divertissement music (see especially the ballets
in Act II).

The struggle for Russian national music, begun by Glinka
and Dargomyzhsky, was carried on after 1860 by a group of five
composers: Balakirev, Cui, Musorgsky, Borodin, and Rimsky-
Korsakov.[18] All were amateurs; only Rimsky-Korsakov—and he
only at a comparatively late stage of his career—ever had a thorough conventional technical training in composition. Balakirev
wrote no operas. César Antonovich Cui (1835–1918) wrote ten,
but most of them are not Russian in subject or musical style.[19] Of
these ten, the most interesting is the intensely romantic *Vilyam
Ratklif* ("William Ratcliff," 1869), the first opera by one of "the
mighty five" to be staged. Initial reactions to Cui's opera were
decidedly unfavorable and the work was withdrawn from production. The Russian national opera in its highest development,
therefore, is the work of the other three composers of the five.

The lack of the usual technical musical education (which
meant, at that time, a German conservatory training) had the effect of turning the nationalist composers to the resources of their
own country for dramatic and musical material, and to their own

18. Livanova, *Stasov i russkaia klassicheskaia opera*; Seroff, *The Mighty Five*.

19. Cui, *La Musique en Russie* (1880), is the source of many misconceptions concerning
the Russian national school. See Taruskin, *Opera and Drama in Russia*, for a discussion
of Cui as opera reformer, critic, and composer; Abraham, "Heine, Queuille, and *William
Ratcliff*." See also Kyui, *Izbrannye stat'i*.

instincts and national traditions for the means of shaping this material into operatic form. These conditions were especially important for Modest Petrovich Musorgsky (1839–1881),[20] the most original of the group, who in *Boris Godunov* (St. Petersburg, 1874) created one of the great masterpieces of nineteenth-century opera, a monument of much that is most typical in Russian musical drama and at the same time an absolutely personal, inimitable work. *Boris* was first composed in 1868–69 and was then rewritten in 1871–72. In 1896, Rimsky-Korsakov prepared a thoroughly revised version with "corrections" of the harmony, improvements in the orchestration, a different order of scenes, and many cuts; the deleted portions were restored in a second revision (1908), and in this form the opera made its way into the repertoire of all foreign opera houses. After the revolution of 1918, the composer's own score was revived for performances in Russia, and this original version was published in 1928.

The libretto of *Boris Godunov* was prepared by Musorgsky himself, using as sources Pushkin's drama of the same title and N. M. Karamzin's *History of the Russian Empire*. The character of the half-mad emperor Boris (reigned 1598–1605), especially as sung and acted by Fyodor Chaliapin, is one of the most vivid in all opera. An equally potent force in the action is the cruel, anonymous mass of the Russian people—a force visibly present in the mighty crowd scenes but also invisibly working like the relentless pressure of Fate at every step toward the catastrophe of the drama. With grim poetic vision, Musorgsky set this primeval force in the closing scene of the opera over against the figure of the Idiot Boy, who, left alone at the last on a darkened stage, keens his lament: "Weep, ye people; soon the foe shall come, soon the gloom shall fall; woe to our land; weep, Russian folk, weep, hungry folk!"[21] One senses in such scenes the influence of the democratic ideals emerging in Russia during the sixties and

20. Biographies by Calvocoressi, Seroff, and Orlova. See also M. Brown, ed., *Musorgsky: In Memoriam, 1881–1981*; Lloyd-Jones, *Boris Godunov: Critical Commentary*; Leyda and Bertensson, eds. *The Musorgsky Reader*; Godet, *En marge de "Boris Godounof"*; Abraham, "Moussorgsky's *Boris* and Pushkin's"; Hoffmann-Erbrecht, "Grundlagen der Melodiebildung bei Mussorgski"; Szabolosi, *Bausteine zu einer Geschichte der Melodie*.

21. References are to Musorgsky's 1874 version, piano-vocal score published by Chester (London, 1926).

seventies following the liberation of the serfs under Alexander II, ideals so eloquently expounded in the writings of Tolstoy. In comparison to the elemental power of most of Musorgsky's opera, the love episode (Act III) seems both dramatically and musically a pale diversion—as does most of the love interest in Russian opera generally. In form, *Boris Godunov* is a series of detached scenes rather than a coherently developed plot, thus illustrating the Russian habit, in both musical and literary creation (compare Tolstoy's *War and Peace*), of compete absorption in the present moment, leaving the total impression to be achieved by the cumulative impact of many separate effects.

A striking feature of Musorgsky's music is the way in which, in the declamation, the melodic line always manages to convey the emotion of the text in the most direct, compressed, and forcible manner imaginable (example 24.3). Perhaps the best examples of this are the two most familiar scenes of the opera, the last part of Act II (including the "clock scene") and the farewell and death of Boris in Act IV. Here Musorgsky realized the ideal of dramatic, semimelodic recitative which Glinka had foreshadowed in *Ruslan and Ludmila* and which Dargomyzhsky had sought in *The Stone Guest*. Much of the same gloomy power, though with less violence, is displayed in the monastery scene at the beginning of Act I. A more songful idiom, equally characteristic of the composer, is heard in the first part of the inn scene (Act I, scene 2). Still more characteristic are the children's songs in the first part of Act II—examples of a psychological insight and musical style in which Musorgsky is almost unique, and which he had demonstrated in his song cycle *Detskaya* ("The Nursery," composed 1870–72). It is to be noted that in all these songs, whether declamatory or lyrical, the melodic line is the guiding factor. It is a style of melody which, with its peculiar intervals (especially the falling fourth at cadences), monotonous reiteration of patterns, irregularity of phrase structure, and archaic, modal basis, has grown most intimately out of Russian folk song. To this melodic line the harmony is generally a mere added support, but it likewise is of a strongly personal type, blended of modal feeling, impressionistic—often childlike—fondness for the mere sound of certain combinations, an unconventional harmonic training, and (one suspects) the happy outcome of improvisation at the piano.

Example 24.3: *Boris Godunov*, Act II

The harmony remains consonant and tonal; nevertheless any effort to analyze a typical passage of Musorgsky according to textbook principles will show how completely foreign his methods were to the conventional practice of the nineteenth century. Not unrelated to the naïveté of his harmonies is Musorgsky's reveling in raw, massive color effects. This trait is seen most clearly in the great crowd scene of the coronation, the orchestral introduction of which is also an example of the Russian mannerism of alternating chords pivoting on one common tone. The chorus itself in this scene is built on the same traditional tune that Beethoven used in his second "Razumovsky" Quartet.

In 1868, besides beginning the composition of *Boris Godunov*, Musorgsky also completed the piano-vocal score for *Zhenitba* ("The Marriage"), an experimental chamber opera based upon Gogol's comedy of the same title. In his setting of Gogol's colloquial prose, Musorgsky's cardinal aim was realistic expression at all costs: truth before beauty, melodic recitative *"true to life* and not melodic in the classical sense . . . a sort of melody created by (human) speech . . . intelligently justified melody."[22] To this end, he avoided conventional formulae, evolving a style as restrained, economical, and incapable of successful imitation as that of Debussy.

Of Musorgsky's other operas, the principal one is *Khovanshchina*, a "people's drama" upon which he worked devotedly but spasmodically from 1873 until the end of his life, leaving it unfinished after all; completed and orchestrated by Rimsky-Korsakov, it was performed at St. Petersburg in 1886. Musorgsky here took for his subject the conflict of the old feudal regime and the sect of the Old Believers with the new westernizing tendencies in Russia during the first years after the accession of Peter the Great (1689). Both libretto and music are as intensely national as in *Boris*, but the drama moves less vigorously and the musical style in general is less well sustained. Nevertheless, the best numbers—including the prelude, the crowd scenes, Shaklovity's aria in Act III, and especially some of the choruses of the Old Believers, where Musorgsky seems to have distilled the very spirit of

22. Letter to Stasov, December 25, 1876, in Leyda and Bertensson, eds., *The Musorgsky Reader*, p. 353.

ancient Russian church style—are equal to anything elsewhere in his works.

By temperament, Musorgsky was inclined to depict predominantly that side of the Russian character which gives itself over to gloom and mysticism, to the emotions of violence, brutality, and madness which predominate in *Boris Godunov* and *Khovanshchina*. A different, though no less normal, aspect of the national personality comes to life in *Knyaz Igor* ("Prince Igor"), an opera by Alexander Porfirievich Borodin (1833–1887)[23] first performed at St. Petersburg in 1890. The libretto is by the composer, after a plan by the critic Vladimir Stasov;[24] the score, unfinished at Borodin's death, was completed by Alexander Glazunov and Rimsky-Korsakov and orchestrated by the latter. The story is taken from a medieval Russian epic (apparently genuine, though long suspected to be an eighteenth-century forgery), but the central plot is of little importance except to give occasion for the many episodic scenes which make up most of the opera. Some of these scenes are comic, others are love scenes, but a large place is also reserved for spectacle, dances, and choruses (for example, the well-known Polovtsian dances in Act II). The musical ancestor of *Prince Igor* is Glinka's *Ruslan*, and its principal descendant is Rimsky-Korsakov's *Sadko*. The style of *Prince Igor* is predominantly lyric, with many of the arias in conventional Italian forms; there is some arioso writing, but little dramatic recitative in the manner of Dargomyzhsky. Indeed, the music is not dramatic at all in the sense in which *Boris Godunov* is dramatic; it does not so much embody a drama as present a series of musical tableaux to accompany and complete the stage pictures. In technical details also it is less unconventional than Musorgsky's music; the most original portions are the oriental scenes, for which Borodin evolved an idiom partly based on Central Asian themes but fundamentally an outgrowth of an eighteen-year-long absorption in the subject and his study of all available musical and historical material. His ancestry (he was the illegitimate son of a Caucasian prince) may

---

23. Biographies by Abraham and Dianin; see also Habets, *Alexandre Borodine.*

24. The important role played by Stasov in the shaping of cultural ideas in Russia during the second half of the nineteenth century is explored in Olkhovsky, *Vladimir Stasov and Russian National Culture.*

also have given him a particular bent toward this style, which, with its persistent rhythmic patterns, chromatic intervals, and melodic arabesques, dominates the second and third acts of the opera. *Prince Igor*, like *Boris Godunov*, makes some use of recurring motifs, but a more important source of unity is the derivation, unobtrusive but unmistakable, of many of the themes of Acts II and III from phrases in the melody of the first Polovtsian chorus.[25]

If *Boris Godunov* represents a darkly fanatical aspect of the Russian character and *Prince Igor* a cheerful, hearty one, then the picture is completed by the works of Nikolay Andreevich Rimsky-Korsakov (1844–1908),[26] whose most characteristic operas reflect a fairy-tale world of fantasy, romance, and innocent humor. This individual musical and dramatic style of Rimsky-Korsakov was not arrived at without some experimentation, and even after it had been achieved, he still continued to experiment. His first two operas, the grand historical drama *Pskovityanka* ("The Maid of Pskov," 1873) and the peasant-life comedy *Mayskaya noch* ("May Night," 1880), showed the influence of Dargomyzhsky and Glinka.[27] *Snegurochka* ("Snow Maiden," 1882), an opera based on a fairy legend with vaguely symbolic touches, was more spontaneous and original, an indication that Rimsky-Korsakov was exploring new directions. *Mlada* (1892), in which some traces of Wagner may be seen, was adapted from a libretto which was to have been collectively composed by Cui, Musorgsky, Rimsky-Korsakov, and Borodin twenty years before (this joint undertaking was never completed). *Noch pered Rozhdestvom* ("Christmas Eve," 1895) was, like *May Night*, taken from a story by Gogol. Both these works are village tales, with love stories and comic-supernatural additions; in both, folk songs play an important part in shaping the musical material.[28]

25. Abraham, *Studies in Russian Music*, pp. 132–41.

26. N. Rimskii-Korsakov, *Letopis' moei muzykal'noi zhizni*; A. Rimskii-Korsakov, *N. A. Rimskii-Korsakov*; Gozenpud, *N. A. Rimskii-Korsakov*; Hofmann, *Rimski-Korsakov*; Iastrebtsev, *Nikolai Andreevich Rimskii-Korsakov*; USSR, Tsentral'nyi gosudarstvennyi literaturnyi arkhiv, *N. A. Rimskii-Korsakov*; Abraham, *Rimsky-Korsakov*; idem, "Satire and Symbolism in *The Golden Cockerel*"; idem, "*Pskovityanka*."

27. There are three versions of *The Maid of Pskov*, with more than twenty years separating the first (1873) from the third (1895). See Abraham, "Pskovityanka."

28. The subject of *Christmas Eve* is the same as that of Tchaikovsky's *Vakula the Smith*. See Taylor, *Gogolian Interludes*.

In 1898 there appeared Rimsky-Korsakov's masterpiece, *Sadko*,[29] an "opera legend," a typical combination of the epic and fantastic in a libretto adapted jointly by the composer and V. I. Bielsky from an eleventh-century legend and drawing much of the musical material from Rimsky-Korsakov's symphonic poem of the same title (1867, with revisions in 1869 and 1891). The score is rich in orchestral and harmonic effects, with the instrumental evocation of an undulating sea and the whole-tone leitmotif for the sea-king's daughter offering two examples. *Sadko* was followed by several experimental works: *Motsart i Salieri* ("Mozart and Salieri"), *Boyarynya Vera Sheloga* (both 1898), and *Tsarskaya nevesta* ("The Tsar's Bride," 1899), the last a real tragedy with arias and concerted numbers in the Italian style, "the old operatic convention of the first half of the nineteenth century decked out with Wagnerian leit-motives and Dargomyzhskian 'melodic recitative' and mildly flavoured here and there with the Russian folk-idiom."[30] *Skazka o Tsare Saltane* ("The Tale of Tsar Saltan," 1900), another fairy story, returned to distinctive national traits in both libretto and music. *Servilia* (1902) and *Pan Voevoda* (1904) were unsuccessful essays in more dramatic plots, with Wagnerian influence in the music. *Kashchey bessmertny* ("Kaschey the Immortal," 1902) was also Wagnerian in technique, with declamatory lines and constant use of leitmotifs, as well as in the redemption idea woven into the legendary story; the music represents Rimsky-Korsakov's extreme excursion in the direction of chromaticism and dissonance.

The last two operas were, with *Sadko*, the most important: *Skazanie o nevidimom grade Kitezhe i deve Fevronii* ("Legend of the Invisible City of Kitezh and The Maiden Fevroniya," 1907) and *Zolotoy petushok* ("The Golden Cockerel," 1909). They were written in the shadow of the Russo-Japanese War, during a period of intense political and revolutionary turmoil, the effects of which weighed heavily upon the composer's career. In 1905, when students (including those at the St. Petersburg Conservatory) protested against government policies and pressed their demands for reform, Rimsky-Korsakov openly endorsed their actions. This antigovernment stand cost him his teaching position at

29. See Tsukkerman, "*Sadko*".

30. Abraham, *Studies in Russian Music*, p. 248.

the conservatory, but it did not silence his opera productions. *Kitezh* has been called "the Russian Parsifal," because of its mystical and symbolical story, based on two ancient legends. But beyond an evident aspiration to combine features of pagan pantheism and orthodox Christianity in the figure of the heroine Fevroniya, the symbolism is vague and not of fundamental importance. *The Golden Cockerel*, from a humorous-fantastic tale of Pushkin, is more objective and ironic, even satirical, but equally unclear as to the detailed application of its moral.

Other than a gradual growth in complexity of idiom and an increasing skill in the fabrication of piquant harmonic and coloristic effects, there is little that can be called an evolution in Rimsky-Korsakov's musical style through his fifteen operas—nothing remotely comparable to the change in Wagner from *Die Feen* to *Parsifal*. Rimsky-Korsakov was a lyrical and pictorial composer, resembling Mendelssohn in exquisiteness of detail as well as in the absence of strongly emotional and dramatic qualities. The realism of Musorgsky was not for him: art, he once said, was "essentially the most enchanting and intoxicating of lies"[31]— a statement that doubtless explains much in his own music. The dramatic force of the last act of *The Maid of Pskov* and the serious musical characterization of Fevroniya in *Kitezh* are exceptional in his work; his original, personal contribution lies in another realm.

> [He] must be granted the quite peculiar power of evoking a fantastic world entirely his own, half-real, half-supernatural, a world as limited, as distinctive and as delightful as the world of the Grimms' fairy-tales or as Alice's Wonderland. It is a world in which the commonplace and matter-of-fact are inextricably confused with the fantastic, naivete with sophistication, the romantic with the humorous, and beauty with absurdity. He was not its inventor, of course; he owed it in the first place to Pushkin and Gogol. But he gave it a queer touch of his own, linking it with Slavonic antiquity and hinting at pantheistic symbolism, which makes it peculiarly his. And musically, of course, he reigns in it undisputed. He invented the perfect music for such a fantastic world: music insubstantial when it was matched with unreal things, deliciously lyrical

---

31. Quoted in Calvocoressi and Abraham, *Masters of Russian Music*, p. 411.

Scene from *The Golden Cockerel* by N. A. Rimsky-Korsakov.

(From *Design in the Theater*)

when it touched reality, in both cases coloured from the most superb palette musician has ever held.[32]

For Rimsky-Korsakov, an opera was primarily a musical rather than a dramatic-literary work; hence the importance of musical design, which frequently dominates both the poetry and the scenic plan (for example, the rondo form in the fourth tableau of *Sadko*). Along with this there is usually a definite association of certain keys with certain moods and, in most of the operas, a consistent use of recurring motives. These are not, as in Wagner, the material out of which a symphonic fabric is developed but rather are melodic fragments (sometimes only a phrase from a large theme) or even inconspicuous harmonic progressions, woven into the opera in a kind of mosaic pattern; they are as often given to the voices as to the orchestra. In the harmony, two distinct idioms are usually found in each opera: one chromatic, fanciful, cunningly contrived, for the imaginary scenes and characters (example 24.4); and the other diatonic, solid, often modal, for the "real" world. The vocal parts, as usual in Russian opera, alternate between melodic recitative and closed aria-like forms. In his lyrical melodies, Rimsky-Korsakov owes much to the model of Glinka; his own melodies are elegant and graceful, though marked by certain persistently recurring formulae. An important factor in his style is the extensive use of folk tunes, and of original tunes of folk-song type; the source or inspiration for many of these was his own collection of Russian folk songs, made in 1876. Church melodies are also occasionally used, notably in *Kitezh*. The oriental idiom, however, is much less extensive and less significant in Rimsky-Korsakov's music than in that of either Balakirev or Borodin. Like all Russian opera composers, he excelled in the depiction of crowd scenes, especially in *The Maid of Pskov* (Act II), *Sadko*, *Kitezh* (Act II and finale), and the humorous ensembles in *May Night*, *Christmas Eve*, and *Sadko*. Above all, of course, he is distinguished for his mastery of orchestral effects, a virtuosity in the treatment of instrumental color such as few composers in history have equaled.

A number of other Russian opera composers of the late nineteenth and early twentieth centuries can be only briefly men-

32. Ibid., p. 422. Quoted by permission of the publisher.

tioned. Eduard Nápravník (1839–1916), as conductor of the St. Petersburg Opera from 1869, was influential in bringing out the works of the native school; the most successful of his own operas was *Dubrovsky* (1895). A pupil of Rimsky-Korsakov, but influenced in opera by Tchaikovsky, was Anton Stepanovich Arensky

Example 24.4: *Sadho*, sc. 2

(Example 24.4 continued)

(1861–1906), composer of *Rafael* (1894). Also under the influence of Tchaikovsky were the operatic works of Mikhail Mikhailovich Ippolitov-Ivanov (1859–1935), Alexander Tikhonovich Grechaninov (1864–1956), and Sergey Vasilievich Rakhmaninov (1873–1943).[33] Sergey Ivanovich Taneyev (1856–1915) produced *Oresteya* ("The Oresteia," 1895), one of the first Russian operas with classical mythology as its subject. This three-act opera is in a severe contrapuntal style, with admixtures of Rubinstein and Tchaikovsky. Influence from the French "impressionist" movement is reflected in Russian opera in the works of Vladimir Ivanovich Rebikov (1866–1920).

THE UKRAINE. Early composers in the Ukraine were Semyon Gulak-Artemovsky (1813–1873),[34] Pyotr Sokalsky (1832–1887),[35] Petro Nistchynsky (1832–1896), Mykola Lysenko (1842–1912), and Mykola Arkas (1852–1909). Gulak-Artemovsky was one of the finest baritone opera singers of this era; his *Zaporozhets za Dunaem* ("A Cossack Beyond the Danube," 1863), in spoken dialogue with simply harmonized songs and choruses, was long popular. Sokalsky's *Osada Dubno* ("The Siege of Dubno," 1878) was an important example of national opera, strongly influenced by the composer's interest in collecting Russian and Ukrainian folk music, an interest not shown in his *Mazepa* (ca. 1859) and *Mayskaya noch* ("May Night," 1876). Lysenko, founder of the Ukrainian School of Music and the chief creator of Ukrainian national opera, used folk melodies in most of his works.[36] His principal opera was *Taras Bulba*, completed by 1890 and performed in 1903, in the Ukrainian language. In addition to several operas for children, he wrote two operas on librettos adapted from Gogol: *Nich pid Rizdvo* ("Christmas Eve," 1883) and *Utoplennitsa* ("The

---

33. In addition to *Aleko*, a student opera, and *Salammbo*, Rakhmaninov wrote two shorter operas, which premiered on the same program at Moscow in 1906; *Francesca da Rimini* and *Skupoi rytsar* ("The Covetous Knight"). See Boelza, ed., *S. V. Rakhmaninov i russkaia opera*; Briantseva, *S. V. Rakhmaninov*; Norris, *Rakhmaninov*; idem, "Rakhmaninov's Student Opera."

34. Kaufmann, *S. S. Gulak-Artemovsky*.

35. Biography by Karysheva.

36. Skalya-Starytsky, *"Mykola Lysenko"*; Durnev, "Narodnaia osnova Tarasa Bul'bi."

Drowned Woman," 1885). His *Natalka-Poltavka* ("Natalie from Poltava," 1889) was also popular.[37]

ARMENIA. Composers of opera in Armenia during the first half of the twentieth century include Armen Tigran Tigranyan (1879–1950) and Alexander Afanasil Spendiaryan (1871–1928).[38] *Anush* (1912), Tigranyan's first opera, established the basis for an Armenian national opera style. Its folklike musical material intensifies the tragic story of Anush and Saro, victims of social injustice and prejudice. *Anush* was an immediate success and has continued to hold a prominent place in the performance repertoire of opera houses in Yerevan (capital of Armenia), Moscow, and Leningrad. The pride and spirit of Armenian life is also present in *David-Bek*, an opera composed by Tigranyan at the end of his career (1949) and performed at Moscow in 1950. The libretto presents an eighteenth-century conflict between Armenians and Persians. Folk songs and dances associated with the warring factions represented in the opera bring to this heroic subject an expression of national realism. Twenty years earlier, Spendiaryan had used this same eighteenth-century Armenian-Persian conflict for his opera *Almast* (Moscow, 1930).

LATVIA, LITHUANIA, AND ESTONIA. A few national operas were produced in the Baltic states after the First World War. In Latvia, an opera company was organized at Riga in 1919. National composers include Alfreds Kalnins (1879–1951), with *Banuta* (1920), the first Latvian opera, and *Dzimtenes Atmoda* ("The Nation's Awakening," 1933), a historical opera; Jāzeps Mediņš (1877–1947), with *Vaidelote* ("The Priestess," 1927); Jānis Mediņš (1890–1966), *Uguns un Nakts* ("Fire and Night," 1921); and Jānis Kalnins (b. 1904), *Hamlet*, (1936).

The first Lithuanian opera, *Biruté*, was composed by

---

37. General works on Ukranian opera are Arkhymovych, *Ukraïns'ka klasychna opera;* idem, *Shiakhy rozvytku ukraïns'koi radians'koi opery;* Dovzhenko, *Narysy z istorii ukrains'koi radians'koi muzyky.* Music in *Ukrainskaia klassicheskaia muzyka: Antologiia klassicheskoi muzyki narodov SSSR* (Moscow: Muzgiz, 1955, no. 1).

38. See At'ayan and Muradian, *Armen Tigranian;* Tigranov, *Aleksandr Spendiarov.* A general work on opera in Armenia is Tigranov, *Armianskii muzykal'nyi teatr.*

Mikas Petrauskas (1873–1937) and staged at Vilnius in 1906. Petrauskas, known primarily for his operettas and Lithuanian revolutionary songs,[39] was forced to leave his homeland for several years because of political unrest. During this period of exile, he visited the United States, where his opera *Egle, Queen of the Snakes* was produced in 1918. The first Lithuanian performance of *Egle* occurred in 1939 at the opera house in Kraunas, where a resident opera company had been established toward the end of 1920. Other Lithuanian operas have been composed by Jurgio Karnavicĭus (b. 1885), whose *Gražina* (1933) is considered the first national opera of Lithuania, and by Antanas Račiūnas (b. 1905), whose *Maryté* (1953) is based on the life of Maryté Melnikaité, a hero of the Soviet Union. Estonian operas have been composed by Arthur Lemba (1885–1963): *Armastus ja Surm* ("Love and Death," Tallinn, 1933, and *Elga* (1934).

Central and Southeastern Europe

POLAND. The early history of opera in Poland is similar to that in Russia, except that the importation of Italian operas began as early as 1628; the first regular court opera was organized five years later and presented a dozen Italian operas and ballets before 1646.[40] A public opera theater was constructed at Warsaw in 1724, but the opere serie of Hasse and other Italian composers failed to win a large following. After 1765, however, a repertoire of French opéra comique and Italian opera (sometimes in Polish translation) in the renamed "National Public Theater" proved more

39. See Gaudrimas, "M. Petrauskas," and the article on Petrauskas in *Great Soviet Encyclopedia*.

40. General works on the history of Polish music include Jachimecki, *Historia muzyki polskiej w zarysie*; idem, *Muzyka polska*; Reiss, *Najpiękniejsza ze wszystkich jest muzyka polska*; Opieński, *La Musique polonaise*. General histories of opera in Poland are Karasowski, *Rys historyczny opery polskiej*; Reiss, *Muzyka w Krakowie w XIX wieku*; Michałowski *Opery polskie* (catalogue and chronology, 1788–1953); Glowacki, "The History of Polish Opera." On the period before Moniuszko, see Bernacki, *Teatr, dramat i muzyka za Stanisława Augusta*; Zetowski, "Teoria polskiej opery narodowej"; Wierzbicka, *Źródła ł do historii teatru warszawskiego*; Opieński, "Les Premiers Opéras polonais".

attractive. The influence of an intense national spirit was evident in Polish opera from the 1770s onward. As in Russia, the first operas in Poland on national themes were in the form of spoken dialogue with songs interspersed. The earliest of such works was *Nedza uszczesliwiona* ("Misery Made Happy"), by Mathias Kamienski (1734–1821), produced at Warsaw in 1778. Another notable early Polish opera was *Cud mniemany czyli Krakowiacy i Górale* ("The Supposed Miracle, or Krakovians and Mountaineers," 1794), by Jan Stafani (1746–1829);[41] this remained popular to the end of the nineteenth century and has been revived several times since; and some of its melodies using Polish dance rhythms (the polonaise in particular) have passed into the realm of national folk song. A prolific if not especially distinguished composer was Jozef Antoni Elsner (1769–1854),[42] whose *Król Lokietek* ("King Lokietek," 1818) is a rescue opera with a libretto reminiscent of *Les Deux Journées*. Elsner, who was Chopin's teacher, held an important position at the Opera in Warsaw, through which he extended his influence in the development of Polish opera. Another influential personage in the early nineteenth century was Karol Kurpiński (1785–1857),[43] with *Jadwiga Królowa Polska* ("Jadwiga, Queen of Poland," 1814), a historical opera on an original Polish libretto, and *Zabobon, czyli Krakowiacy i Górale*, also known by an alternative title, *Nowe Krakowiaki* ("Superstition, or Krakovians and Mountaineers," or "The New Cracovians," 1816), a work in popular style that was quite successful and important in establishing the national style.

The definitive creation of a Polish national school of opera, however, is owed to Stanisław Moniuszko (1819–1872),[44] whose famous *Halka*—first produced at Vilna privately in 1848, them publicly with a staged performance in 1854, and in its final four-act version at Warsaw in 1858—has remained a staple of the Polish opera theater to this day. Curiously, the music of *Halka*

41. See Karasowski, "Jan Stefani"; Niewiadomski, "Z przeszlošci opery polskiej"; Stromenger, "Jan Stefani."

42. Biography by Nowak-Romanowicz.

43. Biography by Pomorska; see also Reiss, "Koryfeusz muzyki polskiej."

44. Biographies by Walicki, Jachimecki, Opieński, Kaczyński, Prosnak, and Rudziński. See also studies by Karasowski, Pozniak, and Rudziński.

does not sound markedly "Polish," at least to a foreigner. The style is rather that of early nineteenth-century romanticism, remarkable for lyric grace of melody, with expressive but unsensational harmonies and transparent instrumentation; yet *Halka*, for all its disarming naïveté, is not devoid of real dramatic force. The conventional recitative-aria form of Moniuszko's operas is modified by the use of transitional passages and recurring themes. Other works by Moniuszko include *Flis* ("The Raftsman," 1858), the comedy *Hrabrina* ("The Countess," 1860), and the semicomic opera *Straszny dwór* ("The Haunted Manor," 1865), next to *Halka* his best and most popular work and one that makes considerable use of recurring motives and places increased emphasis upon choral writing.

Owing to unfavorable political conditions, the promising work begun by Moniuszko did not come to complete fruition in the later part of the nineteenth century. One of the principal composers in this period was Władisław Żeleński (1837–1921),[45] with *Konrad Wallenrod* (1885), a grand opera on a historical subject; *Goplana* (1896), a romantic fairy-tale opera with lyrical melodies and delicate orchestral colors; and *Stara baśń* ("An Old Fairy Tale," 1907), in which the influence of both Weber and Wagner is conspicuous. Others who came to a greater or lesser degree under the Wagnerian spell were Zygmunt Noskowski (1846–1909),[46] Henryk Jarecki (1846–1918), and Roman Statkowski (1859–1925). Jarecki, conductor at the important opera theater of Lwów, continued the nationalistic spirit of his teacher, Moniuszko, by writing operas based upon Polish literature and history. Most of Jarecki's scores, however, are no longer available for study. Noskowski, remembered especially for his writing of symphonic poems, moved into the realm of the music drama with his *Hanusia, lub Dia świętej* ("Hanusia, or For the Holy Country,") produced at Warsaw in 1890. His *Livia Quintilla*, performed at Lwów in 1898, was also successful. Statkowski's *Filenis* (1903), a prize-winning work in an international competition, and *Maria* (1906) exhibit a style that was somewhere between pre-Wagnerian and the Wagnerian music drama. This same genera-

---

45. Biographies by Szopski and Jachimecki. See also Paderewski, *"Konrad Wallenrod"*; Niewiadomski, "W. Żeleński i jego *Goplana.*"

46. Chybiński, "Zygmunt Noskowski"; Sutkowski, *Zygmunt Noskowski.*

tion of composers also included Ignace Jan Paderewski (1860–1941), more celebrated as a pianist than for his one opera, *Manru* (1901),[47] and Miecyslaw Soltys (1863–1929). A new generation showing more progressive tendencies began to be heard from after the restoration of Polish independence in 1919.

CZECHOSLOVAKIA. The father of Bohemian music was Bedřich Smetana (1824–1884), whose first great success came in 1866 with *Prodaná nevěsta* ("The Bartered Bride").[48] This melodious comic opera, so permeated with the rhythms and spirit of national music, has become famous all over the world. Although Smetana did not begin writing operas until late in his career, he nevertheless produced a wide variety of stage works, ranging from singspiel to tragedy. *Hubička* ("The Kiss," 1876) and *Tajemstvi* ("The Secret," 1878), both comic operas, showed advances in technical skill and were almost as successful in the composer's own country as *The Bartered Bride*. Smetana's serious operas, especially *Dalibor* (1868) and *Libuše* (composed 1872, performed 1881), were attacked by patriotic critics because of their use of certain procedures associated with Wagner, such as leitmotifs and the declamatory character of the vocal parts. But the alleged Wagnerisms hardly ever penetrated to the substance of the music, which remained stoutly individual. *Libuše*, in particular, was very nationalistic; its subject concerned the founding of the Bohemian dynasty and proclaimed the glory of the Czech nation.[49]

The leader of the next generation of Bohemian composers, Antonin Dvořák (1841–1904),[50] was primarily a symphonic rather than a dramatic musician, though several of his ten operas

47. Niewiadomski, *"Manru."*

48. Pražák, *Smetanovy zpěvohry*; Nejedlý, *Bedřich Smetana*; idem, *Zpěvohry Smetanovy*; Smetana, *Smetana in Briefen*; Abraham, "The Genesis of *The Bartered Bride*"; Large, *Smetana*; Clapham, *Smetana*.

49. General histories of Czech music include Hostinský, *Die Musik in Böhmen*; Soubies, *Histoire de la musique en Bohême*; Helfert, *Geschichte der Musik in der tschechoslovakischen Republik*; Nejedlý, *Dějiny opery Národního divadla*. General works on Czech opera: Teuber, *Geschichte des Prager Theaters*; Hnilička, *Kontury vývoje hudby poklasické v Čechách*; Boelza, *Cheshskaia opernaia klassika*; Hoza, *Opera na Slovensku*. Principal composers before Smetana were František Skroup (1801–1862), František Skuherský (1830–1892), Karel Sebor (1845–1903), Karel Bendl (1838–1897), and Vilém Blodek (1834–1874). For others, see Alder, *Handbuch der Musikgeschichte*, 2:925.

50. See Šourek, *Život a dílo Antonína Dvořáka*, and studies in English by Fischl, ed., Robertson, Sourek, and Clapham.

were successful at Prague. *Šelma sedlák* ("The Cunning Peasant," 1878) was inspired by Smetana's *The Bartered Bride*. *Čert a Káča* ("The Devil and Kate," 1899) was Dvořák's most popular work in the comic style. In serious opera, he underwent the influence first of Meyerbeer and then of Wagner; the height of his achievement in this field was attained in a late work, *Rusalka* (1901), the libretto of which was well adapted to his lyrical powers. Another important figure in Bohemian music was Zdenko Fibich (1850–1900),[51] a prolific composer who, more internationally minded than either Smetana or Dvořák, came fully under the influence of romanticism and the Wagnerian music drama. He was noted especially for the classical trilogy *Hippodamie* (1890–91), set entirely as a melodrama—that is, orchestral music accompanying or alternating with a spoken text, a form established by the eighteenth-century Bohemian composer Georg Benda (see chapter 15). Two of his best operas were *Nevěsta mesinská* ("The Bride of Messima," 1884), considered the finest Czech tragedy of the nineteenth century, and *Šárka* (1897), based on a story from Czech mythology. Other composers of this generation were Vojtěch Hřímalý (1842–1908), with *Zakletý princ* ("The Enchanted Prince," 1872); Joseph Nešvera (1842–1914), with *Lesni vzduch* ("Woodland Air," 1897); and Hanuš Trneček (1858–1914), whose *Die Geigenmacher von Cremona* ("The Violin Maker of Cremona") was performed at the Schwerin court in 1886.

Bohemian composers of the late nineteenth and early twentieth centuries include Joseph Bohuslav Foerster (1859–1951),[52] whose most successful operas were *Eva* (1889) and *Jessika* (1905). Four pupils of Fibich also made their mark in Bohemian opera: Karl Kovařovic (1862–1920), with *Na starém belidle* ("The Old Bleaching House," 1901); and Karel Weis (1862–1944), Antonin Horák (1875–1910), and Otakar Ostrčil (1879–1949), with *Poupě* ("The Bud," 1912). An influential composer and teacher was Vitězlav Novák (1870–1949),[53] with four operas, of which the most important was *Zvikovský rarášek* ("The Imp of Zvikov," 1915).

51. Rektorys, ed., *Zdeněk Fibich*; Hudec, *Zdeněk Fibich* (with extensive bibliography).

52. Foerster, *Der Pilger* and *J. B. Foerster*.

52. Štěpán, *Novák a Suk*; see also Newmarch, *The Music of Czechoslovakia*.

HUNGARY. The founder of opera in Hungary was Ferenc Erkel (1810–1893), whose *Hunyady László* (1844) holds the same position in its country as do *A Life for the Tsar* in Russia and *Halka* in Poland; and Erkel's other operas were almost equally popular, especially *Bánk bán* (1861).[54] Another important national composer was Mihály Mosonyi (1814–1870), whose chief opera, *Szép Ilonka* ("Fair Ilonka"), was produced in 1861. Others of the early nationalist group were Andreas Bartay (1798–1856), whose *Csel* ("The Trick," 1839) was the first original Hungarian comic opera; and August von Adelburg (1830–1873), with the successful opera *Zrinyi* in 1868. Later nationalists included Jenö Hubay (1858–1937), a celebrated violinist and prolific composer, whose principal opera, *A Cremonai Hegedüs* ("The Luthier of Cremona," 1894), is still given; and Ede Poldini (1869–1957), with the comic opera *A csavargó és királylány* ("The Vagabond and the Princess," 1903). The works of Odön Mihalovich (1842–1929) were Germanic and Wagnerian in musical style, even when on Hungarian librettos, such as *Toldi szerelme* ("Toldi's Love," 1893); and a pronounced flavor of German romanticism is heard in the operas of Géza Zichy (1849–1924), whose most ambitious undertaking was a trilogy on the life of Rákóczi (produced at Budapest, 1905–1912).[55]

ROMANIA AND YUGOSLAVIA. The principal opera composers of Romania have been Eduard Caudella (1841–1924), whose *Petra Rareş* (1889) was one of the first Romanian national operas; Sabin Drăgoi (1894–1968), a pupil of Dvořák and Janáček, with a sophisticated modern use of Romanian folk song in *Napasta* ("The Plague," 1927); Georges Enesco (1881–1955), with one opera, *Oedipe* (1931); and Paul Constantinescu (1909–1963), with *O noapte furtunoasă* ("O Stormy Night," 1934).[56]

One of the first composers of Croatian opera was Vatroslav Lisinskij (1819–1854), with *Ljubav i Zloba* ("Love and

54. See Eősze, *Az opera útja*, pp. 465–96; Ábrányi, *Erkel Ferenc élete és müködese*; Bónis, *Mosonyi Mihály*; idem, "Die ungarischen Opern M. Mosonyi's"; and articles in *Zenetudományi tanulmanyok* (1954), 2:25–174, 175–218; (1955), 4:211–72; (1961), 9:81–158, 169–96.

55. Zichy, *Aus meinem Leben*.

56. See Cosma, *Opera romînească*.

Malice," 1846) and *Porin* (composed, 1851; staged, 1897). Ivan Zajc (1832–1914), known also as Giovanni von Zaytz, was director of opera at Zagreb for more than three decades. Representative of his several hundred works for the stage is *Nikola Subic Zrinsk* (1876). Other composers include Petar Konjović (1883–1970), with *Kostana* (1931); Krešimir Baranović (1894–1975), with *Striženo-Košeno* ("Shorn-Head," 1932); and Jukov Gotovac (b. 1895), with *Morana* (1930) and *Ero s onoga svijeta* ("Ero the Joker," 1935).

Among opera composers of importance in Serbia were Davorin Jenko (1835–1914),[57] whose many works for the theater include *Vračara* ("The Sorceress," 1882), the first Serbian operetta, and *Pribislav i Božana* (1894), a melodrama; Alexander Savine (1881–1949), with *Xenia*, (1919); and Stanislav Biničik (1872–1942), whose *Na uranku* ("At Dawn," 1903) is considered the first Serbian national opera.

GREECE AND TURKEY. A nationalist of Greece was Manolis Kalomiris (1883–1962), whose *Protomastoros* ("The Master Builder," 1916) was the first opera by a Greek on a Greek subject; his later works include *To dachtylidi tis manas* ("Mother's Ring," 1917; revised, 1939) and a festival opera with choruses on a historical subject, *Constantinos o Palaeologos*—the last Byzantine emperor, who ruled from 1448 to 1453—first performed in the theater of Herod Atticus at Athens in the summer of 1962.

The first Turkish operas, *Tas Babek* and *Kerem*, by Ahmed Adnan Saygun (b. 1907), were produced at Ankara in 1934 and 1957, respectively.

The Low Countries and Scandinavia

THE NETHERLANDS. The earliest Dutch opera, *De Triomferende min* ("Love's Triumph"), by Carolus Hacquart (ca. 1649–ca. 1730), was published in 1680, but its first performance took place only

---

57. Cvetko, *Davorin Jenko.*

in 1920 at Arnhem. During the nineteenth century, when the Netherlands was largely under the musical domination of Germany, a few national operas were produced.[58] Among composers of this period were Richard Hol (1825–1904), with *Floris V* (1892); Cornelis van der Linden (1839–1918), *Leiden ontzet* ("The Relief of Leiden," 1893); Henry Brandts-Buys (1851–1905), *Albrecht Beiling* (1881); Karl Dibbern (b. 1855), *Odja* (1901); Emile van Brucken-Fock (1857–1944), *Seleneia* (1895); Cornelis Dopper (1870–1939), *Het Eerekruis* ("The Cross of Honor," 1903); and Charles Grelinger (1873–ca. 1943), with the successful opera *Op Hoop van Zegen* ("On Board the 'Hope of Blessing'," 1907). Jan Brandts-Buys (1868–1933)—*Die Schneider von Schönau* ("The Tailors of Schönau," Dresden, 1916)—was more German than Dutch, but national traits appeared in the realistic-satiric operas of Hol's pupil Johan Wagenaar (1862–1941); his *Doge van Venetie* ("The Doge of Venice," 1904) and *De Cid* (1916) are serious operas.

BELGIUM. Flemish opera composers of the nineteenth and early twentieth centuries were: Joseph Mertens (1834–1901), *De zwaarte Kapitein* ("The Stalwart Captain," 1877); Peter Benoit (1834–1901), *Le Roi des Aulnes* ("The King of Aulnes," 1859) and *Isa* (1867); Jan Blockx (1851–1912),[59] *De Herbergprinses* (1896) and *De Bruid der Zee* ("The Bride of the Sea," 1901); Paul Gilson (1865–1942), *Prinses Zonneschijn* (1903); and Auguste de Boeck (1865–1937), *La Route d'Emeraude* ("The Emerald Route," 1921).[60]

DENMARK. Denmark, like Holland, has been to a large extent a musical province of Germany. The German composer Franz Gläser (1798–1861) wrote three operas to Danish texts. The earliest national opera composers were Johan Hartmann (1805–1900), with *Liden Kirsten* (1846); Henrik Rung (1807–1871), *Stormen paa København* (1845); Siegried Saloman (1816–1899), *Diamant-*

---

58. Reeser, *Een eeuw Nederlandse muziek*; Bottenheim, *De opera in Nederland*; Dresden, *Het muziekleven in Nederland sinds 1880.*

59. See Van den Borren, *Peter Benoit*; F. Blockx, *Jan Blockx.*

60. Closson and Van den Borren, eds., *La Musique en Belgique*; Corbet, ed., *De vlaamse Muziek sedert Benoit.*

korset (1847); and Peter Arnold Heise (1830–1879), *Drot og marsk* ("King and Marshal," 1878). Four operas by Peter Erasmus Lange-Müller (1850–1926) were produced at Copenhagen, including *Spanske studenter* ("The Spanish Students, 1883). One of the most successful Danish comic operas was *Maskarade* (1906), Carl August Nielsen (1865–1931).[61] The most prolific Danish opera composer was August Enna (1859–1939); representative works are *Heksen* ("The Witch," 1892), *Kleopatra* (1894), and *Den lille pige med svovlstik-kerne* ("The Match Girl," 1897).

NORWAY. The first Norwegian opera was *Fjeldeventyret* ("A Mountain Adventure," 1825), an opéra comique by Waldemar Thrane (1790–1828).[62] Several decades later came *Fredkulla* ("The Peacemaker," 1858) and *Junkeren og Flubergrosen* ("The Knight and the Fluberg Sprite," 1867), by Martin Andreas Udbye (1820–1899), and in 1894 *Fra gamle Dage* ("Of Golden Days"), the first of five operas by Johannes Haarklou (1847–1925). Ole Olsen (1850–1927) wrote four operas, one of which, *Lajla*, was performed at Christiania (now Oslo) in 1908. Gerhard Schjelderup (1859–1933), though of Norwegian birth, composed most of his operas to German texts; the same is true of Sigwardt Aspestrand (1856–1941). Catherinus Elling (1858–1942) wrote one opera, *Kosakkerne* ("The Cossacks," 1897).

SWEDEN. Sweden from the seventeenth century had been in touch with the general development of opera in Europe.[63] Italian, French, and German subjects and musical styles, as might be expected, dominated Swedish opera houses in the late eighteenth and early nineteenth centuries. The earliest attempt at an opera on a Swedish historical subject was made by Carl Stenborg, in *Konung Gustaf Adolphs Jagt* ("King Gustavus Adolphus's Hunting Party") in 1777, a "comedy mingled with songs," imitated from Collet's opéra comique *La Partie de chasse de Henri* IV, part of which had been used by Weisse and Hiller for their popular singspiel

---

61. Biographies of Nielsen by Meyer and Dolleris. See also Fabricius, *Carl Nielsen*.

62. Kindem, *Den norske operas historie*; Benestad, *Waldemar Thrane*.

63. See Moberg, "Essais d'opéras en Suède"; Engländer, *Joseph Martin Kraus*; Sundström, "Franz Berwalds Operor."

Die Jagd in 1770.[64] The first grand opera in Swedish was *Thetis och Pelée* (1773), by the Italian composer Francesco Antonio Uttini (1723–1795). Swedish opera composers in the early and middle nineteenth century included Franz Berwald (1796–1868),[65] J. N. Ahlström (1805–1857), Adolf Lindblad (1801–1878), and Johan August Södermann (1832–1876). Some German composers in this period also occasionally wrote operas to Swedish texts.

A more definitely national type of Swedish opera, using native legends and folk melodies, appeared toward the end of the nineteenth century in the works of Ivar Hallström (1826–1901); one of his works was *Den Bergtagna* ("The Mountain Ghost," 1874). Nationalism was temporarily pushed aside by the desire to emulate the Wagnerian music drama, as in the early operas of Andreas Hallén (1846–1925), such as *Harald Viking* (Leipzig, 1881), though more independent traits are evident in his *Waldemarsskatten* ("Waldemar's Treasure"), written for the opening of the Stockholm Opera House in 1899. A Wagner propagandist in Sweden was Richard Henneberg (1853–1925), who wrote a comic opera, *Drottningen's Pilgrimage*, in 1882. A combination of the Wagner style with national melodies is found in the operas of Wilhelm Stenhammar (1871–1927): *Tirfing*, 1898, and *Gildet på Solhaug* ("The Festival at Solhaug," Stuttgart, 1899). A more decisive step toward national opera, though still on a Wagnerian basis, was *Arnljot* (1910), with text and music by Olof Wilhelm Peterson-Berger (1867–1942).[66] Both Natanaël Berg (1879–1957) and Kurt Atterberg (1887–1974) produced operas, though they were distinguished chiefly in the field of the symphony. A notable opera composer of their generation was Ture Rangström (1884–1947), who wrote *Kronbruden* ("The Crown Bride," Stuttgart, 1919, and Stockholm, 1922), based on a drama by Strindberg.

FINLAND. In Finland there was no national opera before the twentieth century. *Kung Carls Jakt* ("King Charles's Hunting Party"), by Fredrik Pacius (1809–1891), performed at Helsinki in 1852 and sometimes called the "first Finnish opera," was by a

64. See Lindström, "Vårt första nationalla Sångspel."
65. Biography by Layton.
66. Biography by Carlberg.

German-born composer and on a Swedish text.[67] The first opera composed to Finnish words was *Pohjan Neiti* ("The Maid of Bothnia"), by Oskar Merikanto (1868–1924);[68] it was performed at Viipuri in 1908. Merikanto's subsequent works, *Elinan Surma* ("Elina's Death," 1910) and *Regina von Emmeritz* (1920), were somewhat influenced by Italian verismo methods. Other composers of this period were Erkki Gustaf Melartin (1875–1937), with *Aino* (1909), and Selim Palmgren (1878–1951), *Daniel Hjort* (1910), on a Swedish text. A more distinctly national style, with folk melodies and recitative rhythms adapted to the Finnish language, was exemplified by Armas Launis (1884–1959) in *Seitsemän veljestä* ("The Seven Brothers," 1913 and *Kullervo*, 1917). Another Finnish folk-song scholar, Ilmari Krohn (1867–1960), produced the opera *Tuhotulva* ("The Deluge") at Helsinki in 1928. Important Finnish operas by Leevi Madetoja (1887–1947), a pupil of D'Indy, are *Pohjalaisia* ("The East Bothnians," 1924) and *Juha* (1935).[69]

Spain and Latin America

SPAIN. With the demise of the zarzuela in favor of the tonadilla in the last half of the eighteenth century and the subsequent disappearance of the tonadilla in the first half of the nineteenth century (see chapter 15), Spanish national opera went into an eclipse from which it did not emerge until about 1850.[70] The first signs of reaction against the reign of Italian opera and French opéra comique in Spanish theaters appeared in the satirical writings of Manuel Breton de los Herreros and in the works of a resident Italian composer, Basilio Basili, who in the late thirties and early

67. See Loewenberg, *Annals of Opera.*

68. Biography by Suomalainen.

69. Several Finnish opera composers were represented at the Metropolitan Opera in the summer of 1983: Joonas Kokkonen, Aulis Sallinen, and Einojuhani Rautavaara.

70. For general surveys, see Chase, *The Music of Spain;* Salazar, *La música contemporánea en España;* Trend, *A Picture of Modern Spain;* Peña y Goñi, *La ópera española;* Subirá, *Historia y anecdotario del Teatro Real;* idem, *El Teatro del Real Palacio;* Muñoz, *Historia de la zarzuela.* See also the references in chap. 15.

forties brought out at Madrid a number of comic operas in Spanish. These two men, in collaboration, produced *El novio y el concierto* (1839), a one-act farcical composition labeled a "zarzuela-comedia," thus reviving the ancient Spanish designation. Other farcical zarzuelas by Basili followed and within a decade the new zarzuela was flourishing, in a form derived from the eighteenth-century tonadilla, using music of a light, popular, national style with admixture of some French and Italian elements. Many of the early librettos were from French sources—an instance of the influence which France has constantly exerted on national Spanish music.

The leading composer of this first period of the revival was Francisco Asenjo Barbieri (1823–1894), who produced over seventy zarzuelas between 1850 and 1880, including the classic work of this type, *Pan y toros* ("Bread and Bulls," 1864).[71] This and other zarzuelas of Barbieri were long popular and have been influential on the development of national music in both Spain and South America. The principal contemporaries of Barbieri were Rafael José María Hernando (1822–1888), Joaquin Gaztambide (1822–1870), Emilio Arriete y Corera (1823–1894), and Cristóbal Oudrid y Segura (1829–1877), who produced in *El molinero de Subiza* ("The Miller of Subiza," 1870) one of the most popular works of that year.

In 1857, the Teatro de la Zarzuela was founded by a group of writers in Madrid to enhance and encourage performance of their works. Two distinct types of zarzuela developed at Madrid, corresponding to the two types of French opéra comique that evolved during the nineteenth century.[72] One was the *zarzuela grande*, usually in three acts, which might be on a serious subject and even in some cases approach the scale and style of grand opera. Barbieri's *Jugar con fuego* ("To Play with Fire," 1851) is an important early example. The other type was the *género chico*—comic, popular, informal, often quite ephemeral pieces in one act, which were produced in immense numbers throughout the century and indeed have continued up to the present day. Most composers of the later nineteenth century wrote zarzuelas of

71. Biography by Salcedo.
72. Mindlin, *Die Zarzuela*.

both types. Some of the most popular works of the genero chico were *La gran vía* ("The Great Road," 1886), by Federico Chueca (1846–1908) in collaboration with Joaquín Valverde (1846–1910); *La viejecita* ("The Old Woman," 1897), by Manuel Fernandez-Caballero (1835–1906); *La bruja* ("The Witch," 1887) and *La revoltosa* ("The Revolutionary Girl," 1897), by Ruperto Chapí y Lorente (1851–1909); and above all *La verbena de la paloma* ("The Festival of Our Lady of the Dove," 1894) by Tomas Bretón y Hernández (1850–1923).[73]

Along with the rise of the popular zarzuela came a growing desire for a national serious opera in Spain. Spanish composers of the earlier nineteenth century had rarely used Spanish texts or national subjects, and their music seldom had anything differentiating it from the contemporary Italian style. A solitary early crusader for Spanish opera was Joaquín Espín y Guillén (1812–1881), one act of whose *Padilla, o El asedio de Medina* ("Padilla; or, The Siege of Medina") was performed at Madrid in 1845. Later in the century, however, the zarzuela composers interested themselves in the task of creating a more permanent and artistic form of national lyric drama than could be made of the género chico pieces to which they owed their popular success. Barbieri had definite ideas on the subject; Arriete, who had composed a number of Italian operas, expanded his two-act zarzuela *Marina* (1855) into a three-act Spanish opera with recitatives (1871). Chapí wrote several serious zarzuelas, including *La tempestad* ("The Tempest," 1882) and *Curro Vargas* ("Vargas the Dandy," 1898), as well as operas—e.g., *Margarita la tornera* ("Margarita, the Nunnery Doorkeeper," 1909), but his genius was for the comic rather than the serious, although the popularity of his serious zarzuelas has endured into the 1980s. Bretón, who had also written Italian operas, composed a Spanish opera, *La Dolores*, in 1895. Still another composer of this period was Emilio Serrano y Ruiz (1850–1939), with the operas *Irene de Otranto* in 1891 and *Gonzalo de Córdoba* (to his own text) in 1898.

The honorable title of "father of modern Spanish music" belongs to Felipe Pedrell (1841–1922), distinguished scholar, composer of operas and symphonic and choral works, and teacher

---

73. Salcedo, *Tomás Bretón*.

or mentor of most of the Spanish composers of the following generation.[74] Pedrell combined a deep feeling for the qualities of Spanish folk song and the great Spanish music of the past with a romantic-mystical temperament which led him frequently onto paths where the general public could not follow. He was a greater idealist than composer, and his beneficent influence on Spanish music is out of all proportion to the very slight outward success of his own works. He was dubbed "the Spanish Wagner" and his most successful opera was called "the Spanish *Tristan*." These encomiums exaggerate the resemblance of his work to Wagner's. That there was some influence is unquestionable, but the examples of Glinka, Musorgsky, and the other Russian opera composers were at least equally potent. As a matter of fact, if comparisons must be made, the composer whom Pedrell most closely resembles is D'Indy. The likeness is one of both temperament and musical style: each was irresistibly drawn into the orbit of Wagner; each, being an ardent nationalist and an artist of high ethical purpose, adapted the technique of the music drama for his own aims; and each succeeded in being individual in spite of this debt. D'Indy was a better technician than Pedrell and was more at home in the realm of purely musical expression; Pedrell, on the other hand, drew his musical idiom from more varied sources.

Pedrell wrote ten operas,[75] the most important of which is *Los Pirineos* ("The Pyrenees"), a trilogy in three acts with prologue, composed to a Catalan text by Victor Balaguer in 1890–91 and first performed in Italian translation at Barcelona in 1902.[76] The poem offers a number of effective scenes, but on the whole its nature is more that of an epic than of a dramatic work. Pedrell's setting is unified by the use of leitmotifs. An idea of his style may be gained from example 24.5, part of the funeral march in the second act. The orchestra has a much less conspicuous position than in Wagner, and the voice parts are nearly always me-

74. Studies by Tebaldini, Curzon, and Istel; Pedrell, *Jornadas postreras* (autobiography) and *Jornadas de arte*; catalogue by Reiff, "Ein Katalog"; Subirá, "Felipe Pedrell."

75. Two of his comedies, *Eda* (1884) and *Little Carmen* (in English), were commissioned for performances in New York City.

76. Pedrell was so anxious to have this trilogy understood that he wrote a book to explain the opera: *Por nuestra música*, The prologue received its initial performance in 1897 in Venice.

Example 24.5: *Los Pirineos*, Act II

lodic. An important proportion of the score is given over to set pieces, which appear in great variety. The composer's scholarly conscience is shown in his evident care to reproduce as authentically as possible the oriental idiom in the solos of the heroine, "Moon-Ray"; the scene of the Love Court in Act I offers modern adaptations of trouvère and troubadour art forms—*tenso, lai,* and *sirventes.* There are quotations from plainsong and from sixteenth-century Spanish church composers, and the excellent choral writing throughout the opera should be especially mentioned. The prologue in particular would make a very effective concert number for a choral society.

It is too much to claim that Pedrell is to be numbered among the greatest opera composers. His dramatic sense often failed him. Too many pages of *Los Pirineos* are thin in inspiration, repetitious, and lacking in rhythmic vitality and variety. But, out of a sincere artist's soul, enough moments of greatness have emerged to make his work an honor to its composer and country and to entitle it to at least an occasional performance, even if in a shortened version.

The national spirit which Pedrell did so much to inspire achieved worldwide recognition in the piano music of two of his pupils, Isaac Albéniz (1860–1909) and Enrique Granados (1867–1916).[77] Both these composers essayed opera, but without important results. Albéniz, apparently under a mistaken notion of his own gifts, and also instigated by a wealthy English patron who fancied himself a dramatic author, devoted several years to writing operas in a heavy, pseudo-Wagnerian style but finally obtained a moderate success with a comic work, *Pepita Jiménez* (1896). Granados, like many of his contemporaries, was interested in trying to re-create the spirit of Madrid as typified in Goya, and the music of his principal opera, *Goyescas* (New York, 1916), was expanded from a series of piano pieces of the same title. The plot of this opera has a strong tinge of Italian verismo.

In addition to his influence on what may be called the main stream of modern Spanish opera, Pedrell is also the founder of the regional school of Catalonia. The leading figure in this school was Jaime Pahissa (1880–1969), composer of *La presó de Lleida* ("The Prison of Lérida," 1906), which was rewritten as a three-act opera, *La Princesa Margarida*, and *Gala Placidia* (1913). Other Catalan composers are Enric Morera (1865–1942),[78] with *Emporium*, (1906); Juan Lamote de Grignon (1872–1949, *Hesperia* (1907); and Juan Manén (1883–1971), *Nerón y Acté*, 1928.

Independent regional development is characteristic of Spanish music, but the only extensive regional opera outside Catalonia is found in the Basque country. The oustanding composer here was José María Usandizaga ;(1887–1915), with the nationalistic *Mendi-Mendyian* (1910) and the successful Puccinian melodramatic opera *Las golondrinas* ("The Swallows," 1914). Another Basque composer was Jesús Guridi (1886–1961), whose national folk opera *Mirentxu* (1915) was followed by a more ambitious work

77. Laplane, *Albéniz*; Collet, *Albéniz et Granados*; and studies by Boladeres Ibern and Subirá.

78. Biography by Iglesias.

with some Wagnerian traits, *Amaya*, and a successful zarzuela, *El Caserio* ("The Hamlet"), in 1926.[79]

PORTUGAL. The early history of dramatic music in Portugal is similar to that of Spain, except that there was no distinct national form of as great importance as the tonadilla.[80] The first opera in Portuguese was *La vida do grande D. Quixote de la Mancha* (1733), by Antonio José da Silva (1705–1739), an isolated attempt which led to nothing. Italian opera came to Portugal as early as 1682, but its flourishing period began only in about 1720. Of the Portuguese composers who devoted themselves to writing in the Italian style, the chief was Marcos Antonio Portugal (1762–1830), whose thirty-five operas were widely performed in Europe in the late eighteenth and early nineteenth centuries. He was also the composer of twenty-one comic operas to Portuguese texts. Italian and French opera continued to dominate the Portuguese stage throughout the nineteenth century; *Eurico* (1870), by Miguel Pereira (1843–1901), with Italian text arranged from a Portuguese novel, is typical of this tendency. Native composers only occasionally adopted their own language or musical idiom, except for comic pieces. In this genre, however, there were successful works by Antonio Luiz Miró (d. 1853), *A marqueza* (1848); Guilherme Cossoul (1828–80), *A cisterna do diablo* ("The Devil's Cistern," 1850); Francisco Alves Rente (1851–1891), *Verde gaio* ("Light Yellow," 1876); and Domingo Cyriaco de Cardoso (1846–1900), *O burro do Senhor Alcaide* ("The Mayor's Donkey," 1891). An outstanding nationalist composer was Alfredo Keil (1850–1907). Three of his operas—*Susana* (1883), *Donna Bianca* (1888), and *Irene* (1893)—have Italian texts; *Serrana* (1899), an *ópera cómica*, has a Portuguese libretto, the first major opera to use that language. The principal later composer of operas in Portugal was Rui Coelho (b. 1892), whose works span the period from 1913 to 1970.

79. See Arozamena, *Jesús Guridi*.

80. See *Theatro comico portuguez*; "The Music of Portugal," in Chase, *Music in Spain*, chap. 28; Vieira, *Diccionario biographico de musicos portuguezes*; Fonseco Benevides, *O real theatro de S. Carlos de Lisboa*; Lavignac, *Encyclopédie*, 4:2422–35, 2447–57.

LATIN AMERICA. Opera in Spanish America has been for the most part an offshoot of Italian and Spanish opera.[81] In the colonial period, missionaries promoted plays with music, and at large centers (for example, Lima) there were performances with music of the works of Calderón and other Spanish dramatists. The earliest extant opera composed in the New World seems to have been *La púrpura de la rosa* ("The Purple of the Rose"),[82] a one-act multiscene work based on a libretto by Calderón with music by Tomás de Torrejón y Velasco (1644–1728).[83] *La púrpura de la rosa*, commissioned to celebrate the birthday of Philip V, was performed in 1701 at the viceroyal palace in Lima. The beginning of the eighteenth century also saw the introduction of Italian opera, interesting examples of which include *El mejor escudo de Perseo* (Lima, 1708), by Rogue Ceruti (ca. 1683–1760), and *La partenope* (Mexico City, 1711) with libretto by Silvio Stampiglia and music by Manuel de Zumaya (ca. 1678–1756).[84] A few tonadillas were brought from Spain during this colonial period, but they exerted little influence over the Italian-dominated theatrical events.

Regular seasons of opera did not begin in Latin America

81. Chase, *A Guide to the Music of Latin America*; Béhague, *Music in Latin America* (with annotated bibliography); Kuss, *Latin American Music: An Annotated Bibliography*; Slonimsky, *Music of Latin America*; Stevenson, *Music in Mexico*; idem, "Opera Beginnings in the New World"; idem, *The Music of Peru*; Fiorda Kelly, *Cronología de las óperas*; Acquarone, *História da música brasileira*; Corrêa de Azevedo, *150 anos de música no Brasil*; Ayesterán, *Crónica de una temporada musical en el Montevideo de 1830*; Abascal Brunet, *Apuntes para la historia del teatro en Chile*; Abascal Brunet and Pereira Salas, *Pepe Vila [1861–1936]: La zarzuela chica en Chile*; Salas and Feo Calcaño, *Sesquicentenario de la ópera en Caracas*; Sixto Prieto, "El Perú en la música escénica" (with bibliography of scores and librettos of operas, ballets, etc., the subjects of which relate to Peru); Saldívar, *História de la música en México*; Romero, *La ópera en Yucatán*; Maria y Campos, *Una temporada de ópera italiana en Oaxaca*; Tolón and González, *Operas cubanas y sus autores*; Sáez, *El teatro en Puerto Rico*. See also *Handbook of Latin American Studies*; *Boletín latino-americano de música*; *Rivista brasileira de música*; *Latin American Music Review*; *Yearbook for Inter-American Musical Research*.

82. Stevenson, *Foundations of New World Opera* (includes a facsimile and transcription of the opera).

83. Another opera based upon the same libretto is *Celos aun del aire matan* (1660) by Juan Hidalgo. (See chap. 15.)

84. The libretto for the 1711 production was printed in Italian and Spanish; the score for this full-length opera has not survived. For an interesting comparison of early eighteenth-century versions of *La partenope*, see Freeman, "The Travels of Partenope." See also Baqueiro Fóster, "La Música" (part 3), for a survey of opera in Mexico from 1711 to 1960.

before the second quarter of the nineteenth century, a period marked by expression of national independence. Italian opera continued to dominate the stage during the first half of the century, but at the same time the production of operas by native composers increased significantly. In Brazil, the initial phase of this nationalistic activity was sparked by *Le due gemelle* (1809), by José Mauricio (1767–1830),[85] which is the earliest example (no longer extant) of an opera by a Brazilian composer, and by Marcos Portugal's revivals of his Italian operas created originally for Lisbon and other cities of Europe. These revivals included *L'oro non compra amore* ("Gold Does Not Buy Love") in 1811, the year of Portugal's arrival in Brazil, and *Artaserse* in 1812. Portugal, well known on both sides of the Atlantic for his Portuguese comic operas, wrote *A saloia namorada* ("A Country Girl in Love") specifically for production in Brazil in 1812.

The establishment of a national opera company in 1857 moved Brazil closer to its goal of presenting operas by native composers, as evidenced by the 1860 production of *A noite de São João* ("The Night of St. John"), by Elias Alvares Lôbo (1834–1901). The most famous Latin America opera composer of the nineteenth century was Carlos Gomes (1836–1896), a Brazilian who studied in Italy and produced at Milan in 1870 his masterpiece, *Il Guarany*, a work still given in Brazil and Italy.[86] Although Gomes chose national subjects for some of his operas and endeavored also to introduce national elements in his music—for example, in *Lo schiavo* ("The Slave," Rio de Janeiro, 1889)—he was too strongly inclined to the Italian style to be entirely successful. A like inclination is evident in the music of Henrique Eulalio Gurjão (1833–1885), whose best-known opera was *Idalia* (1881). Leopold Miguez (1850–1902) was influenced by Wagner in *Os Saldunes* (1901). Even the nationalistic composer Alberto Nepomuceno (1864–1920), whose instrumental works promoted a national musical identity for Brazil, did not develop an independent musical style in his operas.

---

85. The composer is also known by his full name: José Mauricio Nunes Garcia.

86. Biographies by Gomes Vaz de Carvalho and by Brito. See also studies by Seidl, Marchant, Andrade, and Corrêa de Azevedo. *Rivista brasileira de música* published a special issue (1936) dedicated to Carlos Gomes.

In Argentina, tonadillas and zarzuelas were produced in the eighteenth-century theaters of Buenos Aires, but by the second decade of the next century, Italian and French operas were vying for the public's attention. Despite the foreign influence in the theater, a number of Argentine composers were successful in their use of national subjects and Spanish American settings, as in *La indigena* ("The Native Girl," 1862) by Vinceslao Fumi (1823–1880), and in *Pampa* (1897) and *Yupanki* (1899), by Arturo Berutti (1862–1938). Francisco Hargreaves (1849–1900) made extensive use of folk-music material in both *La gatta bianca* ("The White Cat," Milan, 1875) and *El vampiro* (1876). Justin Clérice (1863–1908), a native of Argentina, won recognition in Europe for his French comic operas and ballets.

Early Mexican composers of Italian operas were Luis Baca (1826–1855); Cenobio Paniagua (1821–1882), with *Catalina di Guisa* (1864); and Melesio Morales (1838–1908), whose principal works were *Ildegonda* (1866), *Cleopatra* (1891), and *Anita*, a one-act opera in verismo style (never performed). German romanticism is characteristic of the music of Ricardo Castro (1864–1907) in *La Légende de Rudel*, though national themes had appeared in his earlier *Atzimba*. With the advent of Mexican independence in 1821, national elements began to appear in operas that otherwise reflected the traditional Italian models. *Guatimotzín* (1871), by Aniceto Ortega (1823–1875), is one of the first examples in this category, a distinguished national opera on an Aztec subject, using popular melodies. A more recent national historical opera was *Tata Vasco* (1941), by Miguel Bernal Jiménez (b. 1910); it includes many choral scenes and draws musical material from diverse sources, including Gregorian chant and Indian melodies.[87]

Most of the favorite Spanish zarzuelas were brought to the New World and inspired similar works by local composers in all Latin American countries. Thus, the Venezuelan José Angel Montero (1839–1881) produced fifteen zarzuelas, as well as an opera, *Virginia* (1873). In Columbia, zarzuelas and similar pieces were composed by Juan Crisóstomo Osorio y Ricaurte (1863–1887) and Santos Cifuentes (1870–1932); in Mexico there was a popular

87. See Stevenson, *Music in Mexico*, chap. 4 and pp. 262–64; Barros Sierra, "*Tata Vasco y su partitura.*"

comic opera, *Keofar* (1893), by Felipe Villanueva (1862–1893). Other Latin American opera composers in this period were: in Columbia, Augusto Azzali, *Lhidiac* (1893) and José María Ponce de León (1846–1882), *Ester*, and *Florinda*; in Peru, Daniel Alomias Robles (1871–1942), *Illa-Cori*, and Teodoro Valcárcel (1900–1942), *Suray-Surita*, a ballet opera; in Chile, Eleodoro Ortíz de Zarate (1865–1953), *La fioraia di Lugano* (1895), with Italian text; and in Cuba, Eduardo Sanches de Fuentes (1874–1944), *Dolorosa* (1910) and *Kabelia* (1942).[88]

The national musical renaissance that occurred in Latin America during the first half of the twentieth century did not bring forth operas comparable in either number or importance to the music produced in other forms. In Argentina, where there was more native opera than anywhere else, the Italian influence was still predominant. This was especially the case with Ettore Panizza (1875–1967), a distinguished conductor whose works include *Il fidnazato del mare* ("The Bridegroom of the Sea," 1897); *Medioevo latino* (1900), three one-act operas, each placed in a different Latin country and a different medieval century; *Aurora* (1908), commissioned for the opening of the Teatro Colón at Buenos Aires; and *Bisanzio* (1939). It is also the case with *Tabaré* (1925), by Alfredo Schiuma (1885–1963), which was closely patterned after Verdi's *Il Forza del destino* and was very successful. Another highly praised work of Schiuma is *Las vírgenes del sol* ("The Virgins of the Sun," 1939).[89] A more definitely national group is represented by Felipe Boero (1884–1958). In *Raquela* (1923), Boero gave native dances a prominent role, and in *El matrero* ("The Rogue," 1929), he explored the folklore tradition of the gauchos. Pascual de Rogatis (b. 1881) made an important contribution to Argentine opera with *Huemac* (1916), based on a Toltec legend,[90] and *La novia del hereje* ("The Heretic's Bride," 1935), colored by elements of the Afro–River Plate region. Other composers in this group include Raul Espoile (b. 1889), Enrique Casella (1891–1948), Carlos Lopez Buchardo (1881–1948), Floro

88. See Chase, "Some Notes on Afro-Cuban Music and Dancing."

89. Ferrari Nicolay, "En torno a *Las Vírgenes*."

90. Kuss, "*Huemac* by Pascual de Rogatis."

Ugarte (1884–1975), Gilardo Gilardi (1889–1963), and Athos Palma (1891–1951).[91]

In Brazil, the new nationalism was evident in the music of Oscar Lorenzo Fernandez (1897–1948), Francisco Mignone (b. 1897), and Camargo Guarnieri (b. 1907), but most of their works were not designed for the stage. Important exceptions were two operas composed in the 1930s: *Malazarte*, by Fernandez, and *Pedro Malazarte*, a one-act comedy by Guarnieri. Heitor Villa-Lobos (1887–1959),[92] one of the most famous of recent South American composers, wrote several operas but only two were ever performed: *Izaht* (composed 1918) was heard first in 1940 in a concert version and then staged at Rio de Janeiro in 1958; *Yerma* (composed 1955) was performed at Sante Fe in 1971.

The British Isles and the United States

BRITISH ISLES. Little need to be added to what has already been said in chapter 19 about English opera in the nineteenth century.[93] It was a time when serious opera was universally understood to mean Italian opera, that "exotic and irrational entertainment" which the British had been patronizing ever since the days of Dr. Johnson.[94] Almost the only English musical stage works to have any success at all in the nineteenth century were those of the light variety, by such composers as Balfe, Wallace, Benedict, and (later) Sullivan. The Carl Rosa Opera Company, beginning in 1875, commissioned a few English works, including some from Arthur Goring Thomas (1850–1892), whose *Esmeralda* and *Nadeshda* were given at London in 1883 and 1885, respectively. The vogue for Wagner—signalized by the establishment of a London

91. See Caamaño, ed., *La historia del Teatro Colón*, for information about opera in Buenos Aires.

92. Biographies by Muricy, Mariz, and Peppercorn.

93. But see Walker, *History of Music in England*; E. W. White, *The Rise of English Opera*; idem, *The History of English Opera*; Temperley, *Music in Britain*.

94. See Mapleson, *The Mapleson Memoirs*; Carlyle, "The Opera."

branch of the Wagner Society, which published a periodical entitled *Meister* from 1888 to 1895, and furthered by the circumstance that most of the leading English composers of the generation of the 1840s and 1850s received their training in Germany—was reflected in the numerous English operas on national historical or "Nordic" legendary subjects and in a musical style obviously inspired from Bayreuth. Perhaps the most zealous English disciple of Wagner was Frederick Corder (1852–1932), who wrote *Nordisca* (1887) and *Ossian* (1905). Sullivan's *Ivanhoe* made a great stir at its first production in 1891 but has fortunately long since disappeared from the stage. Other operas of a German-romantic cast were produced in England (and in some instances also in Germany) by Sir Frederic Cowen (1852–1935),[95] Sir Alexander Campbell Mackenzie (1847–1935), and Sir Charles Villiers Stanford (1852–1924). Cowen's *Pauline* (1876) was commissioned by the Carl Rosa company; his *Thorgrim* and two others of similar titles were produced at London in the 1890s. Mackenzie's *Colomba*, first heard at London in 1883, was later produced in Germany; his most successful opera was *The Cricket on the Hearth*, composed around 1900 and first performed in 1914. Stanford attempted to create an English *Meistersinger* in *The Canterbury Pilgrims* (1884), but was better known for his comic opera *Shamus O'Brien* (1896); his *Much Ado About Nothing* made a favorable impression at its first performance in 1901 and was revived in 1935.[96]

The revival of Celtic literature in the late nineteenth and early twentieth centuries led to a number of operas on Celtic legends. Most notable among these was the mythological Welsh trilogy *The Cauldron of Anwen*, by Josef Holbrooke (1878–1958).[97] It was broadly conceived along Wagnerian lines and written in a neoromantic musical style strongly influenced by Wagner. Welsh subjects also attracted Joseph Parry (1841–1903); Granville Bantock (1868–1946), in *Caedmar* (1892) and *The Seal Woman* (1924); and George Lloyd (b. 1913). Scottish stories or legends were used

95. Cowen, *My Art and My Friends*.

96. On Stanford, see Fuller-Maitland, *The Music of Parry and Stanford*, chap. 9, and Greene, *Charles Villiers Stanford*.

97. Biography by Lowe; see also the symposium edited by Holbrooke.

by Hamish MacCunn (1868–1916) in *Jeanie Deans* (Edinburgh, 1894), from Scott's *Heart of Midlothian*, and in *Diarmid* (London, 1897), as well as by Alick Maclean, in *Quentin Durward* (Newcastle-on-Tyne, 1920); and Irish subjects appear in *Eithne*, by Robert O'Dwyer (1862–1949), set to a Gaelic text, and in *Sruth na Maoile* ("The Sea of Moyle," Dublin, 1923), by Geoffrey Palmer (b. 1882).

English operetta and light opera of this period were represented by Alfred Cellier (1844–1891); Edward Soloman (1853–1895); George H. Clutsam (1866–1951); Sidney Jones (1861–1946), with *The Geisha* (1896); Sir Edward German (1862–1936), *Merrie England* (1902); Ivan Caryll (1861–1921), *The Duchess of Dantzic* (1903); Edward Naylor (1867–1934), *The Angelus* (1909); and Hubert Bath (1883–1945), *Bubbles* (1923).

UNITED STATES. The early history of opera in the United States is similar to that in the other nations of the Western Hemisphere.[98] It began in colonial times with the importation of comic operas from Europe (in this case, English ballad opera instead of the Spanish zarzuela); during the nineteenth and early twentieth centuries, fashion successively favored Italian opera, French grand opera, and German music drama. Tentative and unsuccessful efforts were made by native composers to imitate the musical style currently in vogue, sometimes applying it to "American" subjects, the Indians and the Puritan colonists being the two commonest sources of material for librettos. Prizes were offered and awarded; new operas by American composers were produced with fanfare, given a few performances, then shelved and forgotten. A few experimental works on a small scale were produced, but the American public showed little interest in them, preferring to hear *Il barbiere di Siviglia*, *Il trovatore*, *Les Huguenots*, or *Die Walküre*

---

98. General works include Chase, *America's Music*; Krehbiel, *Chapters of Opera*; Hitchcock, *Music in the United States*; Hamm, *Music in the New World*; Hipsher, *American Opera*; Ewen, *Complete Book of the American Musical Theater*; Ritter, *Music in America*; Howard, *Our American Music*. See also Virga, *The American Opera to 1790*; Sonneck, *Bibliography of Early Secular American Music*; idem, *Early Concert Life in America*; idem, *Early Opera in America*; Wegelin, *Micah Hawkins*; idem, *Early American Plays*; Seilhamer, *History of the American Theatre*; Mates, *The American Musical Stage Before 1800*. For regionally specialized studies, see Carson, Davis, Gagey, Kolodin, Mattfeld, and Moore.

in sumptuous settings and sung by expensive foreign stars. In a word, American opera remained, until well into the twentieth century, simply a longed-for but unrealized ideal.

It is possible that the first opera performance in the United States took place as early as 1703, but the earliest date which can so far be substantiated is 1735, when John Hippesley's *Flora*, a ballad opera first heard at London in 1729, was presented at Charleston, South Carolina. The following year, Charles Coffey's *The Devil to Pay* was presented in the same city. *The Beggar's Opera* and several similar works were presented in New York in 1750–51, and a like repertoire was heard in Annapolis and Upper Marlborough, Maryland, in 1752. In the same year, ballad operas were given at Williamsburg, Virginia. Philadelphia followed two years later. All during the latter half of the eighteenth century there were seasons of opera, fairly regularly at New York and sporadically at other places; the total number in proportion to the population was actually greater than at any period since. Most of the works so presented were English comic operas (Shield, Storace, Dibdin, and others), but there were also a few French opéras comiques (Grétry, Monsigny, Philidor), usually in translation and with the music more or less extensively altered and adapted by English and American arrangers, besides many pantomimes and ballets. French opera, both grand and comic, flourished at New Orleans from 1791 until the Civil War and even afterwards.[99] The first season of regular Italian opera in New York was in 1825. From that time on, the uneven career of foreign opera in the United States becomes too complicated to follow here even in outline, the more so since our chief concern is not with "opera in America" but "American opera."

Examples of American opera did not appear until the second half of the eighteenth century. One of the earliest was *The Disappointment; or, The Force of Credulity*, a comic opera in two acts by Andrew Barton of Philadelphia. It was published in 1767 and was scheduled for performance that same year, but the production was canceled. Among the very few American "operas" to be staged in the eighteenth-century were *May Day in Town* (1787) by Royall Tyler (1757–1826), and *Darby's Return* by William

99. Kmen, *Music in New Orleans*.

Dunlap (1766–1839), the New York premiere of which, on November 24, 1789, was attended by the newly elected president, George Washington.

The American operas of this early period were of a type similar to *The Beggar's Opera*, with characters and dialects appropriate to the American locale. Toward the end of the century there were imitations and adaptations of popular plays, such as Dunlap's *The Archers* (1796), with music by the English-born composer Benjamin Carr (1768–1831). Still other "entertainments" were on patriotic themes, with battle scenes and allegorical tableaux. None of these pieces had continuous music; most, in fact, were merely plays with incidental songs. The composers (or arrangers) included Francis Hopkinson (1737–1791),[100] James Hewitt (1770–1827), and Victor Pelissier (ca. 1740–ca. 1820), a native of France who came to America around 1792 and produced several plays with music, among them *Edwin and Angelina* at New York in 1796. In 1808, an "operatic melo-drame" by J. N. Barker entitled *The Indian Princess* was performed at Philadelphia; like the earlier examples mentioned, this was a play (the first extant one on the popular story of Pocahontas and Captain John Smith) with musical numbers, composed by John Bray (1782–1822) and including descriptive instrumental pieces, songs, and choruses.[101] A similar work, *The Enterprise*, with music by Arthur Clifton (b. ca. 1784), was given at Baltimore in 1822.[102] These are but two examples of many such homemade semioperatic entertainments that dot the history of the American stage in the early part of the nineteenth century.

The first publicly performed opera with continuous music by a native American composer was *Leonora* by William Henry Fry (1813–1864),[103] given at Philadelphia in 1845 and in a revised version at New York in 1858—a work of considerable competence and musical interest, modeled on the styles of Donizetti and Meyerbeer. Fry's next opera, *Notre-Dame de Paris*, was given at

---

100. Hopkinson's *America Independent; or, the Temple of Minerva* (1781), an "oratorical entertainment," does have continuous music but apparently was not intended for the stage.

101. The opera is published in Hitchcock, ed., *Earlier American Music Series*, vol. 11.

102. Gettel, "Arthur Clifton's *Enterprise*."

103. Biography by Upton; see also E. Smith, "William Henry Fry's *Leonora*."

Philadelphia in 1864. Another American composer of this period was George Frederick Bristow (1825–1898), whose *Rip Van Winkle* (New York, 1855) was arranged from Washington Irving's tale, with added love scenes and other episodes.[104] This opera has some spoken dialogue; the music is conventional and undistinguished, a lame imitation of the fashionable European light-opera style. *Uncle Remus*, by Henry F. Gilbert (1868–1962), also shares a place in the history of American opera on native themes. Although the opera was never completed, the extant materials (dating from 1905 to 1912) clearly demonstrate the successful role folk tales and music could have in the creation of an art-form for the stage. The libretto (also incomplete), by Charles Johnston, was drawn from the "Uncle Remus" stories of Joel Chandler Harris. It was designed as a series of set-numbers with spoken dialogue and required a narrator (Uncle Remus), an enigmatic personification of Nature (Miss Meadows), and a cast of animal characters. Black song and Afro-American melodies are incorporated into Gilbert's score (portions of which survive in other works, such as his 1909 *Comedy Overture on Negro Themes*), providing a suitable accompaniment for the regional dialect retained in the text.[105]

Of the many German-descended or German-trained American composers in the later nineteenth century, the most important in the field of opera was Walter Damrosch (1862–1950),[106] whose first success with *The Scarlet Letter* (1896) was hardly equaled by his two later works, *Cyrano* (1913) and *The Man without a Country* (1937). Damrosch's music is pleasantly put together and technically well fashioned, but it does not depart from the style of late nineteenth-century German romanticism. A rather more original score, though one still strongly suggestive of Wagner, is that by John Knowles Paine (1839–1906) for *Azara*, published in 1901 but performed only in concert version (1907). The operas of George Whitefield Chadwick (1854–1931) attracted little attention outside his native Boston, but those of his pupils Con-

104. For a reprint of the score and libretto, see Hitchcock, ed., *Earlier American Music Series*, vol. 25.

105. Longyear and Longyear, "Henry F. Gilbert's Unfinished *Uncle Remus* Opera."

106. Damrosch, *My Musical Life*.

verse, Hadley, and Parker were more widely recognized (see Chapter 25).[107]

The dependence of American composers on foreign (usually German) models in the nineteenth century, and the lack of any sustained movement toward a national musical style, are painfully illustrated in the operas mentioned above and also in those of lesser composers of the same period. Two early opera composers of German birth were Eduard de Sobolewski (1808–1872); who wrote *Mohega* (Milwaukee, 1859), and Johann Heinrich Bonawitz (1839–1917); *Ostrolenka* (Philadelphia, 1875). With this group may also be listed the Americans Frederick Grant Gleason (1848–1903), with *Otho Visconti* (Chicago, 1907), and Louis Adolphe Coerne (1870–1922), of whose three operas the only one ever performed was *Zenobia* (Bremen, 1905—the first opera by an American composer to be staged in Germany). To the same generation as Coerne belong Arthur Finley Nevin (1871–1943), with *Poia* (Berlin, 1910) and *The Daughter of the Forest* (Chicago, 1918); Joseph Carl Breil (1870–1926), *The Legend* (New York, 1919); and John Adam Hugo (1873–1945), *The Temple Dancer* (New York, 1919).

American operetta and comic opera may be traced from the works of the German-born Julius Eichberg (1824–93), including *The Doctor of Alcantara* (Boston, 1862) through those of Dudley Buck (1839–1909), *Deseret* (New York, 1880), Edgar Stillman Kelley (1857–1944), *Puritania* (Boston, 1892), and John Philip Sousa (1854–1932), *El Capitan* (Boston, 1896) to Reginald De Koven (1859–1920), *Robin Hood* (Chicago, 1890) and Victor Herbert (1859–1924), *Babes in Toyland* (1903). Both De Koven and Herbert attempted grand opera, but without much success: De Koven wrote *The Canterbury Pilgrims* (New York, 1917) and *Rip van Winkle* (Chicago, 1920), and Herbert, *Natoma* (Philadelphia, 1911) and *Madeleine* (New York, 1914).

In light opera and musical comedy after the First World War, the two leading figures were Jerome Kern (1885–1945, with works such as *Sally* (1920), and George Gershwin (1898–1937), *Of Thee I Sing* (1931). Each of these composers has written one

107. Yellin, "The Life and Operatic Works of George Whitefield Chadwick."

distinguished work in more serious style: Kern, *Show Boat* (1927), and Gershwin, *Porty and Bess* (1935); both works have become practically American folk operas. Notable musical comedies of later vintage were Rodgers and Hammerstein's *Oklahoma!* (1943) and *South Pacific* (1949) and Lerner and Loewe's *My Fair Lady* (1956), based on George Bernard Shaw's *Pygmalion*.[108]

China

Chinese opera, or *xiqu*,[109] is an all-encompassing term that refers to several hundred regional forms of theatrical entertainment, the earliest of which evolved from the music-dramas of the Sung (960–1279) and Yuan (1279–1368) dynasties. The genre represents a synthesis of art-forms whose distinguishing characteristics vary according to regional preferences of performance practice, dialect, instrumentation, literary sources, and folk songs. Stylization of regional forms has produced two main categories of opera: *wen* (civilian) and *wu* (military), the former placing emphasis on love stories and the latter on heroic tales, replete with humorous pantomime and acrobatic displays. Operas associated with the regions of Sichuan, Fukien, Shanghai, Canton, and Beijing were particularly influential in establishing within China an important national tradition, the impact of which was felt in Western countries as early as the mid-nineteenth century.[110]

Regional opera advanced to a dominating position by eclipsing its chief competitor, *kunqu*, a form of music-drama in

108. C. Smith, *Musical Comedy in America*; Green, *The World of Musical Comedy*; Bordman, *American Musical Comedy*; idem, *American Operetta*. See also chap. 25.

109. The *pinyin* system of romanization, adopted in China in 1979 for foreign-language publications, is used here whenever possible instead of the Wade-Giles system.

110. See Lieberman, *Chinese Music: An Annotated Bibliography*; Alley, *Peking Opera*; Schönfelder, *Die Musik der Peking-Oper*; Crump and Malm, eds., *Chinese and Japanese Music-Dramas*; Mackerras, *The Rise of the Peking Opera (1770–1870)*; idem, *The Performing Arts in Contemporary China*; idem, "Chinese Opera After the Cultural Revolution (1970–72)"; idem, ed., *Chinese Theater from Its Origins to the Present Day*; Yang, "The Reform of Peking Opera Under the Communists." See also articles in *Peking Review* (1958–1978) and *Beijing Review* (1979–   ); "China," in *The New Grove Dictionary*.

vogue among the educated elite during the late Ming (1368–1644) and Qing (1644–1911) dynasties. Court poets and musicians were responsible for creating the kunqu repertoire; they relied heavily upon preexisting literature and music for their source materials. Well-known examples of kunqu include *Changsheng dian* ("The Palace of Eternal Youth," 1689), composed by Hong Sheng (1645–1704); *Taohua shan* ("The Peach Blossom Fan," 1699), by Kong Shangren (1648–1718); and *Leifeng ta* ("Leifeng Pagoda"), by an anonymous eighteenth-century writer.[111] Contemporary accounts of kunqu performances describe the vocal style as "delicate," supported instrumentally by flutes (side-blown and vertical), wooden clappers, and traditional string instruments of the period.

In sharp contrast to kunqu works with their written-out librettos and notated musical scores, regional opera developed from an improvised form of rural entertainment, produced for the masses by amateurs or professionals whose stature in society was of the lowest rank. Stock characters and a standardized scenario provided the theatrical participants with a skeletal structure (reminiscent of the commedia dell' arte) around which text and music were improvised according to stated rules of performance.[112] Heightened speech and songs paired with instrumental music and choreographed movements (ranging from a gesture code to acrobatics) produced a stylized expression of daily life.

The particular form of Chinese opera known as the Beijing (Peking) style *(pihuang)* represents a comparatively late development in the history of the genre. It originated in the final decades of the eighteenth century as a composite of two regional melodic styles, *erhuang* and *xipi*, which actors from the southern provinces had been staging in the capital city. The style, which retained erhuang and xipi as its two main categories of melodies, blossomed into an honored national tradition that has continued in various guises for more than one hundred years.

111. Mackerras, ed., *Chinese Theater*, chap. 4. During the past two decades, kunqu operas have been revived by such celebrated troupes as that of the Jiangsu Province Kunqu Institute, which exhibited this style at the West Berlin Arts Festival in the summer of 1985.

112. Traditional regional operas tend to be fairly short (one hour or less), with dramatic expositions limited to a single incident or to one chapter of a novel. The names of the librettists and composers are rarely mentioned. Operas composed or revised for performance after 1949 are considered to be the "collective" creations of anonymous professionals.

Beijing opera was originally staged in banquet halls, courtyards, private homes, and especially in teahouse-theaters. It has four distinct role categories: *dan* (female), *sheng* (male), *jing* (warrior), and *chou* (comic actor).[113] Prior to the twentieth century, all roles were played by male actors who specialized in one of the four categories cited.[114] Costumes were ornate and colorful, more than compensating for the otherwise stark stage, usually devoid of scenery and elaborate props. Spoken dialogue (sometimes deliberately aligned with the continuous steady beats of the clappers) alternated with highly organized aria-types—interjective, narrative, declamatory, dramatic, lyric, and animated—differentiated primarily by their rhythmic patterns. A repeated rhymed couplet provided the basic poetical structure for the arias. The initial four lines of this pattern, consisting of seven or ten syllables each, cadenced according to predetermined textural and melodic formulas.[115] Audiences were so conditioned in their expectation of multiple repetitions of these cadential formulae that any deviation from the pattern within the course of an aria served to heighten dramatic tension. The nature of the word tones in the Chinese language presented special problems for achieving a satisfactory union of text and music. Priority was given to the word tone or stressed word within the couplet before segments of preexisting melodies were superimposed upon the text. Adjustments to either the text or the melody were freely made to insure a satisfactory piece of entertainment.

The singing in Beijing opera is also highly stylized. Its peculiar nasal quality, coupled with a shrill falsetto used for the dan roles, produces a harshness that is disturbing to those unaccustomed to this art-form. The high-pitched vocal timbre is duplicated by an ensemble of traditional Chinese string instruments

113. *Sheng* roles include the distinguished statesman, scholar, or general; *jing* roles (nicknamed "painted-face" roles because of the make-up which defines the characters) represent men of action and supernatural beings. One of the most famous *dan* actors was Mei Lanfang (1894–1961).

114. In some provinces, all-female casts were active in opera productions. Casts with both male and female actors appeared in the early years of this century, but they were not used on a regular basis until after 1949. See Mackerras, *The Rise of the Peking Opera.*

115. Pian, "Aria Structural Patterns in the Peking Opera."

(huqin, erhu, yueqin),[116] reinforcing and embellishing the vocal melodies at the unison or octave. Articulation of the dramatic action is regulated by percussion instruments (gongs, cymbals, clappers, drums). The entrance and exit of characters, the delineation of musical and dramatic sections, the mime activities (dance, acrobatics)—in short, the pacing of the opera—are marked by the percussionists, whose leader is also the director of the entire production.

The prominent position accorded to Beijing opera in the twentieth century has tended to obscure the historical importance and great popularity of many other regional styles, with Cantonese opera and the "clapper operas" of the northern (Shanxi) and southwestern (Sichuan) provinces providing but two interesting examples. Clapper operas, as the name suggests, place special emphasis on percussion instruments, sometimes even excluding all other instruments, as is the case with one particular type of Sichuan opera. An early clapper opera popular in the northern provinces was *Mai yanzhi* ("Selling Cosmetics"), later adapted for the Beijing repertoire. Differences among regional styles are subtle and not easily discerned by Western audiences. In Cantonese opera, there is at least one aspect of the style that does not escape notice. It is the emphasis upon middle (alto-tenor) registers rather than upon the extremely high tessitura of the Beijing style; this produces a more pleasing, mellow quality in the musical material. A further extension of this quality is made possible by the inclusion of a violin in the relatively small instrumental ensemble.[117]

Cantonese opera was flourishing in the mid-nineteenth century, but its continuation as a regional form of entertainment was jeopardized during the Taiping Rebellion (1851–1864). Adverse social and political conditions had forced suspension of the-

116. For concise descriptions and illustrations of the instruments used in opera orchestras, see "China," *The New Grove Dictionary.*

117. The instrumental ensemble varies in size from six to twelve members. It is positioned at the rear of the stage facing the audience, though more recent practice has the ensemble placed stage right behind a screen or slightly offstage. In addition to the violin, Cantonese ensembles sometimes included a saxophone or clarinet, but since the 1960s, most productions have been performed solely with Chinese instruments.

atrical activities and prompted many Chinese men to seek their livelihood overseas. Wealthy merchants who had been financially supporting resident opera companies turned their attention to sponsoring traveling troupes in Europe and the United States. In October 1852, a Cantonese opera, *The Eight Genii,* was presented at San Francisco's American Theatre by a traveling troupe numbering more than 100 performers.[118] With over 20,000 Chinese immigrants already settled in California by that time, it is understandable why there were eager audiences at these productions night after night. As the number of Chinese immigrants increased, so did the number of visiting troupes and performances.

Cantonese opera was banned in the People's Republic of China during the Cultural Revolution of the late 1960s, reinstated with modifications in the early 1970s, and restored to its previous provincial domain after 1977. Through all the turmoil affecting regional opera styles in the course of the twentieth century, Cantonese opera preserved itself without compromise in Hong Kong, where it continues to be a popular form of entertainment.[119]

With the demise of the Qing dynasty in 1911, China embarked on a new political course, one which initiated important changes in its cultural environment. Some of these changes came from within the society; others came directly from the West. For example, a significant addition to the realm of entertainment was the spoken drama *(huaju),* an art-form unknown to Chinese audiences prior to the twentieth century. Other Western forms staged in China were the sung drama *(geju),* which combined traditional Chinese theater with western opera styles, and the dance-drama *(wuju),* with styles as diverse as Western ballet and Chinese folk-dancing. Western forms of classical music, along with Western instruments, not only were permitted to be performed; after 1949, they gradually dominated the educational curriculum of the music schools.

---

118. Riddle, *Flying Dragons, Flowing Streams,* p. 18. Riddle quotes eyewitness accounts of other San Francisco productions in the 1850s. For an excellent photographic record of these staged events from 1852 to 1983, see Renouf, *Pear Garden in the West,* with photographs by Wylie Wong and commentary by Jack Chen. See also Yung, "The Music of Cantonese Opera."

119. Hong Kong's *SINOCAST* radio performances of Cantonese opera are heard in major cities of the United States and Canada.

Foreign pressure upon the life style of China provoked a strong nationalistic reaction, which manifested itself most effectively in the traditional art-forms. In 1937, the All-China Theater World Association was founded to present Beijing and other regional opera styles along with various forms of traditional entertainment as a means of promoting resistance to foreign domination. Seven years later, Mao Zedong, leader of the Chinese Communist Party, delivered his famous "Talks at the Yenan Forum on Literature and Art." [120] He argued that literature and art can be used to unify and educate a nation, to disseminate information to the masses, and to serve as a propaganda weapon against the foreign invasion of China's culture. The advent of the People's Republic of China in 1949 brought into sharp focus the power which could be channeled through the theater arts to create an unprecedented degree of nationalistic fervor. [121]

Tracing the development of Beijing opera in the second half of the twentieth century is complicated by the waxing and waning of various ideological theories. Since drama productions are supposed to reflect the current theories, the operas are constantly being revised to keep pace with the changing political and cultural doctrines set forth by leaders of both the party and state. *Hongdeng ji* ("The Story of the Red Lantern") provides an interesting example of this situation. The opera was originally created as a regional work for the Shanghai repertoire. It was later adapted for Beijing and then was included among the revolutionary works presented at the First Festival of Beijing Operas on Contemporary Themes, organized in 1964 by Jiang Qing, wife of Mao Zedong and leader of what later came to be called the "gang of four." The opera underwent further revisions to strengthen the "class struggle" image and to add emphasis to the role of the hero. By 1970, *Red Lantern* was declared a "model revolutionary opera," one of approximately eight which had earned Jiang Qing's stamp of approval. [122] When pressure mounted to restore the re-

120. Zedong, "Talks at the Yenan Forum."

121. A campaign to preserve native folk music was begun in the 1950s and included the collecting, cataloging, and recording of folk songs from all of the provinces.

122. The story concerns a railway switchman who is charged with the task of relaying a secret code to guerrillas engaged in the war of resistance against Japan (1937–1945). The

gional styles, banned in 1964, Jiang Qing responded with a Cantonese-style version of *Red Lantern*, which was prepared for production in 1972.

The period since the establishment of the Communist regime can be divided into three phases. The first phase, from 1949 to 1964, was that of the "liberation" movement, when traditional theater was viewed as a "utilitarian and practical" medium for the education and entertainment of the masses. The government assumed ownership of private theater companies in 1954 and established new troupes, such as the Beijing Opera Company of China. The primary objective was to control the content of presentations and to bring professional theater to rural audiences. Throughout this phase, regional styles of traditional opera flourished. *Zhiqu Weihu shan* ("Taking Tiger Mountain by Strategy," Beijing, 1958) is representative of operas staged in the late 1950s. The hero of the fast-paced drama is a member of the People's Liberation Army; his victorious assault on an enemy stronghold is credited to the loyal support of the masses in behalf of Mao's objectives.

The second phase, from 1964 to 1977, embraced the era of the Cultural Revolution, beginning around the time of the Festival of Beijing Operas and drawing to a close shortly after the death of Mao Zedong and the silencing of the gang of four. It was dominated by the radical cultural policies set forth by Jiang Qing. Expressed in simplest terms, "modern" attitudes were to replace "traditional" ones. Theater works staged between 1949 and 1966 were condemned as valueless. This included the traditional regional operas as well as the foreign varieties of music-drama. In their place were staged a few "model revolutionary operas," which, in reality, were little more than revisions of existing Beijing operas. Among those that qualified as "models" were *Lung-chiang sung* ("Ode to Dragon River"), *Hai-kang* ("On the Docks"), and *Red Lantern* and *Taking Tiger Mountain by Strategy*. Modernization of the operas involved, among other things, the introduc-

---

hero is tortured by the Japanese general but the code is not revealed. The adopted grandmother of the hero and her daughter are similarly interrogated. As punishment for their resistance, the hero and grandmother are executed; the daughter is freed and she succeeds in delivering the code. For a comparison of the 1964 and 1970 versions, see Mackerras, "Chinese Opera After the Cultural Revolution (1970–72)."

Scene from *White Snake* (Pantages Theater, Los Angeles 1980).
(With kind permission of the photographer, Kathleen A. Bick)

tion of elaborate scenery and a reshaping of the musical material. A more natural speaking and singing style was adopted by the performers, which permitted them to express emotions realistically, and the orchestral ensemble was greatly expanded to include Western instruments, which sometimes dominated the scoring.[123]

During the third phase, which began in 1977, many policies imposed during the Cultural Revolution were reversed.[124] Traditional regional operas of the pre-1966 era were once again performed and operas that had undergone extensive revisions between 1966 and 1976 were restored to their original status. New operas were composed using historical settings and themes along with traditional patterns of performance; others were created with contemporary themes and modern staging, combining Chinese and Western aspects of music and acting techniques.[125] Topics ranged from love stories (which had been banned in the second phase) to patriotic missions, from mythology to fairy tales, from historical biography to comedy. Also back in vogue were the various forms of spoken, sung, and dance-dramas (huaju, geju, and wuju). Variety and novelty in entertainment transformed the cultural offerings in China; they also prompted serious debate over questions of the "new" versus the "traditional," the "West" versus "China."[126]

A representative sample of operas that currently comprise the performing repertoire in Beijing would include *Bishang Liangshan* ("Forced up Mt. Liang"), a traditional revolutionary

123. The scoring for operas staged after 1966 continued to use a combination of Chinese and Western instruments. According to Chou Wen-Chung, "To Create a New Chinese Musical Idiom," the functions of these instruments were clearly differentiated, the Chinese instruments accompanying the singers and the Western instruments, located in the orchestra pit, playing the instrumental interludes. Mackerras, "Chinese Opera After the Cultural Revolution," p. 486, presents a different interpretation of how the Chinese and Western elements were utilized. The reader can investigate this further by comparing opera recordings made before and after 1966.

124. See, in particular, Mackerras, *The Performing Arts in Contemporary China* and Mackerras, ed., *Chinese Theater*.

125. Texts written in Chinese characters are projected on a screen located to one side of the stage, thereby allowing the "message" of the operas to be comprehended by audiences speaking various regional dialects.

126. Traditional operas have been made into films; children's theater offers puppetry and spoken plays; symphony orchestras using western instruments have been organized.

opera based upon the novel *Shuiku zhuan* ("The Water Margin"); it premiered in 1943 and was the first of the traditional works to be performed in China (1977) after the fall of the gang of four. *The Water Margin*, with its stories of rebels overpowering arrogant landlords during the Song dynasty (960–1279), was also the source for other operas; *Sanda Zhujiazhuang* ("Three Attacks on the Zhu Family Village") is an important and very successful new example. Several operas center upon the problems of women in society: *Qin Xianglian, Yangmen nujiang* ("Women Generals of the Yang Family"), *Hongzhu nu* ("The Red Pearl Girl"), and *Baishe zhuan* ("The White Snake"). This last-named is based on an ancient fairy tale about a white snake which was turned into a beautiful young lady. The story was popularized by an anonymous writer in the eighteenth century in the famous kunqu entitled *Leifeng Pagoda* (mentioned above), adapted to the Beijing repertoire, reworked into a ballet, and now once again appears as a traditional opera. In the numerous comic and military operas, long sections of dialogue and fancy feats of acrobatics greatly minimize the need for sung arias.

Both the new wave of creativity and the restoration of traditional works have sought to preserve xiqu as a truly national phenomenon. At the same time, there has been renewed interest in European opera, and students are encouraged by professional musicians to study the operatic roles of the standard repertoire. If the present trend continues, theatrical entertainment in China may follow a pattern not unlike that established by Japan during this century.

Japan

The development of modern opera in Japan (as distinct from that nation's traditional musical-dramatic forms, the *nō* and *kabuki*) followed a course similar in many respects to that in the countries of eastern Europe.[127] Apparently the first Western opera to be

127. For the information presented here, I am indebted to the courtesy of Professor Kozo Hattori of the University of Arts, Tokyo.

staged in Japan was Gounod's *Faust* (Act I only) at Tokyo in 1894. Gluck's *Orfeo*, in Japanese translation and with a Japanese cast, was heard at Tokyo in 1903. The first opera by a Japanese composer was *Hagoromo* ("Magic Clothes of an Angel," 1906), based on a national legend and set to music by Kōsuke Komatsu (b. 1884). Subsequent composers sought to amalgamate the tradition of Japanese musical drama with that of Western opera. Representative works in this line are *Kurofune* ("Black Ships," 1940) by Kōsaku Yamada (1886–1965); *Yūzuru* ("Crane of Twilight") by Ikuma Dan (b. 1924), first produced at Tokyo in 1952 and known in the West from performances at Zurich in 1957; and *Shuzenji-monogatari* ("A Tale at Shuzenji," Tokyo, 1954, and Los Angeles, 1962), by Osamu Shimizu (b. 1911). The libretto of *Kurofune* uses a national historical subject; that of *Yūzuru* is based on a national folk tale, while *Shuzenji-monogatari* simply takes over a kabuki drama without altering so much as a word. In these and other modern operas, national subjects—and to a certain extent also national musical materials—are blended with various Western musical styles from Puccini to the most advanced contemporary idioms.

PART VI

The Twentieth Century

CHAPTER
TWENTY-FIVE

The First Half of the Century

Of all musical forms, opera is the most immediately sensitive to changes in political, economic, social, and general cultural conditions. Its very nature as a complex and costly public spectacle largely dependent on official patronage or private subsidy makes it especially vulnerable to political dictates and economic vicissitudes; its subject matter reflects, positively or negatively, current human preoccupations; its form, content, and idiom are all affected by changing ideals of dramatic and musical style. Two world wars, a worldwide economic depression, and the emergence of political systems committed to strict control of art in the interest of the state were the salient external factors in the first half of the twentieth century.[1] Widespread emigration of authors and composers in the 1930s affected the development of opera in the United States and elsewhere. The passionately felt need of the artist to come to grips with contemporary issues in contemporary terms stimulated new uses of traditional techniques and experiments with new dramatic and musical means. Technological developments also played a part: radio, television, and the long-playing phonograph record immensely increased the actual and potential audience, bringing the traditional repertoire and style of opera within

---

1. General works on the music of this period are Wörner, *Neue Musik in der Entscheidung*; Collaer, *La Musique moderne*; Slonimsky, *Music Since 1900*; Austin, *Music in the Twentieth Century from Debussy through Stravinsky*; Salzman, *Twentieth-Century Music: An Introduction*; Mordden, *Opera in the Twentieth Century*. See also articles in *MQ* (especially the "Current Chronicle" section), *Opera News* (1936–), *American Composers Alliance Bulletin* (1938, 1952–), *Perspectives of New Music*.

everyone's reach and making it possible, to some extent at least, for the public to become acquainted with newer developments. As a result, opera has become of interest to a larger number of people than ever before in its history. Free pursuit of the new, together with an enlarged and diverse public, accounts for an unprecedented diversity of operatic styles in our time—the "polyphonic" or "many-voiced century," as one writer has called it.[2]

As in all periods, the subject matter of twentieth-century opera has been drawn variously from imagined dramatic interactions of human personalities, from history, myth, legend, or folklore, or from the circumstances of contemporary life; treatment has been serious or light, earnest or satirical or playful, as of timeless significance or as applicable peculiarly to the present moment. The aims have been equally varied: mere amusement or entertainment (whether of a general public or of special groups, as, for example, opera for children); instruction and conversion—that is, propaganda; comedy with contemporary social application; or high tragedy in the Aristotelian sense: "the imitation of an action that is serious and also, as having magnitude, complete in itself . . . with incidents arousing pity and fear, wherewith to accomplish its catharsis of such emotions"[3]—the kind of drama that invites the audience to contemplate heroic greatness of deed or character, in some instances being more or less overtly directed toward confirmation of religious faith.

We may recall that the twentieth century inherited, along with the timeless and unchanging line of light or "entertainment" opera, two fundamentally contrasting conceptions of serious musical drama. Stated in simplest terms, these were: (1) the Wagnerian drama of ideas, with personages primarily symbolical and with music in a continuous orchestral texture organized by means of leitmotifs, the vocal lines being of declamatory or arioso character; and (2) the Verdian drama of typical human beings in psychological interaction, with music in the form of distinct numbers connected by recitatives and a texture of emotionally expressive vocal melody sustained by orchestral accompaniment. By and large,

2. Honolka, *Das vielstimmige Jahrhundert.*

3. *Aristotle's Art of Poetry*, trans. Ingram Bywater (Oxford: Clarendon, 1920), chap. 6 (1449b20).

composers at the beginning of the twentieth century adhered to one or the other of these two basic conceptions, even if with compromises or modifications: Strauss in *Salome* and *Electra* (and later in *Die Frau ohne Schatten*) was in the line of descent from Wagner, as was essentially also Debussy in *Pelléas et Mélisande* despite its un-Wagnerian harmonies and dynamics; on the other hand, Puccini and the composers of the verismo school descended (in both senses of the word) from Verdi. Meanwhile, a new conception was growing up, or rather an old one was being revived: the eighteenth-century classical idea of an opera as primarily a musical entity, with poetry "the obedient daughter of music," as Mozart had expressed it. This new-old conception involved, as a rule, the use of distinct musical numbers in definite form, objectivity of expression, and a tendency to let the music develop in its own way, following the dramatic action in broad lines but not attempting to mirror it in detail. This conception of opera, an early example of which is Strauss's *Ariadne,* has influenced many twentieth-century composers—Falla, Ravel and most of the French, some Germans (notably Hindemith), and Stravinsky, especially in *The Rake's Progress.*

"Comic opera," in the twentieth century as in earlier periods, is a designation embracing many different types. At one end of the scale are frankly popular works—musical comedies, operettas, and the like—that seek to entertain a large public by means of (1) music in a style familiar enough to be enjoyed without much effort or close attention but containing some novelty in details; and (2) a dramatic content uncomplicated, superficial (in the sense of carrying no "message"), humorous or sentimental or both, and possibly enlivened by reference to current vogues or topics in the news. Other kinds of comic opera may be distinguished by music in a more advanced style, greater sophistication of plot and subtlety of characterization, or evidence of some aim (for example, satire) in addition to that of entertainment. Most successful writers of light popular works produce nothing of significance outside that special field. Examples of more sophisticated kinds of comic opera, however, have come from nearly every composer for the theater in the present century, including some who are equally competent in the "serious" realm—Alfano, Poulenc, Britten, and Menotti, among others.

One development that attracted much attention in the 1920s and 1930s was the opera of social protest, conspicuous first in Germany and later in the United States. To be sure, the theme of social protest had occurred in opera before, but now it became explicit and central instead of only incidental.

Another phenomenon of the period since 1920 has been the tendency to combine the traditional form of opera with certain features of the oratorio, such as a narrator or a contemplative or didactic chorus. Introduction of oratorio-like elements has occurred typically in large-scale works on historical or legendary subjects, such as Stravinsky's *Oedipus rex*, Milhaud's *Christophe Colomb*, Hindemith's *Mathis der Maler*, Egk's *Columbus*, Schoenberg's *Moses und Aron*, and Orff's *Antigonae*. A like infiltration of oratorio or cantata technique is found in some stage works of smaller scale, such as Falla's *Retablo de Maese Pedro*, Vaughan Williams' *Pilgrim's Progress*, and Britten's *Rape of Lucretia*. Forerunners of the opera-oratorio may be found in Wagner's *Parsifal* and Pfitzner's *Palestrina*, but the combination is especially characteristic of the mid-twentieth century.

Likewise characteristic of this period is the importance of ballet, especially ballet with dramatic elements (Bartók, Stravinsky, Prokofiev) and the incorporation of choreographic (often also choral) spectacle in opera (as in many of the works mentioned above), or even a fusion of opera and ballet, as in Casella's "choreographic comedy" *La giara* (1924) or Henze's *Boulevard Solitude* (1952). Still another feature of the twentieth century is the unprecedented extent to which composers have worked in smaller forms—"chamber" or "workshop" opera, requiring few performers, sometimes written specifically for amateurs or for children. This movement, the result of special conditions, has been particularly prominent in England and the United States but is not by any means confined to those countries. Finally may be mentioned the rise of opera for the new media of radio and television, the writing of incidental music for films as well as for stage plays, and the rise of electronic music, whose special possibilities for opera have begun to be explored with considerable success.

No single one of the typical twentieth-century operatic phenomena (except for the last named) can be called completely "new." What is new, as has already been said, is the unprecedented diversity of operatic styles existing in one and the same period. In part, of course, that diversity is an illusion caused by our nearness to events, our lack of historical perspective; but even discounting this (insofar as possible), the diversity remains.

From 1900 to 1920

The most radical influence on musical style in the first fifteen years of the present century was impressionism, which originated in France with Debussy and gradually made itself felt nearly everywhere from 1900 on. Another source of change was the development of the post-Wagnerian late romantic style in Germany and Austria, evident in Mahler, early Schoenberg, and Richard Strauss. A third set of influences came from composers who carried on with the national movements already begun in the nineteenth century. The effects of these forces appeared in varying degrees and combinations, but underlying all change was the conservative power of tradition, still inescapable and still respected: progress, not revolution, was the ruling ideal, and even "advanced" experiments soon slipped into the central current of evolution without causing too much disturbance.

FRENCH OPERA

The most important French opera of the early twentieth century was *Pelléas et Mélisande*, by Claude Debussy (1862–1918),[4] on a text by Maurice Maeterlinck. It is the only work Debussy completed for the stage, with the exception of the miracle drama *Le Martyre de Saint-Sébastien* (1911, based on D'Annunzio's play) and an early cantata, *L'Enfant prodigue*, which has sometimes been given in operatic form. The first sketches for *Pelléas et Mélisande* are dated 1893, and Debussy revised the score continually.

4. Biographies by Vallas, Lockspeiser, and Nichols. See also Debussy, *Monsieur Croche*; studies of *Pelléas et Mélisande* by Gilman, Emmanuel, Ackere, and Abbate; Myers, "The Opera That Never Was"; Holloway, *Debussy and Wagner*; *Avant-scène opéra*.

The first performance took place at the Opéra-Comique on April 30, 1902—"one of the three or four red-letter days in the history of our lyric stage," as Romain Rolland has said.[5]

It is customary, and in the main correct, to regard *Pelléas et Mélisande* as a monument to French operatic reaction from Wagner; but this opera is at the same time a focal point of French dramatic music, gathering up many essential national traits and giving them exceptionally clear and perfect expression, though colored by the individual genius of Debussy. The personal qualities of the music are so salient that they tend to usurp attention, and it is therefore well to emphasize that *Pelléas* is characteristic not only of Debussy but also of France.

Four things have marked French opera from the beginning of its history. First is the belief that an opera is fundamentally a drama in words to which music has been added; from this doctrine comes the insistence on clear and realistic declamation of the text. Both the contemporary admiration for Lully's recitative and Rousseau's later objections to it as "mannered" came from the same interest in the text as basic to the drama and hence to the opera. In no other country has so much attention been given to this issue. The flourishing of the opéra comique with its spoken dialogue was a constant witness that the French were willing to do without music rather than let it interfere with the understanding of the words. *Pelléas et Mélisande* conforms to this ideal. It is one of the rare instances of a long play, not expressly made for music, being turned into an opera with practically no rearranging.[6] In most places the music is no more than an iridescent veil covering the text: the orchestral background is shadowy, evanescent, almost a suggestion of sound rather than sound itself; and the voice part, with its independence of the bar line, narrow range, small intervals, and frequent chanting on one tone, adheres as closely as possible to the melody of French speech. Only in a few places, as in Mélisande's song at the beginning of Act III or in the love duet in Act IV, scene 4, does the melody become

---

5. Rolland, *Musicians of Today* (trans. Blaiklock), p. 234.

6. The following scenes in the play are omitted in the opera: Act I, sc. 1; Act II, sc. 4; Act III, sc. 1; and Act V, sc. 1. There are many other small omissions, ranging from a single phrase to a dozen lines. There are also numerous alterations in wording, including the addition of words, especially in Act III, sc. 1.

really lyric. How typical this narrow melodic line is of French music may be realized by comparing the contours of French folk-song melodies with those of German or English folk songs, the instrumental themes of Saint-Saëns or César Franck with those of a German like Richard Strauss, or French nineteenth-century recitative in general with the wide ranging arioso of Verdi or Wagner. The use of the Wagnerian type of melody with French words, such as we find in the operas of Chabrier and D'Indy (and, to a lesser extent, in Bruneau and Charpentier), was soon felt to be unnatural. In the return to a more natural declamation and in the damping of orchestral sonorities, therefore, Debussy was in accord not only with traditional French practice but with an even more ancient ideal, that of the early Florentine founders of opera, Peri, Caccini, and Gagliano.

The second historical feature of French opera is its tendency to center the musical interest not in the continuous orchestra or in the solo aria but in the divertissements—that is, interludes in the action where music might be enjoyed without the attention being divided by the necessity of following the drama at the same time. In early French opera and through the nineteenth century, the common form of divertissement was the ballet with choruses. There are no ballets in *Pelléas*, and only one quite brief chorus, but the function of the divertissement is fulfilled by the orchestral preludes and the interludes which are played for changes of scene. Here, and here only, music has the foreground, and the full symphonic resources are employed. But the interludes are not independent of the action; rather, they continue in wordless and concentrated form what has just passed and by gradual transition prepare for what is to come. Thus, Debussy combines the Lullian form of opera with the nineteenth-century practice of treating every detail as a means of accomplishing the central dramatic purpose.

Still another constant feature of French opera has been the deliberate choice of measured, objective, well-proportioned, and rational dramatic actions. The French have not been misled, except momentarily, either by the desire to be forceful at any cost or by the attractions of metaphysical speculation. Not that French opera is as direct and uninhibited in its approach as the Italian; but the French prefer to suggest a hidden meaning by subtle juxtaposition of facts, trusting to stimulate the imagination rather than overwhelm it with exhaustive details, as Wagner tended to do. The quintessence of this indirect, suggestive method in literature is found in the movement known as symbolism, of which Maeterlinck's five-act drama *Pelléas et Mélisande* (1892) is an outstanding example. The story is purposely vague and seems slight indeed when reduced to a bare summary. But the whole effect is in the manner, not the matter. As Edmund Gosse has said:

> Maeterlinck is exclusively occupied in revealing, or indicating, the mystery which lies, only just out of sight, beneath the surface of ordinary life. In order to produce this effect of the mysterious he aims at an extreme simplicity of diction, and a symbolism so realistic as to be almost bare. He allows life itself to astonish us by its strangeness, by its inexplicable elements. Many of his plays are really highly pathetic records of unseen emotion; they are occupied with the spiritual adventures of souls, and the ordinary facts of time and space have no influence upon the movements of the characters. We know not who these orphan princesses, these blind persons, these pale Arthurian knights, these aged guardians of desolate castles, may be; we are not informed whence they come, not whither they go; there is nothing concrete or circumstantial about them. Their life is intense and consistent, but it is wholly of a spiritual character; they are mysterious with the mystery of the movements of a soul.[7]

Debussy's music perfectly supports the mysterious, spiritual character of the drama, doing everything by understatement and whispered suggestion. The full orchestra is hardly ever heard outside the interludes. Instrumental doubling is voided; solo timbres and small combinations are the rule, while the strings are often muted and divided. There are only four fortissimos in the whole score. Debussy's almost excessive "genius for good taste," to use Rolland's words again,[8] is apparent if we contrast the wild greeting of the lovers in the second act of *Tristan* with the meeting of Pelléas and Mélisande in Act IV (example 25.1), or the touching scene of Mélisande's death in Act V with Isolde's Liebestod.

However, soft music is not of necessity better than loud

7. Gosse, "Maeterlinck," in *Encyclopaedia Britannica* (11th ed.), 17:299a. Quoted by permission.

8. Rolland, *Musicians of Today* (trans. Blaiklock), p. 244.

Example 25.1: *Pelléas et Mélisande*, Act IV, sc. 4

music; restraint is of no artistic value unless we are made aware that there is something to be restrained. And here we come to the fourth and last quality characteristic of French opera, which Debussy carries to the ultimate degree, namely, a capacity for the appreciation of the most refined and complex sensory stimuli. In the quality of its acceptances as well as of its refusals, French opera has always tended to be aristocratic. The style of musical impressionism which *Pelléas et Mélisande* exemplifies is essentially one of aristocratic sensualism, treating sounds as of primary value for themselves irrespective of accepted grammatical forms, and creating moods by reiterated minute impacts of motifs, harmonies, and timbres. These elements in *Pelléas* sounded so completely unprecedented in themselves, and so completely detached from the familiar system of musical progressions, that audiences were at first bewildered; but they soon learned to associate the musical moods with those of the poetry and discovered a marvelous correspondence between the two. For as Maeterlinck's drama moved in a realm outside ordinary time and space, so Debussy's music moved in a realm outside the then known tonal system; lacking any strong formal associations within the field of music itself, his harmonies were irresistibly attracted to the similarly free images of the poet. Never was a happier marriage of music and verse. The technical methods of Debussy are familiar to all students of music and may be only briefly indicated here.[9] Modal, whole-tone, or pentatonic melodies and harmonies suggest the far-off, dreamlike character of the play. The free enchainment of seventh and ninth chords, often in organum-like parallel movement, and the blurring of tonality by complex harmonic relationships are also typical. Certain motifs recur and are transformed and harmonically varied, but they are not treated in the continuous symphonic manner of Wagner. D'Indy has well expressed their function by the term "pivot themes."[10]

The influence of Wagner on Debussy is felt chiefly in a negative fashion—that is, by the care Debussy took to avoid writing like Wagner. In those days it was not easy. Debussy complained of his first draft of the duet in Act IV that "the ghost of old Klingsor, alias R. Wagner, keeps peeping out."[11] But the final score owes little to Wagner beyond the orchestral continuity, the use of recurring motifs, and the exclusion of all merely ornamental details; in technique, idiom, feeling, and declamation, it is Debussy's own. Whatever he had learned from *Tristan* or from Musorgsky's *Boris Godunov*, from Massenet or Grieg, or from oriental music had been completely assimilated. So peculiarly was the musical style fitted to Maeterlinck's drama that it is no wonder Debussy was never able to find another suitable libretto. *Pelléas et Mélisande*, like *Fidelio*, remains an isolated masterpiece of its composer in the field of opera.

The next notable French opera of the twentieth century was Paul Dukas' (1865–1935)[12] *Ariane et Barbe-Bleue* ("Ariadne and Bluebeard," 1907)—like *Pelléas*, the composer's only opera and likewise on a symbolist drama by Maeterlinck. The influence of Debussy is apparent in the declamation and in some details of the harmony, but the recitative is less supple and poetic than Debussy's. The orchestration is sonorous, using the brasses with brilliant effect, and the musical style on the whole is anything but

---

9. See further Emmanuel, *"Pelléas et Mélisande"*, pp. 97–114.

10. D'Indy, *Richard Wagner*, p. 81.

11. Letter to Ernest Chausson, quoted in Abraham, *A Hundred Years of Music*, p. 278. Cf. Abbate, *"Tristan in the Composition of Pelléas."*

12. Studies by Samazeuilh and Favre; see also [Dukas], special issue of *RM* (1936).

impressionistic. Dukas was a composer of great technical attainment whose strong point was the development of ideas in large symphonic forms. Unfortunately, his themes are too often undistinguished in themselves, and their development marked less by inspiration than by system and perseverance; for example, the constant practice of repeating the exposition of a theme immediately in a new key (compare the exposition in the first movement of César Franck's symphony) becomes almost a mannerism. Dukas's harmony is subtle, but here again one sometimes feels the absence of any compelling musical or dramatic reason for some of his complicated chord progressions. Another defect is the excessive reliance on the augmented triad in association with the whole-tone scale, a device which has lost the attraction of novelty since 1907. So much must be stated by way of negative criticism of *Ariane et Barbe-Bleue*; on the other hand, its many excellences must be emphasized. The work is less an opera than a huge symphony with the addition of choruses (essential to the drama, not mere embellishments) and solo voices. Cyclical recurrence and transformation of themes are used to create an architectural structure of grand proportions. The large coda that forms the end of Act III is particularly impressive, summing up with Beethovenian finality all the principal themes of the opera and rounding off the whole with the theme which was first heard in the opening measures of the prelude to Act I. Among the many fine details of the score is the song of the "five daughters of Orlamonde," a folksonglike melody from which many of the motifs of the opera are derived (example 25.2). Altogether, *Ariane de Barbe-Bleue* is the most important French lyric drama of the early twentieth century next to *Pelléas et Mélisande*—important, that is, if measured in terms of artistic qualities rather than popular following. It is none the less significant musically for lacking those traits that led to the success of Massenet and Charpentier.

Several more operas of this period merit special mention, each being in its own way a distinctive contribution. Déodat de Séverac's (1872–1921)[13] *Cœur du moulin* ("The Heart of the Mill," 1909), a simple and poignant love story in a pastoral setting, has a musical score in which the influence of Debussy is

13. Biography by Selva.

Example 25.2: *Ariane et Barbe-Bleue*, Act I

modified by an original gift for direct, spontaneous expression and a charming regional flavor of southern France, evident especially in the choruses. Although its individual features were acclaimed by critics, *Le Cœur du moulin* has not had any popular success.

Other operas by Séverac include *Héliogabale* (1910), designed as a regional work with some parts suitable for folk musicians and local villagers; *La Fille de la Terre* ("The Daughter of the Earth," 1913), and *Le Roi Pinard* ("King Pinard," 1919), an opéra bouffe.

Better known are the two operas of Maurice Ravel (1875–1937).[14] *L'Heure espagnole* ("The Spanish Hour," 1911), a one-act opera buffa based on a comedy by Franc-Nohain, is a tour de force of rhythm and orchestration, varied and witty in declamation, with a libretto in which the art of the double-entendre is carried to a height worthy of Favart. The vocal lines are suggestive of Richard Strauss, while under them the orchestra carries on a suite of Spanish dances, ending with a mock-grand "scena and habañera." The scene, set in a clockmaker's shop, gives occasion for many charming and clever sound effects, among which the cuckoo motive is, of course, prominent. The strength of this opera is in just those qualities which Dukas' *Ariane* lacks: piquant details and a sense of lightness, gaiety, and improvisation. Ravel's "lyrical fantasy" *L'Enfant et les sortilèges* ("The Child and the Sorceries"), on a libretto by Colette, was first performed at Monte Carlo in 1925. It is a charming score, one worthy of the composer of *Ma Mère l'Oye*, lighter in texture than *L'Heure espagnole* but equally rich in ingenious orchestral and vocal effects.

Le Pays ("The Country," 1913), by J. Guy Ropartz (1864–1955),[15] is a dramatic and well-proportioned score with symphonic treatment of the orchestra, original in inspiration and evidencing the sound classical training its composer received from César Franck. One can detect a modified Wagnerianism in the opera's melody and harmony, as well as the then fashionable obsession with the sound of the augmented fifth chord. A special position must be assigned to the operas of Gabriel-Urbain Fauré (1845–1924),[16] the most important of which are *Prométhée* (1900) and *Pénélope* (1913). The latter particularly is a beautiful example of the composer's exquisite harmonic style, which lends to the classical subject matter an appropriate atmosphere of repose and

14. Roland-Manuel, *Maurice Ravel* and *Maurice Ravel et son oeuvre dramatique*; biographies by Orenstein and Myers; [Ravel], special issues of *RM* (1925 and 1938).

15. Biographies by Lamy and Kornprobst.

16. Biographies and studies by Koechlin, Suckling, Vuillermoz, and Orledge; [Fauré], special issue of *RM* (1922).

remoteness, evoking the feeling of the antique world as no more common idiom could. From the viewpoint of theatrical effectiveness, *Pénélope* is perhaps too refined; the slow tempo of the action (in Acts I and II especially) emphasizes the statuesque quality which is both the greatest musical beauty and the most serious dramatic weakness of this opera.

In sum, the dominant tendency of late nineteenth- and early twentieth-century French opera was idealistic; the noble, if somewhat vague, striving of *Fervaal* and *L'Étranger*, the mood of meditation on destiny in *Pelléas* and *Ariane*, the naïve religious faith of *Le Jongleur de Notre Dame*, the moral earnestness of *Le Cœur du moulin* and *Le Pays*, the serene, contemplative beauty of *Pénélope*—all show this. Even the so-called naturalistic operas of Bruneau and Charpentier used realism largely as a means of calling forth idealistic sentiment. Thus motivated, composers sought to bring into the theater the finest and most comprehensive resources of a highly developed musical art—resources enriched after 1900 by the new techniques of impressionism—aspiring toward universality of expression, freely using any and all means to which they found themselves attracted. Viewed from a later age, theirs seems an art of leisure and luxury, such as is possible only in a time of prosperity and peace. Leisure gave time for the unfolding of ideals, while luxury provided the material means for their realization on a scale which we have not seen since and probably shall not see again in the near future.

Among the minor composers of French serious opera in this period were Gabriel Pierné (1863–1937), with *La Fille de Tabarin* (1901); Alexandre Georges (1850–1938), *Charlotte Corday* (1901); Xavier Leroux (1863–1919), *La Reine Fiamette* (1903), influenced by Puccini and Massenet, and *Le Chemineau* (1907); Henri Février (1875–1957), *Monna Vanna* (1909); and Jean Noguès (1875–1932), whose *Quo Vadis* (1909) is a mild blend of Massenet and Fauré. Distinguished especially for works in a lighter vein were the Venezuelan-French Reynaldo Hahn (1875–1947), *La Carmélite* (1902), and Camille Erlanger (1863–1919), *Le Juif polonaise* (1909) and *Aphrodite* (1906). More individual in style was Raoul Laparra (1876–1943), with his operas on Spanish subjects, the most popular being *La Habañera* (1908) and *L'Illustre Fregona* (1931).

The music of *Macbeth* (1910), by Ernest Bloch (1880–1959), strongly influenced by Debussy, has declamatory vocal lines, much parallelism in the orchestral texture, and a monotonously constant use of the augmented 5–7 chord, which seems to have fascinated opera composers of this period as much as the diminished seventh had fascinated their predecessors a hundred years earlier. *Macbeth* was severely criticized on account of its "modernistic" harmonies and rhythms and soon dropped out of the repertoire, but it has been occasionally revived. Sylvio Lazzari (1857–1944), with *La Lépreuse* (1912), and Louis Aubert (1877–1968), with La Forêt bleue (Geneva, 1913) had no great success, but the oriental opéra comique *Mârouf, savetier de Caire* ("Marouf, Cobbler of Cairo," 1914), a witty, brilliantly scored work by Henri Rabaud (1873–1949), has become a favorite both in Paris and abroad. It is undoubtedly one of the finest modern comic operas, a worthy descendant of the long French line of works in this style and on similar subjects. Another oriental opera was *Antar*, by Gabriel Dupont (1878–1914), finished in 1914 but not performed until 1921. The Belgian Albert Dupuis (1877–1967) in his operas, such as *La Passion* (Monte Carlo, 1916), reverted to the style of Massenet.

It must be remembered that throughout the period we have been considering, the semidramatic form of the ballet occupied much of the attention of French composers. Lalo's *Namouna* (1882) never received the recognition it merited, but in the early twentieth century the performances of such works as Florent Schmitt's mimodrama *La Tragédie de Salomé* (1907), Ravel's *Daphnis et Chloé* (1912), and Stravinsky's *Firebird, Petrouchka,* and *The Rite of Spring* (1910, 1911, and 1913, respectively) were important musical events.

THE ITALIAN TRADITIONS

Opera in Italy during the early 1900s continued without any noticeable break along the lines already drawn before the turn of the century. The leading composer at this time was Puccini, whose work has already been discussed (see chapter 23). Along with the passing of the fashion for verismo, more and more Italian composers began to take interest in other forms of composition as well as opera and to become more susceptible to the influence of current tendencies from abroad. It was a period of internationalism, even a certain amount of eclecticism. After Wagner came Strauss, Debussy, and Stravinsky in turn to stamp their impress, more or less distinctly, on Italian composers. Interest was aroused in symphonic and chamber music, as evidenced in the output of such men as Giuseppe Martucci (1856–1909) and Giovanni Sgambati (1841–1914), while an important renewal of church music was led by Don Lorenzo Perosi (1872–1956) and Enrico Bossi (1861–1925).

Three Italian composers of the early twentieth century deserve particular notice: Ermanno Wolf-Ferrari (1876–1948), Riccardo Zandonai (1883–1944), and Italo Montemezzi (1875–1952). The special talent of the German-Italian Wolf-Ferrari was for comedy, with librettos either adapted from the eighteenth-century Goldoni or of a similar type.[17] These include *Le donne curiose* ("The Curious Ladies," Munich, 1903) and *Il segreto di Susanna* ("The Secret of Suzanne," Munich, 1909), his most famous work. His only tragic opera, an experiment with some of the methods of verismo, was *I gioielli della Madonna* ("The Jewels of the Madonna," Berlin, 1911), a work strongly suggestive of Donizetti with modern trimmings in harmony and rhythm. The serenade in Act II, perhaps the best-known number in the opera, is a good illustration of the vivacity and rather superficial harmonic cleverness of the style. Zandonai, a pupil of Mascagni, was one of the last composers of the verismo school, and his work is full of the old traditional Italian opera devices.[18] Of his nine operas, *Francesca da Rimini* (1914) is his most important and has maintained a consistent presence in the repertoire of Italian companies, and has even had an occasional international revival.[19] The tragic thirteenth-century love story, retold by Dante in Canto V of the *Inferno* and dramatized by Gabriele d'Annunzio, was reshaped into a libretto by Tito Ricordi. Zandonai's score is smoothly

---

17. Biographies by Rensis and Grisson; Pfannkuch, "Das Opernschaffen Ermanno Wolf-Ferraris."

18. Bonajuti Tarquini, *Riccardo Zandonai*; Chiesa, ed., *Riccardo Zandonai*.

19. For a discussion of the 1983 revival at the Metropolitan Opera, see *Opera News* (March 1984).

Scene from *Francesca da Rimini* (Turin 1914) by R. Zandonai.
(From *Das Theater* [1914] 5:415)

contrived as a mediant between symphony and theater, with its rich orchestration balanced by its reliance on highly skilled acting, and it is effectively designed to accentuate the passion and violence of the medieval romance.

The decline of verismo and the effort to combine some of its features with the neoromantic or exotic type of opera found in Puccini, Giordano, and others is one symptom of a new spirit in Italian musical life. Particular evidence is found in the operas of Montemezzi, especially *L'amore dei tre rè* ("The Love of the Three Kings," 1913) and *La nave* ("The Ship, 1918), where the influence of both Wagner and Debussy is blended with a native Italian lyricism to produce music sound in workmanship, rich in instrumental color, conservative in idiom though not merely imitative, and of enduring beauty.[20] *L'amore dei tre rè* is one of the best Italian tragic operas since Verdi's *Otello*. Notable is the refinement of style: chromaticism is handled with intelligence and restraint, intensifying the expression of feeling by the very refusal to dwell on obvious tricks of theatrical effect. There are memorable moments of classic breadth, as at the end of the love duet in Act II (example 25.3). The voice line is an admirable adjustment of vocal melody to a continuous symphonic texture; recurring motifs and a carefully worked out key scheme make a formal whole of satisfying proportions. Altogether this opera, with its night-shrouded castle, its lovers swooning in sensual ecstasy, and the tragic figure of the blind Archibaldo, with its music which seems from beginning to end one low cry of voluptuous pain, of delicately scented agony and hopeless fatalism, is a work which exemplifies well the course of Italian opera at the end of the romantic period: the ripe fruit of a dying age, the sunset of a long and glorious day.

Some less well-known Italian composers of opera in the first half of the twentieth century may be mentioned here. Ottorino Respighi (1879–1936),[21] especially noted for his symphonic poems, wrote a number of operas in a neoromantic idiom strongly influenced by impressionism: the comic and colorful *Belfagor*

20. Tretti and Fiumi, eds., *Omaggio a Italo Montemezzi*; Mordden, *Opera in the Twentieth Century*, pp. 95–99.

21. Biography by E. Respighi.

Example 25.3: *L'amore dei tre rè*, Act II

MONTEMEZZI

(1923), *La campana sommersa* ("The Sunken Bell," 1927), the spectacular biblical ballet *Belkis* (1930), the mystery play *Maria Egiziaca* (1932), and *La fiamma* ("The Flame," 1934), with a sumptuous orchestral texture. Riccardo Pick-Mangiagalli (1882–1949) had some operas performed successfully at Rome, and his *Ospite inatteso* ("The Unexpected Guest," 1931) was the first opera to have a world premiere broadcast by radio. The operas of Felice Lattuada (1882–1962) were conventional in the main. Operas by Mario Castelnuovo-Tedesco (1895–1968) include *La mandragola* (1926) and some later works in miniature style. Adriano Lualdi (1885–1971) wrote his most popular opera, *La figlia del rè* ("The King's Daughter"), in 1922. One of the most prolific Italian composers was Lodovico Rocca (b. 1895) whose works include *Il dibuc* (1934) and *L'uragano* (1952).

OPERA IN GERMANY AND AUSTRIA

The influence of the French musical style made its mark in Germany with Franz Schreker (1878–1934),[22] whose first opera, *Der ferne Klang* ("The Distant Tone"), was composed between 1903 and 1909, though not performed until 1912.[23] The first notable feature of Schreker's music is the harmony, which basically is like that of Debussy: seventh and ninth chords as consonant units; free use, singly or in combination, of chromatic alteration, pedal points, and organum-like parallel progressions; and treatment of sensuous effect as an end in itself. But it is the Debussy of *L'Après-midi d'un faune* and *La Mer*, rather than of the subdued *Pelléas et Mélisande*, who is Schreker's model. His texture is exceedingly full, often having complicated decorative rhythmic motifs within the beat, or making use of several separated tone masses (as in the opening of Act II of *Der ferne Klang*). All this is supported by an orchestration of corresponding richness, in which harps, muted strings and horns, glissandi, tremolos, and similar effects are prominent. The feeling of tone impressions *(Klang)* in Schreker's operas is so strong as to lead naturally

22. Studies by Bekker, Kapp, Neuwirth, and Hoffman; and numerous articles in *Musikblätter des Anbruch* (see especially vols. 2, 6, and 10). See also Heinsheimer, "Schreker Centennial," and studies by Neuwirth.

23. Alban Berg created a piano reduction of the vocal score.

to a symbolism in which sounds become the embodiment of ideal, mystic forces. There are other signs of the late romantic period as well: occasional Straussian *Sturm und Drang* in the harmony, reminiscences of Verdi in the melodic line, and traces of Puccini's declamation and orchestral treatment.

The whole, nevertheless, is not mere patchwork but an original and very effective theatrical style, which made Schreker, during the years of the First World War and the decade after, one of the most highly regarded opera composers in Germany. His librettos (written by himself) have been criticized for awkwardness of language and for their preoccupation with sex in exaggerated, pathological forms. *Die Gezeichneten* ("The Stigmatized Ones," 1918), a Renaissance subject, has this feature to an extreme degree. His chief work, *Der Schatzgräber* ("The Treasure Digger," 1920), shows a tendency toward more triadic harmony, with much parallelism and a somewhat less complicated texture. The leitmotif system is less prominent here than in his earlier works, and in *Irrelohe* ("Flames of Madness," 1924) it is abandoned altogether. Meanwhile, *Das Spielwerk und die Prinzessin* ("The Playthings and the Princess"), considerably revised in 1920 from the original version of 1913, experimented with pandiatonicism and other new harmonic devices. In marked contrast to the enthusiastic reception accorded Schreker's early operas, the later ones—*Irrelohe*, *Der singende Teufel* ("The Singing Devil, 1928), and *Der Schmied von Gent* ("The Blacksmith of Ghent," 1932)— were staged by his friends and with great reluctance. Although Schreker had been publicly acclaimed as a composer "akin to Wagner,"[24] this rapid decline in popularity dealt his career a crushing blow.

While the Wagnerian movement found some echo in Italy, the influence of verismo in turn was felt in Germany. Its methods are evident in *Tiefland* ("The Lowlands") by Eugen d'Albert (1864–1932), first produced at Prague in 1903 and the most successful of this composer's twenty operas.[25] *Tiefland* is a

---

24. This assessment of Schreker's talent was made by Paul Bekker (1882–1937), a highly regarded music critic in Frankfurt, where the premieres of *Der ferne Klang* and *Der Schatzgräber* took place. See *Musikblätter des Anbruch* (1920), 2:3.

25. Schmitz, "Eugen d'Albert als Opernkomponist"; see also the biography by Raupp.

brutally realistic drama in an effective musical setting that combines Italian-style recitative with Wagnerian harmonies and recurrent motifs in the manner of Puccini. Another popular veristic opera in Germany was *Mona Lisa* (1915), by Max von Schillings (1868–1933),[26] murder and melodrama against a Renaissance background, with a modern frame of prologue and epilogue. The music lies strongly under the influence of Puccini in melody and instrumentation and apparently also of early Debussy in the harmony, and there is some tendency toward separate musical numbers instead of the symphonic continuity of Von Schillings' earlier operas, although recurring motives are still present. Still another German opera of the realist school was *Oberst Chabert* (1912), by Wolfgang von Walterschausen (1882–1954). It is written in a nonmelodic declamatory style, with the dramatic situations underlined by rapidly fluctuating harmonies in which the constant alternation of two triads at the interval of an augmented fourth has the effect of a persistently recurring motif.[27]

A certain eclectic tendency, not unlike that found in Italy, was manifest in German opera of the early twentieth century. The influences of impressionism and verismo already noted in the work of some German composers were combined with other features inherited from the post-Wagnerian and late romantic style. Representative of a more purely German tradition—though explicitly conservative and romantic—was Hans Pfitzner (1869–1949),[28] in whose works a musical language deriving fundamentally from Wagner came to be modified by more diatonic melody, asceticism of feeling, long dwelling on mystical, subjective moods, and frequently dissonant, contrapuntal texture with long-breathed melodic lines (example 25.4). *Der arme Heinrich* (1896) of Pfitzner had a pronounced success, surpassed only by that of his masterpiece, the "musical legend" *Palestrina* in 1917. The latter is a version of Baini's romantic but unfounded story of the way Pales-

---

26. Biography by Raupp.

27. Sailer, "Waltershausen und die Oper." See also Waltershausen's writings on music.

28. Biographies and studies by Dent, Abendroth, Valentin, Müller-Blattau, and Rutz. See also Riezler, *Hans Pfitzner und die deutsche Bühne*; Halusa, "Hans Pfitzners musikdramatisches Schaffen"; Bahle, *Hans Pfitzner und der geniale Mensch*; and Pfitzner's own writings. See also studies of separate operas by Louis (*Die Rose vom Liebesgarten*) and by Hirtler and Berrsche (*Der arme Heinrich*).

Example 25.4: *Palestrina*, Prelude

trina "rescued" polyphonic church music by composing his "Pope
Marcellus" Mass for the Council of Trent; musical motifs from
this mass are incorporated in Pfitzner's score. It does not require
any great penetration to perceive that Pfitzner (who in this one
instance was his own librettist) has treated the legend with reference to his own position as defender of the ancient, good tradition
of music against the modernists and Philistines. This implication,

not unrelated to the dramatic idea of Wagner's *Meistersinger*, was doubtless responsible in part for the favor *Palestrina* enjoyed for a time with the German public, a favor which died out after a couple of decades and which seldom found any echo in other countries. A more advanced harmonic style and partial return to the form of separate numbers was apparent in Pfitzner's later opera, *Das Herz* ("The Heart," 1931).

Contemporary with Pfitzner was the Viennese Alexander von Zemlinsky (1872–1942);[29] of the six operas of his that were produced between 1897 and 1933, the most successful was *Es war einmal* ("Once upon a Time," 1900), but his influence has also been felt through the work of two of his distinguished pupils, Arnold Schoenberg (who will be discussed later) and Erich Wolfgang Korngold (1897–1957). Upon the successful productions of *Violanta* (1916) and *Die tote Stadt* ("The Dead City," 1920), Korngold gained international recognition for his operas.[30] Another Viennese composer of this generation was Franz Schmidt (1874–1939),[31] a pupil of Bruckner and esteemed in Austria as a symphonist, who had some success with the first of his two operas, *Notre Dame* (composed 1902–4, first performed 1914). Other contemporaries whose work for the theater was mostly conservative in musical style include Paul Graener (1872–1944) with *Friedemann Bach* (1931); Max Ettinger (1874–1951), *Frühlings Erwachen* (1928); Joseph Haas (1879–1960),[32] *Tobias Wunderlich* (1937); Julius Weismann (1879–1950), *Leonce und Lena* (1925); Walter Braunfels (1882–1954), *Die Vögel* (1920); and Paul von Klenau (1883–1946); *Rembrandt van Rijn* (1937).

A solitary and enigmatic figure in music of the early twentieth century was Ferruccio Busoni (1866–1924).[33] Of mixed German and Italian ancestry, one of the foremost concert pianists of his day, a scholar and philosopher, he reminds one of an artist

29. See special number of *Der Auftakt* (Prague, 1921).

30. Zemlinsky's *Eine Florentinische Tragödie* (1917) and Korngold's *Violanta* (1916) were revived in a double-bill production by the Santa Fe Opera in 1984.

31. Biography by Liess.

32. Biography by Laux.

33. Biographies by Dent, Guerrini, and Giazotto. See also Bekker, *Klang und Eros*; Gatti, "The Stage Works of Ferruccio Busoni"; Busoni's own writings and "Nota bio-bibliografica."

of the Renaissance in the breadth of his outlook. His aesthetic views, which involved rejection of Wagner and adherence to the operatic ideals of Mozart, made him an important early protagonist of the neoclassic movement. His first opera, *Die Brautwahl* ("The Bridal Choice," 1912), revived the classical principle of set numbers, though the libretto and music still retained many romantic traits. The one-act *Arlecchino* (1917) is an ironical comedy making use of the old commedia dell' arte masks and including some spoken dialogue. The score of *Turandot* (two acts; first performed on the same program with *Arlecchino*) was arranged from earlier incidental music to Gozzi's play. *Doktor Faust*, completed by Busoni's disciple, Philipp Jarnach, and produced posthumously in 1925, is the composer's principal opera and one of the most significant musical treatments of this subject in the twentieth century. Busoni (here as always his own librettist) went back not to Goethe but to the medieval version of the Faust legend, adapting it to his own mystical and symbolical intentions. The score is cast in large musical forms, skillfully using both conventional set numbers and complex polyphony, the whole worked out with uncompromising idealism and making exceptional demands on an audience's attention. It may be true, as Dent has said, that "one cannot apply to *Doctor Faust* the ordinary standards of operatic criticism. It moves on a plane of spiritual experience far beyond that of even the greatest of musical works for the stage."[34] Nevertheless, like many another high plane of "spiritual experience," this one is sometimes dull for outsiders. Despite moments of dramatic force and musical beauty, the general style of *Doktor Faust* is so compressed, so complex in both its dramatic and harmonic implications, and so rooted fundamentally in the late German romantic sound-world that the opera is unlikely ever to become a work in the standard repertoire.

We have traced hitherto the different movements in Germany that may be understood as being, in one way or another, attempts to break away from the potent spell of Wagner: in the fairy-tale opera, by the choice of a different kind of subject matter while retaining to varying degrees the Wagnerian idiom, the technique of leitmotifs, and the general idea of the Gesamtkunst-

34. Dent, *Ferruccio Busoni*, p. 304.

werk; in the Volksoper, by radical simplicity of both subject matter and music; in the "realistic" operas of D'Albert and others, by returning to dramas of uncomplicated human passion without metaphysical implications in a musical style influenced by the methods of Italian verismo; and in the operas of some other composers (notably Schreker), by infusing into the Wagnerian form some of the methods of French impressionism. After the first decade of the twentieth century, there became evident a rather general antiromantic tendency, evidenced by changing ideals as to both the form and the content of opera: in form, a movement of return to the eighteenth-century principle of separate musical numbers, with the device of recurring motives playing only a subordinate role (as in the later works of Von Schillings, Pfitzner, and Schreker); in content, by a return to purely human drama—historical or other—and a musical idiom emphasizing melody, clarity of texture, basically diatonic harmony, and formal structure governed by purely musical principles. This general neoclassic tendency was of course subject to all sorts of exceptions and modifications in individual cases, and after 1920 it found itself in competition with more radical movements, which will be described in the next section; nevertheless, it persisted until well into the twentieth century. Its chief representative is Richard Strauss (1864–1949), whose work is an epitome of the movement from post-Wagner to anti-Wagner in Germany.[35]

Strauss had already produced two operas—*Guntram* (1894) and *Feuersnot* ("Fire-Famine," 1901)[36]—and most of his symphonic poems before he attracted the horrified attention of the entire operatic world with *Salome* in 1905. Oscar Wilde's drama, originally written in French, translated into German by Hedwig Lachmann, and then considerably compressed and revised by Strauss himself, formed the libretto. Its peculiar atmosphere of oriental, sensuous, decadent luxuriance was perfectly

35. See Del Mar, *Richard Strauss: A Critical Commentary on His Life and Works*; Krüger, *Hugo von Hofmannsthal und Richard Strauss*; Schuh, *Über Opern von Richard Strauss*; idem, *Hugo von Hofmannsthal und Richard Strauss*; R. Strauss, *Betrachtungen und Erinnerungen*; correspondence of Strauss and Rolland, Hofmannsthal, Gregor, and Zweig; and studies by Hartmann, Kennedy, Krause, Mann, and Trenner.

36. A concert performance of *Guntram* in 1982 at New York was its United States premiere.

captured in the music, which describes the necrophiliac ecstasy of Salome as vividly as Wagner had once described the agonies of the suffering Amfortas. The final scene of *Salome* was one of the first—perhaps the very first—in which the suggestive power of music had been successfully applied to such a subject, yet it is only one instance of Strauss's amazing skill in musical characterization.

Formally, *Salome* is in the Wagnerian style: the orchestra is dominant, the music is continuous throughout the one act, there is a system of leitmotifs, the texture is uniformly thick and polyphonic, the rhythms are nonperiodic, and the voice parts are mostly of an arioso character. Strauss's mastery of orchestral effect, the individuality and variety of his instrumental coloring, are as evident in the operas as in the symphonic poems. His harmony, which sounded so daring and dissonant at the turn of the century, is no longer novel, but just for this reason we can now better appreciate how appropriate it is for the dramatic purposes. Technically it may be regarded as a continuation of Wagner, with progressions generally conditioned by chromatic voice leading but less bound up with romantic expressiveness, more remote and sudden in its modulations, and much more dissonant. It is a kind of harmony which assumes a familiarity with Wagner on the listener's part, and which as it were telescopes the characteristic Wagner progressions in a manner analogous to the treatment of a fugue subject in stretto. (We have already noticed a similar evolution from the Verdi melodic style in Puccini's operas.) The melodies in *Salome* are of two sorts: either declamatory, with many unusual intervals rising out of the harmonic progressions, or else long-sustained, impassioned outpourings, marked by a very wide range and wide leaps. Strauss managed to combine the characteristics of the music-drama with the striking dramatic quality of Italian verismo and also to introduce some features of grand opera (for example, the Dance of the Seven Veils).

The characteristics of *Salome* are pushed even further in *Elektra* (1909), the first opera Strauss wrote in collaboration with his principal librettist, the Austrian poet and dramatist Hugo von Hofmannsthal (1874–1929). In *Elektra*, the central passion is the heroine's insane thirst for vengeance on the murderers of her father, and here again Strauss has matched the somber horrors of the libretto with music of fearful dissonance, lurid melodramatic power, and a harmonic idiom in which for long stretches polytonality is the normal state. Perhaps the most noticeable feature of the score is the contrast between this dissonant idiom and the occasional stretches of lush, late-romantic sentimentality, with cloying sevenths, ninths, chromatic alterations, and suspensions. Whatever the composer's intentions may have been, these portions give a final dreadful touch of spiritual abnormality to the whole action; they are like something familiar suddenly seen in a ghastly, strange light.

With *Der Rosenkavalier* ("The Rose-Bearer," 1911), a "comedy for music," Strauss and Hofmannsthal achieved an enduring success not equaled by any of their other joint creations.[37] This romantic comedy of Viennese life around the time of Maria Theresa—the mid-eighteenth century—forms a perfect libretto, with humor, farce, sentiment, swiftly moving action, variety of scenes, and superb characterizations. The music is as varied as the drama. In some portions it is no less complex (though considerably less dissonant) than that of *Salome* and *Elektra*. The erotic quality of the love music in the first part of Act I is equal to Strauss's best in this vein. For the most part, however, the style of *Der Rosenkavalier* is more simple and tuneful than that of his earlier operas. The famous waltzes are anachronistic; the waltzes of Schubert, Lanner, and J. Strauss, which these imitate, were not, of course, a feature of eighteenth-century Vienna. But this is of little importance, and it is still less important that Strauss has seen fit to decorate the waltz themes with some of his own harmonic twists. The best musical characterizations are those of the Princess, a figure of mingled humor, wisdom, and pathos, and her country cousin, Baron Ochs, a type of comic boor drawn, at Strauss's insistence, rather more coarsely than Hofmannsthal would have preferred. Sophie and Octavian, the young lovers, are by comparison colorless; their music is that of situations and sentiment rather than of personalities, and any possible realism in their relationship is prevented by making Octavian's part a *Hosenrolle*, a "trouser role"—that is, a man's part sung by a woman, like Mozart's Cherubino. The scene of their first meeting and the presentation of the silver rose thus moves in an atmosphere of ideal,

37. Pörnbacher, *Hugo von Hofmannsthal, Richard Strauss*; Schuh, "*Der Rosenkavalier*": *Vier Studien*.

magical, passionless beauty, unsurpassed anywhere in the whole realm of opera. It is remarkable that here Strauss writes in an almost purely diatonic idiom, even emphasizing the triads by outlining them in the melodies; one of the composer's happiest inspirations, the theme of the silver rose (high, dissonant appoggiatura triads with celesta, flutes, harps, and three solo violins), tinkles against this background.

The ensembles of *Der Rosenkavalier* are virtuoso creations, particularly the scene of the levee in Act I: a dissolution and at the same time an apotheosis of the eighteenth-century opera buffa ensemble, bringing together all the elements of this form in seeming confusion and yet with a curious illusion of realism; the introduction of a stylized Italian tenor aria, a veritable interpolated number in this scene, is accomplished in the spirit of sporting with the formal technique. The first two-thirds of Act III forms another long ensemble of broad farcical nature with elements of the old Viennese popular theater, laid on musically with a rather heavy hand, but of an irresistible comic dash which can be compared only to the ending of the second act of *Die Meistersinger* or the finale of *Falstaff*. After all this hurly-burly follows one of those transformations of mood which are so characteristic of *Der Rosenkavalier*. The trio for three soprano voices (Sophie, the Princess, and Octavian) is another superlative number, a melting baroque texture of long-spun, interweaving lines above simple diatonic harmonies. The long decrescendo continues: the last song is a duet in G major, two strophes of a lyric melody in thirds and sixths, in the style of the old German singspiel. The themes of the silver rose and the lovers' first meeting sound once more. The opera closes with a pantomime of the Princess' little black pageboy, to the same music which was heard at his first appearance near the beginning of Act I. This masterly finale was largely shaped by Strauss's demands. Hofmannsthal at one time feared it would be feeble in effect, but Strauss wrote: "It is at the conclusion that a musician, if he has any ideas at all, can achieve his best and supreme effects—so you may safely leave this for me to judge . . . from the Baron's exit onwards, I'll *guarantee* that, provided you undertake to guarantee the rest of the work." [38]

38. Letter of September 12 (?), 1910, in Strauss and Hofmannsthal, *A Working Friendship*, pp. 67–68. Quoted by permission.

Der Rosenkavalier was hardly finished before Strausss and Hofmannsthal were at work on their next collaborative effort, Ariadne auf Naxos (1912), designed as a pendant to a German version of Molière's Bourgeois Gentilhomme. This one-act piece is a profoundly poetic, sensitive treatment of the myth of Ariadne and Bacchus, in form and spirit suggesting the pastorales and ballets of Lully and Molière, which were likewise usually enclosed within a comedy;[39] and like those models, it introduces comic-satirical elements through personages borrowed from the Italian commedia dell' arte. Strauss's music continues the trend toward diatonicism and simplicity that had been evident in Der Rosenkavalier; harmonically, it starts from the point which the composer had reached in the silver-rose scene of the earlier opera and becomes progressively less and less chromatic. The trio in scene 3 for three sopranos is similar to the trio in the last act of Der Rosenkavalier and is likewise followed by a simple folklike song. A new element is the light, swift, parlando style of the comic scenes and of the prologue, which was added in 1916, when Ariadne was taken out of its original setting in the Molière play.[40] In this prologue, a comedy and an opera seria are being prepared for palace entertainment. As a time-saving device, the master of the palace orders both works to be performed simultaneously, thereby avoiding a delay in the fireworks display that is to conclude the festivities. Thus unfolds before the audience a combined comic-tragic spectacle. One especially difficult role, that of Zerbinetta, is written for a high coloratura soprano; there is a trouser-role, that of the Composer, for a soprano. The leitmotif technique is used to a slight extent, but the orchestra (only thirty-six players) is subordinated to the voices,[41] and there is a distinct tendency toward division into separate numbers.

Ariadne auf Naxos was the definitive stage of Strauss's conversion to a Mozartean style, an intimate opera in which the musical idiom is refined to a more nearly classic purity than in

39. The analogy will be seen most clearly by comparison with the following works of Molière: La Princesse d'Elide (1664), Psyché (a tragédie-ballet, 1671), the pastorale in La Comtesse d'Escarbagnas (1671), and the pastoral intermèdes in Georges Dandin (1668) and Le Malade imaginaire (1673), music by M. A. Charpentier.

40. For a detailed study of the two versions of the work, see Forsyth, "Ariadne auf Naxos".

41. Although the reduced size of the orchestra suggests a chamber-style orchestration, the effects that Strauss is able to achieve are related more to his symphonic poems. See, for example, the orchestral accompaniment to Bacchus' final solo.

the earlier works.[42] From this point on, Strauss remained musically conservative. He had summed up in his own career the transition from Wagnerian music drama to the new anti-Wagnerian opera. But the flame of inspiration no longer burned quite so steadily; moreover, Strauss's later operas, while no less perfect in construction and technical realization than his earlier ones, fell coldly on the ears of a changed postwar world, a world which could only hear his music as something out of a vanished and irrecoverable past. This historical misfortune has deprived the opera-going public, especially outside Germany, of acquaintance with some works that well deserve to be better known.

One of these is *Die Frau ohne Schatten* ("The Woman Without a Shadow"), composed during the years of the First World War on a libretto by Hofmannsthal based on one of his prose tales, and first performed at Vienna in 1919. *Die Frau ohne Schatten* is a symbolic drama with a complex score of grandiose proportions, rich in orchestral effects, embodying contrasting musical styles and recurring motives.[43] The title role is portrayed by a beguiling fairy who has been transformed from a gazelle into an Empress. To make complete her human identity, the Empress must acquire a shadow. Failure to do so within the time limit of three days will bring a curse upon the Emperor: he will be turned to stone. Tensions mount throughout the melodrama section (beginning of Act III), as the Empress realizes that the only way to escape the curse is to inflict disaster upon a childless couple, the dyer Barak and his wife, whom she has come to love. She refuses this course of action, emphatically declaring: "Ich—will—nicht!" (example 25.5). To her surprise, her decision releases the Emperor from his semipetrified state and restores happiness to Barak and his wife (example 25.6). Strauss concludes the opera in a very subdued manner. In the epilogue, voices rise from different areas of the theater (six solo voices from the orchestra pit; the chorus of Unborn Children from offstage and from the balconies and aisles), their chorale-like expression hovering in a faint pianissimo

---

42. There is in the 1916 *Ariadne* score considerable variety of musical style. Compare the overture and incidental music with the expansive design of scene 3.

43. Although the merits of this opera have been hotly contested since its creation, the Metropolitan Opera production in 1981 left no doubt that it can win acclaim from critics and public alike. Cf. Pantle, *"Die Frau ohne Schatten"*; Lehmann, *Five Operas and Richard Strauss*; Hofmannsthal, *Erzählung*.

Example 25.5: *Die Frau ohne Schatten*, Act III

R. STRAUSS

Example 25.6: *Die Frau ohne Schatten*, Act III

R. STRAUSS

above the harmonic support of the organ, harps, celestes, and arpeggiated strings.

On a more intimate scale is *Intermezzo* (1924), a "middle-class comedy with symphonic interludes," on a libretto by the composer in an autobiographical vein reminiscent of his *Sinfonia domestica*, and a real virtuoso piece for the soprano. With *Die ägyptische Helena* (1928, revised version 1933) Strauss and Hofmannsthal returned, not altogether successfully, to the realm of mythology. The best of their postwar operas was the "lyrical comedy" *Arabella*, similar in atomsphere and general sound to *Der Rosenkavalier*, with a plot verging on operetta but handled with delicacy and spontaneous lyric warmth, a happy blending of Strauss's full orchestral sonorities and fine details of chamber music style.

Die schweigsame Frau ("The Silent Woman," 1935), on a libretto by Stefan Zweig after Ben Jonson, is a comedy that includes spoken dialogue, recitatives, lyric passages, and many ensembles, and a few musical quotations from older composers and Strauss himself. *Friedenstag* ("Day of Peace," 1938) is an exceptional one-act work in subject, style, and spirit. The libretto, sketched by Zweig and completed by Josef Gregor, decries the horrors of war and promotes a message of peace. Strauss wanted this opera performed in Germany as a witness to his belief in pacifism and as a statement of resistance to Nazi domination of the arts. He achieved uncensored performances in Nazi Germany by deliberately creating a Wagnerian-style score that gave the impression of being highly nationalistic and politically acceptable. He even included quotations from Martin Luther's chorale tune, "Ein feste Burg," with one such statement occurring in the stirring finale where love, hope, and peace triumph over the destruction and hatred of armed conflict.[44] Josef Gregor also delivered the librettos of Strauss's next two operas, both on mythological themes: *Daphne* (1938), a "bucolic tragedy,"[45] and *Die Liebe der Danae* ("The Love of Danae"), a "merry mythological tale" composed in 1938–40 but not performed until 1952.

Strauss's last opera, *Capriccio* (1942), is a one-act "con-

---

44. See Potter, "Strauss's *Friedenstag*."

45. The United States premiere occurred at the Santa Fe Opera in 1981.

versation piece for music" on a libretto by Clemens Krauss—"no work for the public, only a fine dish for connoisseurs," the composer said. With only a pretext of a plot, *Capriccio* revolves about a discussion (which never reaches a positive conclusion) of certain "theoretical questions of art," especially the relation of words,

Example 25.7: *Capriccio*, sc. 6 ("The Sonnet")

(Example 25.7 continued)

music, and staging in opera; yet for all the lack of dramatic movement, the personages are no mere shadows, but fully drawn human characters. The scene is laid in Paris at the time of the Gluck-
Piccinni quarrel (see chapter 14), which gives Strauss occasion to
quote now and then a musical phrase from operas by these two
composers. *Capriccio* completes a cycle which *Ariadne* began. Ap-

propriately to its period, the score is of a stylized rococo quality and is held throughout in the mood of chamber music. A full orchestra is required but is used for the most part only in small combinations; the sonority of the string sextet, first heard in the introduction, runs like a thread through the opera. The words are made to come clearly through the polyphonic orchestral texture,[46] being conveyed in lifelike dialogue and broadly designed ensembles; the principal aria, a number of central importance in the score, is a lyrical setting of a sonnet translated from Ronsard's sixteenth-century *Continuation des Amours* (example 25.7). Altogether, *Capriccio* must be regarded as among the very best of Strauss's operas, the musical testament of an artist in the matured wisdom of age: in this, as in other respects, a worthy companion to Verdi's *Falstaff*.

OTHER COUNTRIES

The sources of the main stream of operatic production in the early part of the twentieth century were still the three nations of Italy, France, and Germany. At the same time, the nationalist movement continued more or less vigorously in other lands, although as time went on, the earlier marked national quality of the music tended to become somewhat overlaid by foreign elements and opera thus more nearly approached a common international style.

The most famous opera to come out of Hungary in the early twentieth century is *A Kékszakállú herceg vára* ("Duke Bluebeard's Castle"), by Béla Bartók (1881–1945),[47] composed in 1911 and first performed at Budapest in 1918—"the first genuinely Hungarian and at the same time modern opera."[48] The libretto by Béla Balász, inspired by Maeterlinck's version of the ancient tale and published in 1910 as a "mystery play," involves only two characters and contains hardly any external action; the

46. This was always an important consideration with Strauss; see his prefaces to this opera and *Intermezzo*, and also his correspondence with Hofmannsthal.

47. Biographies by Stevens and Moreux. See also *Béla Bartók: A Memorial Review*; Kroó, *Bartok Béla szinpadi müvei* and "*Duke Bluebeard's Castle*"; Lendvai, "A kékszakállú herceg vára" (important musical analysis); studies by Crow, ed., Lendvai, and Zieliński.

48. Kroó, "*Duke Bluebeard's Castle*," p. 340.

inner, symbolic drama proceeds with the opening, one after another, of the seven doors that lead into the hall of Bluebeard's castle. Bartók's music, like Debussy's for *Pelléas*, seems a perfect and inimitable embodiment of the mysterious text. The music flows

Example 25.8: *Duke Bluebeard's Castle*

(Example 25.8 continued)

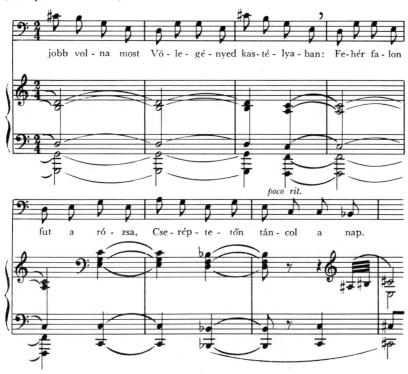

jobb vol - na most Vö - le - gé - nyed kas - té - lya - ban: Fe-hér fa - lon

poco rit.

fut a ró - zsa, Cse - rép - te - tőn tán - col a nap.

unbrokenly throughout the single act, its continuity emphasized by the recurrence of "pivot" motives and themes. The orchestral color and harmony, impressionistic in essence but stamped everywhere with Bartók's individuality, supports a vocal line consisting for the most part of irregular declamatory phrases whose melodic and rhythmic outlines derive from Hungarian folk song (example 25.8).

Equally imbued with Hungarian national feeling, though far less radical in musical idiom than *Bluebeard,* are the stage works of Zoltán Kodály (1882–1967),[49] which combine spoken dialogue with songs and choruses either borrowed from or composed in the style of folk music: *Háry János* (1926), on the adventures of a comic character from national folklore; the ballad opera *Székely fonó* ("The Spinning-Room," 1932, revised from the

49. Biographies by Eősze and Young.

original version of 1924); and *Czinka Panna*, composed for a national centennial celebration and produced at Budapest in 1948.

A more international romantic style is characteristic of the music by the noted pianist-composer Ernst von Dohnányi (1877–1960), as is evident in his three-act opera, *A Vajda tornya* ("The Tower of the Voyvod"), produced at Budapest in 1932. Dohnányi is perhaps best remembered for *Der Tenor* (Budapest, 1929), one of the finest comic operas written in the first half of the twentieth century.[50]

The two principal Polish opera composers of the early twentieth century were Ludomir Różycki (1883–1953) and Karol Szymanowski (1882–1937).[51] Różycki, though regarded in Poland as a nationalist composer, had absorbed Western influences from Germany. His works include *Eros i Psyche* (1917), the comic opera *Casanova* (1923), *Beatrix Cenci* (1927), and *Pani Walewska* ("Madame Walewska," composed 1945), as well as a successful ballet, *Pan Twardowski* (1921). Szymanowski, the leading Polish composer of this period, worked primarily in symphonic and choral forms and wrote only two operas. *Hagith* (composed 1912–14) was influenced in subject matter and construction by Strauss's *Elektra* and in harmony largely by the music of Ravel. Particularly important is Szymanowski's *Król Roger* ("King Roger," 1926), a monumental dramatic work on a libretto somewhat similar to Schreker's *Der ferne Klang*. The music is harmonically rich in a neoimpressionistic idiom, with national influences in the melody; the solo lines range freely from declamatory-arioso phrases to ample melodic arches. The choral writing is particularly effective; some of the choral sonorities are derived from Russian church style, with full texture, doubling of the parts, and parallel movement of the voices (example 25.9). The ballets in Act II introduce oriental motives.

A group of Polish composers who for the most part came to recognition only after the establishment of national independence in 1919 includes Henryk Melcer (1869–1928), with *Marja* (1904); Emil Mlynarski (1870–1935), *Noc letnia* ("Summer Night," 1924); Henryk Opienski (1870–1942), *Jakub lutnista* ("Jacob the

---

50. See Vázsonyi, *Dohnányi Ernő*.

51. On Różycki, see the biography by Wieniawski, the study by Chybiński, and Różycki's own writings. The standard biography of Szymanowski is by Łobaczewska; other biographies by Jachimecki and Golachowski. See also studies by Jachimecki, Iwaszkiewicz, Chylińska, and Wightman.

Lutenist," 1927); Tadeusz Joteyko (1872–1932), *Zygmund August* (1925); Felix Nowowiejski (1877–1946), *Legenda Bałtyku* ("Baltic Legend," 1924);[52] and Adam Tadeusz Wieniawski (1879–1950), *Megae* (1912).

Example 25.9: *King Roger*, Act I

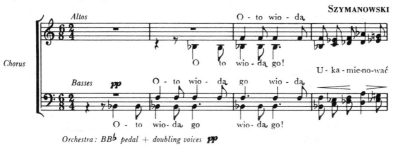

52. Kamieński, *"Legenda Bałtyku."*

(Example 25.9 continued)

(Example 25.9 continued)

In Russia, a singularly different "opera" came to the stage during this period. *Victory Over the Sun*, first performed at St. Petersburg in 1913, is unusual in the sense that it intentionally accentuates visual rather than dramatic or musical impulses. It evolved from a collaboration of Velimir Khlebnikov and Alexei Kruchenykh, Futurist writers; Kasimir Malevich, a Cubist artist; and Mikhail Matiushin, a musician who was also a painter and an art historian. The libretto for *Victory Over the Sun* is written in a "language" that replaces conventional word structure with pure "sounds" to evoke verbal images. While the language may at times be incomprehensible, the theme of the libretto is unmistakably clear: the Sun, symbol of the present, must be captured so that one may experience the future—even a sunless future, which would be preferable to the boring present. This synthesis of art forms produces a unique staged phenomenon to which audiences then and now have responded with a degree of enthusiasm that is best described as wild and exuberant.[53]

A notable figure in Spanish opera of the early twentieth century was Manuel de Falla (1876–1946),[54] although, like Szymanowski, Bartók, and Kodály, he worked mainly in other forms of composition. His principal opera is the charming little marionette piece *El retablo di Maese Pedro* ("Master Peter's Puppet Show," 1923), for three singing parts and an orchestra of twenty-five players, on an episode from *Don Quixote*, using a boy soprano as narrator and in a musical style that cleverly combines archaic features with modern harmonies in an austere but appropriate texture. Falla's earlier opera, *La vida breve* ("Life Is Short"), composed in 1905 and first performed in 1913, is less notable for its dramatic qualities than for the ballets in Act II; Falla's other ballets, *El amor brujo* and *El sombrero de tres picos*, are important works in this form.

During the last twenty years of his life Falla was continually occupied with what he intended to be his masterwork, *La Altántida* ("Atlantis"). Although this vast "scenic cantata" was left unfinished, the music was put together from the composer's

53. Recent performances have been given in Los Angeles (1980), Washington (1981), Berlin (1983), and Brooklyn (1984).

54. Biographies by Pahissa, Demarquez, and Franco; see also Viu, "The Mystery of . . . *La Atlántida.*

sketches by his devoted pupil Ernesto Halffter (b. 1905). Portions of *La Atlántida* were performed in public for the first time, without staging, at Barcelona on November 24, 1961. The first stage production (with the words in Italian translation) took place at La Scala in Milan on June 18, 1962, and a concert version (incomplete) was given at New York on September 29 and 30, 1962. Halffter's final revision of *La Atlántida* was presented in concert at the 1976 Lucerne festival. Subsequent performances of Halffter's definitive version have also taken place in concert halls, even though Falla had wanted this work performed in a religious setting, with its narrative portions illustrated by large paintings.

The text of *La Atlántida* is taken from an epic poem published in 1878 by Mossén Jacinto Verdaguer. Within a framework of half-pagan, half-Christian mythology, it ranges from the remote geological past over the legendary history of the Spanish peninsula, recounting the exploits of Hercules, the Gardens of the Hesperides, the opening of the Straits of Gibraltar, the destruction of Atlantis, and the founding of Cadiz and Barcelona, and culminating with a prophetic vision of Columbus's voyages and the establishment of a Spanish empire in America. In form as well as in some aspects of the subject, the work is reminiscent of Milhaud's *Christophe Colomb* (see below). *Atlántida* is a monumental combination of oratorio and opera, some three hours in length, requiring for full performance a narrator, a dozen soloists, two choruses, and a huge orchestra. The music has extraordinary variety and breadth; the style in general is markedly different from that of Falla's earlier works and has an austere, archaic grandeur (especially in the many choral portions) that recalls the spirit of the great sixteenth-century Spanish church composers.

Some other continental European composers of opera in the first part of the twentieth century will be briefly noted. In Spain, the disciples of Pedrell include Angel Barrios (1822–1964) and Conrado del Campo y Zabaleta (1879–1953), with a jointly composed opera, *El Avapiés* (1919—the title is the name of a quarter in Madrid), and Amadeo Vives (1871–1932), composer of the "lyric eclogue" *Maruxa* (1914) and the popular comic opera *Doña Francisquita* (1923). Joaquín Turina (1882–1949) composed the operas *Margot* (1914) and *Jardín de orienta* ("Oriental Garden," 1923). A notable composer of Holland was Willem Pijper

(1894–1947), whose only completed opera, *Halewijn*, was given at Amsterdam in 1933. In Switzerland, Othmar Schoeck (1886–1957), distinguished especially as a writer of songs, produced a number of operas, the most successful of which was *Penthesilea* (1927). Another important composer in Switzerland is Heinrich Sutermeister (b. 1910), who combines a pleasing melodic style with good feeling for the theater, exemplified in the tragic operas *Romeo und Julia* (1940) and *Raskolnikoff* (1948); after Dostoyevsky's *Crime and Punishment*, as well as in various short works of lighter character written for radio and later revised for regular theater performance.

The situation in England in the early part of the twentieth century is interesting because of the contrast between the work of continentally oriented composers and the efforts of others to create a viable opera of distinctly English character. To the former group belongs the successful woman opera composer, Dame Ethel Smyth (1858–1944).[55] Following two early operas brought out in Germany, her principal stage work, *The Wreckers*, written originally on a French libretto, was produced in a German translation (as *Strandrecht*) at Leipzig in 1906 and finally played in English at London in 1909; it has been revived there with success since 1939. Her next opera was a comedy, *The Boatswain's Mate*, which had a fair success in England; two further one-act operas appeared in 1923 and 1925. Other comic operas by English composers include Lord Berner's (1883–1950) *Carosse du Saint-Sacrement* (Paris, 1921) and Arthur Benjamin's (1893–1960) *The Devil Take Her* (1932)—both witty one-act pieces in a fluent modern style.

A virtual expatriate was Frederick Delius (1862–1934).[56] Born in England of German parentage, he lived most of his life abroad—first in Florida, then for a period of study in Leipzig, and from 1888 in France. Three of his six operas came to performance, all first in Germany. The best known of them, *A Village*

---

55. Biography by St. John. See also Smyth's memoirs, *Impressions That Remained*, and Capell, "Dame Ethel Smyth's Operas."

56. Biographies by Warlock and Jefferson. See also Hutchings, "Delius's Operas"; Lowe, ed., *Frederick Delius 1862–1934: A Catalogue of the Music Archives of the Delius Trust*; Redwood, ed., *A Delius Companion*.

Romeo and Juliet (1907), might from the story almost have been entitled "A Village Tristan and Isolde." It is full of lovely music in a late romantic style—rich in texture, chromatic, with long expressive lines for the solo voices and some fine choral scenes. Celtic folk-song idiom is apparent in some places, for example in Vreli's song at the opening of scene 4; the familiar orchestral selection "The Walk to the Paradise Garden" (from the end of scene 5) is typical of the style.

Among other early twentieth-century composers of serious opera in English were John Edmund Barkworth (1858–1921), with *Romeo and Juliet* (1916), and Ernest Bryson (1867–1942), *The Leper's Flute* (1926). Philip Napier Miles (1865–1935),[57] active promoter of opera in England, composed *Westward Ho!* (1913) and *Markheim* (1924). Well constructed and worked out, though conservative in musical style, were the operas of Nicholas Comyn Gatty (1874–1946): *Greysteel* (1906), *Duke or Devil* (1909), the romantic Shakespearean *Tempest* (1920), and the charming fairy opera *Prince Ferelon* (1921). Sir Eugene Goossens (1893–1958) had some success with his two operas on texts by Arnold Bennett: *Judith* (1929) and *Don Juan de Mañera* (1937). Others in this period were Sir Donald Francis Tovey (1875–1940), with *The Bride of Dionysus* (1932); Colin Macleod Campbell (1890–1953), *Thais and Talmaae* (1921); and Lawrance Arthur Collingwood (b. 1887), *Macbeth* (1934). The only one of the three operas by Albert Coates (1882–1953) to be produced in England was *Pickwick* (1936).

About 1908, Rutland Boughton (1878–1960), an ardent disciple of Wagner's theories and himself a composer of frankly romantic tendencies, conceived the idea of founding an English equivalent of Bayreuth. One outcome of this project was the establishment of the Glastonbury Festival in 1914 and the production there in 1916 of Boughton's *The Round Table*, designed to be the first music-drama in an Arthurian tetralogy. (*The Birth of Arthur*, the prologue, had been heard earlier, with a piano substituting for the orchestra.) Boughton completed the tetralogy, but only the second part *(The Lily Maid)* was performed, in 1934.

---

57. Colles, "Philip Napier Miles."

Meanwhile, the composer had achieved an unexpected success with a less ambitious but appealing opera, *The Immoral Hour* (1914).[58]

In American music, German influences were still preponderant at the beginning of the twentieth century, but by this time composers were more thoroughly trained, more ambitious, versatile, and productive, and they were speaking a more authoritative musical language. Nevertheless, it is worth remarking that neither of the two leading figures in this generation, Charles Martin Loeffler and Edward MacDowell, wrote an opera. The principal composers who did write for the theater were three pupils of Chadwick: Frederick Shepherd Converse (1871–1940), Henry Hadley (1871–1937), and Horatio Parker (1863–1919).[59] Converse's *The Pipe of Desire* (Boston, 1906) was the first American opera to be presented at the Metropolitan (1910)—a pleasant, tuneful score showing some influence of impressionism. Another opera, *The Sacrifice*, was given at Boston in 1911. Hadley's chief successes, in a sound conservative style, were *Azora, Daughter of Montezuma* (Chicago, 1917) and *Cleopatra's Night* (New York, 1920).

Parker's two price-winning operas, *Mona* (New York, 1912) and *Fairyland* (Los Angeles, 1915), are regarded by many as significant American operas that have been unjustly ignored. The neglect is certainly not due to any technical shortcomings in the scores, which are sound in craftsmanship, large in conception, distinguished in musical ideas, and well planned for theatrical effect. But the librettos are sadly old-fashioned: *Mona*, a sufficiently good drama in essence, is markedly in the romantic style of its day, with a scene laid in ancient Britain and the whole obviously owing much to *Tristan und Isolde*. *Fairyland* is one of those combinations of whimsy, symbolism, and vague pantheistic aspiration such as are found in the fairy operas of Rimsky-Korsakov or in Converse's *Pipe of Desire*; and Parker's music is likewise typical of the late romantic period. *Mona* is a slightly modernized *Tristan*, with the same sort of continuous symphonic

58. See Boughton's own writings; Hurd, *Immortal Hour*; Antcliffe, "A British School of Music-Drama."

59. On Hadley, see the biography by Boardman and the monograph by Berthoud. On Parker, see Chadwick, *Horatio Parker*; D. Smith, "A Study of Horatio Parker; memoir by Semler.

structure, system of leitmotifs, opulent harmony, chromatic melody, and avoidance of cadences that characterize its model; *Fairyland* is somewhat lighter in texture and more diatonic in harmony—Wagner leavened by a dash of late Strauss. Musically, the gravest accusation that can be made against either opera is that the same things had been said before; and it may be regretted that these works had the misfortune to come at a moment when tastes in musical matters were on the verge of radical change.

From 1920 to 1950

The first half of the twentieth-century was—or at any rate so it appears to us now—anything but conservative in music. The composers whose names dominate the period were innovators, many of them self-consciously so and some to such a degree as to be quite incomprehensible to the vast majority of the music-listening public. To be sure, most of their music sounds less radical to us than it did to their immediate contemporaries; but the gap between the twentieth-century composer and the public is still wide.

Roughly speaking, the development of Western musical style since 1915 may be summarized as follows: A period lasting until about 1930 was marked by diverse experiments with all the elements of composition, including rhythm but especially looking toward either a radical extension of the classical concept of tonality or the complete transcendence of that concept. After about 1930, two main directions were discernible. The first was toward a replacement of tonality by other systems of order, typically some form of organization stemming from the "twelve-tone" principles developed by Schoenberg in the 1920s. Composers who followed this direction generally retained some elements of traditional music, though in the more extreme manifestations connection with the past, as well as the idea of music as a sensuous language of communication, seems to have disappeared. The second aimed at a reconciliation with tonality in a modern musical idiom, moderation of extreme dissonance, maintenance of communication, and in general some degree of attachment to tradition. The composers who followed this direction sought inspiration largely from pre-romantic Western art music. Of course, the two tendencies inter-acted in practice and moreover were accompanied by various experiments in timbre, rhythm, and form and by occasional exotic influences.

GERMANY AND AUSTRIA

In the early part of the twentieth century, the expressionist movement was reflected in opera most clearly in the works of Arnold Schoenberg (1874–1951)[60] and his pupil, Alban Berg (1885–1935).[61] Schoenberg's *Erwartung* ("Expectation") and *Die glückliche Hand* ("The Lucky Hand") were composed in 1909 and 1913, respectively, though not performed until 1924. Both call for a large orchestra, usually subdivided so that only a few instruments are playing at one time, and both are in the dissonant, thick Schoenbergian harmonic style of the prewar period. The voice lines are wide in range, with large, ultraexpressive intervals, occasionally going over into *Sprechgesang (Sprechstimme)*—that is, a kind of vocal utterance halfway between speaking and singing, with exactly notated rhythm but only approximately notated pitch. Both dramas are essentially subjective, the scenery and action being symbolical; both are, in scale, cantatas rather than operas. *Erwartung* is a monodrama: a woman seeking her lover finds only his dead body, over which she sings a long monologue, a modernistic Liebestod. *Die glückliche Hand* has three soloists with a chorus of twelve voices, and uses colors symbolically in scenery, costumes, and lighting. Schoenberg's later one-act comic opera, *Von Heute auf Morgen* ("From Today until Tomorrow," 1930), is completely in the twelve-tone technique, with distinct recitatives and arias, thus following the general trend of the post-

60. Biographies by Stuckenschmidt and Reich. See also Rufer, *The Works of Arnold Schoenberg: A Catalogue*; Neighbour, "Schoenberg" (with extensive bibliography); Wörner, *Gotteswort und Magie*; idem, "Arnold Schoenberg and the Theater"; H. Keller, "Schoenberg's *Moses and Aaron*"; idem, "Schoenberg's Comic Opera"; Babbitt, "An Introduction to the Music [of Schoenberg's *Moses und Aron*]"; P. White, *Schoenberg and the God-Idea*.

61. Biographies and studies by Reich and Redlich; Leibowitz, "Alban Berg et l'essence de l'opéra"; Reich, "A Guide to *Wozzeck*"; Kerman, "Terror and Self-Pity"; Jouve and Fano, "*Wozzeck*" *ou le nouvel opéra*; and the studies of *Wozzeck* and *Lulu* by Perle.

From a set of sketches for *Wozzeck* by A. Berg.

From a set of sketches for *Wozzeck* by A. Berg.

war period toward the number opera. Of the three works, *Erwartung* is the most successful; in both dramatic technique and musical style it may be regarded as a foretaste of Berg's *Wozzeck*.

Schoenberg's one large work for the theater is *Moses und Aron*, for which he wrote the entire libretto and had composed the music of the first two acts by 1932 (only a few sketches exist for the music of Act III); a radio performance was given in 1954 and the first stage performance in 1957. *Moses und Aron* is an opera-oratorio, in which Schoenberg has used the biblical material for a dramatic presentation of the tragic abyss (tragic, because unbridgeable by good will) that lies between wisdom and action: Moses, the philosopher-lawgiver, cannot communicate his vision; Aaron, the man of action, can only misunderstand and falsify it. Schoenberg's profound drama is united to a musical score of fearful difficulty (he himself doubted whether a performance would actually be possible), towering in conception, masterly in realization, and of overwhelming dramatic effect. Within the unity imposed by consistent use of a single tone row is endless variety of expression and sound, from the (symbolical) Sprechgesang of Moses' role to the gorgeous oriental colors and wild dance rhythms in the scene of the worship of the Golden Calf. *Moses und Aron*, though unfinished—and its very incompleteness may also be symbolic—is one of the great works of twentieth-century opera, and one that will remain significant for many generations.

In contrast to the oratorio-like character of so many contemporary operas, the character of Berg's operas is purely theatrical. *Wozzeck*, composed between 1914 and 1922 and first performed at Berlin in 1925,[62] is based on a "dramatic fragment" by Georg Büchner (1813–1837), the original twenty-five scenes being reduced by Berg to fifteen and grouped in three acts of five scenes each. Wozzeck, the hero, is a representative of what he himself calls "Wir arme Leut' " ("We poor folk"), tormented by circumstances, suffering but unconscious of guilt, finally murdering his mistress and drowning himself, driven always by forces he never thinks of questioning or resisting. Despite the date of Büchner's drama, *Wozzeck* is thoroughly typical of the postwar period in

---

62. During this period, Berg served three and a half years in the Austrian army, an experience that permitted him close identification with the title character.

Germany; its atmosphere seems as though infected by the morbid, bitter, neurotic mood of that time. Yet it is not merely topical: Wozzeck is a universal figure, symbol of the oppressed and, in a larger sense, of man in his naked helplessness before blind powers that care nothing about his fate. Since the expressionist technique makes every external object a projection of Wozzeck's own soul, the scenes, characters, and events of the opera have an unearthly quality, like a nightmarish puppet show; and Berg's music belongs to this nightmare world as surely as Debussy's belongs to the dream world of *Pelléas et Mélisande*. The harmonic style of *Wozzeck* is in most places atonal, full of strange, wonderful color effects (for example, the scene of Wozzeck's suicide) and distorted reminiscences of the normal "waking" world (for example, the "folk song" in Act I, the caricature of the *Rosenkavalier* waltzes in Act II). The vocal lines, mostly in sharply pointed declamation with abrupt, wide intervals, alternate between ordinary speech, Sprechgesang, and song. These are a few recurring motives, notably Wozzeck's "Wir arme Leut' " (see example 25.10), but the chief means of unity is the organization of each act and scene in set musical forms derived from classical patterns. These patterns reveal themselves, however, only on analysis; it is no part of the composer's intention that the auditor should perceive them, unless subliminally. Sometimes they have a direct dramatic function: there is a grim fitness, for example, in the choice of the learned passacaglia form for the scene (Act I, scene 4) in which Wozzeck submits himself to a doctor as a subject for scientific experiments. The scenes within each act are connected by orchestral interludes; the longest of these, in Act III, recapitulates the themes of the entire drama in climax before leading into the brief coda-like final scene. Initial productions of *Wozzeck*, in German and in translations, provoked mixed and often hostile reactions. Now that the sound of the music has become more familiar, it has come to be generally recognized not only as a powerful drama in music but also as one of the few really successful operas in a fully modern style.

Berg's second opera, *Lulu*, was completed in substance before the composer's death in 1935, but the orchestration had been finished only through the first two acts and a small part of the third. The first two acts, and two fragments of the third, were performed in 1937 in Zurich, and frequent revivals of this truncated version appeared for several decades. Berg's widow pos-

Example 25.10: *Wozzeck*, Act I, sc. 1

sessed a reconstruction of the third act, but it was withheld from the public until her death in 1976. The first complete production of *Lulu* took place in 1979 at the Paris Opéra, and in this form it has now come into the repertoire of the world's major opera companies. Although the addition of the reconstructed third act lengthens the performance to four hours, it nevertheless restores a requisite balance to the opera and clarifies the inner motivations of the drama itself. Berg created his libretto, with some cuts, from two plays by Frank Wedekind. The central personage, Lulu, is conceived as the incarnation of the "primal woman-spirit," and the drama is concerned with the fatal effects of her attraction for various lovers, finally ending with her own doom. Although externally occupied with the most realistic details, the work is not essentially realistic but rather expressionistic, sometimes grotesquely and extravagantly so. The drama is in two parts, the division occurring between the rigidly symmetrical first and second scenes of Act II. Separating parts 1 and 2 is a musical interlude (built on the principle of a crab canon) paired with a three-minute silent film which portrays the intervening action—the arrest, conviction, and imprisonment of Lulu and her subsequent escape from a hospital where she had been confined because of illness. The close relationship between the two parts is underlined by the dual roles assigned to three of the singers: Lulu's murder victims in Act I become her clients in Act III.

Both musically and dramatically, the opera is notoriously complex. Notwithstanding this complexity, *Lulu* is marvelously effective in the theater. The changing flow of the drama and the intensity of its emotional expression are always controlled by the composer's intellectual power in wielding musical forms.[63] Certain motives, harmonies, tone series, and combinations are associated with particular characters and scenes. The opera is not, as has often been stated, based throughout on a single tone row, but its felt musical unity is the result of interconnections among the different formal elements. Such subtle relationships may be no more consciously grasped by the audience than are the comparable relationships in *Wozzeck*, but the formal unity and the dramatic import of both works can be sensed in the theater without a knowledge of their technical construction.

Within the general orbit of the Schoenbergian musical style was *Alkestis* (1924), by Egon Wellesz (1885–1974),[64] a one-act setting of a text by Hofmannsthal (after Euripides) in a series of broad tableaux in a rather austere, monolithic idiom. The important position of the chorus in this work was even more emphasized in the composer's later opera, *Die Bakchantinnen* (1931).

Representative of the same Central European school are two operas by Ernst Krenek (b. 1900): *Das Leben des Orest* ("The Life of Orestes," 1930), a half-satirical treatment of the Orestes

---

63. Although the score is conceived as a number opera, Berg superimposes a specific musical form upon each act: sonata (I), rondo (II), theme and variations (III). See Perle, "Alban Berg."

64. Beer, "Egon Wellesz und die Oper"; Redlich, "Egon Wellesz"; Schollum, *Egon Wellesz*.

myth cycle, and the large historical opera *Karl V* (1938). Krenek began his remarkable career at Vienna in the composition classes of Franz Schreker, and when, in 1921, Schreker assumed the directorship of the Academy of Music at Berlin, Krenek followed him there to complete his education. While still a student, Krenek brought forth the first of his twenty operas, *Zwingburg* ("The Tyrant's Castle," 1922). Its political implications are immediately apparent: a tyrant rules from within a castle (which looks suspiciously like a factory) unseen by his subjects, who, with jerky gesticulations, execute monotonous routines to the musical accompaniment of an organ-grinder, who is cursed to play unceasingly. For one day only, the tyrant offers release from this mode of mechanical existence. To bring about this liberation, the organ-grinder is tied to a pole to prevent him from playing. As the people move about in a trancelike state enjoying themselves, they take pity on the organ-grinder and untie him so that he, too, can enjoy freedom. Unfortunately, his freedom means a return to the status quo: the music resumes and the people are once again under the tyrant's spell.

The problem of personal freedom with its attendant autobiographical overtones became, by Krenek's own admission, a dominant theme in his works for the stage.[65] After the satiric farce of *Der Sprung über den Schatten* ("The Leap over the Shadow," 1924), with its variegated musical styles—including jazz elements—integrated into an atonal structure, Krenek brought forth a conspicuous "hit," one which contrasts the life style of an intellectually restrained Central European composer with that of a carefree American jazz musician. It was *Jonny spielt auf* ("Johnny Strikes Up the Band," 1927), a combination of fantasy and gross realism set to exuberant rhythms and catchy tunes in jazz style with just enough dissonance to give the impression of daring "modernism."[66] Considerable variety of mood was achieved within this general idiom, from the gaudily vulgar strains of a restaurant

65. Krenek, *Horizons Circled*, p. 37. See also the composer's other writings, especially *Music Here and Now* and *Exploring Music (Zur Sprache gebracht)*, and Rogge, *Ernst Kreneks Opern*.

66. Initially, there was some resistance to this opera, but it soon became an international success; performances were given at major opera houses, including the Metropolitan in New York.

orchestra to romantic expressiveness and the final apotheosis of Johnny, the black band leader, symbol of the vigorous optimistic new world "conquering Europe with the dance." Krenek intended *Jonny* to be taken seriously, but audiences for the most part regarded it as a comedy or satire, and—whether or not owing to this misunderstanding—it had a brilliant though short-lived success.

Not long after Krenek returned to his native Vienna in 1927, Austria's independence began to be undermined by Nazi aggression in the guise of a new nationalism. His response to the impending crisis was made in an opera, *Karl V*, commissioned by the Vienna State Opera House. It proved to be one of his most important works for the theater, remarkable for a nobility of style well suited to the grandeur of the subject. The libretto focuses upon the ruler of the Holy Roman Empire in the sixteenth century, Charles V, in the period following his abdication of power; the dialogue between Charles and his confessor-monk provides Krenek with an appropriate forum in which to raise questions of current interest, in particular the issue of an individual's freedom to choose allegiance to God and the Church universal instead of fealty to a nation. Using the twelve-tone technique, Krenek created an opera that was "explicitly anti-Nazi, pro-Austrian, and Catholic."[67] For obvious reasons, it was banned from Vienna during the preliminary rehearsals in 1934. The message intended for his fellow Viennese was heard first in Prague at the 1938 premiere; shortly thereafter, Krenek emigrated to the United States.

Except for a few chamber operas, Krenek did not return to writing a full-scale work for the state until *Pallas Athene weint* ("Pallas Athene Weeps," 1955), which presents scenes of the war between Athens and Sparta with application to the modern issue of how to defend freedom without succumbing to tyranny; the music is based on an adaptation of the twelve-tone technique. A somewhat similar technique is used in *Bell Tower* (1957), an expertly wrought, dramatically and musically satisfying setting of a libretto by the composer based on a story by Herman Melville. He followed this one-act opera with *Der goldene Bock* ("The Golden Ram," 1963), which shows his preoccupation with serialism and

67. Krenek, *Horizons Circled*, p. 114.

the theater of the absurd; two operas written specifically for television, and *Sardakai* (1970), a farce of mistaken identities and disguises that pokes fun at some of the sacred conventions of his generation.

ITALIAN AND FRENCH OPERA

Despite many well-publicized experiments and innovations, a large proportion of operas produced after 1920—including some of the best as well as most popular works of this period—kept recognizably close to traditional forms and subjects and avoided any radical departure from accepted musical styles. In the favorable environment of Italy, the tradition was carried on by Franco Alfano (1876–1954), the choice of whom to complete the unfinished score of Puccini's *Turandot* was symbolical of his intermediary position in the history of Italian opera.[68] Alfano had become known as early as 1904 for his *Risurrezione* ("Resurrection"); his most significant later works were *La leggenda di Sakuntala* (1921), a heavily tragic work of grand-opera proportions, and the one-act neo-Puccinian lyrical comedy *Madonna Imperia* (1927), whose vocal lines, alternating smoothly between melodic phrases and a lively, expressive arioso, are supported by luscious harmonies in impressionistic orchestral colors—a perfect match for the refinedly voluptuous text. Alfano's *L'ultimo Lord* (1930), a vivacious comic work, and *Il dottor Antonio* (1949) continued in the same essentially conservative style.

The operas of Ildebrando Pizzetti (1880–1968) are somewhat less conservative in their harmonies than those of Alfano.[69] They have a continuous, full-bodied orchestral texture in a mosaic of recurring motifs, are primarily lyrical in expression, with flexible speechlike vocal melodies, and are characterized by extensive dramatic use of choruses in a sensitive polyphonic style inspired by classical Italian models. The most important of Pizzetti's early operas, and one of his best scores, is *Fedra* (1915),

---

68. *Cinquanta anni di opera e balletto in Italia*; Gatti, "Franco Alfano"; idem, "Recent Italian Operas"; Della Corte, *Ritratto di Franco Alfano*.

69. Biography by Gatti; La Morgia, ed., *La città dannunziana di Ildebrando Pizzetti*; *Musica moderna* (1967), vol. 1, special issue on Pizzetti.

on a text by Gabriele D'Annunzio. A group of works to his own librettos consists of *Debora e Jaele* (1922), *Fra Gherardo* (1928), and *Lo straniero* ("The Stranger," 1930). In all three of these operas, the dramatic action is conveyed by heightened declamation, the result of an almost perfect union of text and music. Pizzetti's later operas include *Orséolo* (1935), *L'oro* ("Gold," 1947), *Vanna Lupa* (1949), *Ifigenia* (first given in radio broadcast, 1950), and *Cagliostro* (1953); *La figlia di Iorio* ("Iorio's Daughter"), a "pastoral tragedy" by D'Annunzio (1954); *Assassinio nella cattedrale* ("Murder in the Cathedral," 1958), based on a translation and adaptation of T. S. Eliot's play; and *Clitennestra* (1965).

Comedy on contemporary subject matter was not a prominent feature of Italian opera under the Fascist government. Composers rather sought material in the safe and distant past, producing such works as *Tre commedie goldoniane* (1926), by Gian Francesco Malipiero (1882–1973),[70] three short comedies after Goldoni in concentrated musical settings, for the most part in lively parlando recitative over a continuous orchestra; and *La donna serpente* ("The Snake Woman," 1932), by Alfredo Casella (1883–1947),[71] based on a tale by Carlo Gozzi. These operas exemplify well the Italian neoclassical movement. The trend away from operas of gigantic size and toward a revival of classical subjects, light balletlike pieces, and eighteenth-century opera buffa is particularly evident in Malipiero's trilogy *L'Orfeide* (1925) and Casella's one-act *Favola d'Orfeo* (1932), both using the Orpheus theme. Malipiero's trilogy is most interesting formally: the middle section consists of seven short detached scenes *(sette canzoni)*, preceded by a prologue in the style of the opera buffa and followed by a semisatirical epilogue, in which a puppet show is introduced. A similar technique of brief, concentrated action is found in Malipiero's *Torneo Notturno* ("Night Tournament," 1930), seven night scenes that revolve around the two principal characters, Desperate Man and Carefree Man.

Expressions of the current political milieu can be found

---

70. Bontempelli, *Gian Francesco Malipiero*; Gatti, ed., *L'opera di Gian Francesco Malipiero*; Waterhouse, "The Emergence of Modern Italian Music"; Messinis, ed., *Omaggio a Malipiero*.

71. D'Amico and Gatti, eds., *Alfredo Casella*; see also Casella's memoirs, *I segreti della giara*.

in other operas by these same two composers. Casella's *Il deserto tentato* ("The Conquest of the Desert," 1937), a "mystery in one act" inspired by Mussolini's Ethiopian adventure, aimed at reflecting the "poetic exaltation of the civilizing mission of a great nation" in music of rather simple oratorio-like style with massive choral sections. Malipiero's *Giulio Cesare* (1936), based on Shakespeare's play, was also conceived at least in part as a gesture of acclaim to Mussolini. Its heroic subject and longer continuous structure are to be found also in Malipiero's *Antonio e Cleopatra* (1938). His basically diatonic writing in *I capricci di Callot* (1942) contrasts with the more dissonantly complex sounds of his postwar *Venere prigioniera* (1957), reminiscent of the first phase of his works for the stage. In his final phase, Malipiero reviewed the varied styles of his operas in *Gli eroi di Bonaventura* (1969), an anthology of excerpts from earlier works, designed perhaps to signal the composer's farewell to the theater. Other operas followed, however, and his stage career concluded with *L'Iscariota* (1971).

In France, conditions after the First World War were less favorable than in Italy for new serious operas in styles so closely related to tradition as were those of Alfano and Pizzetti. Paris, the principal and virtually the only important operatic center, readily accepted new pieces in the lighter forms, but the public for serious opera either remained content with the standard old repertoire or centered its attention on composers of distinctly "modern" tendencies. Thus, a quite exceptional event was the production in 1939 of *Chartreuse de Parme*, by Henri Sauguet (b. 1901),[72] a work conforming in every external detail to the pattern of nineteenth-century singers' opera and couched in simple—though far from unsophisticated—musical idiom that might have traced its lineage from Erik Satie.

The combination of drama and choreography, so typical in the history of French opera, is illustrated in an important opera-ballet, *Padmâvati*, by Albert Roussel (1869–1937),[73] produced at Paris in 1923. *Padmâvati* is a large work, scenically splendid, with fascinating rhythms and beautiful choral writing.

72. Biographies by Schneider and Bril.

73. *RM* (1929), special issue on Roussel; biography by Deane.

Roussel's complex, highly refined harmonic style incorporates Hindu scales and melodic formulae so perfectly as to make the exotic quality an inherent part of the music, not a mere external adornment. In the same way, within a smaller framework, Roussel uses Greek scales in the one-act lyric opera *La Naissance de la lyre* ("The Birth of the Lyre," 1925), on a libretto adapted by Theodore Reinach from Sophocles' *Ichneutai*.

   Among the composers of comic opera in France during the interwar years were Charles Levadé (1869–1948); with *La Rôtisserie de la Reine Pédauque* (1920) and *La Peau de Chagrin* (1929); Marcel Samuel-Rousseau (1882–1955), *Le Bon Roi Dagobert* (1927); and especially Jacques Ibert (1890–1962). Ibert's *Angélique* (1927) is a one-act farce with spoken dialogue, the music scintillating and epigrammatic, using polytonal chords, dance rhythms, and conventional melodies dressed up with dissonant harmonies—a twentieth-century revival of the old spirit of the Paris vaudevilles. Later operatic works of Ibert include *Le Roi d'Yvetot* (1930); *L'Aiglon* and *Les Petites Cardinal* (1937 and 1938), both in collaboration with Honegger; and a radio opera, *Barbe-Bleue* (1943). Other notable French comic operas were *Le Plumet du colonel* (1924) and *La Gaguere imprévue* ("The Unexpected Wager," 1944), by Sauguet; Milhaud's three *"opéras minutes"* (1927); and Honegger's *Les Aventures du Roi Pausole* (1930).

   Arthur Honegger (1892–1955), Swiss-born but resident in Paris most of his life (he was a member of the group known as "les six," which also included Darius Milhaud and Francis Poulenc), was a major composer of French opera, though he also wrote many ballets and much music for films.[74] *Judith* (1926), rewritten as an opera from the incidental music to René Morax's biblical drama produced in 1925, has the characteristic traits of Honegger's style at this period: fervid declamatory phrases in incisive rhythms over percussive harmonies, the progressions of which are actuated by contrapuntal, chromatically moving lines generally in contrary motion, with much use of ostinato figures. The chorus functions chiefly as a background for the soloists' singing, except in the last scene, with its strong closing fugue, "Gloire au dieu tout puissant Jehovah des armées." Honegger's *Antigone* (1927),

---

74. Honegger, *Je suis compositeur*; biographies by Delannoy and Tappolet.

to a text by Jean Cocteau "freely adapted from Sophocles," is a concentrated, continuous symphonic setting of the drama, without word repetitions, arias, ballets, or any other diversionary matter. The vocal lines are constantly in a type of recitative analogous to that of Lully (that is, deriving its pace, accent, and contour immediately and in detail from the words), but of course much more varied in rhythm and melodic pattern than Lully's. An unusual feature of the declamation is the placing of first syllables on the accented beat instead of treating them in the usual way as anacruses, resulting in a singular vehemence of expression (example 25.11). The orchestral part is dissonant and percussive; the effect

Example 25.11: *Antigone*, sc. 4

is altogether stark, quite in keeping with the grim, swift-moving text.

Honegger is especially notable as a composer of the typical twentieth-century combination form of opera-oratorio. His *Le Roi David* ("King David," 1921) is a work of this type, as are also, in different ways, the "stage oratorio" *Cris du monde* (1931) and the "dramatic legend" *Nicolas de Flue* (1941). Most important in this category, however, is *Jeanne d'Arc au bûcher* ("Joan of Arc at the Stake," 1938), on a text by Paul Claudel. As in all his serious dramatic works, Honegger is here concerned with basic social and moral conflicts of man in the modern world, dramatized in historic-legendary characters of heroic stature. Like a medieval cathedral, *Jeanne d'Arc* unites sacred and secular, great and small, ascetic and sensuous, the solemn and the grotesque, profundity and naïveté, in one vast structure of poetic and musical architecture: solos, choruses, and ballets, Gregorian chants, dance tunes, and medieval and modern folk songs, mingle in the complex, highly colored, music of Honegger; five speaking and five solo parts, a mixed chorus, and a children's chorus are required, in addition to a full orchestra.

A minor but far from negligible French opera composer was Honegger's pupil Marcel Delannoy (1898–1962), whose most successful stage work, *Le Poirier de Misère* ("Misère's Peartree," 1927), is a "Flemish legend" set to music in the restless, dissonant style of the time.

The dramatic works of Darius Milhaud (1892–1974), most prolific of all the twentieth-century French composers,[75] may be divided into three groups: (1) Opera-oratorios: a trilogy, *Orestie* (composed 1913–24), consisting of the operas *Agamemnon* (1927), *Les Choéphores* ("The Libation-Bearers," 1919 in concert form, 1935 on the stage), and *Les Euménides* (1927); *Christophe Colomb* (1930); *David* (1954); and *Saint Louis, roi de France* (1972). (2) Short operas, surrealistic, ironic, comic, or satirical, all composed in the period from 1924 to 1926: *Les Malheurs d'Orphée* ("The Misfortunes of Orpheus," 1926); the opéra-bouffe *Esther de Carpentras* (1938); *Le Pauvre Matelot* ("The Poor Sailor," 1927); the previously mentioned "opéras minutes," each ten to fifteen minutes long—*L'Enlèvement d' Europe* ("The Kidnaping of Europa," 1927), *L'Abandon d'Ariane* ("The Desertion of Ariadne," 1928), and *La Délivrance de Thésée* ("The Rescue of Theseus," 1928); and *Fiesta* (1958). (3) The heroic operas: *Maximilien* (1932), *Médée* (1939), and *Bolivar* (1950). To these may be added an early opera, *La Brebis égarée* ("The Lost Lamb," composed 1910–15, performed 1923), the scenic cantata *La Sagesse* (1945), the mystery play *Le Jeu de Robin et Marion* (1951), and the three-act comedy *La Mère coupable* ("The Guilty Mother," 1965), besides ballets and incidental music to plays.

Le Pauvre Matelot, Milhaud's first big success, is a setting of a short three-act play by Jean Cocteau about a sailor who, returning home rich after an absence of many years, decides to test his wife's fidelity by telling her he is a rich friend of her husband who, he says, is about to return home in utter poverty;

---

75. Studies by Collaer, Beck, Palmer, and Roy; Milhaud, *Notes sans musique*; Rostand, "The Operas of Darius Milhaud."

the wife, not recognizing him, murders the supposed stranger in order to get his money for her husband. The peculiar unreality of Cocteau's text is heightened by Milhaud's music, which is in a half-serious, ironic manner, constantly tuneful with sophisticated dissonant harmonies (see example 25.12). Similar musical procedures, in a more mocking spirit, are evident in the three opéras

Example 25.12: *Le Pauvre Matelot*, Act II

(Example 25.12 continued)

minutes, parodies of Greek myths in the fashion of the old Théâtre de la Foire. *Esther de Carpentras*, a modern, lightly satirical version of the biblical Esther story, is especially remarkable for the comic ensembles of Act I and the vivid crowd scenes of Act II.

Of the operas of the *Orestie* trilogy (the dramas of Aeschylus in a translation by Paul Claudel), only *Les Euménides* is set entirely to music. All three include massive choral portions, constantly polytonal in a dissonant texture of blended ostinato figures; extremely sonorous and effective are the places in *Les Choéphores* where the chorus, instead of singing, speaks in powerful rhythmic measures sustained by a large battery of percussion.

Similar technical procedures mark *Christophe Colomb*. Its two parts and twenty-seven scenes call for ten principal soloists, thirty-five other solo parts, three speaking parts, a chorus, and an orchestra reinforced by a special percussion section. Claudel's drama is conceived in epic-allegorical form, with a Narrator and other external personages, presented in a series of tableaux which are explained, commented on, and connected by choral and spoken interludes with percussion accompaniment. The mystical interpretation of Christopher Columbus is always at the forefront as the various scenes in his career unfold. The climax of Part I is a mutiny on board Columbus's ship; this part ends with a gigantic setting (in Latin) of the Sanctus. Part II takes us back to the inn at Valladolid, where the action began after the prologue, and there is an epilogue ending with a choral Alleluia.

Much of the music is in planar polytonal harmony—that is, with free dissonance arising from superposing motifs (often chord streams) in different tonalities, though as a rule no one motif is completely in a single key. The usual method of construction, except in the longest scenes, is to introduce one theme, establish it by ostinato-like repetition, then add successively one, two, or more themes, each of which is also usually treated in ostinato fashion. The various planes of harmony are kept distinct to some degree by contrasting timbres; and there is compensation for the static harmonic effect produced by constant complex dissonance in the variety and vitality of Milhaud's rhythmic patterns as well as in the monumental impression produced by this type of musical construction. Moreover, when the long-continued dissonance finally resolves to a simple chord at the end of a section, the intensity of the resolution is magnified. An example of this is the mutiny scene in Part I, where after a climax of four tonalities in the chorus and four in the orchestra (a total of seven different keys at once, one being duplicated), the whole resolves on a closing climactic triad of B-flat major.

Milhaud applied similar techniques to *Maximilien*, a historical opera based on a drama by Franz Werfel. Here, however, the degree of stylization surpasses that of any previous works: action, melodies, rhythms, all are ritualistic; even church hymns and military marches are indicated in formal, antirealistic outline as parts of a tonal design rather than representations of actual happenings. But in *Médée* there is less of the monumental, less dissonance, more lyricism, and more interest in the individual figures of the drama. The restrained dramatic force of the scene of the preparation of the enchantments is remarkable. Most expressive are the slow, melismatic, long lines in the soprano role of the suffering Creusa, innocent victim of Medea's cruelty. *Bolivar,* with *Christophe Colomb* and *Maximilien,* completed a trilogy of operas on Latin American subjects; like *Médée,* it concentrates on characterizing the persons of the drama, and it continues the composer's gradual trend away from the revolutionary character of his earlier works. *David* was commissioned to celebrate the 3,000th anniversary of Jerusalem as the capital of David's kingdom; its music seems like a final summing up of Milhaud's operatic development, a synthesis in which all elements of his style appear, now transfigured and calm within the broad framework of this festival opera-oratorio.

One of the outstanding French operas of the mid twentieth century was *Dialogues des Carmélites,* by Francis Poulenc (1899–1963),[76] performed at Milan in January 1957 and at Paris in June of the same year. In contrast to the composer's earlier satirical, surrealist comic opera *Les Mamelles de Tirésias* ("The Breasts of Tiresias," 1947) and his later tense monodrama *La Voix humaine* ("The Human Voice," 1959), *Carmélites* presents no ostentatiously novel features either in subject, form, or musical idiom. The theme of its libretto—written by Georges Bernanos after a novella by Gertrude von Le Fort—is the conquest of fear by divine grace. The central personage is a timorous young Carmelite nun caught in the religious persecutions under the Reign of Terror; the drama, developed with fine psychological perception and excellent balance between inner and outer action, had obvious and terrible implications for conditions in France in the 1940s, but its topical features are less important than its universal significance. The latter is powerfully communicated by Poulenc's music, selflessly devoted to the text and bound with it in a union no less perfect than that which Debussy had accomplished in *Pelléas.* These two operas are furthermore alike in the way they achieve profoundly dramatic results through restraint in the use of resources. Like Debussy, Poulenc connects the scenes within each act by means of instrumental interludes and makes unobtrusive use of recurring themes. The vocal solo lines, cast for the most part in quasi-melodic declamation (see example 25.13), are

76. Hell, *Francis Poulenc;* Poulenc, *Entretiens avec Claude Rostand;* idem, "Comment j'ai composé les *Dialogues des Carmélites*"; La Maestre, "Francis Poulenc und seine Bernanos-Oper"; Daniel, *Francis Poulenc: His Artistic Development and Musical Style.*

com - me l'en - fant de la vieil - les - se, et aus-

si la plus ha - sar - dé - e, la plus me - na - cé - e.

Pour dé - tour - ner cet - te me - na - ce, j'au - rais bien don-

- né ma pau - vre vi - e,

kept in clear relief above the continuous, ever-changing, but always lucid and evocative orchestral sonorities. The chorus, used only sparingly throughout most of the opera, comes into the foreground at the dramatic, moving final scene. Altogether, *Dialogues des Carmélites* takes a worthy and, one may hope, a permanently honored place in the history of French opera.

OPERAS ON SOCIAL THEMES

In the seventeenth and eighteenth centuries, operas were used in schools for teaching moral and religious doctrines; in the twentieth century, in like manner, operas were used for teaching left-wing political doctrines. In both cases, the method was to clothe the teachings in easily understood, popularly accessible music. The principal early twentieth-century examples stemmed from the "epic theater" movement in Germany, headed by Bertolt Brecht (1898–1956).[77] Foremost among them were two settings of Brecht's librettos by Kurt Weill (1900–1950):[78] *Die Dreigroschenoper* ("The Threepenny Opera," 1928) and *Aufstieg und Fall der Stadt Mahagonny* ("The Rise and Fall of the City of Mahagonny," 1927; extended version, 1930), both of which remain popular in spite of political changes that have made many parts of their original librettos outdated. Similar in political aim were Weill's school opera *Der Jasager* ("The One Who Consents," 1930) and a larger work, *Die Bürgschaft* ("The Surety," 1932), his last opera to be presented in Germany before the coming of the Nazi regime. Weill later had a second career in the United States as a composer of operas and musical comedies, including *Knickerbocker Holiday* (1938), the "folk opera" *Down in the Valley* (1938), *Street Scene* (1947), and *Lost in the Stars* (1949).

The opera of social protest with music in popular style was echoed in the United States, chiefly in a work by Marc Blitzstein (1905–1964), *The Cradle Will Rock* (1937), in which spoken dialogue alternates with recitatives and songs in a cultured and clever jazz idiom. Blitzstein's *No for an Answer* (1941) is similar

77. See, in addition to Brecht's own writings, Schumacher, *Die dramatischen Versuche Bertolt Brechts*; Hartung, "Zur epischen Oper Brechts und Weills"; Drew, "Topicality and the Universal"; articles in *The Score* (July 1958), no. 23.

78. Kowalke, *Kurt Weill in Europe.*

in aim and general musical style, though with a wider range of expression, and includes some fine choral portions. Both works were presented in commercial theaters on Broadway, a further manifestation of Weill's contention that music should be made accessible to the public. With *Regina* (1949) and his translation (a revised, "Americanized" text) and adaptation of *The Threepenny Opera* (1952), Blitzstein secured for himself a significant place in the annals of American opera.

THE OPERAS OF HINDEMITH AND STRAVINSKY. The satirical tendencies fashionable in Germany during the late 1920s are well illustrated in the comic operas of Paul Hindemith (1895–1963).[79] *Hin und Zurück* ("There and Back," 1927) is a one-act tour de force in which the second half reverses the action of the first, so that at the end the situation is exactly the same as at the beginning; the music correspondingly reverses the order of its themes and movements, though without going into the intricacies of strict retrograde canon. The work is scored for an orchestra of seven wind instruments and two pianos; the music, in various styles by turns but unified in effect nevertheless, is decidedly clever and successful in performance. *Neues vom Tage* ("News of the Day," 1929; revised 1954), the last opera of Hindemith to be produced in Germany before the war, is a longer work, a witty revue about a married couple who, through their efforts to obtain evidence for a divorce, become "the news of the day," with characters so firmly established in the minds of their public that they no longer have any right of private action and cannot even drop their divorce proceedings although they wish to. On this plot are strung several amusing episodes, including a bathroom scene and a chorus of stenographers to the rhythmic accompaniment of clacking typewriters. The music, like most of Hindemith's in this period, is linear in texture and strongly rhythmic, well suited to the lively action. There is also a jazz scene, and the final chorus is a fugue. One of Hindemith's most charming stage works is a children's opera, *Wir bauen eine Stadt* ("We Build a Town"), in straightforward, simple melodic style, first performed at Oxford in 1931.

79. Hindemith, *A Composer's World*; Rösner, *Paul Hindemith*. See also biographies by Strobel, Kemp, Briner, and Skelton.

Several other important works by Hindemith date from the 1920s, among them the opera *Cardillac* (1926; revised 1952) on an excellent tragic libretto by Ferdinand Lyon.[80] No opera of this period more clearly exemplifies the classical principle of separate musical numbers; each number, moreover, is constructed according to purely musical laws, the themes being straightforwardly developed in the manner of a concerto, undeflected by any attempt to illustrate mere details of the text: music and drama run parallel but without interpenetration. The "absolute," instrumental character of the music is reinforced by the prevailing texture, highly rhythmic and contrapuntal; the voice is treated in the late baroque manner as one melodic line among concertizing instruments. In addition to this characteristic linear style, two other idioms are occasionally used: a kind of accompanied recitative in which the vocal declamation is set against a single rhapsodic line in the orchestra; and a quieter, chordal, neoromantic style which foreshadows some aspects of Hindemith's later development (for example, the recitative and aria "Die Zeit vergeht," in Act I, scene 2). The chorus writing is vigorous, idiomatic, and effective, especially in the closing scene.

Hindemith began as an iconoclast but later modified his style, softening harmonic asperities and clarifying tonal relationships. Such changes were incorporated into the revised versions of *Cardillac* and *Neues von Tage* and influenced the composition of *Mathis der Maler* ("Matthias the Painter," 1938). This opera-oratorio is a long and complex work embracing a great variety of musical styles, among which suggestions of medieval modality are prominent. (The most familiar portions of *Mathis* are those arranged by Hindemith as an orchestral suite.) Hindemith's libretto is based on the life of Matthias Grünewald, the sixteenth-century German painter who became famous for his Isenheim altarpiece. Matthias, torn between allegiance to his art and support for the peasants' revolt and subsequent war of 1525, has reason to question the efficacy of artistic creation as a meaningful response to the call for social and political action. Convinced by Paul the Apostle of the immortality of art, Matthias allows his canvas to become a powerful weapon of protest.

The neobaroque trend in Hindemith's music culminates

---

80. Willms, *Führer zur Oper "Cardillac"*.

in *Die Harmonie der Welt* ("The Harmony of the World," 1957), a work similar to *Mathis* but on an even grander scale.[81] There are eleven solo roles, in addition to choruses; a full orchestra is supplemented by a second orchestra on the stage; and many of the sets require a divided stage. Each of the fourteen scenes in the five acts represents an episode in the life and philosophy of the astronomer Johannes Kepler, the title of whose treatise *Harmonices mundi* (1619) Hindemith adopted for his opera. The drama of *Mathis der Maler* had dealt with the position of the artist in society; *Die Harmonie der Welt* was conceived rather as an exemplification of Hindemith's views—going back to medieval teachings—of the order in a work of music as being symbolical of an all-embracing order in the physical and spiritual universe. Consequently, the events and characters have a symbolic function as well as a dramatic one, and this entails both a certain static quality in the development of the drama and an occasional impression that some of the persons are more like allegorical figures than real human beings. The monumental, oratorio-like character of *Die Harmonie der Welt*, in addition to the enormous resources required for its presentation, will doubtless prevent it from ever becoming fixed in the operatic repertoire—which is a misfortune. A richly polyphonic orchestral texture is the basis of the musical structure. As in many twentieth-century operas, classical instrumental forms play a large role in the musical development. Examples are the "scherzo" in 7/8 time in Act II; the "variations on an old war song" in Act V; and especially the closing scene, reminiscent of the grandiose finales in baroque opera, which introduces the earth, sun, and planets (each represented by the personage who was its mystical incarnation in the drama) in a magnificent apotheosis, to a sonorous, orchestral-choral passacaglia on a theme made up of the tones shown in example 25.14.

Another important work of the opera-oratorio type during this period was Igor Stravinsky's *Oedipus Rex* (1927 in concert form; 1928 in a stage production).[82] Its Latin text is a translation of Cocteau's French version of Sophocles' drama. *Oedipus*

81. Briner, "Eine Bekenntnisoper Paul Hindemith."

82. Stravinsky, *Chroniques de ma vie*; idem, *Memories and Commentaries*; idem, "On *Oedipus Rex*"; idem, *Poetics*; Stravinsky and Craft, *Conversations* (and subsequent volumes published between 1959 and 1969); Ramuz, *Souvenirs*; Vlad, *Strawinsky*; E. White, *Stravinsky*; E. White and Noble, "Igor Stravinsky" (with extensive bibliography).

Example 25.14: Tones of passacaglia theme from *Die Harmonie der Welt*

HINDEMITH

rex is more oratorio than opera: all the "action" is narrated between the several "scenes," which consist of stark, blocklike solo and choral numbers that magically convey the feeling of the ancient tragedy, antique, impersonal, yet eternally significant. An earlier one-act opera by Stravinsky, *Mavra* (1922), is a short comic piece, stylized almost to the point of burlesque, with puppetlike characters, the action running from beginning to end in as it were a single breath of swift song over continuous music, eccentrically rhythmic and brilliantly scored for a small group of solo instruments.

Stravinsky's only full-length opera is *The Rake's Progress* (1951), on a libretto by W. H. Auden and Chester Kallman, inspired by Hogarth's prints of the same title.[83] This work, like everything else of Stravinsky's, has been so much written about that little need be said here. It is the most thorough example in modern times of a return to classical opera. Not only does it consist of separate solo (or ensemble) vocal numbers with accompaniment by a small orchestra; its whole texture, and the harmonic and melodic idiom of the music itself, are neo-Mozartean. A harpsichord accompanies the recitatives; there is a closing "moral," as in *Don Giovanni*; and the mingled tone of spoofing and sentiment throughout is reminiscent of *Figaro* or *Così fan tutte*. Part of the charm of *The Rake's Progress* comes from our being kept constantly aware that its eighteenth-century costume is a disguise which only half conceals the sophisticated complexity of the drama and music—a mask which can be enjoyed for its own inanimate beauty but which at the same time shields the oversensitive spectator from direct contact with the emotions of laughter and pity, thereby allowing him to enjoy those emotions behind an unmoving mask of his own. But the disguise is forgotten when we come to the dialogue between Tom and Nick in Act III and the pathetic closing scenes in Bedlam, including Anne's tender farewell lullaby (example 25.15).

83. Griffiths, *Igor Stravinsky: "The Rake's Progress"*. See also Kerman, "Opera à la mode," and other articles on *The Rake's Progress* by E. White, Mason, Schuh, Craft, and Cooke.

Example 25.15: *The Rake's Progress*, Act III

SOVIET COMPOSERS

In the Soviet Union in the 1920s, there were two principal kinds of new operas being performed: the progressive, avant-
garde works promoted by the Association for Contemporary Music, and the traditional, conservative works supported by the
Russian Association of Proletarian Musicians. The latter group

included operas commemorating battles and revolutions (e.g., *For Red Petrograde*, 1925, and *The Storming of Perekop*, 1927) and operas from the international repertoire revised to capture the revolutionary spirit (e.g. *Tosca* revised as *The Struggle of the Commune*, 1924). The other group involved works by both Soviet composers who were truly innovative and outstanding non-Soviet composers such as Berg and Krenek. An opera that certainly moved away from any traditional mold was *Nos* ("The Nose"), by Dmitri Shostakovich (1906–1975),[84] first performed on January 18, 1930, at Leningrad. This satirical comedy, based upon a story from Gogol's *St. Petersburg Tales*, concerns a government official who has lost his nose. In its detached state, the Nose assumes an elusive identity, appearing in the most improbable situations. Ultimately, the Nose is caught, returned to its owner, and restored to its proper position. The score conveys the witty and eccentric text with its fast-paced recitatives, angular and rhythmically complex vocal material, sparsely scored music for the orchestra which explores the extremes of range and timbre, and harsh dissonances. Although recent performances of *The Nose* have shown it to be a brilliant theatrical entertainment, the initial performances of the opera met with mixed reactions, causing it to be eliminated from the stage until the Moscow revival in 1974.

The formation of the Composers Union in 1932, essentially a merging of the two organizations mentioned above, allowed the Soviet Union to exercise the ubiquitous power of the state on behalf of certain kinds of music and opera.[85] This influence, together with the manner in which the musical life of the country was organized, tended to produce a body of Soviet music cut off from, and apparently largely indifferent to, the various contemporary "advanced" currents in Western Europe and the Americas. The officially promoted ideals required, among other things, that music should be treated as the possession of the entire

84. Biographies by Martynov and Rabinovich; Norris, ed., *Shostakovich*; Pribegina, ed., *D. Shostakovich o vremeni i o sebe*; Shostakovich, *The Power of Music*; Volkov, ed., *Testimony: The Memoirs of D. Shostakovich*; Brown, ed., Russian and Soviet Music.

85. General works on music and opera in the Soviet Union are *Sovetskaia opera*; Kulikovich, *Sovetskaia opera na sluzhbe partii*; Abraham, *Eight Soviet Composers*; Laux, *Die Musik in Russland*; Moisenco, *Realist Music*; Olkhovsky, *Music Under the Soviets*; Schwarz, *Music and Musical Life in Soviet Russia 1917–1970*. See also books published in the Russian Music Studies Series of the UMI Research Press.

people rather than of a musical elite only; that its material should be sought in, or shaped by, the music of the people of its own country or region; that it should emphasize melody and be written in a style not too difficult for general comprehension; that it should be "optimistic" in spirit; and that its subject matter—where a text was involved—should affirm socialist ideals. This policy naturally encouraged production of a great many symphonic poems, ballets, choruses, and operas distinguished rather for massive size and suitable political intentions than for musical vitality. On the other hand, official policy also aimed at stimulating the development of popular and especially of regional musical life within the Soviet Union and thus at enriching the musical language of the country from genuine Eastern folkloristic sources. Among the many non-Russian national operas performed since 1930 may be mentioned *Shah-Senem* (1934), by Reinhold Glière (1875–1956), based on Caucasian legends and including musical elements from Caucasian and Iranian sources; *Buran* (1939), by Sergey Vasilenko (1872–1956), with colors and rhythms derived from Uzbek music; operas in the Tatar language by Nazib Zhiganov (b. 1911), particularly *Jalil* (1957); *Aïchurek* (1939), by Abdylas Maldybaev (b. 1906), based on a Kirghiz epic poem and using national melodies; and operas by two leading composers from the Ukraine, Boris Liatoshinsky (1895–1968: *Schors*, 1938) and Y. S. Meitus (b. 1903: *The Young Guard*, 1950).

A work long regarded as a model for Soviet opera was *Tikhy Don* ("The Quiet Don"), by Ivan Dzerzhinsky (1909–1978), first performed at Leningrad in 1935 and subsequently with great success all over the country. This work appears to hold a position in the history of Soviet opera comparable to that of Moniuszko's *Halka* in Poland or Erkel's *Hunyady László* in Hungary: its patriotic subject is treated in accordance with Dzerzhinsky's conviction that "everything that is lived by the people" can be expressed in opera but that this must be done "in artistically generalized, typified figures, avoiding the pitfalls of naturalism,"[86] and the music is technically naïve, simple in texture, predominantly lyric, containing many melodies that suggest folk song without actual cita-

---

86. Symposium on Soviet opera in *Sovetskaia muzyka* (May 1939), quoted in Abraham, *Eight Soviet Composers*, p. 82.

tion, and having a few "modern" touches of harmony and rhythm. A similar work, once even more highly regarded by Soviet critics, was Dzerzhinsky's second opera, *Podnyataya tselina* ("Virgin Soil Upturned," 1937). Dzerzhinsky's early works were representative of a trend in the 1930s toward the "song opera," of which one of the best examples was *V buryu* ("Into the Storm," 1939), by Tikhon Khrennikov (b. 1913).[87] The song opera as a type, however, was subject to certain inherent weaknesses, principally the lack of clear, individual characterization through recitatives and ensembles and the general absence of sharply defined dramatic contrasts.

Stalin's pointed approval of *The Quiet Don* coincided with a blast of offical wrath at Shostakovich's second opera, *Ledi Makbet Mtsenskogo uezda* ("Lady Macbeth of the Mtsensk District").[88] When this tragic-satirical opera in four acts was presented in 1934, it was praised at home and soon made its way abroad (being staged, for example, at Cleveland in 1935 and at London in 1936). Initial comments about the opera ranged from "a work of genius" and "high artistic worth" to "a reflection of correct Party policy" and "a creation that surpasses art in capitalist countries."[89] Two years later, following a performance of *Lady Macbeth* attended by Stalin, an article in *Pravda* denounced it as "confusion instead of natural human music," unmelodic, fidgety, and neurasthenic, and moreover bad in that it tried to present a wicked and degenerate heroine as a sympathetic character. What had apparently shocked Stalin was the sexually explicit language and equally explicit music.

The libretto for *Lady Macbeth of Mtsensk* comes from an 1865 novella of the same title by Nikolay Leskov. The central character, Katerina Izmailova, is a merchant's wife whose frustrations with Russian provincial life lead her to commit adultery, murder, and finally suicide. Shostakovich softens Leskov's tale and projects the highly emotional but deeply sensitive Katerina

---

87. Other notable operas by these two composers include Dzerzhinsky's *Fate of a Man* (1962) and Khrennikov's (Mother (1958), the latter based on a novel by Maxim Gorky.

88. Shostakovich, "My Opera *Lady Macbeth of Mtsensk*."

89. As quoted in Abraham, *Eight Soviet Composers*, p. 25, and Schwarz, *Music and Musical Life in Soviet Russia*, p. 120.

through a lyrically intense vocal line, a lyricism that is meant to clash with the music portraying the other characters which is brutal, lusty, vivid in the suggestion of cruelty and horror, full of driving rhythm and willful dissonance. As in other works of his early period, Shostakovich excels here in two idioms: a nervously energetic presto, thin textured, tonally erratic, and rhythmically irregular; and a long-spun adagio, mounting with clashing contrapuntal lines to sonorous climaxes. The orchestra serves as an equal partner with the voice; the interludes are dramatically important, binding one scene to another and unifying the whole opera. There are some fine choral scenes (particularly in the last act), and some of the aria melodies are related to folk-song idiom, though the solo lines for the most part are declamatory and interwoven with the orchestral texture.

Needless to say, *Lady Macbeth* promptly disappeared from Soviet theaters. The early wholesale condemnation of the opera gave way to a more discriminating evaluation by later Soviet critics, especially since a marked change in Shostakovich's style was signalized in his Fifth Symphony (1937)—a change that mirrored the transition from the revolutionary and experimental period in Soviet music to a period of stricter control under party directives. Similar but less acute crises of policy occurred afterwards, notably in 1948, when criticism of *Velikaya druzhba* ("The Great Friendship,") an opera by Vano Muradeli (1908–1970), caused it to be withdrawn and brought forth an official decree warning against "formalism" and "antipopular" tendencies in Soviet music.[90] Objections were made also to the historical opera *Bogdan Khmelnitsky*, by Konstantin Dankevich (b. 1905), when it came out in 1951, but a new version two years later was more favorably received. A similar fate awaited Shostakovich's 1956 reworking of *Lady Macbeth of Mtsensk*. His revisions, however, were so extensive that, in essence, Shostakovich created a new opera, acknowledged not only by a change in title, to *Katerina Izmailova*, but also by a new opus number. The new version toned

---

90. A translation of the statement issued by the Central Committee of the Communist Party is printed in Olkhovsky, *Music Under the Soviets*, pp. 280–85. After Stalin's death in 1953, the cultural climate moderated, and in 1958 this decree was rescinded. It was also in 1958 that Shostakovich's comic operetta *Moskva, Cheremushki* was composed; it was performed in Moscow one year later.

down the explicit passages in both libretto and score; when the opera was given in Moscow (1962) and London (1963), critical opinion of the musical revisions was generally favorable. More recently, opera houses have been staging the 1934 *Lady Macbeth*, discovering it to be one of the most powerful works of the twentieth century. The success of this revival in the 1980s will surely diminish the likelihood that *Katerina Izmailova* will remain in the performance repertoire.

Another outstanding name among the composers of the Soviet Union is that of Sergey Prokofiev (1891–1953).[91] Neither his life nor his music can be called typical for a Soviet composer. From 1918 to 1932, he lived abroad, chiefly in Paris; an early opera, *Igrok* ("The Gambler"), composed between 1915 and 1917, was first performed (in a revised version) at Brussels in 1929.[92] *Lyubov k term apelsinam* ("The Love for Three Oranges," Chicago, 1921) has a merrily lunatic plot based on a fantastic tale by Gozzi, well suited to Prokofiev's sharp rhythmic style of this period and to his talents for humor and grotesquerie. Choruses, external to the action, intervene capriciously; the solo parts make a mosaic of detached phrases over sparse but colorful orchestration; the only extended tunes are the well-known march and scherzo.

Prokofiev's next opera was *Ognenny angel* ("The Fiery [or Flaming] Angel," composed 1919–1927; first stage performance, Venice, 1955). Another fantastic libretto—this time a tragedy, laid in Germany of the sixteenth century, full of superstition, evil magic, ecstatic visions, hallucination, and horror—gave occasion for a complex but theatrically effective score, with arioso vocal lines over rather heavy orchestral accompaniment and some impressive choral scenes forming the climax of the last act. *The Fiery Angel*, being sadly deficient in optimistic proletarian spirit, has been welcomed only in the decadent West.

---

91. See Prokofiev's own writings. See also Nest'ev, *Prokof'ev*; Jahn, "Von *Spieler* zur *Erzählung vom wahren Menschen*"; McAllister, "The Operas of Sergei Prokofiev"; Porter, "Prokofiev's Late Operas"; Mitchell, "Prokofieff's *Three Oranges*"; Swarsenski, "Sergei Prokofieff: *The Flaming Angel*."

92. Prokofiev wrote the libretto, which is based upon Dostoevsky's novella. See Robinson, "Dostoevsky and Opera"; Taruskin, "Tone, Style, and Form in Prokofiev's Soviet Operas."

In 1932, Prokofiev returned to Russia and began the long and difficult process of adapting his earlier pungent, ironic, often dissonant style to the requirements of his own country. He busied himself with ballets and other semidramatic compositions (including *Lieutenant Kije*, the "symphonic tale" *Peter and the Wolf*, and the cantata *Alexander Nevsky*) and finally a new opera, *Semyon Kotko* (1940), based on scenes from the life of a hero of the revolution of 1918. Here the composer's typical declamatory prose style was relieved by some tuneful episodes, but both libretto (written, as usual, by Prokofiev himself) and music were adversely criticized; *Semyon* was soon withdrawn, but it was revived in a concert performance in 1957 and on the stage at Perm and Leningrad in 1960. Another opera on a contemporary subject, *Povest o nastoyashchem cheloveke* ("The Story of a Real Man") was withdrawn after a private performance in 1948; its first public performance took place at Moscow in 1960.

More successful was the comic opera *Obruchenie v monastyre* ("The Betrothal in a Monastery"), performed at Leningrad in 1946 and revived at Moscow in 1959. The libretto, adapted from Richard Sheridan's eighteenth-century play *The Duenna* (by which name it is often known outside the Soviet Union), gave Prokofiev ample scope for comedy and satire as well as for lyrical expression, providing likewise "an opportunity to introduce many formal vocal numbers—serenades, ariettas, duets, quartets and large ensembles—without interrupting the action."[93] These "formal vocal numbers" are scattered throughout the score; many of them alternate kaleidoscopically with fragments of dialogue in short, tuneful phrases or strict recitative, all held together by a continuous pulsatile accompaniment with countermelodies and mildly dissonant harmonies. The whole spirit and structure of the work, as well as the plot and characters, make it a charming modern descendant of the classical opera buffa.

In 1955 at Leningrad there occurred the premiere of Prokofiev's operatic masterpiece, *Voyna i mir* ("War and Peace"). Based on Tolstoy's novel and composed largely under the patriotic emotions of the war years (a partial performance of the first version took place in 1946), this is a historical grand opera

93. The composer's words, quoted in Nest'ev, *Prokofiev* (in English), p. 323.

Example 25.16: *War and Peace*, Act I, sc. 1

PROKOFIEV

of heroic proportions, consisting in its final form of thirteen scenes and a choral prologue.[94] The epic range of incidents and emotions is matched by music of corresponding variety and convincing dramatic power. As in his previous operas, Prokofiev makes some use of recurrent themes as a unifying device, and in the vocal writing maintains a balance between flexible declamation and lyrical closed forms, both solo and ensemble (see example 25.16). Choruses contribute to the grandeur of the whole, though not so conspicuously as to overshadow the individual characters. The score is particularly rich in expressive (not sentimental) melodies, and the distinctly national character of the melodic writing is unmistakable; the harmonic style is tonal, prevailingly diatonic and consonant, but with a quality of originality that reminds one of Musorgsky. More than any of his other works for the theater, *War and Peace* places Prokofiev in the great tradition of Russian opera: profoundly national in inspiration and musical style but also profoundly human and therefore transcending national limitations.

EASTERN EUROPE

Leoš Janáček (1854–1928), the leading composer in Czechoslovakia in the first quarter of the twentieth century, may be called a nationalist in the sense that all his operas were written to texts in his own language and his melodic idiom was one that grew organically out of the rhythms and inflections of national speech and folk song. But his style, particularly in the late works, was so individual and his genius for dramatic characterization so exceptional as to make him a figure of more than national importance.[95] His first major opera,[96] *Jenůfa*, produced at Brno in 1904

94. There are several versions of this opera, each designed to shorten the performance time of the original.

95. J. Vogel, *Leoš Janáček* (with an extensive bibliography); M. Evans, *Janáček's Tragic Operas*; Tyrrell, *Leoš Janáček: Kát'a Kabanová*. See also Brod, *Leoš Janáček*; Holländer, "Leos Janáček in seinen Opern"; Racek, "Der Dramatiker Janáček"; Shawe-Taylor, "The Operas of Leoš Janáček"; and Janáček's correspondence.

96. His first two operas were *Šarka* (1887) and *The Beginning of a Romance* (1891), the latter an experiment in integrating folk songs into an art form. Janáček spent the period between these two operas in traveling throughout his native Moravia, notating the indigenous folk songs and dances. *Jenůfa* and *Osud* were followed by the satires of *Mr. Brouček's Excursion to the Moon* and the sequel, *Mr. Brouček's Excursion to the Fifteenth Century*.

but ignored elsewhere until after a lavish production at Prague in 1916, is a tragedy. Its central themes of love, death, and regeneration are common to Janáček's final four tragic operas, all written after the birth of the Czechoslovak republic in 1918. In *Jenůfa*, the sufferings of the heroine, falsely accused of murdering

Example 25.17: *Kát'a Kabanová*, Act III

(Example 25.17 continued)

Všichni jdou spat tak leh-ce. i já jdu! A-le

cresc.

f

jak bych se do mo-hy-ly kla-dla. Ta

Più mosso *f*

sfz

hrů - za po tmě!

sfz

sfz

Ně-ja-ký hluk!

sfz

rit.

Fl.

ff

Vla.

rit.

(Example 25.17 continued)

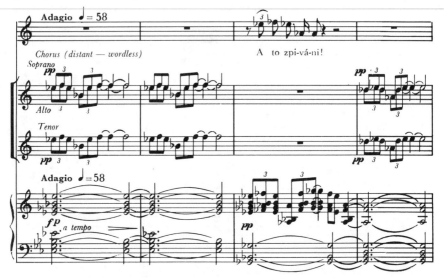

her illegitimate child, awaken in the three principal characters an awareness of a higher level of moral integrity, one which transcends the conventions of village life and rituals. *Jenůfa* stands apart from Janáček's later works because of its structural dependence upon set-numbers, including ensembles and choruses. At the same time, along with expansive melodies of a more conventional romantic sort, there are already passages showing distinctive shapes and concise rhythms arising out of speech intonation. Greater concentration of both drama and music is found in the beautifully poetic, moving *Kát'a Kabanová* (1921)—a work equally remarkable for sensitive characterizations, fine orchestral colorings, and an indescribable poignancy of expression in the melodic outlines (see example 25.17)—one of the masterpieces of twentieth-century opera. It is in this opera that Janáček begins to develop his own unique interpretation of operatic conventions. The conciseness of his libretto allows the action to proceed at breathless speed. Monologues become more numerous; recurring motives add an important orchestral dimension; the chorus, no longer needed as a visible protagonist, assumes an offstage location and functions as a collective symbolic force with its interjections of wordless and mysterious sounds.

The circularity of life forms the key philosophical point of Janáček's next opera, *Přihodylišky Bystroušky* ("The Cunning Little Vixen," 1924). Tender and strange, blended of humor and pity, this unusual opera requires a cast of talking animals and humans. Janáček based his tale upon R. Téšnohlídek's novel *Vixen Sharp-Ears* (1920), which sets forth a nineteenth-century Moravian folk tale about the adventures of a fox and a forester. In the opera, the forester comes to an awareness of the sadness of old age tempered by the miracle of nature's renewal in the forest. "Here in these woods," sings Janáček's Forester (see example 25.18), "life renews itself, and the nightingales return with each returning Spring to find their nests, and Love . . . always the same: where then was parting, now is meeting."[97] *The Cunning Little Vixen* is a work which may be regarded as complementary to *Kát'a Kabanová* but is even more original in style, despite some impressionistic influences in the harmony and orchestration.

Věc Makropulos ("The Makropulos Affair," 1926), based upon Karel Capek's play, shows Janáček on the way to the final stage of his style, reached in the *Glagolitic Mass* of 1927 and the opera *Z mrtvého domu* ("From the House of the Dead"), composed in 1928 and first performed in 1930. In *The Makropulos Affair*, an eternally beautiful woman returns to Vienna seeking the formula for a longevity potion which has preserved her for more than 300 years. Her mysterious sensuality is signaled orchestrally by the introduction of a viola d'amore, an instrument Janáček used with similar connotations in the first version of *Osud* ("Fate," 1903–5) and in *Kát'a Kabanová*.[98] By contrast, her perversion of natural life evokes a musical response that is harsh, dissonant, angular—a cruelness thrust upon the audience in the opening orchestral prelude. *From the House of the Dead* has no plot, properly speaking; its scenes are taken from Dostoevsky's memoirs of his prison life in Siberia. Except for a few measures in Act II sung by the old prostitute, the opera is scored for male voices, collectively assembled as a chorus from which individual

97. Paraphrase of Max Brod's German version of Janáček's text.

98. The scoring for Charpentier's *Louise* and Puccini's *Madama Butterfly*, among others, calls for the viola d'amore. See Tyrrell, "Janáček and the viola d'amore" in his *Leoš Janáček: Kát'a Kabanová*.

Example 25.18: *The Cunning Little Vixen*, Act III

(Example 25.18 continued)

(Example 25.18 continued)

sl - zet poh-nu-tím   nad shle-dá - ním!

soloists step forward to relate their brutal experiences. Only once
does a fleeting moment of hope penetrate the bleakness of the
penal camp—the moment when a wounded eagle is released and
the prisoners sing of freedom. Janáček's music for *From the House
of the Dead* is intensely concentrated, stark, primitive, violent,
with rough harmonies and raw orchestral colors—a grim finale
for a composer whose four greatest operas were all written after
the age of sixty-five.

Other important Czech operas include Otakar Zich's *Guilt*
(1922), Rudolf Karel's *Godmother's Death* (1933), Jaroslav Křička's
White Ghost (1929), and Eugen Suchon's *The Whirlpool* (1949).[99]
Three operas by Alois Hába (1893–1973) also deserve to be mentioned: *The Mother* (1927–29), using quarter-tones; *The New Land*
(1934–36); and *Thy Kingdom Come* (1932–42), using sixth-tones.

99. See Clapham, *"The Whirlpool."*

Hába's interest in quarter- and sixth-tones led to the founding of a department of microtonal music at Prague Conservatory in 1924. His music also prompted the construction of instruments which could execute the unusual requirements of the microtones.[100] A Czech composer who ran his own experimental theater in Prague was Emil Frantisek Burian (1904–1959). Of his six operas, the most important is *Maryša*, a tragedy centering on a peasant girl who is forced to marry against her will.

Comic operas of a robust and popular character were also appearing around this time in Czechoslovakia. *Schwanda the Bagpiper*, by Jaromir Weinberger (1896–1967), first performed at Prague in 1927, is doubtless the most widely known of these. Bohuslav Martinů (1890–1959), a native of Czechoslovakia who from 1923 lived in Paris and later in the United States, has been heard mainly in symphonic and chamber compositions; but he also wrote twelve operas, both comic and serious, which remain little known.[101] They include *Comedy on the Bridge* (1937) and *Greek Passion* (1954). The latter is Martinů's final opera, a large-scaled tragedy based upon Nikos Kazantzakis' novel *Christ Recrucified*, the story of humble Greek peasants who reenact the drama of Christ's Passion and in so doing begin to assume in real life the traits of the biblical characters they had portrayed.

The leading Polish opera composer of the mid-twentieth century was Tadeusz Szeligowsky (1896–1963), whose *Bunt Zakow* ("The Revolt of the Zaks") was produced at Warsaw in 1951 and shortly thereafter at other Polish cities and at Moscow.[102] Its plot is based on an incident at the University of Cracow in 1549: the "Zaks"—students of peasant birth who received their education in return for performing menial duties—rebelled because of ill treatment and left the university and the town in a body. A love story and some comic episodes are added to make up the libretto, but the main emphasis is on the stirring choral scenes. Szeligowsky's music, though harmonically conservative, is very well adapted to the requirements of the theater. Many of the tunes and rhythms have a definite national folk character; in keeping with

100. See studies of Hába and his music by Vysloužil.

101. Šafránek, "Bohuslav Martinů und das musikalische Theater."

102. Lissa, "Pierwsza opera w Polsce Ludowej. *(Bunt żaków)*."

the historical background are some stylized or literal references to Polish poetry and music of the sixteenth century.

ENGLAND AND THE UNITED STATES

The two leading English composers of the early twentieth century, Gustav Holst (1874–1934) and Ralph Vaughan Williams (1872–1958), made significant contributions to opera.[103] Holst's *Savitri* (composed 1908, performed 1916) is a chamber opera of exquisite tenderness and simple emotion, in a musical style that suggests the Eastern setting of the story without attempting literal imitation of Hindu melodies; it contains some beautiful writing for women's chorus. Holst's principal opera, the one-act comedy *The Perfect Fool*, had successful performances at Covent Garden in 1923; the music shows the composer fully emancipated from the neo-Wagnerian tendencies of his earlier dramatic works. *At the Boar's Head* (1925) is a Shakespearean intermezzo with words from *Henry IV*, a jolly work made up largely of traditional English tunes, somewhat in the manner of ballad opera. The influence of these works is not to be reckoned so much by their outward success as by the fact that they represent the serious, original, and uncompromising efforts of a first-rank English composer in the restricted and rather thankless field of native opera. Much the same may be said of Vaughan Williams' six dramatic works. *The Shepherds of the Delectable Mountains*, a pastoral episode after Bunyan, has been frequently revived in England since its first performance in 1922. *Hugh the Drover; or, Love in the Stocks* (1924) is a ballad-type opera with continuous music, containing allusions to a number of traditional tunes without direct quotation, and as thoroughly English in spirit as anything by Gilbert and Sullivan, *Sir John in Love* (1929), based on Shakespeare's *Merry Wives of Windsor*, is the composer's biggest work for the stage (four acts); the music is similar to that of *Hugh the Drover*, but more highly developed both formally and harmonically—a truly English *Falstaff*, not unworthy of comparison with Verdi's Italian

---

103. See the biography of Holst and a study of his music by his daughter, Imogen Holst. On Vaughan Williams, see biographies by Dickinson and U. Vaughan Williams; studies by Howes, Kennedy, and Gordon.

one. The Gilbert and Sullivan tradition lives on in *The Poisoned Kiss* (1936), a tuneful comic opera with spoken dialogue. *Riders to the Sea* (1937) is a restrained but moving setting (in one act) of Synge's play, the vocal parts in flexibly declaimed melodies and the harmonies in neomodal style with much parallel chord progression, the whole having a subdued intensity of feeling that accords well with the peculiar atmosphere of the drama.

Of American operas in conservative style, designed for full-scale production, the most successful were two by Deems Taylor (1885–1966): [104] *The King's Henchman* (New York, 1927) and *Peter Ibbetson* (New York, 1931), smooth, expert works in a mild late-romantic style with modern trimmings, well molded to the taste of that large majority of the opera-going public who are pleased with expressive melodies and sensuous harmonies that pleasantly stimulate without disturbing. Other American operas at the Metropolitan have been less enthusiastically received—for example, *Caponsacchi* (1937, after a first performance in German translation at Freiburg in 1932), by Richard Hageman (1882–1966). Among American operas that have been produced under respectable auspices and gone their way without leaving a mark may be mentioned *The White Bird* (Chicago, 1924), by Ernest Carter (1866–1953), and the prize-winning *In the Pasha's Garden* (New York, 1935), by John Laurence Seymour (b. 1893). [105]

National scenes and subjects, as might be expected, have been frequently tried. An opera by Charles Wakefield Cadman (1881–1946), *The Robin Woman (Shanewis)*, given at the Metropolitan in 1918, uses a number of authentic Indian tunes and has an attractive, if superficial, melodic vein, but is slight in substance and awkward in dramatic details. The same composer's *A Witch of Salem* (Chicago, 1926) has had a modest number of performances. An important American historical opera was *Merry Mount*, by Howard Hanson (1896–1981), [106] commissioned by the Metropolitan and produced there in 1934. The score incorporates many ballets and choruses in a wild, implausible story of Puritan

104. See Howard, *Studies in Contemporary American Composers: Deems Taylor.*

105. For fuller lists, see Hipsher, *American Opera;* Howard, *Our Contemporary Composers.*

106. See Tuthill, "Howard Hanson."

New England. It may be the extravagance of the libretto which has interfered with the full success of *Merry Mount*, or it may be a somewhat stiff, oratorio-like, undramatic quality and the generally static harmonic and melodic style of much of the music. Yet there is considerable variety of idiom: the love strains of Bradford's aria "Rise up, my love" and the following duet, and the "Walpurgisnacht" ballets in Act II, are particularly remarkable; and the work as a whole is able, serious, and uncompromising—a compliment of the sort that opera audiences do not always seem to appreciate.

Other American operas staged in the 1930s include *Emperor Jones* (1933), a work by Louis Gruenberg (1884–1964) based on Eugene O'Neill's play and exploiting a neoprimitive orchestra with drum rhythms and choral interludes. George Antheil (1900–1959), an American living abroad, created a momentary sensation in Germany with the 1930 premiere of his *Transatlantic*, one of the first American operas accorded a major production in Europe. The subject of Antheil's satirical jazz opera focuses upon an American presidential campaign with its correlative political vices.[107] Two unique and enduring examples from this decade are *Porgy and Bess* (1935), by George Gershwin (1898–1937),[108] and *Four Saints in Three Acts* (1934), by Virgil Thomson (1896–1984);[109] coincidentally, both operas had all-black casts and both were commercially presented on Broadway. Gershwin's *Porgy and Bess* is true folk opera, the vernacular of the black culture skillfully communicated in sung recitative and spirituals. The hymnlike dignity and tuneful simplicity of Thomson's *Four Saints in Three Acts* glimpses a vernacular of a different hue. Gertrude Stein's text, written expressly for Thomson, represents an abstract threading together of words, out of which evolves a plotless libretto in praise of Spanish saints in general and of Saint Theresa of Avila in particular. Stein viewed words as independent en-

107. Other works by Antheil include *Helen Retires* (1934) and four operas written in the 1950s: *Volpone, The Brothers, The Wish,* and *Venus in Africa.*

108. See biographies and studies of Gershwin's music by Armitage, Ewen, Thomson, and Goldberg. See also Durham, *DuBose Heyward: The Man Who Wrote Porgy.*

109. See Hoover and Cage, *Virgil Thomson;* Helm, "Virgil Thomson's *Four Saints in Three Acts*"; Jackson, "The Operas of Gertrude Stein and Virgil Thomson"; and Thomson's own writings.

tities divorced from contextual association, mere sounds which, when placed in proper sequential configurations, would evoke meaningful interpretations. The following line from *Four Saints in Three Acts* is indicative of her style of writing: "Saint Therese [*sic*] in a storm in Avila there can be rain and warm snow and warm that is the water is warm the river is not warm the sun is not warm and if to stay to cry."[110] Why, one might rightfully query, did Thomson use an all-black cast for an opera about Catholic saints and the Counter-Reformation? The composer provided this answer: "Blacks sing so beautifully, and they look so beautiful."[111]

The 1930s also saw the first operas by Aaron Copland (b. 1900), *The Second Hurricane* (1937),[112] and by Douglas Moore (1893–1969), *The Devil and Daniel Webster* (1939).[113] The latter work is in one long act, a continuation of the folk-opera tradition with a mixture of folk song, hymn, and spoken dialogue to aid in the painting of a New England scene. Stephen Vincent Benet's libretto focuses upon Jabez Stone, who has sold his soul to the devil. On the day of reckoning, Stone's case is argued by Daniel Webster before a judge and jury representing the devil's interests. In an appeal to the patriotic spirit of the assembled court, Webster successfully argues in the name of liberty and freedom— a distinctively American subject, presented with Moore's penchant for good theatrical craftsmanship, characteristics of his subsequent contributions to American opera (see chapter 26).

110. Quoted in P. Smith, *The Tenth Muse*, p. 399.

111. Quoted in Libby, "How the 'Saints' Came Together in Paris."

112. See Berger, *Aaron Copland*, and Copland's own writings.

113. Weitzel, "A Melodic Analysis of Selected Vocal Solos in the Operas of Douglas Moore"; Edmunds and Boelzner, *Some Twentieth-Century American Composers*.

CHAPTER
TWENTY-SIX

The Recent Past

Varying Tendencies in European Opera

In the face of the general tendency toward sophistication or massiveness in opera music of the 1930s, a move in a different direction, toward radical simplification, was undertaken by Carl Orff (1895–1982).[1] The resulting works aroused more comment, favorable or otherwise, than any other operas of the time—to begin with, because none are operas in the traditional sense of the word, and none are so named in their subtitles. *Carmina burana* (1937), *Catulli carmina* (1943), and *Trionfo di Afrodite* (1953) are essentially combinations of cantata and ballet; so also, but in a different manner and with greater use of spoken dialogue, are *Die Bernauerin* (1947) and *Astutuli* (1953). More like operas in the ordinary sense are *Der Mond* ("The Moon," 1939) and *Die Kluge* ("The Wise Woman," 1943), though it would perhaps be more accurate to designate these as "folk plays with music." The typical idiom in *Die Kluge* is a narrow-ranged, strongly accented melody with many repeated notes and with the phrases reiterated over and over in ostinato fashion; and this melody is accompanied by the simplest possible harmonies, statically persistent, from a small orchestra, with emphasis on percussion instruments and percussive rhythmic sound.

This type of percussive-ostinato background, with still

---

1. Orff, "Gedanken über Musik"; Lindlar, ed., *Die Stimme der Komponisten*; Liess, *Carl Orff*; studies by Kiekert, Helm, Stäblein, W. Keller, and Willnauer. See Also Munich, Bayerische Staatsbibliothek, *Carl Orff: Das Bühnenwerk*.

Scene from the original production of *Oedipus der Tyrann* (Stuttgart 1959) by C. Orff; designed by Caspar Neher, and staged by Günther Rennert.

further simplification of harmony and melody, is applied to a totally different kind of dramatic material in Orff's *Antigonae* (1949) and *Oedipus der Tyrann* (1959), both settings of Hölderlin's translations from Sophocles. In these, there are five gradations of vocal delivery for both soloists and chorus: (1) ordinary speech; (2) rhythmic semispeech, similar to Berg's Sprechgesang; (3) a form of stylized speech consisting of rhythmic chanting centered on one tone but punctuated by melodic deflections to nearby tones and occasional wide leaps; (4) the same, but expanding into a longer quasi-melodic chant; and (5) a combination of (3) or (4) with sweeping stepwise fast impassioned melismatic outbursts, characteristically placed at the beginning of a phrase (example 26.1). The voices may be either unaccompanied or accompanied by ostinato rhythmic patterns in many different combinations of percussion, either without fixed pitch or in static harmonies. The chorus constantly participates in the action and each scene is in a clearly outlined musical form.

No description can do more than suggest the unique effects produced by the composer's peculiar choice of means. Music, reduced nearly to the primal elements of rhythm and single tones, enters into a union with language that conjures up for the imagination a far-off mythical stage in the history of human speech. The variety of sounds and the varying degrees of dramatic tension that Orff manages to achieve within his self-imposed musical limitations are remarkable; nevertheless, the very intensity of the idiom tends to limit the length of time for which it can be effective, and for this reason perhaps *Oedipus*, being shorter than *Antigonae*, is the more successful of the two works. Orff continued with this style of writing for the theater in *Prometheus* (1968) and *De temporum fine comoedia* ("The Play of the End of the World," 1973), the latter with a text in Greek and Latin.[2]

Emil Frantisek Burian (1904–1959), a Czech composer, dramatist, and producer, was strongly influenced by Orff. Of his six operas, the best known is the tragedy *Maryša*, a peasant opera about an ill-fated marriage. First produced outside Burian's native country at Lübeck (1964), the score of *Maryša* exhibits the pulsating rhythmic ostinatos characteristic of Orff's style, along

2. See Thomas, *Carl Orff.*

Example 26.1: *Oedipus der Tyrann*

Copyright information appears on p. 914.

with native folk material and elements reminiscent of Janáček's operas.

A Bavarian contemporary of Orff was Werner Egk (1901–1983).[3] His *Columbus*, originally written for radio broadcast in

3. Egk, *Musik, Wort, Bild.*

1933 and frequently performed since then on German stages in a revised version dating from 1942, is a rather static combination of opera and epic; a later and possibly better mixture of these elements is found in *Irische Legende* (1955; revised version, 1970). *Die Zaubergeige* ("The Magic Violin," 1935), also designed for radio broadcast, immediately preceded the most memorable of Egk's operas, *Peer Gynt* (1938), a straightforward human drama adapted from Ibsen, with a musical score of considerable variety, color, and melodic interest. Other operas by Egk include *Der Revisor* ("The Inspector," 1957), *Kirke* (1948, revised version, 1966), and *Der Verlobung in San Domingo* ("The Engagement in San Domingo," 1963).

The composer who probably best represents the continuing central tradition in opera in the German-speaking countries at the beginning of the postwar era is an Austrian, Gottfried von Einem (b. 1918). In his music, often piercing harmonic dissonances and sharp variegated rhythms are contained within an essentially tonal and romantic framework of expression with singable melodic lines, the whole enlivened by original thematic ideas and handled with a natural flair for stage effect. Von Einem's early works for the theater include, in addition to ballets, the two operas *Dantons Tod* ("Danton's Death," 1947), on a libretto adapted from Georg Büchner's drama of the same title, a work notable for its tumultuous crowd scenes; and *Der Prozess* ("The Trial," 1953), based on Franz Kafka's novel, a score in which each scene constitutes a musical unit with its own characteristic rhythms and its own singing (or speaking) style, instrumental color, and formal pattern. Among his later works are *Der Zerissene* ("The Man Torn Apart," 1964); a neoclassical singspiel, *Der Besuch der alten Dame* ("The Old Lady's Visit," 1971); and *Kabale und Liebe* (1976). *Der Besuch der alten Dame*, based upon Friedrich Dürrenmatt's play with that title, concerns a very wealthy lady who returns to her home town in Switzerland and offers the townsfolk huge sums of money if they will murder her former lover; her offer is accepted and the repulsive deed is accomplished. The horror of the crowd's willingness to comply is skillfully communicated by Von Einem's score.[4]

Von Einem's composition teacher and librettist was Boris

---

4. See Stuckenschmidt, *Die grossen Komponisten*; idem, "Von Einem's *Der Besuch*."

Blacher (1903–1975), a prolific and popular composer in his own right.[5] Blacher's music is as varied as the many styles with which he experimented, including folk, jazz, and electronic. Two of his best-known operas are *Preussiches Märchen* ("Prussian Fairy Tale," 1952), a comedy, and *Abstract Opera No. 1* (1953), on a text of meaningless syllables in a lightly satirical vein.

Interesting experiments in form as well as in subject matter and musical idiom were not the exclusive prerogative of composers working in Germany. Equally adventurous works, in different directions, had been appearing in other countries, especially since the 1940s. Particular mention may be made of Riccardo Malipiero (b. 1914, a nephew of G. F. Malipiero) in Italy, with his comic operas *Minnie la candida* ("Candid Minnie," 1942) and *La donna é mobile* ("Woman Is Fickle," 1954), and a bitterly satirical television opera, *Battono alla porta* ("They Beat on the Door," 1961), which uses electronic effects.[6] Aural-spatial experiments came from Sweden's Lars Johann Werle (b. 1926) in his *Drömmen om Thérèse* ("Dreaming of Therese," 1964), an opera staged in the round with electronic music, and from Karl-Birger Blomdahl (1916–1968) in *Aniara* (1959), in which electronic music was used to create unearthly sounds for a drama on a space ship out of control, falling endlessly into the interstellar depths. This setting by Blomdahl of Harry Martinson's epic poem has become one of the most popular works ever staged at the Stockholm Opera. Its success has been attributed to the familiarity of the text and the variety of musical material, including a textless vocalise sung by the blind Poetess. Other stage works by Blomdahl include *Herr von Hancken* (1964), an opera buffa based on a novel by Hjalmar Bergman, and his unfinished *Sagan om den stora datan* ("The Tale of the Great Computer"), on a book by Hanner Alfvén, in which he planned for electronic sound to take over from the live vocal and instrumental music used at the beginning of the score, paralleling the scenario in which computers render obsolete the roles of human beings.[7]

Adventurous, too, were the politically motivated works.

5. Blacher, "Neuland Rhythmus"; Stuckenschmidt, *Boris Blacher*.

6. Sartori, *Riccardo Malipiero*.

7. Aiken, "Karl-Birger Blomdahl"; articles by Inglefield and Wallner.

Conspicuous among postwar examples was *Intolleranza 1960* by the Italian composer Luigi Nono (b. 1924), first performed at Venice in 1961.[8] It is a "scenic action" on a libretto which, while incorporating Communist quotations and slogans, is nevertheless conceived as a protest against authoritarianism rather than as party-line propaganda. The music, as is typical for Nono, includes various novel sound effects and is in an "advanced" style markedly incongruous with the officially sponsored ideals of Moscow during that era.

Since 1945, an increasing number of composers in every country have adopted some form of twelve-tone technique, either using it as the basis of all their writing or blending or combining it with other techniques and styles. One of the most successful strict applications of twelve-tone technique to opera is heard in *Il prigioniero* ("The Prisoner," 1950), by Luigi Dallapiccola (1904–1975)[9]—successful, because the technical method is perfectly absorbed into the musical content: gradations of dissonance, with all the subtle sonorities, function for expressive ends, and the solo parts are conceived, in good Italian tradition, as singing human voices rather than as abstract contrapuntal lines. Four soloists, a large orchestra (including saxophones, vibraphone, and other "extra" woodwinds and percussion), with brass, bells, and organ and large and small choruses on stage, make up the performing forces. There are four scenes, with a prologue and two choral interludes on Latin liturgical texts. The drama centers around the condition of a Prisoner tortured by hope, "the ultimate torture," but destined never in this world to escape; this Prisoner (nameless, like all the other characters) is the type of modern man. Dallapiccola's thought was occupied with the same theme of imprisonment and escape in his *Canti di prigionia* ("Songs of the Prison," 1941) and *Canti di liberazione* ("Songs of Liberation," 1955). The music of *Il prigioniero* makes use at times of fixed

---

8. The opera was revised as *Intolleranza 1970* and performed at Florence in 1974. See Stenzl, ed., *Luigi Nono: Texte: Studien zu seiner Musik*. For a discussion of Nono's second opera, *Al gran sole carico d'amore*, completed in 1974, see Francesco Degrada's introduction to the published edition.

9. Vlad, "Dallapicola 1948–1955"; Nathan, "The Twelve-Tone Compositions of Luigi Dallapiccola"; Dallapiccola, "The Genesis of the *Canti di prigionia* and *Il prigioniero*"; D'Amico, "Luigi Dallapiccola."

Example 26.2: *Il prigioniero,* sc. 3

forms and often approaches the effect of conventional tonality (especially in the second choral interlude). An idea of the style can be obtained from a portion of the second "ricercare" from scene 3, based on a recurrent motive associated with the ironic word "fratello" ("brother") by which his jailers always address the Prisoner (example 26.2).

A more broadly conceived use of the twelve-tone technique can be found in the operas of many postwar German composers. The leading composer and teacher of this generation was Wolfgang Fortner (b. 1907), distinguished for symphonic and choral works as well as operas. His best-known opera is *Die Bluthochzeit* ("Blood Wedding," 1957), a melodious, clean-textured setting of García Lorca's tragedy *Bodas de sangre*. His other works for the stage include *In Seinem Garten Liebt Don Perlimplin* ("Don Perlimplin, in His Garden," 1962), also based on a play by Lorca, and *Elisabeth Tudor* (1972).[10]

Other postwar composers in Germany who have attracted particular notice for their operas include the Swiss-born Rolf Liebermann (b. 1910), Paul Dessau (1894–1979), Hanns Eisler (1898–1962), Bernd Alois Zimmermann (1918–1970), and Hans Werner Henze (b. 1926). Liebermann, in *Lenore 40/45* (1952) and *Penelope* (1954), has juxtaposed contrasting musical styles for a novel treatment, half realistic and half fantastic-satirical, of contemporary subject matter. His *School for Wives* (1955), with music in a tonal style, is a witty modern version of Molière's comedy.[11] Eisler, an East German composer who lived in the United States from 1933 to 1948, is best remembered for his collaborations with Bertolt Brecht, including the opera *Die Massnahme* ("The Measures Taken," 1930). Two other plays by Brecht were given musical settings by Dessau: *Die Verurteilung des Lukullus* ("The Condemnation of Lucullus," 1951) and *Herr Puntila und Sein Knecht Matti* ("Lord Puntila and His Servant Matti," 1966), a comedy. Questions of moral responsibility pervade the material Dessau brought to the stage, a reflection of his intense involve-

10. Fortner's association with the summer symposiums on contemporary music at Darmstadt brought him to the attention of many of Germany's younger composers. See, in particular, the composer's writings on his music.

11. Klein, "Rolf Liebermann als dramatischer Komponist"; Glanville-Hicks, "Some Reflections on Opera."

ment with political and social issues.[12] *Lukullus*, an internationally successful opera, focuses upon the career of a Roman general whose acts of brutality, committed under the cloak of military expediency, are judged to be crimes against humanity, punishable by banishment into eternal "nothingness." *Einstein* (1974), Dessau's last opera, addresses the question of a scientist's responsibility to society for his inventions; a biographical sketch of the title character is supported by a mixture of musical styles ranging from electronic tape to quotations from J. S. Bach's works, and from jazz to twelve-tone technique.

A powerfully expressive score composed during the postwar era is Zimmermann's *Die Soldaten* (1965), a Janus-faced work that looks back to Berg's *Wozzeck* and points forward to Henze's *We Come to the River*.[13] The story of *Die Soldaten* comes from an eighteenth-century play by Jakob Lenz, whose depiction of the military "establishment" in Prussian society can be read as an indictment of the military in the twentieth century as well. Zimmermann viewed the mini-scenes of the Lenz drama not as a linear progression of the past, present, and future actions of the protagonists but as a whirling sphere of events occurring in an aleatory fashion. In his original designs for the opera, Zimmermann mirrored this conception by positioning the audience in a circle on swivel chairs surrounded by multiple stages. The revised designs, reflecting his submission to practicality, call for a multilayered set consisting of five levels, on which simultaneous staging of scenes can take place. The dramatic possibilities of this set are well exemplified in the layered staging of three scenes, involving different times and places, in which (1) Stolzius receives Marie's letter of rejection, (2) Marie's grandmother sits weeping, anticipating her granddaughter's downfall, and (3) Baron Desportes seduces Marie. This collage of time, space, and action is reinforced by Zimmermann's score, with its variety of instrumental groupings and its pluralism of musical material, such as the *Dies irae* and Bach chorales. From the loud crashing tone clusters in the overture to the introspective recitation of the Lord's Prayer in the concluding scene (example 26.3a, b), *Die Soldaten* makes its

12. Hennenberg, *Paul Dessau*; Schaefer, "Paul Dessaus *Einstein* Oper."

13. Zimmermann composed the score for *Die Soldaten*, including the revisions, between 1958 and 1964. See Seipt, "*Die Soldaten*"; Mordden, *Opera in the Twentieth Century*, pp. 334–36.

Example 26.3a: *Die Soldaten*

ZIMMERMANN

Example 26.3b: *Die Soldaten*

moral statement in a unique manner that has been imitated but seldom duplicated.

In sharp contrast to Zimmermann, who composed only one opera, Hans Werner Henze has emerged as one of the more

Scene from *Don Rodrigo* (New York City Opera, 1967) by A. Ginastera.

prolific opera composers since the end of the Second World War. From his first one-act comedy, *Das Wundertheater* ("The Miracle Theater," 1948), which reveals his serialist training with Wolfgang Fortner and his association with a like-minded group of composers in Darmstadt, to *The English Cat* (Stuttgart, 1983), Henze has engaged himself with a wide variety of literary and musical materials. In *Boulevard Solitude* (1952), he presented a realistic adaptation of the Manon Lescaut story, in which each of the separate scenes is accompanied by a stylized modern dance. He next produced in 1953 *Das Ende einer Welt* ("The End of a World"), composed for radio broadcast, and *Ein Landarzt* ("A Country Doctor"), based on Kafka's story, with music in a style deriving from Berg's *Lulu*.

At that point in his career, Henze moved to Italy, where he acquired a new perspective on the ingredients that help create successful compositions for the stage. Two major works are associated with this Italian sojourn: *Der König Hirsch* ("King Stag," 1956; revised version, 1962), a fairy-tale opera with a long, elaborate, and variegated score, and *Der Prinz von Homburg* (1960), adapted from Heinrich von Kleist's drama, a full-scale grand opera with choruses. From opera in the grand manner, Henze turned to composing a chamber opera, *Elegy for Young Lovers* (1961), a twelve-tonescore for a libretto in English by W. H. Auden and Chester Kallman. A full-scale comedy, *Der Junge Lord* ("The Young Lord," 1965) appeared next, followed by *The Bassarids* (1966), an adaptation by Auden and Kallman of Euripides' *The Bacchae*. The score for this last-named opera is structured as a four-movement symphony, with a specific form for each movement: sonata, scherzo, adagio and fugue, and passacaglia.[14]

In the ten years between *The Bassarids* and *We Come to the River* (1976), Henze became increasingly involved as a left-wing political activist, but his writings and music of this period show that his advocacy of world revolution was tempered by a strong defense of artistic individualism.[15] *We Come to the River*, on an original libretto by Edward Bond, is another antiwar op-

14. Griffiths, "*The Bassarids*"; D. de la Motte, *Hans Werner Henze: "Der Prinz von Homburg*"; Geitel, *Hans Werner Henze*.

15. Henze, *Essays* and *Music and Politics: Collected Writings 1953–1981*.

era, which makes its attack on the militaristic values of a capitalistic society with the harshness of an atonal score and the weight of more than one hundred roles accompanied by three orchestras positioned on three separate stage levels.[16]

From the Argentinian Alberto Ginastera (1916–1983) came three operas, all serial compositions: *Don Rodrigo* (1964), *Bomarzo* (1967), and *Beatrix Cenci* (1971). The libretto for *Don Rodrigo* is taken from a Spanish legend encompassing a period of Moslem rule from the defeat of the Visigoth king in the battle of Guadalete in 711 to the restoration of Christian rule after the conquest of Granada in 1492. The central theme of the legend, heroism, is associated with the complete basic series of the tone row which forms a unifying thread for the entire opera. Ginastera fragments the basic series into several smaller segments, which in turn delineate the actions and feelings of the principal protagonists, Rodrigo and Florinda. Although the score is meticulously contrived through serial techniques and highly structured in conventional musical forms, its musical material is not so cerebral that it cannot communicate with an audience. This is especially true in the final scene, when twenty-four bells peal forth from different parts of the theater in proclamation of the rebirth of Christian Spain. With *Bomarzo* and *Beatrix Cenci*, Ginastera crossed over into a different phase of his career. Both these operas, commissioned and first performed in Washington, D.C., have overtly explicit scenes of sex and violence which have shocked audiences and dismayed critics, causing some to turn away from further contact with Ginastera's concept of musical theater.[17]

England and Canada

Of unquestionable importance for the history of twentieth-century opera is one of England's most versatile composers,

16. The American premiere of this opera took place at Santa Fe in 1984.

17. Chase, "Alberto Ginastera"; Suárez Urtubey, *Alberto Ginastera*; Lowens, "Ginastera's *Beatrix Cenci*"; Orrego-Salas, "An Opera in Latin America: *Don Rodrigo*"; and studies by Kuss.

Benjamin Britten (1913–1976).[18] In June 1945, his *Peter Grimes* was staged at the Sadler's Wells Theatre in London, with Peter Pears singing the title role. That occasion, viewed in retrospect, heralded a new era in English opera, one which continues to be favored with artistic achievements at home and abroad. Britten selected the story of Peter Grimes as told in George Crabbe's multisectional poem *The Borough* (1810), and he had Montagu Slater fashion a libretto about this fisherman from the seacoast town of Aldeburgh. Britten's opera presents an admirably constructed drama, with music in separate numbers linked by orchestral interludes and a few recurring themes, in an idiom permeated with the spirit of English folk song while unobtrusively incorporating Britten's own traits of color, rhythm, and harmony. An outstanding feature is the sensitive declamation of the text, and the expertly handled choral sonorities play an important part in creating the stark dramatic atmosphere of the work. Most effective is Britten's simultaneous use of foreground and background sounds to achieve a telescoping of dramatic events, as in Act II, scene 1, when Ellen and Peter are arguing on the beach against the singing of the liturgy in the church (example 26.4). He also used crossfading techniques to simulate an uninterrupted flow of musical material. A good example of this is the implied continuation of the raging storm in Act I, scene 2. Each time the door to the inn is opened by townsfolk seeking shelter, a fragment of the music associated with the storm (which had been heard in its entirety in interlude 2) is played. Throughout the vocal passages of the score, the orchestra is kept in a subordinate, accompanying role or is silenced altogether as in Grimes' soliloquy (Act III, scene 2); it rises to prominence, however, in the six interludes, communicating a cyclic design of village life, the moods and events of the sea, and a return (through repetition of the orchestral music of Act I) to village life.

Britten's next large-scale opera was *Billy Budd*, the libretto an adapation by E. M. Forster and Eric Crozier of Herman Melville's posthumous novel, *Billy Budd, Foretopman*. The

---

18. See the essays in Mitchell and Keller, eds., *Benjamin Britten*, and in Palmer, ed., *The Britten Companion*. See also the studies of Britten and his music by Holst, P. Evans, Headington, Mitchell, and E. White.

Example 26.4: *Peter Grimes*, Act 1, sc. 2

BRITTEN

B.&H. 18675

Peter Grimes—Benjamin Britten. Libretto by Montague Slater. © Copyright 1945 by Boosey & Hawkes, Ltd.; renewed 1972. Reprinted by permission of Boosey & Hawkes, Inc.

(Example 26.4 continued)

Peter Grimes—Benjamin Britten. Libretto by Montague Slater. © Copyright 1945 by Boosey & Hawkes, Ltd.; renewed 1972. Reprinted by permission of Boosey & Hawkes, Inc.

1960 version of the opera, restructured from the original four acts (1951), consists of a prologue, two acts, and an epilogue. Captain Vere and the crew of the *Indomitable* comprise the all-male cast: seventeen characters, a main-deck chorus of thirty-six voices, a quarter-deck chorus, and a quartet of Midshipmen. The prologue and epilogue allow the audience to see the Billy Budd story through the eyes of Captain Vere, who, in his old age, comes to an understanding of the universal power that one human being can exercise over another. He has had to live out his days haunted by the memory of that fateful day when he chose not to exercise his authority to save an innocent person from death. That person was Billy Budd, a handsome youth falsely accused of plotting mutiny aboard ship. In defense of his innocence, Billy Budd struck his superior officer, the fatal blow witnessed by Captain Vere. Punishment for Billy's action is decided by the drumhead court, its verdict told to Billy, off stage, by the Captain. During this meeting in Billy's cabin, the stage remains empty. The orchestra fills the void, with a slowly moving progression of whole-note chords, each played at a specific dynamic level by different groupings of instruments (brass, woodwinds, strings, tutti), to portray the drama of that confrontation. Before Billy is put to death, he forgives the Captain for following the dictates of naval law rather than those of the heart. The inner struggle of the drama—the opposition of "innocence and infamy"—is manifested in the bitonal clashes and in the juxtaposition of recurring themes.

A Midsummer Night's Dream (1960) is based on Shakespeare's play; Britten and Pears retained the original text (though abbreviating it considerably) to create a delightful fairy-tale atmosphere, complete with an opera within the opera (Act III). Each group of characters is associated with different kinds of textures and orchestral colors. In addition, the division between natural and supernatural characters is clarified by having the latter assigned high voice roles. Some beautiful numbers in the score include the duets in Act I, the comic rehearsal of the rustics in the first scene of Act II, and the ensemble for six boys at the end of the same act. But some of the mannerisms, such as glissandi in the double basses and ostinato techniques generally, are overworked, and a certain monotony of effect results from the prevailing color of high voices; in particular, the countertenor role of Oberon is dramatically unconvincing.

Britten's operas for smaller performing groups include the tragic *Rape of Lucretia* (1946), which uses a commentative "chorus" consisting of two solo voices; the comic *Albert Herring* (1947); and an unusual work, *The Turn of the Screw* (1954), a dramatization of Henry James' tale with music in the form of fifteen variations on a tone row—which, however, is treated as a theme rather than by the usual twelve-tone techniques of construction and moreover is so conceived and harmonized as to produce an effect not far removed from conventional tonality. The music successfully captures the supernatural mood of the story (conveyed here by the black-note keys) in contrast to the natural world (with its seven white-note keys), but the dramatic material is perhaps too subtle to be effectively projected in the theater. Another work by Henry James, his short story *Owen Wingrave*, provided the basis for Britten's opera of the same title, which was commissioned by the British Broadcastiing Corporation and premiered as a television opera in 1971. *Owen Wingrave* is a story about the futility of war as seen through the lives of a professional military family, an attitude with which Britten, an avowed pacifist, could readily sympathize.

For more than thirty years, Britten had shared the spotlight of his illustrious career with his lifelong friend, Peter Pears. Not only had Pears sung the tenor roles in most of Britten's operas; he had also performed as part of their celebrated piano-vocal duo. As a tribute to this artistic partnership, Britten created for Pears the role of Gustav von Aschenbach in his last opera, *Death in Venice* (1973).[19] The libretto written by Myfanwy Piper and based upon Thomas Mann's novella of the same name, is in two acts of seventeen scenes. The central figure of the opera is Aschenbach, a "famous master-writer," who seeks a life of fulfillment after having lived for years under the constraints of his own creative activity. His quest for a new life brings him to Venice, where various incarnations of Fate, each portrayed by the

---

19. In this same year, Britten returned to his first stage work, *Paul Bunyan* (1941), and prepared it for performance at the 1976 Aldeburgh Festival.

same bass-baritone, guide him to his inevitable dissolution and death. In the course of this journey, Aschenbach is ravaged by two forces, fear and friendship. The former is associated with the plague, the latter with his interest in a young boy, Tadzio, whose Apollonian realm is expressed in dance and mime and articulated by the exotic gamelan-like sounds of vibraphone and percussion. In Britten's setting of the text, he relied heavily upon various styles of recitative, including one in which the pitches are notated but the rhythmic interpretation is entrusted to the singer. He also made effective use of orchestral writing to communicate the nonverbal aspects of the story, as in the overture, which bridges the time interval between the second and third scenes of Act I, and in the instrumental postlude, which sustains the final moments of the opera while Aschenbach silently slips from life into death.

Britten wrote two operas for children, *The Little Sweep* (1949) and *Noye's Fludde* (1958). The latter provided a model for a set of three one-act operas with all-male casts written for church performance: *Curfew River* (1964), based on a Japanese nō play; *The Burning Fiery Furnace* (1966), derived from the Old Testament; and *The Prodigal Son* (1968), from the New Testament. All in all, there can be no question as to Britten's signal importance in contemporary English opera or his significance as an original, skillful, and idealistic composer adapting himself without sacrifice of integrity to the practical conditions of his place and time.

Opera in England had indeed taken on new life immediately after the Second World War. The period was marked by a number of other important works. They include *Nelson* (1951) and a humorous chamber opera, *The Dinner Engagement* (1954), both by Lennox Berkeley (b. 1903); *A Tale of Two Cities* (1953), by Arthur Benjamin (1893–1960); *Infidelio* (1954), a chamber opera showing Schoenbergian influence, by Elizabeth Lutyens (1906–1983); and *Troilus and Cressida* (1954), a large-scale opera in an ultraconservative style, by William Walton (1902–1983).[20]

In the next decade, Lutyens composed several more works for the stage, including *The Numbered* (1965–67), in which the characters know at what age they will die but are sworn to keep their age a secret from each other, and *Time Off?—Not a Ghost*

20. Howes, *The Music of William Walton.*

of a Chance! (1967–68).[21] In this same decade, Walton produced a second opera, *The Bear* (1967), an extravaganza which has become an international success. The libretto was fashioned by Paul Dehn from a one-act "vaudeville" by Chekhov and is a humorous caricature of three distinct types of Russian people, represented by the widow Popova (mezzo-soprano), her servant Luka (bass), and the gentleman visitor Smirnov (baritone). Walton mirrors the comic actions of the protagonists with musical parody and clichés. His scoring for chamber ensemble (strings, woodwinds, piano, harp, horn, trumpet, trombone, and percussion) enhances the fast-paced delivery of the text, which is often expressed in accompanied recitative.

A composer highly regarded by his fellow musicians is Alun Dudley Bush (b. 1900), who wrote four major operas—*Wat Tyler* (1951), which won a prize in Britain's Arts Council Festival, *Men of Blackmoor* (1955), *The Sugar Reapers* (1960), and *Joe Hill* (1970)—in addition to several operas for children. His impact on English opera, however, was considerably less than it might have been had his major works received professionally staged performances on his native soil. The reason they did not was more political than musical. Bush had become a member of the Communist party in 1935, and he used his operas as a forum for expounding political views. Potential audiences at home did not share these views, forcing Bush to look elsewhere—namely, to Leipzig and other East German cities—for productions which proved successful and brought him public acclaim.

Throughout the postwar era, there has been growing predilection among British composers for writing operas in a more simplified mode of musical expression to complement the dramatic portrayal of commonplace events. Britten's operas underscore this generalization; those of Michael Tippett (b. 1905) controvert it. Tippett, author of all his opera librettos, is clearly influenced by contemporary theatrical works.[22] By means of symbolism and allegory, he places before his audience a world of myths, dreams, and fantasies. His characters divorce themselves from the "com-

21. Henderson, "Elisabeth Lutyens"; Walsh, *"Time Off* and *The Scene Machine"*; Bradshaw, "The Music of Elisabeth Lutyens."

22. See studies by Bowen, Kemp, E. White, and Whittall, and articles by Clements, Warrack, and Dickinson.

monplace" and become absorbed into the primordial depths of ritualism. The premiere of *The Midsummer Marriage* in 1955 generated few laudatory remarks; a similar fate greeted *King Priam* (1962), *The Knot Garden* (1970), and *The Ice Break* (1977). Subsequent performances have altered those initial reactions and, with the passage of time, Tippett's operas have achieved a prominent place in the twentieth-century repertoire.[23]

The Midsummer Marriage, the longest of the four operas, has the usual complement of arias, duets, and ensembles, but what is distinctive is Tippett's emphasis upon ballet. In the course of the opera, subjective hindrances to eventual marriage are explored and overcome through ritual dance. The path traversed by the lovers from ignorance to enlightenment about themselves is musically conveyed by brilliant orchestration and a directness of vocal declamation. The theme of *King Priam*, a tragedy that draws its characters from the epic realm of Homer, is unavoidable destiny. Numerous monologues allow each character to set forth a particular situation that involves a conflict of choice, especially a conflict between desire and duty. In the orchestration, Tippet uses strings sparingly, even eliminating them (except for the guitar) in Act II.

The Knot Garden has no real plot. Seven characters move through the ritual maze of the garden, seeking transformation from a state of noncommunication to one of reconciliation which will inherently permit communication. The transformation, however, is not realized in the opera, and thus *The Knot Garden*, with its preponderance of duos and trios depicting collective rather than individual communication, might best be viewed as a prelude to the next phase of life, one that begins immediately after the last note of the score has sounded. Tippett's preoccupation with "ritual rebirth" continues in *The Ice Break*. This fast-paced score uses music of the blues, in jolting contrast to the violence of amplified sounds and extensive percussion passages. The chorus, always masked, reinforces the violent mood with its terrifying shouts. Unexpected combinations of instruments and offstage choral and

23. Two ballad operas and an opera for children, all written by Tippett before the Second World War, remain unpublished.

orchestral sounds further contribute to what has been termed Tippett's "'surrealist approach" to opera.

Representative of a younger generation of composers in the British Isles are Iain Hamilton (b. 1922), Thea Musgrave (b. 1928), Alun Hoddinott (b. 1929), William Mathias (b. 1934), and Peter Maxwell Davies (b. 1934). Hamilton's *The Royal Hunt of the Sun* (1977), based on a play of the same name by Peter Schaffer, tells a tale of atrocities committed against the Incas during the Spanish conquest of Peru. His score is composed in a basically tonal style; it calls for two mute roles played by women, one spoken role, and the remaining roles to be sung by male voices, the whole supported by a large orchestra and chorus.

From the Welsh composer, Hoddinott, have come five operas for stage and television which have enjoyed considerable success: *The Beach of Falesá* (1974), *Murder the Magician* (1976), *What the Old Man Does Is Always Right* (1977), *The Rajah's Diamond* (1979), and *The Trumpet Major* (1981).[24] His librettist for three of these operas was Myfanwy Piper, skilled in writing original librettos as well as in fashioning them from other literary sources (in this case, the short stories of Robert Louis Stevenson and a novel by Thomas Hardy). Also from Wales comes Mathias, who wrote *The Servants* (1980) on a story derived from Iris Murdoch's play *The Servants and the Snow*. The action is set in Central Europe at the beginning of this century and focuses upon the ambivalent roles of servant and master on a wealthy landowner's estate. Composed in the tradition of a number opera, in the sense that whole sections can be performed as separate units, the score places considerable importance upon the chorus, which functions as an active protagonist.

Thea Musgrave, who has resided in the United States since the 1970s, uses serial techniques to shape the atonal materials of her opera scores, from *The Decision* (1967), a three-act tragedy about a mine disaster in Scotland, to *Harriet, the Woman Called Moses* (1985), based on the life of an American, Harriet Tubman, and her activities with the underground railroad. The most melodic of Musgrave's opera scores is *A Christmas Carol*

24. Wynne, "Alun Hoddinott"; Boyd, *"The Beach of Falesá"*; Deane, *Alun Hoddinott*.

(1979), which includes quotations from recognizable tunes, such as "God Rest You Merry Gentlemen." The most dramatic is *Mary, Queen of Scots* (1977), a vivid portrayal of sixteenth-century events surrounding the life of Mary Stuart, widow of the king of France, who returns to Scotland and briefly lays claim to the throne. The opera concludes with the Protestant Scots demanding that the Catholic queen abdicate. *The Voice of Ariadne* (1974), dedicated to Benjamin Britten, shows another aspect of Musgrave's serialism. This amusing chamber opera was inspired by Henry James' *The Last of the Valerii*, a short story about a count who becomes enamoured with the spirit of a recently excavated statue to the extent that he ignores his own wife. Not until the statue is buried once again does his interest in the countess resume. Amalie Elguera's libretto adapts the James' retelling of the legend with an important variation: there is no statue to attract the count, only the voice of Ariadne (on prerecorded tape off stage). No one but the count can hear this voice, a situation that provokes some very humorous episodes.[25]

Within the past two decades, Peter Maxwell Davies has produced several operas, including *The Martyrdom of St. Magnus* (1977), *Le Jongleur de Notre Dame* (1978), and *The Lighthouse* (1980), but the one that best exemplifies his personality as a composer is *Taverner* (1972).[26] Davies began formulating ideas for this opera as early as 1956, when he first contemplated writing a libretto on the life of the noted English church composer, John Taverner (1495–1545). The score was completed in 1968, but not before Davies had experimented with the integration of Taverner's music with his own in the *First Fantasia on In Nomine of John Taverner for Orchestra* (1962).[27] The opera explores the conflict between religious faith and artistic freedom as experienced by Taverner when he, in an act of self-fulfillment, agreed to create music for the Roman Catholic church, thereby tacitly affirming Christian dogma which he would later find intolerable.

25. Heinsheimer, "Mistress Musgrave"; Hixon, *Thea Musgrave*; Walsh, "Musgrave's *The Voice of Ariadne*"; Musgrave, "*Mary, Queen of Scots*."

26. Griffiths, *Peter Maxwell Davies*; Pruslin, ed., *Peter Maxwell Davies: Studies from Two Decades* (containing many important articles that originally were printed in *Tempo*).

27. His *Second Fantasia on In Nomine of John Taverner for Orchestra* (1964) grew out of the completed first act of *Taverner*. See Griffiths, *Peter Maxwell Davies*, p. 141.

A characteristic of Davies' style of composition is his penchant for expanding an already unique vocabulary with pre-Baroque sources. In *Taverner*, this characteristic manifests itself in the use of Renaissance instruments to evoke the courtly atmosphere of six-teenth-century England and in the musical quotations from litur-gical plainchant and from Taverner's festal mass, *Gloria Tibi Trinitas*. Seldom can these quotations be readily discerned by an audience, for Davies intentionally distorts his borrowings to sug-gest, symbolically, spiritual and emotional transformations in his principal protagonist.[28]

The Canadian counterpart to this generation of British composers is represented by John Beckwith (b. 1927), Gabriel Charpentier (b. 1925), R. Murray Schafer (b. 1933), Harry So-mers (b. 1925), and Charles Wilson (b. 1931).[29] Although opera has long been a part of Canada's cultural tradition, with perfor-mances of the earliest Canadian score dating from 1790,[30] the rep-ertoire has been limited primarily to nineteenth-century Euro-pean works. Not until the 1960s, a decade that saw the construction of many new theaters and the establishment of resident opera companies, did this situation show signs of change. The Canadian Opera Company's performance in 1966 of the revised *Deirdre* by Healey Willan (1880–1968) paved the way for production of other Canadian operas, with some of the more successful ones designed specifically for radio and television audiences. One of the most important operas to emerge from this period was Harry Somers' *Louis Riel*, commissioned by the Canadian Opera Company in 1967.

Of the composers cited above, R. Murray Schafer may be the best known internationally, not only for his musical com-positions but also for his writings about music.[31] His vocal works

28. See for example, the solo viola passage in Act II, sc. 3, which represents a quotation in inversion from the *In Nomine* section of Taverner's mass.

29. For the most comprehensive view of Canadian music in general and Canadian opera in particular, see the *Encyclopedia of Music in Canada*. See also Proctor, *Canadian Music of the Twentieth Century*; Cherney, *Harry Somers*; MacMillan and Beckwith, eds., *Con-temporary Canadian Composers*; and *Opera Canada*, a journal published quarterly.

30. *Colas et Colinette*, by Joseph Quesnel (1746–1809), which bears a strong resemblance to *Le devin du village* by Rousseau, is considered the earliest surviving Canadian opera.

31. Schafer is the editor of *Ezra Pound and Music* and of Ezra Pound's opera, *Le Tes-tament de François Villon*. For a comprehensive survey of Schafer's life and works as well as an extensive examination of his writings, see Adams, *R. Murray Schafer*.

reveal an intense interest in the special properties of language. In his nonstage works can be found a selection of Tibetan, Egyptian, and Persian texts; in his operas, the librettos are often written in two languages, one of which is the vernacular of the country where the performance is staged. By introducing the vernacular, Schafer can heighten the dramatic immediacy of the events portrayed. This is certainly the case in *Toi* ("Loving," 1965) and in *Patria*, a trilogy of operas focusing upon problems of loneliness and isolation caused by language barriers, from those of the immigrant who discovers his "vernacular" can not be understood by the other characters to those of the mental patient who is daily confronted with the medical jargon of a hospital staff.

The United States

In the United States, the ultraconservative style in opera was represented at midcentury by *Vanessa*, a large-scale, four-act work which premiered at the Metropolitan Opera in 1958 and for which the composer, Samuel Barber (1910–1981), was awarded a Pulitzer Prize.[32] *Vanessa* was so well suited for the stage and contained so many excellent musical numbers that it was not unreasonable for the public to expect Barber's next major opera, commissioned for the gala opening of the Metropolitan's new home at Lincoln Center, also to be theatrically and musically effective. Unfortunately, the inaugural production of *Anthony and Cleopatra* (1966) did not satisfy the public's expectations and the opera was withdrawn. It was later revised and presented at Juilliard School of Music in 1973, but the revision did little to change the public's evaluation of the opera.

More varied and adventurous, though still not involving any radical break with tradition, has been the work of Samuel Barber's close friend and colleague, Gian Carlo Menotti (b. 1911), a theater composer of the order of Puccini and the verismo school. Menotti's musical style is eclectic, drawing upon heterogeneous

32. See Broder, *Samuel Barber*.

elements with a single eye to dramatic effect, of which he is an unerring master.[33] He writes his own librettos,[34] and he often serves as director for his musical productions. Conspicuous among his many successful works for the stage are *The Medium* (1946), an unashamed melodrama perfectly matched by equally melodramatic music; a short comic opera, *The Telephone* (1947); and his first full-length opera, *The Consul* (1950), a compelling treatment of the tragedy of homeless persons in an indifferent world. *Amahl and the Night Visitors*, originally produced on television in 1951, has become a popular classic. It is not necessary to make extravagant claims for Menotti's musical originality in order to recognize that he was one of the very few serious opera composers on the American scene in the 1950s who thoroughly understood the requirements of the theater and made a consistent, sincere attempt to reach the large opera-loving public; his success is a testimonial to the continuing validity of a long and respectable operatic tradition. Critics of Menotti contend that he reached a peak of creativity with *The Saint of Bleecker Street* (1954) and that his subsequent works for the theater—*Help! Help! The Globolinks!* (1969), *The Most Important Man* (1971), *Tamu-Tamu* (1973), and *The Hero* (1976)—provided only a faint reminder of the mastery he had achieved in earlier years. Menotti, undaunted by adverse criticism, has continued to compose new operas, his latest planned for production in 1986.

Leonard Bernstein (b. 1918), well known as a conductor and as the composer of *West Side Story*, considers the Broadway musical theater idiom to be a wellspring for the creation of American national opera.[35] In 1952, Bernstein produced his first opera, *Trouble in Tahiti*; thirty years later he composed his second, *A Quiet Place*, intended as a sequel to *Trouble in Tahiti*. Bernstein originally planned to have both operas produced as a double bill, using a before-and-after format to show changes in family relationships over a twenty-five-year period, but the juxtaposition of the two operas in a production in Houston did not achieve the

---

33. Gruen, *Menotti: A Biography*; Ardoin, *The Stages of Menotti*.

34. He also wrote the libretto for Barber's *Vanessa*.

35. Recent productions from the Broadway repertoire by the Metropolitan Opera and New York City Opera companies support this opinion. See, for example, *Porgy and Bess* by Gershwin and *Sweeney Todd* by Stephen Sondheim.

kind of emotional and psychological impact that he had envisioned. Bernstein withdrew the operas and revised *A Quiet Place* so that it could totally envelop the earlier opera: Act I is derived solely from *A Quiet Place*; Act II begins with the first half of *Trouble in Tahiti*, continues with a brief section from *A Quiet Place*, and concludes with the remaining sections of *Trouble in Tahiti*; Act III is from *A Quiet Place*. The revised opera, entitled *A Quiet Place and Trouble in Tahiti*, was staged first in Milan (1984), where it was heralded as "the most American of American operas," and then in Washington, D.C., where it was reviewed as a possible first step toward the "Great American Opera."[36]

With the end of the Second World War, the production of operas by American composers increased significantly, enhanced by the marked rise of local opera groups, both amateur and professional, and the generally favorable opportunities for performance of new works in the United States. In the forefront of this postwar activity was Douglas Moore (see chapter 25), who continued to write operas that combined distinctly American subject matter and musical idiom with good theatrical craftsmanship. This is especially true of his highly successful opera, *The Ballad of Baby Doe* (1956), which is based upon an actual event that occurred in the gold-rush days of the nineteenth century. Other operas by Moore are *Giants in the Earth* (1951), which glorifies the pioneer spirit of the Norwegian settlers in the Dakotas, and *Carrie Nation* (1966), which focuses upon a prohibitionist's crusade in Kansas. Another uniquely American subject, the career of Susan B. Anthony and the issue of women's suffrage, provides the scenario for *The Mother of Us All* (1947), by Virgil Thomson in another collaboration with Gertrude Stein.

Among other more or less successful works by composers in the United States that were produced in the postwar decades are *The Warrior* (1947) and *The Veil* (1950), by Bernard Rogers (1893–1968); *The Jumping Frog of Calaveras County* (1950), by Lukas Foss (b. 1922); *The Mighty Casey* (1953), by William Schuman (b. 1910); *The Tender Land* (1954), by Aaron Copland (b. 1900); *The Ruby* (1955) and *The Trial at Rouen* (1956), by Norman Dello Joio (b. 1913); *The Wife of Martin Guerre* (1956), by

36. Gruen, "Reworking *A Quiet Place* for La Scala."

William Bergsma (b. 1921); *Good Soldier Schweik* (1958), by the talented American-born Czech composer Robert Kurka (1921–1957); *The Crucible* (1961), by Robert Ward (b. 1917); *The Alcestiad* (1962), by Louise Talma (b. 1906), the first American woman to have an opera premiered in Europe by a major performing company; and *Lizzie Borden* (1965), by Jack Beeson (b. 1921).

Over the course of the past thirty years, Carlisle Floyd (b. 1926) has emerged as one of the major contributors to the repertoire of American opera, his dozen or more works bringing to the stage important themes of Americana. A recent work in this vein is *Citizen of Paradise* (1983), a "monodrama" on the life of Emily Dickinson, commissioned for the opening of a new arts center at Dickinson College (Pennsylvania). The libretto is a selection of Dickinson's poems, which Floyd skillfully arranged as a prologue, four episodes, ("Self," "Friendship and Society," "Nature," "Death and Solitude"), and an epilogue to create a dramatically intense and musically effective piece for the theater.

Floyd first gained recognition as an opera composer with *Susannah* (1955), an immediately popular work which continues to hold the stage, and *Wuthering Heights* (1959).[37] Among his later works which have received national attention are two full-length operas: *Of Mice and Men* (1970), adapted by Floyd from John Steinbeck's "play" rather than from the novel of 1937; and *Willie Stark* (1981), based on Robert Penn Warren's novel *All the King's Men*, which dates from 1946.

Roger Sessions (1896–1985) and Hugo Weisgall (b. 1912) offer another aspect of American opera, although their works have yet to be fully appreciated by the public. Sessions composed two operas, *The Trial of Lucullus* (1947) and *Montezuma*, the latter a monumental atonal score performed first in Berlin (1964) and then in Boston (1976) under the direction of Sarah Caldwell. These avant-garde creations did little to influence a younger generation of composers. What did influence them was Sessions' teaching and his high regard for the rich heritage of Western music.

This influence can be felt in the music of Weisgall, who studied with Sessions, for each of Weisgall's operas shows an allegiance to the grand operatic tradition while at the same time

37. See articles by Eyer and Sabin.

exploring new literary and musical territory. He composed eight operas between 1952 and 1978. *The Stronger* (1952), a mono-drama after Strindberg; *Six Characters in Search of an Author* (1959), on a play of the same title by Pirandello; *Nine Rivers from Jordan* (1968), a lengthy work in three acts; and *Jenny, or The Hundred Nights* (1976), on a Japanese nō play, represent well the characteristics of Weisgall's style. These include florid, soaring vocal lines (example 26.5); quotations of familiar tunes,

Example 26.5: *Six Characters in Search of an Author*

Do you think this a-ri-a is high e-nough for____ so - pra no?

such as "Believe Me If All Those Endearing Young Charms," which appears in a violin descant in *The Hundred Nights*; and excellent ensemble writing—all set forth in a very dissonant and rhythmically alive medium.[38]

Throughout his career, Weisgall has been a strong advocate of chamber opera, composing them (e.g., *Gardens of Adonis*, 1980) and organizing groups to specialize in their production. Many composers share his interest and have enjoyed considerable success with smaller-scaled works. A masterpiece in this category is one by Stephen Paulus (b. 1949), *The Village Singer* (1979), a one-act opera that paved the way for acceptance of the composer's full-length opera, *The Postman Always Rings Twice* (1982). Other operas that deserve to be mentioned are *Full Moon in March* (1979), by John Harbison (b. 1938), and *Women in the Garden* (1978), by Vivian Fine (b. 1913), with a libretto drawn from the life and writings of four women: Virginia Woolf, Gertrude Stein, Isadora Duncan, and Emily Dickinson.

Twentieth-century opera has certainly not lacked composers willing to experiment with new musical and dramatic forms, but seldom have any achieved the kind of box-office success which Philip Glass (b. 1937) has done with all three of his major operas.

38. Saylor, "The Music of Hugo Weisgall"; Blumenfeld, "Hugo Weisgall's 66th Birthday and the new *Gardens of Adonis*"; Rochberg, "Hugo Weisgall."

Scene from Act IV, sc. 3C of *Einstein on the Beach* (BAM, Brooklyn 1984) by Philip Glass; designed by Robert Wilson.

(Photo by Babette Mangolte, courtesy of Brooklyn Academy of Music)

The 1976 production of *Einstein on the Beach*, created by Glass in collaboration with the playwright/director Robert Wilson, initiated a new movement in modern opera, which favors an eclectic style embracing classical, popular, and non-Western traditions.[39] Glass's compositional format depends upon maximal repetitions of minimal musical segments tempered with romantic emotionalism. In other words, this "minimalist" style, as it is sometimes called, involves the continuous repetition of melodic cells while at the same time subjecting these cells to alteration through barely perceptible changes in texture, harmony, and especially rhythm. Unfortunately, the terms "minimalist" and "maximalist" which are applied to Glass's manner of composing are far too restrictive to define a style of opera that is closely tied to the visual arts of stage design and governed by the textual sounds derived from archaic languages. Nor do these terms adequately describe a style of composing that seems to be in a constant state of development, for each of the operas marks a different plateau in Glass's career.

Einstein on the Beach is an allegory of the atomic age communicated to an audience through a stream-of-consciousness technique held together by the biographical events of the scientist's life. For more than four hours without interruption (there are no intermissions), the audience concentrates upon a three-tiered cubic design containing personages who repeat words and sounds (solfège syllables, a paragraph read forty-three times) to the amplified accompaniment of synthesizers, woodwinds, and chorus.

The second opera in Glass's triptych of portraits about men whose revolutionary ideas affected the world in which they lived is *Satyagraha* (1981), an epic about nonviolence as expressed by one episode in the life of Mahatma Gandhi: his struggle for Indian civil liberties in South Africa during the period from 1893 to 1914. The opera is sung in Sanskrit, the language of the *Bhagavad-Gita*, from which Constance DeJong derived her libretto, and is scored for a normal orchestra, but without brass or percussion. Each of the three acts is associated with a figure (silently positioned high on a platform) who symbolizes the spirit

39. Coe, "Philip Glass Breaks Through"; Griffiths, *Modern Music*; Mertens, *American Minimal Music*.

of nonviolence that has pulsated through other times and other places: Leo Tolstoy, Rabindranath Tagore, and Martin Luther King, Jr. So closely related is the minimal technique to Indian music that the score gives the illusion of presenting Indian ragas, as in the 140 repetitions of the opening four-chord progression by the lower strings. Staging and music combine in *Satyagraha* to produce a hypnotic effect on the audience to the extent that Gandhi's final blessing, repeated over every one of his thirty comrades, becomes a "sound gesture" which audiences take with them as they depart from the theater.

Akhnaten (1984), the third opera of the triptych, chronicles the rise and fall of an Egyptian pharaoh whose reign (ca. 1375–1358 B.C.) was marked by religious, judicial, and cultural reforms. Akhnaten, son of King Amenhotep III, was crowned pharaoh upon his father's death. Declaring himself a descendant of Aten, a sun god, Akhnaten decreed that his subjects should worship that god exclusively and ordered a city built in the god's honor. He resided in that city with his wife, Nefertiti, and became so immersed in religious devotions that his kingdom crumbled from neglect. He lost the throne and the city was ultimately destroyed, and in the final scene of the opera the ruins are visited by tourists and the ghost of Akhnaten. The opera is sung in the original languages of the quoted materials that comprise the libretto—Egyptian, Hebrew, and Akkadian; the narrator of the opera's action speaks in the vernacular of the audience in attendance. The score, which calls for an orchestra without violins, exhibits the same minimalist style of Glass's earlier compositions, with the endlessly repeated melodic patterns sustained by slowly changing harmonies giving a sense of time transcended.

The attention devoted to Glass's compositions and productions in both Europe and the United States has almost overshadowed the appearance of another important contribution to twentieth-century opera: namely, *Saint François d'Assise* (1983), by Olivier Messiaen (b. 1980). This is the only opera Messiaen has composed in the course of his long and illustrious career, and it bears the unmistakable stamp of his style.[40] His episodic retelling

40. Samuel, *Conversations with Olivier Messiaen*; Hold, "Messiaen's Birds"; and studies by Bell, Johnson, and Nichols. See also Messiaen, *The Technique of My Musical Language*.

of the life of St. Francis takes more than five hours to perform and requires a large chorus and orchestra, the latter augmented by extra brass, woodwinds, and three electronic instruments called *Ondes Martenot*. Messiaen's abundance of melodic motives incorporating bird songs and plainchant combines with rhythmically complex patterns to produce a serenely beautiful score which, nevertheless, is one of the most difficult to perform in the entire literature.

Here our survey of the history of opera ends. It is sad to think that so much beauty lies buried in the silence of the past, that so much of what pleased our forebears has been all but submerged in the inexorable flow of history. Operas of the past, however, need not disappear. They can live again, not only in our imagination, but also on the stage, where their movement, color, and sound can still exalt us. But we must not be satisfied merely to have "the past, like an inspired rhapsodist, fill the theatre of everlasting generations with her harmony."[41] The old should be balanced by the new, for history is both a return and a beginning. As we restore the past, we must also listen to the future. It is there that, out of a meeting of East and West and in the rhythms of new life together, as yet unheard sounds of the operatic realm are being fashioned.

41. The words of Shelley, as quoted in the preface to Altman et al., *Theater Pictorial*.

LIST OF ABBREVIATIONS

AfMF	*Archiv für Musikforschung*
AfMw	*Archiv für Musikwissenschaft*
AMZ	*Allgemeine musikalische Zeitung*
C.E.	Collected Edition
C.F.	*Chefs-d'oeuvre de l'opéra français*
CMc	*Current Musicology*
DdT	*Denkmäler deutscher Tonkunst*
DJbM	*Deutsches Jahrbuch der Musikwissenschaft*
DTB	*Denkmäler der Tonkunst in Bayern*
DTOe	*Denkmäler der Tonkunst in Oesterreich*
EMTA	*Echo Muzyczne, Teatralne i Artystyczne*
HAM	*Historical Anthology of Music*
JAMS	*Journal of the American Musicological Society*
JMP	*Jahrbuch der Musikbibliothek Peters*
K	Köchel, *Chronologisch-thematisches Verzeichnis sämtlicher Tonwerke . . . Mozarts.*
M	*Musica* (Kassel, 1947–)
MA	*Musical Antiquary*
MD	*Musica disciplina*
Mf	*Musikforschung*
MfMg	*Monatshefte für Musikgeschichte*
MGG	*Musik in Geschichte und Gegenwart*
M&L	*Music & Letters*
MLA Notes	*Music Library Association Notes*
MM	*Mercure muscial*
MMR	*Monthly Musical Record*
MMus	*Modern Music*

MQ	*Musical Quarterly*
MR	*Music Review*
MSD	*Musicological Studies and Documents*
MT	*Musical Times*
MTNA	*Proceedings of the Music Teachers National Association*
MuG	*Musik und Gesellschaft*
NM	*Nuestra música*
NOHM	*New Oxford History of Music*
NZfM	*Neue Zeitschrift für Musik*
OeM	*Oesterreichische Musikzeitschrift*
OHM	*Oxford History of Music*
perf.	performed, performance
PRMA	*Proceedings of the Royal Musical Association* (London)
RassM	*Rassegna musicale*
RBM	*Revue belge de musicologie*
RdM	*Revue de musicologie*
RHCM	*Revue d'histoire et de critique musicales* (with no. 10 of vol. 2, became *SIM Revue musicale*)
RIdM	*Revue internationale de musique*
RM	*Revue musicale* (Paris, 1920–)
RMI	*Rivista musicale italiana*
SB	Schering, *Geschichte der Musik in Beispielen*
SchwM	*Schweizerische Musikzeitung*
SIM	*Société internationale de musique*
SIMG	*Sammelbände der internationalen Musikgesellschaft*
SovM	*Sovetskaia muzyka*
STM	*Svensk Tidskrift för Musikforskning*
SzMw	*Studien zur Musikwissenschaft* (Beihefte der DTOe)
VfMw	*Vierteljahrsschrift für Musikwissenschaft*
ZfMw	*Zeitschrift für Musikwissenschaft*
ZIMG	*Zeitschrift der internationalen Musikgesellschaft*

BIBLIOGRAPHY

This bibliography is an abridgement of the one which appeared in the second edition. However, it contains full bibliographical information for all the works cited in the footnotes to this edition. Interested readers should consult the Bibliography in the second (English) edition for additional works published before 1965.

General

Abert, Hermann. *Gesammelte Schriften und Vorträge*. Halle an der Saale: Niemeyer, 1929.

Abry, Emile. *Histoire illustrée de la littérature française*. Paris: Didier, 1935.

Adler, Guido. *Handbuch der Musikgeschichte unter Mitwirkung von Fachgenossen*. Frankfurt am Main: Frankfurter Verlags-Anstalt, 1924.

Ambros, August Wilhelm. *Geschichte der Musik*. Vol. 4. 3rd ed., rev. and enl. by Hugo Leichtentritt. Leipzig: Leuchart, 1909.

Barrenechea, Mariano Antonio. *Historia estética de la música, con dos estudios mas sobre consideraciones históricas y técnicas acerca del canto y la obra maestra del teatro melodramático*. Buenos Aires: Editorial Claridad, 1941.

Bekker, Paul. *Klang und Eros*. Stuttgart and Berlin: Deutsche Verlags-Anstalt, 1922.

Blume, Friedrich. *Classic and Romantic Music*. Trans. by M. D. Herter Norton. New York: Norton, 1970.

Botstiber, Hugo. *Geschichte der Ouvertüre und der freien Orchesterformen*. Leipzig: Breitkopf & Härtel, 1913.

Bruneau, Alfred. *La Musique française: Rapport sur la musique en France du XIIIe au XXe siècles; la musique à Paris en 1900*. Paris: Fasquelle, 1901.

Bücken, Ernst. *Der heroische Stil in der Oper*. Leipzig: Kistner & Siegel, 1924.

Bustico, Guido. *Bibliografia delle storie e cronistorie dei teatri italiani*. Milan: Bollettino bibliografico musicale, 1929.

Chavarri, Eduardo López. *Historia de la música*. 3rd ed. Barcelona: Imprenta elzeviriana, 1929.

Chouquet, Gustave. *Histoire de la musique dramatique en France*. Paris: Firmin-Didot, 1873.

Clément, Félix. *Dictionnaire des opéras (dictionnaire lyrique), rev. et mis à jour par Arthur Pougin*. Paris: Larousse, [1905].

Combarieu, Jules. *Histoire de la musique*. 3rd ed. 3 vols. Paris: Colin, 1920.

Cone, Edward T. "Music: A View from Delft." *MQ* (1961), 47:439–53.

Conrad, Peter. *Romantic Opera and Literary Form*. Berkeley and Los Angeles: University of California Press, 1977.

Covent Garden Opera Series. London: Boosey & Hawkes, 1947(?)—.

Cross, Milton. *Complete Stories of the Great Operas*. Garden City, N.Y.: Doubleday, 1955.

Dahlhaus, Carl. *Neues Handbuch der Musikwissenschaft*. Wiesbaden: Akademische Verlagsgesellschaft Athenaion, 1980–.

Dahlhaus, Carl and Dietrich Mack. *Handbuch des Musiktheaters*. Munich: Piper Verlag, 1985.

Denkmäler des Theaters: Inszenierung, Dekoration, Kostüm des Theaters. Vienna: Nationalbibliothek; Munich: R. Piper, 1925–30. In 12 parts; plates (some colored) in portfolios, with explanatory text. Trans. as: *Monumenta scenica: The Art of the Theatre*. London: Batsford, 1925–31.

Dent, Edward J. "The Nomenclature of Opera." *M&L* (1944), 25:132–40, 213–26.

Donington, Robert. *The Opera*. New York: Harcourt Brace Jovanovich, 1978.

Eitner, Robert, ed. *Publikationen älterer praktischer und theoretischer Musikwerke, vorzugsweise des XV. XVI. Jahrhunderts*. Leipzig: Breitkopf & Härtel, 1873–1905.

Enciclopedia della spettacolo. Rome: Casa Editrice Le Machere, 1954–.

Flaherty, Gloria. *Opera in the Development of German Critical Thought*. Princeton: Princeton University Press, 1978.

Fuld, James. *The Book of World-Famous Libretti: The Musical Theater from 1598 to Today*. New York: Pendragon, 1984.

Gradenwitz, Peter. *Wege zur Musik der Gegenwart*. Stuttgart, 1963.

Grout, Donald Jay. *A Short History of Opera*. New York: Columbia University Press, 1949; 2nd ed., 1965.

——. *Breve storia dell' opera*. Trans. by Caterina D'Amico de Carvalho. Milan: Rusconi, 1985.

——. *A History of Western Music*. 3rd ed., with Claude Palisca. New York: Norton, 1980.

Grove, Sir George. *Dictionary of Music and Musicians*. Ed. by Eric Blom. 5th ed. 9 vols. London: Macmillan, 1954. *Supplementary Volume*. New York: St. Martin's, 1961. [For 6th ed., see *The New Grove*.]

Haas, Robert M. *Afführungspraxis der Musik*. Wildpark-Potsdam: Athenaion, [1931].

——. "Geschichtliche Opernbezeichnungen." In *Festschrift Hermann Kretzschmar zum 70. Geburtstag*. Leipzig: Peters, 1918. 43–45.

Hamm, Charles. *Opera*. New York: Da Capo, 1980.

Haweis, Hugh Reginald. *Music and Morals*. New York: Harper, 1872.

Jacobs, Arthur and Stanley Sadie. *Opera: A Modern Guide*. New York: Drake, 1972.

Keller, Otto. *Die Operette in ihrer geschichtlichen Entwicklung*. Vienna: Stein-Verlag, 1926.

Kerman, Joseph. *Opera as Drama*. New York: Knopf, 1956.

Kinsky, Georg. *A History of Music in Pictures*. London: Dent, [1937].

Kobbé, Gustav. *Kobbé's Complete Opera Book*. Ed. and rev. by the Earl of Harewood. New York: Putnam, 1976.

Krehbiel, Henry Edward. *A Book of Operas*. New York: Macmillan, 1928. [2 vols. in one, combining "A Book of Operas" and "A Second Book of Operas."]

Kretzschmar, Hermann. *Geschichte der Oper*. Leipzig: Breitkopf & Härtel, 1919.

———. *Geschichte des neuen deutschen Liedes. I. Teil: von Albert bis Zelter*. Leipzig: Breitkopf & Härtel, 1911.

Lajarte, Théodore de. *Bibliothèque musicale du théâtre de l'opéra*. 2 vols. Paris: Librairie des bibliophiles, 1878.

Lang, Paul Henry. *Music in Western Civilization*. New York: Norton, [1941].

Lavignac, Alexandre Jean Albert, ed. *Encyclopédie de la musique et Dictionnaire du Conservatoire. Première Partie: Histoire de la musique*. 5 vols. Paris: Delagrave, 1913–22.

Leichtentritt, Hugo. *Music, History, and Ideas*. Cambridge: Harvard University Press, 1938.

Loewenberg, Alfred, comp. *Annals of Opera, 1597–1940: Compiled from the Original Sources*. 2nd ed. 2 vols. Geneva: Societas Bibliographica, [1955].

Mantzius, Karl. *A History of Theatrical Art in Ancient and Modern Times*. 6 vols. London: Duckworth, 1903–21.

Marco, Guy A. *Opera: A Research and Information Guide*. New York: Garland, 1984.

Marco, Guy A., Ann Garfield, and Sharon Ferris. *Information on Music: A Handbook of Reference Sources in European Languages*. 3 vols. Littleton, Colo.: Libraries Unlimited, 1984.

Monaldi, Gino. *Cantanti evirati celebri del teatro italiano*. Rome: Ausonia, 1920.

Morrden, Ethan. *The Splendid Art of Opera*. New York: Methuen, 1980.

Moser, Hans Joachim. *Geschichte der deutschen Musik*. 3 vols. Stuttgart and Berlin: Cotta, 1920–24.

Die Musik in Geschichte und Gegenwart. Ed. by Friedrich Blume. 14 vols. Kassel and Basel: Bärenreiter, 1949–68.

Neumann, Frederick. *Essays in Performance Practice*. Ann Arbor, Mich.: UMI Research, 1982.

The New Grove Dictionary of Music and Musicians. Ed. by Stanley Sadie. 20 vols. London: Macmillan, 1980.

The New Oxford History of Music. London: Oxford University Press, 1954–.

Nicoll, Allardyce. *The Development of the Theatre*. 4th ed. New York: Harcourt, Brace, 1958.

Orrey, Leslie. *A Concise History of Opera*. London: Scribner's, 1972.

Parsons, Charles H., ed. *The Opera Reference Index*. 22 vols. Lewiston, N.Y.: Mellen. Forthcoming.

Pastor, Ludwig. *The History of the Popes, from the Close of the Middle Ages*. Vols. 29, 30, and 31. London: Kegan Paul, 1938–40.

Pirrotta, Nino. *Music and Culture in Italy from the Middle Ages to the Baroque.*
Cambridge: Harvard University Press, 1984.

Riemann, Hugo. *Handbuch der Musikgeschichte.* 2nd ed. 2 vols. in 5 parts.
Leipzig: Breitkopf & Härtel, 1919–22.

Rolland, Romain. *Musiciens d'autrefois.* 9th ed. Paris: Hachette, 1924. Trans.
as: *Some Musicians of Former Days.* London: Kegan Paul, 1915.

Rosenthal, Harold and John Warrack. *Concise Oxford Dictionary of Opera.*
New York: Oxford University Press, 1979.

Saint-Evremond, Charles de Marguetel de St. Denis. *Œuvres meslées.* 3 vols.
2nd ed. London: Tonson, 1709.

Schering, Arnold. *Geschichte des Instrumentalkonzerts.* 2nd ed. Leipzig: Breitkopf & Härtel, 1927.

———. *Musikgeschichte Leipzigs.* 3 vols. Leipzig: Kistner & Siegel, 1926.

Schering, Arnold, ed. *Geschichte der Musik in Beispielen.* Leipzig: Breitkopf &
Härtel, 1931; reprint, 1950.

Schmidgall, Gary. *Literature as Opera.* New York: Oxford University Press,
1977.

Scholz, János, ed. *Baroque and Romantic Stage Design.* New ed. New York:
Beechhurst, [1955].

Schünemann, Georg. *Geschichte der deutschen Schulmusik.* Leipzig: Kistner &
Siegel, 1928.

Smith, Patrick J. *The Tenth Muse: A Historical Study of the Opera Libretto.*
New York: Knopf, 1970.

Solerti, Angelo, comp. and ed. *Le origini del melodramma: Testimonianze dei
contemporanei.* Turin: Bocca, 1903.

Storia dell' Opera. 3 vols. Turin: UTET, 1977.

Strunk, Oliver, ed. *Source Readings in Music History.* New York: Norton, 1950.

*Theatrical Designs from the Baroque through Neo-Classicism: Unpublished Ma-
terial from American Private Collections.* 3 vols. New York: Bittner, 1940.

Thrane, Carl. *Danske Komponister.* Copenhagen: Forlagsbureaunet, 1875.

Tittmann, Julius. *Kleine Schriften zur deutschen Literatur und Kulturgeschichte.*
Göttingen: Dieterischen, 1847.

U.S. Library of Congress. Division of Music. *Catalogue of Opera Librettos Printed
Before 1800.* Prepared by Oscar George Theodore Sonneck. 2 vols. Washington: D.C.: Government Printing Office, 1914.

———. *Dramatic Music (Class M 1500, 1510, 1520): Catalogue of Full Scores.*
Comp. by O. G. T. Sonneck. Washington, D.C.: Government Printing Office, 1908.

Van Witsen, Leo. *Costuming for Opera: Who Wears What and Why.* Bloomington: Indiana University Press, 1981.

Walker, Ernest. *A History of Music in England.* 3rd ed., rev. by J. A. Westrup.
Oxford: Clarendon, 1952.

Wellesz, Egon, *Essays on Opera.* Trans. by Patricia Kean. London: Dobson,
[1950].

Wolff, Hellmuth Christian. *Oper: Szene und Darstellung von 1600 bis 1900.*
Leipzig: Deutscher Verlag für Musik, 1968.

Part I: Music and Drama
to the End of the Sixteenth Century

Adam de la Halle. *Œuvres complètes du trouvère Adam de la Halle, poésies et musique: Publiées . . . par E. de Coussemaker.* Paris: Durand & Pedone-Lauriel, 1872.

Adler, Guido. (See general bibliography.)

Alaleona, Domenico. "Su Emilio de' Cavalieri." *La nuova musica* (1905), nos. 113–14, pp. 35–38, 47–50.

Ambros, August Wilhelm. (See general bibliography.)

Anthony, James R. *French Baroque Music from Beaujoyeulx to Rameau.* New York: Norton, 1974.

Apollonio, Mario. *Storia della commedia dell' arte.* Rome: Augustea, 1930.

Aristotle. *Poetics.* Trans. by Thomas Twining as: *Aristotle's Treatise on Poetry.* London: Payne, 1789.

Atti dell' accademia del R. Istituto musicale di Firenze, anno XXXIII: Commemorazione della riforma melodrammatica. Florence: Galletti e Cocci, 1895.

Axton, Richard, comp. *Medieval French Plays.* Trans. by Richard Axton and John Stevens. New York: Barnes & Noble, 1971.

Bartholomaeis, Vincenzo de, ed. *Laude drammatiche e rappresentazioni sacre.* 3 vols. Florence: Le Monnier, 1943; reprint, 1967.

Beat, Janet. "Monteverdi and the Opera Orchestra of His Time." In *The Monteverdi Companion.* Ed. by Denis Arnold and Nigel Fortune. New York: Norton, 1968. 277–301.

Beaujoyeulx, Balthasar de, ed., et al. *Circe ou le Balet comique de la royne.* Paris, 1582; facsimile eds. by Carol MacClintock and Lander MacClintock, (n.p.), 1971; Margaret McGowan, Binghamton, N.Y., 1982.

Becherini, Bianca. "La musica nelle 'Sacre rappresentazioni' Fiorentine." *RMI* (1951), 53:193–241.

Bohn, [Emil?]. "Theophilus: Niederdeutsches Schauspiel aus einer Handschrift des 15. Jahrhunderts." *MfMg* (1877), 9:3–4, 24–25.

Bonfantini, Mario, ed. *Le sacre rappresentazioni italiane: Raccolta di testi dal secolo XIII al secolo XVI.* [Milan]: Bompiani, [1942].

Bowles, Edmund A. "The Role of Musical Instruments in Medieval Sacred Drama." *MQ* (1959), 45:67–84.

Brand, C. P. *Torquato Tasso: A Study of the Poet and of His Contribution to English Literature.* Cambridge: Cambridge University Press, 1965.

Brown, Howard Mayer. *Music in the French Secular Theater, 1400–1550.* Cambridge: Harvard University Press, 1963.

Burney, Charles. *The Present State of Music in France and Italy.* London: Becket, 1771.

Caccini, Giulio. *Le nuove musiche.* 1601; reprint, Rome: Raccolte Claudio Monteverdi, 1930.

——. *Le nuove musiche*. Ed. by H. Wiley Hitchcock. Recent Researches in the Music of the Baroque Era, vol. 9. Madison, Wis.: A-R Editions, 1970.

Camillucci, Guido. "*L'Amfiparnaso*, commedia harmonica." *RMI* (1951), 53:42–60.

Chailley, Jacques. "La Nature musicale du *Jeu de Robin et Marion*." In *Mélanges d'histoire du théâtre du moyen-âge et de la renaissance, offerts à Gustave Cohen*. Paris: Librairie Nizet, 1950. 111–17.

Chambers, E. K. *The Medieval Stage*. 2 vols. London: Oxford University Press, 1903.

Christout, Marie F. *Le Ballet de cour de Louis XIV, 1643–1672, mises en scène*. Paris: Picard, 1967.

Cohen, Gustave. *Histoire de la mise en scène dans le théâtre réligieux français du moyen âge*. New ed. Paris: Champion, 1926.

Cohen, Gustave, ed. *Recueil de farces françaises inédites du XVe siècle*. Cambridge, Mass.: Medieval Academy of America, 1949.

Collins, Fletcher. *Medieval Church Music-Dramas: A Repertory of Complete Plays*. Charlottesville: University Press of Virginia, 1976.

——. *The Production of Medieval Church Music-Drama*. Charlottesville: University Press of Virginia, 1972.

Coussemaker, Edmond de. *Drames liturgiques du moyen âge*. Rennes: Vatar, 1860; Paris: Didron, 1861.

Crescimbeni, Giovanni M. *Commentarii intorno all' "Istoria della poesia italiana"*. vol 2. London: Becket, 1803.

D'Ancona, Alessandro. *Origini del teatro italiano*. 2nd ed. 2 vols. Turin: Loescher, 1891.

——. *Sacre rappresentazioni dei secoli XIV, XV e XVI*. 3 vols. Florence: Successori Le Monnier, 1872.

Demuth, Norman. *French Opera: Its Development to the Revolution*. Sussex: Artemis, 1963.

Dent, Edward J. "The *Amfiparnaso* of Orazio Vecchi." *MMR* (1906), 36:50–52, 74–75.

——. "Notes on the *Amfiparnaso* of Orazio Vecchi." *SIMG* (1910–11), 12:330–47.

Doni, Giovanni Battista. *Compendio del trattato de' generi de' modi della musica*. Rome: Fei, 1635. [Abstract of a larger work which was never published; portions of this work are quoted in Solerti, ed., *Le origini del melodramma*, under the title "Trattato della musica scenica."]

——. *Lyra Barberina ΑΜΦΙΧΟΡΔΟΣ: Accedunt eisudem opera, pleaque nondum edita ad veterem musicam illustrandam pertinentia*. 2 vols. Florentiae typis Caesareis, 1763.

Donington, Robert. *The Rise of Opera*. New York: Scribner's, 1981.

Einstein, Alfred. *The Italian Madrigal*. 2 vols. Princeton: Princeton University Press, 1949.

Fano, Fabio, ed. *La camerata fiorentina: Vincenzo Galilei*. Milan: Ricordi, 1934.

Les Fêtes du mariage de Ferdinand de Médicis et de Christine de Lorraine,

Florence 1589. Paris: Editions du Centre national de la recherche scientifique, 1963.

Flanigan, C. Clifford. "The Liturgical Context of the *Quem quaeritis* Trope." In *Studies in Medieval Literature in Honor of William L. Smoldon on His 82nd Birthday*. Kalamazoo: Western Michigan University Press, 1974; reprint from *Comparative Drama* (1974).

Flecha, Mateo. *Las ensaladas*. [Praga, 1581.] Transcribed by Higinio Anglès. Barcelona: Biblioteca Central, 1954.

Flemming, Willi. *Geschichte des Jesuitentheaters in den Landen deutscher Zunge*. Berlin: Gesellschaft für Theatergeschichte, 1923.

Galilei, Vincenzo. *Dialogo della musica antica, et della moderna*. Fiorenza: Marescotti, 1581; facsimile reprint, Rome: R. Accademia d'Italia, 1934.

Ghisi, Federico. "Un Aspect inédit des intermèdes de 1589 à la cour medicéenne et le développement de courses masquées et des ballets équestres durant les premières décades du XVIIe siècle." In *Les Fêtes de la Renaissance*. Paris: Editions du Centre national de la recherche scientifique, 1956. 145–52.

——. *Feste musicali della Firenze Medicea*. Florence: Vallecchi, 1939; reprint, 1969.

——. "L'orchestra in Monteverdi." In *Karl Gustav Fellerer zum 60. Geburtstag*. Ed. by Heinrich Hüschen. Regensburg: Bosse, 1962.

Greenburg, Noah, ed. *The Play of Daniel*. [Br. Mus. Egerton 2615.] New York: Oxford University Press, 1959.

Greg, Walter W. *Pastoral Poetry and Pastoral Drama*. London: Bullen, 1906.

Guarini, Giambattista. *Compendio della poesia tragicomica (1599)*. Trans. in *Literary Criticism*. Ed. by A. Gilbert. New York: American Book, 1940.

Guy, Henri, *Essai sur la vie et les oeuvres littéraires du trouvère Adan de le Hale*. Paris: Hachette, 1898.

Hamilton, Edith. "The Greek Chorus, Fifteen or Fifty?" *Theatre Arts Monthly* (1933), 17:459.

Hardison, O. B. *Christian Rite and Christian Drama in the Middle Ages*. Baltimore: The Johns Hopkins University Press, 1965.

——. "Gregorian Easter Vespers and Early Liturgical Drama." In *The Medieval Drama and its Claudelian Revival*. Ed. E. C. Dunn. Washington, D.C.: The Catholic University of America Press, 1970. 27-40.

Harris, Ellen T. *Handel and the Pastoral Tradition*. London: Oxford University Press, 1980.

Henderson, William James. *Some Forerunners of the Italian Opera*. London: John Murray, 1911.

Hoffmann von Fallersleben, August Heinrich. *In dulci jubilo . . . ein Beitrag zur Geschichte der deutschen Poesie*. Hanover: Rumpler, 1854.

Hol, Joan C. "Horatio Vecchi et l'évolution créatrice." In *Gedenkboek Dr. D. F. Scheurleer*. The Hague: Nijhoff, 1925. 159–67.

Ingegneri, Angelo. *Della poesia rappresentativa e del modo di rappresentare le favole sceniche*. Ferrara: Baldini, 1598.

Jeppesen, Knud, ed. *Die Mehrstimmige italienische Laude um 1500*. Leipzig: Breitkopf & Härtel; Copenhagen: Levin & Munksgaard, 1935.

Jubinal, Achille, ed. *Mystères inédits du quinzième siècle*. 2 vols. Paris: Téchener, 1837.

Kaufman, Henry W. "Music for a Favola Pastorale (1554)." In *A Musical Offering: Essays in Honor of Martin Bernstein*. Ed. by E. H. Clinkscale and Claire Brook. New York: Pendragon, 1977. 163–82.

Krieg, Eduard. *Das lateinische Osterspiel von Tours*. (With Anhang: "Das lateinische Osterspiel aus der Handschrift 927 [Ff. 1–8] der Stadtibibliothek von Tours.") Würzburg: Triltsch, 1956.

Kühl, Gustav. "Die Bordesholmer Marienklage, herausgegeben und eingeleitet." *Jahrbuch des Vereins für niederdeutsche Sprachforschung* (1898), 24:1–75, and Musikbeilage of 14 pages.

Lacroix, Paul, comp. *Ballets et mascarades de cour de Henri III à Louis XIV (1581–1652)*. 6 vols. Geneva: Gay, 1868–70; reprint, 1968.

Landi, Antonio. *Il commodo, commedia d'Antonio Landi con i suoi intermedi*. Florence: Giunti, 1566. [The *intermedi* are by G. B. Strozzi the elder.] Earlier ed., 1539.

Lucianus Samosatensis. *Lucian*. Trans. by A. M. Harmon. 8 vols. New York: Macmillan, 1913–36. Contains "On the Dance," 5:209–89.

McGee, Timothy J. "The Liturgical Placements of the *Quem quaeritis* Dialogue." *JAMS* (1976), 29:1–29.

McGowan, Margaret M. *L'Art du ballet de cour en France, 1581–1643*. Paris: Editions du Centre national de la recherche scientifique, 1963.

Mantica, Francesco, ed. *Prime fioriture del melodramma italiano*. 2 vols. Rome: Casa editrice Claudio Monteverdi, 1912–30.

Mantzius, Karl. (See general bibliography.)

Martin, Henriette. "La 'Camerata' du Comte Bardi et la musique florentine du xvie siècle." *RdM* (1932), 13:63–74, 152–61, 227–34; (1933), 14:92–100, 141–51.

Mathiesen, Thomas. "New Fragments of Ancient Greek Music." *Acta musicologica* (1981), 53:14–32.

Moser, Hans Joachim. (See general bibliography.)

Mountford, J. F. "Greek Music in the Papyri and Inscriptions." In *New Chapters in the History of Greek Literature, Second Series*. Ed. by J. Powell and E. Barber. London: Oxford University Press, 1929. 146–83.

Müller-Blattau, Joseph M., ed. *Die Kompositionslehre Heinrich Schützens in der Fassung seines Schülers Christoph Bernhard*. Leipzig: Breitkopf & Härtel, 1926.

Neri, Achille. "Gli intermezzi del *Pastor fido*." *Giornale storico della letteratura italiana* (1888), 11:405–15.

Nicoll, Allardyce. (See general bibliography.)

Nolhac, Pierre and Angelo Solerti. *Il viaggio in Italia de Enrico III re di Francia, e le feste a Venezia, Ferrara, Mantova, e Torino*. Turin: Roux, 1890.

Palisca, Claude V. "The *Alterati* of Florence, Pioneers in the Theory of Dramatic Music." In *New Looks at Italian Opera: Essays in Honor of Donald*

J. Grout. Ed. by William Austin. Ithaca, N.Y.: Cornell University Press, 1968. 9–38.

——. "Girolamo Mei: Mentor to the Florentine Camerata." *MQ* (1954), 40:1–20.

——. "Vincenzo Galilei and Some Links Between 'Pseudo-Monody' and Monody." *MQ* (1960), 46:344–60.

Palisca, Claude V., ed. *Girolamo Mei (1519–1594): Letters on Ancient and Modern Music to Vincenzo Galilei and Giovanni Bardi. A Study with Annotated Texts.* [Rome]: American Institute of Musicology, 1960.

Pedrell, Felipe. "*La Festa d'Elche* ou le drame lyrique liturgique, *La Mort et l'assomption de la Vierge.*" *SIMG* (1900–1901), 2:203–52.

Pirrotta, Nino. "*Commedia dell' arte* and Opera." *MQ* (1955), 41:305–324.

——. *Li due Orfei.* Torino: Eri, 1969.

——. "Temperaments and Tendencies in the Florentine Camerata." *MQ* (1954), 40:169–89. [Originally published in Italian in *Le manifestazioni culturali dell' Accademia nazionale di Santa Cecilia.* Rome: 1953.]

——. "Tragédie et comédie dans la 'Camerata fiorentina.' " In *Musique et poésie au XVIe siècle.* Paris: Editions du Centre national de la recherche scientifique, 1954. 287–97.

Pirrotta, Nino (with Elena Pavoledo). *Music and Theatre from Poliziano to Monteverdi.* Trans. by Karen Eales. New York: Cambridge University Press, 1982.

Poliziano [Angelo Ambrogini]. *Orfeo.* In *"La favola di Orfeo," opera in un atto di Messer Angelo Ambrogini detto 'Poliziano.'* Ed. by Alfredo Casella. Milan: Carisch, [1934].

——. *Le stanze, l'Orfeo e le rime.* Florence: Barbera, 1863.

Porter, William V. "Peri and Corsi's *Dafne:* Some New Discoveries and Observations." *JAMS* (1965), 18:170–196.

Reese, Gustave. *Music in the Middle Ages.* New York: Norton, [1940].

——. *Music in the Renaissance.* New York: Norton, 1959.

Richter, L. "Das Musikfragment aus dem Euripiderschen Orestes." *DJbM* (1973), 16:111–49.

Rolland, Romain. *Musiciens d'autrefois.* (See general bibliography.)

——. "Les Origines de l'opéra et les travaux de M. Angelo Solerti." *RHCM* (1903), 3:127–29, 280–82.

Ronga, Luigi. "Lettura storica dell' *Amfiparnaso.*" *RassM* (1953), 23:101–15.

Rothschild, James, Baron de, ed. *Le Mistère du Viel Testament.* 6 vols. Paris: Firmin-Didot, 1878–91.

Rubsamen, Walter. *Literary Sources of Secular Music in Italy (ca. 1500).* Berkeley and Los Angeles: University of California Press, 1943.

Sachs, Curt. *Die Musik der Antike.* Potsdam: Athenaion, [1928].

Sacre rappresentazioni nel manoscritto 201 della Bibliothèque municipale di Orléans. Ed. by Giampiero Tintori and Raffaello Monterosso. Cremona: Athenaeum Cremonense, 1958.

Schering, Arnold. *Aufführungspraxis alter Musik.* Leipzig: Quelle & Meyer, 1931.

——. "Zur Geschichte des begleiteten Sologesangs im 16. Jahrhundert." *ZIMG* (1911–12), 13:190–96.

Schrade, Leo. "Les Fêtes du mariage de Francesco dei Medici et de Bianca Cappello [1579]." In *Les Fêtes de la Renaissance*. Paris: Editions du Centre national de la recherche scientifique, 1956. 107–31.

——. *La Représentation d' "Edipo Tiranno" au Teatro Olimpico (Vicenze 1585)*. Paris: Editions du Centre national de la recherche scientifique, 1960.

Smits van Waesberghe, Jos. "A Dutch Easter Play." *MD* (1953), 7:15–37.

Smoldon, William L. *The Music of the Medieval Church Dramas*. Ed. by Cynthia Bourgeault. London: Oxford University Press, 1980.

Smoldon, William L. and Noah Greenberg, eds. *The Play of Herod*. New York: Oxford University Press, 1965.

Solerti, Angelo. *Gli albori del melodramma*. 3 vols. Milan: Sandron, [1905].

——. *Musica, ballo e drammatica alla corte Medicea dal 1600 al 1637*. Florence: Bemporad, 1905.

——. "Precedenti del melodramma." *RMI* (1903), 10:207–33, 466–84.

——. "Primi saggi del melodramma giocoso." *RMI* (1905), 12:814–38; (1906), 13:91–112.

——. *Vita di Torquato Tasso*. 3 vols. Rome: Loescher, 1895.

Solerti, Angelo, ed. *Ferrara e la corte Estense nella seconda metà del secolo decimosesto: I discorsi di Annibale Romei, gentiluomo ferrarese*. Città di Castello: Lapi, 1891.

Solerti, Angelo, comp. and ed. *Le origini del melodramma: Testimonianze dei contemporanei*. Turin: Bocca, 1903.

Sonneck, Oscar George Theodore. "A Description of Alessandro Striggio and Francesco Corteccia's Intermedi *Psyche and Amore*, 1565." *MA* (1911), 3:40–53.

——. *Miscellaneous Studies in the History of Music*. New York: Macmillan, 1921.

Sternfeld, Frederick W. "The Birth of Opera: Ovid, Poliziano, and the *lieto fine*." In *Analecta musicologica*. Cologne: Arno Volk Verlag Hans Gerig, 1979. 19:30–51.

——. "The First Printed Libretto." *M&L* (1978), 59:121–38.

Stevens, John. "Medieval Drama." *The New Grove Dictionary*, 12:21–58.

Strunk, Oliver, ed. (See general bibliography.)

Symonds, John Addington. *Renaissance in Italy: Italian Literature*. 2 vols. New York: Holt, 1882.

Tasso, Torquato. *Dialoghi*. Ed. by Ezio Raimondi. 3 vols. Florence: Sansoni, 1958.

Trend, John Brande. "The Mystery of Elche." *M&L* (1920), 1:145–57.

Vecchi, Giuseppe. *Uffici drammatici padovani*. Florence: Olschki, 1954.

Vecchi, Orazio. *L'Amfiparnaso*. Ed. by Bonaventura Somma. Rome: De Santis, [1953].

——. *L'Amfiparnaso, commedia harmonica*. Ed. by Cecil Adkins. Chapel Hill: University of North Carolina Press, 1977.

Walker, D. P. "La Musique des intermèdes florentins de 1589 et l'humanisme."

In *Les Fêtes de la Renaissance*. Paris: Editions du Centre national de la recherche scientifique, 1956. 133–44.

Webster, T. B. L. *The Greek Chorus*. London: Methuen, 1970.

Yates, Frances A. *The French Academies of the Sixteenth Century*. [London]: Warburg Institute, University of London, 1947.

———. "Poésie et musique pour les magnificences du mariage du Duc de Joyeuse, Paris, 1581." In *Musique et poésie au XVIe siècle*. Paris: Editions du Centre national de la recherche scientifique, 1954. 241–64.

———. *The Valois Tapestries*. 2nd ed. London: Routledge & Kegan Paul, 1975.

Young, Karl. *The Drama of the Medieval Church*. 2 vols. Oxford: Clarendon, 1933.

Zarlino, Gioseffo. *Le istituzioni harmoniche*. Venice: [Pietro da Fino?], 1558; reprint of part 4, Yale University Press, 1983; reprint of Venice 1573 edition, Gregg, 1966.

Zinar, Ruth. "The Use of Greek Tragedy in the History of Opera." *CMc* (1971), no. 12, pp. 80–95.

Part II: The Seventeenth Century

Abert, Anna Amalie. *Claudio Monteverdi und das musikalische Drama*. Lippstadt: Kistner & Siegel, 1954.

Ademollo, Alessandro. *I primi fasti del teatro di via della Pergola in Firenze (1657–1661)*. Milan: Ricordi, [1885].

———. *I teatri di Roma nel secolo decimosettimo*. Rome: Pasqualucci, 1888; reprint, 1969.

Adler, Guido. *Handbuch der Musikgeschichte*. (See general bibliography.)

———. "Die Kaiser Ferdinand III., Leopold I., Joseph I. und Karl VI. als Tonsetzer und Förderer der Musik." *VfMw* (1892), 8:252–74.

Aldrich, Putnam C. "The Principal Agréments of the Seventeenth and Eighteenth Centuries: A Study in Musical Ornamentation." Ph.D. diss., Harvard University, 1942.

Allam, Edward. "Alessandro Stradella." *PRMA* (1954), 80:29–42.

Ambros, August Wilhelm. (See general bibliography.)

Anthony, James R. *French Baroque Music*. (See part 1 bibliography.)

———. "Printed Editions of André Campra's *L'Europe galante*." *MQ* (1970), 46:54–73.

Arnold, Denis and Nigel Fortune, eds. *The Monteverdi Companion*. New York: Norton, 1968.

Arnold, Frank T. *The Art of Accompaniment from a Thorough-Bass as Practiced in the XVIIth and XVIIIth Centuries*. 2 vols. 2nd ed. New York: Dover, 1965.

Atti dell' accademia. (See part 1 bibliography.)

Austin, William W., ed. *New Looks at Italian Opera: Essays in Honor of Donald Jay Grout.* Ithaca, N.Y.: Cornell University Press, 1968.

Bannard, Yorke. "Music of the Commonwealth." *M&L* (1922), 3:394–401.

Barclay Squire. (See Squire, William Barclay.)

Barthélemy, Maurice. *André Campra, sa vie et son oeuvre (1660–1744).* Paris: Picard, 1957.

———. "Les Opéras de Marin Marais." *RBM* (1953), 7:136–46.

Bauer, Anton. *Opern und Operetten in Wien: Verzeichnis ihrer Erstaufführungen in der Zeit von 1629 bis zur Gengenwart.* Graz, Cologne, Vienna: Hermann Böhlaus Nachfolge, 1955.

Bauman, Thomas. "Benda, the Germans, and Simple Recitative." *JAMS* (1981), 34:119–131.

Baxter, William Hubbard, Jr. "Agostino Steffani: A Study of the Man and His Work." 2 vols. Ph.D. diss., University of Rochester, 1957.

Beat, Janet. (See part 1 bibliography.)

Beaujoyeulx, Baltasar de. (See part 1 bibliography.)

Becker, Heinz. "[Review of:] Hellmuth Christian Wolff, *Die Barockoper in Hamburg (1678–1738).*" *Mf* (1960), 13:211–14.

Berend, Fritz. *Nicolaus Adam Strungk.* Hanover: Homann, [1915].

Bianconi, Lorenzo and Thomas Walker. "Dalla *Finta pazza* alla *Veremonde:* Storie de Febiarmonici." *RIM* (1975), 10:379–454.

Bjurström, Per. *Giacomo Torelli and Baroque Stage Design.* 2nd ed. Stockholm: National Museum, 1961.

Blaze, [François Henri Joseph], called Castil-Blaze. *De l'opéra en France.* Paris: Janet & Cotelle, 1820.

Bolte, Johannes. *Die Singspiele der englischen Komödianten und ihrer Nachfolger in Deutschland, Holland und Skandinavia.* Hamburg and Leipzig: Voss, 1893.

Bonlini, G. C. *Le glorie della poesie e della musica contenute nell' esatta notizia de' teatri della città di Venezia.* Venice, [1730].

Borland, John E. "French Opera Before 1750." *PRMA* (1907), 33:133–57.

Borrel, Eugène. *Jean-Baptiste Lully: Le cadre, la vie, la personnalité, le rayonnement, les oeuvres, bibliographie.* Paris: Colombe, 1949.

Bragaglia, Anton Giulio. "Celebrazioni Marchigiane: Giacomo Torelli da Fano." *Il giornale di politica e di letteratura* (1934), 10:331–62; (1935), 11:69–80.

Briganti, Francesco. *Gio. Andrea Angelini-Bontempi (1624–1705), musicista, letterato, architetto: Perugia-Dresda.* Florence: Olschki, 1956.

Brockpähler, Renate. *Handbuch zur Geschichte der Barockoper in Deutschland.* Emsdetten and Westfalen: Lechte, 1964.

Brook, Barry, ed. *French Opera in the Seventeenth and Eighteenth Centuries.* 75 vols. New York: Pendragon 1983–.

Brown, Howard Mayer. "How Opera Began: An Introduction to Jacopo Peri's *Euridici* (1600)." In *The Late Renaissance, 1525–1630.* Ed. by Eric Cochrane. New York: Harper & Row, 1970. 401–43.

Brown, Howard Mayer, ed. *Italian Opera, 1640–1770.* 97 vols. New York: Garland, 1979–84.

Bücken, Ernst. (See general bibliography.)

Burney, Charles. *A General History of Music from the Earliest Ages to the Present Period.* 4 vols. London: Printed for the Author, 1776–89.

Bustico, Guido. (See general bibliography.)

Caccini, Francesca. *La liberazione di Ruggiero dall' Isola d'Alcina.* Ed. by Doris Silbert. Smith College Music Archives (1945), no. 7. Northampton, Mass.: Smith College.

Caccini, Giulio. (See part 1 bibliography.)

Campardon, Emile. *L'Académie royale de musique au XVIIIe siècle.* 2 vols. Paris: Berger-Levrault, 1884.

Carfagno, Simon A. "The Life and Dramatic Music of Stefano Landi, with a Transliteration and Orchestration of the Opera *Sant' Alessio.*" 2 vols. in 4. Ph.D. diss., University of California, Los Angeles, 1960.

Carter, Tim. "Jacopo Peri." *M&L* (1980), 61:121–35.

Castil-Blaze. (See Blaze, François Henri Joseph.)

Catelani, Angelo. *Delle opere di Alessandro Stradella esistente nel l'archivio musicale della R. Biblioteca Palatina di Modena.* Modena: Vincenzi, 1866.

Cesti, Pietro Antonio. *L'Orontea.* Ed. by William C. Holmes. Wellesley Edition, no. 11. Wellesley, Mass.: Wellesley College, 1973.

Chiarelli, Alessandra. "*L'incoronazione di Poppea* e *Il Nerone:* Problemi di filologia testuale." *RIM* (1974), 9:117–51.

Chouquet, Gustave. (See general bibliography.)

Chrysander, Friedrich. "Eine englische Serenata von J. Sigismund Kusser um 1710." *AMZ* (1879), 14:408–12, 417–22.

——. "Die Feier des zweihundertjährigen Bestandes der Oper in Hamburg." *AMZ* (1878), 13:113–15, 129–32, 145–48.

——. *G. F. Händel.* 3 vols. Leipzig: Breitkopf & Härtel, 1858–67.

Clarke, Henry Leland. "Dr. John Blow (1649–1708), Last Composer of an Era." Ph.D. diss., Harvard University, 1947.

Collaer, Paul. "L'orchestra di Claudio Monteverdi." *Musica* (1934), 2:86–104.

Coradini, Francesco. "P. Antonio Cesti: Nuove notizie biografiche." *RMI* (1923), 30:371–88.

Corte, Andrea della. (See Della Corte, Andrea.)

Covell, Roger David. "Monteverdi's *L'incoronazione di Poppea:* The Musical and Dramatic Structure." Ph.D. diss., University of New South Wales, 1977.

Crussard, Claude. "Marc-Antoine Charpentier, théoricien." *RdM* (1945), 27:49–68.

——. *Un Musicien français oublié: Marc-Antoine Charpentier.* Paris: Floury, 1945.

Culley, Thomas D. *Jesuits and Music: A Study of Musicians Connected with the German College in Rome During the Seventeenth Century and Their Activities in Northern Europe.* St. Louis: Jesuit Historical Institute, 1970.

Cutts, John. "Le Rôle de la musique dans les masques de Ben Jonson et notammement dans *Oberon* (1610–1611)." In *Les Fêtes de la Renaissance.* Paris: Editions du Centre national de la recherche scientifique, 1956. 285–303.

Day, Christine J. "The Theater of SS. Giovanni e Paolo and Monteverdi's *L'in-coronazione di Poppea.*" *CMc* (1978), pp. 22–38.

DeLage, Joseph O., Jr., "The Overture in Seventeenth-Century Italian Opera." Ann Arbor, Mich.: University Microfilms, 1961.

Della Corte, Andrea. "*La forza d'amor paterno* di Alessandro Stradella." *Musica d'oggi* (1931), 13:389–94.

Denkmäler des Theaters. (See general bibliography.)

Dent, Edward J. *Alessandro Scarlatti: His Life and Works.* New ed., with preface and additional notes by Frank Walker. London: Arnold, [1960]. [First published in 1905.]

——. *Foundations of English Opera.* Cambridge: Cambridge University Press, 1928.

——. "Italian Chamber Cantatas." *MA* (1911), 2:142–53, 185–99.

De Rensis, Raffaello. "Un musicista diplomatico del Settecento: Agostino Steffani." *Musica d'oggi* (1921), 3:129–32.

Doni, Giovanni Battista. (See part 1 bibliography.)

Donington, Robert. (See part 1 bibliography.)

Ehrichs, Alfred. *Giulio Caccini.* Leipzig: Hesse & Becker, 1908.

Einstein, Alfred. "Agostino Steffani." *Kirchenmusikalisches Jahrbuch* (1910), 23:1–36.

——. "Agostino Steffani." *Neue Musik-Zeitung* (1928), 49:316–19.

——. *The Italian Madrigal.* (See part 1 bibliography.)

Eitner, Robert, ed. (See general bibliography.)

Emslie, McDonald. "Nicholas Lanier's Innovations in English Song." *M&L* (1960), 41:13–27.

Engländer, Richard. "Zur Frage der *Dafne* (1671) von G. A. Bontempi und M. G. Peranda." *Acta musicologica* (1941), 13:59–77.

Epstein, Peter. "Dichtung und Musik in Monteverdi's *Lamento d'Arianna.*" *ZfMw* (1927–28), 10:216–22.

Evans, Herbert Arthur, ed. *English Masques.* Glasgow: Blackie, 1897.

Evans, Willa McClung. *Ben Jonson and Elizabethan Music.* Lancaster, Pa.: Lancaster Press, 1929.

Evelyn, John. *Diary.* 2 vols. London: J. M. Dent, 1907.

Fabbri, Paolo. *Monteverdi.* Turin: Musica Torino, 1985.

Fassini, Sesto. "Gli albori del melodramma italiano a Londra." *Giornale storico della letteratura italiana* (1912), 60:340–76.

Finney, Gretchen Ludke. "*Comus*, Dramma per Musica." *Studies in Philology* (1940), 37:483–500.

Fischer, Georg. *Musik in Hannover.* 2nd enlarged ed. of *Opern und Concerte im Hoftheater zu Hannover bis 1866.* Hanover: Hahn, 1903.

Flemming, Willi. (See part 1 bibliography.)

Flemming, Willi, ed. *Die Oper.* Leipzig: Reclam, 1933.

Flood, W. H. Grattan. "Quelques précisions nouvelles sur Cambert et Grabu à Londres." *RM* (1928), 9:351–61.

Fogaccia, Piero. *Giovanni Legrenzi.* Bergamo: Orobiche, [1954].

Forsyth, Cecil. *Music and Nationalism: A Study of English Opera.* London: Macmillan, 1911.

Gentili, Alberto. "Alessandro Stradella." In *Miscellanea della Facoltà di Lettere e Filosofia, Serie Prima*. Turin: R. Università di Torino, 1936. 155–76.

Gérold, Theodore. *L'Art du chant en France au XVIIe siècle*. Strassburg: Fischbach, 1921.

Gherardi, Evaristo, comp. *Le Théâtre italien de Gherardi*. 5th ed. 6 vols. Amsterdam: Cene, 1721.

Ghisi, Federico. "L'orchestra in Monteverdi." (See part 1 bibliography.)

Ghislanzoni, Alberto. *Luigi Rossi (Aloysius de Rubeis), biografia e analisi delle composizioni*. Rome: Bocca, [1954].

Gianturco, Carolyn. "Nuove considerazioni sul *Tedio del Recitativo*." *RIM* (1982), 18:212–39.

——. "The Operas of Alessandro Stradella (1644–1682)." Ph.D. diss., Oxford University, 1970.

——. "A Possible Date for Stradella's *Il trespolo tutore*." *M&L* (1973). 54:25–37.

——. "Stradella e Pasquini: Due approcci al libretto comico del *Trespolo tutore*." In *L'opera comica nei sei-settecenti a Venezia e in Italia*. Venice, 1975.

Giazotto, Remo. *Vita di Alessandro Stradella*. 2 vols. [Milan]: Curci, [1962].

Glover, Jane. *Cavalli*. New York: St. Martin's, 1978.

Goldschmidt, Hugo. "Cavalli als dramatischer Komponist." *MfMg* (1893), 25:45–48, 53–58, 61–111.

——. "Francesco Provenzale als Dramatiker." *SIMG* (1905–6), 7:608–34.

——. "Die Instrumentalbegleitung der italienischen Musikdramen in der ersten Hälfte des XVII. Jahrhunderts." *MfMg* (1895), 27:52–62.

——. *Die Lehre von der vokalen Ornamentik*. Vol. 1 of *Das 17. und 18. Jahrhundert bis in die Zeit Glucks*. Charlottenburg: Lehsten, 1907.

——. *Studien zur Geschichte der italienischen Oper im 17. Jahrhundert*. 2 vols. Leipzig: Breitkopf & Härtel, 1901–4. [Review by R. Rolland, *RHCM* (1902), 2:20–29.]

Gombosi, Otto. "Some Musical Aspects of the English Court Masque." *JAMS* (1948), 1:3–19.

Groppo, Antonio. *Catalogo di tutti i drammi per musica recitati ne' teatri di Venezia dall' anno 1637 sin all' anno presente 1745*. Venice: A. Groppo, [1745?].

Gros, Etienne. *Philippe Quinault*. Paris: Champion, 1926.

Grout, Donald Jay. "The Chorus in Early Opera." In *Festschrift Friedrich Blume*. Kassel: Bärenreiter, 1963. 151–61.

——. "Some Forerunners of the Lully Opera." *M&L* (1941), 22:1–25.

Haar, James. "Astral Music in Seventeenth-Century Nuremberg: The *Tungendsterne* of Harsdörffer and Staden." *MD* (1962), 16:175–89.

Haas, Robert M. *Aufführungspraxis*. (See general bibliography.)

——. *Die Musik des Barocks*. Potsdam: Athenaion, [1934].

——. "Die Oper in Deutschland bis 1750." In *Handbuch der Musikgeschichte unter Mitwirkung von Fachgenossen*. Ed. by Guido Adler. Frankfurt am Main: Frankfurter Verlags-Anstalt, 1924.

——. *Die Wiener Oper*. Vienna and Budapest: Eligius, 1926.

Hadamowsky, Franz. *Barocktheater am Wiener Kaiserhof: Mit einem Spielplan (1625–1740)*. Vienna: Sexl, 1955. [Reprinted from *Jahrbuch der Gesellschaft für Wiener Theaterforschung* (1951–52).]

Hanning, Barbara R. *Of Poetry and Music's Power: Humanism and the Creation of Opera*. Ann Arbor, Mich.: UMI Research, 1980.

Harris, Ellen T. (See part 1 bibliography.)

Hartmann, Fritz. *Sechs Bücher Braunschweigischer Theatergeschichte*. Wolfenbüttel: Zwissler, 1905.

Hawkins, John. *A General History of the Science and Practice of Music*. 5 vols. London: Payne, 1776.

[Hawkins, John?] *Memoirs of the Life of Sig. Agostino Steffani*. [London (?), 17–.]

Hess, Heinz. *Zur Geschichte des musikalischen Dramas im Seicento: Die Opern Alessandro Stradellas*. Leipzig: Breitkopf & Härtel, 1906.

Heuss, Alfred. *Die Instrumental-Stücks des 'Orfeo' und die venetianischen Opern-Sinfonien*. Leipzig: Breitkopf & Härtel, 1903.

Hjelmborg, Bjørg. "Aspects of the Aira in the Early Operas of Francesco Cavalli." In *Natalicia musicologica Knud Jeppesen*. Copenhagen: Hansen, 1962. 173–98.

Holmes, William C. (See Cesti, Pietro Antonio.)

——. "Comedy–Opera–Comic Opera." *Analecta musicologica* (1968), 5:92.

Holst, Imogen, ed. *Henry Purcell, 1659–1695: Essays on His Music*. London: Oxford University Press, 1959.

Howard, Patricia. "The Operas of Lully." Ph.D. diss., University of Surrey, 1974.

Huber, Wolfgang. "Das Textbuch der frühdeutschen Oper: Untersuchung über literarische Voraussetzung, stoffliche Grundlagen und Quellen." Ph.D. diss., University of Munich, 1957.

[Hunold, Christian Friedrich.] *Die allerneueste Art, zur reinen und galanten Poesie zu gelangen*. Hamburg: Liebernickel, 1707.

Isherwood, R.M. *Music in the Service of the King: France in the Seventeenth Century*. Ithaca, N.Y.: Cornell University Press, 1973.

Jander, Owen H. *A Catalogue of the Manuscripts of Compositions by Alessandro Stradella Found in European and American Libraries*. Rev. ed. Wellesley, Mass.: Wellesley College, 1962.

——. "The Prologues and Intermezzos of Alessandro Stradella." *Analecta musicologica*. Vol. 7. Cologne: Böhlau, 1969. 87–111.

Jeffrey, Peter. "The Autograph Manuscripts of Francesco Cavalli." Ph.D. diss., Princeton University, 1980.

Jeppesen, Knud, ed. (See part 1 bibliography.)

Johnson, Margaret. "Agazzari's *Eumelio, a Dramma Pastorale*." *MQ* (1971), 57:491–505.

Keller, P. "Stadens Oper *Seelewig*." Ph.D. diss., University of Zurich, 1970.

Keppler, Philip. "Agostino Steffani's Hannover Operas." In *Studies in Music History: Essays for Oliver Strunk*. Princeton: Princeton University Press, 1968. 341–55.

Kinsky, Georg. (See general bibliography.)

Klages, Richard. *Johann Wolfgang Franck*. Hamburg, 1937.

Kleefeld, Wilhelm. "Das Orchester der Hamburger Oper, 1678–1738." *SIMG* (1899–1900), 1:219–89.

Köchel, Ludwig von. *Johann Josef Fux*. Vienna: Hölder, 1872.

——. *Die kaiserliche Hofmusikkapelle in Wien von 1543 bis 1867*. Vienna: Beck, 1869.

Kreidler, Walter. *Heinrich Schütz und der Stile concitato von Claudio Monteverdi*. Kassel: Bärenreiter, 1934.

Kretzschmar, Hermann. "Beiträge zur Geschichte der venetianischen Oper." *JMP* (1907), 14:71–81; (1910), 17:61–71; (1911), 18:49–61.

——. "Einige Bemerkungen über den Vortrag alter Musik." *JMP* (1900) 7:53–68.

——. *Geschichte der Oper*. (See general bibliography.)

——. "Monteverdi's *Incoronazione di Poppea*." *VfMw* (1894), 10:483–530.

——. "Die venetianische Oper und die Werke Cavalli's und Cesti's." *VfMw* (1892), 8:1–76.

Lajarte, Theodore de. (See general bibliography.)

La Laurencie, Lionel de. *Les Créateurs de l'opéra français*. Paris: Alcan, 1930.

——. *Lully*. Paris: Alcan, 1911.

Lang, Paul Henry. "The Literary Aspects of the History of the Opera in France." Ph.D. diss., Cornell University, 1935.

Lawrence, William John. "Notes on a Collection of Masque Music." *M&L* (1922), 3:49–58.

[Le Cerf de la Viéville, Jean Laurent.] *Comparaison de la musique italienne et de la musique françoise*. 3 vols. Brussels: Foppens, 1704–6. [Also forms vols. 2–4 of Jacques Bonnet, *Histoire de la musique et de ses effets*. Amsterdam: Royer, 17–.]

Lewis, Anthony. "Purcell and Blow's *Venus and Adonis*." *M&L* (1963), 44:266–69.

Liliencron, Rochus. "Die Chorgesänge des lateinischen–deutschen Schuldramas im 16. Jahrhundert." *VfMw* (1890), 6:309–87.

[Limojon de St. Didier, Alexandre Toussaint.] *La Ville et la république de Venise*. Paris: De Luyne, 1680. Trans. as: *The City and Republick of Venice*. London: Brome, 1699.

Lindgren, Lowell. "The Three Great Noises 'Fatal to the Interest of Bononcini'." *MQ* (1975), 41:560–83.

Lindner, Ernst Otto. *Die erste stehende deutsche Oper*. 2 vols. Berlin: Schlesinger, 1855.

Liuzzi, Fernando. *I musicisti in Francia*. Vol. 1, *Dalle origini al secolo XVII*. Rome: Edizioni d'Arte Dansei, 1946.

Lowens, Irving. "The *Touch-Stone* (1728): A Neglected View of London Opera." *MQ* (1959), 45:325–42.

Luckett, Richard. "Exotick but Rational Entertainments: The English Dramatick Operas." In *English Drama: Forms and Development*. Ed. by Marie Axton and Raymond Williams. Cambridge: Cambridge University Press, 1977. 123–41.

Lully et l'opéra français. *RM* (January 1925), vol. 6, special number.

McManaway, J. G. "Songs and Masques in *The Tempest.*" In *Luttrell Society Reprints* (1953), no. 14, pp. 71–96.

Malipiero, Gian Francesco. *Claudio Monteverdi.* Milan: Treves, 1929.

Mark, Jeffrey. "The Jonsonian Masque." *M&L* (1922), 3:358–71.

Marmontel, Jean François. *Elémens de littérature.* 6 vols. Paris: Née de la Rochelle, 1787.

Marx, Hans Joachim. "Geschichte der Hamburger Barock Oper: Ein Forschungsbericht." *Hamburger Jahrbuch für Musikwissenschaft* (1978), 3:7–34.

Mattheson, [Johann]. *Grundlage einer Ehrenpforte.* Hamburg: In Verlegung des Verfassers, 1740. New ed., Berlin: Liepmanssohn, 1910; reprint, 1969.

——. *Die neueste Untersuchung der Singspiele.* Hamburg: Herold, 1744.

Maugars, André. "Response faite à un curieux sur le sentiment de la musique d'Italie, écrite à Rome le premier octobre 1639 . . . in deutscher Uebersetzung mitgetheilt von W. J. von Wasialewski." *MfMg* (1878), 10:1–9, 17–23.

Meer, J. H. van der. *Johann Josef Fux als Opernkomponist.* 3 vols. and music supplement. Bilthoven: Creyghton, 1961.

Ménestrier, Claude François. *Des Ballets anciens et modernes.* Paris: Guignard, 1682.

Mercure de France. Paris, 1672–1820.

Misson, Maximilien. *A New Voyage to Italy.* 2 vols. London: Bonwicke, 1714.

Moller, Johannes. *Cimbria literata.* 3 vols. Havniae: Kisel, 1744.

Monteverdi, Claudio. *The Letters of Claudio Monteverdi.* Trans. by Denis Stevens. New York: Cambridge University Press, 1980.

——. *Orfeo.* Orchestral score by Ottorino Respighi. Piano-vocal score by Giovanni Salviucci. Milan: Carisch, 1935.

Moore, Robert Etheridge. *Henry Purcell and the Restoration Theatre.* London: Heinemann, [1961].

Moser, Hans Joachim. (See general bibliography.)

Muffat, Georg. *Florilequim secundum. Passovii.* N. p.: Höller, 1698. (Reprinted in DTOe, vol. 4.)

Murata, Margaret K. *Operas for the Papal Court 1631–1668.* Ann Arbor, Mich.: UMI Research, 1981.

Nalbach, Daniel. *The King's Theatre 1704–1867.* London: Society for Theatre Research, 1972.

Narciss, Georg Adolf. *Studien zu den Frauenzimmergesprächspielen Georg Phillipp Harsdörfers.* Leipzig: Eichblatt, 1928.

Nettl, Paul. "Exzerpte aus der Raudnitzer Textbüchersammlung." *SzMw* (1920), 7:143–44.

——. "Zur Geschichte der kaiserlichen Hofkapelle von 1636–1680." *SfMw* (1929), 16:70–85; (1930), 17:95–104; (1931), 18:23–35; (1932), 19:33–40.

Neuhaus, Max. "Antonio Draghi." *SzMw* (1913), 1:104–92.

Neumann, Frederick. (See general bibliography.)

Neumann, Friedrich-Heinrich. *Die Aesthetik des Rezitativs: Zur Theorie des Rezitativs im 17. und 18. Jahrhundert.* Strassburg: Heitz, 1962.

Newman, Joyce. *Jean-Baptiste de Lully and His Tragédies lyriques.* Ann Arbor, Mich.: UMI Research 1979.

Nicoll, Allardyce. *The Development of the Theatre*. (See general bibliography.)

——. "Italian Opera in England: The First Five Years." *Angelia* (1922), 46:257–81.

Noyes, Robert Gale. *Ben Jonson on the English Stage, 1660–1776*. Cambridge: Harvard University Press, 1935.

Osthoff, Wolfgang. *Das dramatische Spätwerk Claudio Monteverdis*. Tutzing: Schneider, 1960.

——. "Neue Beobachtungen zu Quellen und Geschichte von Monteverdis *Incoronazione di Poppea*." *Mf* (1958), 11:129–38.

——. "Zur Bologneser Aufführung von Monteverdis *Ritorno d'Ulisse* in Jahre 1640." In *Oesterreichische Akademie der Wissenschaftern: Anzeiger der Phil.-hist. Klasse* (1958), vol. 95.

Palisca, Claudio V. "The First Performance of *Euridice*." In *Queens College Twenty-Fifth Anniversary Festschrift*. New York: Queens College of CUNY, 1964.

Paoli, Rodolfo. "Difesa del primo melodramma." *RassM* (1950), 20:93–100.

Parry, C[harles] Hubert H[astings]. *The Music of the Seventeenth Century*. 2nd ed. London: Oxford University Press, 1938.

Pastor, Ludwig. (See general bibliography.)

Pepys, Samuel. *The Diary of Samuel Pepys*. 8 vols. London: Bell; New York: Harcourt, Brace, 1924–26.

Petrobelli, Pierluigi. "Francesco Manelli: Documenti e osservazioni." *Chigiana* (1967), 24:43.

Pirrotta, Nino. "*Commedia dell' arte* and Opera." (See part 1 bibliography.)

——. "Early Opera and Aria." In *New Looks at Italian Opera*, ed. by Austin. 39–107.

Pirrotta, with Pavoledo. *Music and Theatre*. (See part 1 bibliography.)

Pougin, Arthur. *Les Vrais Créateurs de l'opéra français, Perrin et Cambert*. Paris: Charvay, 1881.

Prendergast, Arthur H. "The Masque of the Seventeenth Century." *PRMA* (1897), 23:113–31.

Price, Curtis. *Henry Purcell and the London Stage*. Cambridge: Cambridge University Press, 1984.

——. *Music in the Restoration Theatre: With a Catalogue of Instrumental Music in the Plays 1665–1713*. Ann Arbor, Mich.: UMI Research, 1979.

Prunières, Henry. *Le Ballet de cour en France avant Benserade et Lully*. Paris: Laurens, 1914.

——. *Cavalli et l'opéra vénitien au XVIIIe siècle*. Paris: Reider, [1931].

——. "Notes sur les origines de l'ouverture française." *SIMG* (1910–11), 12:565–85.

——. *L'Opéra italien en France avant Lulli*. Paris: Champion, 1913. [Review by R. Rolland, *MM* (1914), 10:6–15.

——. "Les Représentations du *Palazzo l'Atlante* à Rome (1642) d'après des documents inédits." *SIMG* (1912–13), 14:218–26.

——. *La Vie illustre et libertine de Jean-Baptiste Lully*. Paris: Plon-Nourrit, [1929].

Quinault, Philippe. *Théâtre.* 5 vols. Paris: Compagnie des Libraires, 1739.

Rau, Carl August. *Loreto Vittori.* Munich: Verlag für moderne Musik, 1916].

Redlich, Hans Ferdinand. *Claudio Monteverdi, Leben und Werk.* Olten: Walter, 1949. Trans. as: *Claudio Monteverdi: Life and Works.* London: Oxford University Press, 1952.

——. "Notationsprobleme in Cl. Monteverdis *Incoronazione di Poppea.*" *Acta musicologica* (1938), 10:129–32.

Reiner, Stuart. "Collaboration in *Chi soffre speri.*" *MR* (1961), 22:265–82.

Reyher, Paul. *Les Masques anglais.* Paris: Hachette, 1909.

Richard, Pierre. "Stradella et les Contarini: Episode des moeurs vénitiennes au XVIIe siècle. *Le Ménestrel* (1864–65), vol. 32, and (1865–66), vol. 33, passim.

Riemann, Hugo. "*Basso ostinato* und *Basso* quasi *ostinato:* Eine Anregung." In *Festschrift Liliencron.* Leipzig: Breitkopf & Härtel, 1910. 193–202.

——. *Handbuch.* (See general bibliography.)

Riley, Maurice W. *The History of the Viola.* Ann Arbor, Mich.: Braun-Brunfield, 1980.

Rolland, Romain. *Musiciens d'autrefois.* (See general bibliography.)

——. "L'Opéra populaire à Venise: Francesco Cavalli." *MM* (1906), 2:61–70, 151–60.

——. "La Première Représentation du *San Alessio* de Stefano Landi en 1632, à Rome, d'après le journal manuscrit de Jean Jacques Bouchard." *RHCM* (1902), 2:29–36, 74–75.

Rommel, Otto. *Die Alt-Wiener Volkskomödie: Ihre Geschichte vom barocken Welt-Theater bis zum Tode Nestroys.* Vienna: Schroll, [1952].

Roncaglia, Gino. *Le composizioni di Alessandro Stradella esistenti presso la R. Biblioteca Estense di Modena.* Milan: Bocca, 1942.

——. "*Il Trespolo tutore* di Alessandro Stradella, 'la prima opera buffa.' " *RMI* (1954), 56:326–32.

Rosand, Ellen. "The Descending Tetrachord: An Emblem of Lament." *MQ* (1979), 65:346–59.

——. "Seneca and the Interpretation of *L'incoronazione di Poppea.*" *JAMS* (1985), 37:34–71.

Sabbatini, Nicola. *Pratica di fabricar scene, e machine ne' teatri.* Ravenna: Pietro de Paoli, 1638. German ed.: *Anleitung Dekorationen und Theatermaschinen herzustellen.* Ed. by Willi Flemming. Weimar: Gesellschaft der Bibliophilen, 1926.

Sachs, Curt. "Die Ansbacher Hofkapelle unter Markgraf Johann Friedrich (1672–86)." *SIMG* (1909–10), 11:105–37.

[Salvioli, Giovanni.] *I teatri musicali di Venezia nel secolo XVII.* Milan: Ricordi, [1879].

Salza, Abd-el-kader. "Drammi inediti di Giulio Rospigliosi." *RMI* (1907), 14:473–508.

Samuel, Harold E. "John Sigismond Kusser in London and Dublin." *M&L* (1980), 61:158–71.

Sandberger, Adolf. "Beziehungen der Königin Christine von Schweden zur italienischen Oper und Musik, insbesondere zu M. A. Cesti: Mit einem Anhang über Cestis Innsbrucker Aufenthalt." *Bulletin de la Société union musicologique* (1925), 5:121–73.

Sartori, Claudio. *Monteverdi*. Brescia: Scuola, 1953.

Schering, Arnold. *Geschichte des Instrumentalkonzerts*. (See general bibliography.)

Schering, Arnold, ed. *Geschichte der Musik in Beispielen*. (See general bibliography.)

Schiedermair, Ludwig. *Die deutsche Oper: Grundzüge ihres Werdens und Wesens*. 3rd ed. Berlin: Dümmlers, 1943.

Schletterer, Hans Michael. *Das deutsche Singspiel von seinen ersten Anfängen bis auf die neueste Zeit*. Leipzig: Breitkopf & Härtel, [1863?].

——. *Vorgeschichte und erste Versuche der französischen Oper*. Vol. 3 of *Studien zur Geschichte der französischen Musik*. Berlin: Damköhler, 1885.

Schmidt, Carl B. "Antonio Cesti's *Il pomo d'oro*: A Re-examination of a Famous Hapsburg Court Spectacle." *JAMS* (1976), 29:381–412.

——. "Antonio Cesti's *La Dori*: A Study of Sources, Performance Traditions, and Musical Styles." *RIM* (1975), 10:455–98.

——. "The Operas of Antonio Cesti." Ph.D. diss., Harvard University, 1973.

Schmidt, Günther. *Die Musik am Hofe der Markgrafen von Brandenburg-Ansbach vom ausgehenden Mittelalter bis 1806*. Kassel: Bärenreiter, 1956.

Schmidt, Gustav Friedrich. *Die frühdeutsche Oper und die musikdramatische Kunst Georg Caspar Schürmann's*. 2 vols. Regensburg: Bosse, 1933.

——. "Johann Wolfgang Francks Singspiel *Die drey Töchter Cecrops*." *AfMf* (1939), 4:257–316.

——. "Zur Geschichte, Dramaturgie und Statistik der frühdeutschen Oper (1627–1750)." *ZfMw* (1922–23), 5:582–97, 642–65; (1923–24), 6:129–57, 496–530.

Schmitz, Eugen. "Zur musikgeschichtlichen Bedeutung der Harsdörfferschen 'Frauenzimmergesprächspiel.'" In *Festschrift Liliencron*. Leipzig: Breitkopf & Härtel, 1910. 254–77.

Scholes, Percy. *The Puritans and Music in England and New England*. London: Oxford University Press, 1934.

Scholz, Hans. *Johann Sigismund Kusser*. Leipzig: Röder, 1911.

Schrade, Leo. *Monteverdi, Creator of Modern Music*. New York: Norton, 1950.

Schreiber, Irmtraud. *Dichtung und Musik der deutschen Opernarien 1680–1700*. Bottrop: Postberg, 1934.

Schünemann, Georg. (See general bibliography.)

Seifert, Herbert. *Neues zu Antonio Draghis Weltlichen Werken*. Vienna: Oesterreichischen Akademie der Wissenschaften, 1978.

Silbert, Doris. "Francesca Caccini, Called La Cecchina." *MQ* (1946), 32:50–62.

Silin, Charles I. *Benserade and His Ballets de Cour*. Baltimore: The Johns Hopkins University Press, 1940.

Solerti, Angelo. *Musica, ballo e drammatica*. (See part 1 bibliography.)

——. "I rappresentazioni musicali di Venezia dal 1571 al 1605." *RMI* (1902), 9:503–58.

Solerti, Angelo, comp. and ed. (See part 1 bibliography.)

Spitta, Philipp. *Johann Sebastian Bach*. 4th ed. 2 vols. Leipzig: Breitkopf & Härtel, 1930.

Spitz, Charlotte. "Die Entwicklung des 'stilo recitative.' " *AfMw* (1921), 3:237–44.

Squire, William Barclay. "J. W. Franck in England." *MA* (1911–12), 3:181–90.

Stalnaker, W. P., Jr. "The Beginnings of Opera in Naples." Ph.D. diss., Princeton University, 1968.

Strainchamps, Edmund. "New Light on the *Accademia degli Elevati* of Florence." *MQ* (1976), 62:507–535.

Strunk, Oliver, ed. (See general bibliography.)

Tessier, André. "Robert Cambert à Londres." *RM* (1927), 4:101–22.

Tittmann, Julius. (See general bibliography.)

Tomlinson, Gary. "Madrigal, Monody, and Monteverdi's *Via naturale alla immitatione.*" *JAMS* (1981), 1:145–57.

Torchi, Luigi. "L'accompagnamento degli istrumenti nei melodrammi italiani della prima metà del Seicento." *RMI* (1894), 1:7–38; (1895), 2:666–71.

Torrefranca, Fausto. "Il *grande stregone* Giacomo Torelli e la scenografia del Seicento." *Scenario* (1934), 3:473–80.

[Truinet, Charles Louis Etienne and A. E. Roquet (Thoinan).] *Les Origines de l'opéra français*. Paris: Plon-Nourrit, 1886.

Untersteiner, Alfredo. "Agostino Steffani," *RMI* (1907), 14:509–34.

Vallas, Léon. *Un Siècle de musique et de théâtre à Lyon (1688–1789)*. Lyon: Masson, 1932.

Vogel, Emil. "Marco da Gagliano," *VfMw* (1889), 5:396–442, 509–68.

Weaver, Robert Lamar. "Florentine Comic Operas of the Seventeenth Century." Ann Arbor, Mich.: University Microfilms, 1958.

——. "Sixteenth-Century Instrumentation," *MQ* (1961), 47:363–78.

Weaver, Robert and Norma Weaver. *A Chronology of Music in the Florentine Theater 1590–1750*. Detroit: Information Coordinators, 1978.

Weilen, Alexander von. *Geschichte des Wiener Theaterwesens von den ältesten Zeiten bis zu den Anfängen der Hoftheater*. Vienna: Gesellschaft für vervielfältigende Kunst, 1899.

——. *Zur Wiener Theatergeschichte: Die vom Jahre 1629 bis zum Jahre 1740 am Wiener Hofe zur Aufführung gelangten Werke theatralischen Charakters und Oratorien*. Vienna: Hölder, 1901. [An important supplement to Köchel, *Kaiserliche Hofmusikkapelle*; see corrections in Nettl, "Exzerpte aus der Raudnitzer Textbüchersammlung." *SzMw* (1920), 7:143–44.]

Wellesz, Egon. "Die Aussetzung des Basso Continuo in der italienischen Oper." In *International Musical Society, Fourth Congress Report*. London: Novello, 1912. 282–85.

——. "Cavalli und der Stil der venetianischen Oper von 1640–1660." *SzMw* (1913), vol. 1.

——. *Essays on Opera*. (See general bibliography.)

——. "Die Opern und Oratorien in Wien von 1660–1708," *SzMw* (1919), 6:5–138.

——. "Zwei Studien zur Geschichte der Oper im 17. Jahrhundert." *SIMG* (1913), 15:124–54.

Werner, Theodor Wilhelm. "Agostino Steffanis Operntheater in Hannover." *AfMf* (1938), 3:65–79.

West, Dorothy Irene. "Italian Opera In England (1660–1740) and Some of Its Relationships to English Literature." Ph.D. diss., University of Illinois, 1937.

Westrup, Jack Allan. "The Cadence in Baroque Recitative," In *Natalicia musicologica Knud Jeppesen*. Copenhagen: Hansen, 1962. 243–52.

——. "Monteverdi and the Orchestra." *M&L* (1940), 21:230–45.

——. *Purcell*. London: Dent, [1937]. 8th rev. ed., London: Dent, 1980.

White, Eric Walter. *The History of English Opera*. London: Faber & Faber, 1983.

——. "New Light on *Dido and Aeneas*." In *Henry Purcell*, ed. by Holst.

——. *The Rise of English Opera*. London: Lehmann, 1951.

Wiedemann, Carla. *Leben und Wirken des Johann Philipp Förtsch, 1652–1732*. Kassel and Basel: Bärenreiter, 1955.

Wiel, Taddeo. *I codici musicali contariniani del secolo XVII nella R. Biblioteca di S. Marco in Venezia*. Venice: Ongania, 1888.

——. "Francesco Cavalli." *MA* (1912–13), 4:1–19.

Witzenmann, Wolfgang. "Domenico Mazzochi, 1592–1665: Dokumente und Interpretationen," In *Analecta musicologica* (1970), 8:1–283.

——. "Die römische Barockoper *La vita humana ovvero Il trionfo della Pietà*." In *Analecta musicologica* (1975), 15:158–201.

Wolff, Hellmuth Christian. *Die Barockoper in Hamburg (1678–1738)*. 2 vols. Wolfenbüttel: Möseler, 1957.

——. *Oper: Szene und Darstellung*. (See general bibliography.)

——. *Die venezianische Oper in der zweiten Hälfte des 17. Jahrhunderts*. Berlin: Elsner, 1937.

Worsthorne, Simon Towneley. *Venetian Opera in the Seventeenth Century*. Oxford: Clarendon, 1954.

Zelle, Friedrich. *Johann Philipp Förtsch*. Berlin: Gaertner, 1893.

——. *Johann Theile und Nikolaus Adam Strungk*. Berlin: Gaertner, 1891.

——. *Johann Wolfgang Franck*. Berlin: Gaertner, 1889.

Zelm, Klaus. "Die Sänger der Hamburger Gänsemarkt-Oper." *Hamburger Jahrbuch für Musikwissenschaft* (1978), 3:35–73.

Zimmerman, F. B. *Henry Purcell: His Life and Times*. New York: St. Martin's, 1967.

Zorzi, Ludovico et al. *I teatri pubblici di Venezia (secoli XVII–XVIII)*. Venice: Biennale di Venezia, 1971.

Zucker, Paul. *Die Theaterdekoration des Barock*. Berlin: Kaemmerer, 1925.

Part III: The Eighteenth Century

Abert, Anna Amalie. *Christoph Willibald Gluck*. Munich: Bong, [1960].

Abert, Hermann. *Gesammelte Schriften*. (See general bibliography.)

——. "Johann Christian Bach's italienische Opern und ihr Einfluss auf Mozart." *ZfMw* (1918–19), 1:313–28.

——. *Mozart's "Don Giovanni"*. London: Eulenberg, 1981.

——. *Niccolo Jommelli als Opernkomponist, mit einer Biographie*. Halle an der Saale: Niemeyer, 1908.

——. *W. A. Mozart*. Rev. and enlarged by Otto Jahn as *Mozart*. Ed. by Anna A. Abert. 7th ed. 2 vols. Leipzig: Breitkopf & Härtel, 1956.

——. "Zur Geschichte der Oper in Württemberg." In *III. Kongress der Internationalen Musikgesellschaft . . . Bericht*. Vienna: Artaria; Leipzig: Breitkopf & Härtel, 1909. 186–93.

Abraham, Gerald. "The Operas." In *The Mozart Companion*. Ed. by H. C. Robbins Landon and Donald Mitchell. New York: Oxford University Press, 1956. (2nd ed., 1965.) 283–323.

Abraham, Gerald, ed. *Handel: A Symposium*. London: Oxford University Press, 1954.

Adimari, Lodovico. "Satira quarta: Contro alcuni vizi delle donne, e particolamente control le cantatrice." In *Satire del marchese Lodovico Adimari*. London: Masi, 1788. 183–253.

Adler, Guido. *Handbuch der Musikgeschichte*. (See general bibliography.)

Ahnell, Emil Gustave. "The Concept of Tonality in the Operas of Jean-Philippe Rameau." Ph.D. diss., University of Illinois, 1958.

Aldrich, Putnam C. (See part 2 bibliography.)

Alfieri, Pietro. *Notizie biografiche di Niccolò Jommelli de Aversa*. Rome: Tip. delle belle arte, 1845.

Allanbrook, Wye Jamison. *Rhythmic Gesture in Mozart: "Le nozze di Figaro" and "Don Giovanni"*. Chicago: University of Chicago Press, 1983.

Anderson, Emily, ed. *The Letters of Mozart and His Family Chronologically Arranged*. Trans. by C. B. Oldman. 3 vols. London: Macmillan, 1938.

Angermüller, Rudolf. *Antonio Salieri: Sein Leben und seine weltlichen Werke, unter besonderer Berücksichtigung seiner "grossen" Opern*. 3 vols. Munich: Katzbichler, 1971–72.

——. "Wer war der Librettist von *La finta giardiniera?*" *Mozart-Jahrbuch 1976–77*, pp. 1–8.

Anthony, James R. *French Baroque Music*. (See part 1 bibliography.)

——. "The French Opéra-Ballet in the Early Eighteenth Century: Problems of Definition and Classification." *JAMS* (1965), 18:197–206.

Arnheim, Amalie. "*Le Devin du village* von Jean-Jacques Rousseau und die Parodie *Les Amours de Bastien et Bastienne*." *SIMG* (1902–3), 4:686–727.

Arnoldson, Louise Parkinson. *Sedaine et les musiciens de son temps*. Paris: Entente, 1934.

Asenjo y Barbieri, Francisco. *Cancionero musical de los siglos XV y XVI*. Madrid: Tip. de los huérfanos, [1890].

Babcock, Robert W. "Francis Coleman's *Register of Operas*, 1712–1734." *M&L* (1943), 24:155–58. [Supplemented and corrected in a letter by O. E. Deutsch, *M&L* (1944), 25:126.]

Barbaret, Vincent. *Lesage et le théâtre de la foire*. Nancy, 1887.

Bartha, Dénes and László Somfai. *Haydn als Opernkapellmeister: Die Haydn-Dokumente der Esterházy-Opernsammlung.* Mainz: Schott, 1960.

Bauman, Thomas. *North German Opera in the Age of Goethe.* Cambridge: Cambridge University Press, 1985.

Bauman, Thomas, ed. *German Opera 1770–1800.* 22 vols. New York: Garland, 1985.

Beare, Mary. *The German Popular Play "Atis" and the Venetian Opera.* Cambridge: Cambridge University Press, 1938.

Beau, A. Eduard. "Die Musik im Werk des Gil Vicente," *Volkstum und Kultur der Romanen* (1936), 9:177–201.

Beechey, Gwilym. "Thomas Linley, Junior, 1756–1778." *MQ* (1974), 60:74–82.

Behrend, William. "Weyse und Kuhlau: Studie zur Geschichte der dänischen Musik." *Die Musik* (1904), 3:272–86.

[Benjamin, Lewis Saul.] *Life and Letters of John Gay . . . by Lewis Melville [pseud.].* London: D. O'Connor, 1921.

Berger. Arthur V. "*The Beggar's Opera,* the Burlesque, and Italian Opera," *M&L* (1936), 17:93–105.

Bianconi, Lorenzo. "Funktionen des Operntheaters in Neapel bis 1700 und die Rolle Alessandro Scarlattis." In *Colloquium Alessandro Scarlatti, Würzburg 1975.* Tutzing: Schneider, 1979. 13–116.

Bobillier, Marie [Michel Brenet, pseud.]. "Grétry, sa vie et ses oeuvres." In *Mémoires couronnés et autres mémoires publiés par l'Académie royale . . . de Belgique.* (1884), vol. 36.

Bollert, Werner. *Die Buffoopern Baldassare Galuppis.* Bottrop: Postberg, 1935.

Bolte, Johannes. (See part 2 bibliography.)

Bonnet, George Edgar. *Philidor et l'évolution de la musique française au XVIIe siècle.* Paris: Delagrave, 1921.

Borrel, Eugene. "Un Paradoxe musical au XVIIIe siècle." In *Mélanges de musicologie.* Paris: Droz, 1933. 217–21.

Borren, Charles van den. *Alessandro Scarlatti et l'esthétique de l'opéra napolitain.* Paris: Editions de la Renaissance, 1921.

Böse, F. "Ariosti und Bonocini am Berliner Hof." *AfMw* (1965), 22:56.

Botstiber, Hugo. (See general bibliography.)

Bötther, Friedrich. *Die "Comédie-Ballet" von Molière-Lully.* Berlin: Graphisches Institut P. Funk, 1931.

Boyer, Noel. *La Guerre des bouffons et la musique française (1752–1754).* Paris: Editions de la Nouvelle France, [1945].

Breitholtz, Lennart. *Studier i operan "Gustaf Wasa."* Uppsala: Lundequistska, [1954].

Brook, Barry, ed. *The Symphony 1720–1840.* 60 vols. New York: Garland, 1979–85.

Brook, Barry S. and Marvin E. Paymer. "The Pergolesi Hand: A Calligraphic Study." *MLA Notes* (1982), 38:550–78.

Brosses, Charles de. *Lettres familières sur l'Italie.* Ed. by Yvonne Besand. 2 vols. Paris: Firmin-Didot, 1931.

Brown, Bruce Alan. "Gluck's *Rencontre Imprévue* and Its Revisions." *JAMS* (1983), 36:498–518.

Brown, Howard Mayer, ed. (See part 2 bibliography.)

Brown, John. *Letters on the Italian Opera*. 2nd ed. London: T. Cadell, 1791.

Brück, Paul. "Glucks *Orpheus und Euridike*." *AfMw* (1925), 7:436–76.

Brückner, Fritz. *Georg Benda und das deutsche Singspiel*. Leipzig: Breitkopf & Härtel, 1904. Also *SIMG* (1903–4), 5:571–621.

———. "Zum Thema 'Georg Benda und das Monodram.' " *SIMG* (1904–5), 6:496–500.

Brunelli, Bruno, ed. *Tutte le opere di Pietro Metastasio*. Milan: A. Mondadori, 1943–54.

Bücken, Ernst. *Die Musik des Rokoko und Klassik*. Wildpark-Potsdam, 1927.

Buelow, George J. "An Evaluation of Johann Mattheson's Opera, *Cleopatra* (Hamburg, 1704)." In Landon, ed., *Studies in Eighteenth-Century Music*. 92–107.

———. "A Lesson in Operatic Performance Practice by Madame Faustina Bordoni." In *Essays in Honor of Martin Bernstein*. Ed. by E. H. Clinkscale and C. Brook. New York: Pendragon, 1977.

Burney, Charles. *A General History of Music*. (See part 2 bibliography.)

———. *Memoirs of the Life and Writings of the Abate Metastasio; in Which Are Incorporated Translations of His Principal Letters*. 3 vols. London: Robinson, 1796.

———. *The Present State of Music in France and Italy*. (See part 1 bibliography.)

———. *The Present State of Music in Germany, the Netherlands, and Provinces*. 2 vols. London: Becket, 1773.

Burt, Nathaniel. "Opera in Arcadia." *MQ* (1955), 41:145–70.

Bussey, William M. *French and Italian Influence on the Zarzuela 1700–1770*. Ann Arbor, Mich.: UMI Research, 1980.

Callegari, Matelda. "Il melodramma e Pietro Metastasio." *RMI* (1919), 26:518–44; (1920), 27:31–59, 458–76.

Calmus, Georgy. *Die ersten deutschen Singspiele von Standfuss und Hiller*. Leipzig: Breitkopf & Härtel, 1908.

———. *Zwei Opernburlesken aus der Rokokozeit*. Berlin: Liepmannssohn, 1912.

Calzabigi, Ranieri de'. "Dissertazione . . . su le poesie drammatiche del Sig. Abate Pietro Metastasio." In *Poesie del Signor Abate Pietro Metastasio*. Paris: Vedova Quillan, 1755–69. 1:xix–cciv.

Cametti, Alberto. "Critiche e satire teatrali romane del '700." *RMI* (1902), 9:1–35.

———. "Saggio cronologico delle opere teatrali (1754–1794) di Nicolò Piccinni." *RMI* (1901), 8:75–100.

Campanini, Naborre. *Un precursore del Metastasio*. Vol. 43 of *Biblioteca critica della letteratura italiana*. Florence: Sansoni, 1904.

Campardon, Emile. *Les Comédien du roi de la troupe italienne*. 2 vols. Paris: Berger-Levrault, 1880.

———. *Les Spectacles des foires . . . depuis 1595 jusqu'à 1791*. 2 vols. Paris: Berger-Levrault, 1877.

Cannon, Beekman C. *Johann Mattheson, Spectator in Music*. New Haven: Yale University Press, 1947.

Carmena y Millán, Luis. *Crónica de la ópera italiana en Madrid desde el año 1738 hasta nuestros dias.* Madrid: Minuesa de los Rios, 1878.

Carmody, Francis J. *Le Repertoire de l'opéra-comique en vaudevilles de 1708 à 1764.* Berkeley and Los Angeles: University of California Press, 1933.

Carreras y Bulbena, José Rafael. *Domenech Terradellas.* Barcelona: Altés, 1908.

Carroll, Charles Michael. "François-André Danican-Philidor: His Life and Dramatic Art." 2 vols. Ann Arbor, Mich.: University Microfilms, 1960.

Casavola, Franco. *Tommaso Traetta di Bitonto (1727–1779): La vita e le opere.* Bari: Società di Storia Patria per la Puglia, 1957.

Chailley, Jacques. *"The Magic Flute," Masonic Opera: An Interpretation of the Libretto and the Music.* Trans. by H. Weinstock. New York: Da Capo, 1982.

Chailly, Luciano. *Il matrimonio segreto.* [Milan]: Istituto d'Alta Cultura, [1949].

Chantavoine, Jean. *Mozart dans Mozart.* Paris: Desclée de Brouwer, [1948].

Chase, Gilbert. *The Music of Spain.* 2nd ed. New York: Dover, [1958].

Chatfield-Taylor, H. C. *Goldoni: A Biography.* New York: Duffield, 1913.

Chavarri, Eduardo López. (See general bibliography.)

Chigiana (1975), vols. 29–30 (special issues devoted to Gluck).

Chouquet, Gustave. (See general bibliography.)

Chrysander, Friedrich. *G. F. Händel.* (See part 2 bibliography.)

——. "Die Oper *Don Giovanni* von Gazzaniga und von Mozart." *VfMw* (1888), 4:351–435.

[Cimarosa, Domenico.] *Per il bicentario della nascità di Domenico Cimarosa.* Aversa: Comitato per le Celebrazione, 1949.

Clercx, Suzanne. *Grétry, 1741–1813.* Brussels: Editions La Renaissance, [1944].

Clive, Geoffrey. "The Demonic in Mozart." *M&L* (1956), 37:1–13.

Conrad, Leopold. *Mozarts Dramaturgie der Oper.* Würzburg: Triltsch, 1943.

Cooper, Martin. *Gluck.* New York: Oxford University Press, 1935.

——. *Opéra comique.* New York: Chanticleer, [1949].

Corte, Andrea della. (See Della Corte, Andrea.)

Cortese, Nino. "Un' autobiografia inedita di Giovanni Paisiello." *RassM* (1930), 3:123–35.

Cotarelo y Mori, Emilio. *Historia de la zarzuela o sea El drama lírico en España, desde su origen a fines del siglo XIX.* Madrid: Archivos, 1934.

——. *Orígenes y establecimiento de la ópera en España hasta 1800.* Madrid: Revista de archivos, 1917.

Cotarelo y Mori, Emilio, ed. *Colección de entremeses, loas, bailes, jácaras y mojingangas desde fines del siglo XVI á medíados del XVII.* Madrid: Bailly-Baillière, 1911.

Croce, Benedetto. *I teatri di Napoli, secolo XV–XVIII.* Naples: L. Pierro, 1891. New ed., 1916.

Croll, Gerhard. "Gluckforschung und Gluck-Gesamtausgabe." In *Musik und Verlag: Karl Vötterle zum 65. Geburtstag.* Kassel, 1968. 192ff.

Cross, Eric. *The Late Operas of Antonio Vivaldi 1727–1738.* Ann Arbor, Mich.: UMI Research, 1981.

Crussard, Claude. (See part 2 bibliography.)

Cucuel, Georges. *Les Créateurs de l'opéra-comique français*. Paris: Alcan, 1914.

——. "La Critique musicale dans les 'revues' du XVIIIe siècle." *L'Année musicale* (1912), 2:127–203.

——. "Notes sur la comédie italienne de 1717 à 1789." *SIMG* (1913–14), 15:154–66.

——. "Les Opéras de Gluck dans les parodies du XVIIIe siècle." *RM* (1922), vol. 3, no. 5, 201–21; no. 6, 51–68.

——. "Sources et documents pour servir à l'histoire de l'opéra-comique en France. *L'Année musicale* (1913), 3:247–82.

Curzon, Henri de. *Grétry*. Paris: Laurens, [1907].

Cyr, Mary. "Rameau's *Les fêtes d'Hébé*." Ph.D. diss., University of California, Berkeley, 1975.

D'Accone, Frank. *Alessandro Scarlatti's "Gli equivoci nel sembiante": The History of a Baroque Opera*. New York: Pendragon, 1985.

Damerini, Adelmo. "Tommaso Traetta: Cenni biografici." *Bollettino bibliografico musicale* (July 1927), 2:1–13.

D'Angeli, Andrea. *Benedetto Marcello, vita e opere*. Milan: Bocca, 1940.

Da Ponte, Lorenzo. *Memorie*. 2 vols. New York: Lorenzo e Carlo Da Ponte, 1823. English trans. by Elisabeth Abbott; ed. and annotated by Arthur Livingston. Philadelphia: Lippincott, 1929.

D'Arienzo, Nicola. "Le origini dell' opera comica." *RMI* (1895), 2:597–628; (1897), 4:421–59; (1899), 6:473–95; (1900), 7:1–33.

Dean, Winton. *Handel and the Opera Seria*. Berkeley and Los Angeles: University of California Press, 1969.

——. *Handel's Dramatic Oratorios and Masques*. London: Oxford University Press, 1959.

——. "The Recovery of Handel's Operas." In Hogwood and Luckett, eds., *Music in Eighteenth-Century England*. 103–13.

——. "Vocal Embellishment in a Handel Aria." In *Studies in Eighteenth-Century Music*. Ed. by Landon. 151–59.

Degrada, Francesco. "L'opera napoletana." In *Storia dell' Opera*, 1:237–332.

Della Corte, Andrea. "Appunti sull' estetica musicala di Pietro Metastasio." *RMI* (1921), 28:94–119.

——. *Baldassare Galuppi: Profilo critico*. Siena, 1948.

——. *L'opera comica italiana nel 1700*. 2 vols. Bari: Laterza, 1923.

——. *Paisiello: Con una tavola tematica. L'estetica musicale di P. Metastasio*. Turin: Bocca, 1922.

——. *Piccinni (Settecento italiano): Con frammenti musicali inediti e due ritratti*. Bari: Laterza, 1928.

Dent, Edward J. *Alessandro Scarlatti*. (See part 2 bibliography.)

——. "Emanuel Schikaneder." *M&L* (1956), 37:14–21.

——. "Ensembles and Finales in 18th-Century Italian Opera." *SIMG* (1909–10), 11:543–69; (1910–11), 12:112–38.

——. *Foundations of English Opera*. Cambridge: Cambridge University Press, 1928.

——. *Handel*. London: Duckworth, [1934].

———. *Mozart's Operas: A Critical Study*. London: Chatto & Windus; New York: McBride, Nast, 1913. 2nd ed., New York: Oxford University Press, 1947.

———. *Mozart's Opera "The Magic Flute": Its History and Interpretation*. Cambridge: W. Heffer, 1911.

———. "Notes on Leonardo Vinci." *MA* (1912–13), 4:193–201.

[Desboulmiers, Jean Auguste Julien.] *Histoire anecdotique et raisonée du théâtre italien, depuis son rétablissement en France jusqu'à l'année 1769*. 7 vols. Paris: Lacombe, 1769.

Desnoiresterres, Gustave. *Gluck et Piccinni, 1774–1800*. 2nd ed. Paris: Didier, 1875.

Deutsch, Otto Erich. *Handel: A Documentary Biography*. London: Black; New York: Norton, 1955.

———. *Mozart: A Documentary Biography*. 2nd ed. Stanford, Cal.: Stanford University Press, 1966.

———. *Mozart und die Wiener Logen: Zur Geschichte seiner Freimaurer-Kompositionen*. Vienna: Wiener Freimaurer-Zeitung, 1932.

DiChiera, David. "The Life and Operas of Gian Francesco di Majo." Ph.D. diss., University of California, Los Angeles, 1962.

Diderot, Denis. *Le Neveu de Rameau: Satyre publiée pour la première fois sur le manuscrit original autographe*. Paris: Plon, Nourrit, 1891.

Dietz, Max. *Geschichte des musikalischen Dramas in Frankreich während der Revolution bis zum Directorium (1787 bis 1795)*. Vienna: Groscher & Blaha, 1885. 2nd ed., Leipzig: Breitkopf & Härtel, 1893.

Di Giacomo, Salvatore. *Il conservatorio dei poveri di Gesu Cristo e quello di S. M. di Loreto*. Palermo: Sandron, 1928.

———. *Il conservatorio di Sant' Onofrio a Capuana e quello di S. M. della Pietà dei Turchini*. Naples: Sandron, 1924.

[Ditters] von Dittersdorf, Karl. *Karl von Dittersdorfs Lebensbeschreibung: Seinem Sohne in die Feder diktiert*. Leipzig: Breitkopf & Härtel, 1801. Trans. as: *The Autobiography of Karl von Dittersdorf*. London: Bentley, 1896.

Donath, Gustav. "Florian Gassmann als Opernkomponist." *SzMw* (1914), 2:34–211.

Doran, John. *"Mann" and Manners at the Court of Florence, 1740–1786: Founded on the Letters of Horace Mann to Horace Walpole*. 2 vols. London: Bentley, 1876.

Downes, Edward E. D. "The Neapolitan Tradition in Opera." In *International Musicological Society, Report of the Eighth Congress, New York 1961*. Kassel: Bärenreiter, 1961. 1:277–84.

———. "The Operas of Johann Christian Bach as a Reflection of the Dominant Trends in Opera Seria 1750–1780." Ph.D. diss., Harvard University, 1958.

———. "*Secco* Recitative in Early Classical Opera Seria (1720–80)." *JAMS* (1961), 14:50–69.

Druilhe, Paule. *Monsigny*. Paris: Colombe, [1955].

DuBos, Jean Baptiste. *Critical Reflections on Poetry, Painting, and Music*. Trans. from the French 5th ed. 3 vols. London: J. Nourse, 1748.

Du Gérard, N. B. *Tables alphabetique & chronologique de pieces representées sur l'ancien Théâtre italien, depuis son establissement jusqu'en 1697*. Paris: Prault, 1750.

Early Music (1983), vol. 11, no. 4 (Rameau tercentenary issue).

Ebert, Alfred. *Attilio Ariosti in Berlin (1697–1703)*. Leipzig: Giesecke & Devrient, 1905.

Eckermann, Johann Peter. *Gespräche mit Goethe*. 2 vols. Berlin: Bong, [1916].

Einstein, Alfred. *Gluck*. London: Dent; New York: Dutton, [1936]. 2nd ed., 1964.

———. *Gluck: Sein Leben, seine Werke*. Zurich and Stuttgart: Pan-Verlag, [1954]. English trans., London: J. M. Dent, [1954].

———. *Mozart, His Character, His Work*. New York: Oxford University Press, 1945.

Eitner, Robert. "Die deutsche komische Oper." *MfMg* (1892), 24:37–92.

Engel, Hans. "Die Finali der Mozartschen Opern." *Mozart-Jahrbuch 1954* (1955), 113–34.

Engländer, Richard. "Glucks *Cinesi* und *Orfano della China*." *Gluck-Jahrbuch* (1913), 1:54–81.

———. *Johann Gottlieb Naumann als Opernkomponist*. Leipzig: Breitkopf & Härtel, 1922; reprint, 1970.

Fassini, Sesto. "Il melodramma italiano a Londra ai tempi del Rolli," *RMI* (1912), 29:35–74, 575–636.

Faustini-Fasini, Eugenio. *Opere teatrali, oratori e cantate di Giovanni Paisiello (1764–1808): Saggio storico-cronologico*. Bari: Laterza, 1940.

Favart, Charles Simon. *Mémoires et correspondances littéraires, dramatiques et anecdotiques*. 3 vols. Paris: Collin, 1808.

———. *Théâtre*. 10 vols. Paris: DuChesne, 1763–[77].

Feder, Georg. "A Special Feature of Neapolitan Opera Tradition in Haydn's Vocal Works." In *Haydn Studies*. Ed. by J. Larsen et al. New York: Norton, 1975.

Federhofer, Hellmut. "Die Harmonik als Dramatischer Ausdrucksfaktor in Mozarts Meisteropern." *Mozart-Jahrbuch (1968–1970)*.

Fehr, Max. *Apostolo Zeno, 1668–1750, und seine Reform des Operntextes*. Zurich: Tschopp, 1912.

Felix, Werner. *Christoph Willibald Gluck*. Leipzig: P. Reclam Jun., 1965.

Festschrift zur Händel-Ehrung der Deutschen Demokratischen Republik 1959. Leipzig: Deutsche Verlag für Musik, [1959].

Fiske, Roger. *English Theatre Music in the Eighteenth Century*. London: Oxford University Press, 1973.

———. "The Operas of Stephen Storace." *PRMA* (1959–60), 86:29–44.

———. "A Score for *The Duenna*." *M&L* (1961), 42:132–41.

Fitzlyon, April. *The Libertine Librettist: A Biography of Mozart's Librettist Lorenzo da Ponte*. London: Calder, [1955].

Flemming, Willi, ed. (See part 2 bibliography.)

Flögel, Bruno. "Studien zur Arientechnik in den Opern Händels." *Händel-Jahrbuch* (1929), 2:50–156.

Florimo, Francesco. *La scuola musicale di Napoli e i suoi conservatori*. 2nd ed. 4 vols. Naples: Morano, 1880–82.

Floros, C. "Das 'Programm' in Mozarts Meisterouvertüren." *SzMw* (1964), 26:140–86.

Flower, Newman. *George Frideric Handel: His Personality and His Times*. New and rev. ed. London: Cassell, 1959.

Font, Auguste. *Favart, l'opéra-comique et la comédie-vaudeville aux XVIIe et XVIIIe siècles*. Paris: Fischbacher, 1894.

Ford, A. "Music and Drama in the Operas of Giovanni Bononcini." *PRMA* (1974–75), 101:107.

Foscolo, Ugo. *Dei sepolcri*. Verona: Gambaretti, 1807.

Franklin, Benjamin. "The Ephemera: An Emblem of Human Life." In *The Writings of Benjamin Franklin*. Ed. by Albert Henry Smith. New York: Macmillan, 1907. 7:206–9.

Frati, Lodovico. "Attilio Ottavio Ariosti." *RMI* (1926), 33:551–57.

———. "Satire di musicisti." *RMI* (1915), 22:560–66.

Freeman, Robert S. *Opera Without Drama*. Ann Arbor, Mich.: UMI Research, 1967.

Friedländer, Max. *Das deutsche Lied im 18. Jahrhundert*. 3 parts in 2 vols. Stuttgart and Berlin: Cotta, 1902.

Fuchs, Marianne. "Die Entwicklung des Finales in der italienischen Opera Buffa vor Mozart." Ph.D. diss., University of Vienna, 1932.

Gagey, Edmond M. *Ballad Opera*. New York: Columbia University Press, 1937.

Garrett, Edith Vogl. "Georg Benda, the Pioneer of the Melodrama." In *Studies in Eighteenth-Century Music*. Ed. by Landon. 236–42.

Geiringer, Karl. *The Bach Family: Seven Generations of Creative Genius*. New York: Oxford University Press, 1954.

———. *Joseph Haydn: Der schöpferische Werdegang eines Meisters der Klassik*. Mainz: Schott 1959.

Genest, Emile. *L'Opéra-comique connu et inconnu*. Paris: Fischbacher, 1925.

Gerber, Rudolf. *Christoph Willibald Gluck*. Potsdam: Athenaion, [1950].

———. *Der Operntypus Johann Adolf Hasses und seine textlichen Grundlage*. Leipzig: Kistner & Siegel, 1925.

Geulette, Thomas Simon. *Notes et souvenirs sur le théâtre-italien au XVIII siècle*. Paris: Praz, 1938.

Gherardi, Evaristo, comp. *Le Théâtre italien de Gherardi*. 6 vols. 5th ed. Amsterdam: M. C. le Cene, 1721.

Gianturco, Carolyn. *Mozart's Early Operas*. London: Batsford, 1981.

Giazotto, Remo. "Apostolo Zeno, Pietro Metastasio e la critica del Settecento." *RMI* (1946), 48:324–60; (1947), 49:46–56; (1948), 50:39–65, 248–58; (1949), 51:43–66, 130–61.

———. *Poesia melodrammatica e pensiero critico nel Settecento*. Milan: Bocca, [1952].

Giornale de' letterati d'Italia, vol. 38, part 2. Venice: Hertz, 1733.

Girdlestone, Cuthbert. *Jean-Philippe Rameau: His Life and Work*. London: Cassel, [1957] (2nd ed., 1969).

Glossy, Blanka and Robert Haas, eds. *Wiener Komödienlieder aus drei Jahrhunderten*. Vienna: Schroll, 1924.

Gluck, Christoph Willibald. *Collected Correspondence and Papers*. Ed. by Hedwig Mueller von Asow and E. H. Mueller von Asow; trans. by Stewart Thomson. London: Barrie and Rockliff, [1962].

Gluck-Jahrbuch. Ed. by H. Abert. Jahrgang I-IV, Leipzig: Breitkopf & Härtel, 1913, 1915, 1917, 1918.

Gmeyner, Alice. "Die Opern Antonio Caldaras." Ph.D., diss., University of Vienna, 1935.

Godwin, Joscelyn. "Layers of Meaning in *The Magic Flute.*" *MQ* (1979), 65:471–92.

Goldoni, Carlo. *Mémoires.* 3 vols. Paris: Veuve Duchesne, 1787. Trans. as: *Memoirs of Goldoni.* 2 vols. London: Colburn, 1814.

Goldschmidt, Hugo. *Die Lehre von der vokalen Ornamentik.* (See part 2 bibliography.)

——. *Die Musikästhetik des 18. Jahrhunderts und ihre Beziehungen zu seinen Kunstschaffen.* Zurich: Rascher, 1915. See also review by A. Schering, *ZfMw* (1918–19), 1:298–308.

——. "Die Reform der italienischen Oper des 18. Jahrhunderts und ihre Beziehungen zur musikalischen Aesthetik." In *III. Kongress der Internationalen Musikgesellschaft . . . Bericht.* Leipzig: Breitkopf & Härtel, 1909. 196–207.

Gómez, Julio. "Don Blas de Laserna: Un capítulo de la historia del teatro lírico español." *Revista de la biblioteca, archivo, y museo del ayunta-miento de Madrid* (1925).

Gottsched, Johann Christoph. *Versuch einer kritischen Dichtkunst vor die Deutschen.* Leipzig: B. C. Breitkopf, 1730. 2nd ed., 1737.

Goudar, Ange [Jean Jacques Sonette, pseud.]. *Le Brigandage de la musique italienne.* 1777.

Grannis, Valleria Belt. *Dramatic Parody in Eighteenth-Century France.* New York: Institute of French Studies, 1931.

Graves, Richard. "English Comic Opera: 1760–1800." *MMR* (1957), 87:208–15.

Grétry, André Ernest Modeste. *Mémoires, ou essais sur la musique.* 3 vols. Paris: Imprimerie de la république, [1797]. (First published in 1789.)

——. *Oeuvres complètes: Réflexions d'un solitaire.* 4 vols. Brussels and Paris: Von Oest, 1919–22.

Griffin, Thomas Edward. "The Late Baroque Serenata in Rome and Naples: A Documentary Study with Emphasis on Alessandro Scarlatti." Ph.D. diss., University of California, Los Angeles, 1983.

Grimm, Friedrich Melchior von. "Lettre sur Omphale." In *Correspondance littéraire, philosophique et critique.* 16 vols. Paris: Garnier, 1877–82. 16:287–309.

——. *Le Petit Prophète de Boemischbroda.* Paris, 1753.

——. "Poëme lyrique." In *Encyclopédie ou Dictionnaire raisonné.* Neuchâtel: S. Faulche, 1765. 12:822–36.

[Grosley, Pierre Jean.] *New Observations on Italy and Its Inhabitants.* 2 vols. London: Davis & Reymers, 1769.

Grout, Donald Jay. *Alessandro Scarlatti.* Berkeley: University of California Press, 1979.

——. "The Origins of the Opéra-comique." Ph.D. diss., Harvard University, 1939.

Grout, Donald Jay, ed. *The Operas of Alessandro Scarlatti.* 9 vols. Cambridge: Harvard University Press, 1974–.

——. "The Music of the Italian Theatre at Paris, 1682–1697," in *Papers of the American Musicological Society, Annual Meeting, 1941.* Ed. by G. Reese. Printed by the Society, [1946], pp. 158–70.

——. "Seventeenth-Century Parodies of French Opera." *MQ* (1941), 27:211–19, 514–26.

Guingené, Pierre Louis. *Notice sur la vie et les ouvrages de Nicolas Piccinni.* Paris: Panckoucke, [1801].

Haas, Robert M. *Aufführungspraxis.* (See general bibliography.)

——. *Gluck und Durazzo im Burgtheater.* Zurich: Amalthea, 1925.

——. "Die Musik in der Wiener deutscher Stegreifkomödie." *SzMw* (1925), 12:1–64.

——. "Die Wiener Ballet-Pantomime im 18. Jahrhundert und Glucks *Don Juan.*" *SzMw* (1923), 10:3–36.

——. "Wiener deutsche Parodieopern um 1730." *ZfMw* (1925–26), 8:201–25.

Haberl, Franz X. "Johann Mattheson: Biographische Skizze." *Caecilien Kalender* (1885), 53–60.

Haböck, Franz. *Die Gesangskunst der Kastraten: Erster Notenbuch A. Die Kunst des Cavaliere Carlo Broschi Farinelli.* Vienna: Universal, [1923].

——. *Die Kastraten und ihre Gesangskunst.* Stuttgart: Deutsche Verlags-Anstalt, 1927.

Händel-Festspiele . . . 1922: Veranstaltet vom Universitätsbund. Göttingen: Lange, 1922.

Händel-Jahrbuch. Leipzig: Breitkopf & Härtel, 1928–.

Hammelmann, H. and M. Rose. "New Light on Calzabigi and Gluck." *MT* (1969), 110:604.

Hardie, Graham Hood. "Leonardo Leo (1694–1744) and His Comic Operas *Amor vuol sofferenza* and *Alidoro.*" Ph.D. diss., Cornell University, 1973.

Harich, J. "Das Repertoire des Opernkapellmeisters Joseph Haydn in Eszterháza (1780–1790)." *The Haydn Yearbook* (1962), 1:9–110.

Harris, Ellen. *Handel and the Pastoral Tradition.* (See part 1 bibliography.)

——. "The Italian in Handel." *JAMS* (1980), 33:458–500.

Hauger, George. "William Shield." *M&L* (1950), 31:337–42.

Hawkins, John. *A General History.* (See part 2 bibliography.)

Heartz, Daniel. "The Creation of the *buffo* Finale in Italian Opera." *PRMA* (1977–78), 68ff.

——. "The Genesis of Mozart's *Idomeneo.*" *MQ* (1969), 55:1–19.

——. "Goldoni, Don Giovanni, and *Dramma Giocoso.*" *The Musical Times* (1979), 993–98.

——. "The Great Quartet in Mozart's *Idomeneo,*" In *The Music Forum.* Ed. by Felix Salzer. New York: Columbia University Press, 1980. 5:233–56.

——. "Hasse, Galuppi, and Metastasio." In *Venezia e il melodramma nel Settecento.* Venice, 1975.

——. "Mozart and His Italian Contemporaries: *La clemenza di Tito.*" *Mozart-Jahrbuch* (1978–79), 275ff.

——. "Mozart's Overture to *Titus* as Dramatic Argument." *MQ* (1978), 64:29–49.

——. "*Orfeo ed Euridice:* Some Criticisms, Revisions, and Stage-Realizations During Gluck's Lifetime." *Chigiana* (1975).

——. "Raaff's Last Aria: A Mozartian Idyll in the Spirit of Hasse." *MQ* (1974), 60:517–43.

Helfert, W. "Zur Geschichte des Wiener Singspiels." *ZfMw* (1922–23), 5:194–209.

Hell, Helmut. *Die Neapolitanische Opernsinfonie in der ersten Hälfte des 18. Jahrhunderts.* Tutzing: Schneider, 1971.

Helm, Ernest Eugene. *Music at the Court of Frederick the Great.* Norman: University of Oklahoma Press, 1960.

Henderson, Donald G. "The *Magic Flute* of Peter Winter." *M&L* (1983), 64:193–205.

Heriot, Angus. *The Castrati in Opera.* London: Secker & Warburg, 1956.

Heuss, Alfred. "Das dämonische Element in Mozarts Werken." *ZIMG* (1906), 7:175–86.

——. "Mozarts *Idomeneo* als Quelle für *Don Giovanni* and *Die Zauberflöte.*" *ZfMw* (1930–31), 13:177–99.

——. *Die Instrumental-Stücke.* (See part 2 bibliography.)

Hiller, Johann Adam. *Johann Adam Hiller.* Leipzig: Siegel, [1915].

Hirschberg, Eugen. *Die Enzyklopädisten und die französische Oper im 18. Jahrhundert.* Leipzig: Breitkopf & Härtel, 1903.

Hodermann, Richard. *Georg Benda.* Coburg: Wechsung, 1895.

——. *Geschichte des Gothaischen Hoftheaters 1725–1779.* Hamburg: Voss, 1894.

Hoffmann, Ernst Theodor Amadeus. "*Don Giovanni:* A Marvelous Adventure Which Befell a Traveling Enthusiast." Trans. by Abram Loft. *MQ* (1945), 31:504–16.

Hoffmann von Fallersleben, August Heinrich. *Unsere volkstümlichen Lieder.* 4th ed. Leipzig: Engelmann, 1900.

Hogarth, George. *Memoirs of the Musical Drama.* 2 vols. London: Bentley, 1838. New ed. as: *Memoirs of the Opera in Italy, France, Germany, and England.* 2 vols. London: Bentley, 1851.

Hogwood, Charles and Richard Luckett, eds. *Music in Eighteenth-Century England: Essays in Memory of Charles Cudworth.* Cambridge: Cambridge University Press, 1983.

Holl, Karl. *Carl Ditters von Dittersdorfs Opern für das wiederhergestellte Johannisberger Theater.* Heidelberg: Winter, 1913.

Holmes, William C. "Pamela Transformed." *MQ* (1952), 38:581–94.

——. "*La Statira*" *by Pietro Ottoboni and Alessandro Scarlatti: The Textual Sources with a Documentary Postscript.* New York: Pendragon 1983.

Holzer, Ludmilla. "Die komische Opern Glucks." *SzMw* (1926), 13:3–37.

Hopkinson, Cecil. *A Bibliography of the Works of C. W. von Gluck, 1714–1787.* London: Printed for the author, 1959 (2nd ed., 1967).

Hortschansky, Klaus. "Mozarts *Ascanio in Alba* und der Typus der Serenata." *Analecta musicologica* (1978), 18:148–58.

——. *Parodie und Entlehnung im Schaffen Christoph Willibald Glucks.* Cologne: Volk, 1973.

Howard, Patricia. *Gluck and the Birth of Modern Opera.* London: Barrie & Rockliff, 1963.

Hucke, Helmuth. "Die neapolitanische Tradition in der Oper." In *International Musicological Society, Report of the Eighth Congress, New York, 1961.* Kassel: Bärenreiter, 1961. 1:253–77.

Hughes, Charles W. "John Christopher Pepusch." *MQ* (1945), 31:54–70.

Hunt, Jno Leland. *Giovanni Paisiello: His Life as an Opera Composer.* New York: National Opera Association, 1975.

Hunter, Richard Hugh. "Comic Scenes in Selected Operas of Alessandro Scarlatti." Master's thesis, Cornell University, 1968.

Iacuzzi, Alfred. *The European Vogue of Favart: The Diffusion of the Opéra-Comique.* New York: Institute of French Studies, 1932.

Istel, Edgar. *Die Entstehung des deutschen Melodrams.* Berlin: Schuster & Loeffler, 1906.

——. *Studien zur Geschichte des Melodrams.* Vol. 1, *Jean Jacques Rousseau als Komponist seiner lyrischen Szene "Pygmalion".* Leipzig: Breitkopf & Härtel, 1901. Continued in *Annals de la Société Jean Jacques Rousseau* (1905), 1:141–72, (1906), 2, entire volume; (1907), 3:119–55.

Jackson, Paul J. "The Operas of David Perez." Ph.D. diss., Stanford University, 1967.

Jobe, R. D. "The Operas of André-Ernest-Modeste Grétry." Ph.D. diss., University of Michigan, 1965.

Jouve, Pierre Jean. *Le Don Juan de Mozart.* Freiburg: Librairie de l'Université, 1942. Trans. as: *Mozart's Don Juan.* London: Stuart, 1957.

Jullien, Adolphe. *La Cour et l'opéra sous Louis XVI.* Paris: Didier, 1878.

Kelly, Michael. *Reminiscences of the King's Theatre.* 2 vols. London: Colburn, 1826.

Kephart, Carolyn. "An Unnoticed Forerunner of *The Beggar's Opera*." *M&L* (1980), 61:266–71.

Kidson, Frank. *"The Beggar's Opera": Its Predecessors and Successors.* Cambridge: Cambridge University Press, 1922.

Kierkegaard, Sóren. "The Immediate Stages of the Erotic or the Musical Erotic." In *Either/Or, a Fragment of Life,* vol. 1. Trans. by David F. Swenson and Lillian Marvin Swenson. Princeton: Princeton University Press, 1944.

King, Alexander Hyatt. *Mozart in Retrospect: Studies in Criticism and Bibliography.* Westport, Conn: Greenwood Press, 1976.

Kirkendale, Ursula. *Antonio Caldara: La Vita.* Florence: Olschki, 1971.

Köchel, Ludwig von. *Chronologisch-thematisches Verzeichnis sämtlicher Tonwerke Wolfgang Amadeus Mozarts.* 3rd ed. Ann Arbor, Mich.: Edwards, 1947; 6th ed., Wiesbaden: Breitkopf & Härtel, 1964.

Kolneder, Walter. *Antonio Vivaldi: His Life and Work.* Trans. by Bill Hopkins. Berkeley: University of California Press, 1970.

BIBLIOGRAPHY

Komorzyński, Egon von. *Emmanuel Schikaneder*. Berlin: Behr, 1901.

———. *Emmanuel Schikaneder: Ein Beitrag zur Geschichte des deutschen Theaters*. Vienna: Doblinger, [1951].

———. *Mozart: Sendung und Schicksal*. 2nd ed. Vienna: Kremayr & Scheriau, [1955].

Krebs, Carl. *Dittersdorfiana*. Berlin: Gerbrüder Paetel, 1900.

Kretzschmar, Hermann. "Allgemeines und Besonderes zur Affektenlehre." *JMP* (1911), 18:63–77; (1912), 19:65–78.

———. "Die *Correspondance littéraire* als musikgeschichtliche Quelle," *JMP* (1903), 10:77–92. (Also in his *Gesammelte Aufsätze*, 2:210–25.)

———. *Geschichte der Oper*. (See general bibliography.)

———. *Geschichte des neuen deutschen Liedes*. (See general bibliography.)

———. "Zwei Opern Nicolo Logroscinos." *JMP* (1908), 15:47–68.

Krogh, Torben Thorberg. *Zur Geschichte des dänischen Singspiels im 18. Jahrhundert*. Copenhagen: Levin & Munksgaard, 1924.

Krone, Walter. *Wenzel Müller*. Berlin: Ebering, 1906.

Kurth, Ernst. "Die Jugendopern Glucks bis *Orfeo*," *SzMw* (1913), 1:193–277.

La Gorce, Jérôme de. "Twenty Set Models for the Paris Opéra in the Time of Rameau." *Early Music* (1983), 11:429–40.

Lalande, Joseph Jérôme Lefrançais de. *Voyage d'un François en Italie, fait dans les années 1765 & 1766*. 8 vols. Paris: Desaint, 1769.

La Laurencie, Lionel de. "La Grande Saison italienne de 1752: Les Bouffons." *MM* (1912), no. 6, pp. 18–33; nos. 7–8, pp. 13–22. (Also published as: *Les Bouffons (1752–1754)*. Paris: Revue SIM, 1912.)

———. *Rameau, biographie critique*. Paris: Laurens, [1908].

Landon, H. C. Robbins. "Haydn's Marionette Operas." *The Haydn Yearbook* (1962), 1:111–97.

———. "Out of Haydn." *Opera News* (August 1982).

Landon, H. C. Robbins, ed. *Studies in Eighteenth-Century Music: A Tribute to Karl Geiringer on His Seventieth Birthday*. London: Allen & Unwin, 1970.

Lang, Paul Henry. *George Frideric Handel*. New York: Norton, 1966.

La Rotella, Pasquale. *Niccolo Piccinni*. Bari: Cressati, 1928.

Larsen, Jens Peter. *Die Haydn-Ueberlieferungen*. Copenhagen: Munksgaard, 1939.

Lauppert, Albert von. *Die Musikästhetik Wilhelm Heinses: Zugleich eine Quellenstudie zur Hildegard von Hohenthal*. Greifswald: Abel, 1912.

Lawner, George. "Form and Drama in the Operas of Joseph Haydn." Ph.D. diss., University of Chicago, 1959.

Lazarevich, Gordana. "Haydn and the Italian Comic Intermezzo Tradition." In *Kongressbericht: Joseph Haydn Kongress*. Vienna, 1982.

———. "J. A. Hasse as a Comic Dramatist: The Neapolitan Intermezzi." *Analecta musicologica* (1985).

———. "Pasticcio Revisited: J. A. Hasse and His Parti Buffe." In *Music and Civilization: Essays in Honor of Paul Henry Lang*. Ed. by E. Strainchamps and M. Maniates. New York: Norton, 1984.

———. "The Role of the Neapolitan Intermezzo in the Evolution of Eighteenth-

Century Musical Style: Literary, Symphonic, and Dramatic Aspects, 1685–1745." Ph.D. diss., Columbia University, 1970.

Leclerc, Hélène. "*Les Indes galantes* (1735–1952): Les sources de l'opéra-ballet, l'exotisme orientalisant, les conditions matérielles du spectacle." *Revue d'histoire du théâtre* (1953), 5:259–85.

Lee, Vernon [Violet Paget]. *Studies of the Eighteenth Century in Italy.* London: Satchell, 1880.

Leichtentritt, Hugo. *Händel.* Stuttgart and Berlin: Deutsche Verlags-Anstalt, 1924.

——. "Handel's Harmonic Art." *MQ* (1935), 21:208–23.

——. *Music, History, and Ideas.* (See general bibliography.)

——. *Reinhard Keiser in seinen Opern.* Berlin: Tessarotypie-Actien-Gesellschaft, 1901.

Leo, Giacomo. *Leonardo Leo, celebre musicista del secolo XVIII, ed il suo omonimo Leonardo Leo di Corrado: Nota storica.* Naples: Cozzolino, 1901.

——. *Leonardo Leo . . . e le sue opere musicali.* Naples: Melfi & Joele, 1905.

Lert, Ernst. *Mozart auf dem Theater.* Berlin: Schuster & Loeffler, 1918.

Le Sage, Alain René. *Le Théâtre de la foire ou l'Opéra-comique.* 10 vols. Paris: P. Gandouin, 1724–37.

Leux, Irmgard. *Christian Gottlob Neefe.* Leipzig: Kistner & Siegel, 1925.

Levallois, Andrée and Anne Souriau. "Caractérologie musicale (les personnages du *Don Juan* de Mozart)." *Revue d'esthétique* (1954), 7:157–82.

Levarie, Siegmund. *Mozart's "Le Nozze di Figaro": A Critical Analysis.* Chicago: University of Chicago Press, 1952.

Lewis, C. S. *The Allegory of Love.* Oxford: Clarendon, 1936.

Lincoln, Stoddard. "The First Setting of Congreve's *Semele,*" *M&L* (1963), 44:103–17.

Lindgren, Lowell. "Ariosti's London Years, 1716–29." *M&L* (1981), 62:331–51.

——. "A Bibliographic Scrutiny of Dramatic Works set by Giovanni and His Brother Antonio Maria Bononcini." Ph.D. diss., Harvard University, 1972.

——. "Le opere drammatiche *romane* di Francesco Gasparini (1689–1699)." In *Atti del Primo Convegno Internazionale.* Florence: Olschki, 1981. 167–82.

——. "The Three Great Noises." (See part 2 bibliography.)

——. "I trionfi di Camillo." *Stadi musicali* (1977), 6:89–159.

Lindner, Ernst Otto. (See part 2 bibliography.)

Lippmann, Friedrich, ed. *Colloquium 'Mozart und Italien' (Rom 1974).* Cologne: Arno Volk, 1978.

Livermore, Ann Lapraik. "The Spanish Dramatists and Their Use of Music." *M&L* (1944), 25:140–49.

Loewenberg, Alfred. *Annals of Opera.* (See general bibliography.)

The London Stage, 1660–1800: A Calendar of Plays, Entertainments, and Afterpieces, Together with Casts, Box-Receipts, and Contemporary Comment. Part 1 (1660–1700), ed. by W. Van Lennep; part 2 (1700–1719), 2 vols., ed. by E. L. Avery; part 3 (1729–1747), 2 vols., ed. by A. H. Scouten; part 4 (1747–1776), 3 vols., ed. by G. W. Stone; part 5 (1776–1880), 3 vols., ed. by C. B. Hogan. Carbondale: Southern Illinois University Press, 1960–68.

Longyear, Rey M. "Schiller and Opera." *MQ* (1966), 52:171–82.

Lorenz, Alfred Ottokar. *Alessandro Scarlattis Jugendoper.* 2 vols. Augsburg: Benno Filser, 1927.

——. "Das Finale in Mozarts Meisteropern." *Die Musik* (June 1927), 19:621–32.

Lowinsky, Edward E. "Taste, Style, and Ideology in Eighteenth-Century Music." In *Aspects of the Eighteenth Century.* Ed. by E. R. Wasserman. Baltimore: The Johns Hopkins University Press, 1965. 163–205.

Lüthge, Kurt. *Die deutsche Spieloper.* Brunswick: W. Piepenschneider, 1924.

McClymonds, Marita P. *Niccolo Jommelli: The Last Years 1769–1774.* Ann Arbor, Mich.: UMI Research, 1980.

Magnani, Giuseppe. *Antonio Salieri: Musicista legnaghese (1750–1825).* Legnago: Edito a cura del comune di Legnago, 1934.

Maier, Johann Christoph. *Beschreibung von Venedig.* 2nd ed. 4 vols. Leipzig: J. A. Barth, 1795.

[Mainwaring, John.] *Memoirs of the Life of the Late George Frederic Handel.* London: R. & J. Dodsley, 1760.

Mann, William. *The Operas of Mozart.* New York: Oxford University Press, 1977.

[Marcello, Benedetto.] *Il teatro alla moda, osia metodo sicuro, e facile per ben comporre, & esequire l'Opere Italiane in Musica all' uso moderno.* [Venice]: Licante, [ca. 1720]. English trans. *MQ* (1948), 34:371–403; (1949), 35:85–105.

Marmontel, Jean François. (See part 2 bibliography.)

Martens, Heinrich. *Das Melodram.* Berlin: Vieweg, 1932.

Martienssen, C. A. "*Holger Danske*, Oper von Fr. L. Ae. Kunzen." *ZIMG* (1911–12), 13:225–32.

Marx, Adolf Bernhard. *Gluck und die Oper.* 2 vols. Berlin: Janke, 1863; reprint, 1970.

Mason, James Frederick. "The Melodrama in France from the Revolution to the Beginning of Romantic Drama." Ph.D. diss., The Johns Hopkins University, 1911. [Chap. 1 published: Baltimore: Furst, 1912.]

Masson, Paul-Marie. "Les Idées de Rousseau sur la musique." *RHCM* (1912), vol. 8, no.6, pp. 1–17; nos. 7–8, pp. 23–32.

——. *L'Opéra de Rameau.* Paris: Laurens, 1930.

——. "Rameau and Wagner." *MQ* (1939), 25:466–78.

Mattei, Saverio. *Memorie per servire alla vita di Metastasio.* Colle: A. M. Martini, 1785.

Mattheson, [Johann]. *Grundlage einer Ehrenpforte.* (See part 2 bibliography.)

——. *Die neueste Untersuchung.* (See part 2 bibliography.)

Maurer, Julius. *Anton Schweitzer als dramatischer Komponist.* Leipzig: Breitkopf & Härtel, 1912.

Mayer-Reinach, Albert. "Carl Heinrich Graun als Opernkomponist." *SIMG* (1899–1900), 1:446–529.

——. "Zur Herausgabe des *Montezuma* von Carl Heinrich Graun in den Denkmälern deutscher Tonkunst." *MfMg* (1905), 37:20–31.

Meikle, Robert Burns. "Leonardo Vinci's *Artaserse:* An Edition, with an Editorial and Critical Commentary." Ph.D. diss., Cornell University, 1970.

Meinardus, Ludwig. "Johann Mattheson und seine Verdienste um die deutsche Tonkunst." In *Sammlung musikalischer Vorträge.* Ed. by Paul Waldersee. Leipzig: Breitkopf & Härtel, 1879–98. 1:215–72.

Menke, Werner. *Das Vocalwerk Georg Philipp Telemanns.* Kassel: Bärenreiter, 1942.

Mennicke, Karl. *Hasse und die Brüder Graun als Sinfoniker.* Leipzig: Breitkopf & Härtel, 1906.

——. "Johann Adolph Hasse: Eine biographische Skizze." *SIMG* (1903–4), 5:230–44, 469–75.

Meyer, Ralph. *Die Behandlung des Rezitatives in Glucks italienischen Reformopern.* Leipzig: Breitkopf & Härtel, 1919.

Millner, Frederick L. *The Operas of Johann Adolf Hasse.* Ann Arbor, Mich.: UMI Research, 1979.

Minor, Jakob. *Christian Felix Weisse.* Innsbruck: Wagner, 1880.

Mitjana y Gordón, Rafael. *Histoire du développement du théâtre dramatique et musical en Espagne des origines au commencement du XIXe siècle.* Uppsala: Almqvist & Wiksell, 1906.

Moberly, Robert B. "The Influence of French Classical Drama on Mozart's *La Clemenza di Tito.*" *M&L* (1974), 54:291–298.

——. "Mozart and His Librettists." *M&L* (1973), 54:161–69.

Monaldi, Gino. (See general bibliography.)

Monnet, Jean. *Mémoires.* Paris: Louis-Michaud, [1884].

Monnier, Philippe. *Venise au XVIIIe siècle.* Paris: Perrin, 1907. Trans. as: *Venice in the Eighteenth Century.* London: Chatto & Windus, 1910.

Montagu, Lady Mary [Pierrepont] Wortley. *The Letters and Works of Lady Mary Wortley Montagu.* 2 vols. London: Bickers, [1861].

Mooser, Robert Aloys. *Annales de la musique et des musiciens en Russie au XVIIIe siècle.* 3 vols. Geneva: Mont-Blanc, 1948–51.

——. "Un Musicien espagnol en Russie à la fin du XVIIIe siècle." *RMI* (1936), 40:432–49.

Mosel, Ignaz Franz. *Ueber das Legen und die Werke des Anton Salieri.* Vienna: J. B. Wallishausser, 1827.

Moser, Hans Joachim. *Christoph Willibald Gluck.* Stuttgart: Cotta, 1940.

——. *Geschichte der deutschen Musik.* (See general bibliography.)

Mozart: Briefe und Aufzeichnungen. Comp. and annotated by Wilhelm A. Bauer and Otto Erich Deutsch. 7 vols. Kassel: Bärenreiter, 1971.

Mozart: Die Dokumente seines Lebens. Comp. and ed. by Otto Erich Deutsch. In *Mozart: Neue Ausgabe sämtlicher Werke,* ser. 10. Kassel: Bärenreiter, 1955.

Mozart-Jahrbuch. Ed. by Abert. 3 vols. Munich: Drei Masken, 1923–24, 1929; 1951–.

Mozart und seine Welt in zeitgenössischen Bildern. In *Mozart: Neue Ausgabe sämtlicher Werke,* ser. 10. Kassel: Bärenreiter, 1955.

Muratori, Lodovico Antonio. *Della perfetta poesia italiana, spiegata e dimostrata con varie osservazioni.* 2 vols. Venice: S. Colete, 1724.

Negri, Francesco. *La vita di Apostolo Zeno.* Venice: Alvisopoli, 1816.

Nettl, Paul. "An English Musician at the Court of Charles VI." *MQ* (1942), 28:318–28.

——. *Mozart and Masonry.* New York: Philosophical Library, [1957].

Neues Mozart-Jahrbuch. Ed. by Erich Valentin. 3 Jahrgänge. Regensburg: G. Bosse, 1941–43.

Newman, Ernest. *Gluck and the Opera.* London: Dobell, 1895; reprint, 1967.

Nin [y Castellano], J[oachin]. *Sept Chansons picaresques espagnoles anciennes, librement harmonisées et précédées d'une étude sur les classiques espagnols du chant.* Paris: Eschig, 1926.

——. *Sept Chants lyriques espagnols anciens, librement harmonisés et précédés d'une étude sur les classiques espagnols du chant.* Paris: Eschig, 1926.

Noack, Friedrich. "Die Opern von Christoph Graupner in Darmstadt." In *Bericht über den I. Musikwissenschaftlichen Kongress der Deutschen Musikgesellschaft.* Leipzig: Breitkopf & Härtel, 1926. 252–59.

Noske, Frits R. "*Don Giovanni:* An Interpretation." *Theatre Research* (1973), 13:60–74.

Nouveau Théâtre italien, Le. New ed. Paris: Briasson, 1733–53.

Noverre, Jean-Georges. *Lettres sur la danse, et sur les ballets.* Lyon: Delaroche, 1760.

Nuovo, Antonio. *Tommaso Traetta.* Bitonto: Amendolagine, 1938.

Oliver, Alfred Richard. *The Encylopedists as Critics of Music.* New York: Columbia University Press, 1947.

[Origny, Abraham Jean Baptiste Antoine d'.] *Annales du théâtre-italien.* 3 vols. Paris: Duchesne, 1788.

Osthoff, Wolfgang. "Mozarts Cavatinen und ihre Tradition." In *Osthoff Festschrift.* Ed. by W. Stauder, A. Aarburg, and P. Cahn. Tutzing: Schneider, 1969. 139–77.

Ottzenn, Curt. *Telemann als Opernkomponist.* Berlin: Ebering, 1902.

Pagano, Robert and Lino Bianchi. *Alessandro Scarlatti.* Turin: Edizioni RAI, 1972.

[Parfaict, François.] *Histoire de l'ancien théâtre italien depuis son origine en France, jusqu'à sa suppression en l'année 1697.* Paris: Lambert, 1753.

——. *Mémoires pour servir à l'histoire des spectacles de la foire.* Paris: Briasson, 1743.

Parini, Giuseppe. "La evirazione (La musica) [Ode]," in his *Le odi, il giorno e poesie minore, con note di Guido Mazzoni.* New ed. Florence: Barbèra, 1947. pp. 50–57.

Parkinson, J. A. *An Index to the Vocal Works of Thomas Augustine Arne and Michael Arne.* Detroit: Information Coordinators, 1972.

Les Parodies du nouveau théâtre italien . . . avec les airs gravés. New ed. Paris: Briasson, 1738.

Parolari, Cornelio. "Giambattista Velluti." *RMI* (1932), 39:263–98.

Pascazio, Nicola. *L'uomo Piccinni e la querelle célèbre.* Bari: Laterza, 1951.

Pastore, Giuseppe A. *Leonardo Leo.* Galatina: Pajano, 1957.

Pauly, Reinhard G. "Benedetto Marcello's Satire on Early 18th Century Opera." *MQ* (1948), 34:222–33.

Peckham, Mary. "The Operas of Georg Philipp Telemann." Ph.D. diss., Columbia University, 1969.

Pedrell, Felipe. *Cancionero musical popular español.* 4 vols. Valls: Castells, [1918–22].

———. *Teatro lírico español anterior al siglo XIX.* 5 vols. La Coruña: Berea, [1897–]1898.

Peiser, Karl. *Johann Adam Hiller.* Leipzig: Hug, 1894.

Pendle, Karen. "The Opéras Comiques of Grétry and Marmontel." *MQ* (1976), 62:409–34.

Pergolesi, Giovanni Battista. *Complete Works.* Ed. by Barry Brook et al. New York: Pendragon, 1985–.

Petty, Frederick. *Italian Opera in London 1760–1800.* Ann Arbor, Mich.: UMI Research, 1980.

Pincherle, Marc. *Vivaldi.* Paris: Librairie Plon, [1955]. Trans. as : *Vivaldi: Genius of the Baroque.* New York: Norton, [1957].

Piovano, Francesco. "Baldassare Galuppi: Note bio-bibliografiche." *RMI* (1906), 13:676–726; (1907), 14:333–65; (1908), 15:233–74.

Pirrotta, Nino. "Falsirena e la più antica delle cavatine." *Collectanea historiae musicae* (1957), 2:355–66.

Pitts, R. E. L. "Don Juan Hidalgo, Seventeenth-Century Spanish Composer." Ph.D. diss., George Peabody College for Teachers (Nashville, Tenn.), 1968.

Poladian, Sirvart. "Handel as an Opera Composer." Ann Arbor, Mich.: University Microfilms, 1958.

Pougin, Arthur. *Jean-Jacques Rousseau, musicien.* Paris: Fischbacher, 1901.

———. *Madame Favart: Étude théâtrale, 1727–1772.* Paris: Fischbacher, 1912.

———. *Monsigny et son temps.* Paris: Fischbacher, 1908.

———. *L'Opéra-comique pendant la révolution de 1788 à 1801.* Paris: A. Savine, 1891.

Powers, Harold S. "*Il Serse trasformato.*" *MQ* (1961), 47:481–92; (1962), 48:73–92.

Preibisch, Walter. "Quellenstudien zu Mozarts *Entführung aus dem Serail:* Ein Beitrag zur Geschichte der Türkenoper." *SIMG* (1908–9), 10:430–76.

Prota-Giurleo, Ulisse. *Alessandro Scarlatti, 'il Palermitano' (la patria & la famiglia).* Naples: L'autore, 1926.

———. *Nicola Logroscino, 'il dio dell' opera buffa.'* Naples: L'autore, 1927.

Pupino-Carbonelli, Giuseppe. *Paisiello.* Naples: Tocco, 1908.

Quadrio, Francesco Saverio. *Della storia e della ragione d'ogni poesia.* 4 vols. Bologna: Pisarri, 1739–49.

Quantz, Johann Joachim. *Versuch einer Anweisung die Flöte traversiere zu spielen.* Berlin: Voss, 1752; reprint, Leipzig: Kahnt, 1906.

Raab, Leopold. *Wenzel Müller.* Boden bei Wien: Verein der N.-Oe. Landesfreunde in Boden, 1928.

Rabany, Charles. *Carlo Goldoni: Le théâtre et la vie en Italie au XVIIIe siècle.* Paris: Berger-Levrault, 1896.

Radiciotti, Giuseppe. *Pergolesi.* Milan: Treves, [1935]. German ed.: *Giovanni*

Battista Pergolesi: Leben und Werk. Enlarged and rev. by Antoine E. Cherbuliez. Zurich: Pan-Verlag, [1954].

Raeli, V. "The Bi-Centenary of Tommaso Traetta." *The Chesterian* (1926–27), 8:217–23.

———. "Tommaso Traetta." *Rivista nazionale di musica* (March 1827).

[Raguenet, François.] *Défense du parallèle des Italiens et des François en ce qui regarde la musique et l'opéra.* Paris: Barben, 1705.

———. *Paralele des Italiens et des François en ce qui regarde la musique et les opéras.* Paris: J. Moreau, 1702.

Reichel, Eugen. "Gottsched und Johann Adolph Scheibe." *SIMG* (1900–1901), 2:654–68.

Reiff, A. "Die Anfänge der Oper in Spanien, mit Textproben." *Spanien, Zeitschrift für Auslandskunde* (1919). Vol. 1, no. 3.

Richebourg, Louisette. *Contribution à l'histoire de la 'Querelle des Bouffons.'* Paris: Nizet, 1937.

Riedinger, Lothar. "Karl von Dittersdorf als Opernkomponist." *SzMw* (1914), 2:212–349.

Riley, Maurice. (See part 2 bibliography.)

Rivalta, Camillo. *Giuseppe Sarti.* Faenza: Lega, 1928.

Roberti, Giuseppe. "La musica in Italia nel secolo XVIII secondo le impressioni di viaggiatori stranieri." *RMI* (1900), 7:698-729; (1901), 8:519-59.

Roberts, John H., ed. *Handel Sources: An Anthology of the Sources of Handel's Borrowings.* 9 vols. New York: Garland, 1985.

Robinson, Michael. *Naples and Neapolitan Opera.* London: Oxford University Press, 1972.

Rockstro, William Smyth. *The Life of George Frederick Handel.* London: Macmillan, 1883.

Rolland, Romain. "L'Autobiographie d'un illustre oublié: Telemann." In *Voyage musical au pays du passé.* Paris: Eduard-Joseph, 1919.

———. *Haendel.* New ed. Paris: Michel, [1951].

———. "Métastase, précurseur de Gluck." *MM* (1912), vol. 8, no. 4, pp. 1–10.

Roncaglia, Gino. *Il melodioso settecento italiano.* Milan: Hoepli, 1935.

Rosa, Salvator. "La musica." In [Johann] Mattheson, *Mithridat.* Hamburg: Geissler, 1749. i–lvi (with German translation).

Rossell, Denton. "The Formal Construction of Mozart's Operatic Ensembles and Finales." 2 vols. Ann Arbor, Mich.: University Microfilms, 1956.

Roth, Hermann, "Händels Ballettmusiken." *Neue Musik-Zeitung* (1928), 49:245–52.

Rousseau, Jean Jacques. *Dictionnaire de musique.* 2 vols. Amsterdam: Rey, 1768. Trans. as: *A Complete Dictionary of Music.* London: J. Murray, 1779.

———. *Œuvres complètes.* 25 vols. Paris: P. Dupont, 1823–26. Contains "Confessions," vols. 14–16; writings on music, vols. 11–13.

Rowell, Lewis E., Jr. "Four Operas of Antonio Vivaldi." Ph.D. diss., University of Rochester, 1958.

Rubsamen, Walter. "Mr. Seedo, Ballad Opera, and the Singspiel." In *Miscelánea en homenaje a Mons. Higinio Anglés.* Barcelona: Consejo superior de investigaciones científicas, 1958–61. 2:776–809.

Rubsamen, Walter, ed. *The Ballad Opera: A Collection of 171 Original Texts of Musical Plays printed in Photo-facsimile*. 28 vols. New York: Garland, 1974.

Rushton, Julian G. "*Iphigénie en Tauride:* The Operas of Gluck and Piccinni." *M&L* (1972), 53:411–30.

——. "Music and Drama at the Académie Royale de Musique, Paris, 1774–1789," Ph.D. diss., Oxford University, 1970.

——. *W. A. Mozart's "Don Giovanni"*. Cambridge: Cambridge University Press, 1981.

Ryom, Peter. "La Situation actuelle de la musicologie vivaldienne." *Acta musicologica* (1981), 120–44.

Sadie, Stanley. *The New Grove Mozart*. New York: Norton, 1983.

Sage, Jack. "Nouvelles lumières sur la genèse de l'opéra et la zarzuela en Espagne." *Journées internationales d'étude du Baroque* (1970), 4:170.

Schenk, Johann Baptist. ["Autobiographische Skizze."] *SzMw* (1924), 11:75–85.

Scherillo, Michele. *L'opera buffa napoletana durante il Settecento: Storia letteraria*. 2nd ed. [Milan]: Sandron, [1917]. (First published as: *Storia letteraria dell' opera buffa napolitana dalle origini al principio del secolo XIX*. Naples: R. Università, 1883; reprint, 1969.)

Schering, Arnold. *Musikgeschichte Leipzigs*. (See general bibliography.)

——. "Zwei Singspiele des Sperontes." *ZfMw* (1924–25), 7:214–20.

Schletterer, Hans Michael. *Das deutsche Singspiel*. (See part 2 bibliography.)

——. "Die Opernhäuser Neapels." *MfMg* (1882), 14:175–81, 183–89; (1883), 15:12–19.

Schlitzer, Franco, ed. *Tommaso Traetta, Leonardo Leo, Vincenzo Bellini: Notizie e documenti raccolti in occasione della 'IX Settimana Musicale Senese' 16–22 settembre 1952*. Siena: Ticci, 1952.

Schmid, Anton. *Christoph Willibald Ritter von Gluck*. Leipzig: Fleischer, 1854.

Schmid, Ernst Fritz. "Mozart und Monsigny." *Mozart-Jahrbuch 1957* (1958), 57–62.

Schmidt, Gustav Friedrich. *Die frühdeutsche Oper*. (See part 2 bibliography.)

Schmidt, Heinrich. *Johann Mattheson, ein Förderer der deutschen Tonkunst, im Lichte seiner Werke*. Leipzig: Breitkopf & Härtel, 1897.

Schmidt, Leopold. *Zur Geschichte der Märchenoper*. Halle: Hendel, 1895.

Schmitz, Eugen. "Formgesetze in Mozarts *Zauberflöte*." In *Festschrift Max Schneider zum 80. Geburtstage*. Leipzig: Deutscher Verlag für Musik, [1955]. 209–14.

Schneider, Max. "Die Begleitung des Secco-Rezitativs um 1750." *Gluck-Jahrbuch* (1917), 3:88–107.

Schultz, William Eben. *Gay's "Beggar's Opera": Its Content, History, and Influence*. New Haven: Yale University Press, 1923. 2nd ed., 1967.

——. "The Music of *The Beggar's Opera* in Print, 1728–1923." *MTNA* (1934), 19:87–99.

Schwarz, Max. "Johann Christian Bach." *SIMG* (1900–1901), 2:401–54.

Scudo, Pierre. *Le Chevalier Sarti*. Paris: Hachette, 1857.

Sear, H. G. "Charles Dibdin: 1745–1814." *M&L* (1945), 26:61–65.

Shergold, Norman D. *A History of the Spanish Stage.* Oxford: Clarendon, 1967.

Siegmund-Schultze, Walther. *Georg Friedrich Händel: Leben und Werk.* Leipzig: Deutscher Verlag für Musik, 1954.

Silva, G. Silvestri. *Illustri musicisti calabresi: Leonardo Vinci.* Genoa: Nazionale, [1935].

Smith, Kent M. "The Life and Music of Egidio R. Duni: His Role in the Establishment of the Opéra Comique." Ph.D. diss., Cornell University, 1980.

Sonneck, Oscar George Theodore. "Ciampi's *Bertoldo, Bertoldino e Cacasenno* and Favart's *Ninette à la cour.*" *SIMG* (1911), 12:525–64.

Soriano Fuertes, Mariano. *Historia de la música española.* 4 vols. Madrid: Martín y Salazar; Barcelona: Ramírez, 1856–59.

The Spectator (London, 1711–14). 4 vols. London and Toronto: Dent, 1919–26.

Speziale, G. "Ancora per Paisiello." *RassM* (1931), 4:1–16.

Spinelli, Alessandro Giuseppe. *Bibliografia goldoniana.* Milan: Dumolard, 1884.

Spitta, Philipp. *Johann Sebastian Bach.* (See part 2 bibliography.)

Spitz, Charlotte. *Antonio Lotti in seiner Bedeutung als Opernkomponist.* Borna and Leipzig: Noske, 1918.

———. "Die Opern *Ottone* von G. F. Händel (London 1722) und *Teofane* von A. Lotti (Dresden 1719): Ein Stilvergleich." In *Festschrift Adolf Sandberger.* Munich: Zierfuss, 1918. 265–71.

Squire, William Barclay. "An Index of Tunes in the Ballad-Operas." *MA* (1910–11), 2:1–17.

Steglich, Rudolf. "Das deutsche Händelfest in Leipzig." *ZfMw* (1924–25), 7:587–92.

———. "Göttinger Händelfestspiele 1924." *Zeitschrift für Musik* (1924), 91:496–98.

———. "Göttinger Händel-Opern Festspiele 1927." *Zeitschrift für Musik* (1927), 94:424–26.

———. "Die Händel-Opern-Festspiele in Göttingen." *ZfMw* (1920–21), 3:615–20.

———. "Händels Oper *Rodelinde* und ihre neue Göttinger Bühnenfassung." *ZfMw* (1920–21), 3:518–34.

———. "Die neue Händel-Opern-Bewegung." *Händel-Jahrbuch* (1928), 1:71–158.

Stendhal, pseud. [Marie Henri Beyle]. *Vies de Haydn, de Mozart et de Métastase.* Ed. by Daniel Muller. Paris: Champion, 1914.

Strauss, J. F. "Jean Jacques Rousseau: Musician." *MQ* (1978), 64:474–482.

Streatfeild, Richard Alexander. "Handel, Rolli, and Italian Opera in London in the Eighteenth Century." *MQ* (1917), 3:428–45.

Strohm, Reinhard. "Händel in Italia: Nuovi contributi." *RMI* (1974), 9:152–74.

Strunk, Oliver, ed. (See general bibliography.)

Subirá, Josá. *El compositor Iriarte (1750–1791) y el cultivo español del melólogo (melodrama).* 2 vols. Madrid: Consejo superior de investigaciones científicas, Instituto español de musicología, 1949–50.

———. *Historia de la música teatral en España.* Barcelona: Editorial Labor, 1945.

———. *Los maestros de la tonadilla escénica.* Barcelona: Editorial Labor, 1933.

———. *La música en la casa de Alba.* Madrid: [Sucesores de Rivadeneyra], 1927.

———. *La participación musical en el antiguo teatro español.* Barcelona: Diputación provincial, 1930.

———. "Le Style dans la musique théâtrale espagnole." *Acta musicologica* (1932), 4:67–75.

———. *La tonadilla escénica.* 3 vols. Madrid: Tipografía de archivos, 1928–30.

———. *Tonadillas teatrales inéditas.* Madrid: Tipografía de archivos, 1932.

Subirá, José, ed. *Celos aun del aire matan.* Barcelona: Institut d'Estudias Catalans, 1933.

Symonds, John Addington. *Renaissance in Italy: The Revival of Learning.* 2nd ed. London: Smith, Elder, 1883.

Szabolsci, Bence. "Exoticisms in Mozart." *M&L* (1956), 37:323–32.

———. "Mozart et la comédie populaire." In *Studia musicologica* (Budapest, Hungarian Academy of Sciences, 1961), 1:65–91. (Originally published in Hungarian: Budapest, 1957.)

Terry, Charles Stanford. *Johann Christian Bach.* London: Oxford University Press, 1929.

Testa, Susan. "Il binomio Gluck-Angiolini e la realizzazione balletto 'Don Juan'." *Chigiana* (1975), 29/30:535ff.

Theater-Kalendar auf das Jahr . . . (Reichard). Vols. 1–25. Gotha: 1775–1800.

Thierstein, E. A. "Five French Operas of Sacchini." Ph.D. diss., University of Cincinnati, 1974.

Thrane, Carl. *Danske Komponister.* (See general bibliography.)

Tibaldi Chiesa, Mary. *Cimarosa e il suo tempo.* [Milan]: Garzanti, [1939].

Tiersot, Julien. "Étude sur *Orphée* de Gluck." *Le Ménestrel* (1896), 62:273–386.

———. *Jean-Jacques Rousseau.* Paris: Alcan, 1912.

———. "La Musique des comédies de Molière à la Comédie-française." *RdM* (1922), 6:20–28.

Torre, Arnaldo della. *Saggio di una bibliografia delle opere intorno a Carlo Goldoni (1793–1907).* Florence: Alfani e Venturi, 1908.

Tosi, Pietro Francesco. *Opinioni de' cantori antichi, e moderni, o sieno Osservazioni sopra il canto figurato.* [Bologna: L. dalla Volpe, 1723.] Trans. as: *Observations on the Florid Song; or, Sentiments on the Ancient and Modern Singers.* London: J. Wilcox, 1742.

Troy, Charles. *The Comic Intermezzo: A Study in the History of Eighteenth-Century Italian Opera.* Ann Arbor, Mich.: UMI Research, 1979.

Tufts, G. "Ballad Operas: A List and Some Notes." *MA* (1913), 4:61.

Tyson, Alan. "*La clemenza di Tito* and Its Chronology." *The Musical Times* (1975), 116:221–27.

Unger, Max. "Zur Entstehungsgeschichte des *Trionfo di Clelia*." *NZfM* (1915), 82:269.

Ursprung, Otto. "*Celos* usw., Text von Calderón, Musik von Hidalgo: Die älteste erhaltene spanische Oper." In *Festschrift Arnold Schering.* Berlin: Glas, 1937. 223–40.

Valdrighi, Luigi Francesco. *I Bononcini da Modena.* Modena: Vincenzi, 1882.

Valentin, Erich. *Georg Philipp Telemann.* Burg: Hopfer, [1931].

Vélez de Guevara, Juan Crisóstomo. *Los celos hacen estrellas*. Ed. by Jack E. Varey. London: Tamesis, 1970.

Vetter, Walther. "Deutschland und das Formgefühl Italiens: Betrachtungen über die Metastasianische Oper." *Deutsches Jahrbuch der Musikwissenschaft* (1960), 5:7–37.

Villarosa, Carlo Antonio de Rosa. *Memorie dei compositori di musica del regno di Napoli*. Naples: Stamperia reale, 1840.

[Villeneuve, Josse de.] *Lettre sur le méchanisme de l'opéra italien*. Paris: Duchesne; Florence and Paris: Lambert, 1756. German trans. by R. Haas, *ZfMw* (1924–25) 7:129–63.

Viollier, Renée. *Jean-Joseph Mouret, le musicien des grâces, 1682–1738*. Paris: Librairie Floury, 1950; reprint, 1976.

Virella Cassañes, Francisco. *La ópera en Barcelona*. Barcelona: Redondo & Xumetra, 1888.

Virga, Patricia H. *The American Opera to 1790*. Ann Arbor, Mich.: UMI Research, 1982.

Vitale, Roberto. *Domenico Cimarosa* Aversa: Noviello, 1929.

Vivaldi, Antonio. *La Griselda*. Vol. 35 of *Italian Opera 1640–1770*. Ed. by Howard M. Brown. New York: Garland, 1977.

Voigt, F. A. "Reinhard Keiser." *VfMw* (1890), 6:151–203.

Volek, T. and M. Skalická. "Vivaldis Beziehungen zu den böhmischen Ländern." *Acta musicologica* (1967), 39:64.

Volkmann, Hans. "Domenico Terradellas." *ZIMG* (1911–12), 13:306–9.

Wagner, Richard. *Gesammelte Schriften und Dichtung*. 5th ed. 12 vols. Leipzig: Breitkopf & Härtel, n.d.

Walker, Frank. "*Orazio*: The History of a Pasticcio." *MQ* (1952), 28:369–83.

Walsh, T. J. *Opera in Dublin 1705–1797*. Dublin: Allen Figgis, 1973.

Warburton, Ernest. "A Study of Johann Christian Bach's Operas." Ph.D. diss., Oxford University, 1969.

Werner, Eric. "Leading or Symbolic Formulas in *The Magic Flute*." *MR* (1957), 18:286–93.

Werner, Theodor Wilhelm. "Zum Neudruck von G. Ph. Telemanns *Pimpinone* in den Reichsdenkmalen." *AfMf* (1936). pp. 361–65.

White, Eric Walter. *The History of English Opera*. (See part 2 bibliography.)

Williams, Hermine W. "Francesco Bartolomeo Conti: His Life and Operas." Ph.D. diss., Columbia University, 1964.

Winckelmann, Johann Joachim. *Sämtliche Werke*. 12 vols. Donauöschingen: Im Verlage deutscher Classiker, 1825–29.

Winesanker, Michael. "The Record of English Musical Drama, 1750–1800." Ph.D. diss., Cornell University, 1944.

Wirth, Helmut. "Johann Christian (Jean Chrétien) Bach." *RIdM* n.s. (Autumn, 1950), no. 8, pp. 133–42.

——. *Joseph Haydn als Dramatiker*. Wolfenbüttel: Kallmeyer, 1940.

——. "The Operas of Joseph Haydn Before *Orfeo*." In *Joseph Haydn Orfeo ed Euridice . . . Analytical Notes*. Boston: Haydn Society, [1951]. 12–48.

Wolf, Robert Peter. "Jean-Philippe Rameau's Comédie Lyrique, *Les Paladins* (1760): A Critical Edition and Study." Ph.D. diss., Yale University, 1977.

Wolff, Hellmuth Christian. *Die Barockoper*. (See part 2 bibliography.)

——. *Die Händel-Oper auf der modernen Bühne: Ein Beitrag zu Geschichte und Praxis der Opern-Bearbeitung und -Inszenierung in der Zeit von 1920 bis 1956.* Leipzig: Deutscher Verlag für Musik, 1957.

Wortsmann, Stephan. *Die deutsche Gluckliteratur*. Nuremberg: Karl Koch, 1914.

Wotquenne, Alfred. *Alphabetisches Verzeichnis der Stücke in Versen aus den dramatischen Werken von Zeno, Metastasio und Goldoni.* Leipzig: Breitkopf & Härtel, 1905.

——. "Baldassare Galuppi (1706–1785): Etude bibliographique sur ses oeuvres dramatiques." *RMI* (1899), 6:561–79.

——. *Catalogue thématique des oeuvres de Chr. W. v. Gluck.* Leipzig: Breitkopf & Härtel, 1904.

Wright, Edward. *Some Observations Made in Travelling Through France, Italy &c in the Years 1720–1721, and 1722.* 2 vols. London: T. Ward and E. Wicksteed, 1730.

Wyzewa, Teodor de and Georges de Saint-Foix. *W.-A. Mozart: Sa vie musicale et son oeuvre.* 5 vols. Paris: Desclée, de Brouwer et Cie., 1912–46.

Yorke-Long, Alan. *Music at Court: Four Eighteenth-Century Studies.* London: Weidenfeld & Nicolson, [1954].

Zeller, Bernhard. *Das recitativo accompagnato in den Opern Johann Adolf Hasses.* Halle: Hohmann, 1911.

Zelm, Klaus. *Die Opern Reinhard Keisers.* Salzburg: Kätzbichler, 1975.

[Zille, Moritz Alexander.] *"Die Zauberflöte": Text-Erläuterung für alle Verehrer Mozarts.* Leipzig: Lissner, 1866.

Zingerle, Hans. "Musik- und Textform in Opernarien Mozarts." *Mozart-Jahrbuch 1953* (1954), 112–15.

Part IV: The Nineteenth Century

Abbate, Carolyn. "The Parisian 'Vénus' and the 'Paris' *Tannhäuser*." *JAMS* (1983), 36:73–123.

Abert, Anna Amalie. "Webers *Euryanthe* und Spohrs *Jessonda* als grosse Opern." In *Festschrift für Walter Wiora.* Kassel: Bärenreiter, 1967. 435–40.

Abert, Hermann. *Gesammelte Schriften* (See general bibliography.)

——. "Robert Schumann's *Genoveva*." *ZIMG* (1909–10), 11:277–89.

Abraham, Gerald. *A Hundred Years of Music.* 4th ed. London: Duckworth, 1974.

——. "Wagner's Second Thoughts." In *Slavonic and Romantic Music.* New York: St. Martin's, 1968. chap. 25.

Abraham, Gerald, ed. *The Music of Schubert*. New York: Norton, 1947; reprint, 1969.

——. *Schumann: A Symposium*. London: Oxford University Press, 1952; reprint, 1977.

Abry, Emile. (See general bibliography.)

Achter, M. J. "Félicien David, Ambroise Thomas, and French Opéra Lyrique, 1850–1870." Ph.D. diss., University of Michigan, 1972.

Adam, Adolphe. *Derniers souvenirs d'un musicien*. Paris: Michal Levy, 1859.

——. *Souvenirs d'un musicien . . . précédés de notes biographiques écrites par lui-meme*. Paris: Calmann-Lévy, 1884.

Adamo, M. R. and F. Lippmann. *Vincenzo Bellini*. Turin, 1981.

Adler, Guido. *Handbuch der Musikgeschichte*. (See general bibliography.)

Almanach der deutschen Musikbücherei auf das Jahr 1924–25. Regensburg: Bosser, 1924.

Almanach des spectacles. Nos. 1–43. Paris, 1874–1913.

Amico, Tomasino d'. *Francesco Cilèa*. Milan: Curci, [1960].

Angermüller, R. "Zwei Selbstbiographien von Joseph Weigl (1766–1846)." *DJbM* (1973), 16:46.

Ashbrook, William. *Donizetti*. London: Cassell, 1965.

——. *Donizetti and His Operas*. Cambridge: Cambridge University Press, 1982.

——. *The Operas of Puccini*. New York: Oxford University Press, 1968.

Ashbrook, William and Julian Budden. "Gaetano Donizetti." In *The New Grove Masters of Italian Opera*. New York: Norton, 1983.

Aubry, Georges Jean. *La Musique française d'aujourdhui*. Paris: Perrin, 1916. Trans. as: *French Music of Today*. London: Paul, 1919.

Augé-Laribé, Michel. *Messager, musicien de théâtre*. Paris: Colombe, [1951].

Bagge, Selmar. "Robert Schumann und seine *Faust*-Scenen." In *Sammlung musikalischer Vorträge*. Ed. by Paul Waldersee. Leipzig: Graf, 1879. 1:121–40.

Bailey, R. "The Genesis of *Tristan und Isolde*, and a Study of Wagner's Sketches and Drafts for the First Act." Ph.D. diss., Princeton University, 1969.

Baily, Leslie. *The Gilbert & Sullivan Book*. London: Cassell, 1952. Rev. ed., London: Spring, 1966.

Ballo, Ferdinando. *Arrigo Boito*. Turin: Edizioni Arione, [1938].

Ballola, G. Carli. "Mercadante e *Il bravo*." In Massimo Mila, *Il melodramma italiano dell' ottocento: Studi e ricerche*. Turin: Einaudi, 1977.

Barblan, Guglielmo. *L'opera di Donizetti nell' età romantica*. Bergamo: Banca Mutua Popolare, 1948.

Barrett, William. *Balfe: His Life and Work*. London: Remington, 1882.

Bartlet, M. Elizabeth C. "Archival Sources for the Opéra-Comique." *19th-Century Music* (1983), 7:119–29.

Barzun, Jacques. *Berlioz and the Romantic Century*. 2 vols. Boston: Little, Brown, 1950.

——. *Darwin, Marx, Wagner: Critique of a Heritage*. Boston: Little, Brown, 1941. 2nd ed. Garden City, N.Y.: Doubleday, 1958.

Bauer, Hans Joachim. *Wagners "Parsifal": Kriterien der Kompositiontechnik.* Munich: Katzbichler, 1977.

Bauer, Oswald Georg. *Richard Wagner: The Stage Designs from the Première to the Present.* Trans. from the German ed. (1982). New York: Rizzzoli International, 1983.

Becker, Heinz. *Der Fall Heine-Meyerbeer: Neue Dokumente revidieren ein Geschichtsurteil.* Berlin: W. de Gruyter, 1958.

——. *Giacomo Meyerbeer in Selbstzeugnissen und Bilddokumenten.* Reinbek: Rowohlt Taschenbuch, 1980.

Becker, Heinz, ed. (*See* Meyerbeer.)

Beckett, Lucy. *Richard Wagner: Parsifal.* Cambridge: Cambridge University Press, 1981.

Bekker, Paul. *Wagner: Das Leben im Werke.* Stuttgart: Deutsche Verlags-Anstalt, 1924. Trans. as: *Richard Wagner: His Life in His Works.* New York: Norton, [1931].

Belardinelli, Alessandro, ed. *Documenti Spontiniani inedite.* 2 vols. Florence: Sansoni Antiquariato, 1955.

Bellasis, Edward. *Cherubini: Memorials Illustrative of His Life.* London: Burns & Oates, 1874.

Bellini, Vincenzo. *Epistolario.* Ed. by Luisa Cambi. Verona: Mondadori, 1943.

Berlioz, Hector. *A Travers Chants: Études musicales.* 2nd ed. Paris: Michel Lévy, 1872.

——. *Mémoires.* Paris: Michel Lévy, 1870. Trans. as: *Memoirs of Hector Berlioz.* Annotated and the translation revised by Ernest Newman. New York: Tudor, [1935].

Besch, Otto. *Engelbert Humperdinck.* Leipzig: Breitkopf & Härtel, 1914.

[Bizet, Georges.] *RdM* (November 1938), vol. 22 (special number devoted to Bizet).

Boito, Arrigo. *Tutti gli scritti, a curo di Piero Nardi.* [Milan]: Mondadori, [1942].

Bollert, Werner. "Joseph Weigl und das deutsche Singspiele." *Aufsätze zur Musikgeschichte.* Bottrop, 1938.

Borren, Charles van den. *L'Oeuvre dramatique de César Franck: "Hulda" et "Ghiselle".* Brussels: Schott, 1907.

Borriello, A. *Mito, poesia e musica nel "Mefistofele" di Arrigo Boito.* Naples: Guida, [1950].

Boschot, Adolphe. *Hector Berlioz: Une vie romantique.* Edition définitive. Paris: Plon, [1951].

——. *L'Histoire d'un romantique: Hector Berlioz.* Vol. 1, *La Jeunesse d'un romantique . . . 1803–1831.* Paris: Plon-Nourrit, 1906. New ed., [1946]. Vol. 2, *Un Romantique sous Louis-Philippe . . . 1831–1842.* Paris: Plon-Nourrit, 1908. Rev. ed., 1948. Vol. 3, *Le Crépuscule d'un romantique . . . 1842–1869.* Paris: Plon-Nourrit, 1913. Rev. ed., [1950].

——. *La Vie et les oeuvres de Alfred Bruneau.* Paris: Fasquelle, [1937].

Brancour, René. *Félicien David.* Paris: Laurens, [190–].

——. *Méhul.* Paris: Laurens, [1912].

Braunstein, Josef. *Beethovens Leonore-Ouvertüren: Eine historisch-stilkritische Untersuchung.* Leipzig: Breitkopf & Härtel, 1927.

Bréville, Pierre de and H. Gauthier-Villars. *"Fervaal": Étude thématique et analytique.* Paris: Durand, 1897.

Brown, Clive. "Spohr's *Jessonda*." *MT* (1980), 121:94-97.

Brown, Maurice J. E. *Essays on Schubert.* New York: St. Martin's, 1966.

——. *Schubert: A Critical Biography.* New York: St. Martin's, 1958.

Bruneau, Alfred. *Massenet.* Paris: Delagrave, 1934.

——. *La Musique française.* (See general bibliography.)

——. *Musiques d'hier et de demain.* Paris: Bibliothéque Charpentier, 1900.

Brunel, P. *Vincenzo Bellini.* Paris: Fayard, 1981.

Bruyas, Florian. *Histoire de l'opérette en France, 1855–1965.* Lyons: Vitte, 1974.

Bücken, Ernest. *Der heroische Stil.* (See general bibliography.)

——. *Die Musik des 19. Jahrhunderts bis zur Moderne.* Wildpark-Potsdam: Akademische Verlagsgesellschaft Athenaion, 1929–32; reprint, New York: Musurgia, ca. 1949.

Budden, Julian. *The Operas of Verdi.* 3 vols. London: Oxford University Press, 1973–81.

Burgmüller, Herbert. *Die Musen darben: Ein Lebensbild Albert Lortzings.* Düsseldorf: Progress-Verlag, [1956].

Burian, Jarka. *Svoboda: Wagner.* Middletown, Conn.: Wesleyan University Press, 1983.

Buschkötter, Wilhelm. "Jean François Le Sueur: Eine Biographie." *SIMG* (1912–13), 14:58–154.

Butler, E. M. *The Fortunes of Faust.* Cambridge: Cambridge University Press, 1952.

Calvocoressi, Michel D. *Vincent d'Indy, "L'Etranger": Le poème, analyse thématique de la partition.* Paris: Courrier musical, [1903].

Carlez, Jules. *Catel.* Caen: Delesques, 1894.

Carner, Mosco. "The Exotic Element in Puccini." *MQ* (1936), 22:45–67.

——. "Giacomo Puccini." In *The New Grove Masters of Italian Opera.* New York: Norton, 1983.

——. *Puccini: A Critical Biography.* 2nd ed. London: Duckworth, 1974.

——. "Puccini's Early Operas." *M&L* (1938), 19:295–307.

Cellamare, Daniele. *Umberto Giordano: La vita e le opere.* [Milan]: Garzanti, [1949].

Chailley, Jacques. *"Parsifal" de Richard Wagner: Opera initiatique.* Paris: Buchet/Chastel, [1979].

Chamberlain, Houston Stewart. *Das Drama Richard Wagners.* 6th ed. Leipzig: Breitkopf & Härtel, 1921. (First published 1892.) Trans. as: *The Wagnerian Drama.* London and New York: Lane, 1915.

Chantavoine, Jean. *Camille Saint-Saëns.* Paris: Richard-Masse, 1947.

Chantavoine, Jean and Jean Gaudefroy-Demombynes. *Le Romantisme dans la musique européenne.* Paris: Michel, 1955.

Charlton, David. *"Ossian, Le Sueur, and Opera." Studies in Music* (Australia, 1977), 11:37–48.

Chop, Max. *August Bungert*. Leipzig: Seemann, 1903.

——. *E. N. V. Reznicek*. Vienna: Universal-Edition, [1920].

Chorley, Henry F. *Modern German Music*. 2 vols. 1854; reprint, New York: Da Capo, 1973.

——. *Thirty Years' Musical Recollections*. New York: Knopf, 1926.

Chouquet, Gustave. (See general bibliography.)

Chusid, Martin. "Notes on the Performance of *Rigoletto*." *Verdi Newsletter* (November 1980), no. 8.

Cinquante Ans de musique française de 1874 à 1925. Paris: Librairie de France, [1925].

Clément, Félix. (See general bibliography.)

Coeuroy, André. *La Musique française moderne*. Paris: Delagrave, 1922.

Cohen, H. R. "Berlioz and the Opera, 1829–1849." Ph.D. diss., New York University, 1973.

Combarieu, Jules. *Histoire de la musique*. (See general bibliography.)

Conati, Marcello. "Between Past and Future: The Dramatic World of Rossini in *Mosè in Egitto* and *Moïse et Pharaon*," *19th Century Music* (1980–81), 4:32–48.

——. *Encounters with Verdi*. Trans. by Richard Stokes. Ithaca, N.Y.: Cornell University Press, 1984.

Confalonieri, Giulio. *Prigionia di un artista (Il romanzo di Luigi Cherubini)*. 2 vols. [Milan]: Genio, [1948].

Cooper, Martin. *French Music: From the Death of Berlioz to the Death of Fauré*. London: Oxford University Press, 1969; reprint, 1974.

——. *Ideas and Music*. London: Barrie & Rockliff, 1965.

Coquis, André. *Léo Delibes: sa vie et son oeuvre (1836–1891)*. Paris: Richard-Masse, 1957.

Cornelius, Carl Maria. *Peter Cornelius, der Wort- und Tondichter*. Regensburg: G. Bosse, [1925].

Cornelius, Peter. *Literarische Werke*. 4 vols. Leipzig: Breitkopf & Härtel, 1904–5.

Coults, J. "Jean-François Le Sueur: A Study of the Composer and Five of His Operas." Ph.D. diss., University of Cardiff, 1966.

Crabbe, John. *Hector Berlioz: Rational Romantic*. London: Kahn & Averill, 1982.

Crosten, William L. *French Grand Opera: An Art and a Business*. New York: King's Crown, 1948.

Cucuel, Georges. *Les Créateurs de l'opéra-comique*. (See part 3 bibliography.)

Curtiss, Mina. *Bizet and His World*. New York: Knopf, 1958.

——. "Fromental Halévy." *MQ* (1953), 39:196–214.

Curzon, Henri de. *Ernest Reyer*. Paris: Perrin, 1924.

——. *La Légende de Sigurd*. Paris: Fischbacher, [1889].

——. *Léo Delibes*. Paris: Legouix, 1926.

Czech, Stan. *Franz Lehár: Weg und Werk*. Berlin: Werk-Verlag, 1942.

Dahlhaus, Carl. *Between Romanticism and Modernism*. Trans. by Mary Whittal. Berkeley and Los Angeles: University of California Press, 1983.

——. *Die Musik des 19. Jahrhunderts.* Vol. 6 of *Neues Handbuch der Musikwissenschaft.* Wiesbaden: Athenaion, 1980.

——. *Richard Wagner's Music Dramas.* Trans. by Mary Whittall. Cambridge: Cambridge University Press, 1979.

——. *Wagners Konzeption des musikalischen Dramas.* Regensburg: G. Bosse, 1971.

Damerini, Adelmo, ed. *Luigi Cherubini nel il centenario della nascita.* Florence, 1962.

Daninger, Josef C. *Sage und Märchen im Musikdrama: Eine ästhetische Untersuchung an der Sagen- und Märchenoper des 19. Jahrhunderts.* Prague: Hoffmanns Witwe, 1916.

Daube, Otto. *Siegfried Wagner und die Märchenoper.* Leipzig: M. Schleppegrell, [1936].

Dauriac, Lionel. *Meyerbeer.* Paris: Alcan, 1913.

Davies, Laurence. *César Franck and His Circle.* Boston: Houghton Mifflin, 1970.

Dean, Winton. "Beethoven and Opera." In *The Beethoven Companion.* Ed. by Denis Arnold and Nigel Fortune. London: Faber, 1971.

——. *Georges Bizet: His Life and Work.* 3rd ed. London: Dent, 1975.

——. "Opera Under the French Revolution." *PRMA* (1967–68), 94:77–96.

Deane, Basil. *Cherubini.* London: Oxford University Press, 1965.

Deathridge, John. *Wagner's "Rienzi": A Reappraisal Based on a Study of the Sketches and Drafts.* Oxford: Clarendon, 1977.

Deathridge, John and Carl Dahlhaus, eds. *The New Grove Wagner.* New York: Norton, 1984.

Decaux, Alain. *Offenbach, roi du second empire.* [Paris]: Amiot, [1958].

Decsey, Ernst. *Hugo Wolf.* 3rd–6th eds., rev. Berlin: Schuster & Loeffler, [1919].

——. *Johann Strauss.* Stuttgart and Berlin: Deutsche Verlags-Anstalt, 1922.

——. *Johann Strauss: Ein wiener Buch.* Vienna: Paul Neff, 1948.

De Donno, Alfredo. *Mascagni nel 900 musicale.* Rome: Casa del libro, [1935].

De Eisner-Eisenhof, A. "Guiseppe Weigl: Una biografia." *RMI* (1904), 11:459–83.

Della Corte, Andrea. *L'opera comica italiana.* (See part 3 bibliography.)

Delmas, Marc. *Gustave Charpentier et le lyrisme français.* Paris: Delagrave, 1931.

De Napoli, Giuseppe de. *Amilcare Ponchielli (1834–1886); La vita, le opera, l'epistolario. . . .* Cremona: Società Editoriale "Cremona Nuova," 1936.

Dent, Edward J. "A Best-Seller in Opera [Flotow's *Martha*]." *M&L* (1941), 22:139–54.

——. *The Rise of the Romantic Opera.* The Messenger Lectures at Cornell University, 1937–38. Ed. by Winton Dean. Cambridge: Cambridge University Press, 1976.

Destranges, Etienne. *"Le Chant de la cloche", de Vincent d'Indy: Etude analytique.* Paris: Tresse et Stock, 1890.

——. *"L'Etranger" de M. Vincent d'Indy: Étude analytique et thématique.* Paris: Fischbacher, 1904.

——. *"Fervaal" de Vincent d'Indy: Étude thématique et analytique.* Paris: A. Durand, 1896.

Deutsch, Otto Erich. *Schubert: A Documentary Biography*. Trans. by Eric Blom. London: Dent, 1946; reprint, 1977.

——. *Schubert: Thematic Catalogue of All His Works*. New York: Norton, [1950].

Dickinson, Alan Edgar Frederic. "The Structural Methods of The Ring." *MMR* (1954), 84:87–92, 124–29.

Donati-Petteni, Giuliano. *Donizetti*. Milan: Treves, 1930.

Donington, Robert. *Wagner's "Ring" and Its Symbols: The Music and the Myth*. 3rd ed. New York: St. Martin's, 1974.

Dorn, Heinrich. *Aus meinem Leben*. 7 vols. Berlin: Behr, 1870–86.

Dufrane, Louis. *Gossec*. Paris: Fischbacher, 1927.

Du Moulin-Eckart, Richard Maria Ferdinand. *Wahnfried*. Leipzig: Kistner & Siegel, 1925.

Dunhill, Thomas F. *Sullivan's Comic Operas: A Critical Appreciation*. New York: Oxford University Press, 1928.

Dünnebeil, Hans, ed. *Carl Maria von Weber, ein Brevier*. Berlin: AFAS-Musik-verlag, 1949.

——. *Schrifttum über Carl Maria von Weber mit Schallplattenverzeichnis*. 4th ed. Berlin: Bote und Bock, 1957.

Du Tillet, Jacques. "A propos du drame lyrique: Une lettre de M. Camille Saint-Saëns," *Revue politique et littéraire* (July 3, 1897), pp. 27–30.

Eckermann, Johann Peter. *Gespräche mit Goethe*. Ed. by Fritz Bergemann. Wiesbaden: Insel-Verlag, 1955.

Ehrenhaus, Martin. *Die Operndichtung der deutschen Romantik: Ein Beitrag zur Geschichte der deutschen Oper*. Vol. 1. Breslau: Hirt, 1911.

Engländer, Richard. "Paërs *Leonora* und Beethovens *Fidelio*," *Neues Beethoven Jährbuch* (1930), 4:118–32.

Favre, Georges. *Boieldieu: Sa vie—son oeuvre*. 2 vols. Paris: Droz, 1944–45.

Février, Henry. *André Messager: Mon maître, mon ami*. Paris: Amiot-Dumont, 1948.

Fischer, Georg. *Marschner-Erinnerungen*. Hanover and Leipzig: Hahn, 1918.

——. *Musik in Hannover*. (See part 2 bibliography.)

Flood, W. H. Grattan. *William Vincent Wallace: A Memoir*. Waterford: The Waterford News, 1912.

Florimo, Francesco. *La scuola musicale*. (See part 3 bibliography.)

Flotow, Rosa. *Friedrich von Flotow's Leben von seiner Witwe*. Leipzig: Breit-kopf & Härtel, 1892.

Folstein, R. L. "A Bibliography on Jacques Offenbach," *CMc* (1971), no. 12, p. 116.

Fouque, Octave. "Le Sueur comme prédécesseur de Berlioz." In *Les Révolution-naires de la musique*. Paris: Calmann-Lévy, 1882. 1–183.

Fragapane, Paolo. *Spontini*. [Bologna]: Sansoni, [1954].

Freeman, James. "Johann Simon Mayr and His *Ifigenia in Aulide*," *MQ* (1971), 59:187–210.

——. "Opera Production in Palermo, 1809–1830: A Theater and a Collection of Scores." Ph.D. diss., Harvard University, 1979.

Frensdorf, Victor Egon. *Peter Winter als Opernkomponist*. Erlangen: Junge, 1908.

Frese, C. *Dramaturgie der grossen Opern Giacomo Meyerbeers*. Berlin: Lienau, 1970.

Fulcher, Jane. "Meyerbeer and the Music of Society." *MQ* (1981), 67:213–29.

Gaartz, Hans. *Die Opern Heinrich Marschners*. Leipzig: Breitkopf & Hartel, 1912.

Gallois, Jean. *Ernest Chausson: l'homme et l'oeuvre*. Paris: Seghers, 1967.

Garlington, Aubrey. "August von Schlegel and the German Romantic Opera." *JAMS* (1977), 30:500–6.

——. "The Concept of the Marvelous in French and German Opera, 1770–1840: A Chapter in the History of Opera Esthetics." Ph. D. diss., University of Illinois, 1965.

——. "E. T. A. Hoffmann's *Der Dichter und der Komponist* and the Creation of the German Romantic Opera," *MQ* (1979), 65:22–47.

——. "German Romantic Opera and the Problems of Origins." *MQ* (1977), 63:247–63.

Gatti, Carlo. *Catalani: La vita e le opere*. [Milan]: Garzanti, [1953].

Gerlach, L. *August Klughardt, sein Leben und seine Werke*. Leipzig: Hug, 1902.

Ghislanzoni, Alberto. *Gaspare Spontini: Studio storico-critico*. Rome: Ateneo, 1951.

Gibson, R. Wayne. "The Ensemble Technique in the Grand Operas of Giacomo Meyerbeer (1791–1864)." Ph.D. diss., Northwestern University, 1975.

Glasenapp, Carl Friedrich. *Siegfried Wagner und seine Kunst*. New Series, 2 vols. Leipzig: Breitkopf & Härtel, 1913, 1919.

Glaser, G. "Franz von Holstein, ein Dichterkomponist des 19. Jahrhunderts." Ph.D. diss., University of Leipzig, 1930.

Glass, Frank W. *The Fertilizing Seed: Wagner's Concept of the Poetic Intent*. Ann Arbor, Mich.: UMI Research, 1983.

Gnirs, Anton. *Hans Heiling*. Carlsbad: Heinich, 1931.

Goldberg, Issac. *The Story of Gilbert and Sullivan*. New York: Simon & Schuster, 1928.

Goldberg, L. "A Hundred Years of Berlioz's *Les Troyens*." Ph.D. diss., University of Rochester, 1973.

Goldmark, Karl. *Erinnerungen aus meinem Leben*. Vienna: Rikola, 1922. Trans. as: *Notes from the Life of a Viennese Composer*. New York: Boni, 1927.

Goslich, Siegfried. *Beiträge zur Geschichte der deutschen romantischen Oper zwischen Spohrs "Faust" und Wagners "Lohengrin"*. Leipzig: Kistner & Siegel, 1937.

——. *Die deutsche romantische Oper*. Tutzing: Schneider, 1975.

Gossett, Philip. "Gioacchino Rossini." In *The New Grove Masters of Italian Opera*. New York: Norton, 1983.

——. "Happy Ending for a Tragic Finale." *Opera News* (October 1977), 42:34–35.

Gossett, Philip, ed. *Italian Opera 1810–1840*. 58 vols. New York: Garland, 1984–.

Gossett, Philip and Charles Rosen, eds. *Early Romantic Opera*. 72 vols. New York: Garland, 1977–85.

Gounod, Charles François. *Mémoires d'un artiste.* 5th ed. Paris: Calmann Lévy, 1896. Trans. as: *Memoirs of an Artist.* New York: Rand, McNally, 1895.

Gradenwitz, Peter. "Félicien David (1810–1876) and French Romantic Orientalism." *MQ* (1976), 62:471–506.

Graedener-Hattingberg, Magda von. *Hugo Wolf.* Vienna: Wancura, 1953.

Greeff, Paul. *E. T. A. Hoffmann als Musiker und Musikschriftsteller.* [Cologne and Krefeld]: Staufen-Verlag, 1948.

Gregor-Dellin, Martin. *Richard Wagner, Sein Leben, Sein Werk. Sein Jahrhundert.* Munich: Piper, 1980.

Grosheim, Georg Christoph. *Selbstbiographie.* Hamburg and Kassel: Settnick, 1925.

Grout, Donald Jay. *A History of Western Music.* (See general bibliography.)

——. *A Short History of Opera.* (See general bibliography.)

Grün, Bernard. *Kulturgeschichte der Operette.* 2nd ed. Berlin: Lied der Zeit [1967].

——. *Prince of Vienna: The Life, the Times, and the Melodies of Oscar Straus.* London: Allen, 1955.

Guest, Ivor. *The Romantic Ballet in Paris.* Middletown, Conn.: Wesleyan University Press, 1966; reprint, 1980.

Gysi, Fritz. *Max Bruch.* Zurich: Orell Füssli, [1922].

Hadamowsky, Franz Heinz Otto. *Die Wiener Operette: Ihre Theater und Wirkungsgeschichte.* Vienna: Bellaria, 1947.

Halévy, François. *Derniers Souvenirs et portraits.* Paris: Lévy, 1863.

——. *Souvenirs et portraits.* Paris: Lévy, 1861.

Hall, Robert A., Jr. "The Psychological Motivation of Wagner's *Götterdämmerung.*" *The German Quarterly* (1963), 36:245–57.

Harding, James. *Folies de Paris: The Rise and Fall of French Operetta.* London: Elm Tree, 1979.

——. *Massenet.* London: Dent, 1970.

Hardy, Joseph. *Rodolphe Kreutzer: Sa jeunesse à Versailles.* Paris: Fischbacher, 1910.

[Harsdörffer, Georg Philipp.] *Frauenzimmer Gesprechspiele so bey ehrund tugendliebenden Gesellschaften mit nutzlicher Ergetzlichkeit beliebet und geübet werden mögen.* 8 vols. Nuremberg: Endtern, 1643–57.

Hartford, Robert. *Bayreuth: The Early Years.* Cambridge: Cambridge University Press, 1980.

Hasse, Max. *Der Dichtermusiker Peter Cornelius.* 2 vols. Leipzig: Breitkopf & Härtel, 1922–23.

——. *Peter Cornelius und sein "Barbier von Bagdad".* Leipzig: Breitkopf & Härtel, 1904.

Hausegger, Siegmund von. *Alexander Ritter: Ein Bild seines Characters und Schaffens.* Berlin: Marquardt, [1907].

Hédouin, Pierre. *Gossec, sa vie et ses ouvrages.* Paris: Prignet, 1852.

Hegel, Georg Wilhelm Friedrich. *Aesthetik.* Vol. 14 of *Sämtliche Werke.* Stuttgart: Frommann, 1927.

Heine, Heinrich. *Sämtliche Werke.* Leipzig: Insel-Verlag, 1910–15.

Hellmer, Elmund, ed. *"Der Corregidor" von Hugo Wolf.* Vienna: Hugo Wolf Verein; Berlin: Fischer, 1900.

Hellouin, Frédéric. *Gossec et la musique française à la fin du XVIIIe siècle.* Paris: Charles, 1903.

———. *Un Musicien oublié: Catel.* Paris: Fischbacher, 1910.

Henderson, Donald G. (See part 3 bibliography.)

Hess, Willy. *Beethovens Oper "Fidelio" und ihre drei Fassungen.* Zurich: Atlantis, [1953].

Heuberger, Richard. *Im Foyer: Gesammelte Essays über das Opernrepertoire der Gegenwart.* Leipzig: H. Seemann, 1901.

Hill, Edward Burlingame. *Modern French Music.* Boston and New York: Houghton Mifflin, 1924.

Himonet, André. *"Louise" de Charpentier: Etude historique et critique, analyse musicale.* Paris: Mellottée, [1922].

Hoechst, Coit Roscoe. *Faust in Music.* Gettysburg, Pa.: Gettysburg Compiler, 1916.

Hoffmann, Ernst Theodor Amadeus. *Musikalische Novellen und Aufsätze: Volständige Gesamtausgabe.* Ed. by Edgar Istel. 2 vols. Regensburg: Bosse, [1921?].

———. *Sämtliche Werke.* Ed. by Eduard Griesebach. 15 vols. in 4. Leipzig: Hesse, 1907.

Hoffmann, Max. *Gustav Albert Lortzing, der Meister der Deutschen Volksoper.* Leipzig: Breitkopf & Härtel, 1956.

Hogarth, George. (See part 3 bibliography.)

Hohenemser, R. *Luigi Cherubini.* Leipzig: Breitkopf & Härtel, 1913.

Holoman, D. Kern. *The Creative Process in the Autograph Musical Documents of Hector Berlioz c. 1818–1840.* Ann Arbor, Mich.: UMI Research, 1980.

Holzer, R. *Die Wiener Vorstadtbühnen.* Vienna: Verlag des Österreichischen Staatsbruckerei, 1951.

Hopkinson, Cecil A. *A Bibliography of the Musical and Literary Works of Hector Berlioz 1803–1869, with Histories of the French Music Publishers Concerned.* 2nd ed. Tunbridge Wells: Macnutt, 1980.

———. *Bibliography of the Works of Gicacomo Puccini, 1858–1924.* New York: Broude, 1968.

Hsu, Dolores M. "Weber on Opera: A Challenge to Eighteenth-Century Tradition." In H. C. Robbins Landon, ed., *Studies in Eighteenth-Century Music: A Tribute to Karl Geiringer on His Seventieth Birthday.* Ed. by H. C. Robbins Landon. London: Allen & Unwin, 1970. 297–309.

Hughes, Gervase. *The Music of Arthur Sullivan.* London: Macmillan, 1960.

Hussey, Dyneley. *Verdi.* London: J. M. Dent, 1948.

Indy, Vincent d'. *César Franck.* Paris: Alcan, 1906. English trans., New York: John Lane, 1910.

———. *Richard Wagner et son influence sur l'art musical français.* Paris: Delagrave, 1930.

Istel, Edgar. *Bizet und "Carmen".* Stuttgart: Engelhorn, 1927.

———. *Die Blütezeit der musikalischen Romantik in Deutschland.* Leipzig: Teubner, 1909. 2nd ed., 1921.

——. "German Opera Since Richard Wagner." *MQ* (1915), 1:260–90.

——. *Die moderne Oper vom Tode Wagners bis zum Weltkrieg.* Leipzig: Teubner, 1915. 2nd ed., 1923.

Jacob, Heinrich Eduard. *Johann Strauss, Father and Son.* [New York]: Greystone, 1940.

——. *Johann Strauss und das neunzehnte Jahrhundert.* Amsterdam: Querido, 1937.

Jacob, Walter. *Der beschwerliche Weg des Peter Cornelius zu Liszt und Wagner.* Mainz: Krach, 1974.

Jacob, Walter, ed. *Leo Blech: Ein Brevier.* Hamburg and Leipzig: Prisman-Verlag, [1931].

Jacobs, Arthur. *Arthur Sullivan: A Victorian Musician.* New York: Oxford University Press, 1984.

Jähns, Friedrich Wilhelm. *Carl Maria von Weber in seinen Werken: Chronologisch-Thematische Verzeichniss seiner sämtlichen Compositionen . . .* Berlin: Leinau, 1891.

Jaspert, Werner. *Johann Strauss.* Berlin: Werk Verlag, [1939].

Jeri, Alfredo. *Mascagni: Quindici opere, mille episodi.* 3rd ed. Cernusco sul Naviglio: Grazanti, 1945.

Jouvin, B[enoît Jean Baptiste]. *Hérold, sa vie et ses oeuvres.* Paris: Au Ménestrel, Heugel, 1868.

Jullien, Adolphe. *Musiciens d'aujourd'hui.* 2 vols. Paris: Librairie de l'Art, 1892–94.

Kapp, Julius. *Meyerbeer.* Berlin: Schuster & Loeffler, [1920]. 8th ed., 1930.

Kastner, Emerich. *Bibliotheca Beethoveniana: Versuch einer Beethoven-Bibliographie.* Leipzig: Breitkopf & Härtel, 1913.

Kaufmann, Walter Arnold, ed. and trans. *Basic Writings of Nietzsche.* New York: Modern Library, 1968.

Keller, Otto. *Franz von Suppé.* Leipzig: Wöpke, 1905.

——. Die Operette. (See general bibliography.)

Kenny, Charles Lamb. *A Memoir of Michael William Balfe.* London: Tinsley, 1875.

Kerman, Joseph. *Opera as Drama.* (See general bibliography.)

——. "Verdi's *Otello,* or Shakespeare Explained." *The Hudson Review* (1953–54, 6:266–77.

Kienzl, Wilhelm. *Meine Lebenswanderung.* Stuttgart: Engelhorn, 1926.

Kienzl-Rosegger: Wilhelm Kienzls 'Lebenswanderung' im Auszug . . . Briefwechsel mit Peter Rosegger. Ed. by Hans Sittner. Zurich and Vienna: Amalthea-Verlag, [1953].

Killer, Hermann. *Albert Lortzing.* Potsdam: Athenaion, 1938.

Kimbell, David R. B. *Verdi in the Age of Italian Romanticism.* Cambridge: Cambridge University Press, 1981.

King, A. Hyatt. "Music for the Stage." In *The Music of Schubert,* ed. by Abraham. 198–216.

Klein, John W. "Alfredo Catalani." *MQ* (1937), 23:287–94.

——. "Alfredo Catalani: 1854–93." *M&L* (1954) 35:40–44.

——. "Catalani and His Operas." *MMR* (1958), 88:67–69, 101–7.

Knappe, Heinrich. *Friedrich Klose*. Munich: Drei Masken, 1921.

[Koch, Lajos.] *Karl Goldmark*. Budapest: Hauptstädtische Hausdruckerei, 1930.

Köhler, Volkmar. "Rezitativ, Szene und Melodram in Heinrich Marchners Opern." In *Gesellschaft für Musikforschung Kongressbericht*. Bonn, 1976. 461.

Kohut, Adolph. *Auber*. Leipzig: Reclam, 1895.

Kracauer, Siegfried. *Orpheus in Paris*. New York: Knopf, 1938. First published as: *Jacques Offenbach und das Paris seiner Zeit*. Amsterdam: De Lange, 1937.

Kraus, Ludwig. "Das deutsche Liederspiel in den Jahren 1800–1830." Ph.D. diss., University of Halle, 1921.

Krehbiel, Henry Edward. (See general bibliography.)

Kretzschmar, Hermann. "Die musikgeschichtliche Bedeutung Simon Mayrs." *JMP* (1904), 11:27–41. (Also in his *Gesammelte Aufsätze*, 2:226–41.)

——. "Über die Bedeutung von Cherubinis Ouvertüren und Hauptopern für die Gegenwart." *JMP* (1906), 13:75–91.

Kreuzhage, Eduard. *Hermann Goetz*. Leipzig: Brietkopf & Härtel, 1916.

Kroll, Erwin. *Carl Maria von Weber*. Potsdam: Athenaion, 1934.

——. *Ernst Theodor Amadeus Hoffmann*. Leipzig: Breitkopf & Härtel, 1923.

Krott, Rudolfine. "Die Singspiele Schuberts." Ph.D. diss., University of Vienna, 1921.

Kroyer, Theodor. "Die circumpolare Oper." *JMP* (1919), 26:16–33.

Kruse, Georg Richard. *Albert Lortzing*. Berlin: Harmonie, 1899.

——. *Hermann Goetz*. Leipzig: Reclam, [1920].

——. *Otto Nicolai*. Berlin: Berlin-Wien, [1911].

——. "Otto Nicolai's italienische Opern," *SIMG* (1910–11), 12:267–96.

Kuckuk, Ludwig. "Peter Winter als deutscher Opernkomponist." Ph.D. diss., University of Heidelberg, 1923.

Kufferath, Maurice. *"Fidelio" de L. van Beethoven*. Paris: Fischbacher, 1913.

Kuhlmann, Hans. *Stil und Form in der Musik von Humperdincks Oper "Hansel und Gretel"*. Borna and Leipzig: Noske, 1930.

Kurth, Ernst. *Romantische Harmonik und ihre Krise in Wagners "Tristan"*. 2nd ed. Berlin: Hesse, 1923.

Lamy, Félix. *Jean-François Le Sueur*. Paris: Fischbacher, 1912.

Landormy, Paul Charles René. *"Faust", de Gounod: Étude et analyse*. Paris: Mellotée, 1944.

Lang, Paul Henry. *The Experience of Opera*. New York: Norton, 1973.

——. "The Literary Aspects." (See part 2 bibliography.)

——. *Music in Western Civilization*. (See general bibliography.)

Langlois, Jacques. *Camille Saint-Saëns*. Moulins: Crépin-Leblond, 1934.

Laue, Hellmuth. *Die Operndichtung Lortzings*. Bonn: Röhrscheid, 1932.

Laux, Karl. *Carl Maria von Weber*. Leipzig: Reclam, 1966.

Lavoix, H[enri], fils. *Histoire de l'instrumentation depuis le seizième siècle jusqu'à nos jours*. Paris: Firmin-Didot, 1878.

Lippmann, Friedrich. "Vincenzo Bellini." In *The New Grove Masters of Italian Opera*. New York: Norton, 1983.

——. *Vincenzo Bellini und die italienische Opera seria seiner Zeit*. Cologne: Böhlau, 1969.

Liszt, Franz. *Dramaturgische Blätter*. Vol. 3 of *Gesammelte Schriften*. Leipzig: Breitkopf & Härtel, 1881.

Locke, Ralph P. "Notice biographique sur Félicien David." In *Célébration du centenaire de la mort de Félicien David*. Cadenet, 1976.

Loewenberg, Alfred. (See general bibliography.)

Longyear, Rey M. "The *Banda sul Palco*: Stage Bands in 19th-Century Opera." *Journal of Band Research* (1978), 13:25–40.

——. "D. F. E. Auber: A Chapter in the History of the Opéra Comique, 1800–1878." Ann Arbor, Mich.: University Microfilms, 1957.

——, "The Ecology of 19th-Century Opera." In *Gesellschaft für Musikforschung: Bericht über den Internationalen musikwissenschaftliche Kongress*. Bonn, 1970.

——. " 'Le Livret bien fait': The Opéra Comique Librettos of Eugène Scribe." *The Southern Quarterly* (1963), 1:169–92.

——. *Nineteenth-Century Romanticism in Music*. 2nd ed. Englewood, N.J.: Prentice Hall, 1973.

——. "Political and Social Criticism in French Opera, 1827–1920." In *Essays on the Music of J. S. Bach and Other Divers Subjects: A Tribute to Gerhard Herz*. Ed. by R. Weaver. Louisville, Ky.: University of Louisville Press, 1981. 245–54.

Loomis, Roger Sherman, ed. *The Romance of Tristram and Ysolt by Thomas of Britain*. New York: Columbia University Press, 1931.

Lorenz, Alfred Ottokar. *Das Geheimnis der Form bei Richard Wagner*. 4 vols. Berlin: Hesse, 1924–33.

Lortzing, Gustav Albert. *Gesammelte Briefe*. Regensburg: Gustav-Bosse, [1913]. 3rd ed., 1947.

Louis, Rudolf. *Die deutsche Musik der Gegenwart*. Munich: Müller, 1909; 3rd ed., 1912.

McCreless, Patricia. *Wagner's "Siegfried": Its Drama, History, and Music*. Ann Arbor, Mich.: UMI Research, 1982.

Malherbe, Charles Théodore. *Auber: Biographie critique*. Paris: Laurens, [1911].

Mann, Thomas. *Leiden und Grösse der Meister*. Berlin: Fischer, 1935. (A condensed English translation of the essay on Wagner in this volume is found in Mann, *Freud, Goethe, Wagner*. New York: Knopf, 1937.)

Mariani, G. *Arrigo Boito*. Parma, 1973.

Marino, Samuel J. "Giacomo Puccini: A Check List of Works by and about the Composer." *Bulletin of the New York Public Library* (February 1955), 59:62–81.

Martineau, René. *Emmanuel Chabrier*. Paris: Dorbon, 1910.

Mascagni, Pietro. *Mascagni parla: Appunti per le memorie de un grande musicista*. Rome: De Carlo, 1945.

Massenet, Jules. *Mes Souvenirs*. Paris: Lafitte, 1912. Trans. as: *My Recollections*. Boston: Small, Maynard, 1919.

Mattheson, Johann. *Die neueste Untersuchung*. (See part 2 bibliography.)

Mayerhofer, Gottfried. *Abermals vom Freischützen: Der Münchener 'Freischütze' von 1812* [by Franz Xavier von Caspar]. Regensburg: Bosse, 1959.

Medici, Mario and Marcello Conati, eds. *Carteggio Verdi-Boito*. Parma: Istituto di Studi Verdiani, 1978.

Meyerbeer, Giacomo. *Briefwechsel und Tagebücher . . . herausgegeben und kommentiert von Heinz Becker*. Vol. 1, *Bis 1824*. Berlin: De Gruyter, [1960].

Mongrédien, Jean. *Catalogue thématique de l'oeuvre complète du compositeur Jean-François Le Sueur*. New York: Pendragon, 1980.

——. *Contribution à l'étude d'un demi-siècle de musique française 1780–1830*. 2 vols. Berne: Peter Lang, 1980.

Monographien moderner Musiker. Ed. by E. Segnitz. 3 vols. Leipzig: Kahnt, 1906–9.

Moser, Hans Joachim. *Carl Maria von Weber: Leben und Werk*. 2nd ed. Leipzig: Breitkopf & Härtel, 1955.

——. *Geschichte der deutschen Musik*. (See general bibliography.)

Moutoz, A. *Rossini et son "Guillaume Tell"*. Paris: Pilon, 1872.

Munter, Friedrich. *Ludwig Thuille*. Munich: Drei Masken, 1923.

Münzer, Georg. *Heinrich Marschner*. Berlin: Harmonie, 1901.

Münzer, Georg, ed. *Das Singebuch des Adam Puschmann, nebst den original-melodien des M. Behaim und Hans Sachs*. Leipzig: Breitkopf & Härtel, 1907.

Myers, Rollo H. *Emmanuel Chabrier and His Circle*. London: Dent, 1969.

——. *Modern French Music*. Oxford: Blackwell, 1971.

Nacamuli, Guido Davide. *Discorso commemorativo su Antonio Smareglia*. Trieste: Guiliana, 1930.

Nardi, Piero. *Vita di Arrigo Boito*. 2nd ed. Milan: Mondadori, 1944.

Neues Beethoven Jahrbuch. Augsburg: B. Filser, 1924–.

Newcomb, Anthony. "The Birth of Music out of the Spirit of Drama." *19th Century Music* (1981), 4:38–66.

Newman, Ernest. *The Life of Richard Wagner*. 4 vols. New York: Knopf, 1933–46; reprint, 1976.

Nicolai, Otto. *Tagebücher*. Ed., with biographical notes, by B. Schröder. Leipzig: Breitkopf & Härtel, 1892. New ed. by Wilhelm Altmann, Regensburg: Bosse, 1937.

Nicolaisen, Jay. *Italian Opera in Transition 1871–1893*. Ann Arbor, Mich.: UMI Research, 1980.

Nietzsche, Friedrich. *Gesammelte Werke*. 23 vols. Munich: Musarion, 1920–29. "Die Geburt der Tragödie," in vol. 3; "Jenseits von Gut und Böse," in vol. 15; "Der Fall Wagner" and "Nietzsche contra Wagner," in vol. 17.

Noske, Frits. "Ritual Scenes in Verdi's Operas." *M&L* (1973), 54:415–39.

Notarnicola, Biagio. *Saverio Mercadante, biografia critica nel 150° dalla nascità (1795–1945)*. Rome: [Poliglotta], 1945.

——. *Saverio Mercadante nella gloria e nella luce*. Rome: Diplomatica, 1948–49.

Odendahl, Laurenz. *Friedrich Heinrich Himmel*. Bonn: Rost, 1917.

Offenbach, Jacques. *Offenbach en Amérique: Notes d'un musicien en voyage*. Paris: Calmann-Lévy, 1877. Trans. as: *Orpheus in America*. Bloomington: Indiana University Press, [1957].

Orrey, L. *Bellini*. London: Dent, 1969.

Osborne, Charles. *The Complete Operas of Puccini*. London: Atheneum, 1982.

Overhoff, Kurt. *Richard Wagners germanisch-christlicher Mythos: Einführungen in den "Ring des Nibelungen" und "Parsifal"*. Dinkelsbühl: Kronos-Verlag, [1955].

Palmer, A. Dean. *Heinrich August Marschner 1795–1861: His Life and Stage Works*. Ann Arbor, Mich: UMI Research 1980.

Pannain, Guido. *Ottocento musicale italiano: Saggi e note*. Milan: Curci, [1952].

Pastura, Francesco. *Bellini secondo la storia*. Parma: Guanda, 1959.

——. *Vincenzo Bellini*. Turin: Società Editrice Internazionale, 1959.

Paul, Charles, B. "Rameau, D'Indy, and French Nationalism." *MQ* (1972), 58:46–56.

Pearson, Hesketh. *Gilbert and Sullivan: A Biography*. New York: Harper, 1935.

Pendle, Karen. *Eugène Scribe and French Opera of the Nineteenth Century*. Ann Arbor, Mich.: UMI Research 1979.

Perris, Arnold. "French Music in the Time of Louis-Philippe: Art as a Substitute for the Heroic Experience." Ph.D. diss., Northwestern University, 1967.

Peteani, Maria von. *Franz Lehár: Seine Musik, sein Leben*. Vienna: Glocken, 1950.

Petzet, Detta and Michael Petzet. *Die Richard Wagner-Bühne, König Ludwigs II*. Munich: Prestel, 1970.

Pierre, Constant. *Les Hymnes et chansons de la révolution: Aperçu général et catalogue avec notes historiques, analytiques et bibliographiques*. Paris: Imprimerie nationale, 1904.

Pilati, Mario. "Francesco Cilèa." *Bollettino bibliografico musicale* (June 1932), 7:5–13. (Followed by unsigned "Bibliografia delle opere musicali di Francesco Cilèa," pp. 14–16.)

Pizzetti, Ildebrando. *La musica italiana dell' Ottocento*. Turin: Palatine, [1947].

Plantinga, Leon. *Romantic Music*. New York: Norton, 1984.

Porges, Heinrich. *Wagner Rehearsing the "Ring"*. Trans. by R. L. Jacobs, Cambridge: Cambridge University Press, 1983.

Porter, Andrew. "Giuseppe Verdi." in *The New Grove Masters of Italian Opera*. New York: Norton, 1983.

Pougin, Arthur. *Adolphe Adam*. Paris: Charpentier, 1877.

——. *F. Halévy, écrivain*. Paris: Clauden, 1865.

——. *Hérold*. Paris: Laurens, [1906].

——. *Méhul*. 2nd ed. Paris: Fischbacher, 1893.

——. *Musiciens français du XVIIIe siècle: Dezèdes*. Paris: Chaix, 1862.

——. "La Première Salle Favart et l'opéra-comique 1801–1838." *Le Ménestrel* (1894), vol. 60, and (1895), vol. 61, passim.

Pretzsch, Paul. *Die Kunst Siegfried Wagners*. Leipzig: Breitkopf & Härtel, 1919.

Primmer, Brian. *The Berlioz Style*. London: Oxford University Press, 1973.

Prod'homme, Jacques Gabriel. *François-Joseph Gossec, 1734–1829: La vie, les oeuvres, l'homme et l'artiste*. Paris: Colombe, 1949.

——. *Gounod*. 2 vols. Paris: Delagrave, [1911].

Radiciotti, Giuseppe. *Gioacchino Rossini*. 3 vols. Tivoli: Chicca, 1927.

Rauh, Adam. *Heinrich Dorn als Opernkomponist*. Neustadt: Schmidt, 1939.

Rayner, Robert Macey. *Wagner and "Die Meistersinger"*. London: Oxford University Press, 1940.

Rebois, Henri. *La Renaissance de Bayreuth de Richard Wagner à son fils Siegfried*. Paris: Fischbacher, 1933.

Reeser, H. Eduard. "Audible Staging: Motion and Gesture in the Music of Richard Wagner." In *Essays on Drama and Theatre: Liber Anicorum Benjamin Hunningher*. Antwerp: Standaard, 1973. 140ff.

Refardt, Edgar. *Hans Huber: Leben und Werk eines Schweizer Musikers*. Zurich: Atlantis-Verlag, [1944].

Reyer, Ernest [Louis Etienne Ernest Rey]. *Notes de musique*. 2nd ed. Paris: Charpentier, 1875.

——. *Quarante Ans de musique*. Paris: Calmann-Lévy, [1909].

Riehl, Wilhelm Heinrich. *Musikalische Charakterköpfe*. 2 vols. Stuttgart: Cotta, 1899.

Rinaldi, Mario. *Musica e verismo*. Rome: De Santis, [1932].

Ringer, Alexander L. "Cherubini's *Médée* and the Spirit of French Revolutionary Opera." In *Essays in Musicology in Honor of Dragan Plamenac*. Ed. by G. Reese and R. J. Snow. Pittsburgh: University of Pittsburgh Press, 1969; reprint, 1977. 281–300.

Robert, Frédéric. *Emmanuel Chabrier: l'homme et son oeuvre*. Paris: Seghers, [1970].

Röder, Erich. *Felix Draeseke: Der Lebens- und Leidensweg eines deutschen Meisters*. 2 vols. Dresden: W. Limpert, [1932–37].

Rodewald, Albert. "The Early Serious Operas of Simone Mayr." Ph.D. diss., University of Pennsylvania. Forthcoming.

Roethe, Gustav. "Zum dramatischen Aufbau der Wagnerschen *Meistersinger*." *Akademie der Wissenschaften, Berlin: Sitzungsberichte* (Jahrgang 1919). 673–708.

Rolland, Romain. *Musiciens d'aujourd'hui*. 5th ed. Paris: Hachette, 1912. Trans. as: *Musicians of Today*. 2nd ed. New York: Holt, 1915.

Roncaglia, Gino. *L'Otello di Giuseppe Verdi*. Florence: Fussi, [1946].

——. "Il 'tema-cardine' nell' opera di Giuseppe Verdi." *RMI* (1943), 57:220–29.

Ruhnke, M. "Die Librettisten des *Fidelio*." In *Opernstudien: Anna Amalie Abert zum 65. Geburtstag*. Ed. by K. Hortschansky. Tutzing: Schneider, 1975. 121–40.

Sachs, Curt. "The Road to Major." *MQ* (1943), 29:381–404.

Saint-Saëns, Charles Camille. *Portraits et souvenirs*. Paris: Société d'édition artistique, [1900]. Trans. as: *Musical Memoirs*. Boston: Small, Maynard, [1919].

Salburg, Edith. *Ludwig Spohr*. Leipzig: Koehler & Amelang, [1936].

Saloman, O. "Aspects of 'Gluckian' Operatic Thought and Practice in France: The Musico-dramatic Vision of Le Sueur and La Cépède (1785–1809) in Relation to Aesthetic and Critical Tradition." Ph.D. diss., Columbia University, 1970.

Sartori, Claudio. *Puccini*. [Milan]: Nuova Accademia, [1958].

Sartori, Claudio, ed. *Giacomo Puccini*. Milan: Ricordi, 1959.

Saunders, William. *Weber*. London: Dent, 1940.

Scarsi, Giovanna. *Rapporto poesia-musica in Arrigo Boito*. Rome: Delia, 1973.

Schafer, R. Murray. *E. T. A. Hoffmann and Music*. Toronto: University of Toronto Press, 1975.

Schelling, Friedrich Wilhelm Joseph von. *Die Philosophie der Kunst*. (*See* Zimmermann, Robert.)

——. *The Philosophy of Art*. Trans. by A. Johnson. London: J. Chapman, 1845.

——. *Sämtliche Werke*. Ed. by K. F. A. Schelling. Stuttgart: Cotta, 1856–1861.

Schemann, Ludwig. *Cherubini*. Stuttgart: Deutsche Verlags-Anstalt, 1925.

Schenk, Erich. *Johann Strauss*. Potsdam: Athenaion, 1940.

Schiedermair, Ludwig. *Beiträge zur Geschichte der Oper um die Wende des 18. und 19. Jahrhunderts*. 2 vols. Leipzig: Breitkopf & Härtel, 1907–10.

——. *Die deutsche Oper*. (See part 2 bibliography.)

Schläder, Jurgen. "*Undine* von E. T. A. Hofmann." In "*Undine*" *auf dem Musiktheater. Zur Entwicklungsgeschichte der deutschen Spieloper*. Bonn and Bad Godesberg, 1979. 232–357.

Schmidt, Gustav Friedrich. *Die frühdeutsche Oper*. (See part 2 bibliography.)

Schmitz, Eugen. "Zur Geschichte des Leitmotivs in der romantischen Oper." *Hochland* (1907), 4:329–43.

Schneider, Louis Hervé. *Charles Lecocq*. Paris: Perrin, 1924.

——. *Massenet*. Paris: L. Carteret, 1908. Rev. ed., Paris: Charpentier, 1926.

Schnoor, Hans. *Weber: Gestalt und Schöpfung*. Dresden: VEB Verlag der Kunst, 1953.

Schopenhauer, Arthur. *Die Welt als Wille und Vorstellung*. Leipzig: Brockhaus, 1819. Trans. as: *The World as Will and Idea*. New York: Scribner, 1950.

Schünemann, Georg. "Mendelssohns Jugendopern." *ZfMw* (1922–23), 5:506–45.

Selden, Margery Stomne. "Cherubini and England." *MQ* (1974), 60:421.

Seré, Octave. *Musiciens français d'aujourd'hui*. Paris: Mercure de France, 1911.

Servières, Georges. *Edouard Lalo*. Paris: H. Laurens, [1925].

——. *Emmanuel Chabrier*. Paris: F. Alcan, 1912.

Slonimsky, Nicolas. *Music Since 1900*. 4th ed. New York: Scribner, 1971.

Smareglia, Ariberto. *Vita ed arte di Antonio Smareglia*. [Lugano: Mazzuconi, 1932.]

Smareglia, Mario, comp. *Antonio Smareglia nella storia del teatro melodrammatico italiano dell' Ottocento attraverso critiche e scritti raccolti da Mario Smareglia*. Pola: Smareglia, [1934].

Smith, Patrick. (See general bibliography.)

Soubies, Albert. *Histoire de l'opéra-comique: La seconde Salle Favart, 1840–[1887]*. 2 vols. Paris: Flammarion, 1892–93.

——. *Histoire du théâtre-lyrique, 1851–1870*. Paris: Fischbacher, 1899.

——. *Le Théâtre-italien de 1801 à 1913*. Paris: Fischbacher, 1913.

Soubies, Albert and Henri de Curzon. *Documents inédits sur le "Faust" de Gounod*. Paris: Fischbacher, 1912.

Specht, Richard. *E. N. v. Rezniček*. Leipzig: Tal, 1923.

——. *Julius Bittner*. Munich: Drei Masken, 1921.

Spitta, Philipp. "Jessonda." In his *Zur Musik*. Berlin: Paetel, 1892. 237–66.

Spohr, Ludwig. *Lebenserinnerungen*. Ed. by Folker Göthel. Tutzing, 1968.

Stebbins, Lucy Poate and Richard Poate Stebbins. *Enchanted Wanderer: The Life of Carl Maria von Weber*. New York: Putnam, [1940].

Stein, Jack M. *Richard Wagner and the Synthesis of the Arts*. Detroit: Wayne State University Press, 1960; reprint, 1973.

Stendhal, pseud. [Marie Henri Beyle]. *Vie de Rossini, suivi des notes d'un dilettante*. Paris: Champion, 1922. Trans. as: *Memoirs of Rossini*. London: Hookham, 1824.

Stomne, Margery. "The French Operas of Luigi Cherubini." Ph.D. diss., Yale University, 1951.

Strobel, Heinrich. "Die Opern von E. N. Méhul." *ZfMw* (1923–24), 6:362–402.

Strunk, Oliver, ed. (See general bibliography.)

Subotnik, Rose R. "Lortzing and the German Romantics: A Dialectical Assessment." *MQ* (1976), 62:241–64.

——. "Popularity and Art in Lortzing's Operas: The Effects of Social Change on a National Operatic Genre." Ph.D. diss., Columbia University, 1973.

Sullivan, Herbert and Newman Flower. *Sir Arthur Sullivan: His Life, Letters, and Diaries*. London: Cassell, [1950].

Suskin, Sylvan. "The Music of Charles-Simon Catel for the Paris Opéra." Ph.D. diss., Yale University, 1970.

Thayer, Alexander Wheelock. *The Life of Ludwig van Beethoven*. Rev. and ed. by Elliot Forbes. 2 vols. Princeton: Princeton University Press, 1967.

Thompson, Herbert. *Wagner and Wagenseil*. London: Oxford University Press, 1927.

Tiersot, Julien. *Un Demi-siècle de musique française*. Paris: Alcan, 1918.

Toye, Francis. *Giuseppe Verdi*. London: Heinemann; New York: Knopf, 1931.

——. *Rossini: A Study in Tragi-Comedy*. New ed. London: Barker, [1954].

——. "Verdi." *PRMA* (1929–30), 56:37–53.

Valentin, Erich. *Hans Sommer: Weg, Werk und Tat eines deutschen Meisters*. Brunswick: Litolff, 1939.

Vallas, Léon. *La Véritable Histoire de César Franck (1822–1890)*. Paris: Flammarion, [1955]. Trans. as: *César Franck*. London: Harrap; New York: Oxford University Press, 1951.

——. *Vincent d'Indy*. 2 vols. Paris: Michel, [1946–50].

[Verdi, Giuseppe.] *I copialettere*. Ed. by G. Cesari and A. Luzio. [Milan: Stucchi Ceretti, 1913.]

Voss, Egon. *Studien zur Instrumentation Richard Wagners*. Regensburg: G. Bosse, 1970.

Wagner, Richard. *The Diary of Richard Wagner 1865–1882*. Annotated by Joachim Bergfeld. Trans. by George Bird. London: Cambridge University Press, 1980.

——. *Gesammelte Schriften*. (See part 3 bibliography.)

——. *Mein Leben: Volks-Ausgabe*. Munich: Bruckmann, 1914.

——. *My Life*. Ed. by Mary Whittall. Trans. by Andrew Grey. Cambridge: Cambridge University Press, 1983.

——. *Opera and Drama*. Trans. by Edwin Evans. New York: C. Scribner, [1913].

——. *Prose Works*. Trans. by William Ashton Ellis. 8 vols. New York: Broude, 1966; reprint, 1979.

——. *Three Wagner Essays: Music of the Future, On Conducting, On Performing Beethoven's Ninth Symphony*. Trans. by Robert L. Jacobs. London: Eulenburg, 1979.

Wagner, Siegfried. *Erinnerungen*. Stuttgart: Engelhorn, 1923.

Wahl, Eduard. *Nicolo Isouard*. Munich: Wolf, 1906.

Walker, Frank. *Hugo Wolf; A Biography*. New York: Knopf, 1952.

——. *The Man Verdi*. New York: Knopf, 1962.

——. "Mercadante and Verdi." *M&L* (1952), 33:311–21: (1953), 34:33–38.

Waltershausen, Hermann Wolfgang Karl Sartorius von. "Zur Dramaturgie des *Fidelio*." *Neues Beethoven Jahrbuch* (1924), 1:142–58.

Warrack, John. *Carl Maria von Weber*. 2nd ed. Cambridge: Cambridge University Press, 1976.

Warrack, John, ed. *Carl Maria von Weber: Critical Writings on Music*. Trans. by M. Cooper. Cambridge: Cambridge University Press, 1981.

Wassermann, Rudolf. *Ludwig Spohr als Opernkomponist*. Munich: Huber, 1909.

Weaver, William, ed. *Verdi: A Documentary Study*. [London]: Thames & Hudson, [1977].

Weber, Carl Maria von. *Sämtliche Schriften*. Ed. by George Kaiser. Berlin and Leipzig: Schuster & Loeffler, 1908.

——. (See also Warrack, ed.)

Weber, Max Maria von. *Carl Maria von Weber*. 3 vols. Leipzig: Keil, 1864–66.

Weber, William. *Music and the Middle Class: The Social Structure of Concert Life in London, Paris, and Vienna*. London: Croom-Helm, 1975.

Weingartner, Felix. *Lebenserinnerungen*. 2 vols. Zurich and Leipzig: Orell Füssli, [1928–29]. Trans. as: *Buffets and Rewards*. London: Hutchinson, [1937].

——. *Die Lehre von der Wiedergeburt des musikalischen Dramas*. Kiel and Leipzig: Lipsius & Fischer, 1895.

Weinstock, Herbert. *Donizetti and the World of Opera in Italy, Paris, and Vienna in the First Half of the Nineteenth Century*. New York: Pantheon, 1964; reprint, 1979.

——. *Rossini: A Biography*. New York: Knopf, 1968.

——. *Vincenzo Bellini: His Life and His Operas*. New York: Knopf, 1971.

Werfel, Franz and Paul Stefan, eds. *Verdi: The Man in His Letters*. Trans. by Edward Downes. New York: Fischer, [1942].

Westernhagen, Curt von. *Richard Wagner: Sein Werk, sein Wesen, sein Welt*. [Zurich]: Atlantis-Verlag, [1956].

——. *Vom Holländer zum Parsifal: Neue Wagner-Studien*. [Freiburg and Zurich]: Atlantis-Verlag, [1962].

——. *Wagner: A Biography*. Trans. by Mary Whittall. 2 vols. Cambridge: Cambridge University Press, 1978.

Williamson, Audrey. *Gilbert & Sullivan Opera: A New Assessment.* 2nd ed. London: Rockliff, 1955.

Willis, Stephen Charles. *Luigi Cherubini: The Middle Years 1795–1815.* Ann Arbor, Mich.: UMI Research, 1975.

Wolzogen, Alfred von and Neuhaus, Hans Paul. *Lebensbilder.* Regensburg: Bosse, 1923.

——. *Thematischer Leitfaden durch die Musik zu Richard Wagners Festspiell "Der Ring des Nibelungen".* Leipzig: Schloemp, 1876.

Zavadini, Guido. *Donizetti: Vita, musiche, epistolario.* Bergamo: Istituto italiano d'arti grafiche, 1948.

Zimmerman, Robert. *Schillings Philosophie der Kunst.* Vienna: K. Gerold, 1875.

Part V: Nationalism and Opera

Abascal Brunet, Manuel. *Apuntes para la historia del teatro en Chile: La zarzuela grande.* 2 vols. Santiago de Chile: Imprenta universitaria, 1940–51.

Abascal Brunet, Manuel and Eugenio Pereira Salas. *Pepe Vila: La zarzuela chica en Chile.* Santiago de Chile: Imprenta universitaria, 1952.

Abraham, Gerald. *Borodin: The Composer and His Music.* London: Reeves, [1927].

——. "The Genesis of *The Bartered Bride*." *M&L* (1947), 28:36–49.

——. "Heine, Queuille, and *William Ratcliff*." In *Musicae Scientiae Collectanea: Festschrift Karl Gustav Fellerer zum 70. Geburtstag.* Ed. by Heinrich Hüschen. Cologne: Volk, 1973.

——. "Moussorgsky's *Boris* and Pushkin's." *M&L* (1945), 26:31–38.

——. *On Russian Music.* New York: Scribner, 1939.

——. "The Operas of Alexei Verstovsky." *19th Century Music* (1984), 7:326–35.

——. "The Operas of Serov." In *Essays Presented to Egon Wellesz.* Ed. by Jack Westrup. Oxford: Clarendon, 1966.

——. "*Pskovityanka*: The Original Version of Rimsky-Korsakov's First Opera." *MQ* (1968), 54:58–73.

——. *Rimsky-Korsakov.* London: Duckworth, [1949].

——. "Satire and Symbolism in *The Golden Cockerel*." *M&L* (1971), 52:46–54.

——. *Studies in Russian Music.* London: Reeves, 1935.

——. "Tchaikovsky's First Opera." In *Festschrift Karl Gustav Fellerer zum 60. Geburtstag.* Ed. by Heinrich Hüschen. Regensburg: Bosse, 1962.

Abrahams, Gerald, ed. *Tchaikovsky: A Symposium.* London: Lindsay Drummond, 1945.

Ábrányi, Kormél. *Erkel Ferenc élete és müködése.* Budapest, 1895.

Acquarone, Francisco. *História da música brasileira.* Rio de Janeiro: Editora Paulo de Azevedo, [n.d.].

Adler, Guido. *Handbuch der Musikgeschichte.* (See general bibliography.)

Akademiia nauk SSSR. Institut istorii iskusstv. *Istoriia russkoi i sovetskoi muzyki.* 4 vols. Moscow: Muzgiz, 1956–60.

——. *Pamiati Glinki, 1857–1957: Issledovaniia i materialy.* Moscow: Akademiia nauk, 1958.

Alexeyev, A. *Anton Rubinshteyn.* Moscow and Leningrad, 1945.

Alley, Rewi. *Peking Opera.* Peking: New World, 1957.

Al'shvang, Arnol'd Aleksandrovich. *P. I. Chaikovskii.* Moscow: Gos. muzykal'noe izd-vo, 1959.

Andrade, Mário de. *Carlos Gomes.* Rio de Janeiro: Pongetti, 1939.

Arkhymovych, Lidiia Borysivna. *Shiakhy rozvytku ukraïns'koï radians'koï opery.* Kiev: Muz. Ukraina, 1970.

——. *Ukraïns'ka klasychna opera.* Kiev: Derzh. vyd-vo obrazotvorchoho mystetstva i muzychnoï lit-ry, 1957.

Arozamena, Jesús María de. *Jesús Guridi: Inventario de su vida y de su música.* Madrid: Nacional, 1967.

Asaf'ev, Boris Vladimirovich. *Izbrannye trudy.* 5 vols. Moscow: Akademiia nauk SSSR, 1952–54.

——. *Russkaia muzyka ot nachala XIX stoletiia.* Moscow and Leningrad: Akademiia nauk SSSR, 1930. Trans. as: *Russian Music from the Beginning of the 19th Century.* Ann Arbor, Mich.: Edwards, [1953].

At'ayan, Rhobert and Matevos Muradian. *Armen Tigranian.* Moscow: Muzyka, 1966.

Ayesterán, Lauro. *Crónica de una temporada musical en el Montevideo de 1830.* Montevideo: Ediciones Ceibo, 1943.

Baker, Jennifer. "Dargomizhsky, Realism, and *The Stone Guest.*" MR (1976), 37:193.

Baqueiro Fóster, Gerónimo. "La Música." In *México: Cincuenta años de revolución.* Mexico City: Fondo de cultura economica, 1963. 4:439–77.

Barenboim, Lev A. *Anton Grigor'evich Rubinshtein.* Leningrad, 1957–62.

Barros Sierra, José. "*Tata Vasco* y su partitura." *Romance* (April [1941]), vol. 2, no. 23.

Baskin, Vladimir S. *A. N. Serov.* Moscow, 1890.

Béhague, Gerard. *Music in Latin America: An Introduction.* Englewood Cliffs, N.J.: Prentice-Hall, 1979.

Benestad, Finn. *Waldemar Thrane: En pionér i norsk musikliv.* Olso: Universitetsforlag, 1961.

Berkov, Pavel Naumovich, ed. *Russkaia komediia i komicheskaia opera XVIII veka.* Moscow: Iskusstvo, 1950.

Berliand-Chernaia, E. S. *Pushkin i Chaikovskii.* [Moscow]: Muzgiz, 1950.

Bernacki, Ludwik. *Teatr, dramat i muzyka za Stanisława Augusta.* 2 vols. Lvov: Zakład narodowy imienia Ossolińskich, 1925.

Bernandt, Grigorii Borisovich. *Slovar' oper.* Moscow: Sovetskii kompozitor, 1962.

Blockx, Frank. *Jan Blockx, 1851–1912.* Brussels: Manteau, [1943].

Boelza, Igor' Fedorovich. *Cheshskaia opernaia klassika.* Moscow: Iskusstvo, 1951.

Boelza, Igor' Fedorovich, ed. *S. V. Rakhmaninov i russkaia opera: Sbornik statei.* Moscow: Vserossiiskoe Teatral'noe Obshchestvo, 1947.

Boladeres Ibern, Guillermo de. *Enrique Granados*. Barcelona: Editorial Arte y letras, [1921].

Bónis, Ferenc. "Die ungarische Opern M. Mosonyi's." *Studia musicologica* (1967), 2:139–88.

———. *Mosonyi Mihály*. Budapest, 1960.

Bordman, Gerald. *American Musical Comedy: From "Adonis" to "Dreamgirls"*. New York: Oxford University Press, 1982.

———. *American Operetta: From "H. M. S. Pinafore" to "Sweeney Todd"*. New York: Oxford University Press, 1981.

Borren, Charles van den. *Peter Benoit*. Antwerp: De Nederlandsche Boekhandel, 1943.

Bottenheim, S. A. M. *De opera in Nederland*. Amsterdam: Van Kampen & Zoon, 1946.

Bowen, Catherine D. and Barbara von Meck. *"Beloved Friend."* New York: Random House, 1937.

Briantseva, Vera. S. *V. Rakhmaninov*. Moscow, 1976.

Brito, J. *Carlos Gomes*. Rio de Janeiro, 1956.

Brown, David. *Glinka: A Biographical and Critical Study*. London: Oxford University Press, 1974.

———. *Tchaikovsky: A Biographical and Critical Study*. Vol. 1, *The Early Years (1840–1874)*. London: Gollancz, 1978.

Brown, Malcolm Hamrick, ed. *Musorgsky: In Memoriam 1881–1981*. Ann Arbor, Mich.: UMI Research, 1982.

———. *Russian and Soviet Music: Essays for Boris Schwarz*. Ann Arbor, Mich.: UMI Research, 1983.

Caamaño, Roberto, ed. *La historia del Teatro Colón*. Buenos Aires: Cinetea, 1969.

Calvocoressi, Michael D. *Glinka*. Paris: Laurens, [1911?].

———. *Modest Mussorgsky: His Life and Works*. Fair Lawn, N.J.: Essential Books, 1956.

Calvocoressi, Michael D. and Gerald Abraham. *Masters of Russian Music*. New York: Knopf, 1936.

Carlberg, Bertil. *Peterson-Berger*. Stockholm: Bonnier, [1950].

Carlyle, Thomas. "The Opera." In *Critical and Miscellaneous Essays*. New York: Scribner, 1904. 4:397–403.

Carson, W. G. B. *St. Louis Goes to the Opera, 1837–1941*. St. Louis: Missouri Historical Society, 1946.

Chaikovskii. (*See* Tchaikovsky.)

Chase, Gilbert. *America's Music: From the Pilgrims to the Present*. New York: McGraw Hill, [1954].

———. *A Guide to the Music of Latin America*. 2nd ed., rev. and enlarged. Washington, D.C.: Pan American Union, 1962.

———. *A The Music of Spain*. (See part 3 bibliography.)

———. "Some Notes on Afro-Cuban Music and Dancing." *Inter-American Monthly* (December 1942), 1:32–33.

Cheshikhin, Vsevolod. *Istoriia russkoi opery (1674–1903)*. St. Petersburg: Jurgenson, 1905.

Chou, Wen-Chung. "To Create a New Chinese Musical Idiom." *The New York Times*, September 9, 1973, p. D23.

Chybiński, A. "Zygmunt Noskowski," *Przegląd Powszechny* (1909), 104:130–36.

Clapham, John. "The Operas of Antonín Dvořák." *PRMA* (1957–58), 84:55–69.

——. *Smetana*. London: Dent, 1972.

Closson, Ernest and Charles Van den Borren, eds. *La Musique en Belgique du Moyen Age á nos jours*. Brussels: La Renaissance du Livre, [1950].

Collet, Henri. *Albéniz et Granados*. New ed. Paris: Libraire Plon, 1948.

Corbet, August, ed. *De vlaamse Muziek sedert Benoit*. Met de medewerking van F. van der Mueren [and others]. Antwerp: Vlaams Economisch Verbond, 1951.

Corrêa de Azevedo, L. H. "Carlos Gomes: Sua verdadeira posição no quadro da ópera italiana no sec. XIX e na evolução da música brasileira." *Boletín latino-americano de música* (1937), 3:83–87.

——. *150 anos de música no Brasil (1800–1950)*. Rio de Janeiro: Libraria José Olympio, 1956.

Cosma, Octavian L. *Opera romînească*. Vol. 2. Bucharest: Editura Muzicala a Uniunii Compozitorilor din R. P. R., 1962.

Cowen, Frederic Hymen. *My Art and My Friends*. London: Arnold, 1913.

Crump, J. I. and William P. Malm, eds. *Chinese and Japanese Music-Dramas*. Ann Arbor, Mich.: University of Michigan Center for Chinese Studies, 1975.

Cui, César. *La Musique en Russie*. Paris: Fischbacher, 1880.

——. *(See also Kyui, Tsezar.)*

Curzon, Henri de. *Felipe Pedrell et "Les Pyrénées"*. Paris: Fischbacher, 1902.

Cvetko, Dragotin. *Davorin Jenko: Doba, življenje, delo*. Ljubljana: Slovenski knjižni zavod, 1955.

Damrosch, Walter. *My Musical Life*. New York: Scribner, 1923.

Davis, Ronald L. "A History of Resident Opera in the American West." Ann Arbor, Mich.: University Microfilms, 1961.

Dianin, Sergei Aleksandrovich. *Borodin: Zhizneopisanie, materialy i dokumenty*. 2nd ed. Moscow: Gos. muzykal'noe izd-vo, 1960.

Dmitriev, A. N. *Muzykal'naia dramaturgiia orkestra M. I. Glinki*. Leningrad, 1957.

Dobrokhotov, B. *A. N. Verstovskii*. Moscow, 1949.

——. *E. I. Fomin*. Moscow and Leningrad, 1949. 2nd ed., 1968.

Dolleris, Ludwig. *Carl Nielsen, en Musikografi*. Odense: Fyns Boghandels Forlag, 1949.

Dovzhensko, Valerian D. *Narysy z istorii ukrains'koï radians'koï muzyky*. Kiev: Derzh. vid-vo obrazotvorchoho mystetstva i muz. lit-ry URSR, 1957. Vol. 1.

Dresden, Sem. *Het muziekleven in Nederland sinds 1880*. Amsterdam: Elsevier, 1923.

Druskin, Mikhail Semenovich. *Ocherki po istorii russkoi muzyki, 1790–1825*. Leningrad: Gos. muzykal'noe izd-vo, 1956.

——. *Voprosy muzykal'noi dramaturgii opery*. Leningrad: Gos. muzykal'noe izd-vo, 1952.

Durnev, I. "Narodnaia osnova *Tarasa Bul'bi.*" *SovM* (1962), no. 10, p. 53.

Engländer, Richard. *Joseph Martin Kraus und die Gustavianische Oper.* Uppsala: Almqvist & Wiksells, 1943.

Eősze, László. *Az opera útja.* Budapest: Zeneműkiadó Vállalat, 1960.

Evans, Edwin. *Tchaikovsky.* New York: Pellegrini & Cudahy, 1949.

Ewen, David. *Complete Book of the American Musical Theater: A Guide to More Than 300 Productions of the American Musical Theater from "The Black Crook" (1866) to the Present, with Plot, Production History, Stars, Composers, Librettists, and Lyricists.* Rev. ed. New York: Holt, [1959].

Fabricius, Johannes. *Carl Nielsen, 1865–1931: A Pictorial Biography.* Copenhagen: Berlingske, 1965.

Ferrari Nicholay, Mauricio. "En torno a *Las Vírgenes del Sol,* la nueva opera argentina." *Estudios* (Buenos Aires), año 29 (1939), 62:29–46.

Findeisen, Nikolai Fedorovich. *A. N. Serov: ego zhizn' i muzykal'naia deiatel'nost'.* St. Petersburg, 1900. 2nd ed., 1904.

——. "The Earliest Russian Operas." *MQ* (1933), 19:331–40.

——. *Ocherki po istorii muzyki v Rossii . . . do kontsa XVIII veka.* Moscow and Leningrad: Gosudarstvennoe izdatel'stvo, Muzsektor, 1928–29.

Fiorda Kelly, Alfredo. *Cronología de las óperas, dramas, líricos, oratorios, himnos, etc. cantados en Buenos Aires.* Buenos Aires: Riera, 1934.

Fischl, Viktor, ed. *Antonin Dvořák, His Achievement.* London: Drummond, [1943].

Foerster, Josef Bohuslav. *Der Pilger: Erinnerungen eines Musikers.* Prague: Artia, 1955.

——. *J. B. Foerster: Jeho životní pouť a tvorba, 1859–1949.* [Prague]: Orbis, [1949].

Fonseco Benevides, Francisco da. *O real theatro de S. Carlos de Lisboa, desde a sua funação em 1793 até á actualidade.* Lisbon: Castro Irmão, [1883].

Freeman, Robert. "The Travels of Partenope." In *Studies in Music History: Essays for Oliver Strunk.* Comp. by Harold Powers, Princeton: Princeton University Press, 1968.

Fuller-Maitland, John Alexander. *The Music of Parry and Stanford.* Cambridge: Heffer, 1934.

Gagey, Edmond McAdoo. *The San Francisco Stage: A History.* New York: Columbia University Press, 1950.

Gaudrimas, Iu. "M. Petrauskas." *Iz istorii litovskoi* (1964), 1:139–75.

Gettel, William D. "Arthur Clifton's *Enterprise.*" *JAMS* (1949) 2:23–35.

Ginzburg, Semen L'vovich, ed. *Russkii muzykal'nyi teatr 1700–1835.* Moscow: Iskusstvo, 1941.

Glinka, Mikhail Ivanovich. *Literaturnoe nasledie.* 2 vols. [Leningrad]: Gos. muzykal'noe izd-vo, 1952–53.

——. *Zapiski.* Leningrad: Gos. muzykal'noe izd-vo, 1953.

Glowacki, John M. "The History of Polish Opera." Ph.D. diss., Boston University, 1952.

Godet, Robert. *En marge de "Boris Godounof": Notes sur les documents iconographiques de l'édition Chester.* Paris: Alcan, 1926.

Gomes Vaz de Carvalho, Itala. *Vida de Carlos Gomes.* 3rd ed. Rio de Janeiro: Noite, 1946.

Gozenpud, Abram Akimovich. *Muzykal'nyi teatr v Rossii: Ot istokov do Glinki.* Leningrad: Gos. muzykal'noe izd-vo, 1959.

——. *N. A. Rimskii-Korsakov: Temy i idei ego opernogo tvorchestva.* Moscow: Gos. muzykal'noe izd-vo, 1957.

——. *Russkii opernyi teatr XIX veka.* 3 vols. Leningrad, 1969–73.

Great Soviet Encyclopedia. Trans. of 3rd ed. of *Bol'shaia Sovetskaia Entsiklopediia.* 32 vols. New York: Macmillan, 1977.

Green, Stanley. *The World of Musical Comedy: The Story of the American Musical Stage As Told Through the Careers of Its Foremost Composers and Lyricists.* New York: Ziff-Davis, [1960].

Greene, Harry Plunket. *Charles Villiers Stanford.* London: Arnold, [1935].

Habets, Alfred. *Alexandre Borodine, d'après la biographie et la correspondance publiées par M. Wladimir Stassof.* Paris: Fischbacher, 1893. Trans. as: *Borodin and Liszt.* London: Digby, Long, [1895].

Hamm, Charles. *Music in the New World.* New York: Norton, 1983.

Handbook of Latin American Studies. Cambridge: Harvard University Press, 1936–.

Hanson, Lawrence and Elisabeth Hanson. *Tchaikovsky: The Man Behind the Music.* New York: Dodd, Mead, 1966.

Helfert, Vladimír. *Geschichte der Musik in der tschechoslovakischen Republik.* Prague: Orbis-Verlag, 1936.

Hipsher, Edward E. *American Opera and Its Composers.* Philadelphia: T. Presser, [1927].

Hitchcock, H. Wiley. *Music in the United States: An Historical Introduction.* 2nd ed. Englewood Cliffs, N.J.: Prentice-Hall, 1974.

Hitchcock, H. Wiley, ed. *Earlier American Music Series.* New York: Da Capo, 1972–.

Hnilič^ka, Alois. *Kontury vývoje hudby poklasické v Čechách.* Prague, 1935.

Hoffmann-Erbrecht, Lothar. "Grundlagen der Melodiebildung bei Mussorgski." In *Bericht über den internationalen musikwissenschaftlichen Kongress Bamberg 1953.* Kassel and Basel: Bärenreiter, [1954]. 292–66.

Hofmann, Rostislav. *Rimski-Korsakov: Sa vie, son oeuvre.* Paris: Flammarion, 1958.

Holbrooke, Josef, ed. *Joseph Holbrooke: Various Appreciations by Many Authors.* London: R. Carte, 1937.

Hostinský, Otakar. *Die Musik in Böhmen.* Vienna: Hof- und Staatsdruckerei, 1894.

Howard, John Tasker. *Our American Music: Three Hundred Years of It.* 3rd ed. New York: Crowell, [1954].

Hoza, Stefan. *Opera na Slovensku.* 2 vols. Martin, Czechoslovakia: Osveta, 1953–54.

Hudec, Vladimir. *Zdeněk Fibich.* Prague: Academia, 1971.

Iakovlev, Vasilii Vasil'evich. *Pushkin i muzyka.* Moscow: Gos. muzykal'noe izd-vo, 1949.

Iarustovskii, B. M. *Dramaturgiia russkoi opernoi klassiki.* Moscow: Muzgiz, 1953. Trans. as: *Die Dramaturgie der klassischen russichen Oper.* Berlin: Henschelverlag, 1957.

——. *Opernaia dramaturgiia Chaikovskogo.* Moscow: Gos. muz. izd-vo, 1947.

Iastrebtsev, Vasilii Vasil'evich. *Nikolai Andreevich Rimskii-Korsakov: Vospominaniia, 1886–1908.* [Leningrad: Gos. muzykal'noe izd-vo, 1959.]

Iglesias, Ignasi. *Enric Morera: Estudi biografie.* Barcelona: Artis, [1921].

Istel, Edgar. "Felipe Pedrell." *MQ* (1925), 11:164–91.

Jachimecki, Zdzisław. *Historia muzyki polskiej w zarysie.* Warsaw: Gebethner i Wolff, [1920].

——. *Muzyka polska w rozwoju historycznym.* 2 vols. Cracow: S. Kamiński, 1948–1951.

——. *Stanisław Moniuszko.* Warsaw: Gebethner i Wolff, 1921.

——. *Władysław Żeleński.* Cracow: Polskie Wyd. Muzyczne, 1952.

Kaczyński, T. *Dzieje sceniczne "Halki" Stanislawa Moniuszki.* Cracow, 1969.

Karasowski, Maurycy. "Jan Stefani." *Ruch Muzyczny* (1857), pp. 210–14, 217–19, 226–29, 237–39.

——. "Moniuszko jako kompozytor dramatyczny." *Biblioteka Warszawska* (1861), 82:261–81.

——. *Rys historyczny opery polskiej, poprzedzony szczegółowym poglądem na dzieje muzyki dramatycznej powszechnej.* Warsaw: Glücksberg, 1859.

Karlinsky, Simon. "Russian Comic Opera in the Age of Catherine the Great." *19th Century Music* (1984), 7:318–25.

Karysheva, T. *P. P. Sokal'skii: Narys pro zhyttia i tvorchist'.* Kiev: Derzh. vid-vo obrazotvorchoho mystetstva i muzychnoï lit-ri URSR, 1959.

Kaufmann, L. S. *S. S. Gulak-Artemovsky.* Kiev, 1962.

Keldysh, Iurii Vsevolodovich. *Istoriia russkoi muzyki.* Vols. 2 and 3. Moscow: Muzgiz, 1947 and 1954.

Kelly, Alfredo. (*See* Fiorda Kelly, Alfredo.)

Khubov, G. *Zhizn' A. Serova.* Moscow and Leningrad, 1950.

Kindem, Ingeborg Eckhoff. *Den norske operas historie.* Olso: Mortensen, 1941.

Kmen, Henry. *Music in New Orleans.* Baton Rouge: Louisiana State University Press, 1966.

Kolodin, Irving. *The Story of the Metropolitan Opera, 1883–1950: A Candid History.* New York: Knopf, 1953.

Krehbiel, Henry. *Chapters of Opera.* New York: Holt, 1909; reprint, New York: Da Capo, 1980.

Kuss, Malena. "*Huemac* by Pascual de Rogatis: Native Identity in the Argentine Lyric Theatre." In *Yearbook for Inter-American Musical Research.* Austin: University of Texas, 1974. 10:68–87.

——. *Latin American Music: An Annotated Bibliography of Reference Sources and Research Materials.* Paris: UNESCO, 1984.

——. "Nativistic Strains in Argentine Operas Premiered at the Teatro Colón (1908–1972)." Ph.D. diss., University of California at Los Angeles, 1976.

Kyui, Tsezar, *Izbrannye stat'i.* Leningrad: Gos. muzykal'noe izd-vo, 1952.

Laplane, Gabriel. *Albéniz: Sa vie, son oeuvre*. [N.p.]: Editions du Milieu du Monde, 1956.

Large, Brian. *Smetana*. New York: Praeger, 1970.

Layton, Robert. *Berwald*. London: Publ. under the auspices of the Anglo-Swedish Literary Foundation [by] Blond, [1959].

Lehmann, Dieter. *Russlands Oper und Singspiel in der zweiten Hälfte des 18. Jahrhunderts*. Leipzig: Breitkopf & Härtel, 1958.

Leyda, Jay and Sergei Bertensson, eds. *The Musorgsky Reader: The Life of Modeste Petrovich Musorgsky in Letters and Documents*. New York: Norton, 1947.

Lieberman, Fredric. *Chinese Music: An Annotated Bibliography*. 2nd ed. New York: Garland, 1979.

Lindström, Sven. "Vårt första nationalla Sångspel." *STM* (1942), 24:68–83.

Livanova, Tamara Nikolaevna. *Ocherki i materialy po istorii russkoi muzykal'noi kul'tury*. Moscow: Iskusstvo, 1938.

——. *Russkaia muzykal'naia kul'tura XVIII veka v ee sviaziakh s literaturoi, teatrom i bytom*. 2 vols. Moscow: Gos. muzykal'noe izd-vo, 1952–53.

——. *Stasov i russkaia klassicheskaia opera*. Moscow: Gos. muzykal'noe izd-vo, 1957.

Livanova, Tamara Nikolaevna, ed. *M. I. Glinka: Sbornik materialov i statei*. Moscow: Gos. muzykal'noe izd-vo, 1950.

Lloyd-Jones, David. *Boris Godunov: Critical Commentary*. London, 1975.

Loewenberg, Alfred, comp. (See general bibliography.)

Longyear, Rey M. and Katherine E. Longyear. "Henry F. Gilbert's Unfinished *Uncle Remus* Opera." In *Yearbook for Inter-American Musical Research*. Austin: University of Texas, 1974. 10:50–67.

Lowe, George. *Josef Holbrooke and His Work*. London: Kegan Paul; New York: Dutton, 1920.

Mackerras, Colin. "Chinese Opera After the Cultural Revolution (1970–1972)." *China Quarterly* (1973), 55:478–510.

——. *The Performing Arts in Contemporary China*. London: Routledge & Kegan Paul, 1981.

——. *The Rise of the Peking Opera (1770–1870): Social Aspects of the Theatre in Manchu China*. Oxford: Clarendon, 1972.

Mackerras, Colin, ed. *Chinese Theater from Its Origins to the Present Day*. Honolulu: University of Hawaii Press, 1983.

Mapleson, James Henry. *The Mapleson Memoirs, 1848–1888*. 2nd ed. 2 vols. London: Remington, 1888.

Marchant, Annie d'Armond. "Carlos Gomes, Great Brazilian Composer." *Bulletin of the Pan American Union* (1936), 70:767–76.

Maria y Campos, Armando de. *Una temporada de ópera italiana en Oaxaca*. Mexico City: Ediciónes populares, 1939.

Mariz, Vasco. *Heitor Villa-Lobos: Life and Work of the Brazilian Composer*. Washington, D.C.: Brazilian American Cultural Institute, 1970. 5th ed., Rio de Janeiro, 1977.

Mates, Julian. *The American Musical Stage Before 1800.* New Brunswick, N.J.: Rutgers University Press, [1962].

Mattfeld, Julius. *A Hundred Years of Grand Opera in New York:, 1825–1925: A Record of Performance.* New York: The New York Public Library, 1927.

Meyer, Torben. *Carl Neilsen, Kunstneren og Mennesket: En Biografi.* 2 vols. Copenhagen: Nyt Nordisk, 1947–48.

Michałowski, Kornel. *Opery polskie.* [Cracow]: Polskie Wydawnictwo Muzyczne, [1954].

Mindlin, Roger. *Die Zarzuela; das spanische Singspiel im 19. und 20. Jahrhundert.* Zurich: Atlantis, 1965.

Moberg, Carl Allan. "Essais d'opéras en Suède, sous Charles XII." In *Mélanges de musicologie.* Paris: Droz, 1933. 123–32.

Montagu-Nathan, Montagu. *Glinka.* London: Constable, 1916.

Moore, Edward C. *Forty Years of Opera in Chicago.* New York: Liveright, 1930.

Mooser, Robert Aloys. *Opéras, intermezzos, ballets, cantates, oratorios joués en Russie durant le 18e siècle. Avec l'indication des oeuvres de compositeurs russes parues en Occident, à la même époque. Essai d'un répertoire alphabétique et chronologique.* 2nd ed. Geneva: Kistner; Monaco: Union Européene d'Editions, 1955.

Muñoz, Matilde. *Historia de la zarzuela y el género chico.* Madrid: Editorial Tesoro, [1946].

Muricy, Andrade. *Villa-Lobos: Una Interpretação.* Rio de Janeiro: Serviço de Documentação do MEC, 1961.

Muzyka: Monografje muzyczne. Ed. by Mateusz Glinski. Vol. 10 (incorrectly called vol. 9), *Opera: Monografia zbiorowa.* Warsaw, [1934].

Muzykal'noe nasledie Chiakovskogo: Iz istorii ego proizvedenii. Moscow: Akademiia nauk SSSR, 1958.

Nejedlý, Zdeněk. *Bedřich Smetana.* 2nd ed. 7 vols. [Prague]: Orbis, 1950–54.

——. *Dějiny opery Národníko divadla.* 2nd ed. [Prague]: Práce, 1949.

——. *Zpěvohry Smetanovy.* 2nd ed. Prague: Státní nakl. politické literatury, 1954.

Newmarch, Rosa. *The Music of Czechoslovakia.* 2nd ed. New York: J. & J. Harper Editions, 1969.

——. *The Russian Opera.* New York: Dutton, [1914]; reprint, 1972.

Niewiadomski, S. "*Manru* [of Paderewski]." *Biblioteka Warszawska* (1901), 243:87–104.

——. "W. Żeleński i jego *Goplana.*" *EMTA* (1897), p. 64.

——. "Z przeszłošci opery polskiej." *Muzyka* (1931), pp. 65–68.

Norris, Geoffrey. *Rakhmaninov.* London: Dent, 1976.

——. "Rakhmaninov's Student Opera." *MQ* (1973), 59:441.

Nowak-Romanowicz, Alina. *Jósef Elsner.* Cracow: Polskie Wydawn ictwo Muzyczne, [1957].

Olkhovsky, Yuri. *Vladimir Stasov and Russian National Culture.* Ann Arbor, Mich.: UMI Research, 1983.

Opieński, Henryk. *La Musique polonaise.* Paris: Gebethner & Woldd, 1929.

———. "Les Premiers Opéras polonais considérés dans leur rapports avec la musique de Chopin." *RdM* (1929), 10:92–98.

———. *Stanisław Moniuszko, życie i dzieła.* Lvov and Poznan: Nakładem wydawn. polskiego, 1924.

Orlova, Alexandra. *Musorgsky's Days and Works: A biography in Documents.* Trans. by Roy J. Guenther. Ann Arbor, Mich.: UMI Research, 1983.

Paderewski, I. J. "*Konrad Wallenrod.*" *Tygodnik Illustrowany* (1885), 1:175–76.

Pedrell, Felipe. *Cancionero musical.* (See part 3 bibliography.)

———. *Jornadas de arte (1841–1891).* Paris: Ollendorf, 1911.

———. *Jornadas postreras.* Valls: Castells, 1922.

———. *Por neustra música: Algunas observaciones sobre la magna cuestión de una escuela lírico nacional.* Barcelona: Heurich, 1891.

Pekelis, Mikhail Samoilovich. *A. S. Dargomyzhskii i ego okruzhenie.* 2 vols. Moscow, 1966–73.

———. *Dargomyzhskii i narodnaia pesnia.* Moscow: Muzgiz, 1951.

Peña y Goñi, Antonio. *España, desde la ópera a la zarzuela.* Madrid: Alianza Editorial, 1967.

———. *La ópera española y la música dramática en España en el siglo XIX.* Madrid: El Liberal, 1881.

Peppercorn, Lisa M. *Heitor Villa-Lobos: Leben und Werk des brasilianischen Komponisten.* Zurich: Atlantis, 1972.

Pian, Rulan Chao. "Aria Structural Patterns in the Peking Opera." In Crump and Malm, eds., *Chinese and Japanese Music-Dramas,* pp. 65–98.

Pomorska, Hanna. *Karol Kurpiński.* [Warsaw]: Czytelnik, 1948.

Pozniak, W. "Niezrealizowane projekty operowe Moniuszki," *Kwartalnik Muzyczny* (1948), nos. 21–22, pp. 234–51.

Pražák, Přemysl. *Smetanovy zpěvohry.* 4 vols. Prague: Za svobodu, 1948.

Prosnak, J. *Stanisław Moniuszko.* Cracow, 1964. 2nd ed., 1969.

Protopopov, Vladimir Vasil'evich. "*Ivan Susanin*" *Glinki: Muzykal'no-teoreticheskoe issledovanie.* Moscow: Izd-vo Akademii nauk SSSR, 1961.

Rabinovich, Aleksandr Semenovich. *Russkaia opera do Glinki.* [Moscow]: Muzgiz, 1948.

Reeser, Eduard. *Een eeuw Nederlandse muziek [1815–1915].* Amsterdam: Querido, 1950.

Reiff, A. "Ein Katalog zu den Werken von Felipe Pedrell." *AfMw* (1921), 3:86–97.

Reiss, J[osef] W[ładysław]. "Koryfeusz muzyki polskiej, Karol Kurpiński." *Wiedza i Zycie* (1949), pp. 1061–69.

———. *Muzyka w Krakowie w XIX wieku.* Cracow: Anczyc, 1931.

———. *Najpiękniejsza ze wszystkich jest muzyka polska.* Cracow: Giescczykiewicz, 1946; Warsaw: Polskie Wydawnictwo Muzyczne, [1958].

Rektorys, Artuš, ed. *Zdeněk Fibich: Sborník dokumentů a studií o jeho životé a díle.* 2 vols. [Prague]: Orbis, 1951–52.

Renouf, Renée. *Pear Garden in the West.* San Francisco: Strawberry Hill, 1984.

Riddle, Ronald. *Flying Dragons, Flowing Streams: Music in the Life of San Francisco's Chinese.* Westport, Conn.: Greenwood, 1983.

Ridenour, Robert C. *Nationalism, Modernism, and Personal Rivalry in Nineteenth-Century Russian Music.* Ann Arbor, Mich.: UMI Research, 1981.

Rimskii-Korsakov, Andrei Nikolaevich. *N. A. Rimskii-Korsakov : Zhizn' i tvorchestvo.* 5 vols. Moscow: Ogiz-Muzgiz, 1933–46.

Rimskii-Korsakov, Nikolai Andreevich. *Letopis' moei muzykal'noi zhizni.* 7th ed. Moscow: Gos. muzykal'noe izd-vo, 1955. 5th ed. (1935) trans. as: *My Musical Life.* New York, 1942.

Ritter, Frédéric Louis. *Music in America.* New York: Scribner, 1883.

Robertson, Alec. *Dvořák.* New York: Pellegrini & Cudahy, 1949.

Romero, Jesús C. *La ópera en Yucatán.* Mexico City: Ediciones Guión de América, 1947.

Rudziński, Witold. *Stanisław Moniuszko.* Cracow, 1954. 4th ed., 1972.

——. "Szkice Moniuszkowskie. IV. Śpiewak domowy." *Muzyka* (1952), no. 9/10 (30–31), pp. 65–76.

Sáez, Antonia. *El teatro en Puerto Rico (notas para su historia).* [San Juan]: Editorial Universitaria, Universidad de Puerto Rico, 1950.

Salas, Carlos and Eduardo Feo Calcaño. *Sesquicentenario de la ópera en Caracas: Relato histórico de ciento cincuenta años de ópera 1808–1958.* Caracas: Vargas, 1960.

Salazar, Adolfo. *La música contemporánea en España.* Madrid: Ediciones La Nave, [1930].

Salcedo, Angel S. *Francisco Asenjo Barbieri: su vida y su obra.* Madrid: Biblioteca Musicos Españoles, [ca. 1920].

——. *Tomás Bretón.* Madrid: Imprenta clasica española, 1924.

Saldívar, Gabriel. *História de la música en México (épocas precortesiana y colonial).* Mexico City: Cultura, 1934.

Schönfelder, Gerd. *Die Musik der Peking-Oper.* Leipzig: Deutscher Verlag für Musik, 1972.

Scott, A. C. *The Classical Theatre of China.* New York: Macmillan, 1957.

Seaman, Gerald. *History of Russian Music.* New York: Praeger, 1967.

——. "The National Element in Early Russian Opera, 1779–1800." *M&L* (1961), 42:252–62.

Seidl, Robert. *Carlos Gomes.* Rio de Janeiro: [Imprensa moderna], 1935.

Seilhamer, George Overcash. *History of the American Theatre.* 3 vols. Philadelphia: Globe, 1888–91.

Selden, Margery Stomne. "Early Roots of Russian Opera." *JAMS* (1962), 15:206–11; see also ibid. (1963), 16:257–60.

Seroff, Victor Ilyitch. *The Mighty Five: The Cradle of Russian National Music.* Freeport, N.Y.: Books for Libraries Press, 1970.

——. *Modest Musorgsky.* New York: Funk & Wagnalls, 1968.

Serov, Aleksandr Nikolaevich. *"Rusalka," opera A. S. Dargomyzhskogo.* Moscow: Gos. muzykal'noe izd-vo, 1953.

Sixto Prieto, Juan. "El Perú en la música escénica." *Fénix* (1953), no. 9, pp. 278–351.

Skalya-Starytsky, M. "Mykola Lysenko 1842–1962." Manuscript (1962) in the British Museum Library, with English translation.

Slonimsky, Nicolas. *Music of Latin America.* New York: Crowell, 1945.

Smetana, Bedřich. *Smetana in Briefen und Erinnerungen.* Ed. František Bartoš. Prague: Artia, 1954. Trans. as: *Letters and Reminiscences.* Prague: Artia, 1955.

Smith, Cecil. *Musical Comedy in America.* New York: Theatre Arts, 1950.

Smith, Edwin. "William Henry Fry's *Leonora.*" D.M.A. diss., University of Kentucky, 1974.

Sonneck, Oscar George Theodore. *A Bibliography of Early Secular American Music (Eighteenth Century).* Washington, D.C.: Library of Congress, Music Division, 1945.

——. *Early Concert Life in America.* Leipzig: Breitkopf & Härtel, 1907.

——. *Early Opera in America.* New York: G. Schirmer, 1915; reprint, New York: Blom, 1963.

——. *Francis Hopkinson, the First American Poet-Composer.* Washington, D.C.: Printed for the Author by H. L. McQueen, 1905.

Soubies, Albert. *Histoire de la musique en Bohême.* Paris: Flammarion, 1898.

Šourek, Otakar. *Antonín Dvořák: His Life and Works.* Prague: Orbis, 1952; New York: Philosophical Library, [1954].

——. *Život a dílo Antonína Dvořáka.* 4 vols. Prague: Hudební matice umělecké besedy, 1922–23.

Sovetskaia muzyka. [Moscow]: Gos. muzykal'noe izd-vo, 1933– .

Stasov, Vladimir Vasil'evich. *Izbrannye stat'i o M. I. Glinke.* Moscow: Gos. muzykal'noe izd-vo, 1955.

——. *Mikhail Ivanovich Glinka.* Moscow: Gos. muzykal'noe izd-vo, 1953.

——. *Selected Essays.* Trans. by Florence Jones. New York: Da Capo, 1968.

Štěpán, Václav. *Novák a Suk.* Prague: Hudební matice umělecké besedy, 1945.

Stevenson, Robert. *Foundations of New World Opera.* Lima: Ediciones Cultura, 1973.

——. *Music in Mexico: A Historical Survey.* New York: Crowell, [1952].

——. *The Music of Peru: Aboriginal and Viceroyal Epochs.* Washington, D.C.: Pan American Union, [1960].

——. "Opera Beginnings in the New World." *MQ* (1959), 45:8–25.

Stromenger, K. "Jan Stefani." *Lódź Teatralna* (1946–47) no. 3, pp. 15–19.

Subirá, José. *Enrique Granados.* Madrid: [Ascasíbar], 1926.

——. "Felipe Pedrell y el teatro musical español," *Anuario musical* (1972), 27: 61–76.

——. *Historia y anecdotario del Teatro Real.* Madrid: Editorial Plus Ultra, [1949].

——. *El Teatro del Real Palacio (1849–1851), con un bosquejo preliminar sobre la música palatina desde Felipe V hasta Isabel II.* Madrid: Consejo superior de investigaciones científicas, Instituto español de musicología, 1950.

Sundström, Einar. "Franz Berwalds Operor." *STM* (1947), 29:16–62.

Suomalainen, Yrjö. *Oskar Merikanto: Suomen kotien jäveltäjä.* Helsinki: Kustannusosakeyhtiö Otava, [1950].

Sutkowski, Adam. *Zygmunt Noskowski.* Cracow: Polskie Wydawnictwo Muzyczne, [1957].

Szabolcsi, Bence. *Bausteine zu einer Geschichte der Melodie.* Budapest: Corviva, [1959].

Szopski, Felicjan. *Władysław Żeleński.* Warsaw: Gebethner i Wolff, 1928.

Taruskin, Richard. *Opera and Drama in Russia As Preached and Practiced in the 1860s.* Ann Arbor, Mich.: UMI Research, 1982.

Taylor, Philip. *Gogolian Interludes: Gogol's Story "Christmas Eve" as the Subject of the Operas by Tchaikovsky and Rimsky-Korsakov.* London: Collets, 1984.

Tchaikovsky, Modest Ilich. *The Life and Letters of Peter Ilich Tchaikovsky.* Ed. and trans. by Rosa Newmarch. London: Lane, 1906.

Tchaikovsky, Peter Ilich. *Diaries.* Trans. by Wladimir Lakond [pseud.]. New York: Norton, 1945.

Tebaldini, Giovanni. "Felipe Pedrell ed il dramma lirico spagnuolo." *RMI* (1897), 4:267–98, 494–524. Also published separately: Turin: Bocca, 1897.

Temperley, Nicholas. *Music in Britain: The Romantic Age, 1800–1914.* London: Athlone, 1981.

Teuber, Oscar. *Geschichte des Prager Theaters.* 3 vols. Prague: Haase, 1883–87.

Theatro comico portuguez, ou Collecção das operas portuguezas, que se representárão na casa do theatro público do Bairro Alto di Lisboa. 4 vols. Lisbon: S. T. Ferreira, 1787–92.

Tigranov, Georgii. *Aleksandr Spendiarov.* Moscow, 1959. 2nd ed., 1971.

———. *Armianskii muzykal'nyi teatr.* 2 vols. Erevan: Armianskoe gos. izd-vo, 1956, 1960. Vol. 2 has imprint: Erevan: Aipetrat, 1960.

Tolón, Edwin T. and Jorge A. González. *Operas cubanas y sus autores.* Havana: [Imprenta Ucar, Garcia], 1943.

Torrejón y Velasco, Tomás. *La púrpura de la rosa.* Ed. by R. L. Stevenson. Lima, 1976.

Trend, John Brande. *A Picture of Modern Spain.* New York: Houghton Mifflin, 1921. *La Trilogía "Los Pireneos" y la crítica.* Barcelona: Oliva, 1901.

Tsukkerman, Viktor Abramovich. "*Sadko": Opera-bylina N. A. Rimskogo-Korsakovo.* Moscow: Muzgiz, 1936.

Upton, William Treat. *William Henry Fry: American Journalist and Composer-Critic.* New York: Crowell, 1954.

USSR. Tsentral'nyi gosudarstvennyi literaturnyi arkhiv. *N. A. Rimskii-Korsakov: Sbornik dokumentov.* Moscow: Gos. muzykal'noe izd-vo, 1951.

Vieira, Ernesto. *Diccionario biographico de musicos portuguezes: Historia e bibliographia da musica em Portugal.* 2 vols. Lisbon: Moreira & Penheiro, 1900.

Virga, Patricia. *The American Opera to 1790.* Ann Arbor, Mich.: UMI Research, 1982.

Walicki, Aleksandr. *Stanisław Moniuszko.* Warsaw: Gebethnera i Wolffa, 1873.

Walker, Ernest. (See general bibliography).

Warrach, John. *Tchaikovsky.* London: Scribner's, 1973.

Wegelin, Oscar. *Early American Plays, 1714–1830.* New York: Dunlap Society, 1900.

———. *Micah Hawkins and the Saw-Mill: A Sketch of the First Successful American Opera and Its Author.* New York: Privately printed, 1917.

White, Eric Walter. (See part 2 bibliography.)

Wierzbicka, Karyna, Żródła do historii teatru warszawskiego od roku 1762 do roku 1833. Warsaw: Zakład narodowy imienia Ossolińskich, 1951.

Yang, Richard R. S. "The Reform of Peking Opera Under the Communists." *China Quarterly* (1962), 11:124–39.

Yellin, Victor. "The Life and Operatic Works of George Whitefield Chadwick." Ph.D. diss., Harvard University, 1957.

Yung, Bell. "The Music of Cantonese Opera." Ph.D. diss., Harvard University, 1976.

Zagiba, Franz. *Tschaikovskij: Leben und Werk.* Zurich, Leipzig, Vienna: Amalthea-Verlag, [1953].

Zedong, Mao. "Talks at the Yenan Forum on Literature and Art." In *Selected Readings from the Works of Mao Tse-tung.* Peking: Foreign Language Press, 1971. 250–86.

Zetowski, S. "Teoria polskiej opery narodowej z końca XVIII i początku XIX wieku." *Muzyka Polska* (1937), pp. 274–80.

Zichy, Géza, *Aus meinem Leben.* 2 vols. Stuttgart: Deutsche Verlags-Anstalt, 1911–13.

Part VI: The Twentieth Century

Abbate, Carolyn. "*Tristan* in the Composition of *Pelléas.*" *19th Century Music* (1981), 5:117–41.

Abendroth, Walter. *Hans Pfitzner.* Munich: Lagen & Muller, 1935.

Abraham, Gerald. *Eight Soviet Composers.* London: Oxford University Press, [1943], reprint, 1970.

———. *A Hundred Years of Music.* (See part 4 bibliography.)

———. "Realism in Janáček's Operas." In his *Slavonic and Romantic Music.* 83–98.

———. *Slavonic and Romantic Music.* New York: St. Martin's, 1968.

Ackere, Jules van. *Maurice Ravel.* [Brussels]: Elsevier, [1957].

———. "*Pelléas et Mélisande,*" ou la recontre miraculeuse d'une poésie et d'une musique. Brussels: Librairie Encyclopédique, 1952.

Adams, Stephen. *R. Murray Schafer.* Toronto: University of Toronto Press, 1983.

Aiken, R. "Karl-Birger Blomdahl." Ph.D. diss., University of Cincinnati, 1968.

Altman, George et al., eds. *Theater Pictorial.* Berkeley and Los Angeles: University of California Press, 1953.

American Composers Alliance Bulletin. New York: 1938, 1952–.

Antcliffe, Herbert. "A British School of Music-Drama: The Work of Rutland Boughton," *MQ* (1918), 4:117–27.

Antheil, George. "Opera—A Way Out," *MMus* (January–February 1934), 9:89–94.

——. "Wanted—Opera by and for Americans," *MMus* (June–July 1930), 7:11–16.

Ardoin, John. *The Stages of Menotti.* Garden City, N.Y.: Doubleday, 1985.

Armitage, Merle. *George Gershwin: Man and Legend.* New York: Duell, Sloan & Pearce, [1958].

Austin, William. *Music in the Twentieth Century from Debussy Through Stravinsky.* New York: Norton, 1966.

Avant-scène opéra (1977), 9:1–145 (special issue on *Pelléas et Mélisande*).

Babbitt, Milton. "An Introduction to the Music [of Schoenberg's *Moses und Aron*]." In brochure accompanying the recording of the opera, Columbia K 3 L–241.

Bahle, Julius. *Hans Pfitzner und der geniale Mensch: Eine psychologische Kulturkritik.* Constance: Weller, [1949].

Beck, Georges. *Darius Milhaud.* Paris: Heugel, 1949. Supplement: *Catalogue chronologique complet de son oeuvre.* Paris: Heugel, [1956].

Beer, Otto Fritz. "Egon Wellesz und die Oper." *Die Musik* (1931), 23:909–12.

Bekker, Paul. *Franz Schreker: Studie zur Kritik der modernen Oper.* Berlin: Schuster & Loeffler, 1919.

——. *Klang und Eros.* (See general bibliography.)

Béla Bartók: A Memorial Review Including Articles on His Life and Works. Reprinted from *Tempo,* New York: Boosey & Hawkes, [1950].

Bell, Carla Huston. *Olivier Messiaen.* Boston: Twayne, 1984.

Berg, Alban. "A Word about *Wozzeck.*" *MMus* (1927), 5:22–24.

Berger, Arthur. *Aaron Copland.* New York: Oxford University Press, 1953.

Berrsche, Alexander. *Kurze Einführung in Hans Pfitzners Musikdrama "Der arme Heinrich".* Leipzig, [1910].

Berthoud, Paul B. *The Musical Works of Dr. Henry Hadley.* New York: National Association for American Composers and Conductors, 1942.

Blacher, Boris. "Neuland Rhythmus." In *Das musikalische Selbstportrait.* Ed. by J. Müller-Marein and H. Reinhardt. Hamburg, 1963.

Blumenfeld, Harold. "Hugo Weisgall's 66th Birthday and the new *Gardens of Adonis.*" *Perspectives of New Music* (Spring–Summer 1979), pp. 156–65.

Boardman, Herbert Russell. *Henry Hadley, Ambassador of Harmony.* Atlanta: Banner Press of Emory University, [1932].

Bonajuti Tarquini, Vittoria. *Riccardo Zandonai, nel ricordo dei suoi intimi.* Milan: Ricordi, 1951.

Bontempelli, Massimo, *Gian Francesco Malipiero.* Milan: Bompiani, [1942].

Boughton, Rutland. *The Death and Resurrection of the Music Festival.* London: Reeves, [1913].

——. *The Glastonbury Festival Movement.* London: [Somerset], 1922.

——. *Music Drama of the Future: "Uther and Igraine", Choral Drama . . . with Essays by the Collaborators.* London: Reeves, 1911.

Bowen, Meirion. *Michael Tippett*. London: Robson, 1982.

Boyd, Malcolm. *"The Beach of Falesá."* MT (1974), 115:207.

Bradshaw, S. "The Music of Elisabeth Lutyens." MT (1971), 112:653.

Brecht, Bertolt. "Two Essays." *The Score* (July 1958), no. 23, pp. 14–26.

Brett, Philip. *"Peter Grimes".* Cambridge: Cambridge University Press, 1983.

Bril, F. Yvonne. *Henri Sauguet*. Paris: Seghers, 1967.

Briner, Andres. "Eine Bekenntnisoper Paul Hindemith: Zu seiner oper *Die Harmonie der Welt*." SchwM (1959), 99:1–5, 50–56.

——. *Paul Hindemith*. Zurich: Atlantis, 1971.

Britten, Benjamin and others. *"The Rape of Lucretia"*: A Symposium by Benjamin Britten, Eric Crozier, John Piper, Henry Boys. London: Lane, 1948.

Brod, Max. *Leoš Janáček*. Vienna: Universal, [1956].

Broder, Nathan. *Samuel Barber*. New York: G. Schirmer, 1954.

Brown, Malcolm H. "Prokofiev's *War and Peace*: A Chronicle." MQ (1977), 63:297–326.

Brown, Malcolm H., ed. *Russian and Soviet Music*, (See part 5 bibliography.)

Busoni, Ferruccio. *Entwurf einer neuen Aesthetik der Tonkunst*. Leipzig: Insel-Verlag, n.d. Trans. as: *Sketch of a New Esthetic of Music*. New York: G. Schirmer, 1911.

——. "Nota bio-bibliografica su Ferruccio Busoni." RassM (1940), 13:82–88.

——. *Über die Möglichkeiten der Oper und über die Partitur des "Doktor Faust"*. Leipzig: Breitkopf & Härtel, 1926.

——. *Von der Einheit der Musik*. Berlin: Hesse, [1923].

——. *Wesen und Einheit der Musik*. Rev. by J. Herrmann. Berlin: Wunsiedel, Hesse, 1956. Trans. as: *The Essence of Music and other Papers*. London: Rockliff, 1957.

Capell, Richard. "Dame Ethel Smyth's Operas at Covent Garden." MMR (1923), 53:197–98.

Casella, Alfredo. *I segreti della giara*. Florence: Sansoni, 1941. Trans. as: *Music in My Time*. Norman: University of Oklahoma Press, [1955].

Chadwick, George. *Horatio Parker*. New Haven: Yale University Press, 1921.

Chase, Gilbert. "Alberto Ginastera: Argentine Composer." MQ (1957), 43:439–60.

Cherney, Brian. *Harry Somers*. Toronto: University of Toronto Press, 1975.

Chiesa, Renato, ed. *Riccardo Zandonai*. Milan: Unicopli, 1984.

Chybiński, A. "L. Różycki jako twórca dramatu muzycznego *Bolesław Śmiały*." *Młoda Muzyka* (1909), no. 7–8.

Chylińska, Teresa. *Szymanowski i jego muzyka*. Warsaw, 1971.

Cinquanta anni di opera e balletto in Italia. Ed. by Guido Gatti. Rome: Carlo Bestetti, 1954.

Clapham, John. "*The Whirlpool*: A Slovak Opera." MR (1958), 19:47–51.

Clements, Andrew. "*The Ice Break*." *Music and Musicians* (1977), 26:42–44.

Coe, Robert. "Philip Glass Breaks Through," *New York Times Magazine* (October 25, 1981), pp. 68ff.

Collaer, Paul. *Darius Milhaud*. Paris: Richard-Masse, 1947.

——. *La Musique moderne, 1905–1955*. Paris and Brussels: Elsevier, 1955.

Colles, H. C. "Philip Napier Miles." *M&L* (1936), 17:357–67.

Cooke, Deryck. *"The Rake* and the 18th Century." *MT* (1962), 103:20–23.

Copland, Aaron. *The New Music 1900–1960.* Rev. ed. New York: Norton, 1968.

———. *Our New Music.* New York: Whittlesey, [1941].

Craft, Robert. "Reflections on *The Rake's Progress.*" *The Score* (September 1954), no. 9, pp. 24–30.

Crow, Todd. *Bartók Studies.* Detroit: Information Coordinators, 1976.

Dallapiccola, Luigi. "The Genesis of the *Canti di prigionia* and *Il prigioniero:* An Autobiographical Fragment." *MQ* (1953), 39:355–72.

D'Amico, Fedele. "Luigi Dallapiccola." *Melos* (1953), 20:69.

D'Amico, Fedele and Guido M. Gatti, eds. *Alfredo Casella.* [Milan]: Ricordi, [1958].

Daniel, Keith W. *Francis Poulenc: His Artistic Development and Musical Style.* Ann Arbor, Mich.: UMI Research, 1982.

Deane, Basil. *Albert Roussel.* London: Barrie and Rockliff, [1961].

———. *Alun Hoddinott.* Cardiff: University of Cardiff, 1977.

Debussy, Claude. *Monsieur Croche, anti-dilettante.* Paris: Dorbon-aîné, 1921.

Delannoy, Marcel. *Honegger.* Paris: Flore, Horay, [1953].

Della Corte, Andrea. *Rittrato di Franco Alfano.* Turin: Paravia, [1935].

Del Mar, Norman. *Richard Strauss: A Critical Commentary on His Life and Works.* 3 vols. Philadelphia: Chilton, 1969–73; reprint, 1978.

Demarquez, Suzanne. *Manuel de Falla.* Paris: Flammarion, 1963; reprint, 1968.

Dent, Edward J. *Ferruccio Busoni: A Biography.* London: Oxford University Press, 1933; 2nd ed., 1984.

———. "Hans Pfitzner." *M&L* (1923), 4:119–32.

Dickinson, A. E. F. "Round About *The Midsummer Marriage.*" *M&L* (1956), 37:50–60.

———. *Vaughan Williams.* London: Faber & Faber, 1963.

Drew, David. "Topicality and the Universal: The Strange Case of Weill's *Die Burgschaft.*" *M&L* (1958), 29:242–55.

[Dukas, Paul.] *RM* (May–June 1936), special issue (contains articles on Dukas's operas).

Durham, Frank. *DuBose Heyward: The Man Who Wrote Porgy.* Columbia: University of South Carolina Press, 1954.

Edmunds, J. and G. Boelzner. *Some Twentieth-Century American Composers.* New York: New York Public Library, 1959–60.

Egk, Werner. *Musik, Wort, Bild. Texte und Anmerkungen: Betrachtungen und Gedanken.* Munich: Langen, Müller, [1960].

Einem, Gottfried von. *"Der Prozess."* *OEM* (1953), 8:198–200.

Emmanuel, Maurice. *"Pelléas et Mélisande"* de Debussy: Etude et analyse. Paris: Mellottée, [1925?]. New ed., 1950.

Encyclopedia of Music in Canada. Toronto: University of Toronto Press, 1981.

Eősze, László. *Kodály Zoltán, életeés munkássága.* Budapest: Zeneműkiadó Vállalat, 1956. Trans. as: *Zoltan Kodaly, His Life and Work.* London: Collet, 1962.

Evans, Michael. *Janáček's Tragic Operas.* Bloomington: Indiana University Press, 1977.

Evans, Peter. *The Music of Benjamin Britten*. Minneapolis: University of Minnesota Press, 1979.

Ewen, David. *Composers Since 1900: First Supplement*. New York: Wilson, 1981.

——. *A Journey to Greatness: The Life and Music of George Gershwin*. New York: Henry Holt, [1956].

Eyer, Ronald. "Carlisle Floyd's *Susannah*." *Tempo* (1956–57), no. 42, pp. 7–11.

[Fauré, Gabriel Urbain.] *RM* (October 1922), special issue.

Favre, Georges. *L'oeuvre de Paul Dukas*. Paris: Colombe, 1969.

Forsyth, Karen. *"Ariadne auf Naxos" by Hugo von Hofmannsthal and Richard Strauss*. Oxford: Oxford University Press, 1982.

Fortner, Wolfgang. "*Bluthochzeit* nach Federico Garcia Lorca." *Melos* (1957), 24:71–73.

——. "Subtilste Verständigung." *Akzente* (1957), 4:121.

——. *Wolfgang Fortner, eine Monographie: Werkanalysen, Aufsätze, Reden*. Rodenkirchen, 1960.

Franco, Enrique. *Manuel de Falla y su obra*. Madrid: Publicaciones Españolas, 1976.

Gatti, Guido Maria. "Franco Alfano." *MQ* (1923), 9:556–77.

——. *Ildebrando Pizzetti*. Turin: G. B. Paravia, [1934]; 2nd ed., Milan: Ricordi, [1955]. English trans., London: Dennis Dobson, 1951.

——. "Recent Italian Operas." *MQ* (1937), 23:77–88.

——. "The Stage Works of Ferruccio Busoni." *MQ* (1934), 20:267–77.

Gatti, Guido M., ed. *L'opera di Gian Francesco Malipiero: Saggi di scrittori italiani e stranieri . . . seguiti dal catalogo delle opere con annotazioni dell' autore e da ricordi e pensieri dello stesso*. [Bologna]: Edizioni di Treviso, 1952.

Geitel, Klaus. *Hans Werner Henze*. Berlin: Rembrandt-Verlag, 1968.

Giazotto, Remo. *Busoni: La vita nell' opera*. [Milan]: Genio, [1947].

Gilman, Lawrence. *Debussy's "Pelléas et Mélisande", a Guide to the Opera*. New York: G. Schirmer, 1907.

Glanville-Hicks, P[eggy]. "Some Reflections on Opera: Rolf Liebermann, a Man of the Theatre," *American Composers Alliance Bulletin* (1957), 6:12–15, 22.

Golachowski, Stanisław. *Karol Szymanowski*. [Cracow]: Polskie Wydawnictwo Muzyczne, [1956].

Goldberg, Isaac. *George Gershwin: A Study in American Music*. Rev. ed. New York: Ungar, [1958].

Goldovsky, Boris. "*Marva*, a Lyric Masterpiece." *Chrysalis* (1951), 4:3–4.

Gordon, Diane Kestin. "Folklore in Modern English Opera." 2 vols. Ph.D. diss., University of California, Los Angeles, 1959.

Griffiths, Paul. "*The Bassarids*: Hans Werner Henze talks to Paul Griffiths." *MT* (1974), 115–831–2.

——. *Igor Stravinsky: "The Rake's Progress"*. Cambridge: Cambridge University Press, 1982.

——. *Modern Music: The Avant-Garde Since 1945*. New York: Braziller, 1981.

——. *Peter Maxwell Davies*. New York: Universe, 1981.

Grisson, Alexandra Carola. *Ermanno Wolf-Ferrari*. Regensburg: Bosse, 1941; 2nd ed. Zurich: Amalthea-Verlag, [1958].

Gruen, John. *Menotti: A Biography*. London: Macmillan, 1978.

——. "Reworking *A Quiet Place* for La Scala." *The New York Times* (July 15, 1984), p. H17.

Guerrini, Guido. *Ferruccio Busoni: La vita, la figura, l'opera*. Florence: Monsalvato, 1944.

Hall, Raymond. "The *Macbeth* of Bloch," *MMus* (May–June 1938), 15:209–15.

Halusa, Karl. "Hans Pfitzners musikdramatisches Schaffen." Ph.D. diss., University of Vienna, 1929.

Hartmann, Rudolf. *Richard Strauss: The Staging of His Operas and Ballets*. Trans. by Graham Davies. New York: Oxford University Press, 1981.

Hartung, Günther. "Zur epischen Oper Brechts und Weills." *Wissenschaftliche Zeitschrift des Martin-Luther-Universität Halle-Wittenberg* (1959), 8:659–73.

Headington, Christopher. *Britten*. New York: Holmes & Meier, 1982.

Heinsheimer, Hans Werner. "Mistress Musgrave: A Woman Composer with Two Premieres." *Opera News* (September 1977), pp. 44–47.

——. "Schreker Centennial." *MQ* (1978), 74:224–249.

Hell, Henri. *Francis Poulenc, musicien français*. Paris: Plon, [1958]. English trans., London: Calder, [1959].

Helm, Everett. "Carl Orff." *MQ* (1955), 41:285–304.

——. "Virgil Thomson's *Four Saints in Three Acts*." *MR* (1954), 15:127–32.

Henderson, Robert. "Elisabeth Lutyens." *MT* (1963), 104:551.

Hennenberg, Fritz. *Paul Dessau: eine Biographie*. Leipzig: Deutscher Verlag für Musik, 1965.

Henze, Hans Werner. *Essays*. Mainz: Schott's Söhne, 1964.

——. *Music and Politics: Collected Writings 1953–1981*. Ithaca: Cornell University Press, 1982.

Hindemith, Paul. *A Composer's World: Horizons and Limitations*. Cambridge: Harvard University Press, 1952.

Hipsher, Edward E. (See part 5 bibliography.)

Hirtler, Franz. *Hans Pfitzners "Armer Heinrich" in seiner Stellung zur Musik des ausgehenden 19. Jahrhunderts*. Würzburg: Triltsch, 1940.

Hixon, Donald L. *Thea Musgrave: A Bio-Bibliography*. Westport, Conn.: Greenwood, 1984.

Hoffman, Rudolf Stephan. *Franz Schreker*. Leipzig: E. P. Tal, 1921.

Hofmannsthal, Hugo von. *Erzählung*. In his *Sämtliche Werke*. Frankfurt am Main: Fischer, 1975.

Hold, Trevor. "Messiaen's Birds." *M&L* (1971), 52:113–122.

Holländer, Hans. "Leoš Janáček in seinen Opern." *NZfM* (1958), 119:425–27.

Holloway, Robin. *Debussy and Wagner*. London: Eulenberg, 1979.

Holst, Imogen. *Britten*. 3rd edition. London: Faber & Faber, 1980.

——. "Britten's *Let's Make an Opera!*" *Tempo* (Winter 1950–51), no. 18, pp. 12–16.

——. *Gustave Holst*. London: Oxford University Press, 1974.

——. *The Music of Gustave Holst.* 2nd ed. London and New York: Oxford University Press, 1968.

Honegger, Arthur. *Je suis compositeur.* Paris: 1951. English trans., New York: St. Martin's, 1966.

Honolka, Kurt. *Das vielstimmige Jahrhundert: Musik in unserer Zeit.* Stuttgart: Cotta, 1960.

Hoover, Kathleen O'Donnell and John Cage. *Virgil Thomson: His Life and Music.* New York: Yoseloff, 1959. 2nd ed., 1970.

Howard, John Tasker. *Our Contemporary Composers: American Music in the Twentieth Century.* New York: Crowell, 1941.

——. *Studies in Contemporary American Composers: Deems Taylor.* New York: J. Fischer, 1927.

Howes, Frank. *The Dramatic Works of Ralph Vaughan Williams.* London: Oxford University Press, 1937.

——. *The Music of Ralph Vaughan Williams.* London: Oxford University Press, 1954.

——. *The Music of William Walton.* 2nd ed. London: Oxford University Press, 1974.

Hurd, Michael. *Immortal Hour: The Life and Period of Rutland Boughton.* London: Routledge & Kegan Paul, [1962].

Hutchings, Arthur. "Delius's Operas," *Tempo* (Winter 1952–53), no. 26, pp. 22–29.

Indy, Vincent d'. *Richard Wagner.* (See part 4 bibliography.)

Inglefield, Ruth K. "Karl-Birger Blomdahl: A Portrait," *MQ* (1972), 57:67–81.

Iwaszkiewicz, J. "Dzieje *Króla Rogera.*" *Muzyka* (1926), pp. 271–72.

Jachimecki, Zdzisław. *Karol Szymanowski.* Cracow: Skład gł. w Ksiegarni Jagiellońskiej (Druk. "Czasu"), 1927.

——. "Karol Szymanowski." *Slavonic and East European Review* (July 1938), 17:174–85.

——. "Operetka Karola Szymanowskiego." *Muzyka* (1952), nos. 3–4, (24–25), pp. 27–39.

Jackson, R. "The Operas of Gertude Stein and Virgil Thomson." Ph.D. diss., Tulane University, 1962.

Jahn, Renate. "Vom *Spieler* zur Erzählung vom wahren Menschen." MuG (1961), 11:232–38.

Janáček, Leoš. *Korespondence Leoše Janáčka s libretisty Vyletů Broučkových.* Prague: Hudebni Matice, 1950.

——. *Korespondence Leoše Janáčka s Marié Calmou a MUDr. Frant. Veselým.* Prague: Orbis, 1951.

——. *Leoš Janáček in Briefen und Erinnerungen.* [Prague]: Artia, [1955]. Trans. as: *Letters and Reminiscences.* Prague: Artia, 1955.

Jarman, Douglas. *The Music of Alban Berg.* Berkeley and Los Angeles: University of California Press, 1979.

Jefferson, Alan. *Delius.* London: Dent, 1972.

Johnson, Robert S. *Messiaen.* Berkeley and Los Angeles: University of California Press, 1975.

Jouve, Pierre Jean and Michel Fano. *"Wozzeck" ou le nouvel opéra.* Paris: Plon, [1953].

Kamieński, L. *"Legenda Bałtyku."* Muzyka (1924), no. 2, 64–68.

Kapp, Julius. *Franz Schreker.* Munich: Drei Masken, 1921.

Keller, Hans. "Schoenberg's Comic Opera [*Von Heute auf Morgen*]." *The Score* (July 1958), no. 23, pp. 27–36.

——. "Schoenberg's *Moses and Aaron.*" *The Score* (October 1957), no. 21, pp. 30–45.

Keller, Wilhelm. *Karl Orff's "Antigonae": Versuch einer Einführung.* Mainz: Schott, [1950].

Kemp, Ian. *Hindemith.* London: Oxford University Press, 1970.

——. *Michael Tippett: The Man and His Work.* New York: Da Capo, 1985.

Kennedy, Michael. *Richard Strauss.* London: Dent, 1976.

——. *The Works of Ralph Vaughan Williams.* London: Oxford University Press, 1964.

Kerman, Joseph. "Grimes and Lucretia." *The Hudson Review* (1949–50), 2:277–84.

——. "Opera à la mode: Stravinsky's *The Rake's Progress.*" *The Hudson Review* (1953–54), 6:560–77.

——. "Terror and Self-Pity: Alban Berg's *Wozzeck.*" *The Hudson Review* (1952–53), 5:408–19.

Kiekert, Ingeborg. *Die musikalische Form in den Werken Carl Orff's.* Regensburg: Bosse, 1957.

Klein, Rudolf. "Rolf Liebermann als dramatischer Komponist." *Melos* (1954), 21:275–80.

Koechlin, Charles Louis Eugène. *Gabriel Fauré: Avec citations musicales dans le texte.* Paris: Plon, [1949].

Kornprobst, Louis. *J. Guy Ropartz: Étude biographique et musicale.* Strassburg: Editions Musicales d'Alsace, [1949].

Kowalke, Kim H. *Kurt Weill in Europe.* Ann Arbor, Mich.: UMI Research, 1979.

Krause, Ernst. *Richard Strauss: Gestalt und Werk.* Leipzig: Breitkopf & Härtel, 1955.

——. *Richard Strauss: The Man and His Work.* Boston: Crescendo, 1969.

Krebs, Stanley Dale. *Soviet Composers and the Development of Soviet Music.* New York: Norton, 1970.

Krenek, Ernst. *Horizons Circled. Reflections on My Music.* Berkeley: University of California Press, 1974.

——. *Music Here and Now.* New York: Norton, [1939].

——. *Zur Sprache gebracht: Essays über Musik.* Munich: Langen/Muller, [1958]. Trans. as: *Exploring Music.* London, 1966.

Króo, György. *Bartók Béla szinpadi müvei.* Budapest, 1962.

——. "Duke Bluebeard's Castle." *Studi Musicologica* (1961), 1:251–340. (English trans. of a chapter from his *Bartók Béla szinpadi müvei.*)

Krüger, Karl Joachim. *Hugo von Hofmannsthal und Richard Strauss.* Berlin: Junker & Dünnhaupt, 1935.

Kulikovich, Mikola. *Sovetskaia opera na sluzhbe partii i pravitel'stva.* Munich, 1955.

Kuss, Malena. *Latin American Music: An Annotated Bibliography of Reference Sources and Research Materials.* Paris: UNESCO, 1984.

——. "Native Idioms in Twentieth-Century Operas from Argentina, Brazil, and Mexico: Towards a Comparative Chronology of Stylistic Change." *Miscellanea Musicologica* (1980), vols. 11–12.

——. "Symbol und Phantasie in Ginasteras *Bomarzo*." In *Alberto Ginastera.* Ed. by F. Spangemacher. Bonn: Boosey & Hawkes, 1984.

——. "Type, Derivation, and Use of Folk Idioms in Ginastera's *Don Rodrigo*." *Latin American Music Review* (1980), 1:176–95.

La Maestre, André Espiau de. "Francis Poulenc und seine Bernanos-Oper." *OeM* (1959), 14:4–9.

La Morgia, Manlio, ed. *La città dannunziana di Ildebrando Pizzetti: Saggi e note.* [Pescara: Comitato Centrale Abruzzese per le Onoranze a I. Pizzetti; Milan: Ricordi], 1958.

Lamy, Fernand. *J. Guy Ropartz: L'homme et l'oeuvre.* Paris: Durand, 1948.

Laux, Karl. *Joseph Haas.* Berlin: Henschelverlag, 1954.

——. *Die Musik in Russland und der Sowjetunion.* Berlin: Henschelverlag, 1958.

Lehmann, Lotte. *Five Operas and Richard Strauss.* Trans. by Ernst Pawel. New York: Da Capo, 1982.

Leibowitz, René. "Alban Berg et l'essence de l'opéra: Réflexions sur la musique dramatique 'sub una specie'." *L'Arche* (February 1946), no. 13, 3e année, 130–34; (March 1946), no. 13, 4e année, 158–66.

Lendvai, Ernő. *Béla Bartók: An Analysis of His Music.* London: Kahn & Averill, 1971.

——. "A kékszakallu herceg vára." *Magyar Zene* (1961), 1:339–87.

Libby, Theodore W., Jr. "How the 'Saints' Came Together in Paris." *The New York Times* (November 8, 1981).

Liess, Andreas. *Carl Orff: Idee und Werk.* [Zurich]: Atlantis-Verlag, [1955]. English trans., 1966; 2nd ed., 1971.

——. *Franz Schmidt, Leben und Schaffen.* Graz: Böhlaus, 1951.

Lindlar, Heinrich, ed. *Die Stimme der Komponisten.* Rodenkirchen: Tonger, 1958.

Lissa, Z. "Pierwsza opera w Polsce Ludowej. (Bunt żaków)." *Muzyka* (1951), no. 10, pp. 3–29.

Łobaczewska, Stefanja. *Karol Szymanowski: Życie i twórczość.* Cracow: Polskie Wydawnictwo Muzyczne, [1950].

Lockspeiser, Edward. *Debussy.* 3rd ed. New York: Pellegrini & Cudahy, 1951.

——. *Debussy: His Life and Mind.* 2 vols. London: Macmillan, 1965–66.

Louis, Rudolf. *Hans Pfitzners "Die Rose vom Liebesgarten".* Munich: Seyfried, 1904.

Lowe, R., ed. *Frederick Delius 1826–1934: A Catalogue of the Music Archives of the Delius Trust.* London, 1974.

Lowens, Irving. "Ginastera's *Beatrix Cenci*." *Tempo* (1973), no. 105, p. 48.

McAllister, Rita. "The Operas of Sergei Prokofiev." Ph.D. diss., Cambridge University, 1970.

MacMillan, Keith and John Beckwith, eds. *Contemporary Canadian Composers.* Toronto: Oxford University Press, 1975.

Mann, William. *Richard Strauss: A Critical Study of the Operas.* London: Cassell, 1964.

Martynov, Ivan I. *Dmitri Shostakovich, the Man and His Work.* Trans. by T. Guralsky. New York: Philosophical Library, [1947].

Mason, Colin. "Stravinsky's Opera." *M&L* (1952), 33:1–9.

Mathis, Alfred. "Stefan Zweig as Librettist and Richard Strauss." *M&L* (1944), 25:163–76, 226–45.

Mertens, Wim. *American Minimal Music.* New York: Broude, 1983.

Messiaen, Olivier. *The Technique of My Musical Language.* Trans. by John Satterfield. 2 vols. Paris: Leduc, 1966.

Messinis, M., ed. *Omaggio a Malipiero.* Florence, 1977.

Milhaud, Darius. *Notes sans musique.* Paris: Juilliard, 1949. Trans. as: *Notes Without Music: An Autobiography.* London: Dennis Dobson, 1952; American ed., with new final chap., rev. and enlarged. New York: Knopf, 1963.

Mitchell, Donald. *Britten and Auden in the Thirties: The Year 1936.* London: Faber & Faber, 1981.

——. "Prokofieff's *Three Oranges:* A Note on Its Musical-Dramatic Organisation." *Tempo* (Autumn 1956), no. 41, pp. 20–24.

Mitchell, Donald and Hans Keller, eds. *Benjamin Britten: A Commentary on His Works, from a Group of Specialists.* London: Rockliff, [1952].

Moisenco, Rena. *Realist Music: 25 Soviet Composers.* London: Meridian, 1949.

Mordden, Ethan. *Opera in the Twentieth Century: Sacred, Profane, Godot.* New York: Oxford University Press, 1978.

Moreux, Serge. *Béla Bartók.* Paris: Richard-Masse, 1955.

Motte, D. de la. *Hans Werner Henze: "Der Prinz von Homburg".* Mainz: Schott, 1963.

Müller-Blattau, Joseph. *Hans Pfitzner.* Potsdam: Athenaion, 1940.

Munich. Bayerische Staatsbibliothek. *Carl Orff: Das Bühnenwerk.* Munich, 1970. [Catalog by R. Munster.]

Musgrave, Thea. "*Mary, Queen of Scots.*" *MT* (1977), 118:625.

Myers, Rollo. "The Opera That Never Was: Debussy's Collaboration with Victor Segalen in the Preparation of *Orphée.*" *MQ* (1978), 64:495–506.

——. *Ravel: His Life and Works.* London: Yoseloff, 1973.

Nathan, Hans. "The Twelve-Tone Compositions of Luigi Dallapiccola." *MQ* (1958), 44:289–310.

Neighbour, Oliver Way. "Schoenberg." In *The New Grove Second Viennese School.* New York: Norton, 1983.

Nest'ev, Izrail' Vladimirovich. *Prokof'ev.* Moscow: Gos. muzykal'noe izd-vo, 1957. English trans., Stanford, Cal.: Stanford University Press, 1960.

Neuwirth, G. *Die Harmonik in der Oper "Die ferne Klang" von Franz Schreker.* Regensburg: Bosse, 1972.

——. *Franz Schreker.* Vienna, 1959.

Nicholas, Roger. *Debussy*. London: Oxford University Press, 1975.
——. *Messaien*. London: Oxford University Press, 1975.
——. *Ravel*. London: Dent, 1977.
Norris, Christopher, ed. *Shostakovich, the Man and His Music*. Boston: Boyars, 1982.
Olkhovsky, Audrey. *Music Under the Soviets: The Agony of an Art*. New York: Praeger, 1955.
Opera Annual. Ed. by Harold Rosenthal. London: Calder, 1954–.
Opera News. New York: Metropolitan Opera Guild, 1936–.
Orenstein, Arbie. *Ravel: Man and Musician*. New York: Columbia University Press, 1975.
Orff, Carl. "Gedanken über Musik mit Kindern und Laien." *Die Musik* (1932), 24:668.
Orledge, Robert. *Gabriel Fauré*. London: Eulenberg, 1979.
Orrego-Salas, Juan. "An Opera in Latin America: *Don Rodrigo* by Ginastera." *Artes hispánicas* (1967), no. 1, pp. 94–133.
Pahissa, Jaime. *Vida y obra de Manuel de Falla*. Buenos Aires: Ricordi Americana, 1947. Trans. as: *Manuel de Falla: His Life and Works*. London: Museum Press, [1954].
Palmer, Christopher. *Milhaud*. London: Duckworth, 1976.
Palmer, Christopher, ed. *The Britten Companion*. Cambridge: Cambridge University Press, 1984.
Pantle, Sherrill H. *"Die Frau ohne Schatten" by Hugo von Hofmannsthal and Richard Strauss: An Analysis of Text, Music, and Their Relationship*. Berne: Lang, 1978.
Perle, George. "Alban Berg." In *The New Grove Second Viennese School*. New York: Norton, 1983.
——. *The Operas of Alban Berg: "Lulu"*. Berkeley and Los Angeles: University of California Press, 1984.
——. *The Operas of Alban Berg: "Wozzeck"*. Berkeley and Los Angeles: University of California Press, 1980.
Pfannkuch, Wilhelm. "Das Opernschaffen Ermanno Wolf-Ferraris." Ph.D. diss., University of Kiel, 1952.
Pfitzner, Hans Erich. *Gesammelte Schriften*. 3 vols. Augsburg: Filser, 1926.
——. *Reden, Schriften, Briefe*. Ed. by Walter Abendroth. [Berlin-Frohnau and Neuwied/Rhein]: Luchterhand, [1955].
——. *Von musikalischen Drama: Gesammelte Aufsätze*. Munich and Leipzig: Suddeutsche Monatshefte, 1915.
Pörnbacher, K. *Hugo von Hofmannsthal, Richard Strauss: "Der Rosenkavalier": Interpretation*. Munich: Oldenbourgh, 1964.
Porter, Andrew. "Prokofiev's Late Operas." *MT* (1967), 108:312.
Potter, Pamela M. "Strauss's *Friedenstag*: A Pacifist Attempt at Political Resistance." *MQ* (1983), 79:408–24.
Poulenc, Francis. "Comment j'ai composé les *Dialogues des Carmélites*." *L'Opéra de Paris* (1957), 34:277–87.
——. *Entretiens avec Claude Rostand*. Paris: Julliard, [1954].

Pribegina, G., ed. *D. Shostakovich o vremeni i o sebe.* Moscow, 1980.

Proctor, George A. *Canadian Music of the Twentieth Century.* Toronto: University of Toronto Press, 1980.

Prokof'ev, Sergei Sergeevich. *Autobiography, Articles, Reminiscences.* [Comp., ed., and annotated by S. Shlifstein; trans. by Rose Prokofieva.] Moscow: Foreign Languages Publishing House, [1959?]. Trans. of: *S. S. Prokof'ev: Materialy, documenty, vospominaniia.* Moscow: Gos. muzykal'noe izd-vo, 1956. 2nd ed., 1961.

———. *Prokofiev by Prokofiev: A Composer's Memoir.* Ed. by David H. Appel. Garden City, N.Y.: Doubleday, 1979.

———. *Sergei Prokofiev: Materials, Articles, Interviews.* Comp. by Vladimir Blok. Moscow: Progress, [1978].

Pruslin, Stephen, ed. *Peter Maxwell Davies: Studies from Two Decades.* London: Boosey & Hawkes, 1977.

Rabinovich, D. *Dmitry Shostakovich, Composer.* Moscow: Foreign Languages Publishing House, 1959.

Racek, Jan. "Der Dramatiker Janáček." *Deutsches Jahrbuch der Musikwissenschaft* (1961), 5:39–57.

Ramuz, Charles Ferdinand. *Souvenirs sur Igor Stravinsky.* Paris: Gallimard, [1929].

Raupp, Wilhelm. *Eugen d'Albert.* Leipzig: Koehler & Amelang, [1930].

———. *Max von Schillings.* Hamburg: Hanseatische Verlagsanstalt, [1935].

[Ravel, Maurice.] *RM* (April 1925 and December 1938), special issues on Ravel.

Redlich, Hans Ferdinand. *Alban Berg: The Man and His Music.* London: Calder; New York: Abelard-Schuman, [1957].

———. *Alban Berg: Versuch einer Würdigung.* Vienna: Universal, 1957.

———. "Egon Wellesz." *MQ* (1940), 26:65–75.

———. "Unveröffentlichte Briefe Alban Bergs an Arnold Schönberg." In *Festschrift Friedrich Blume.* Kassel: Bärenreiter, 1963. 272–80.

Redwood, C., ed. *A Delius Companion.* London, 1976.

Reich, Willi. *Alban Berg.* Vienna: H. Reichner, [1937].

———. "A Guide to *Wozzeck.*" *MQ* (1952), 38:1–21.

———. *Schoenberg: a Critical Biography.* Trans. by Leo Black. London: Longman, 1971.

Reizenstein, Franz. "Walton's *Troilus and Cressida.*" *Tempo* (Winter 1954–55), no. 34, pp. 16–27.

Rensis, Raffaello de. *Ermanno Wolf-Ferrari, la sua vita d'artista.* Milan: Treves, 1937.

Respighi, Elsa. *Ottorino Respighi: Dati biografici ordinati.* [Milan]: Ricordi, [1954].

Riezler, Walter. *Hans Pfitzner und die deutsche Bühne.* Munich: Piper, 1917.

Robinson, Harlow. "Dostoevsky and Opera: Prokofiev's *The Gambler.*" *MQ* (1984), 70:96–106.

Rochberg, George. "Hugo Weisgall." *American Composers Alliance Bulletin* (1958), 7:2–7.

Rogge, W. *Ernst Kreneks Opern: Spiegel der zwanziger Jahre*. Wolfenbüttel: Vera-Verlag, 1970.

Roland-Manuel, pseud. [Alexis Manuel Lévy]. *Maurice Ravel*. London: Dobson, 1947.

———. *Maurice Ravel et son oeuvre dramatique*. Paris: Librairie de France, 1928.

Rolland, Romain. *Musicians of Today*. 2nd ed. New York: Holt, 1915.

———. *Musicians of Today*. Trans. by Mary Blaiklock. London: Kegan Paul, n.d.

Rösner, Helmut. *Paul Hindemith: Katalog seiner Werke, Diskographie, Bibliographie, Einführung in das Schaffen*. Frankfurt, 1970.

Rostand, Claude. "The Operas of Darius Milhaud." *Tempo* (Spring 1951), no. 19, pp. 23–28.

Roy, Jean. *Darius Milhaud*. Paris: Seghers, 1968.

Różycki, L. "Dzieje *Erosa i Psyche*." *Muzyka* (1930), no. 2, pp. 82–85.

———. "Kilka słów o mojej *Beatrix Cenci*." *Muzyka* (1927), pp. 69–70.

———. "O mojej operze *Casanova*." *Muzyka* (1925), pp. 129–30.

Rufer, Josef. *The Works of Arnold Schoenberg: A Catalogue of His Compositions, Writings, and Paintings*. Trans. by Dika Newlin. London: Faber & Faber, 1962.

Rutz, Hans. *Hans Pfitzner: Musik zwischen den Zeiten*. [Vienna]: Humboldt-Verlag. [1949].

———. *Neue Oper: Gottfried Einem und seine Oper "Dantons Tod"*. Vienna: Universal, [1947].

Sabin, Robert. "Carlisle Floyd's *Wuthering Heights*." *Tempo* (Autumn 1961), no. 59, pp. 23–26.

Šafránek, Miloš. *Bohuslav Martinů, the Man and His Music*. New York: Knopf, 1944.

———. "Bohuslav Martinů und das musikalische Theater." *Musica* (1959), 13:550–54.

Sailer, Rudolf. "Waltershausen und die Oper." Ph.D. diss., University of Cologne, 1957.

St. John, Christopher. *Ethel Smyth: A Biography*. Additional chapters by V. Sackville-West and Kathleen Dale. [London]: Longmans, Green, [1959].

Salzman, Eric. *Twentieth Century Music: An Introduction*. 2nd ed. Englewood Cliffs, N.J.: Prentice-Hall, 1974.

Samazeuilh, Gustave. *Paul Dukas*. Paris: Durand, 1913.

Samuel, Claude. *Conversations with Olivier Messiaen*. Trans. by Felix Aprehamian. London: Stainer & Bell, 1976.

Sartori, Claudio. *Riccardo Malipiero*. Milan: Zerboni, 1957. (In English.)

Saylor, Bruce. "The Music of Hugo Weisgall." *MQ* (1973), 59:239–62.

Schaefer, H. "Paul Dessaus *Einstein* Oper." *MuG* (1974), 24:213.

Schafer, R. Murray, ed. *Ezra Pound and Music: The Complete Literature*. New York: New Directions, 1977.

Schmitz, Eugen. "Eugen d'Albert als Opernkomponist." *Hochland* (1909), 6:464–71.

Schneider, Marcel. *Henri Sauguet*. Paris, 1959.

Schollum, Robert. *Egon Wellesz: eine Studie.* Vienna: Österreichische Musik zeitschrift, [1964].

Schuh, Willi. *Hugo von Hofmannsthal und Richard Strauss: Legende und Wirklichkeit.* Munich: Hanser, 1964.

——. *"Der Rosenkavalier": Vier Studien.* Olten: Vereinigung von Freunden der Oltener Liebhaberdrucke, 1968.

——. *Über Opern von Richard Strauss.* Vol. 1 of *Kritiken und Essays.* Zurich: Atlantis-Verlag, [1947].

——. "Zur Harmonik Igor Strawinskys unter besonderer Berücksichtigung von *The Rake's Progress.*" In *Internationaler Musik-Kongress Wien 1952, Bericht.* Vienna: Österreichischer Bundesverlag, 1953, 127–34.

Schumacher, Ernst. *Die dramatischen Versuche Bertolt Brechts, 1918–1933.* Berlin: Rütten & Loening, 1955.

Schwarz, Boris. *Music and Musical Life in Soviet Russia 1917–1970.* New York: Norton, 1972.

Seipt, A. *"Die Soldaten."* In *Neue Musik seit 1945.* Stuttgart, 1972. 360.

Selva, Blanche. *Déodat de Séverac.* Paris: Delagrave, 1930.

Semler, Isabel Parker. *Horatio Parker: A Memoir for His Grandchildren Compiled from Letters and Papers.* New York: Putnam's, 1942.

Seré, Octave. (See part 4 bibliography.)

Shawe-Taylor, Desmond. "The Operas of Leoš Janáček." *PRMA* (1958–59), 85; 49–64.

Shostakovich, Dmitrii. "My Opera, *Lady Macbeth of Mtsensk.*" *MMus* (November–December 1934), 12:23–30.

——. *The Power of Music.* New York: Music Journal, 1968.

Skelton, Geoffrey. *Paul Hindemith: The Man behind the Music.* London: Gollancz, 1975.

Slonimsky, Nicolas. (See part 4 bibliography.)

Smith, David Stanley. "A Study of Horatio Parker." *MQ* (1930), 16:153–69.

Smith, Patrick. (See general bibliography.)

Smyth, Dame Ethel. *Impressions That Remained: Memoirs.* New York: Knopf, 1946. (First published, London: Longmans, Green, 1919.)

Sovetskaia opera: Sbornik kriticheskikh statei. Moscow: Gos. muzykal'noe izd-vo, 1953.

Spangemacher, Friedrich, ed. *Alberto Ginastera.* Bonn: Boosey & Hawkes, 1984.

Stäblein, Bruno. "Schopferische Tonalität: Zum Grossaufbau von Orffs *Antigonae.*" *M* (1952), 6:145–48.

Stenzl, J., ed. *Luigi Nono: Texte: Studien zu seiner Musik.* Zurich, 1975.

Stevens, Halsey. *The Life and Music of Béla Bartók.* New York: Oxford University Press, 1953; 2nd ed., 1963.

Strauss, Richard. *Betrachtungen und Erinnerungen.* 2nd ed. Zurich: Atlantis-Verlag, [1957].

[——.] *Richard Strauss et Romain Rolland: Correspondance, fragments de journal.* Paris: Michel, [1951].

Strauss, Richard and Hugo von Hofmannsthal. *Briefwechsel.* Ed. by Franz Strauss, Alice Strauss, and Willi Schuh. Trans. as: *A Working Friendship:*

The Correspondence between Richard Strauss and Hugo von Hofmannsthal. New York: Random House, [1961].

Strauss, Richard and Joseph Gregor. *Briefwechsel, 1934–1949: Im Auftrag der Wiener Philharmoniker.* Ed. by Roland Tenschert. Salzburg: Müller, [1955].

Strauss, Richard and Stefan Zweig. *Briefwechsel.* Ed. by Willi Schuh. [Frankfurt am Main]: Fischer, 1957.

Stravinsky, Igor Fedorovich. *Chroniques de ma vie.* Paris: Denoël & Steele, [1935]. Trans. as: *Chronicles of My Life.* London: Gollancz, 1936.

———. *Memories and Commentaries.* Garden City, N. Y.: Doubleday, 1960.

———. "On *Oedipus Rex.*" *Encounter* (1962), 18:29–35.

———. *Poetics.* New York: Vintage, 1956.

———. *Poétique musicale sous forme de six leçons.* Cambridge: Harvard University Press, 1942.

———. *RM* (May–June 1939) and *MQ* (vol. 67, 1982), special issues on Stravinsky.

Stravinsky, Igor and Robert Craft. *Conversations with Igor Stravinsky.* Garden City, N.Y.: Doubleday, 1959.

Strobel, Heinrich. *Paul Hindemith.* 3rd ed. Mainz: Schott's Söhne, [1948].

Stuckenschmidt, Hans Heinz. *Arnold Schönberg.* Zurich: Atlantis-Verlag, [1951]. 2nd ed., 1957. English trans., New York: Grove, [1959].

———. *Boris Blacher.* Berlin: Bote & Bock, 1963.

———. *Die grossen Komponisten unseres Jahrhunderts.* Munich: Peper, 1971.

———. "Von Einem's *Der Besuch der alten Dame.*" *Tempo* (1971–72), no. 98, p. 28.

Suárez Urtubey, Pola. *Alberto Ginastera.* Buenos Aires: Ediciones Culturales, 1967.

Suckling, Norman. *Fauré.* London: Dent, 1946.

Swarsenski, Hans. "Sergei Prokofieff: *The Flaming Angel.*" *Tempo* (Spring 1956), no. 39, pp. 16–27.

Tappolet, Willy. *Arthur Honegger.* Zurich: Atlantis-Verlag, [1954].

Taruskin, Richard. "Tone, Style and Form in Prokofiev's Soviet Operas: Some Preliminary Observations." In *Studies in the History of Music*, vol. 2. New York: Broude, 1982.

Thomas, Werner. *Carl Orff: "De temporum fine comoedia"* . . . *eine Interpretation.* Tutzing: Schneider, 1973.

Thomson, Virgil. *American Music Since 1910.* New York: Holt, Rinehart, & Winston. 1971.

———. "George Gershwin." *MMus* (November–December 1935), 13:13–19.

———. *The Musical Scene.* New York: Knopf, 1945.

———. *The State of Music.* New York: Morrow, 1939.

Tippett, Michael. *Moving into Aquarius.* 2nd ed. London: Paladin, 1974.

Trenner, Franz, ed. *Richard Strauss: Dokumente seines Lebens und Schaffens.* Munich: Beck, [1954].

Tretti, Luigi and Leonello Fiumi, eds. *Omaggio a Italo Montemezzi.* Verona: Ghidini & Fiorini, [1952].

Tuthill, Burnet C. "Howard Hanson." *MQ* (1936), 22:140–53.

Tyrrell, John. *Leoš Janáček: Kát'a Kabanová*. Cambridge: Cambridge University Press, 1982.

Valentin, Erich. *Hans Pfitzner*. Regensburg: Bosse, 1939.

Vallas, Léon. *Claude Debussy et son temps*. Paris: Alcan, 1932; Paris: Michel, 1958. Trans. as: *Claude Debussy, His Life and Works*. London: Oxford University Press, 1933.

Vaughan Williams, Ursala. *R. V. W., a Biography*. London: Oxford University Press, 1964.

Vázsonyi, Balint. *Dohnányi Ernō*. Budapest, 1971.

Viu, Vicente Salas. "The Mystery of Manuel de Falla's *La Atlántida*." *Inter-American Music Bulletin* (January 1963), no. 33, pp. 1–6.

Vlad, Roman. "Dallapiccola 1948–1955." *The Score* (March 1956), no. 15, pp. 39–52.

——. *Strawinsky*. [Turin]: Einaudi, 1958. English trans. of 3rd rev. ed., London: Oxford University Press, 1979.

Vogel, Jaroslav. *Leoš Janáček*. Trans. by Karel Janovicky. Rev. and enlarged ed. New York: Norton, 1981.

Volkov, Solomon, ed. *Testimony: The Memoirs of D. Shostakovich*. New York: Harper & Row, 1979.

Vuillermoz, E. *Gabriel Fauré*. Paris, 1960. English trans., 1969.

Vysloužil, Jiří. *Alois Hába*. Brno, 1970.

——. "Alois Hába, Arnold Schönberg und die Tschechische Musik." *Aspekte der neuen Musik*, ed. by W. Burde. Kassel, 1968. 58.

——. "Hába's Idea of Quarter-tone Music." In *Hudební věda* (1968), 5:466.

Wallner, Bo. "Karl-Birger Blomdahl 1916–1968." *Perspectives of New Music* (1969), pp. 186–89.

Walsh, Stephen. "Musgrave's *The Voice of Ariadne*." *MT* (1974), 115:465.

——. "*Time-Off* and *The Scene Machine*." *MT* (1972), 113:137.

Waltershausen, Hermann. "*Der Freischütz*": *Ein Versuch über die musikalische Romantik*. Munich: Bruckmann, 1920.

——. *Das Siegfried-Idyll, oder, Die Rückkehr zur Natur*. Munich: Bruckmann, 1920.

——. "Zur Dramaturgie des *Fidelio*." *Neues Beethoven Jahrbuch* (1924), 1:142–58.

Warlock, Peter, pseud. [Philip Heseltine]. *Frederick Delius*. With additions by Hubert Foss. New York: Oxford University Press, 1952.

Warrack, John. "*The Ice Break*." *MT* (1977), 118:553–56.

Waterhouse, John C. G. "The Emergence of Modern Italian Music (up to 1940)." Ph.D. diss., Oxford University, 1968.

Weitzel, H. "A Melodic Analysis of Selected Vocal Solos in the Operas of Douglas Moore." Ph.D. diss., New York University, 1971.

White, Eric Walter. *Benjamin Britten, His Life and Operas*. 2nd ed. Berkeley and Los Angeles: University of California Press, 1983.

——. *Michael Tippett and His Operas*. London: Barrie & Jenkins, 1979.

——. "The Rake's Progress." *Tempo* (Summer 1951), no. 20, pp. 10–18.

——. *Stravinsky: The Composer and His Works*. 2nd ed. London: Faber, 1979.

White, Eric Walter and Jeremy Noble. "Igor Stravinsky." In *The New Grove Modern Masters.* New York: Norton, 1984. 105–225.

White, John S. *The Salome Motive.* New York: Eloquent, [ca. 1947].

White, Pamela. *Schoenberg and the God-Idea: The Opera "Moses und Aron".* Ann Arbor, Mich.: UMI Research, 1985.

Whittall, Arnold. *Britten and Tippett: Studies in Themes and Techniques.* London: Oxford University Press, 1982.

——. "A War and a Wedding: Two Modern British Operas." *M&L* (1974), 55:299–306.

Wieniawski, Adam. *Ludomir Różycki.* Warsaw: Gebethner & Wolff, [1928].

Wightman, A. "The Music of Karol Szymanowski." Ph.D. diss., University of York, 1972.

Willnauer, Franz, ed. *Prometheus: Myths, Drama, Musik. Beiträge zu Carl Orffs Musikdrama noch Aischylos.* Tübingen: Wunderlich, 1968.

Willms, Franz. *Führer zur Oper "Cardillac" von Paul Hindemith.* Mainz: Schott, [1926].

Wörner, Karl H. "Arnold Schoenberg and the Theater." *MQ* (1962), 48:444–60.

——. *Gotteswort und Magie: Die Oper "Moses und Aron" von Arnold Schönberg.* Heidelberg: Schneider, 1959. Trans. by P. Hamburger as: *Schoenberg's "Moses and Aaron".* London: Faber & Faber, 1963.

——. *Neue Musik in der Entscheidung.* Mainz: Schott's Söhne, [1956].

Wynne, David. "Alun Hoddinott: A Survey." *Welsh Music* (1970), 3:2.

Young, Percy M. *Zoltán Kodály.* London: Benn, 1964.

Zielinski, T. A. *Bartók.* Cracow, 1969. German trans., 1973.

Zuck, Barbara. *A History of Musical Americanism.* Ann Arbor, Mich.: UMI Research, 1980.

SOURCES AND TRANSLATIONS OF MUSICAL EXAMPLES

2.1   Coussemaker, ed. *Oeuvres complètes du trouvère Adam de la Halle.*
Translation: Robin: Yes, and you shall be my love, you shall have my belt, my purse, and my buckle. Shepherdess, sweet girl, give me your rosary. Marion: Gladly, my sweet friend.

3.1   *Circe ou le Balet comique de la royne*, 1582 edition, p. 31. (See also facsimile edition, Turin, 1965.)

3.2   M. Schneider, *Die Anfänge des Basso Continuo* (Leipzig, 1918), pp. 147–48.
Translation: Rejoice, ye mortal throng, happily and gladly rejoice at such a gift, and with music and song allay the fatigue of your toil.

3.3   Solerti, *Gli albori del melodramma.*
Translation: Thou with heavenward-pointing horns fixed in thy broad and spacious forehead: O Lycian Pan!

4.1   *L'Euridice composta in musica in stile rappresentativo da Giulio Caccini Romano* (Florence: G. Marescotti, 1600), p. 15.
Translation: And raising her eyes toward heaven, her lovely face pale and colorless, all her great beauty remained immobile, forzen.

4.2   Kretzschmar, *Geschichte der Oper*, p. 38. Realization omitted.
Translation: Alas! How my heart turns cold in my breast with horror and pity; O miserable beauty, how in an instant, ah! thou art brought low.

4.3   Caccíni, *L'Euridice*, 1600.
Translation: To song, to dance, to the shade, to the flower-decked meadows, to the happy streams run singing, O shepherds, on this blessed day.

4.4   *La Dafne di Marco da Gagliano . . . rappresentata in Mantova* (Florence: G. Marescotti, 1608), pp. 3–4.
Translation: If a heart can find mercy above in the golden cloisters, hear our lamentations and prayers, O monarch and king of Heaven.

5.1   *L'Orfeo favola in musica da Claudio Monteverdi rappresentata in Man-*

tova l'anno 1607 & novamente data in luce (Venice: R. Amadino, 1609), p. 1.

5.2   Monteverdi, C.E. XI, 31. Note values halved, bar lines twice as frequent.
Translation: Remember, O shady thickets, my long and bitter torments.

5.3   Monteverdi, *Orfeo*, facsimile of first ed. Figures in brackets correspond to Malipiero's realization. C.E. XI, 59.
Translation: Messenger: To you I come, Orpheus, unhappy messenger of most unhappy and baneful news. Thy lovely Euridice . . . Orpheus: Alas, what do I hear? Messenger: Thy beloved wife is dead. Orpheus: Alas!

5.4   Monteverdi, *Orfeo*, facsimile of first ed. Last two accidentals under bass notes correspond to Malipiero's realization, C.E. XI, 61.
Translation: Calling to thee, Orpheus! Orpheus! after a deep sigh she breathed her last in my arms and I remained, my heart filled with pity and horror.

6.1   *Il S. Alessio, dramma musicale . . . posto in musica da Stefano Landi Romano* (Rome: P. Masotti, 1634), p. 1.

6.2   *Il S. Alessio . . .* , pp. 1–2.

6.3   Il S. Alessio . . . , p. 107.
Translation: Brief shall be the delay; rest and take hope. And when thou art come to the last hour, do not fear death. Contemplate the dark pass, full of hope to all who have suffered pain.

6.4   *La catena d'Adone posta in musica da Domenico Mazzocchi* (Venice: A. Vincenti, 1627), p. 23. Rome: Bibl. Santa Cecilia, G.C.S. 2. C.6
Translation: The breeze smiles to the fair sky of your divine countenance, and amid dances and songs is revealed to you a smiling new heaven, a new earth, and a new world.

6.5   *La Galatea, dramma del Cav. Loreto Vittori da Spoleti, dal medesimo posto in musica* (Rome: V. Bianchi, 1639), pp. 112–13.
Translation: Weep, O fields and flowers, for the vanished splendors; and thou, O earth, wrap thy breast in a dark mantle and sadly keep company to our plaints.

6.6   Rossi, *Orfeo* (Rome: Biblioteca Apostolica Vaticana, MS Chigi Q. V 58, f. 189).
Translation: Kill me, O sorrows: and while I go with desperate pace amidst these savage rocks seeking how I may die, to you more than to a serpent or a wild beast is due that despicable glory. Kill me: since death knew that Euridice alone was my life, and he does not remember that I still live. Kill me, O sorrows.

6.7   Mazzocchi, *Chi soffre, speri* (Rome: Biblioteca Apostolica Vaticana, MS Barb. lat. 4376, ff. 49ᵛ–50).

Translation: Let each one follow his pleasure, as long as I may live happily on this shady bank where my father, near to death, promised me (may the prophecy be true!) an unexpected outcome of fortunate happenings.

6.8   Abbatini, *Dal male il bene* (Rome: Biblioteca Apostolica Vaticana, MS Barb. lat. 4376, ff. 49ᵛ–50).
Translation: What is the good of searching forever so anxiously to know what others do? Of fretting my brain in my own craze to understand what may be outside of this and that?

7.1   Monteverdi, C.E. XIII. 80–81. Realization omitted.
Translation: Seneca: Reason is the ruler of man and gods. Nero: You—you—you drive me to frenzy!

7.2   Monteverdi, C.E. XIII. 136. Signature changed from one flat: flat omitted under bass C in measures 1, 4, 8.
Translation: When I am with you my heart beats, when you are away I am dull; I long for and constantly think about your beauty.

7.3   Monteverdi, C.E. XIII, 85–86. Realization omitted.
Translation: O my adored one, still in my arms I held thee. Poppea, I hardly breathe: I gaze upon thy lips and, gazing, recover with my eyes the fiery spirit which, embracing thee, O dear one, I diffused into thee.

7.4   Cavalli, *Egisto* (Venice: Biblioteca Nazionale di San Marco, MS It. IV-411, ff. 84–85ᵛ). Time values halved; original time signature C_2^3, no accidentals in signature.
Translation: Rejoice with me, beloved trees; resound with glad harmonies, ye songsters; Lidio returns and leaves Clori.

7.5   Cavalli, *Egisto* (Venice: Biblioteca Nazionale di San Marco. MS It. IV-411, f. 50ᵛ). Time values halved; original signature $\frac{3}{2}$. Bar lines added before measures 5, 9, 16.
Translation: Weep, sorrowing eyes, and let the fountain and river weep to my tearful plaint.

7.6   Cavalli, *Giasone* (Venice: Biblioteca Nazionale di San Marco, MS It. IV-363, ff. 58ᵛ–59). Original time signature $\frac{3}{2}$; time values halved.
Translation: Open to me the creaking hinges of the magic cave and admit me among the shades of the black abode.

7.7   Venice: Biblioteca Nazionale di San Marco, MS It. IV-41, ff. 30–30ᵛ.
Translation: If perfidious Love pierce thee with his arrows . . .

7.8   DTOe VI, 108. Continuo omitted.
Translation: These are the tricks used by madmen and mountebanks.

7.9   Venice: Biblioteca Nazionale di San Marco. MS It. IV-41, f. 33ᵛ.
Translation: The sweet sighs and afflictions are precious to me.

7.10   Rolland, *Les Origines du théâtre lyrique moderne, Supplément musical*, p. 9. Reduced from four staves.
Translation: Let me die, cruel stars.

7.11   Hess, *Zur Geschichte des musikalischen Dramas im Seicento*, pp. 88–89. Introduction omitted (six measures of two parts over continuo).
Translation: What are you thinking of, my heart? Your beloved is lost, and lost is all hope of ever having him back.

8.1   DdT LV, 102. Bass and realization omitted.
Translation: Victory! victory! ect.

8.2   DdT LV, 74. Realization and German text (translation) omitted.
Translation: Cruel lady, you laugh at me but I shall laugh at you. I shall pray to Jupiter that he someday burn with his lightnings the one who has outraged me.

8.3   DTB XII^2, 119–20. Condensed from five staves; realization omitted.
Translation: Cease, O fate, to make me suffer.

8.4   DTB XII^2, 159. Accompaniment (three-part strings) omitted.
Translation: I tremble, and mortal cold runs through my veins.

8.5   DTB XII^2, 163–64. Condensed from five staves; realization omitted.
Translation: The trumpet calls me here.

9.1   MfMg XIII (1881).
Translation: Ah, omnipotent God, worker of miracles, who has led me mercifully through many a plight! Neither in misery nor in happiness would I know what to do without you.

9.2   Franck, *Cara Mustapha*; H. C. Wolff, *Die Barockoper in Hamburg*, II, 40–41.
Translation: Parting, sad parting, forever; ah, how my heart is torn by suffering, all too heavy.

9.3   *Das Erbe deutscher Musik*, ser. 2, II, 147. Realization omitted.
Translation: When one has achieved his goal he should not let any misgivings trouble his happiness, which will be gone before he knows it.

9.4   Kusser, *Erindo*: H. C. Wolff, *Die Barockoper in Hamburg*, II, 68–69.
Translation: Thus, in this longed-for sanctuary, may remembrance and pledge both flourish together.

10.1   SB ex. 232. Accompaniment omitted.
Translation: O death, come and put an end to my sad lot.

10.2a   *Atys, Tragédie mise en musique par Monsieur de Lully* . . . (Paris: Christopher Ballard, 1689), pp. 58–59.
Translation: Is it so wrong to love overmuch that which we find loveable?

10.2b *Atys, Tragédie mise en musique par Monsieur de Lully* . . . , 2nd ed., Oeuvre VI ([Paris]: Christopher Ballard, 1720), pp. 42–43.

10.3 Lully, *Amadis*; H. Prunières, ed., *J. B. Lully: Oeuvres complètes* (Paris, 1930–39), III, 95–96. Condensed from five staves; flat added before last bass note of measure 8.
Translation: Thick woods, redouble your shade; you will never be dark enough, you will never conceal deeply enough my unhappy love.

10.4 Lully, *Phaëton* (1683).

11.1 *Old English Edition*, XXV, 110. Slurs omitted.

11.2 *Old English Edition*, XXV, 21. Reduced from three staves; realization omitted.

11.3 *Old English Edition*, XXV, 130–31. Realization omitted.

11.4 Purcell, C. E. XXVI, 41.

11.5 Purcell, C.E. IX, 17–18. Reduced from four staves; realization omitted.

11.6 Purcell, C.E. XIX, 49. Reduced from two staves; realization omitted.

12.1 A. Scarlatti, *Mitridate Eupatore* (Library of Congress M 1500 .S28M5 case. f. 45–46ᵛ).
Translation: Kind Gods of our fathers, graciously hear my sorrow; as you favored with your help the undertakings of my ancestors, give strength to him who is preparing to punish a traitor.

12.2 Dent, *Alessandro Scarlatti*, p. 110. Realization omitted; figure and accidentals in brackets correspond to Dent's realization.
Translation: O vain hope! O broken faith! O brief, alluring, dolorous, impious happiness! From whom now can I seek aid or consolation? In heaven, on the sea or the earth, in the abyss? Ah! Mithridates is dead!

12.3 Händel, C.E. Supplement VI, 104. Reduced from four staves; names of instruments changed from "violino e flauto dolce"; "(Bassi)" changed to "[Continuo]."
Translation: Babble not so loud. O crystal-silver brook.

12.4 Händel, C.E. Supplement VI, 26.
Translation: Ormena! Ormena, thou settest me on fire!

12.5 DdT XXXVII/XXXVIII, 38. Reduced from five staves; realization omitted; stage direction translated.
Translation: . . . and lovest no other?

12.6 DdT XXXVII/XXXVIII, 202. Reduced from five staves.
Translation: Gods, show pity.

12.7 Händel, C.E. LVII, 72. Accompaniment omitted.
Translation: Let the world fall.

12.8   Händel, C.E. LXVIII, 82–83. Recitative reduced from five staves, aria from six staves.
Translation: (Recitative) What do I hear? O God! Cleopatra will yet die. Vile soul, when wilt thou depart? But still! To avenge myself I shall have . . . (Aria) If you do not feel pity for me, just Heaven, I shall die.

12.9   Rameau, C.E. X, *Appendice*, p. 26.
Translation: Mournful spot, where everything breathes shame and sorrow; dark and cruel realm of despair.

13.1   Händel, C.E. XCII. Three string parts omitted; ornamented version of melody by Dr. Putnam Aldrich.
Translation: Never was shade of plant so dear, precious, and kindly.

13.2   Haas, *Aufführungspraxis*, p. 186. Signature changed from two flats.
Translation: . . . explains the cruelty of fate.

13.3   Vinci, *Artaserse* (Library of Congress M 1500 .V6A6), pp. 17 ff.
Translation: The wave of the sea bathes the valley and the mountain, goes by in the river, is imprisoned in the fountain, murmurs and groans always until it returns to the sea.

13.4   Pergolesi, *L'Olimpiade* (MS copy, Library of Congress M 1500 .P42O6 case).
Translation: While you sleep, Love increases the pleasure of your dreams with the thought of my pleasure.

13.5   Gerber, *Der Operntypus Hasses*, pp. 77–78. Slurs added, other slight changes in notation.
Translation: I will be silent if you desire it, but you are wronging my faithfulness if you call me betrayer.

13.6   DdT XV, 166. Accompaniment reduced from four staves.
Translation: Without regret I leave a greatness which I have known to be all too fragile and fleeting, and which I have possessed without being overcome by pride. A great and strong soul should always be ready to quit those goods from which death one day will separate him. But thou, O faithful wife!

13.7   DTB XIV^1, 146–47. Accompaniment (first and second violins, viola, continuo) omitted; realization and reduction omitted.
Translation: Do not weep for my misfortunes, do not be distressed at my torments.

14.1   DTB XIV^2, 144. Accompaniment (four string parts) omitted.
Translation: As your beautiful flame is lighted in your natal star, so will it shine resplendent.

14.2   DTOe LX, 46–47. Reduced from nine staves.

15.1   *I classici della musica italiana* XXIII, Quaderno 89–90, p. 11.

Translation: And yes and no, and no and yes, and here and there, and up and down—now enough of this: let's have an end of it!

15.2 *I classici della musica italiana* XX, Quaderno 80, pp. 6–7. Reduced from three staves.
Translation: But if Lindoro comes, then, ah! then all is joy, all is well. When I shall see my love . . .

15.3 *Théâtre de la Foire*, vol. I.

15.4 Monsigny, *Le Déserteur*. Piano-vocal score, Paris: Alphonse Leduc, no. A.L. 5204, pp. 10–11.
Translation: Can one give pain to the one he loves? Why try to annoy him? It is just like being spiteful toward oneself.

15.5 Grétry, C.E. I, 43–44. Orchestra parts condensed from seven staves.
Translation: O Richard, O my king! All the world abandons you; only I in all the earth am concerned about you; I alone want to break your chains, and all the rest abandon you.

15.6 *The Beggar's Opera*, 2d ed. (1728), p. [45]. Repeat marks after first double bar omitted to conform with text.

15.7 Hiller, *Die Jagd* (Leipzig, 1772).
Translation: O, that his heart loved me as my heart loves him!

15.8 Dittersdorf, *Das rote Käppchen*. MS Vienna Nationalbibliothek.
Translation: 1. Why, in a word, does Mr. Schulz stay at home and not appear at today's meal? 2. I thank you for the food and drink, when drunken men fall off their chairs. (Refrain) It might go bad with the women, but if one stays at home nothing can happen.

15.9 Subirá, *La tonadilla escénica* III, [16–17].
Translation: Let us go to the market, my dear.

17.1 Cherubini, *Lodoïska* (Paris, [1791?]), pp. 180–83.
Translation: Alas, in this cruel refuge, there was enough of my misfortune. . . . the end of the woes which I have suffered.

17.2 Cherubini, *Les Deux Journées*. Piano-vocal score, Universal Ed. 3157, p. 14. Text underlaid from another ed., Braunschweig: Meyer, [before 1862].
Translation: Good Frenchman, my God reward you; a good deed is never in vain.

17.3 Spontini, *Fernand Cortez*, Leipzig: Hofmeister, plate no. 1135, p. 282. Condensed from three staves.
Translation: Sorrowful presentiments, you do not deceive me; my fate is decided.

18.1 Auber, *La Muette de Portici*, Novello piano-vocal score, p. 137.
Translation: Holy love for our country, give us boldness and pride; to my country I owe life and it owes me liberty.

18.2 Meyerbeer, *L'Africaine*. Edition Peters No. 2773, piano-vocal score, p. 127. Reduced from three staves; indication of instruments omitted.
Translation: How pale she is! What cold runs in my veins!

18.3 Berlioz, *Les Troyens*. Piano-vocal score, Choudens, p. 420. Names of instruments translated; flat added before bass D in measure 11; first eighth rest added in measure 15.
Translation: Farewell, proud city, which generous striving has so quickly built and made to flourish; my loving sister, follower in all my wanderings; farewell, my people, farewell!

19.1 Boieldieu, *Jean de Paris*. Piano-vocal score, Brussels: E. Loweryns, [ca. 1830?], pp. 60–61.
Translation: Remain faithful to Glory, cherish the beauty of ladies: that is the way to act like a true French cavalier.

19.2 Auber, *Les Diamants de la couronne* (Paris: Beck, 1841).

19.3 Auber, *La Part du Diable* (Paris: Boulé, 1843).
Translation: Return, my protectress, help your poor servant; turn from me the rigor of a fate whose caprice I fear.

19.4 Hérold, *Le Pré aux clercs*. Piano score, Paris: Léon Grus, plate no. 1746, pp. 72–73. For this example, the three vocal parts and accompaniment have been further reduced to illustrate Hérold's style.

20.1 Rossini, *Tancredi*. Piano-vocal score, Paris; Launer, plate no. 3237, pp. 50–51.

20.2 Donizetti, *Linda di Chamounix*. Piano-vocal score, Paris: Schonenberger, s.d. [184–?] plate no. S-975, p. 157.
Translation: If our love is so hateful to men, let us break the hard tie of this bitter life: in Heaven above our struggle will be ended.

20.3 Bellini, *La sonnambula*. Novello octavo piano-vocal score.
Translation: Ah, I will not look upon thee, O flower so soon withered; thou hast passed away even as love, which endured but a single day.

20.4 Mercadante, *La Vestale*. Piano-vocal score, [183–?] plate no. v. 12212 v, pp. 155–62.
Translation: Vestal & chorus: Through my being courses the horrid cold of death: surely a God whom the Tiber abhors today gave a sign in Heaven.

20.5 Verdi, *Ernani*. Piano-vocal score, Novello, plate no. 8063, pp. 174–75. Condensed from six staves.
Translation: So thou didst laugh, Lion of Castile, and every mountain of Iberia; every glad echo produced a great roar as once against the oppressing Moor.

20.6 Verdi, *La Traviata*. Piano-vocal score, G. Schirmer, p. 108.
Translation: Love me, Alfredo, love me as I love you.

20.7 Verdi, *Otello*. Piano-vocal score, Ricordi, plate no. 52105, p. 361.
Translation: And thou, how pale thou art! and motionless, and mute, and lovely, blessed creature born under an evil star.

22.1 Wagner, *Das Liebesverbot*. Piano-vocal score. B&H, plate no. E. B. 4520, p. 396.
Translation: Ah, what a death for love and honor; to it I dedicate my youthful strength.

22.2 Wagner, *Tannhäuser*. Eulenburg small score, plate no. E.E. 4850, pp. 648–49. Reduced from six staves.
Translation: With fervor in my heart such as no sinner has ever felt, I sought the road to Rome.

22.3 Wagner, *Lohengrin*. B&H, plate no. 25700, p. 140.
Translation: Never shalt thou ask me, never trouble to know whence I came, nor my name and state.

22.4 Motifs from the *Ring*.

22.5 Motif from *Tristan und Isolde*.

23.1 D'Indy, *L'Étranger*. Piano-vocal score, Durand (1902), pp. 149–50. Some notes enharmonically altered.
Translation: O sea! Sinister sea, seductive in thy raging.

23.2 Puccini, *Tosca*. Piano-vocal score, G. Ricordi & Co., plate no. 109916, p. 1. By kind permission of G. Ricordi & Co., Milan.

23.3 Puccini, *Madama Butterfly*. Piano score, Ricordi, plate no. 110001, p. 123.

23.4 Giordano, *Andrea Chénier*. Piano-vocal score, Sonzogno (1896), plate no. 929, pp. 88–89.
Translation: I have often heard her say with her ardent voice: have faith in love, Chénier! thou art loved!

23.5 Kienzl, *Der Evangelimann*. Bote & Bock, piano-vocal score (1894), plate no. 14035, pp. 66–67. Upper staff of accompaniment omitted.
Translation: You're not hitting anything any more. The bowling ball is too heavy for you.

24.1 Glinka, *A Life for the Tsar*. Piano-vocal score, Moscow, n.d., p. 212. Alto voice and accompaniment omitted.

24.2 Glinka, *Ruslan and Ludmila*. Piano-vocal score, Moscow: P. Jurgenson, s.d., plate no. 30087, pp. 269–70.

24.3 Mussorgsky, *Boris Godunov*. Piano-vocal score, London: J. & W. Chester, plate no. J.W.C. 9722, p. 154. Reproduced by permission of J. & W. Chester, Ltd., London.
Translation: Phew! Give me air! This suffocates my soul! I felt blood

surging upward to my face, then down again like a torrent. O conscience, thou art cruel, merciless thy vengeance!

24.4 Rimsky-Korsakov, *Sadko*. Piano-vocal score, Leipzig: M. P. Balaieff, [1906?] plate no. 1434–1643, pp. 82–83.
Translation: Come out from the blue sea, come out to the green fields; come out, prophetic sisters.

24.5 Pedrell, *Los Pirineos*. Piano-vocal score, J. B. Pujol, plate no. P.25C., pp. 239–40. Time signature, tempo mark, and first "pp" inserted from previous directions.

25.1 Debussy, *Pelléas et Mélisande*. Piano-vocal score, Durand (1907), p. 236.
Translation: Mélisande: Pelléas! Pelléas: Mélisande! Is it thou, Mélisande? Mélisande: Yes. Pelléas: Come here.

25.2 Dukas, *Ariane et Barbe-Bleue*. Piano-vocal score, Durand (1906), pp. 72–74. Reduced from three or five staves to show only essential harmonic outline; recitatives (two soloists) omitted.
Translation: The five daughters of Orlamonde (the black fairy is dead) have sought the gates, have lighted their five lamps, have opened the towers, have traversed three hundred rooms without finding daylight, have opened a well . . .

25.3 Montemezzi, *L'amore dei tre rè*. Piano-vocal score, Ricordi, plate no. 114651, pp. 126–27. Reduced from four staves; first two measures notated with signature of three flats instead of three sharps.
Translation: Take, take her; there thou art, Fiora.

25.4 Pfitzner, *Palestrina*. Piano-vocal score cop. 1916 by Adolph Fürstner (A.7403, 7415, 7418F), p. 5.

25.5 Richard Strauss, *Die Frau ohne Schatten*. Piano-vocal score, Boosey & Hawkes, ed. no. A.7500 F., p. 588. Copyright assigned 1942 to Boosey & Hawkes, Ltd., for all countries, except Germany, Danzig, Italy, Portugal, and the Soviet Union. Reprinted by permission of Boosey & Hawkes, Inc.
Translation: I will not!

25.6 Richard Strauss, *Die Frau ohne Schatten*. Piano-vocal score, Boosey & Hawkes, ed. no. A.7500 F., p. 642. Copyright assigned 1942 to Boosey & Hawkes, Ltd., for all countries, except Germany, Danzig, Italy, Portugal, and the Soviet Union. Reprinted by permission of Boosey & Hawkes, Inc.
Translation: Now will I rejoice as no one has ever rejoiced!

25.7 Richard Strauss, *Capriccio*. Piano-vocal score. Boosey & Hawkes, plate no. 8453, pp. 80–81. Copyright 1942 by Richard Strauss. Reprinted by permission of Boosey & Hawkes Inc., Sole Agents. Translation of Pierre de Ronsard's Sonnet XXVIII from his *Continuation des Amours* (Paris 1555). Pierre de Ronsard, *Oeuvres complètes*, vol. 7, ed. by Paul Laumonier (Paris: Droz, 1934), pp. 145–46:

Je ne saurois aimer autre que vous,
Non, Dame, non, je ne aurois le faire:
Autre que vous ne me sauroit complaire,
Et fust Venus descendue entre nous.
   Vos yeus me sont si gracieus & dous,
Que d'un seul clin ils me peuvent defaire,
D'un autre clin tout soudain me refaire,
Me faisant vivre ou mourir en deux cous.
   Quand je serois cinq cens mille ans en vie,
Autre que vous, ma mignonne m'amie,
Ne me feroit amoureus devenir.
   Il me faudroit refaire d'autres venes,
Les miennes sont de vostre amour si plenes,
Qu'un autre amour n'y sauroit plus tenir.

25.8 Bartók, *Herzog Blaubarts Burg*. Piano-vocal score, Universal Ed., plate no. U.E. 7026, p. 11. Copyright 1921 by Universal Edition. Renewed 1948. Copyright and renewal assigned to Boosey & Hawkes Inc. Reprinted by permission.
Translation: The walls are wet! What moisure is this on my hands? Do the rocks and dungeons weep?—Ah, Judith, better were the bright days of our betrothal, when white walls enclosed the garden of roses and sunshine gilded the gables.

25.9 Szymanowski, *König Roger*. Piano-vocal score, Universal Ed., plate no. U.E. 7750, pp. 23–26. Used by permission of Universal Editions. A.G., Vienna.
Translation: See, there he is! There he comes! Seize the wretch, kill the blasphemer, stone him, stone him!

25.10 Berg, *Wozzeck*. Universal Ed., plate nos. U.E. 7379/U.E. 121000, p. 29. Used by permission of Universal Editions, A.G. Vienna.
Translation: We poor folk! See, Captain: money, money! Those who have no money!

25.11 Honegger, *Antigone*. Piano-vocal score, Senart, plate no. EMS7297, pp. 51–52.
Translation: Neither does justice impose laws of this sort, and I did not believe that your decree could make the caprice of a man prevail over the rule of the immortals, over the laws which are not written.

25.12 Milhaud. *Le Pauvre Matelot*. Piano-vocal score, Paris: Heugel, [no plate no.] pp. 38–40.
Translation: His wife: Come in! The sailor: I come to bring you news, Madame. His wife: Of my husband? The sailor: Yes, indeed, Madame, news of your husband. His wife: He is dead . . . The sailor: No, Madame, he is alive, I saw him three weeks ago.

25.13 Poulenc, *Dialogues des Carmélites*. Piano-vocal score, Ricordi, plate no. R.1471, pp. 80–81. By kind permission of G. Ricordi & Co., Milan.

Translation: . . . like the child of one's old age, and also the most risky, the most threatened. To turn away this threat I would gladly have given my poor life.

25.14 Hindemith, *Die Harmonie der Welt*. Piano-vocal score, Mainz, B. Schott's Söhne, ed. no. 4925.

25.15 Stravinsky, *The Rake's Progress*. Piano-vocal score, Boosey & Hawkes, plate no. 17088, p. 222. © 1949, 1950, 1951 by Boosey & Hawkes, Inc. Reprinted by permission.

25.16 Prokofiev, *War and Peace* (Moscow, 1958, plate no. M 26793ᵃ), pp. 77–79.
Translation: . . . when from the gold-drenched hills the herds are flocking down to the river, and the clamor of their lowing thunders melodiously across the waters; and, his nets hauled in, the fisherman in his boat is shore-bound, sailing alone, framed by bushes . . .

25.17 Janáček, *Kátja Kabanowá*. Piano-vocal score, Universal Ed., plate no. U.E. 7103, pp. 143–45. Used by permission of Universal Editions, A.G., Vienna.
Translation: How kindly my Boris spoke to me, how tenderly! I know no more. The nights are full of terror; everyone goes to rest, but for me it is like sinking into the grave. This fear of the dark! And such a noise!—That is like singing!

25.18 Janáček, *Das schlaue Füchslein*. Piano-vocal score, Universal Ed., plate no. U.E. 7564, pp. 176–78. Used by permission of Universal Editions, A.G., Vienna.

26.1 Orff, *Oedipus der Tyrann*. Piano-vocal score, Mainz, B. Schott's Söhne, ed. no. 4996, p. 234. © 1959 by B. Schott's Soehne, Mainz. Reprinted by permission of the original copyright owners and their U.S. representatives. Associated Music Publishers, Inc., New York.
Translation: Perish the man, whoe'er he was, that loosed me from the cruel fetters on my feet and rescued me from death and saved my life, conferring no kindness thereby! For had I then died, I had not been so sore a woe to my friends or mine own self. (Chorus:) I too could have wished it thus. (E. P. Coleridge's translation.)

26.2 Dallapiccola, *Il prigioniero*. Piano-vocal score, S. Zerboni, plate no. S. 4464 Z., pp. 61–62. By kind permission of Edizioni Suvini Zerboni, Milan.
Translation: I cannot control [myself]. Surprised here, at night, I could not avoid renewed, atrocious sufferings. What to do? Return to my dark cell and wait still, always in vain?

26.3a Zimmermann, *Die Soldaten*. Piano-vocal score, B. Schott's Soehne, ed. 5076, p. 524. © B. Schott's Soehne, Mainz, 1966. All rights reserved. Used by permission of European American Music Distributors Corporation, sole U.S. agent for B. Schott's Soehne.
Translation: Our Father, who is in (heaven).

INDEX